WORDPERFECT FOR THE MACINTOSH

Rob Krumm

MIS: PRESS

MANAGEMENT INFORMATION SOURCE, INC.

COPYRIGHT

Copyright © 1988 by Management Information Source, Inc.
1107 N.W. 14th Avenue
Portland, Oregon 97209
(503) 222-2399

Second Printing

ISBN 0-943518-91-1

Library of Congress Catalog Card Number: 88-14047

All rights reserved. Reproduction or use, without express permission, of editorial or pictorial content, in any manner, is prohibited. No patent liability is assumed with respect to the use of the information contained herein. While every precaution has been taken in the preparation of this book, the publisher assumes no responsibility for errors or omissions. Neither is any liability assumed for damages resulting from the use of the information contained herein.

WordPerfect is a trademark of the WordPerfect Corporation
HyperCard is a trademark of Apple Computer, Inc.

TABLE OF CONTENTS

Introduction v
    WordPerfect 4.2 for the IBM PC v
    Conventions Used in This Book vii
    Command and Menu Summary x

Chapter 1: Editing Skills 1
    Entering Text 2
        Cursor Movement with the Keyboard 3
        Cursor Movement with the Mouse 5
        Inserting and Deleting Text 7
        Starting a New Line 8
        Vertical Movement Using the Keyboard 9
        Deleting Words 11
        Wraparound Typing 13
        Inserting Text in Paragraphs 15
        Hyphenation 16
        Repeating a Character 19
    Enhancing the Text 20
        Changing Print Styles 21
        Inserting the System Date 27
        Spell Checking 29
        Thesaurus 35
    Printing a Document 39
    Saving a Document 40
    Summary 42

Chapter 2: Margins and Formatting 45
    Setting Margins 46
        More Margin Changes 52
    Changing Point Size 58
    Adding a Heading 61
    Changing Fonts 62
    Converting Case 63
    Revising Formatted Documents 65
        WordPerfect Codes 67
    Soft Returns, Hyphens, and Justification 83
    Summary 87

Chapter 3: Tables and Tabs 89
    Full Window Display 90
    Using Tabs 92
    Using Replace 93
    Setting Individual Tabs 97

i

- Entering a Table 103
  - Underline Style 104
  - Table Text 105
  - Deleting Tabs with the Mouse 107
  - Adding Tabs with the Mouse 110
  - Double Underlines 114
  - Tabs with Leader Characters 116
  - Quick Tables 120
  - Cut-and-Paste Tables 124
  - Moving from Table to Table 126
  - Changing Tab Locations 132
  - Changing Tabs from the Menu Display 135
  - Adusting for Font Size Changes 138
- Line Spacing 141
  - Stopping Line Spacing 145
  - Keeping a Block Together 146
- Summary 150

Chapter 4: Special Text Formats 151
- Indents 152
  - Multiple Indents 155
  - Changing an Indent 159
- Creating a New Page 160
- Overhangs 161
  - Creating a Bullet 162
  - Margin Release 166
- Outlines 171
  - Changing Outline Levels 174
  - Stopping the Outline Mode 177
  - Revising an Outline 179
  - Inserting Paragraph Numbers 181
  - Outline Codes 184
  - Outline Styles 187
- Columns 190
  - Parallel Columns 191
  - Newspaper Columns 205
- Previewing the Printing 209
- Zooming the Display 212
- Summary 214

Chapter 5: Page Formats 217
- Opening Files 218
- Adding Page Numbers 220
  - Setting Page Numbers 220
  - Suppressing Page Numbers 225
  - Numbering Sequence 227
  - Mixing Page Number Formats 230
  - Alternating Page Number Positions 234

- Modifying Page Number Positions ... 235
- How Page Numbers Affect Text ... 238
- Headers and Footers ... 239
  - WordPerfect Text Formats ... 243
  - Suppressing Headers ... 250
  - Odd and Even Headers ... 252
- Footnotes and Endnotes ... 264
  - Inserting a Footnote ... 273
  - Endnotes ... 275
  - Editing a Footnote ... 277
  - Footnote/Endnote Styles ... 279
  - Changing Note Styles ... 283
- Page Formats and Margins ... 287
- Summary ... 288

Chapter 6: Multiple Documents and Windows ... 289
- Opening Multiple Documents ... 290
- Changing Windows ... 293
  - The Windows Menu ... 294
  - Transferring Data Between Windows ... 298
  - Showing the Clipboard ... 299
  - Cleaning Up the Display ... 309
  - Moving and Sizing Windows ... 310
  - Zooming a Window ... 315
- Retrieving Text ... 318
  - Appending Text to a File ... 322
- Inserting Graphics ... 325
- Summary ... 334

Chapter 7: Merge Operations ... 335
- Form Letters ... 336
- List Processing ... 337
  - Creating a Shell Document ... 341
  - Creating Field Codes ... 345
  - Creating a List Document ... 354
  - Merging Documents ... 361
  - Adding Attributes to the Shell Letter ... 367
- Reports ... 373
  - Get Next Record ... 375
  - Adding Record Numbers ... 379
  - Parallel Column Reports ... 381
  - Adding Headings to Reports ... 385
- Fill-in Forms ... 391
  - Inserting a Merge Pause ... 393
- Automatic Printing ... 398
- Assembling Documents ... 401
  - Assembling with Merge Codes ... 403
  - Selecting the Work Folder ... 406

iii

    Merge Assembly 410
    Summary 412

Chapter 8: Macros **415**
    Defining a Macro 416
    Typing Macros 417
    More Macros 423
    Single-Key Macros 426
        Outlines with Formats 430
    Enter Key Combinations 443
        Defining an Enter Key Combination 444
    Pausing a Macro 449
    Merge and Macros 450
        Attaching a Macro to a Merge Document 454
        Interactive Macros 458
    Halting a Macro 469
    Chains and Searches 471
    Summary 475

Chapter 9: Reference Tasks **477**
    Tables of Contents 478
        Marking Table of Contents Items 483
    Other Lists 488
    Indexes 489
        Index Subheadings 491
    Defining Lists and Tables 493
    Generating Lists 501
    Revision Marking 503
        Removing the Revision Marks and Text 507
    Summary 510

Chapter 10: Management Tasks **513**
    About Saving 514
        Saving Files 514
        File Format 515
        Password Protection 517
        Saving a Block of Text 520
    File Management 520
    System Defaults 526
    Odds and Ends 530
        Typeover Mode 531
        Widow and Orphan Control 531
        Kerning 531
        Show Position 532
    Summary 533

Index **435**

INTRODUCTION

In the last few years, WordPerfect has taken the word processing world by storm. WordPerfect is currently the leading word processor among the approximately 1.2 million users of IBM PCs and compatibles.

This book is an introduction to WordPerfect for the Macintosh. The goal of this book is to provide you with a solid understanding of WordPerfect and teach you to approach a variety of word processing problems with WordPerfect's tools.

This book is also designed to progress through a series of examples in which you will be exposed to all of WordPerfect's features with the help of specific, detailed examples. Working through these examples will teach you the how and the why of word processing with WordPerfect.

Moving in a logical sequence, this book discusses basic skills first to build a foundation for advanced topics covered later.

WordPerfect for the Macintosh is a powerful and remarkably accessible word processing program. This book should encourage you to learn and use the advanced features of the program. All too often, software users learn a few basic commands and never move beyond that level.

WordPerfect 4.2 for the IBM PC

If you have used WordPerfect 4.1 or 4.2 on an IBM PC or compatible, you will soon find that WordPerfect for the Macintosh preserves many of its popular features. There are, however, a number of differences. Following is a summary of differences between WordPerfect 4.2 for the IBM PC and WordPerfect for the Macintosh. Unless otherwise noted, the term "WordPerfect" throughout this text refers to WordPerfect for the Macintosh.

Codes

WordPerfect uses the familiar system of inserting command codes within the body of the document. On the Macintosh, you can edit the document while codes are displayed.

Introduction

Menus

WordPerfect uses the standard Macintosh system of mouse-activated pull-down menus; you don't need a keyboard template to locate commands. WordPerfect recognizes 61 keyboard shortcut commands that cover most—though not all—standard WordPerfect features.

Windows

Because of the Macintosh interface, WordPerfect allows you to edit more than two documents at one time. The total number of documents that can be edited at one time is determined by the size of the documents and the amount of available memory in your Macintosh.

Fonts

WordPerfect displays on-screen changes in font size and type style.

Measurement

Because it uses multiple font styles and sizes, WordPerfect measures in inches rather than in lines and characters.

Features

WordPerfect retains most text-editing features found in its PC counterpart. The major omission is in the area of math functions; WordPerfect cannot perform calculations of any sort.

Merge operations operate the same as they do in the PC version, but no sorting command is provided. The ^O merge code is eliminated.

PC features not included in the Macintosh version are automatic line-numbering, tables of authorities, document summaries and comments, line drawing, concordance indexing, vertical column operations, and type-through.

Introduction

Conventions Used in This Book

If you are an experienced Macintosh user, you already know the conventions of mouse and keyboard use. In this book, the following typographic conventions are used to refer to specific key and mouse operations.

Key Notations

The names of special keys are enclosed in square brackets. Following are a few examples:

[Return]

indicates that you should press the Return key.

list [Return]

indicates that you should type in the word "list" and then press the return key.

[Enter]n

indicates that you should press the Enter key, release it, and then press the "n" key.

Note: The Return key and the Enter key (in the bottom right corner of the numeric keypad) are used for different purposes in WordPerfect for the Macintosh. See Chapter 1 for more details.

vii

Introduction

Directional arrow keys are represented by the symbol for each arrow. For example,

→

indicates that you should press the right arrow key.

Parenthetical information to the right of commands is only for the reader's clarification and should not be entered. For example,

← (3 times)

indicates that you should press the left arrow key three times.

The Macintosh keyboard includes a key called the **Command** key. The Command key is not labeled "command" but is labeled with an apple or cloverleaf symbol. The Command key appears as **[Apple]** in this book.

WordPerfect requires that you use a number of key combinations. Following are examples of how these combinations are expressed in this book.

[Apple/s]

represents holding down the Apple key and simultaneously pressing the letter "s."

[Apple/Shift/s]

represents holding down the Apple and Shift keys and simultaneously pressing the letter "s."

Introduction

[Apple/Option/s]

represents holding down the Apple and Option keys and simultaneously pressing the letter "s."

Mouse Operations

The following terms represent standard mouse operations:

- **Point** refers to moving the mouse so that the mouse pointer is positioned in a specific word or item.

- **Drag** refers to moving the mouse while holding down the mouse button.

- **Click** refers to pressing the mouse button.

- **Double Click** refers to clicking the mouse button twice in rapid succession.

Introduction

Command and Menu Summary

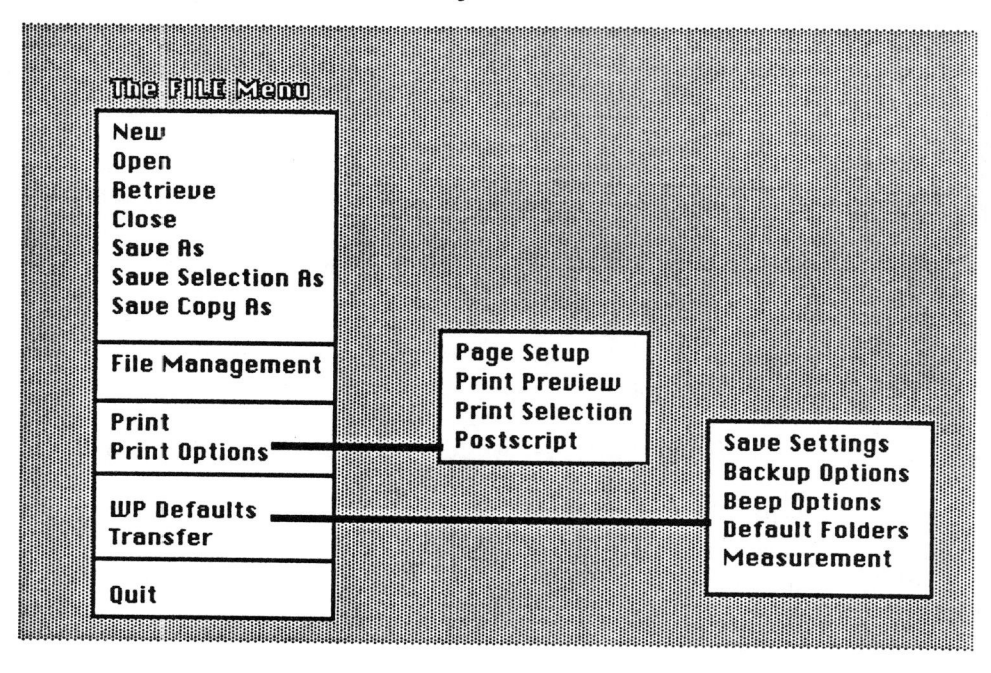

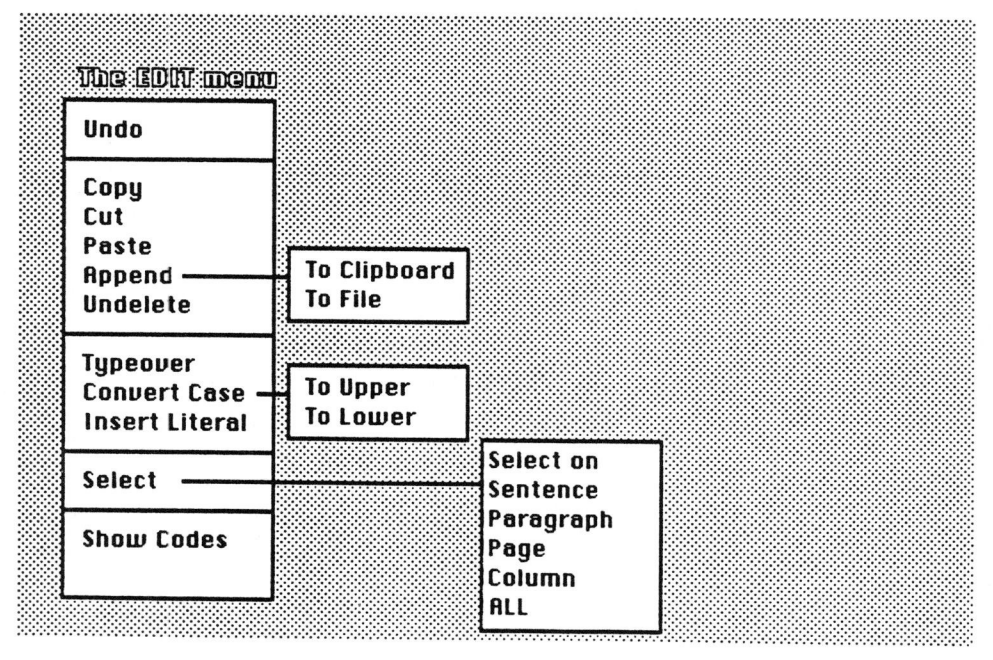

The FILE Menu

- New
- Open
- Retrieve
- Close
- Save As
- Save Selection As
- Save Copy As

- File Management

- Print
- Print Options
  - Page Setup
  - Print Preview
  - Print Selection
  - Postscript

- WP Defaults
  - Save Settings
  - Backup Options
  - Beep Options
  - Default Folders
  - Measurement
- Transfer

- Quit

The EDIT menu

- Undo

- Copy
- Cut
- Paste
- Append
  - To Clipboard
  - To File
- Undelete

- Typeover
- Convert Case
  - To Upper
  - To Lower
- Insert Literal

- Select
  - Select on
  - Sentence
  - Paragraph
  - Page
  - Column
  - ALL

- Show Codes

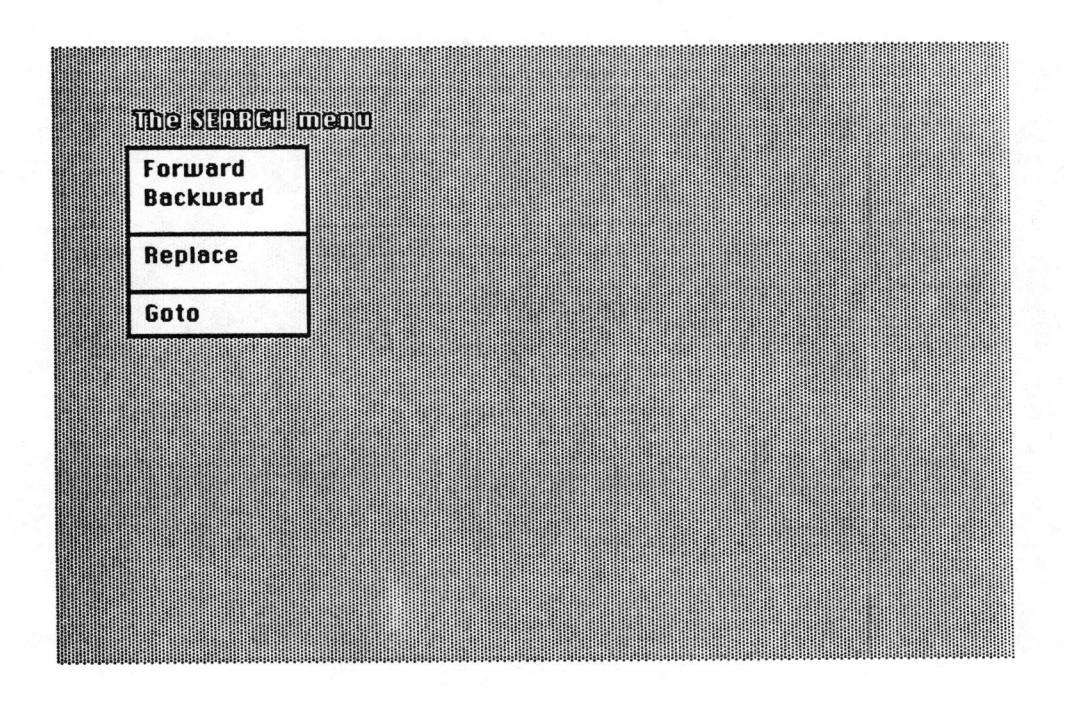

Introduction

The SEARCH menu

- Forward
- Backward
- Replace
- Goto

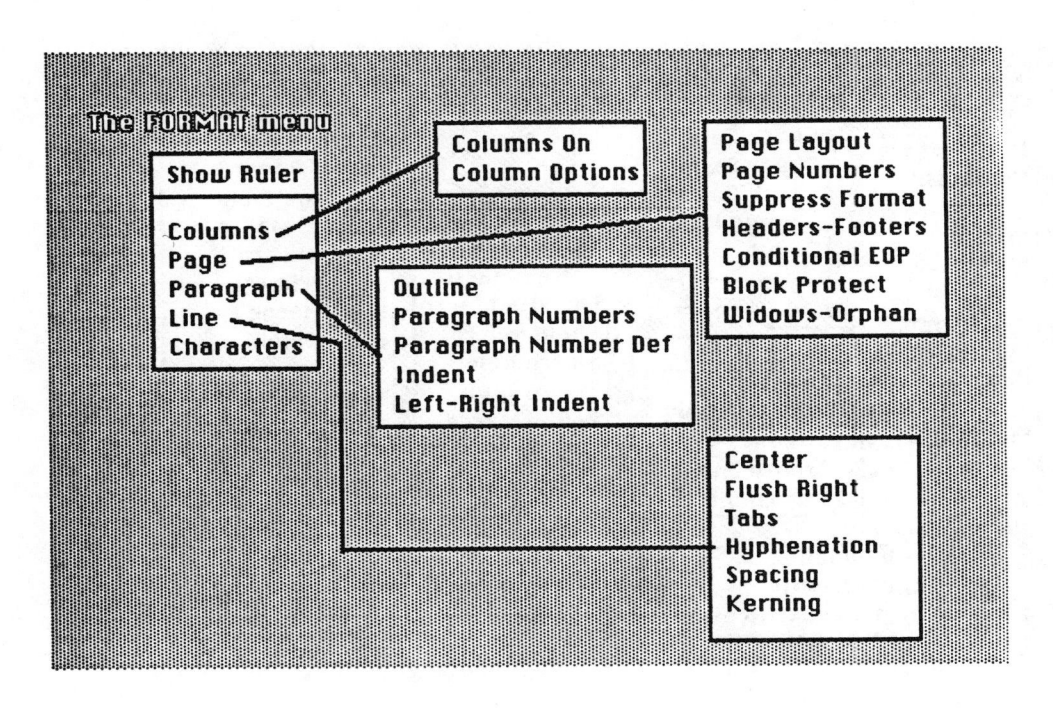

The FORMAT menu

- Show Ruler
- Columns → Columns On, Column Options
- Page → Page Layout, Page Numbers, Suppress Format, Headers-Footers, Conditional EOP, Block Protect, Widows-Orphan
- Paragraph → Outline, Paragraph Numbers, Paragraph Number Def, Indent, Left-Right Indent
- Line → Center, Flush Right, Tabs, Hyphenation, Spacing, Kerning
- Characters

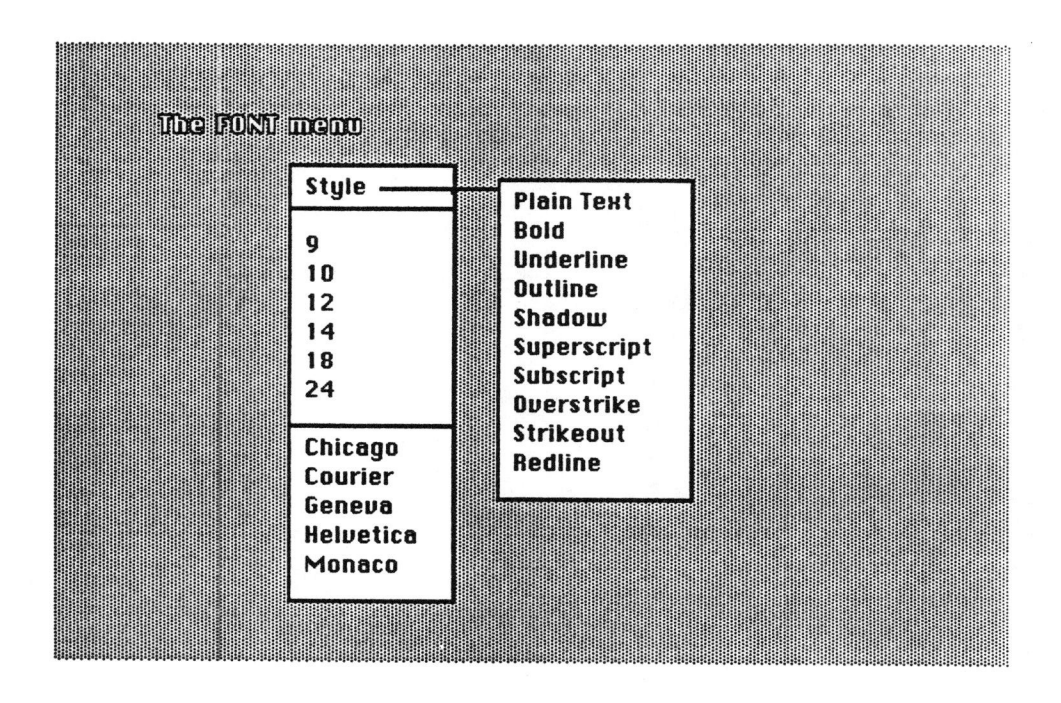

Introduction

The FONT menu

Style
9
10
12
14
18
24
Chicago
Courier
Geneva
Helvetica
Monaco

Plain Text
Bold
Underline
Outline
Shadow
Superscript
Subscript
Overstrike
Strikeout
Redline

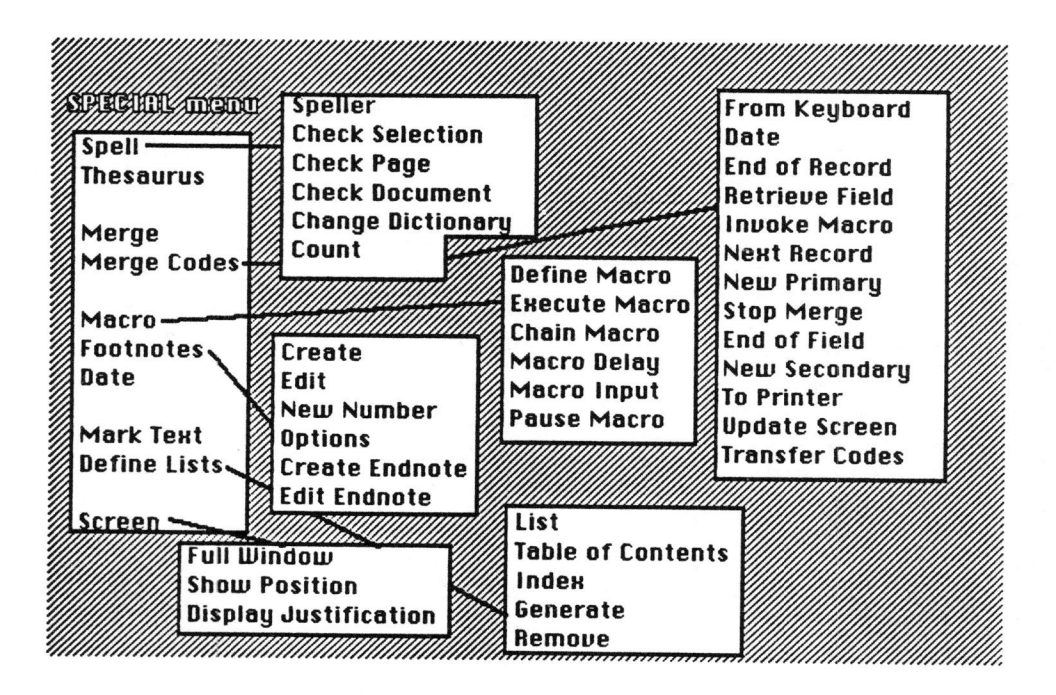

SPECIAL menu

- Spell
- Thesaurus
- Merge
- Merge Codes
- Macro
- Footnotes
- Date
- Mark Text
- Define Lists
- Screen

Speller
Check Selection
Check Page
Check Document
Change Dictionary
Count

Create
Edit
New Number
Options
Create Endnote
Edit Endnote

Full Window
Show Position
Display Justification

Define Macro
Execute Macro
Chain Macro
Macro Delay
Macro Input
Pause Macro

List
Table of Contents
Index
Generate
Remove

From Keyboard
Date
End of Record
Retrieve Field
Invoke Macro
Next Record
New Primary
Stop Merge
End of Field
New Secondary
To Printer
Update Screen
Transfer Codes

Apple Shortcut Commands

⌘ A	Append	⌘ S	Save document
⌘ B	Search Backward	⌘ T	Thesaurus
⌘ C	Copy	⌘ U	Undelete
⌘ D	Insert Date	⌘ V	Paste
⌘ E	Spell Check	⌘ W	Cycle window
⌘ F	Search Forward	⌘ X	Cut
⌘ G	Goto	⌘ Y	Text Style menu
⌘ H	Replace	⌘ Z	Undo
⌘ I	Insert Character	⌘ 1	Column menu
⌘ J	Mark Text menu	⌘ 2	Page Format menu
⌘ K	Close window	⌘ 3	Paragraph menu
⌘ L	File Management	⌘ 4	Line Format menu
⌘ M	Macro menu	⌘ 5	Character menu
⌘ N	New window	⌘ 6	Select menu
⌘ O	Open document	⌘ 7	Display codes
⌘ P	Print document	⌘ 8	Merge menu
⌘ Q	Quit WordPerfect	⌘ 9	Footnote menu
⌘ R	Display Ruler		

Apple-Shift Shortcut Commands

⌘ Shift A	Select All	⌘ Shift S	Shadow text
⌘ Shift B	Bold text	⌘ Shift T	Indent left
⌘ Shift C	Center text	⌘ Shift U	Underline text
⌘ Shift D	Date Function	⌘ Shift V	Overstrike text
⌘ Shift E	End of Record	⌘ Shift W	Spell Check document
⌘ Shift F	Flush Right	⌘ Shift X	Execute macro
⌘ Shift G	Generate indexes	⌘ Shift Y	Outline on/off
⌘ Shift H	Headers-Footers	⌘ Shift Z	Full screen display
⌘ Shift I	Italic text		
⌘ Shift J	Display justified		
⌘ Shift K	Columns on/off		
⌘ Shift L	Indent left/right		
⌘ Shift M	Record Macro		
⌘ Shift N	Select on/off		
⌘ Shift O	Outline		
⌘ Shift P	Preview Print		
⌘ Shift Q	Stop merge code		
⌘ Shift R	End of Field		

CHAPTER 1

EDITING SKILLS

1 Editing Skills

The first task in any word processing program is to learn the basic editing operations and commands. A discussion of editing also serves as an introduction to the fundamental philosophy of the program. In this chapter, you will learn WordPerfect's established editing operations and acquire insight into the philosophy behind them.

ENTERING TEXT

In word processing, you spend most of your time entering text. The operations that allow you to enter, delete, insert, and replace text are part of the editing process. Begin by entering the following text:

Miss M. Moss

Note the short, vertical line blinking next to the letter "s" at the end of the name "Moss." That line — the text cursor — is probably familiar if you have worked with other word processors.

The cursor is important; it identifies the "point of attack" while you are word processing. To perform an operation, you must first consider the location of the cursor in the text.

Observe also that the Macintosh displays a second cursor on the screen. This cursor is the **mouse cursor**, which indicates the current pointing position of the mouse. In WordPerfect, the position of the text cursor takes precedence over the location of the mouse cursor, which means that the location of the text cursor tells WordPerfect where to insert your changes. Remember, the text cursor appears just to the left of the indicated character; thus, a reference to the text cursor being "on" a certain character indicates the character to the cursor's immediate right.

The mouse cursor is used to change the position of the text cursor.

Editing Skills 1

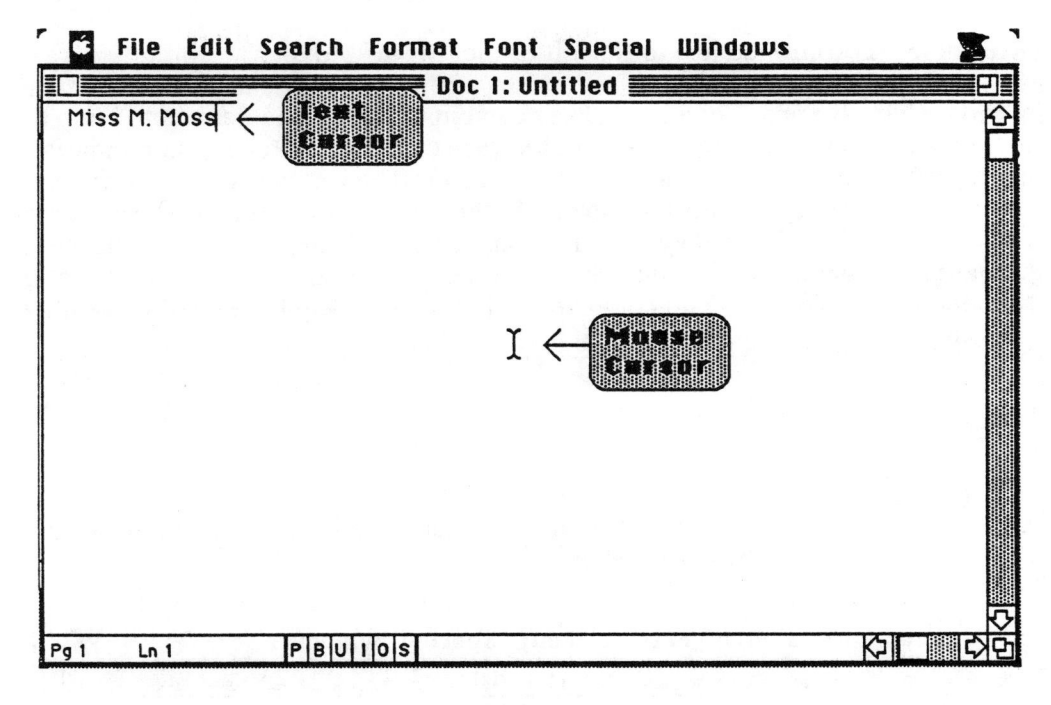

[Figure showing a Mac-style window with menu bar "File Edit Search Format Font Special Windows", titled "Doc 1: Untitled", containing "Miss M. Moss|" with an arrow pointing to a label "Text Cursor", and an I-beam cursor in the middle with an arrow pointing to a label "Mouse Cursor". Status bar shows "Pg 1 Ln 1   P B U I O S".]

Figure 1.1

Cursor Movement with the Keyboard

Because cursor position is so crucial, it is important to learn how to change the position of the cursor on a line. Enter

←

The text cursor moves one character to the left. The arrow keys ← and → move the text cursor one character to the left or right, respectively.

If you want to move word by word, you can combine the arrow keys with the Apple key. Again, the Apple key is used much like the Shift key; when used with another key, it is pressed and held before the other key is pressed. To move to the beginning of the word, enter

[Apple/←]

1 Editing Skills

The cursor is positioned just to the left of the "M" in "Moss."

WordPerfect also provides a special key combination that enables you to jump to the ends of lines. This combination of keys is called an Enter-key combination and is different from an Apple/key combination. The Enter key is also different from the Return key; on the Macintosh SE, the Enter key is found on the numeric keypad. To use an Enter-key combination, press the Enter key; then, release it before pressing the combination key. For example, suppose you want to jump to the left side of the line. The command is [Enter]←. Begin the combination by pressing

[Enter]

Examine the screen area where the mouse cursor was located. The mouse cursor has been replaced by the number 1.

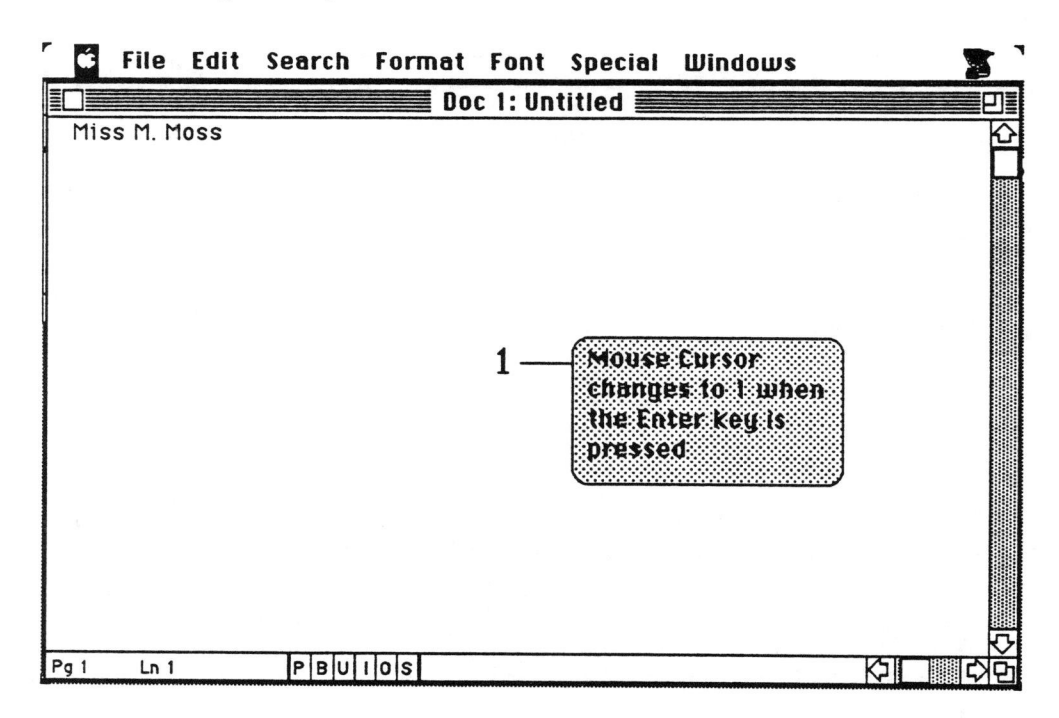

Figure 1.2

Editing Skills 1

The number serves to remind you that you have pressed the Enter key once. Later, you will learn to create your own commands by pressing the Enter key more than once. For now, press the left arrow key:

←

The cursor jumps to the left side of the line. To move to the right, simply substitute the right arrow key for the left arrow key in the previous command. To move one character to the right, enter

→

To move one word to the right, enter

[Apple/→]

To jump to the right end of the line, enter

[Enter]→

Cursor Movement with the Mouse

Another way to change the cursor position in the text is to use the mouse. Simply point the mouse at the position in the text where you want to locate the text cursor, and click. To place the cursor before the middle initial "M,"

Point just to the left of the "M"

5

1 Editing Skills

Your screen should resemble the following:

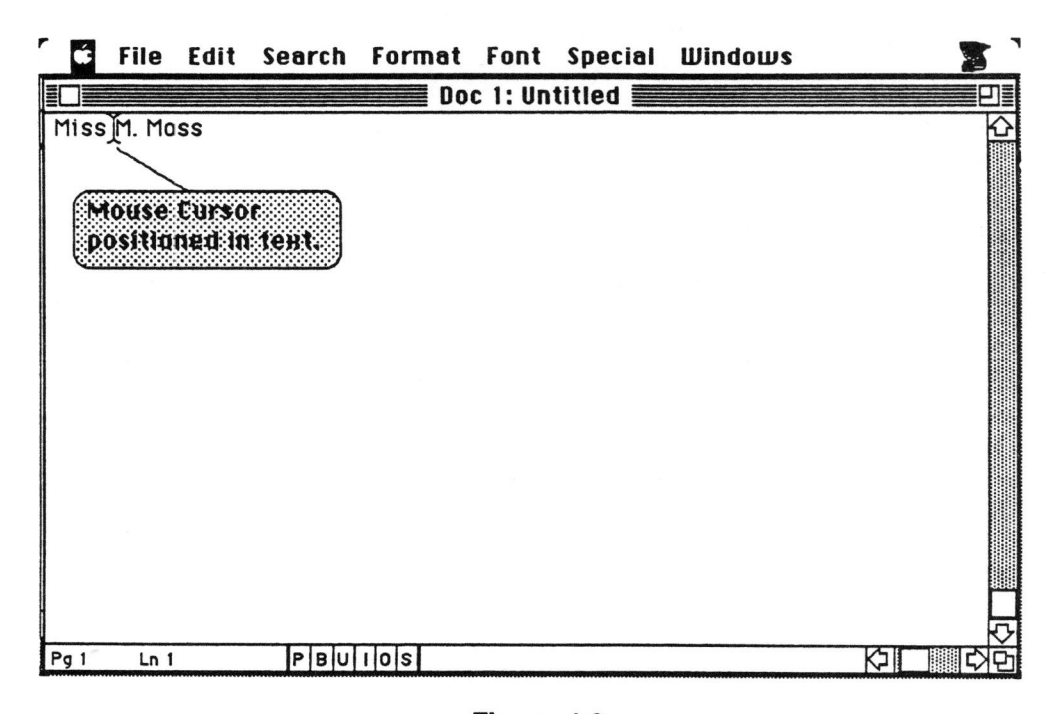

```
┌─────────────────────────────────────────────────┐
│  🍎  File  Edit  Search  Format  Font  Special  Windows   │
│ ══════════════════ Doc 1: Untitled ══════════════│
│ Miss I. Moss                                    │
│        ╭─────────────────╮                      │
│        │  Mouse cursor    │                     │
│        │ positioned in text│                    │
│        ╰─────────────────╯                      │
│                                                 │
│                                                 │
│ Pg 1   Ln 1      P B U I O S                    │
└─────────────────────────────────────────────────┘
```

Figure 1.3

| **Click** the mouse |

The text cursor jumps to the position indicated by the mouse cursor. To position the cursor at the end of the line,

| **Point** at the end of the line |
| **Click** |

Editing Skills 1

The best method for positioning the cursor depends on your purpose. The mouse method makes it easy to jump the cursor from one point to another in the text. If, however, you want to be sure you are positioned exactly at the beginning of a word or line, keyboard commands are more accurate. In this book, both methods will be explained if WordPerfect allows two ways of performing a task. Try both and judge for yourself.

Inserting and Deleting Text

WordPerfect editing takes place in an **insert mode**, which means whatever you type is added to the document. If you add text to the end of the document, the document's length is increased. If you add text to any other part of the document, to make room for the new text, WordPerfect moves the text located on the right of your entry to the right (or down). For example, suppose you want to use the full name "Marilyn" instead of the initial "M."

First, position the cursor on the correct place in the text. Enter

[Apple/→]   (2 times)

The cursor is now on the "M." Because the "M" is part of "Marilyn," position the cursor to the right one character by entering

→

Insert the rest of the name:

arilyn

WordPerfect inserts the new characters and pushes the period to the right to make room. You no longer need the period; it should be removed.

7

1 Editing Skills

WordPerfect allows two ways of deleting characters from text: the Delete key and the Decimal key.

The Delete Key   The Delete key deletes the character to the left of the cursor position. The Delete key functions much like the Backspace key on an electronic typewriter.

The Decimal Key   The Decimal key refers to the decimal-point key on the numeric keypad. Don't confuse the decimal key with the period key next to the ? key on the main keyboard. The decimal key deletes the character on which the cursor is positioned.

These two delete keys may seem confusing at first, but you will become accustomed to their operation in a short while. Remember, the character just to the right of the text cursor is the character the cursor is "on." To delete that character, use the decimal-point key. Enter

[Decimal]

Starting a New Line

When you have finished entering text on a line and want to start a new line, you must position the cursor at the end of the line before you press the Return key. Jump to the end of the line by entering

[Enter]→

Create a new line by entering

[Return]

8

Editing Skills 1

Enter the next line of the address block:

268 Meadow Lane [Return]
Memphis, Tenn. 38101 [Return]

The document should now resemble the following:

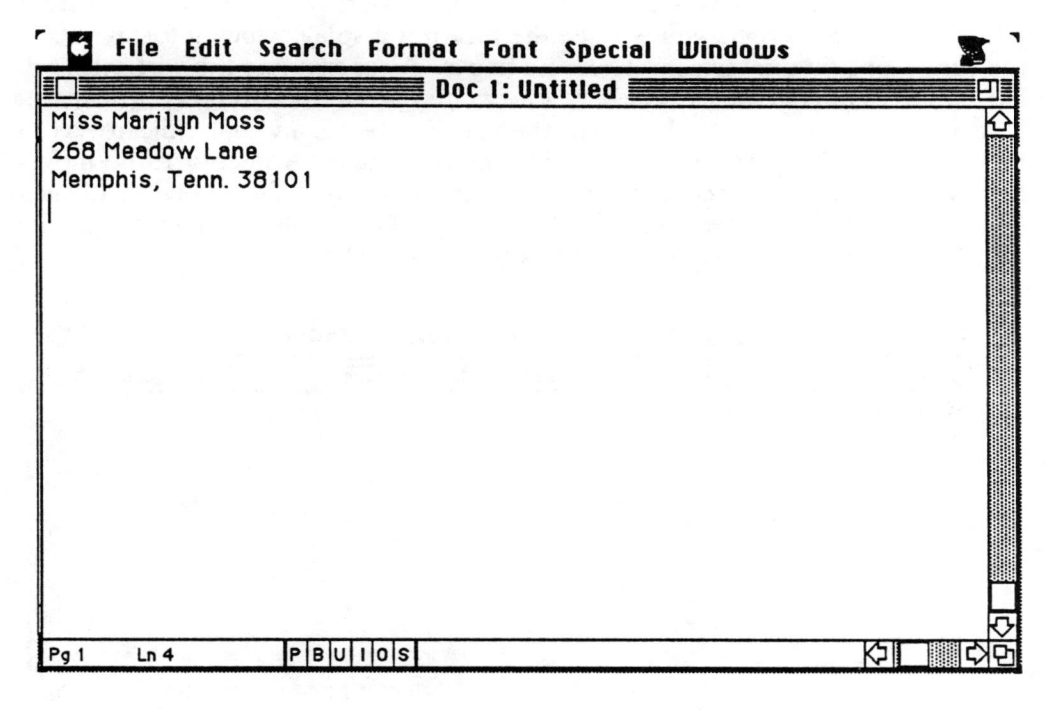

```
 File  Edit  Search  Format  Font  Special  Windows
━━━━━━━━━━━━━━━━━━━ Doc 1: Untitled ━━━━━━━━━━━━━━━━━━━
Miss Marilyn Moss
268 Meadow Lane
Memphis, Tenn. 38101
|
```

Pg 1   Ln 4   P B U I O S

Figure 1.4

Vertical Movement Using the Keyboard

Now that you have created lines, you must learn to change the vertical position of the cursor. The simplest and most instinctive way to move the cursor vertically is with the up arrow and down arrow keys. Each key will move you one line in its respective direction. Enter

↓

1 Editing Skills

The cursor remains stationary because you cannot move the cursor past the last character in the document. Even though the screen shows blank space below the text, that space is not yet part of the document. Enter

↑

This time, the cursor moves up one line to line #3. If you examine the bottom left corner of the screen, you will see the **location display**, which informs you of the cursor position in terms of lines and pages. Also, examine the vertical scroll bar on the right edge of the window. The white box has moved up approximately two-thirds of the way to the top of the bar. The box is a visual indicator as to the relative position of the cursor within the document. Remember, the movement of the scroll bar is relative to the document. In a very short document, each line requires a large move by the box. In a large document, moving a single line may have no perceptible effect on the position of the box.

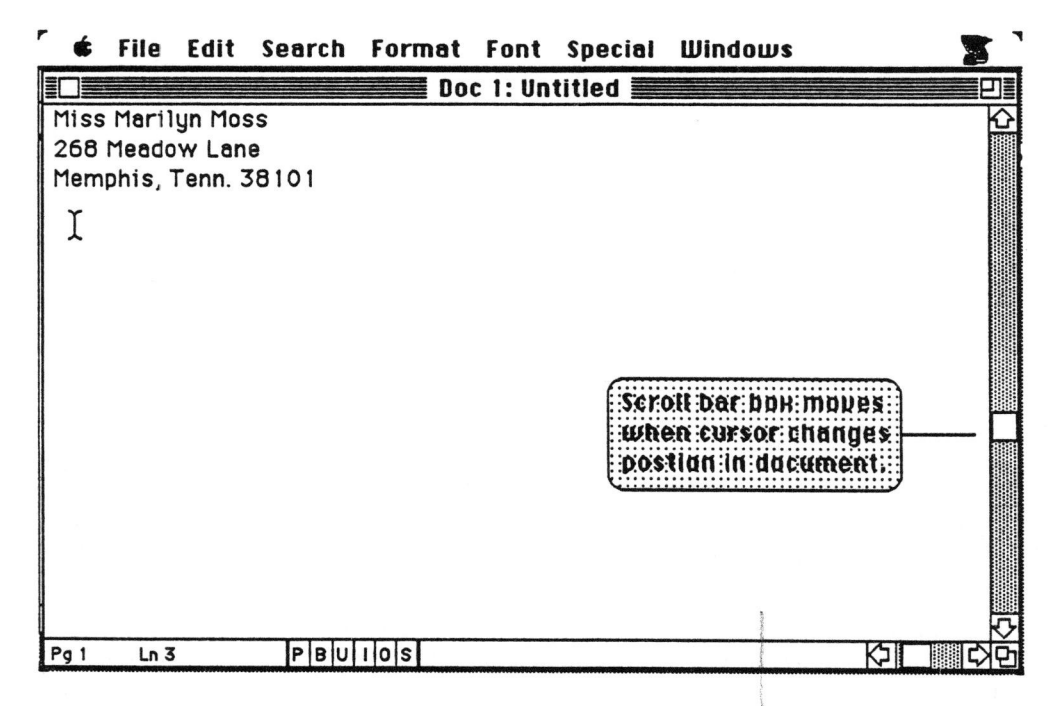

Figure 1.5

Editing Skills 1

If you want to move the cursor to the beginning of the document, press

[Enter] [Enter]

The number 2 now appears, indicating that you pressed the Enter key twice. Complete the instruction by entering

↑

The cursor is now at the top of the document. Pressing the up arrow moves the cursor to the top of the window, which is not necessarily the top of the document. Position the cursor at the end of the document by pressing

[Enter] [Enter]↓

Deleting Words

You may have noticed that the state name has been entered as a four-character abbreviation. The Postal Service prefers two-letter state abbreviations. To conform to that standard, you must remove the four-letter abbreviation and replace it with the two-letter code.

Position the cursor on the word "Tenn" by entering

[Apple/→] (2 times)

To delete the word at the cursor position, enter

[Apple/Delete]

1 Editing Skills

Note that WordPerfect does not remove the period. WordPerfect cannot differentiate between the end of an abbreviation and the end of a sentence because both are terminated with a period. When you delete a word, the period remains — assuming that it is used to mark the end of the sentence. To remove the period, enter

[Decimal]

Type in the two-letter code:

TN

Jump to the end of the document by entering

[Enter] [Enter] ↓

The next part of the document consists of the salutation line. To leave a blank line between the address and the salutation, enter

[Return]

In WordPerfect, blank lines — such as those used to separate paragraphs — are always entered as returns. Enter the salutation of the letter.

Dear Ms. Moss [Return] [Return]

Editing Skills **1**

Wraparound Typing

Until now, all text has been entered in short lines. A short line requires you to manually create a line-ending by pressing the Return key. When you enter paragraphs, however, you need not be concerned about where to end lines. Word-Perfect automatically ends and starts a new line when you have typed sufficient text. This feature is called **wraparound** typing and is found in almost all word processing programs. Now, enter some more text.

Thank you for your order of April 8th for one dozen picture frames, size 12" by 16"

The screen should resemble the following:

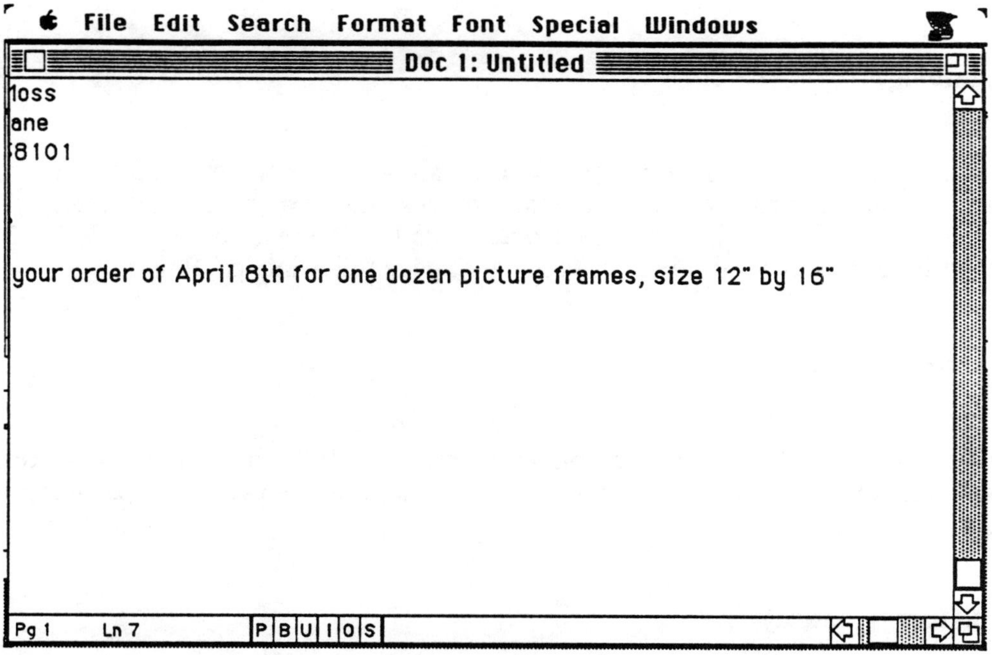

Figure 1.6

13

1 Editing Skills

The current setting of WordPerfect allows you to type lines of text that are wider than can be displayed in the window. (This is true if you are using the Apple ImageWriter. If you are using the Apple LaserWriter or have your system set up as such, you will not encounter this problem. LaserWriter users can ignore sections of this chapter discussing horizontal scrolling problems of the ImageWriter.)

As your text reaches the right side of the window, WordPerfect shifts the screen display to the right, allowing you to see the far right side of the line. This procedure is referred to as **horizontal scrolling**. Horizontal scrolling permits you to create documents that are wider than the display window. WordPerfect normally defaults to a margin setting of 1" for both the left and right margins. It is assumed that you are using a sheet of paper that is 8.5" wide. If 1" is used for the left margin and 1" for the right margin, the total length of the line is 6.5". Unfortunately, the Macintosh screen displays a window slightly smaller than 6.5"—about 6-3/8", which means that when you work at the standard margin size, a small portion of each full line will be cut from view. Continue by entering

, catalog

At this point, you have finally reached the maximum width for a line of text. Word-Perfect automatically ends the line and moves your text to the next line in the document. The width of the line is determined by the margins (see Chapter 3). Continue the entry. Remember to leave a space following "catalog."

number 13-126.

Once the end of the first paragraph has been reached, you must press the Return key. Entering a second Return will leave a blank line between the paragraphs. Enter

[Return] [Return]

Editing Skills 1

Then, enter the following paragraph:

These frames come in three different finishes: ebony, walnut and maple. Please indicate on the enclosed form which finish or finishes you want and return it to us in the enclosed envelope. [Return] [Return]

The screen should resemble the following:

```
 File  Edit  Search  Format  Font  Special  Windows
═══════════════════════ Doc 1: Untitled ═══════════════════════
Miss Marilyn Moss
268 Meadow Lane
Memphis, TN 38101

Dear Ms. Moss,

Thank you for your order of April 8th for one dozen picture frames, size 12" b
catalog number 13-126.

These frames come in three different finishes: ebony, walnut and maple. Pleas
indicate on the enclosed form which finish or finishes you want and return it
in the enclosed envelope.

|

Pg 1   Ln 14      P B U I O S
```

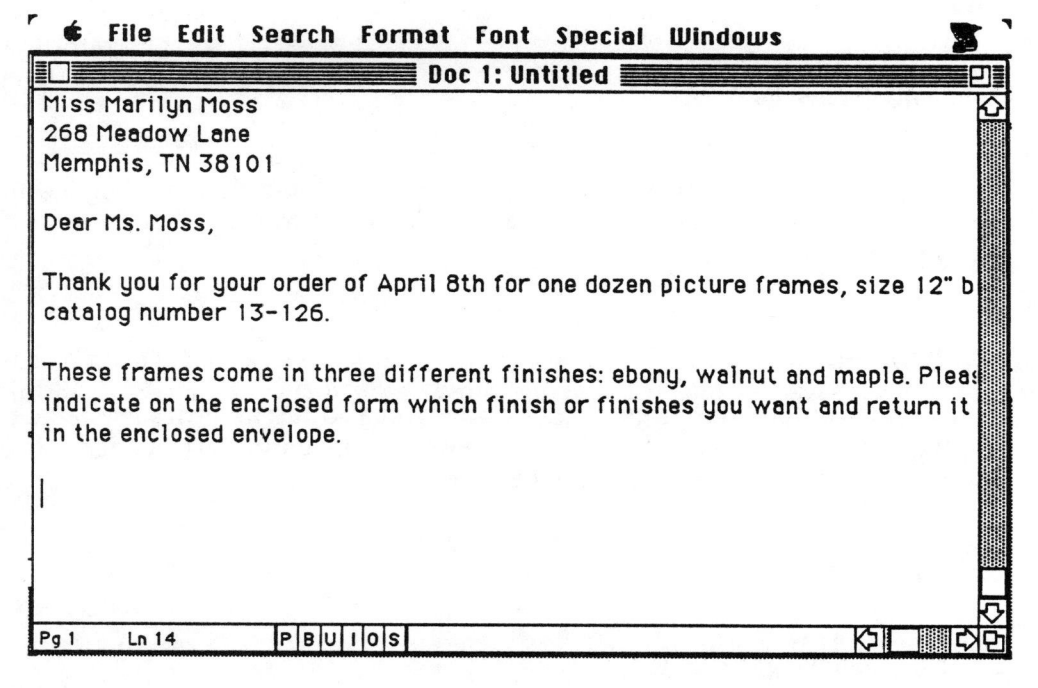

Figure 1.7

Inserting Text in Paragraphs

Earlier, you learned to insert text in short lines. WordPerfect allows you to insert text in paragraphs; doing so, however, may require that you reformat the paragraph to accommodate the new text.

1 Editing Skills

For example, suppose you realize that you forgot to enter another choice—mahogany finish—into the list. At this point, line 11 begins with the word "indicate" and line 12 with the word "in." To change the cursor position:

| **Point** at "e" in "ebony" |
| **Click** |

Enter

mahogany,[space bar]

If you look at the beginning of lines 11 and 12, you will notice that they begin with the new words. WordPerfect automatically adjusts lines when you add new text to any paragraph.

Hyphenation

In addition to automatic line endings, WordPerfect also automatically hyphenates long words that fall at the ends of lines. To make a more uniform right edge, move the cursor to the end of the document by pressing

[Enter] [Enter] ↓

Enter the following text:

Your prompt cooperation in returning the order form will assure you of satisfactory service

This time, something different happened when you entered the words "satisfactory service." WordPerfect split the word "satisfactory" so that part of the word remained on line 14 and part was placed on line 15.

Editing Skills 1

```
  File   Edit   Search   Format   Font   Special   Windows
══════════════════════════ Doc 1: Untitled ══════════════════════════
Miss Marilyn Moss
268 Meadow Lane
Memphis, TN 38101

Dear Ms. Moss,

Thank you for your order of April 8th for one dozen picture frames, size 12" b
catalog number 13-126.

These frames come in three different finishes: ebony, walnut and maple. Pleas
indicate on the enclosed form which finish or finishes you want and return it
in the enclosed envelope.

Your prompt cooperation in returning the order form will assure you of satisf
tory service

Pg 1   Ln 15      P B U I O S
```

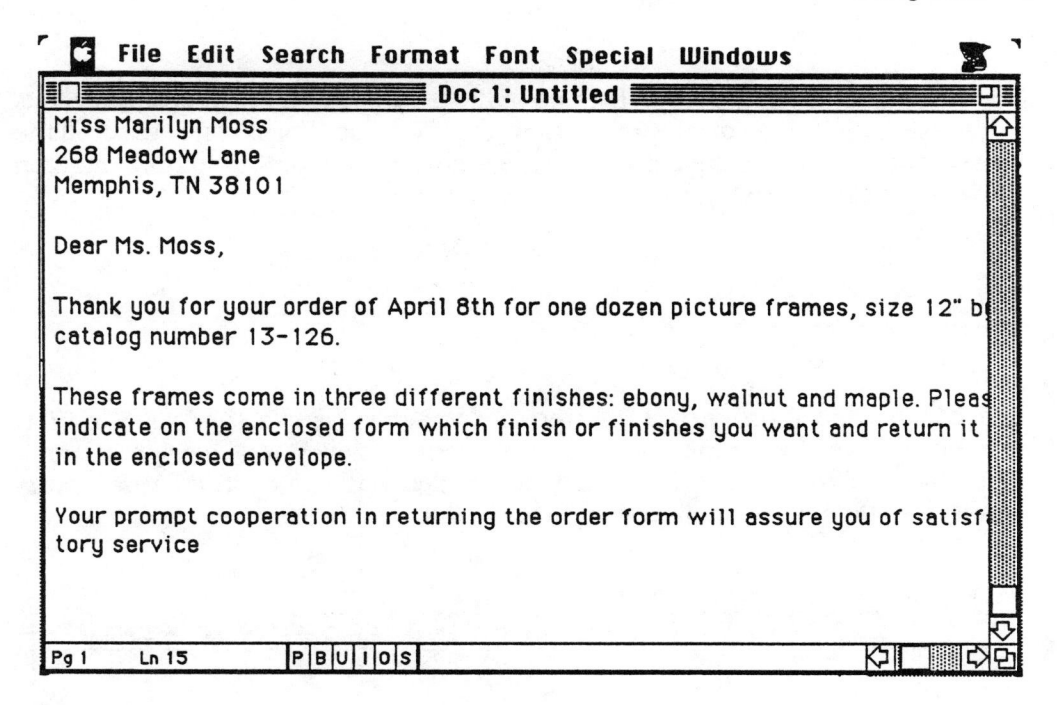

Figure 1.8

To see the hyphen, change the cursor position so that WordPerfect will scroll the screen to the right. Move the cursor to the beginning of the line by entering

[Enter] [Enter] ←

Move the cursor back to the previous line by entering

←

1 Editing Skills

Now the cursor is positioned at the end of the previous line, but WordPerfect has not scrolled the screen display to the far right. To force WordPerfect to scroll the screen, you must move the cursor into the visible portion of the window and then move it back to the right. Enter

    ←   (3 times)
    →   (2 times)

You can see that WordPerfect inserted the hyphen in "satisfactory" so as to fit as much of the word onto the line as possible without going past the right margin. Without hyphenation, the line would have ended with the word "of," and "satisfactory" would have been placed on the next line.

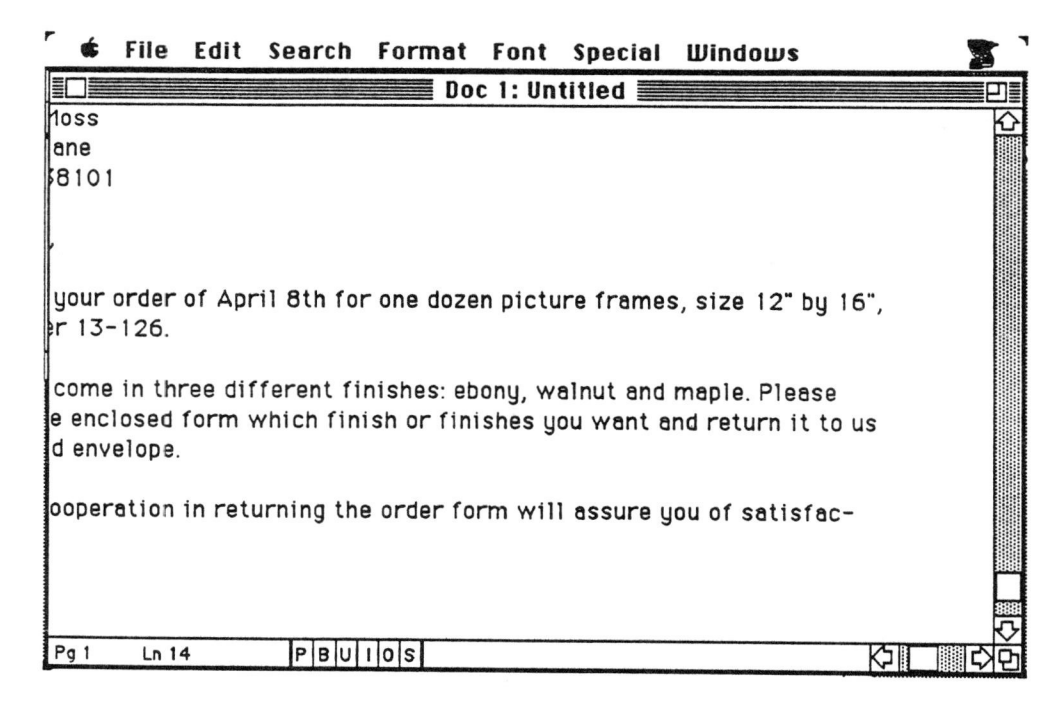

Figure 1.9

Complete the paragraph by moving to the end of the document and entering

[Enter] [Enter] ↓
.   (a period)
[Return] [Return]

Repeating a Character

Now that you are ready to close the letter, indent the text from the left margin. To perform this task, simply enter 50 spaces to fill in part of the line. WordPerfect has a special command — Escape — that will repeat a given character a specified number of times. The first step is to set the repeat command at the proper number — in this case, 50. Enter

[Esc]

Your screen should resemble the following:

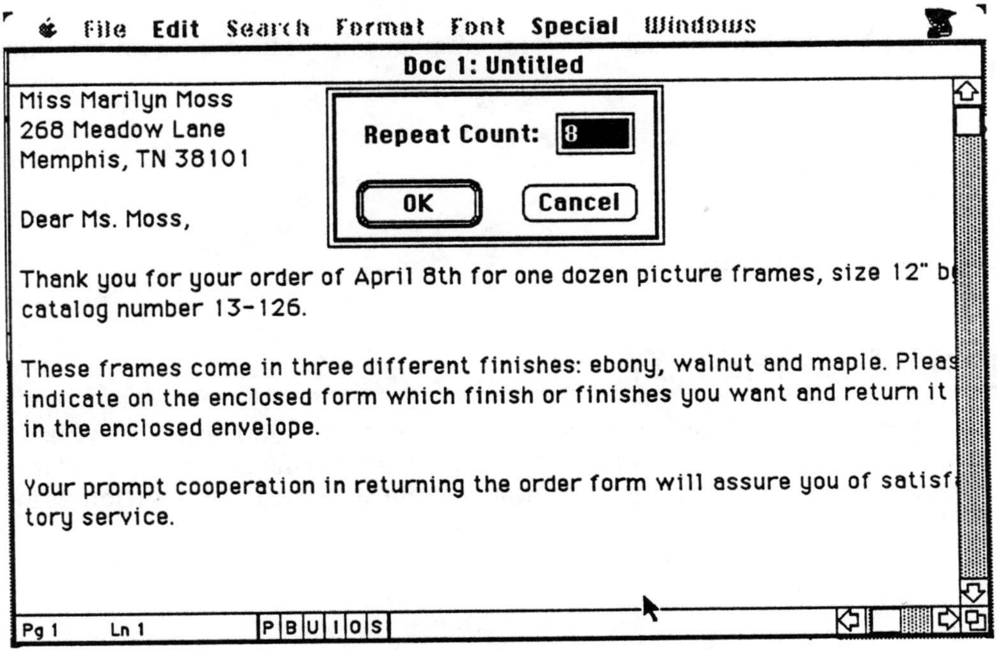

```
 🍎  File  Edit  Search  Format  Font  Special  Windows
┌─────────────────── Doc 1: Untitled ───────────────────┐
│ Miss Marilyn Moss                                     │
│ 268 Meadow Lane      ┌─Repeat Count: [8]─┐            │
│ Memphis, TN 38101    │                   │            │
│                      │   [ OK ]  [Cancel]│            │
│ Dear Ms. Moss,       └───────────────────┘            │
│                                                       │
│ Thank you for your order of April 8th for one dozen picture frames, size 12" b│
│ catalog number 13-126.                                │
│                                                       │
│ These frames come in three different finishes: ebony, walnut and maple. Pleas │
│ indicate on the enclosed form which finish or finishes you want and return it │
│ in the enclosed envelope.                             │
│                                                       │
│ Your prompt cooperation in returning the order form will assure you of satisf │
│ tory service.                                         │
│                                                       │
│ Pg 1   Ln 1        |P|B|U|I|O|S|                      │
└───────────────────────────────────────────────────────┘
```

Figure 1.10

1 Editing Skills

WordPerfect displays a dialog box at the top of the screen showing the **repeat count** for the Escape command. The number of repetitions is normally set to 8. To change that setting to 50, enter

50 [Return]

Now that the count has been set to the proper number, you can enter a block of characters by simply pressing the Esc key and entering the character you want repeated. Unfortunately, the Esc command will not work with the Return key because the Return key is used to set the repeat value. To insert 50 spaces, enter

[Esc] [space bar]

The cursor moves 50 spaces to the right. Enter

Sincerely yours, [Return] [Return] [Return]

Press the Esc key again to add the same number of spaces to the next two lines. Enter

[Esc] [space bar]
Oscar La Fish [Return]
[Esc] [space bar]
Sales Manger [Return]

ENHANCING THE TEXT

Word processors provide a wide variety of operations and features to enhance text. These features go beyond inserting and deleting. There are two major areas in which WordPerfect can help you improve your document: text attributes and reference help.

Editing Skills 1

Text attributes   The Macintosh (with WordPerfect) can provide a variety of character fonts and styles.

Reference tasks   Operations in which WordPerfect functions as a reference to help you find words (Thesaurus), check your spelling (Dictionary), or insert the current time or date (Clock).

Begin by moving the cursor to the top of the document. Enter

[Enter] [Enter] ↑

Most business letters are printed on letterhead stationery embossed with the company's name and address. Suppose, however, that no letterhead is available. Print enhancements available in WordPerfect can help you create a suitable letterhead as part of a document.

The first step is to enter the letterhead's text:

THE HANOVER PICTURE FRAME COMPANY [Return]
1432 Woodland Road [Return]
Nashville, TN 37202 [Return] [Return]

Changing Print Styles

At this point, the letterhead appears much like the text of the document, but WordPerfect allows you to change that format. Return again to the top of the document by entering

[Enter] [Enter] ↑

The key to changing the style of text is to select the text. **Selection** refers to the process in which a portion of the text is highlighted and then modified by style changes. The rest of the document remains as it is. WordPerfect allows you to select text with keyboard commands or with the mouse. To begin, try the mouse method.

21

1 Editing Skills

To select with the mouse, point at the first character you want to select and then drag the mouse to the last character in the group. These characters and all highlighted characters between them constitute the selection.

> **Point** at the "T" in "THE HANOVER"
> **Drag** the mouse to the end of the line
> **Release** the button

The text on the first line will be highlighted. You are now ready to change the style of the text.

Selection Using the Mouse

To make changing type styles as simple as possible, WordPerfect displays a series of "buttons" across the bottom of the window.

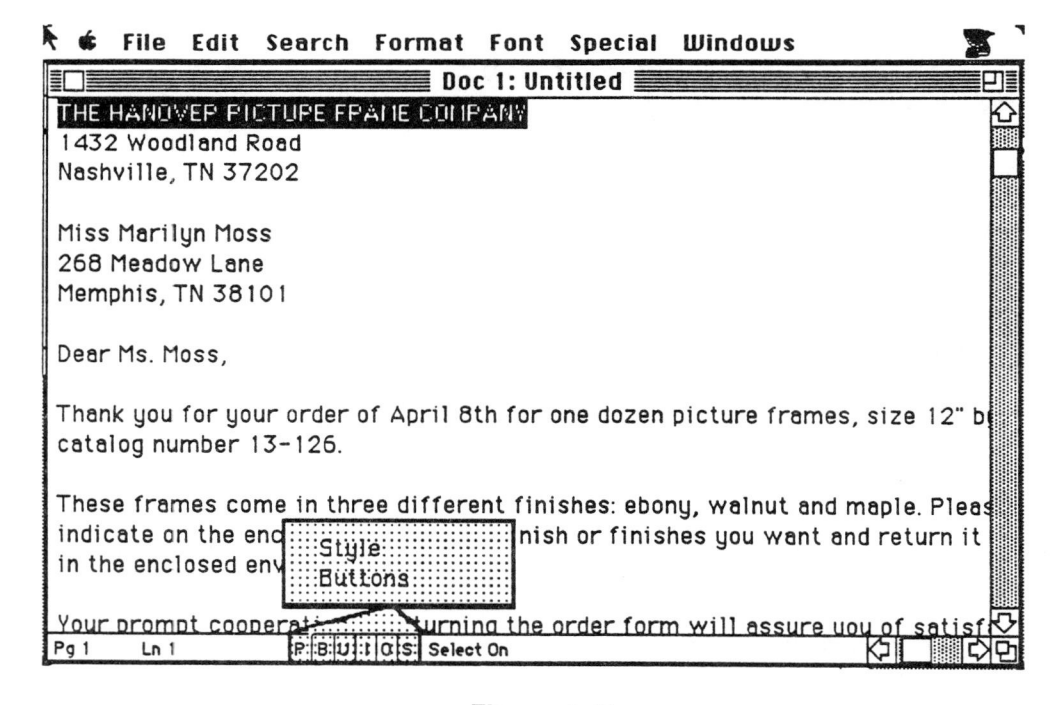

Figure 1.11

Editing Skills **1**

The buttons stand for the following attributes:

P   Plain text. (Use this button to reset text to its original plain style.)
B   Bold print
U   Underlined text
I   Italic print
O   Outline text
S   Shadow print

Suppose you wanted to change the style of the name of the company to shadow text:

```
Point at "S"
Click
```

WordPerfect changes the highlighted text to the outline style.

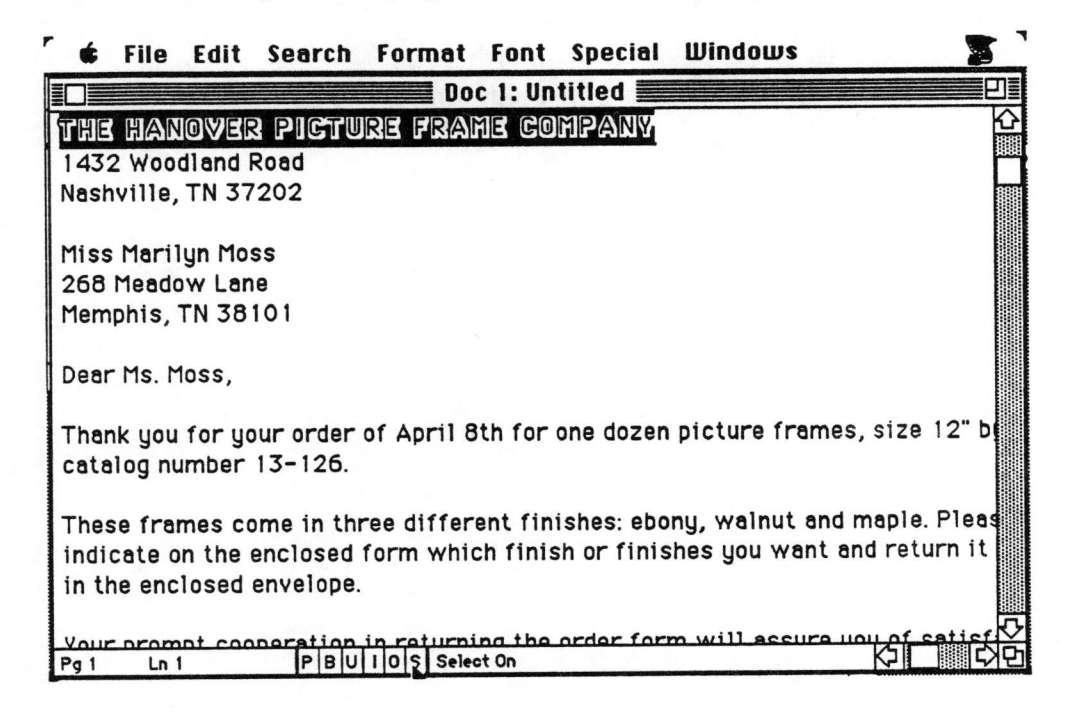

Figure 1.12

1 Editing Skills

You can combine style attributes by clicking additional style characteristics. For example, you can add italics to the shadow:

```
Point at "I"
Click
```

Add bold to the other attributes:

```
Point at "B"
Click
```

To more clearly visualize what the text looks like, remove the selection highlight by entering

→

The document should now resemble the following:

Editing Skills 1

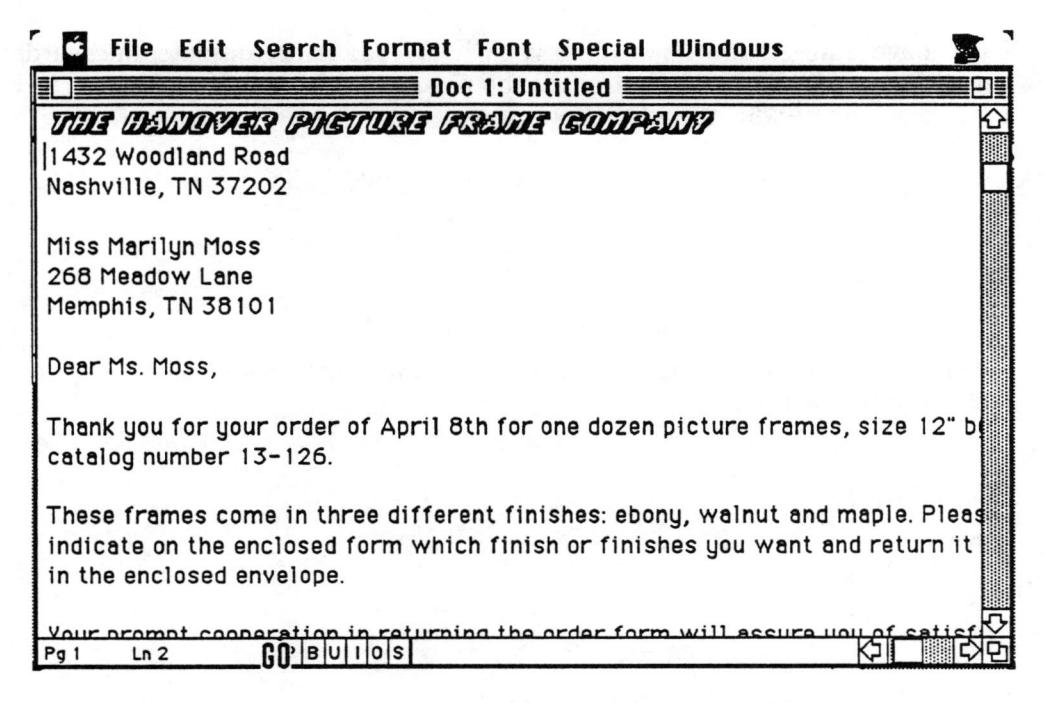

[Screenshot of a WordPerfect document window titled "Doc 1: Untitled" showing a letter from The Hanover Picture Frame Company, 1432 Woodland Road, Nashville, TN 37202, addressed to Miss Marilyn Moss, 268 Meadow Lane, Memphis, TN 38101, beginning "Dear Ms. Moss, Thank you for your order of April 8th for one dozen picture frames..."]

Figure 1.13

Selection Using the Keyboard

While selection with the mouse is quick and easy, WordPerfect also provides a method of selecting text by using the keyboard.

Keyboard selection requires that you turn on the selection, highlight the appropriate area of text by moving the text cursor, perform your operations, and then turn off the selection. The advantage of keyboard selection is that you can use the arrow keys to control the selection by character, word, or line more precisely than you can with the mouse.

To turn the selection on, you must enter a key combination that requires you to simultaneously hold down the Apple key and Shift key and then press the letter "n." Enter

[Apple/Shift/n]

25

1 Editing Skills

If you have entered the keystroke properly, WordPerfect displays the words "Select On" on the bar at the bottom of the window, which tells you that any text cursor movements will expand the selection.

Suppose you want to format the next two lines as bold-italic. Enter

↓↓

The highlight extends over both lines. You can now choose the text attributes you want for that selection:

```
Point at "B"
Click
Point at "I"
Click
```

Turn off the selection by entering the same keystroke that you used to turn on the selection:

[Apple/Shift/n]

The selection highlight is removed from the text. The document resembles the following:

Editing Skills **1**

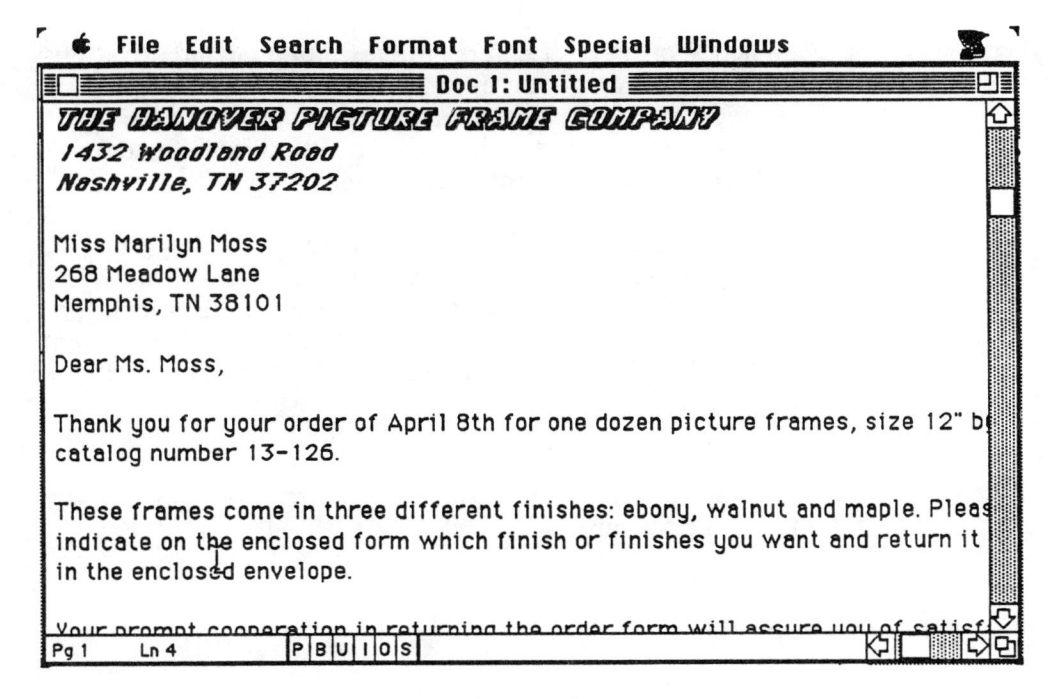

```
 ★  File  Edit  Search  Format  Font  Special  Windows
═══════════════════════ Doc 1: Untitled ═══════════════════════
```
THE HANOVER PICTURE FRAME COMPANY
1432 Woodland Road
Nashville, TN 37202

Miss Marilyn Moss
268 Meadow Lane
Memphis, TN 38101

Dear Ms. Moss,

Thank you for your order of April 8th for one dozen picture frames, size 12" b
catalog number 13-126.

These frames come in three different finishes: ebony, walnut and maple. Plea
indicate on the enclosed form which finish or finishes you want and return it
in the enclosed envelope.

Your prompt cooperation in returning the order form will assure you of satisf

```
Pg 1    Ln 4          P B U I O S
```

Figure 1.14

Inserting the System Date

WordPerfect has a special facility for inserting the current date or time into a document, which is a convenient feature when you are typing a letter. To insert the current date into the letter, add a blank line to separate the date from the company's address. Enter

[Return]

To insert a date, enter

[Apple/d]

WordPerfect displays a menu listing three options at the top of the screen. Dates can be inserted in a document as **date text** or as **date functions**.

27

1 Editing Skills

Date Text   When WordPerfect enters date text, it enters a date based on the current date on the Macintosh's clock. Once inserted, the date text remains the same unless you edit the text. Inserting date text in a document indicates the date that particular document was originally typed.

Date Function   A date function is actually a command instructing WordPerfect to insert the current date into the document, which means that when you store and retrieve the document, the text of the date will be changed automatically. A document with a date function will not retain the original date when it is retrieved.

In this case, insert the date as text so that the date on the letter remains the same if you retrieve the file at a later time.

```
Point at "Insert Text"
Click
```

The date is inserted into the document (of course, your date will be different). Enter another blank line into the letter:

[Return]

The screen should now resemble the following:

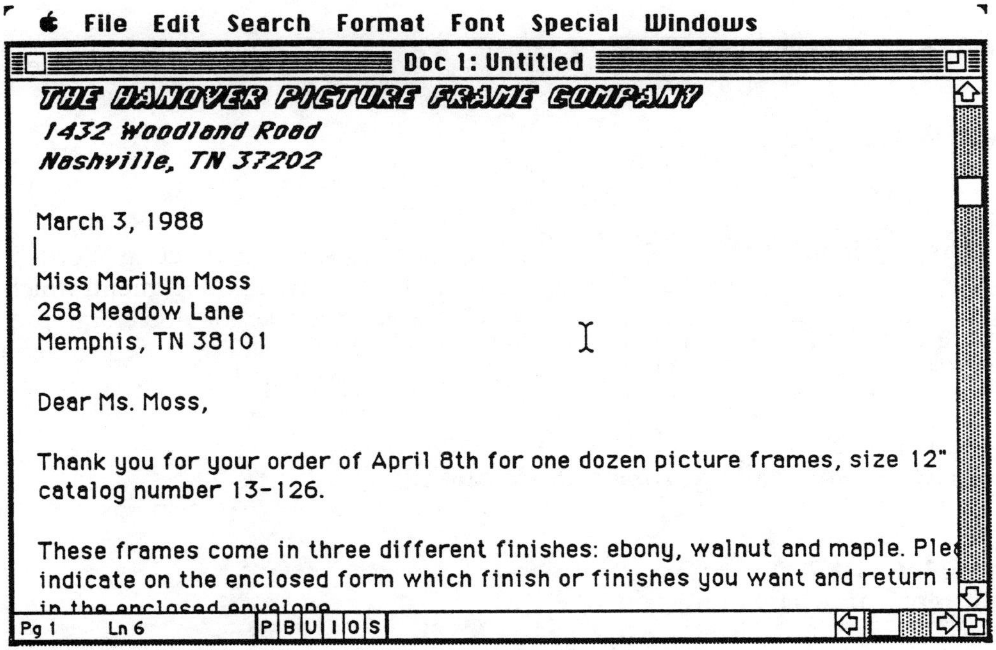

Editing Skills **1**

Figure 1.15

Spell Checking

WordPerfect can also help you catch and correct spelling and typographical errors. To see how a spelling check works, make some intentional mistakes.

Point at the "c" in "catalog"
Click

Delete the word by entering

[Apple/Delete]

29

1 Editing Skills

Enter a misspelled word:

catelog[space bar]

Intentionally misspell another word:

> **Point** at "d" in "different"
> **Click**

Delete the word and replace it with a mistake:

[Apple/delete]
diffrent[space bar]

The Spell check option can be found on the Special menu.

> **Point** at the Special menu
> **Click**
> **Drag** the highlight to Spell
> **Release**

The Spell menu appears on the screen. There are six options — five are currently available. You can choose to check the current page — Check Page — or the entire document — Check Document.

> **Point** at Check Document
> **Click**

When WordPerfect enters the spell check mode, the first word it encounters is "HANOVER."

30

Editing Skills 1

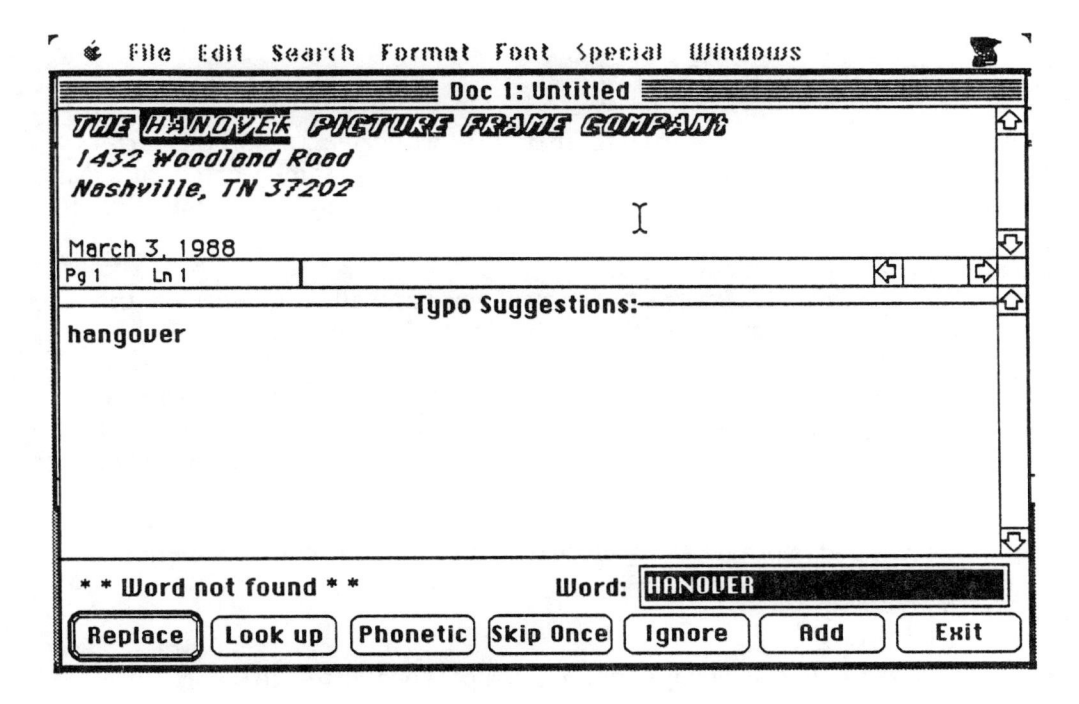

![Figure 1.16 - WordPerfect spell check dialog showing "HANOVER" flagged as word not found, with typo suggestion "hangover" and buttons: Replace, Look up, Phonetic, Skip Once, Ignore, Add, Exit]

Figure 1.16

"HANOVER" — a proper noun — is not found in WordPerfect's dictionary file. In the box labeled Typo Suggestions, WordPerfect lists any words in its dictionary that are close in spelling to the selected word. At the bottom of the display, a series of option buttons is displayed:

Replace This option replaces the highlighted word with one of the words on the list or with a correction that you type in manually.

Look up This option allows you to list words in the dictionary. Look up is helpful when you are not sure about the word or the correct spelling; it allows you to browse through the words in the WordPerfect dictionary in hopes that you will encounter the correct word.

Phonetic This option performs a phonetic search of the dictionary. For example, if you spelled the word with an "f," the phonetic search will locate words that use a "ph."

continued...

1 Editing Skills

...from previous page

Skip Once   This option is used to instruct WordPerfect to skip the current word and continue the spell check. If the same word occurs again in the document, WordPerfect again displays it as a misspelled word.

Ignore   This option skips the current word and all occurrences of the word throughout the remainder of the spell check.

Add   This option adds the current word to the dictionary. The Add option allows you to expand the WordPerfect dictionary to include terms, phrases, and proper nouns that are likely to appear in your documents.

Exit   This option exits spell check and returns to the document.

Because "HANOVER" is a proper noun, instruct WordPerfect to ignore the word.

```
Point at Ignore
Click
```

The program skips the word and continues to search the document for other misspelled words. The next item encountered is "8th." A special box appears at the bottom of the display, informing you that the indicated word contains numbers.

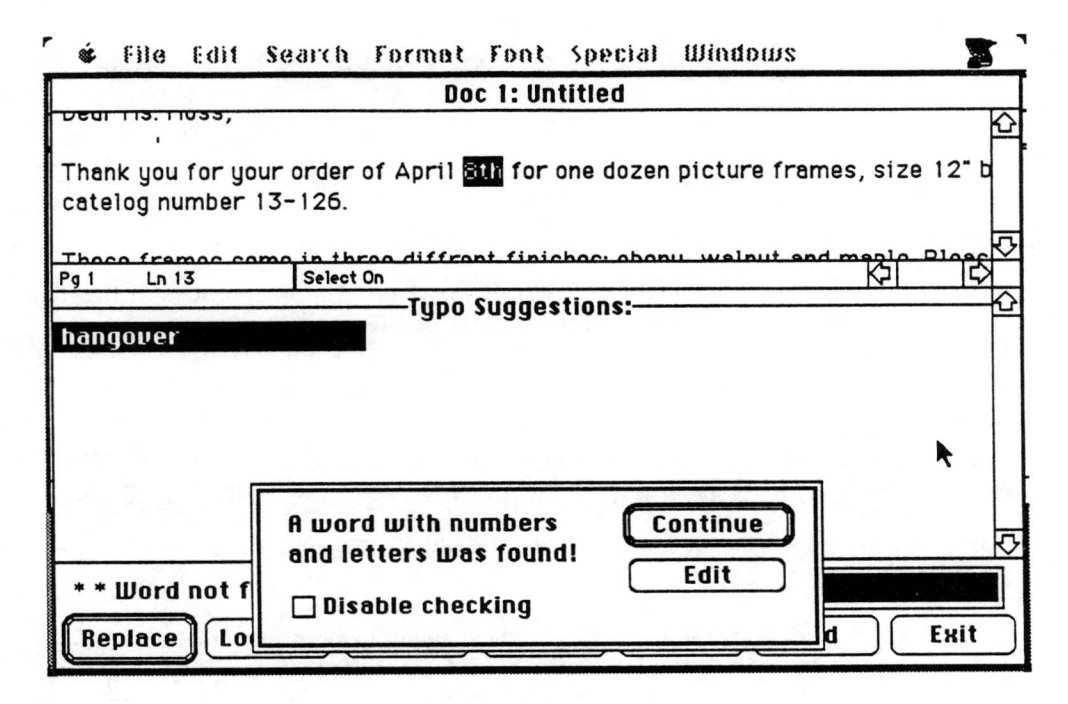

Figure 1.17

Dictionary entries do not contain mixtures of words and numbers. Most word and number combinations are idiosyncratic terms, such as account numbers, and should be excluded from a spell check.

WordPerfect offers three alternatives:

Continue   Instructs WordPerfect to skip the word and continue the spell check.

Edit   Allows you to enter a correction without leaving the spell check.

Disable checking Instructs WordPerfect to ignore all combinations of words and numbers that occur in this document. Choosing this option would tell the program not to stop for other idiosyncratic combinations.

1 Editing Skills

At this point, instruct WordPerfect to skip this word and continue the spell check:

```
Point at Continue
Click
```

As the spell check continues, the program encounters one of the intentional misspellings.

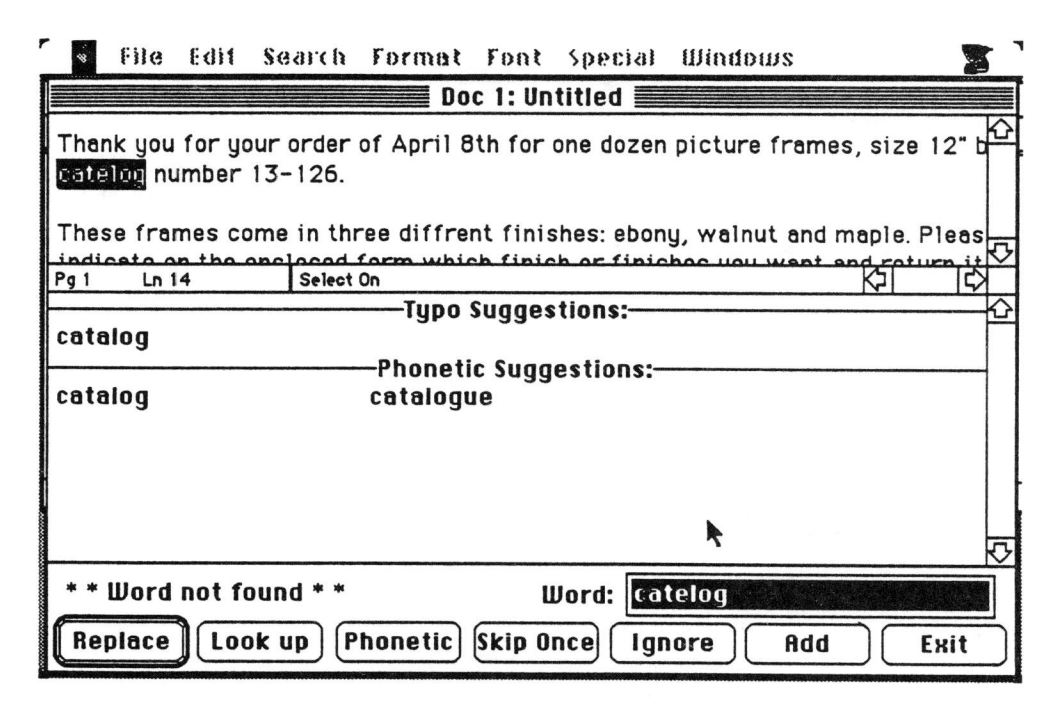

Figure 1.18

WordPerfect has located the misspelled word "catelog." Below the text, two boxes are displayed — one for typographical error corrections, and the other for phonetic corrections. Note that the phonetic corrections include the alternate spelling "catalogue."

Editing Skills **1**

To replace the misspelled word with a correct spelling, select the correction you want to use by clicking on the word:

```
Point at "catalog"
Click
Point at Replace
Click
```

The check continues and stops at the second intentional mistake. WordPerfect displays the correct spelling — "different" — in the typos box. Make the correction:

```
Point at "different"
Click
Point at Replace
Click
```

If you have typed the rest of the document correctly, the spell check reaches the end of the document and displays a message listing the total number of words in the document — 85 in this case. Return to the text entry mode.

```
Point at Exit
Click
```

Note that when the spell check is complete, the cursor remains at the end of the document.

Thesaurus

WordPerfect can also display lists of synonyms. For example, suppose you want to use another word in place of "assure."

The first step is to indicate the word in the document for which you want synonyms displayed.

1 Editing Skills

> **Point** at "assure"
> **Click**

You can place the cursor anywhere in the word. To activate the thesaurus, enter

[Apple/t]

WordPerfect displays three columns at the bottom of the screen. The first column lists words that are synonymous with "assure." Words with dots in front of them are referred to as head words — synonyms for which WordPerfect has additional lists.

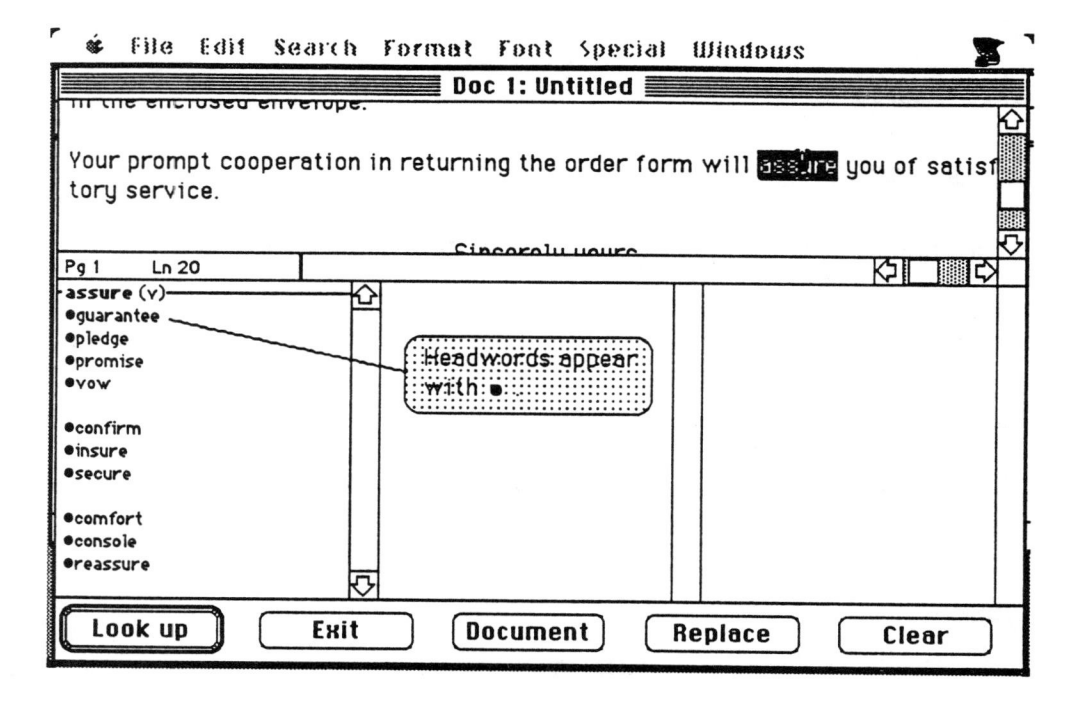

Figure 1.19

Editing Skills **1**

For example, to display additional synonyms for "guarantee,"

> **Point** at "guarantee"
> **Click**

WordPerfect highlights the word. List synonyms for "guarantee," using the Look up option.

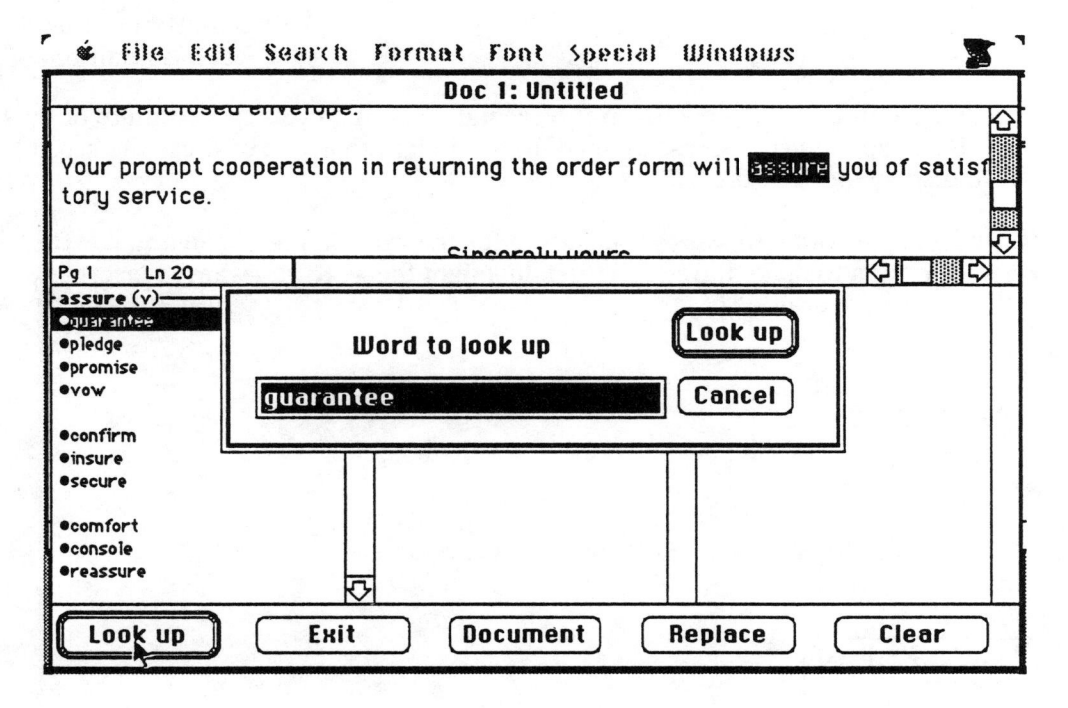

Figure 1.20

37

1 Editing Skills

```
Point at Look up
Click
```

WordPerfect displays another dialog box in the center of the screen. The word "guarantee" is highlighted. For a list of synonyms, use the Look up option in the dialog box (see Figure 1.20).

```
Point at Look up
Click
```

WordPerfect places the new list in the second column so you can examine both lists. Because the list in the second column is longer than the box, use the scroll bar to display more of the list.

If you locate a word you want to substitute for the word in the document, use the Replace option to make the swap. First, highlight the word you want to insert. In this case, use "guarantee."

```
Point at "guarantee"
Click
```

With the word highlighted, select the Replace option.

```
Point at Replace
Click
```

The word "assure" is removed from the text, and the word "guarantee" is inserted in its place.

Editing Skills 1

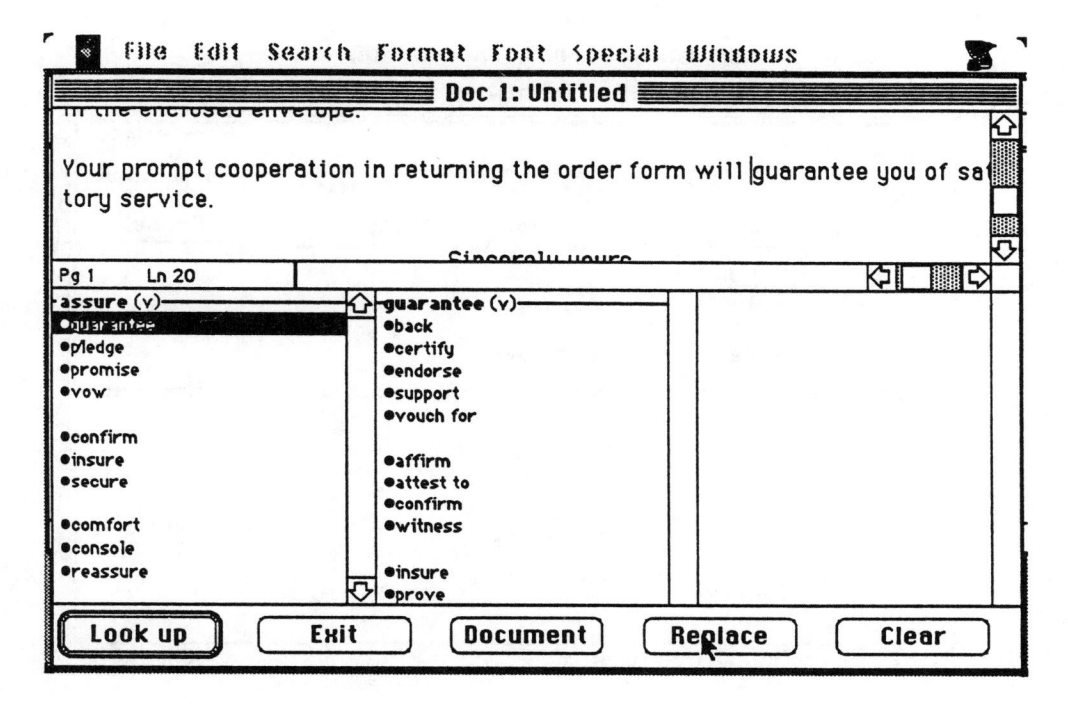

Figure 1.21

To return to the document window, click on the Exit option.

```
Point at Exit
Click
```

PRINTING A DOCUMENT

Once the document is edited and corrected, you can print it. To begin printing, enter

[Apple/p]

WordPerfect displays the menu for the printer:

1 Editing Skills

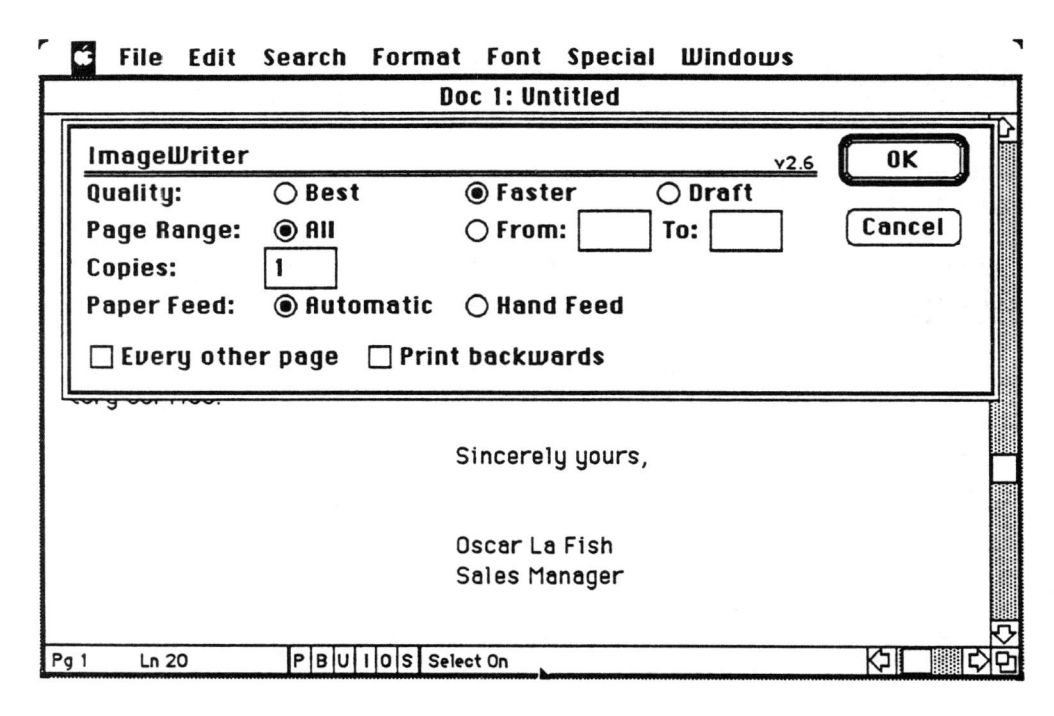

Figure 1.22

To print the document, simply enter

[Return]

The document is sent to the printer. To stop printing, enter

[Apple/.]

SAVING A DOCUMENT

The final step is to save the text file you have created. Up to this point, you have been working with the computer's internal memory. You will now transfer the text in memory to a disk file.

Editing Skills **1**

The Save command is located on the File menu.

> **Point** at File
> **Click**
> **Drag** to Save
> **Release**

WordPerfect displays the Save Document dialog box:

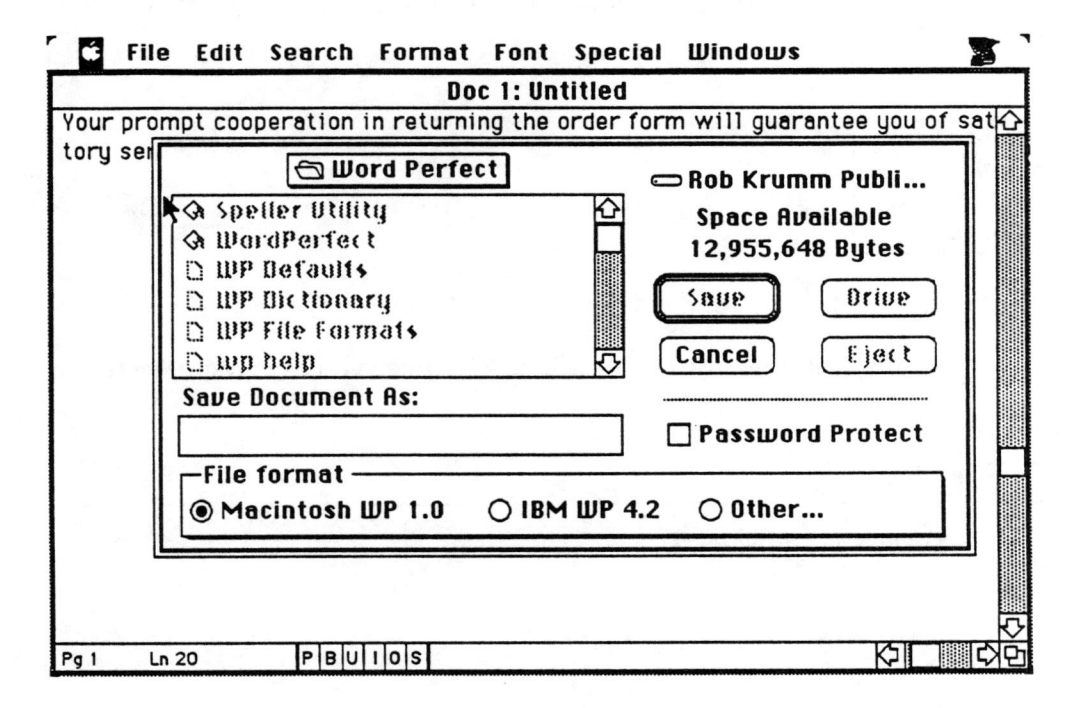

Figure 1.23

To save a file, you must enter a name for the document. Enter

business letter[Return]

41

1 Editing Skills

The text is saved as a disk file, and WordPerfect returns you to the document screen. You can continue to edit, or you can close the window. The Close command is located on the File menu.

Point at File
Click
Drag to Close
Release

To return to the same display that appears when you load the program, open a new document window:

Point at File
Click
Drag to New
Release

The screen displays a new document window in which you can enter new text.

SUMMARY

- **Keyboard Equivalents:**

Move char left	←
Move word left	[Apple/←]
Move end left	[Enter]←
Move char right	→
Move word right	[Apple/→]
Move end right	[Enter]→

- **Insert Text.** WordPerfect operates in an insert mode, which means that all text entered into the document is added, and room is made for that text by extending the length of the document. WordPerfect will add new pages as you fill current pages.

Editing Skills 1

- **Delete Text.** You can delete text by using the Delete or decimal keys.

- **Repeat.** The Esc key is not used to delete or cancel. In WordPerfect, the Esc key is used to repeat a character or directory key a specified number of times.

- **Hyphenation.** WordPerfect automatically hyphenates words that fall into its hyphenation zone. You can turn off hyphenation by using the Line Format command—[Apple/4]5.

- **Enhancements.** WordPerfect allows you to use a variety of styles of text, including bold, italic, underline, shadow, and outline. You can select these styles by using the buttons on the bottom bar or entering keyboard commands such as [Apple/Shift/b] for bold and [Apple/Shift/i] for italic.

- **Spell/Thesaurus.** WordPerfect provides an on-line dictionary and thesaurus. You can invoke the dictionary by pressing [Apple/e] and the Thesaurus by pressing [Apple/t].

CHAPTER 2

MARGINS AND FORMATTING

2 Margins and Formatting

Chapter 1 described the basic editing skills required to create, change, print, and save documents with WordPerfect. This chapter explores the formatting capacities of WordPerfect by demonstrating how to use and control margins to enhance the appearance of your documents.

The assumption is that you have loaded WordPerfect and the Doc 1 window is displayed on your screen. If you have just completed the first chapter, the Doc 1 window should be displayed.

SETTING MARGINS

Previously, you learned that WordPerfect's default margin settings slightly exceed the screen width of the Macintosh and that the screen display scrolls horizontally when you enter lines that occupy the full margin width. WordPerfect uses margins set at a width that makes scrolling necessary because of the default margins used by other versions of WordPerfect, specifically, the MS-DOS versions. Standard MS-DOS screen displays are about 8.5" wide, so a 6.5" line can be fully displayed. WordPerfect is committed to compatibility between all versions of its products.

For this or other reasons, you may want to change the margins used by WordPerfect. WordPerfect includes a Full Screen command that suppresses the display of scroll bars, eliminating the need for horizontal scrolling at the default margins. The Full Screen command is discussed later in this chapter.

To begin this document, you will first create a new set of margins smaller than the default settings for WordPerfect. You can perform this operation from the menu or from the ruler line.

In WordPerfect, margin changes are included in the Page Layout option on the Page Format menu. Display the Page Format menu by entering

[Apple/2]

Option #1 on this menu—Page Layout—controls the margin settings. Enter

1

Margins and Formatting 2

WordPerfect displays the Page Layout dialog box:

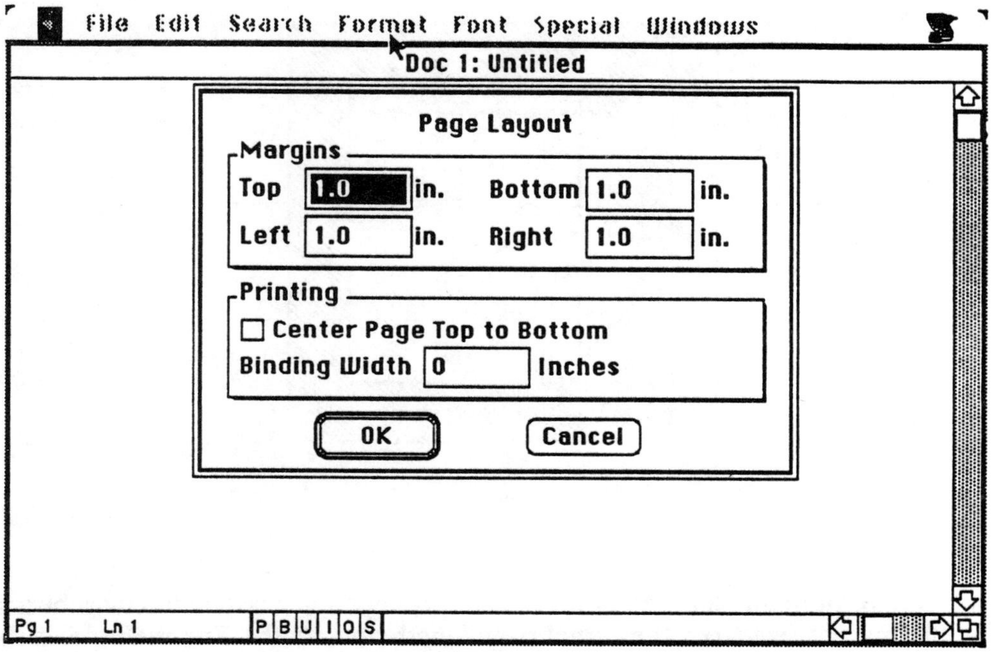

Figure 2.1

The box displays the current values for the left, right, top, and bottom margins. The default setting is 1". WordPerfect assumes that you are printing on standard 8.5" by 11" paper.

2 Margins and Formatting

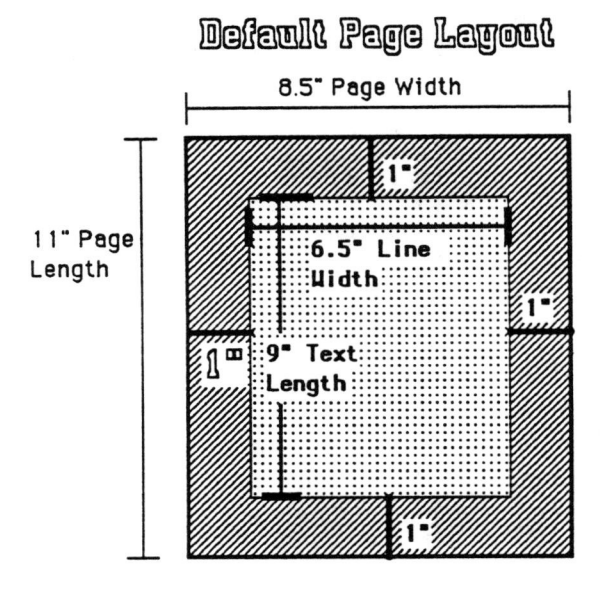

Default Page Layout

Figure 2.2

The actual width and length of the page's working area is calculated by subtracting the margin size from the actual page length and width. For example, if the page width is 8.5" wide, the left margin is 1", and the right margin is 1", then the line width is 6.5".

> Page Width - (Left Margin + Right Margin) = Line Width

In a similar manner, you can determine how long the text on the page is by subtracting the top and bottom margins — 1" each — from the length of the 11" page for a text length of 9".

In this example, increase the left and right margins to 1.25". A new margin is selected by double-clicking on the value:

Point at left margin box
Double Click

48

Margins and Formatting 2

Enter the new value:

1.25

> **Point** at right margin box
> **Double Click**

Enter the new value for the right margin:

1.25 [Return]

The new margins result in a 6" line width that fits on the Macintosh screen without requiring horizontal scrolling.

Now, enter the following paragraph text:

It was only with the advent of computers that people actually tried to create

At this point in the text, you will enter an italic word. To italicize a word, use the print style display at the bottom of the screen. If you are typing text, you might prefer to change print styles with keyboard commands rather than with the mouse. The [Apple/y] key combination displays the Print Style menu. Enter

[Apple/y]

Italic print is listed as option #4. Enter

4

49

2 Margins and Formatting

Enter the word you want italicized:

[space bar]
thinking
[space bar]

To return to normal style text, enter

[Apple/y]
1

Continue by entering the following text:

machines and witnessed

Suppose you want the next word to be bold. WordPerfect provides special keyboard combinations that implement bold, underline, italic, outline, shadow, and overstrike text. The commands are as follows:

Bold	**[Apple/Shift/b]**
Underline	**[Apple/Shift/u]**
Italic	**[Apple/Shift/i]**
Outline	**[Apple/Shift/o]**
Shadow	**[Apple/Shift/s]**
Overstrike	**[Apple/Shift/v]**

To turn on bold text, enter

[Apple/Shift/b]

Margins and Formatting 2

Enter the next phrase in the paragraph:

[space bar]
bizarre variations on
[space bar]

Return to normal text and complete the paragraph. Enter

[Apple/y] 1
the theme of thought. [Return] [Return]

The text resembles the following:

```
 File  Edit  Search  Format  Font  Special  Windows
                    Doc 1: Untitled
It was only with the advent of computers that people actually tried
to create thinking machines and witnessed bizarre variations the
theme of thought.




Pg 1    Ln 5         P B U I O S
```

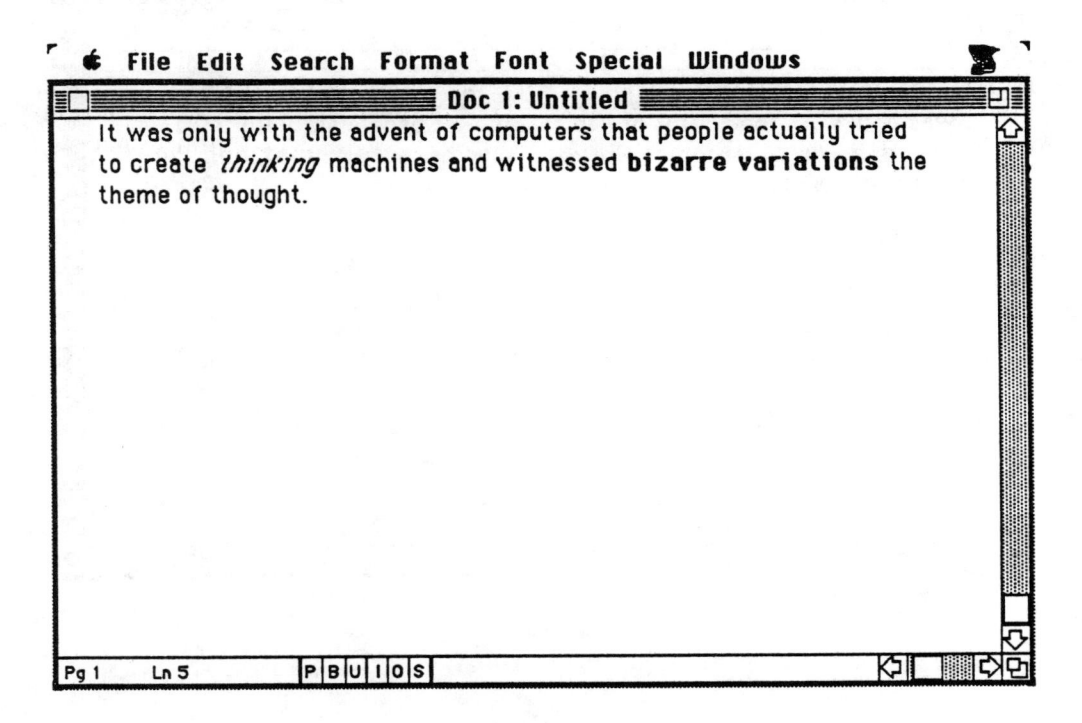

Figure 2.3

2 Margins and Formatting

More Margin Changes

The text you will now enter should be formatted to indicate it is a direct quotation. First, change the margins with the **ruler line**—a special display option that provides a visual method of changing formatting options such as margins and tabs. To maximize the amount of space used for displaying text, WordPerfect does not ordinarily display the ruler line on screen. To display the ruler line, enter

[Apple/r]

The ruler line is inserted at the top of the text display.

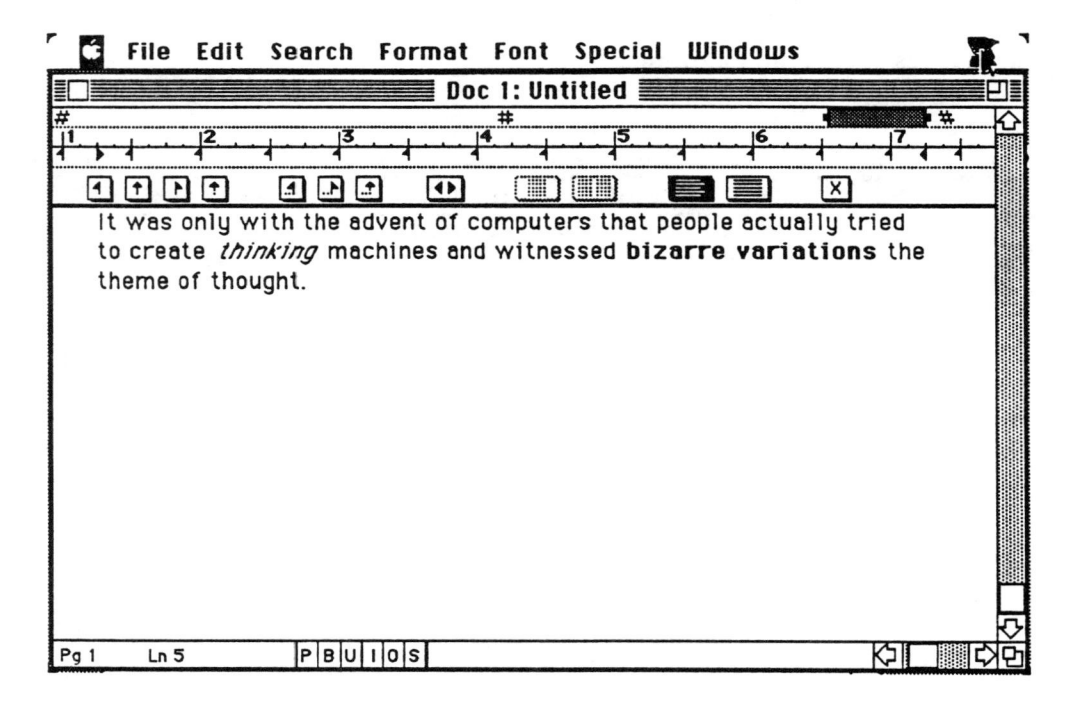

Figure 2.4

The ruler lines display is a very busy one and actually consists of three lines of information.

52

Margins and Formatting **2**

The top line contains # signs to indicate locations for page numbers. You will learn more about page number position in Chapter 4. A dark gray area appears on the right side of the line, marking the H-zone (hyphenation zone). The H-zone is described in detail later in this chapter.

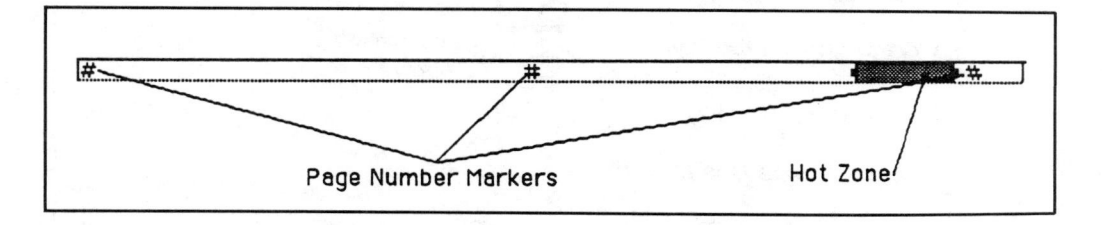

Figure 2.5

The second line of the display looks like a ruler and is marked off in inches, half inches, and quarter inches.

A series of markers appears below the ruler, showing the location of the left margin, the right margin, and current tab stops.

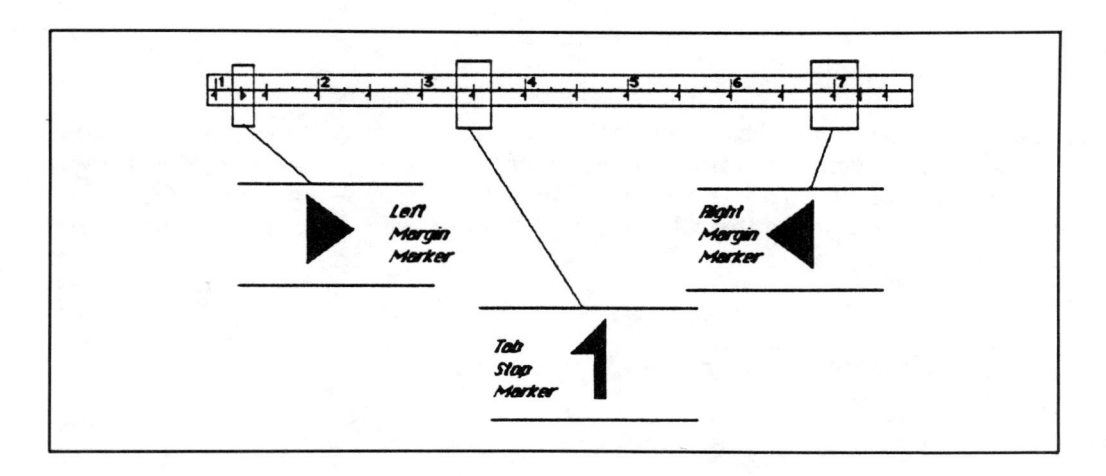

Figure 2.6

53

2 Margins and Formatting

In addition to the three lines, the ruler also displays icons that represent tab, column, and justification operations.

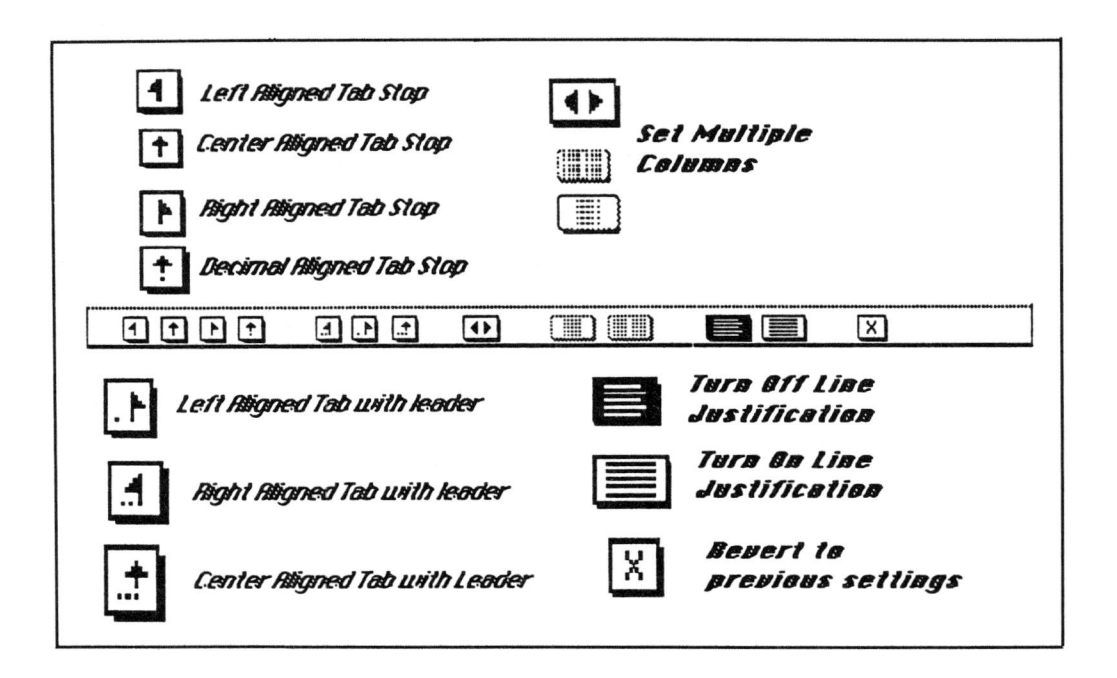

Figure 2.7

Margins can be changed by pointing the mouse at the current margin marker and dragging it to a new position on the ruler line. (When dragging the margin markers, remember that it is the vertical line of the arrow — not the pointed end — that should line up with the ruler marks.) For example, suppose you want to set the new left margin to 2".

> **Point** at left margin marker
> **Drag** the marker to 2 inches

Margins and Formatting **2**

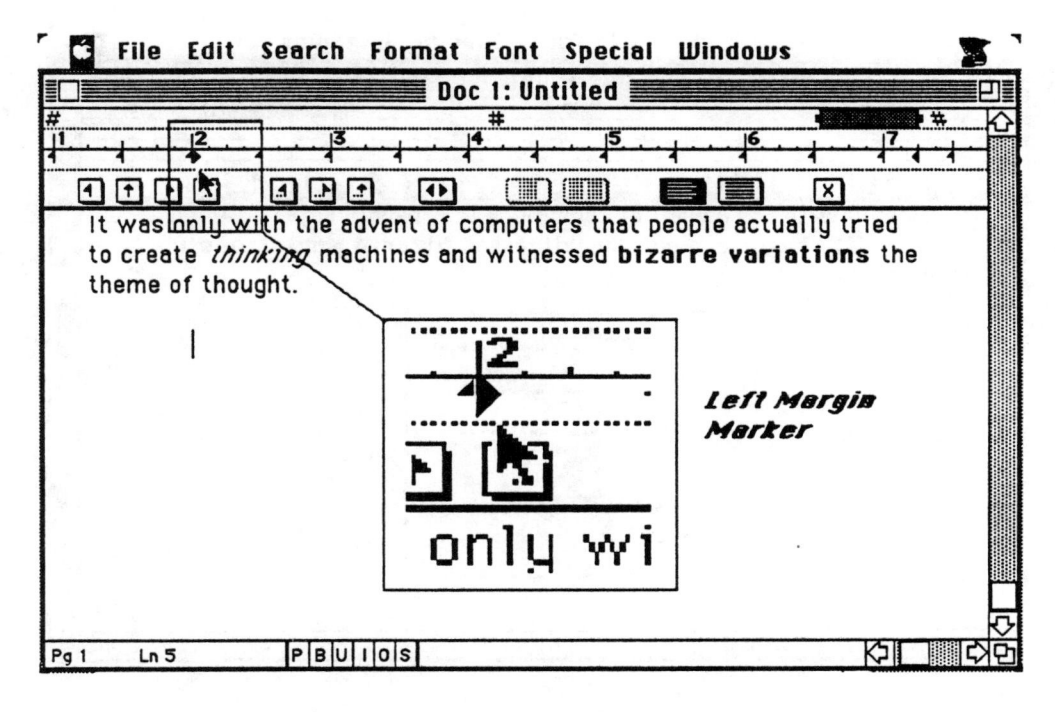

Figure 2.8

Next, use the same method to change the right margin to 6.5".

Point at right margin marker
Drag the marker to 6.5 inches

55

2 Margins and Formatting

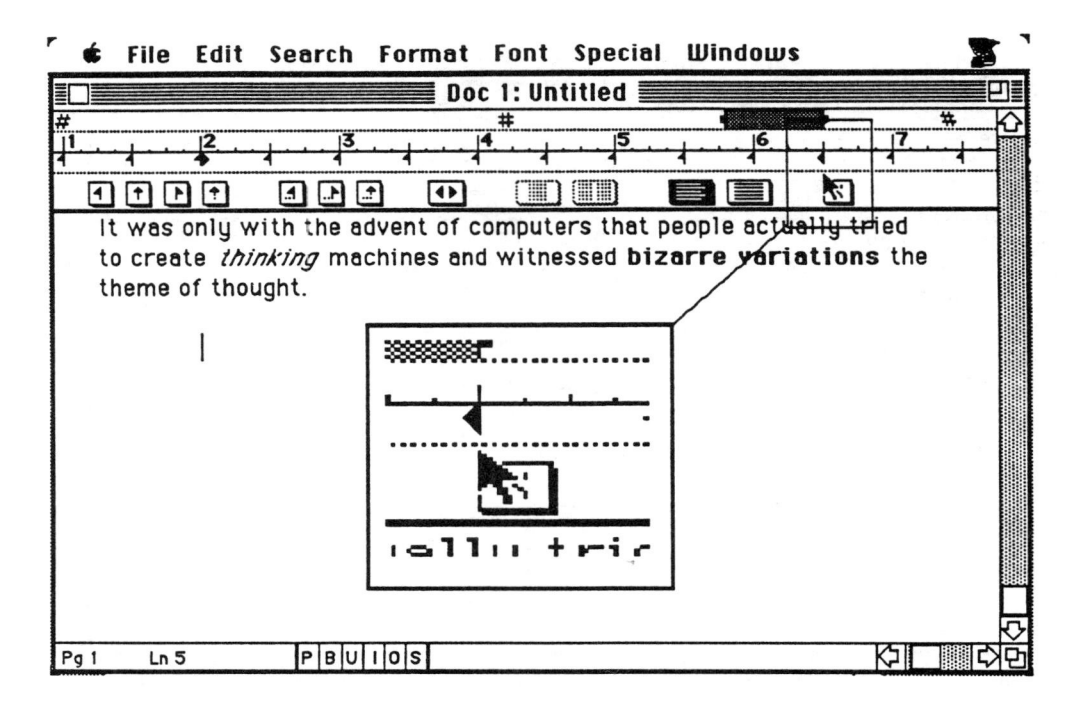

Figure 2.9

Now that you have changed the margins, turn off the ruler display so you can concentrate on text entry. (You can enter text with the ruler displayed if you want.) Enter

[Apple/r]

You have now used both methods of changing margins. While both techniques perform basically the same function, there are important differences between them. In general, it is faster and easier to change margins using the ruler line display. Dragging the margin markers is less precise than entering the exact location. You may have noted that it is not easy to be sure you have aligned the margin marker exactly. Because WordPerfect allows measurements as small as 1/100", it is easy to drag the marker slightly off the mark.

To check the exact location of the margins, use the Page Layout command. Enter

Margins and Formatting **2**

[Apple/2] 1

The display shows the exact location (measured in 1/100ths of an inch) of the current margins. You may find, as shown in Figure 2.10, that your margins are slightly off the 2.00" you intended.

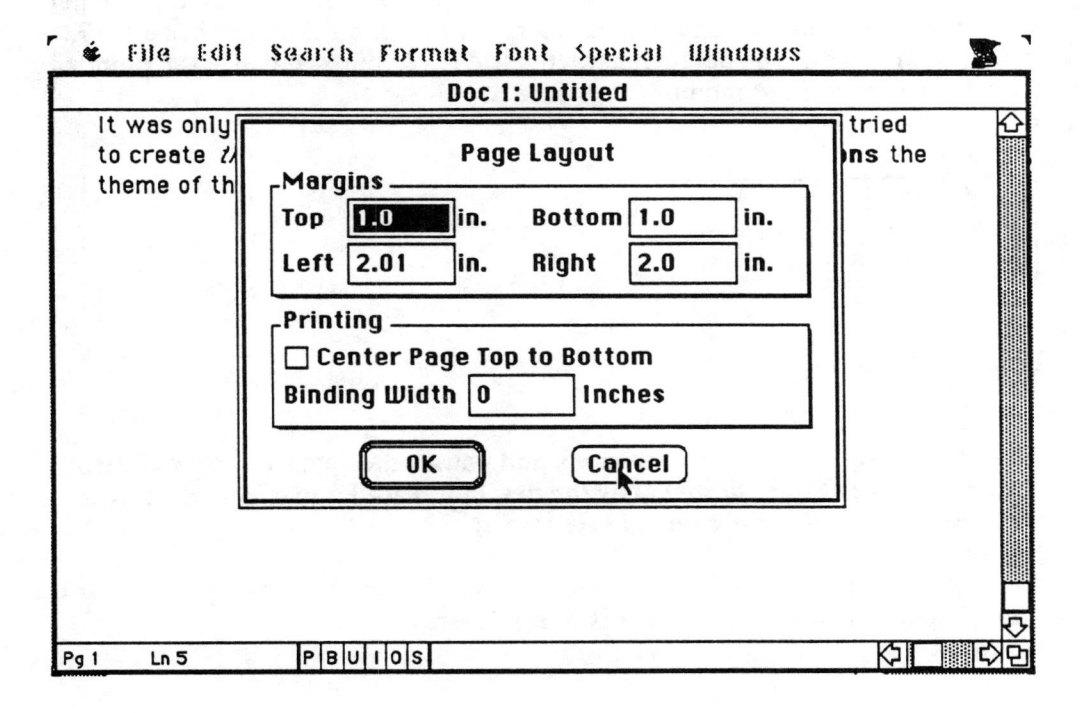

Figure 2.10

It is unlikely that very small errors—such as 1/100"—will have any meaningful effect on your text. For the sake of consistency; however, you might want to change the left and right margins to exactly 2.00".

When you have made these corrections, enter

[Return]

57

2 Margins and Formatting

CHANGING POINT SIZE

In addition to changing margins, you may want to change the size of characters. Making characters larger or smaller adds variety to your document. In this case, reduce the point size of the text, which will allow you to type more text within your margins. **Point size** is a typographical term. Typographers measure the height of characters in points. A point is 1/72" high. Twelve-point characters are 12/72 — or 1/6" — in height. The default character size is 12 points. Change the point size to 10 by using the Font menu.

> **Point** at Font
> **Drag** the mouse to 10
> **Release**

Enter the following text:

All of the idiosyncrasies, the weakness and power, the vagaries and vicissitudes of human thought were hinted at by the new found ability to experiment with the term now called electronic thought. [Return]
[Return]
As a result, we have acquired, in the last twenty years or so, a new perspective on what thought is and what thought is not. [Return]
[Return]

The document should resemble the following:

Margins and Formatting **2**

```
 ⌘  File  Edit  Search  Format  Font  Special  Windows
╞══════════════════ Doc 1: Untitled ══════════════════╡
It was only with the advent of computers that people actually tried
to create *thinking* machines and witnessed **bizarre variations** the
theme of thought.

        All of the idiosyncracies, the weakness and power, the vagaries
        and vicissitudes of human thought were hinted at by the new found
        ability to experiment with the term now called electronic thought.

        As a result, we have acquired, in the last twenty years or so, a new
        perspective on what thought is and what thought is not.

        |

                                                        I

 Pg 1    Ln 1        P B U O S
```

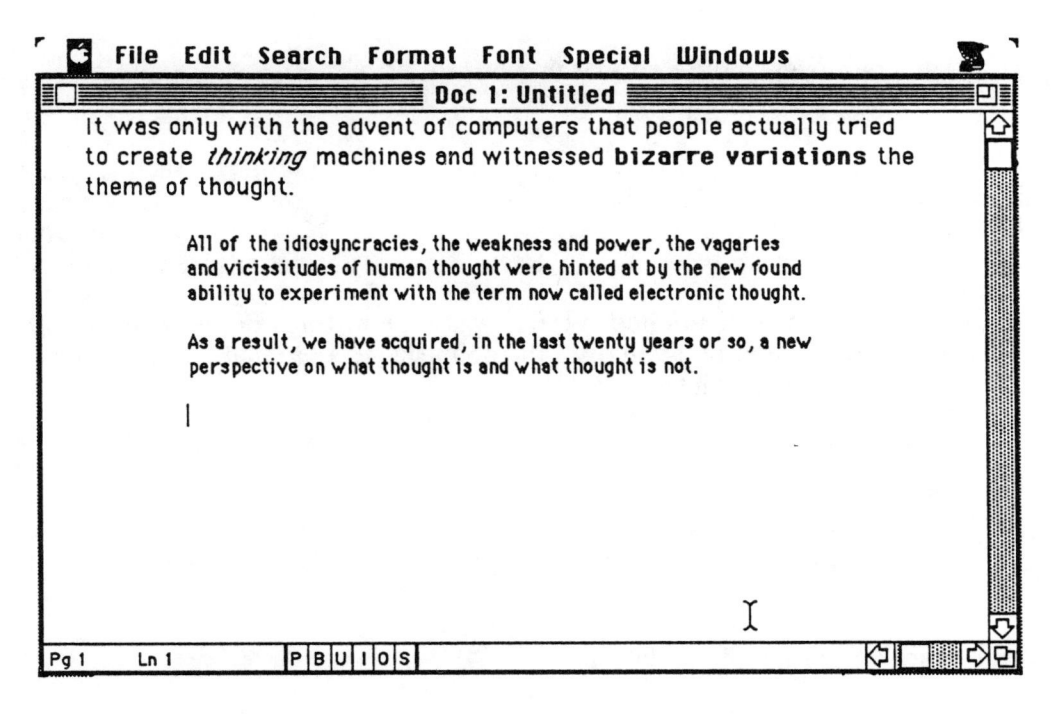

Figure 2.11

You have now reached the end of the quotation. You must change the margins and point size back to the original settings. Begin with the margins. Enter

[Apple/2] 1

You can only make changes in this menu from the keyboard. The Tab key will change the highlight to another margin box. Enter

[Tab]

59

2 Margins and Formatting

The highlight moves to the Left margin box. Enter

1.25
[Tab] [Tab]
1.25 [Return]

The text cursor is now positioned at the new margin setting. Before entering additional text, remember that you reset the point size to 12 to match the point size used in the first paragraph.

> **Point** at Font
> **Drag** to 12
> **Release**

Enter another paragraph:

Computer terminology has become part of our everyday jargon. How often have you heard the word

Change to italicized text by entering

[Apple/Shift/i]
[space bar]
interface
[space bar]

Return to normal text. Enter

[Apple/y] 1

Continue the paragraph by entering

Margins and Formatting **2**

as a synonym for meet, call, or talk.

The document should resemble the following:

```
  File  Edit  Search  Format  Font  Special  Windows
======================= Doc 1: Untitled =======================
It was only with the advent of computers that people actually tried
to create *thinking* machines and witnessed **bizarre variations** the
theme of thought.

        All of the idiosyncracies, the weakness and power, the vagaries
        and vicissitudes of human thought were hinted at by the new found
        ability to experiment with the term now called electronic thought.

        As a result, we have acquired, in the last twenty years or so, a new
        perspective on what thought is and what thought is not.

Computer terminology has become part of our everyday jargon. How
often have you heard the word *interface* used as a synonym for meet,
call or talk.

|
Pg 1   Ln 16      P B U I O S
```

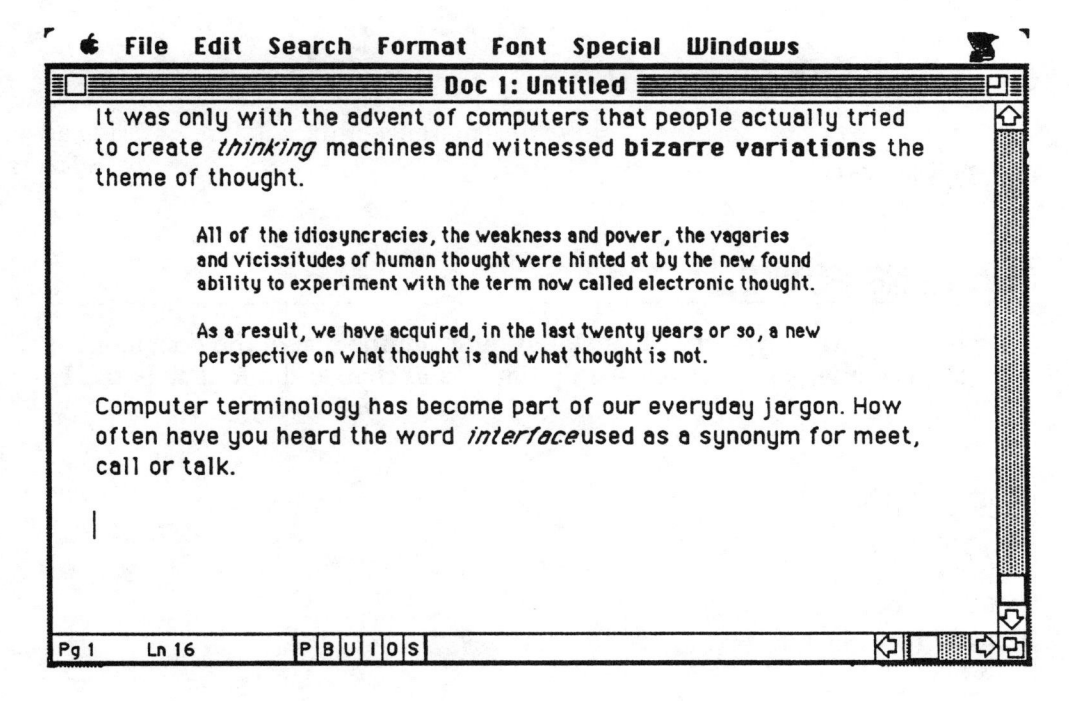

Figure 2.12

ADDING A HEADING

Create a heading for the document. Place the cursor at the beginning of the document. Enter

[Enter] [Enter] ↑

Make room for the heading by entering two blank lines. Enter

[Return] [Return]

61

2 Margins and Formatting

Because the cursor follows along when you enter the returns, move back to the beginning of the document again by entering

[Enter] [Enter] ↑

Create a centered line by entering

[Apple/Shift/c]

CHANGING FONTS

For a heading, use a type style that stands out from the rest of the document. In this case, use a larger point size — 18 points — and change the font style to Helvetica.

```
Point at Font
Drag to 24
Release
Point at Font
Drag to Helvetica
Release
```

Enter the text of the heading:

Perspectives on Thought

As you typed the first letter — "P" — WordPerfect adjusted the height of the line to match the point size. WordPerfect automatically changes the vertical line height to correspond to the new character size.

Margins and Formatting **2**

CONVERTING CASE

WordPerfect includes a command to convert the case of text from uppercase to lowercase, or vice versa. For example, suppose you decide that your heading would look best if it were in all uppercase letters. Select the text you want to convert.

```
Point at "P" in "Perspective"
Click
Drag to the end of the line
Release
```

The Convert command is found on the Edit menu.

```
Point at Edit
Drag to Case Convert
Release
```

WordPerfect displays two options on this menu—To Upper or To Lower. To change to all uppercase, select the To Upper option.

```
Point at To Upper
Click
```

The screen should resemble the following:

2 Margins and Formatting

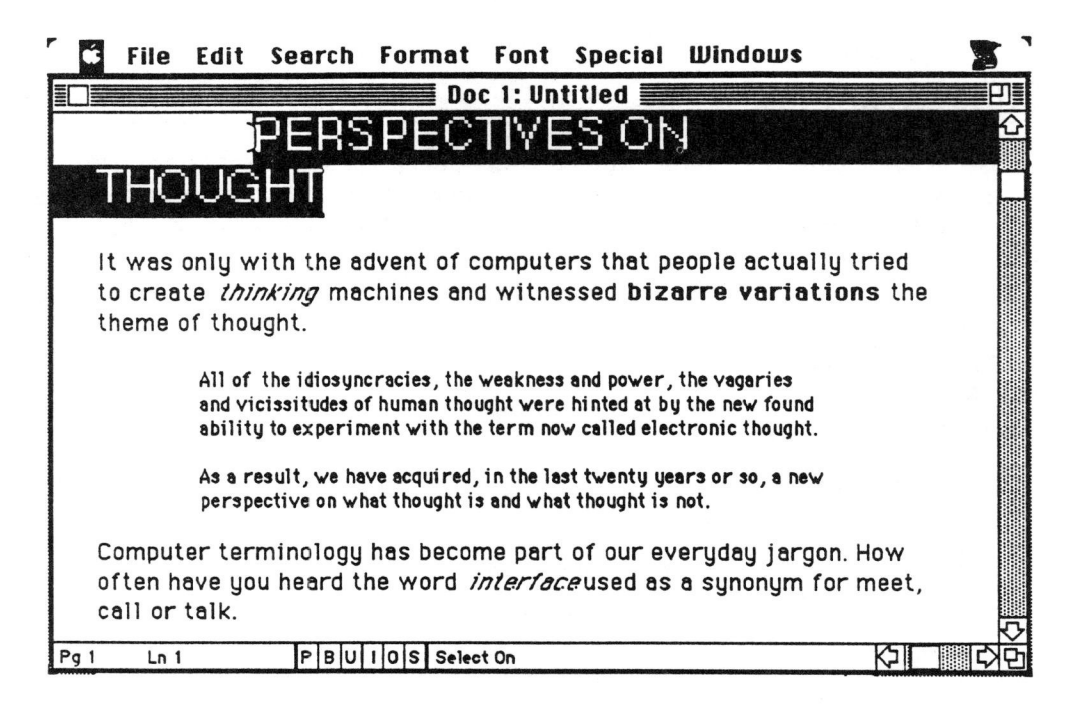

Figure 2.13

WordPerfect carried out your command and converted the title to all uppercase characters, but, in doing so, the program created a problem. In proportionally spaced text, uppercase letters occupy more space than lowercase letters. When you are working with a large point size, the effect of a change in case can dramatically change the width of the line. In this case, WordPerfect was forced to place the word "THOUGHT" on the next line.

There are two options to restore your heading to a single line. You can widen the margins to accomodate the text, or you can change the text to a smaller point size, such as 18. Reduce the point size to 18.

Point at Font
Drag to 18
Release

The heading is reduced in size and now fits within the existing margins.

Margins and Formatting **2**

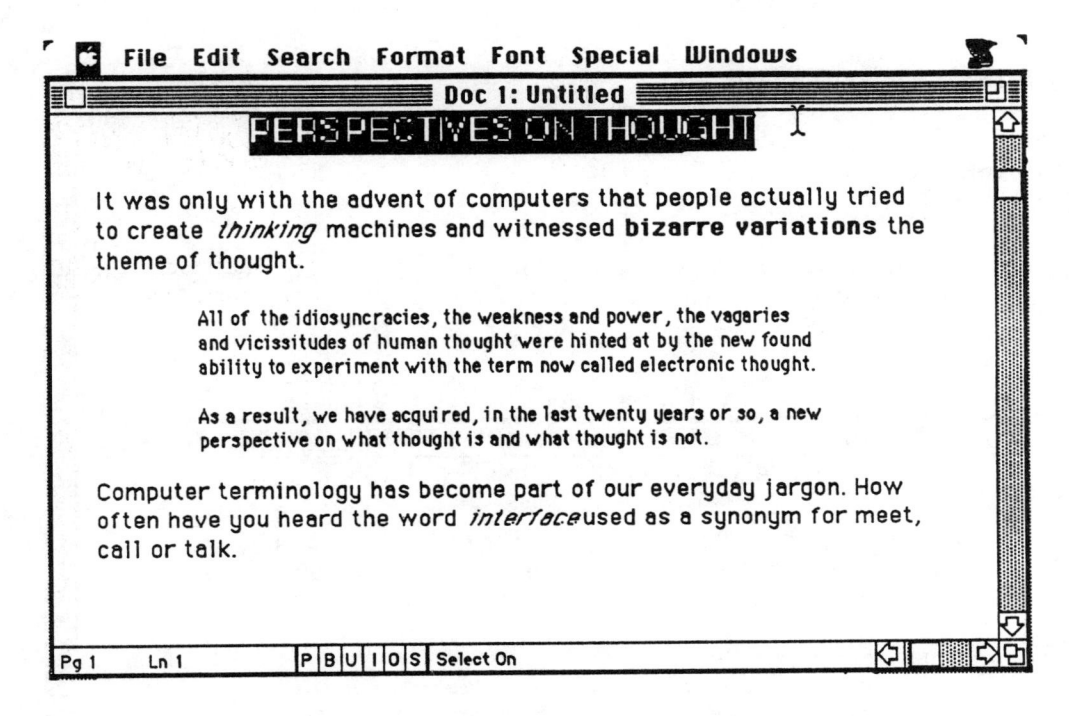

[Screenshot of a document window titled "Doc 1: Untitled" with heading "PERSPECTIVES ON THOUGHT" and body text about computers and thought.]

Figure 2.14

REVISING FORMATTED DOCUMENTS

This current document is different from the business letter created in Chapter 1 because this document contains a variety of formatting changes. The changes affect margins, point size, and text attributes in a variety of combinations. Making changes in a document containing different formats is more complex than revising documents without multiple formats.

As an example, to insert some text at the beginning of "All of the...," use the mouse to position the cursor at the beginning of the paragraph.

Point the mouse just to the left of the letter "A" in the word "All"
Click

65

2 Margins and Formatting

Enter the following text:

Computer based

The new text is added to the document, but it is entered with the wrong margins and character size.

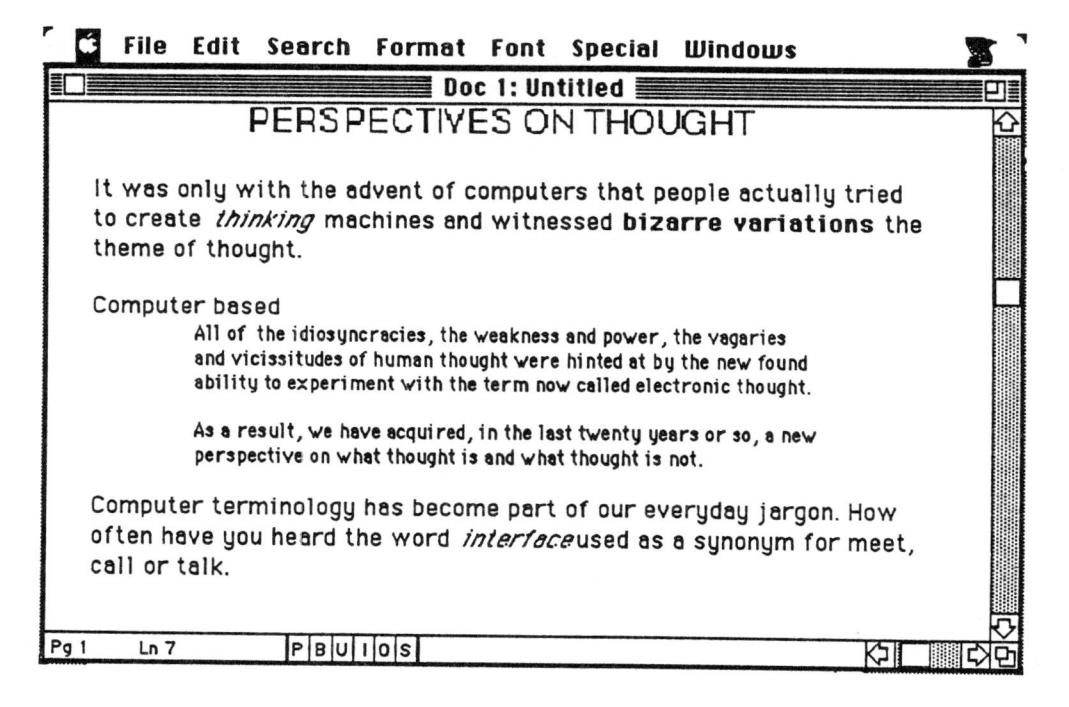

Figure 2.15

Apparently, WordPerfect is using the format of the opening paragraph rather than that of the quotation paragraphs.

WordPerfect Codes

In WordPerfect, all formatting commands, such as margin, font, and point size, result in special **codes** in the text. Codes act as markers that tell WordPerfect how to format a specific section of the document. For example, when you turn on italic text — [Apple/Shift/i] — WordPerfect inserts a code for "begin italic." When you turn off the italic text — [Apple/Shift/i] — WordPerfect inserts a code for "end italic." Each time a command is entered, a code is inserted into the text to record the selected format.

In the normal display mode, WordPerfect does not reveal the location of these codes. To see the codes and their locations, you must use the Reveal Codes display. Enter

[Apple/7]

WordPerfect splits the screen into two windows. The top window shows your document as you are accustomed to seeing it. The bottom window shows a very different type of display.

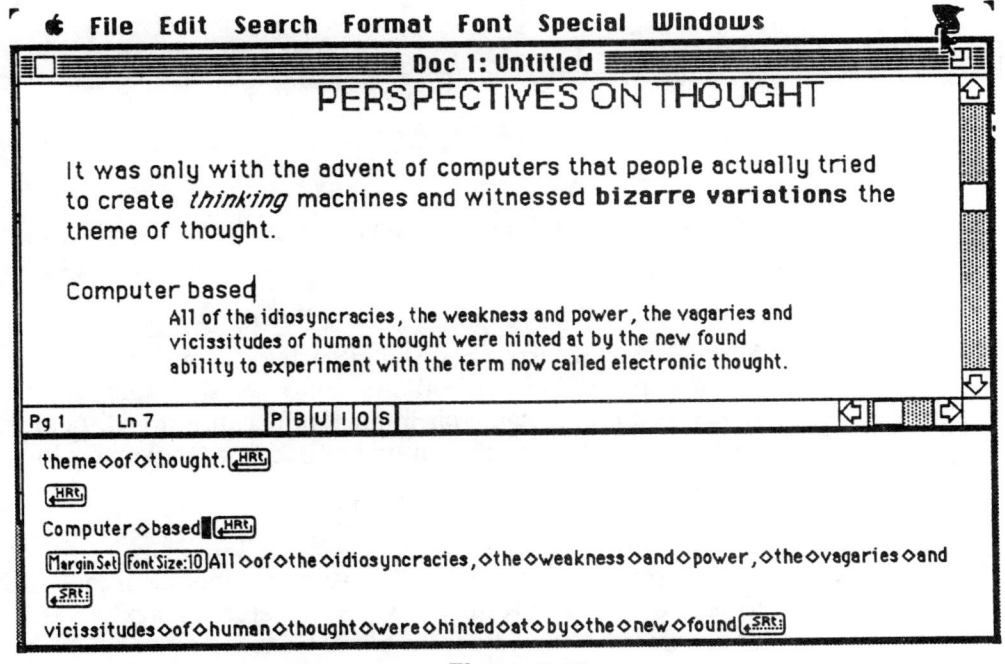

Figure 2.16

2 Margins and Formatting

In the bottom of the screen, the codes display window shows your text and all formatting codes inserted in the text. The codes display usually displays five lines of text: the line on which the cursor is positioned and two lines above and below that location.

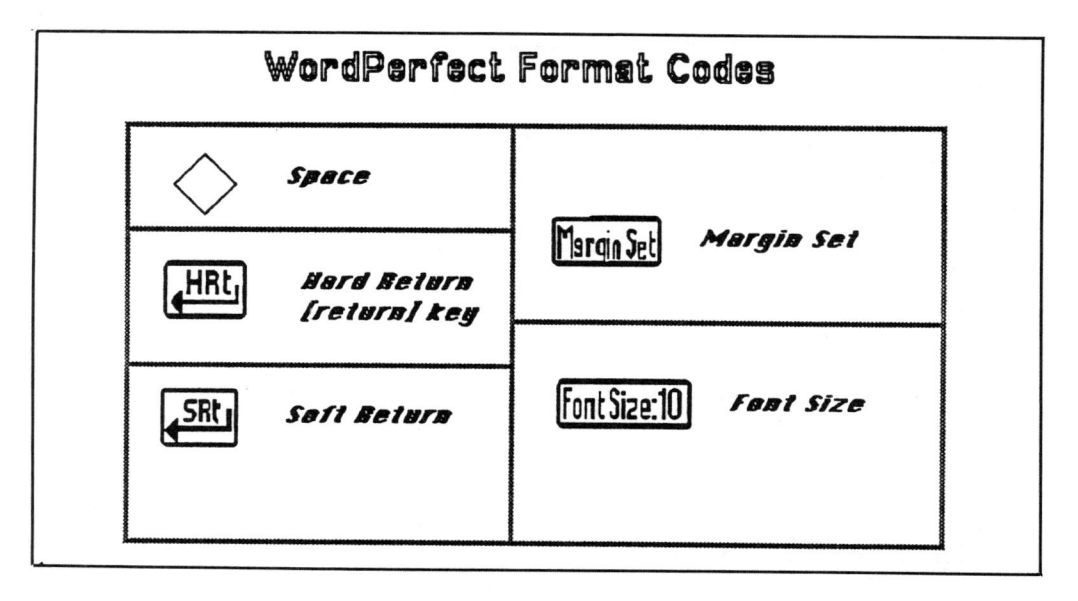

Figure 2.17

WordPerfect displays special codes for the following basic items: spaces, hard returns, and soft returns.

Spaces WordPerfect inserts a code, ◊, in each location in which you typed a space. This code allows you to see the exact number of spaces entered, which is important because it is difficult to determine the number of typed spaces when you are looking at the document display.

Hard Returns A hard return code [HRt] is inserted into the document each time you press the Return key. Hard returns mark the ends of paragraphs, short lines, or blank lines.

68

Margins and Formatting 2

Soft Returns Soft return [SRt] codes are inserted automatically by WordPerfect as you enter paragraph text. When WordPerfect wraps one line to the next, it inserts the [SRt] code. When you add text or change margins or font size, WordPerfect automatically adjusts the location of the [SRt] codes to ensure that the paragraph fits within the current margins.

In addition to these codes, WordPerfect displays codes for formatting changes. For example, the Margin and Font Size commands previously entered created codes in the text.

Margin Set The [Margin Set] code indicates the position in the document in which a margin change has been entered.

Font Size The [Font Size] code records the position in the text at which a font size change was entered. Font size codes also display the size (e.g., 10) of the font that was selected.

Your current cursor location in the codes display is shown as a black square. Currently, the cursor is positioned above the [Margin Set] and [Font Size] codes. This position explains why WordPerfect formatted the new text — "Computer based" — as normal text. When you used the mouse to position the cursor, you did not take into account the exact location in which WordPerfect stored the formatting codes, even though the cursor position appeared to be correct.

In WordPerfect, it is crucial to take into consideration the location of the formatting codes when you have a document that contains many format changes.

With the codes display window open, you can continue to edit your document. An added advantage is the ability to see how the cursor is positioned in terms of formatting codes as well as text.

In this example, you need make sure that the new text you are entering follows the formatting codes. To correct the entry you have made, delete the words "Computer based" from their current location. Move the cursor to the beginning of the line. Enter

[Enter] ←

2 Margins and Formatting

Note that as you move the cursor in the text window, the codes display cursor (the black box) also changes position.

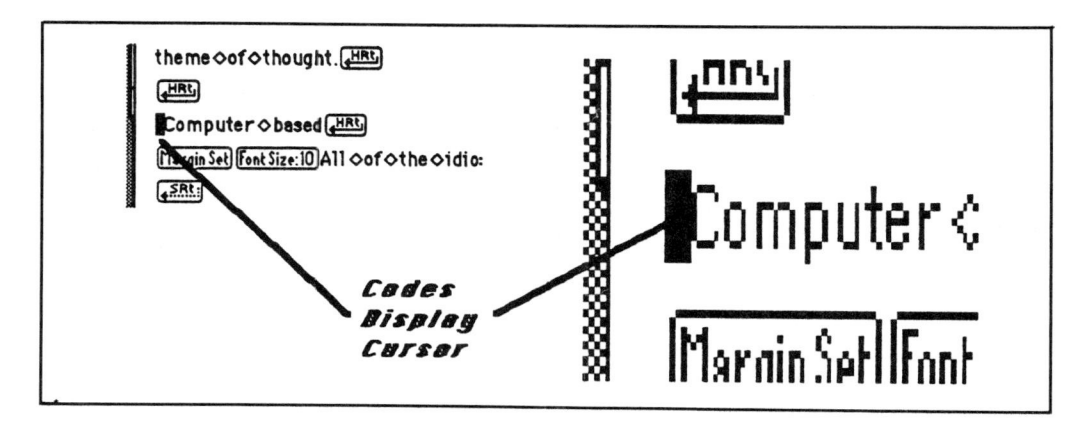

Figure 2.18

Delete this line by using the command [Apple/1]. Be sure to use the 1 on the numeric keypad. The [Apple/1] command that uses the 1 on the top row of the keyboard is the Format Column command, not the Delete Line command. Enter

[Apple/1]

The words are deleted from the line.

Deleting Blank Lines

When you entered the text, WordPerfect added an [HRt] that is still in the document and appears as an extra blank line inserted between the paragraphs. Blank lines, or [HRt] codes, can be deleted and inserted much like any other character. To remove the blank line, enter

[Decimal]

Margins and Formatting 2

To ensure that the text you want to add is formatted as part of the quotation, position the cursor to the right of the formatting codes. Enter

→ →

The cursor is now positioned so that any text entered will be formatted with the quotation section settings. Note that when you look at the text display window, the cursor indicator appears the same way it did when it was positioned to the left of the codes. When you are working near the beginning or end of a formatted section of a document, the only way to correctly position the cursor is to turn on the codes display and pay attention to the location of the formatting codes. Enter

Computer based intelligence

This time, the text is formatted as part of the quotation section. The text appears in both the document and the codes window.

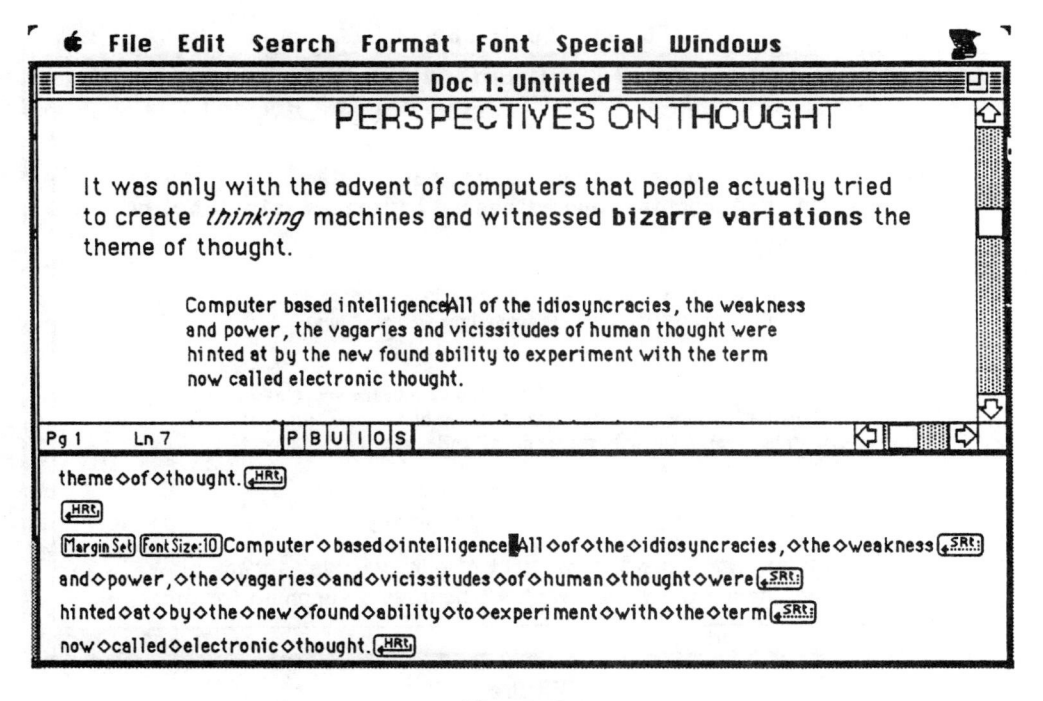

Figure 2.19

71

2 Margins and Formatting

You can perform all of WordPerfect's operations with the codes display window open; however, WordPerfect's operation can be slowed if the program must simultaneously update two windows. Now that you have located the correct position for the entry, you can close the codes window and return to the normal document display. Enter

[Apple/7]

Complete the new paragraph by entering.

[space bar]
has created a debate over the potential for machines to actually perform operations we refer to as thought.
[Return] [Return]

The text should now resemble the following:

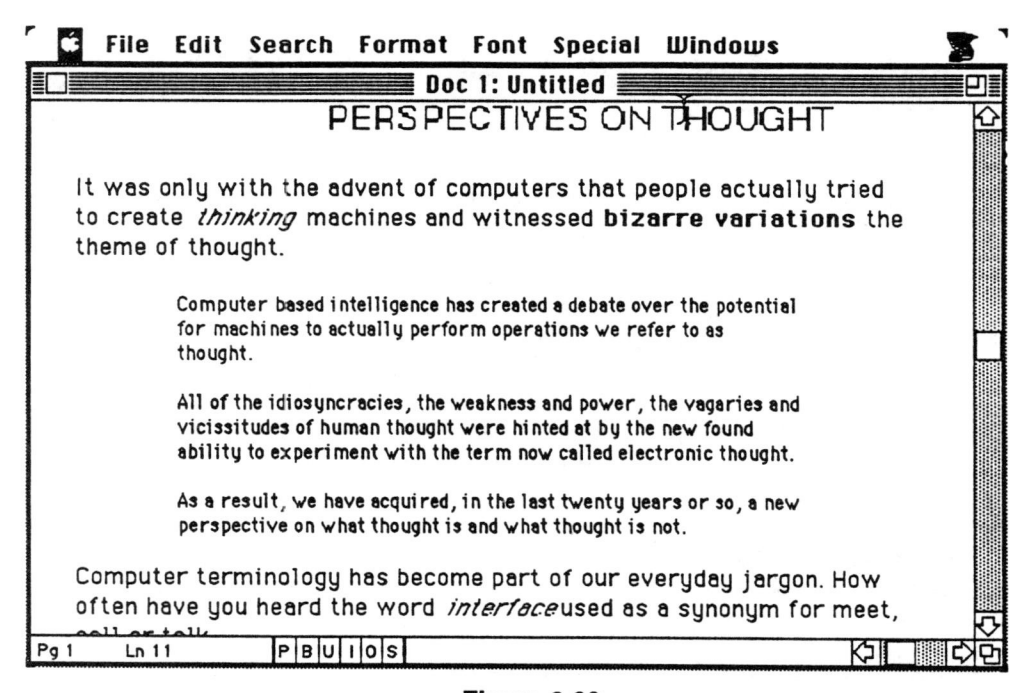

Figure 2.20

72

Margins and Formatting **2**

Searching for Codes

If you decide to insert a paragraph below the quotation, you must locate the next format change code in the text. One way to locate the code is to make your best guess and then open the codes display window to see the exact location of the cursor and the format codes.

The drawback to this method is that you must manually search the text, which is time-consuming when you work with large documents. A better solution is to get WordPerfect to perform the search. WordPerfect can search forward or backward in the document.

```
Point at Search
Drag to Forward
Release
```

The Search menu is displayed:

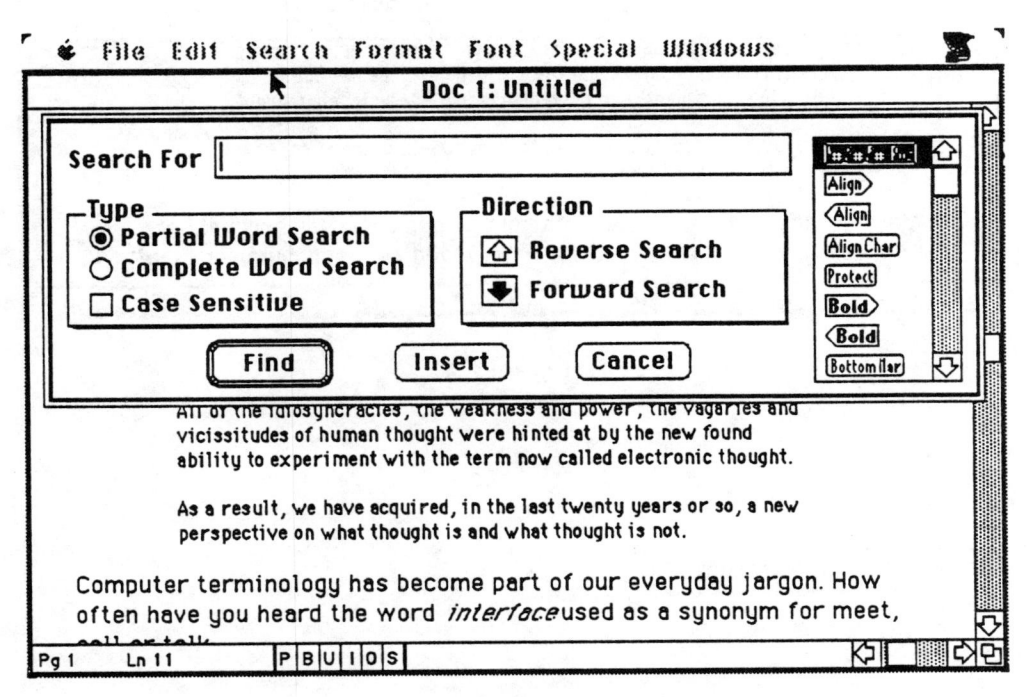

Figure 2.21

73

2 Margins and Formatting

The search function can be used to locate words, phrases, codes, or any combination of words and codes. To search for text, you simply type the text you want to find. To locate a code (as in this case) select one from the scroll box on the right. The formatting codes are listed in alphabetical order.

> **Drag** the bar until you see the [Margin Set] code

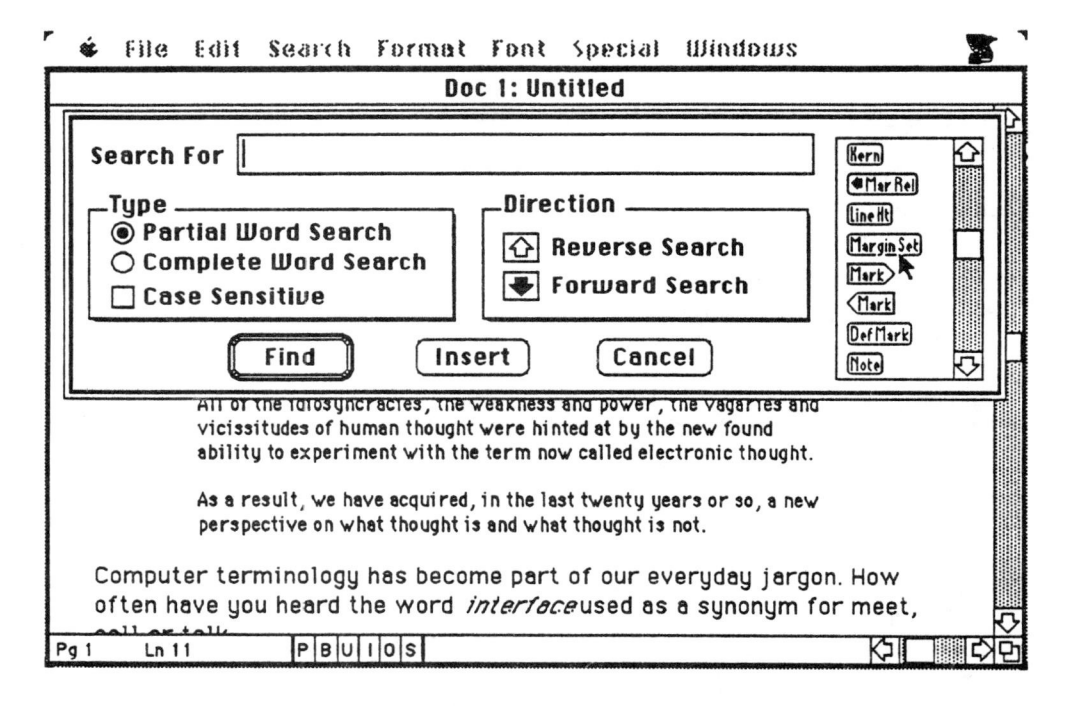

Figure 2.22

Insert the margin code into the search box:

> **Double click** on [Margin Set]

Margins and Formatting **2**

Execute the search.

```
Point at Find
Click
```

The cursor jumps to the word "Computer." Reveal the codes by entering

[Apple/7]

The screen should resemble the following:

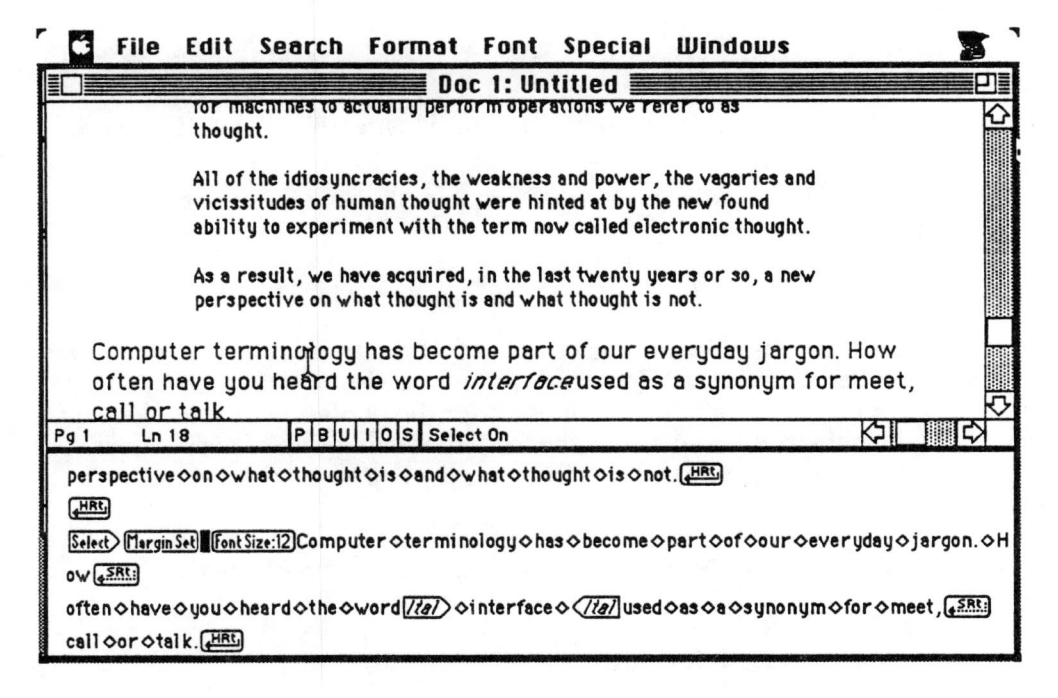

Figure 2.23

2 Margins and Formatting

The cursor is positioned just after the [Margin Set] code; however, this position is not where you want to enter text. The codes display reveals that the cursor is still to the left of the [Font Size:12] code. To move one more position to the right, enter

→

The cursor is now in position to insert text in the correct format. Close the codes window by entering

[Apple/7]

Enter the following paragraph:

Once the subject of mathematician's speculations, artificial intelligence is as familiar as artificial grass.
[Return] [Return]

Removing Codes

WordPerfect's system of formatting codes allows you to treat formatting options as you would text characters. You can insert new codes or delete old codes. For example, to change the margin settings used for the quotation section, locate the margin code in the text that controls the format of that group of paragraphs. The best method for performing this task is to use the Search command to locate the margin format code.

You can also display the Search menu by using keyboard commands:

    [Apple/f] Search forward
    [Apple b] Search backward

To search backward, enter

Margins and Formatting 2

[Apple/b]

The Search menu appears. Notice that WordPerfect remembers the last search item, [Margin Set]. Because you are still searching for the same item, you can leave the search item as it is. Enter

[Return]

The cursor moves to the next [Margin Set] code. Search for the next code by entering

[Apple/b] [Return]

WordPerfect automatically selects the code located by the search. Because the [Margin Set] code is indented from the left margin, the highlight is very wide. The previous [Margin Set] code was also selected, but the highlight was not wide because the code was flush left with the margin.

You can delete the [Margin Set] code by entering

[Delete]

When you delete the margin set code, WordPerfect has no reason to format the quotation paragraphs differently from the other text. The quotation text reverts to the previous margin settings.

2 Margins and Formatting

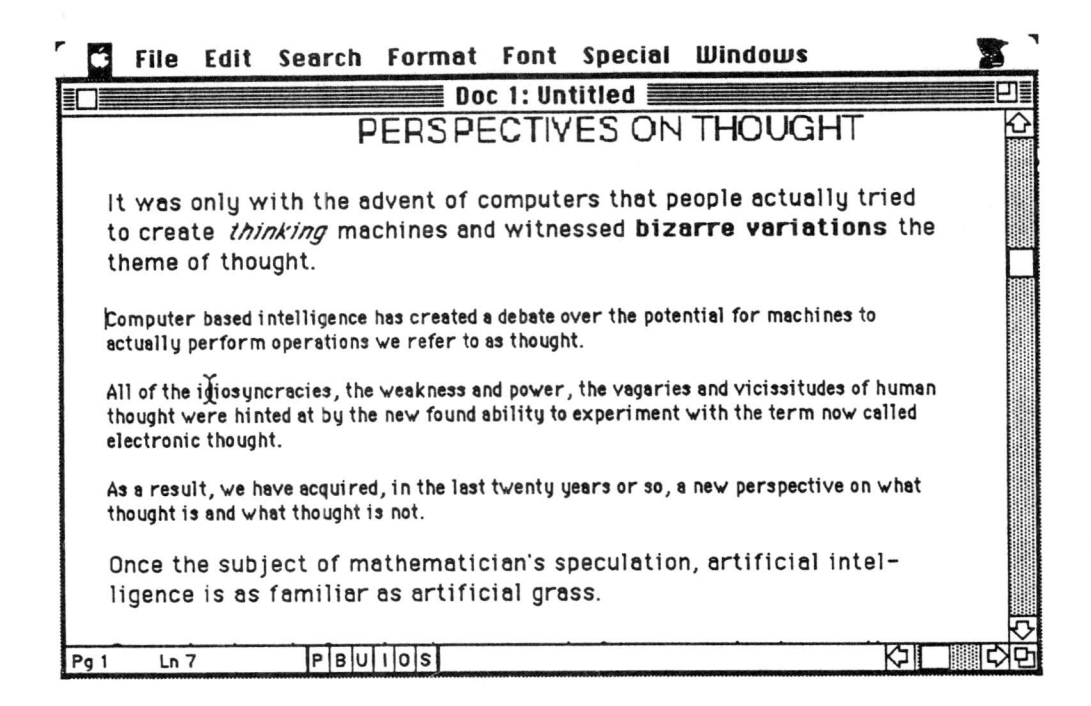

Figure 2.24

Create a new set of margin codes by entering

[Apple/2] 1
[Tab]
2.5 [Tab] [Tab]
2.5 [Return]

WordPerfect reformats the quotation paragraphs to the new margins. Note that the new margins stop at the paragraph that begins with "Once the subject..." because you have already inserted a [Margin Set] code at that point in the text. The new margins — 2.5" left and right — affect all of the text until another code is encountered.

Margins and Formatting 2

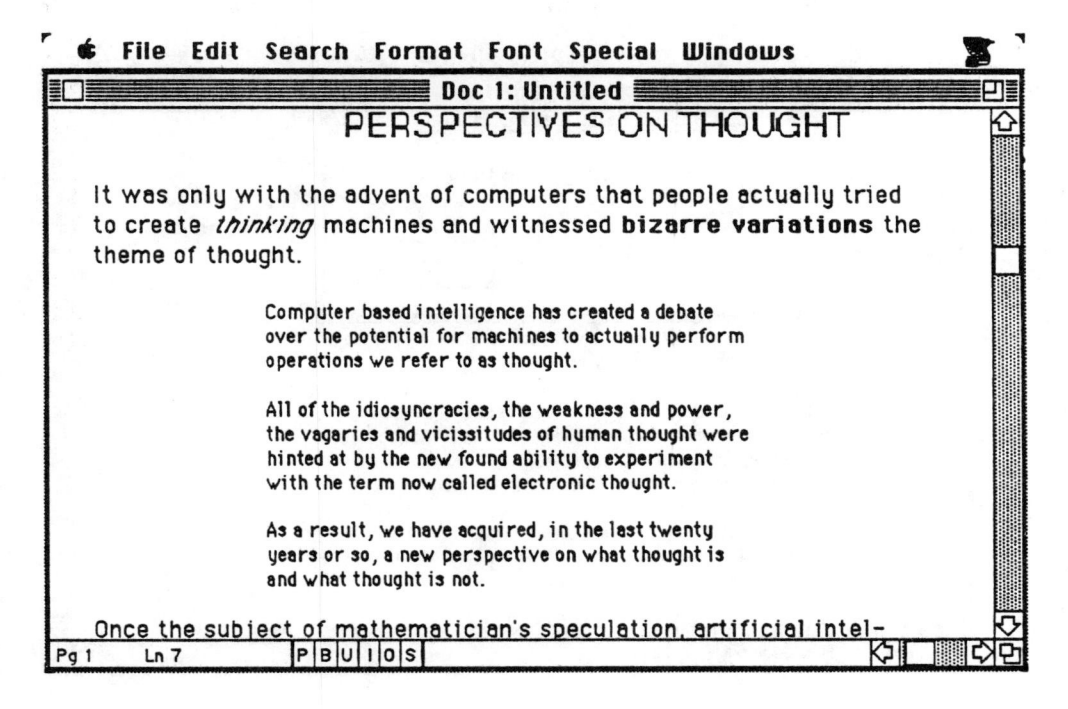

Figure 2.25

Suppose that you decide to change the left and right margins to 2.25". You can delete the [Margin Set] code by entering

[Delete]

This time, WordPerfect displays a warning box:

2 Margins and Formatting

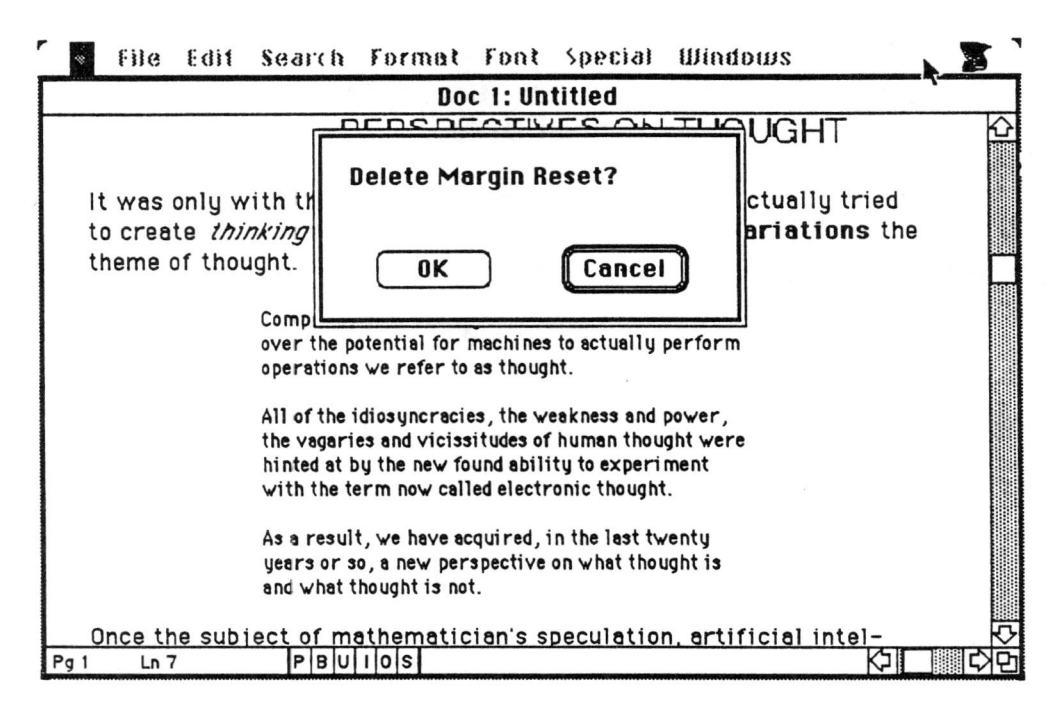

Figure 2.26

If you enter a character in the document window that selects a hidden code for deletion, WordPerfect displays a box warning you that a code is about to be deleted. This is a safety precaution to prevent you from accidentally deleting a formatting code that you would not be able to see unless the codes display window was open. Delete the code:

```
Point at OK
Click
```

Once again, the text is reformatted to the previous margin setting. Create a new margin code for the quotation section by entering

Margins and Formatting 2

[Apple/2] 1
[Tab]
2.25 [Tab] [Tab]
2.25 [Return]

The text is reformatted to conform to the new margin code.

You can see that WordPerfect allows you to change the code settings as many times as you like. Each code affects all text following it until another code is encountered or the end of the document is reached. When a code is deleted, the last previous code is used to reformat the text. If all the codes are removed, WordPerfect reverts to its default settings, such as 1" left and right margins.

It is not strictly necessary to delete the old [Margin Set] code before you enter a new one. Suppose that you decided to change the margins one more time, for example, the left margin to 2.5". Enter

[Apple/2] 1
[Tab]
2.5 [Return]

The new code causes WordPerfect to reformat the text within a 2.5" left margin and a 2.25" right margin. To determine if the other code is still in the document, open the codes display window by entering

[Apple/7]

The codes display shows that there are two [Margin Set] codes next to one another in the text.

2 Margins and Formatting

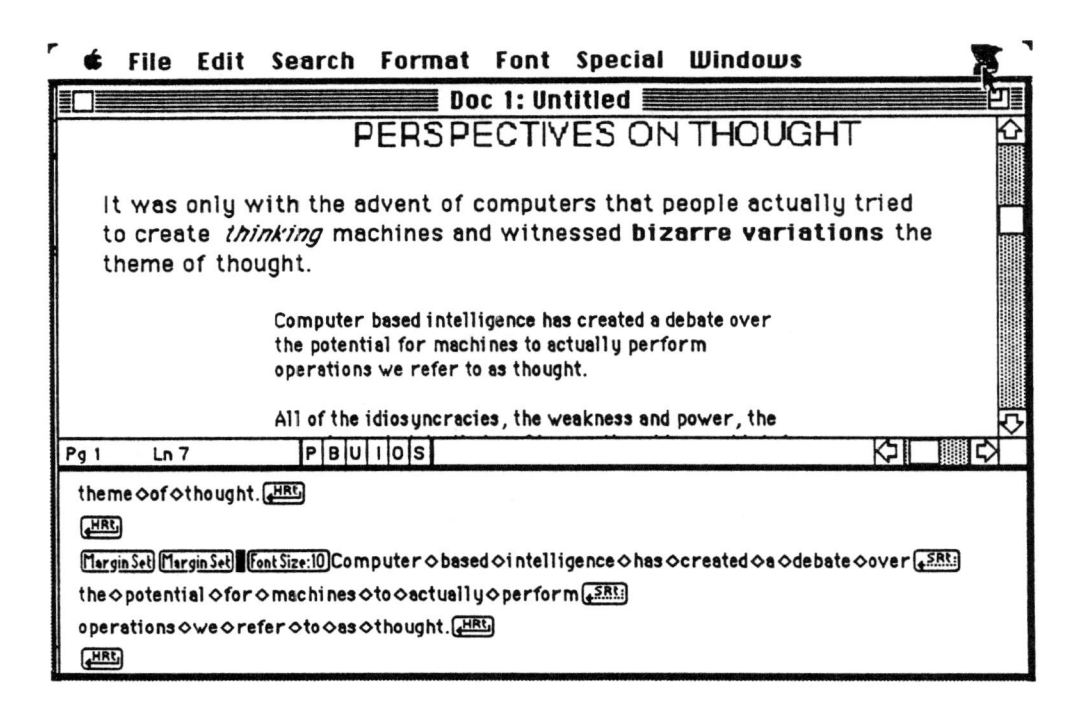

Figure 2.27

If more than one code of the same type appears next to the same code, the last code in the series affects the text. For the moment, the first code has no effect; however, should you delete the last code, the previous code will become active.

Close the codes window by entering

[Apple/7]

Remove the newest [Margin Set] code by entering

[Delete]

WordPerfect displays the warning box.

| Point OK |
| Click |

The paragraph is immediately reformatted to the margins set by the previous code — 2.25" left and right. If you were to delete the code one more time, the text would revert to the margins set at the beginning of the document — 1.25" left and right.

When possible, it is a good idea to remove from the text codes that have been replaced. While they do not cause any actual harm, retaining unneeded codes makes t'.e codes window display harder to read and understand.

Print the document by entering

[Apple/p] [Return]

When printing is complete, save the document by entering

[Apple/s]
margins [Return]

SOFT RETURNS, HYPHENS, AND JUSTIFICATION

Justification — another issue related to margins — refers to the relationship between line endings (specifically, [SRt], or soft return, codes) and the right margin.

The normal procedure for WordPerfect is to place the [SRt] code as close to the right margin as possible without going beyond it; as a result, some lines will be shorter than other lines. The right edge of the text will appear ragged.

2 Margins and Formatting

To minimize the ragged appearance of the right margin, WordPerfect is set to automatically insert hyphens into words that fall within the H-zone. The H-zone, or hyphenation zone, was mentioned earlier in this chapter because it appears as part of the ruler line display. Display the ruler line by entering

[Apple/r]

The dark gray area on the right side of the ruler display's top line shows the current H-zone, which determines when WordPerfect should attempt to hyphenate a word. WordPerfect follows specific rules for hyphenating words that fall at the end of [SRt] codes:

1. If a word begins **inside** the H-zone, the entire word is wrapped to the next line.

2. If a word begins **outside** the H-zone and its length exceeds the right margin, WordPerfect will hyphenate the word.

In this document, the word "intelligence" on line 20 was hyphenated using these rules. You can increase or decrease the size of the H-zone by dragging the button on the left side of the H-zone marker. As a general rule, making the H-zone smaller increases the number of hyphenated words at the ends of lines, and using a larger H-zone decreases the number of hyphenated words in a document.

Despite the use of the H-zone to hyphenate some words, the line endings do not fit exactly on the right margin. WordPerfect offers an option called **full justification,** which causes WordPerfect to adjust the spacing on each line that ends with an [SRt] so that the text aligns perfectly on the right margin. Justified text is available in most word processing programs; it is a matter of taste whether justified text improves the appearance of your document. To see what this document looks like with fully justified text, move the cursor to the beginning of the document:

[Enter] [Enter] ↑

To turn full justification on or off, you must use the icons on the ruler line.

Margins and Formatting 2

Turn on full justification:

> **Point** at Justification On icon
> **Click**

The right ends of the lines now appear aligned exactly on the right margins. To return to nonjustified text, simply delete the justification code inserted in the text. Remember, when you choose an option such as justification, WordPerfect inserts a code in the text that can be deleted. Enter

[Delete]

A box appears, warning you that you are about to delete a Justify Text code.

> **Point** at OK
> **Click**

The text returns to its nonjustified form.

You can justify selected parts of text. To justify only the quotation section of this document,

> **Point** before the "C" in "Computer based"
> **Click**

Turn on the justification:

> **Point** at Justification On icon
> **Click**

85

2 Margins and Formatting

Next, you must turn the justification off at the end of the quotation section. You can position the cursor with the Search command. Enter

[Apple/f]
once [Return]

The cursor highlights the first word in the paragraph after the quotation section. Turn off the hyphenation:

| **Point** at the Justification Off icon |
| **Click** |

The remainder of the text is now unjustified.

Return WordPerfect to its original setup by closing this document and opening a new document window. Enter

[Apple/k]

WordPerfect does not close the window; rather, it displays a box warning you that you have made changes to the document by adding justification. Save the changes.

| **Point** at Yes |
| **Click** |

Open a new document by entering

[Apple/n]

SUMMARY

- **Page Layout**. The Page Layout menu is used to set page margins. The menu can be accessed by entering [Apple/2] 1. Distances in WordPerfect are measured in inches. You can specify margins to within 1/100". Each margin change operation inserts a [Margin Set] code into the text at the current cursor location. The [Margin Set] code controls the margins of all the text following the code until another code, if any, is encountered. If you have consecutive margin codes in the text, the right-most code is the one used by WordPerfect to format the text.

- **Ruler Line.** The ruler line is a visual display that allows you to change many formatting options with the mouse. You can change margins by dragging the left or right margin markers with the mouse. Ruler line margin changes insert a [Margin Set] code in the text at the current cursor location just as menu margin changes do.

- **Font Size.** WordPerfect automatically adjusts line endings when you change the point size of the text.

- **Case Conversion**. You can use WordPerfect to convert selected characters to upper- or lowercase. Case conversion is found on the Edit menu.

- **Shows Codes**. The [Apple/7] command will cause WordPerfect to split the window between the normal text display and a special window called the codes display. The codes display shows special symbols that indicate the location of various formatting codes.

- **Searching for Codes.** The Search command—[Apple/f] for forward search or [Apple/b] for backward search—can locate text and codes within the document. A scroll box displays the code symbols used in WordPerfect.

2 Margins and Formatting

- **Delete Codes.** Codes can be deleted much like text characters. When the codes display is active, the Delete and Decimal keys will delete codes just as they delete characters. When the codes window is closed, WordPerfect displays a warning box when a code is deleted, which allows you to confirm your intentions.

- **Justification**. WordPerfect normally leaves a ragged right edge on lines that end with [SRt] codes. If justification is turned on, WordPerfect adjusts line spacing so that all [SRt] codes fall exactly at the right margin.

- **Delete Codes.** Codes can be deleted in much the same way as text characters. When the codes display is active, the Delete and Decimal keys will delete codes just as they delete characters. When the codes window is closed, WordPerfect displays a warning box when a code is deleted, which allows you to confirm your intentions.

- **Justification**. WordPerfect normally leaves a ragged right edge on lines that end with [SRt] codes. If justification is turned on, WordPerfect adjusts line spacing so that all [SRt] codes fall exactly at the right margin.

CHAPTER 3

TABLES AND TABS

3 Tables and Tabs

This chapter describes how to prepare information organized into tables by using tabs. A **tab** is a designated horizontal indentation used to align text at different intervals along the same horizontal line. If you have never used tabs on a word processor, you will find that they are similar — but much more powerful — than tab settings on a typewriter. If you have used word processing programs, you will learn how WordPerfect implements tabs and what tab-like features are available in the program.

This chapter assumes that you have loaded WordPerfect and have a new document — Doc 1: Untitled — ready for entry.

FULL WINDOW DISPLAY

The WordPerfect Corporation provides as much screen display area as possible for editing in their programs. In the IBM PC version of WordPerfect, only a single line at the bottom of the screen includes status information. The remaining space is for text. On the Macintosh, each window is bordered on top by the menu and window name bars and on the right and bottom by scroll bars. To increase the amount of document space in the window, WordPerfect allows you to choose Full Screen mode. In this mode, the menu, name, and right scroll bars are hidden, which increases the amount of display space available for text. The disadvantage of the full-screen view is that it doesn't allow you to use the right scroll bar to position the document.

The Full Screen option is found under the Special menu.

> **Point** at Special
> **Drag** to Screen
> **Release**

The Screen menu lists four options. The Colors option is active only on Macintosh II computers equipped with color screens. Option #3 — Display justification — is already active, which means that when you select text justification, the lines will appear justified on the screen as well as when printed.

The Show Position option turns on a display that shows, in inches, the horizontal and vertical position of the cursor on the page.

Tables and Tabs **3**

To change to the Full Screen display mode, enter

1

The screen appears completely blank with the exception of the bottom bar. This display is more like the screen display used by WordPerfect on the IBM PC.

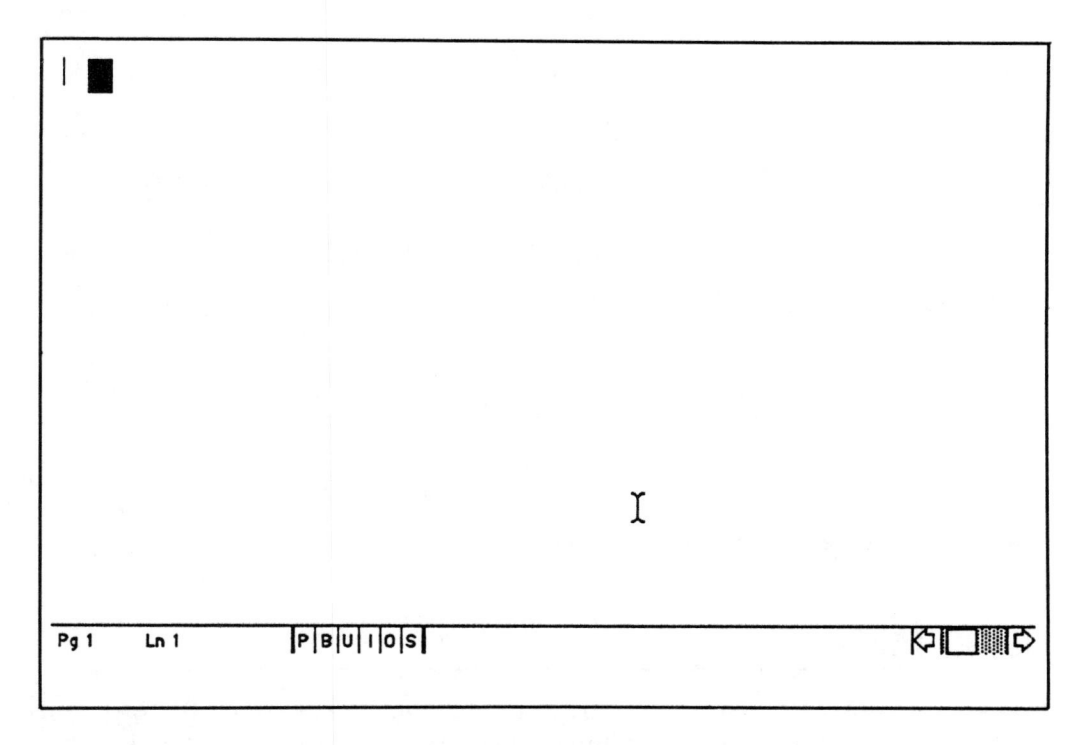

Figure 3.1

Note that the menu bar does not appear on the display.

| **Point** at the top of the screen |

91

3 Tables and Tabs

The menu bar appears.

> Point at center of the screen

The menu bar disappears once again. This display provides the largest screen for text display. So you can return to the normal display, WordPerfect supplies a special keyboard command. Enter

[Apple/Shift/z]

The normal WordPerfect window reappears. Activate the full-screen display again by entering

[Apple/Shift/z]

Create a heading for this document by entering

[Shift/Apple/c]
Macintosh Software Hits [Return] [Return]

USING TABS

It is not necessary to create tab stops to use tabs in WordPerfect; the program automatically defaults to inserting tab stops every 0.5". These tabs are available in every document window and are handy for indenting paragraphs. For example, suppose you want to begin this document with the first line of a paragraph indented 0.5". Enter

[Tab]

The cursor jumps 0.5" to the right. Enter the following text:

Tables and Tabs 3

The following table lists the most popular Macintosh programs as of the Spring of 1988. The data was compiled from the leading Macintosh software distributors. [Return] [Return]

USING REPLACE

The Search command was introduced in the previous chapter as a means to locate codes within a document. A variation on the Search command is the **Replace** command, which searches for a specific word, phrase, or code and can swap the located item with another text or code entry.

For example, the word "Macintosh" is used several times in the text. Suppose you want all references to "Macintosh" in bold. One method for accomplishing this task would be to manually select the words and enter bold commands, but the Replace command offers a faster, more accurate alternative.

The first step is to position the cursor at the beginning of the document. Remember that unlike the Search function, which can search forward or backward through the document, the Replace function only operates in a forward direction. Enter

[Enter] [Enter] ↑

Display the Replace menu by entering

[Apple/h]

Your screen should resemble the following:

93

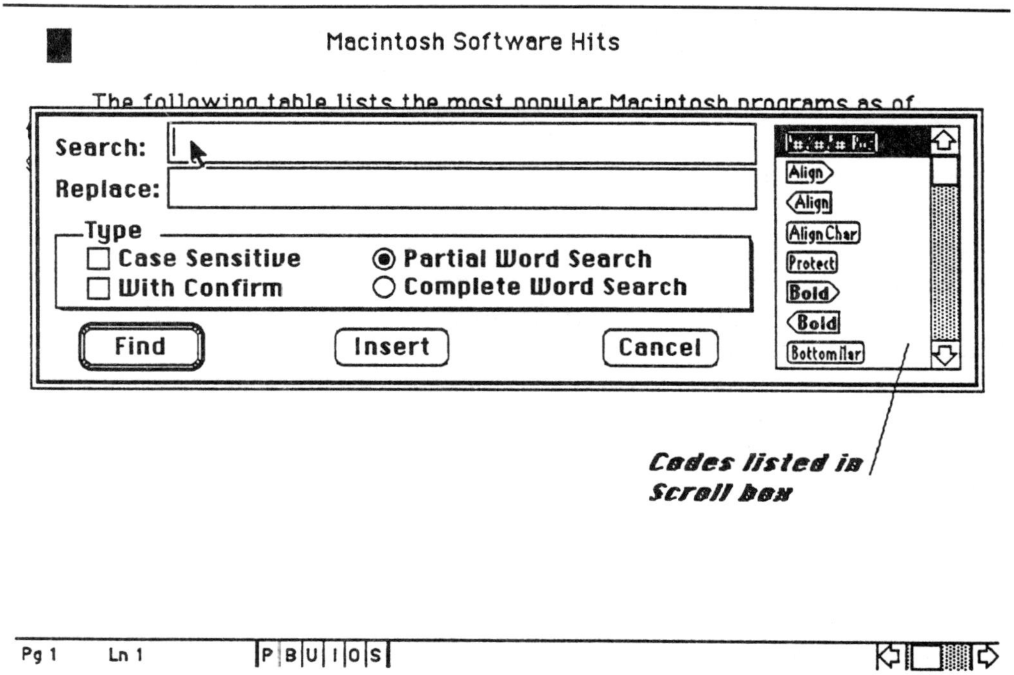

3 Tables and Tabs

[Figure: Macintosh Software Hits window with Search/Replace dialog showing Type options (Case Sensitive, With Confirm, Partial Word Search, Complete Word Search), Find/Insert/Cancel buttons, and a scroll box with codes. Annotation: *Codes listed in Scroll box*]

Figure 3.2

This menu is very similar to the Search menu, but there are two places in which to enter text. The first is the search text; the second is the replace text. In this case, you are searching for "Macintosh." Enter

Macintosh
[Tab]

The Replace text must contain bold codes. If you examine the scroll bar on the right, you will see two bold codes: one for Begin Bold and one for End Bold.

WordPerfect has automatically highlighted the Begin Bold code because it is the first code on the list. Insert the code into the replace line:

94

Tables and Tabs 3

> **Point** at Insert
> **Click**

Enter the following text:

Macintosh

Remember, you must also include an End Bold code to tell WordPerfect to stop the bold following the word "Macintosh."

> **Point** at the second bold code
> **Double Click**

The menu should now resemble the following:

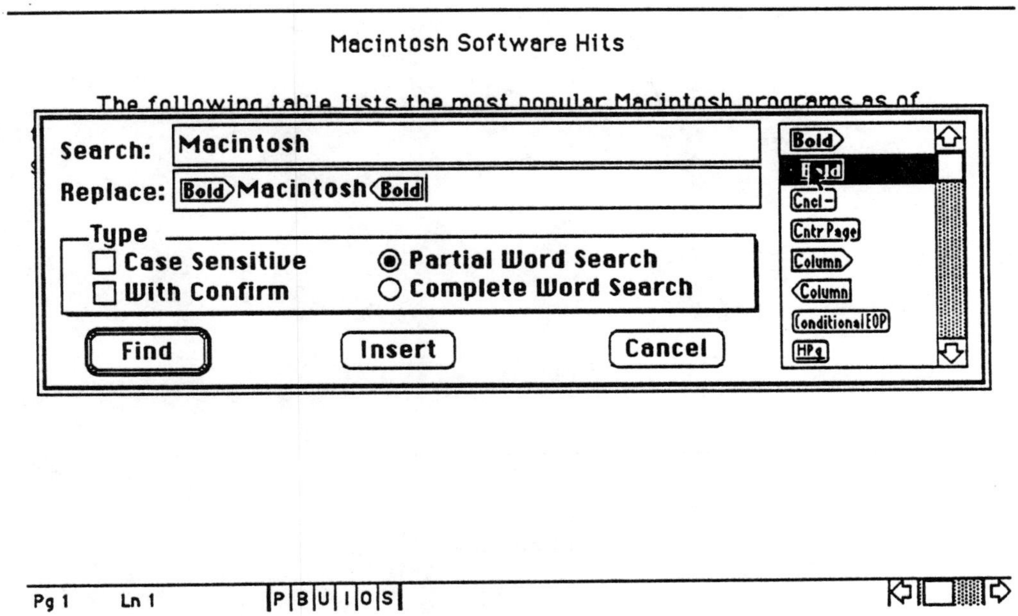

```
                    Macintosh Software Hits

     The following table lists the most popular Macintosh programs as of
    ┌─────────────────────────────────────────────────────────┐
    │  Search:  [Macintosh              ]       [Bold>]    ▲  │
    │                                           [B▼ld]       │
    │  Replace: [<Bold>Macintosh<Bold>]         [Cncl-]       │
    │  ┌Type─────────────────────────────┐      [CntrPage]    │
    │  │ ☐ Case Sensitive  ● Partial Word Search  [Column>]   │
    │  │ ☐ With Confirm    ○ Complete Word Search [<Column]   │
    │                                           [ConditionalEOP]│
    │    ( Find )       ( Insert )   ( Cancel )  [HPg]     ▼  │
    └─────────────────────────────────────────────────────────┘

  Pg 1    Ln 1    |P|B|U|I|O|S|
```

Figure 3.3

3 Tables and Tabs

Execute the operation by entering

[Return]

WordPerfect searches the text and makes the replacements. The top of the document has scrolled off the display. Return to the top by entering

[Enter] [Enter] ↑

You can see that all instances of the word "Macintosh" are now bold:

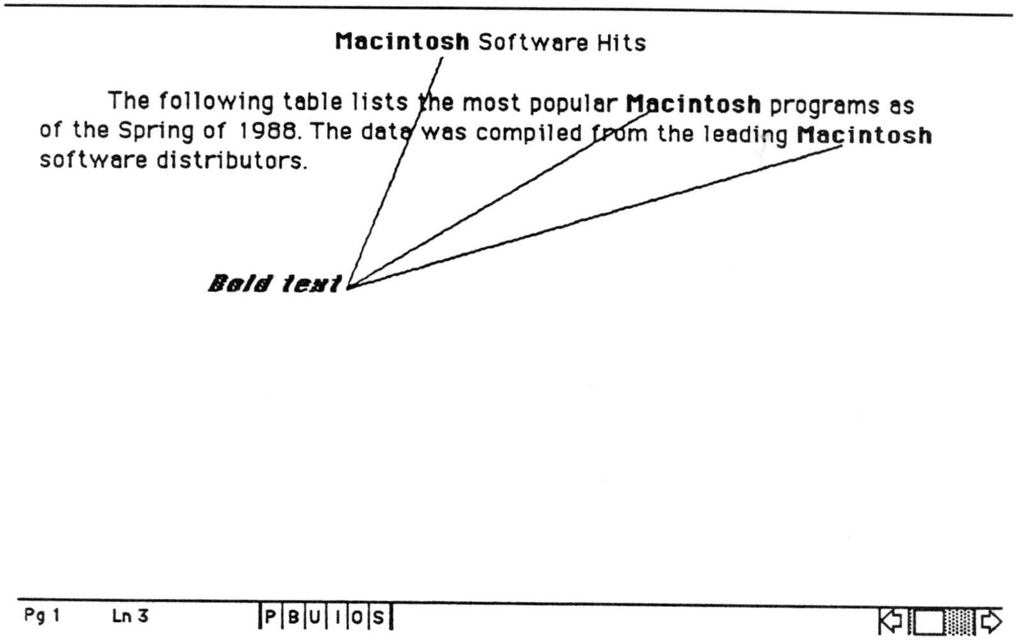

Macintosh Software Hits

The following table lists the most popular **Macintosh** programs as of the Spring of 1988. The data was compiled from the leading **Macintosh** software distributors.

Bold text

Pg 1   Ln 3 |P|B|U|I|O|S|

Figure 3.4

Tables and Tabs **3**

Return the cursor to the end of the document:

[Enter] [Enter] ↓

Return to the normal display by entering

[Apple/Shift/z]

SETTING INDIVIDUAL TABS

The next section of the document includes a table that requires individual tab stops. Tab operations are found on the Line Format menu.

```
Point at Format
Drag to Line
Release
```

To perform tab-related operations, enter

3

The ruler line displays the current settings. Note that there are tab markers every .5".

3 Tables and Tabs

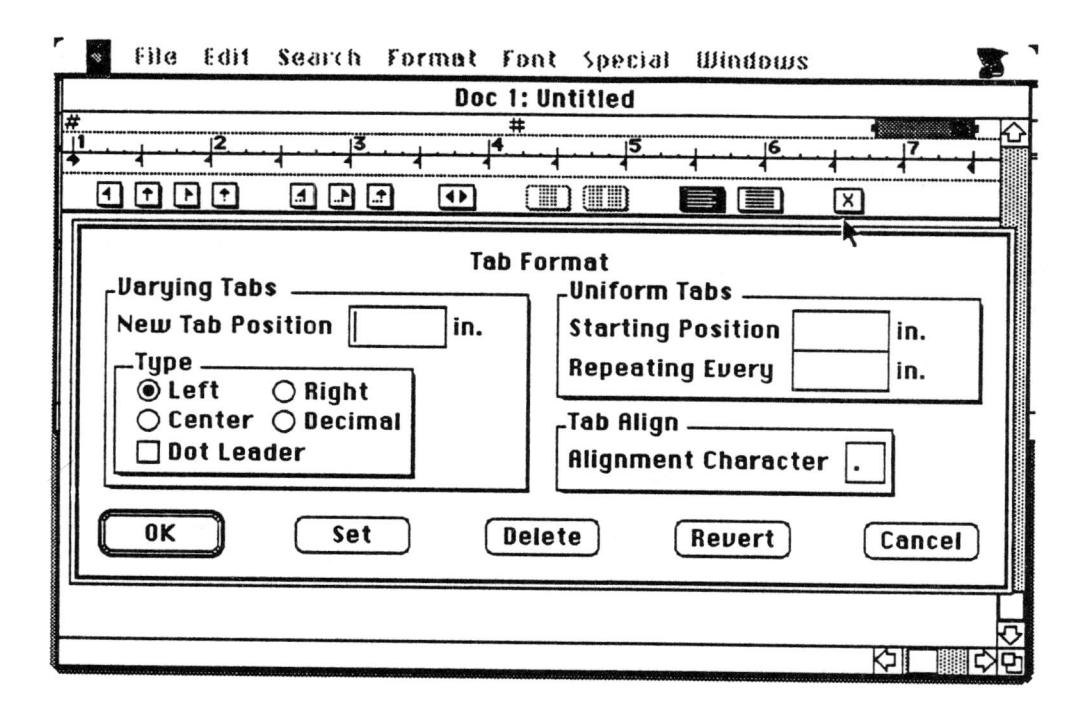

Figure 3.5

You must remove the existing tabs by using the Delete option.

> **Point** at Delete
> **Click**

WordPerfect removes all existing tab markers.

Tables and Tabs 3

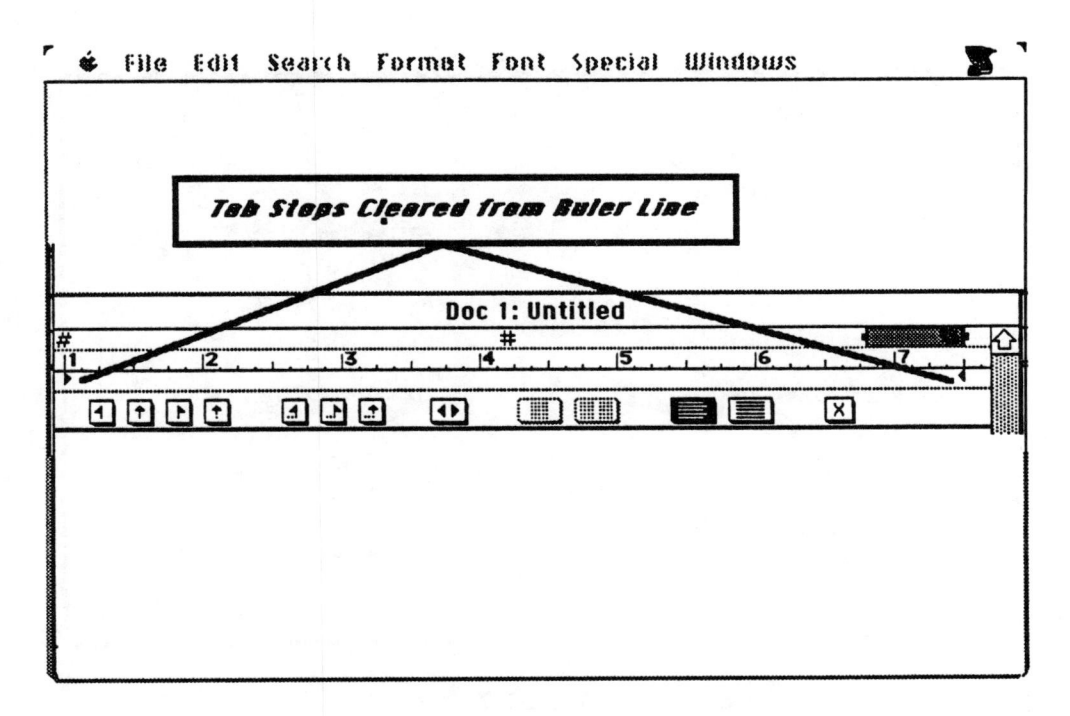

Figure 3.6

Now that the previous tabs have been removed, you can insert new tab stops for the table. First, you must make two decisions.

Location You must enter a value in inches, which tells WordPerfect where to place the tab stop. Locations are always measured from the edge of the page.

Alignment Alignment refers to the way WordPerfect aligns text at a tab stop. WordPerfect allows left-, center-, decimal-, and right-aligned tabs. The default is left alignment.

3 Tables and Tabs

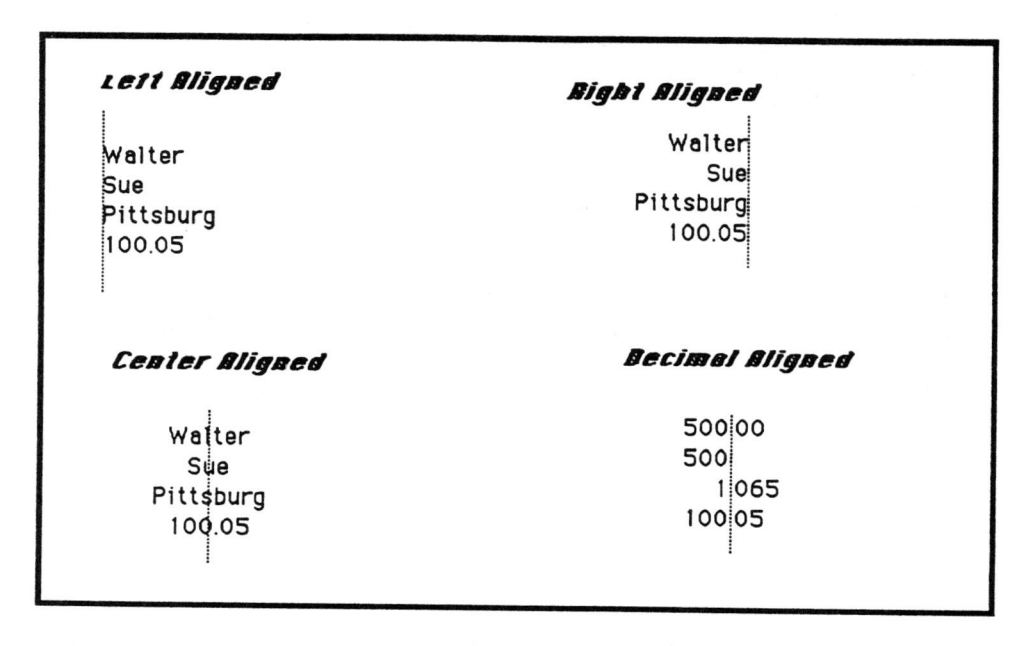

```
     Left Aligned                    Right Aligned

    Walter                                  Walter
    Sue                                        Sue
    Pittsburg                            Pittsburg
    100.05                                  100.05


    Center Aligned                 Decimal Aligned

         Walter                         500 00
          Sue                           500
       Pittsburg                          1 065
        100.05                          100 05
```

Figure 3.7

To start, create a left-aligned tab at 1.5". Enter

1.5

To set the tab, use the mouse:

> **Point** at Set
> **Click**

100

Tables and Tabs 3

A tab marker appears on the ruler line to indicate that a tab has been positioned. Create two more tabs—one at 3.5" and the other at 5". Enter

3.5

> **Point** at Set
> **Click**

Then enter

5

> **Point** at Set
> **Click**

The last tab is to be decimal-aligned at 6.5". Change the alignment to decimal.

> **Point** at the Decimal button
> **Click**

Enter

6.5

> **Point** at Set
> **Click**

101

3 Tables and Tabs

You have created the necessary tabs for the table. Complete the entry:

> **Point** at OK
> **Click**

The document window looks exactly as it did before. To see what has changed, display the codes by entering

[Apple/7]

The codes display shows that you have inserted a Tab Set code into the text. Remember, the location of this code is important. Only text following this code will recognize the four new tabs. Text above the code will align to the standard 0.5" tabs.

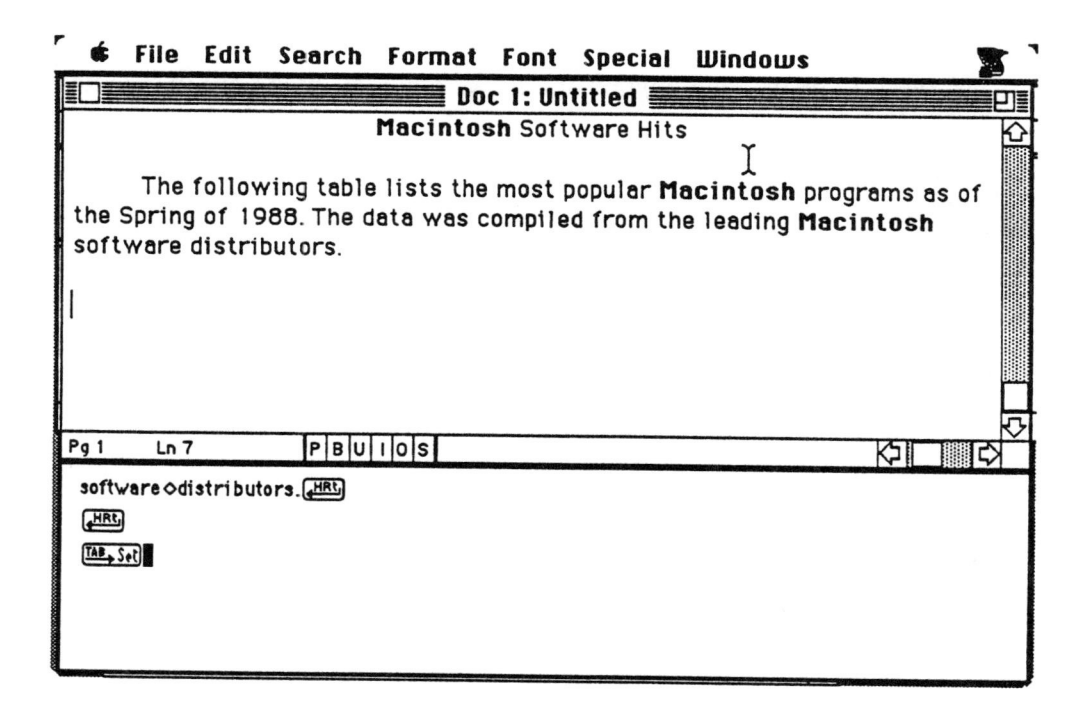

Figure 3.8

Close the codes window by entering

[Apple/7]

ENTERING A TABLE

Tables usually begin with headings. Move to the first tab stop by entering

[Tab]

To set the headings off from the rest of the table, turn on underlining:

> **Point** at U on the bottom bar
> **Click**

Enter the headings:

Program Name[Tab]
Company[Tab]
Type[Tab]
Price

Turn off underlining:

> **Point** at U on the bottom bar
> **Click**

3 Tables and Tabs

Underline Style

As you entered headings, you may have noticed that the underline did not extend to areas between tabs. WordPerfect provides several underline options. The default style of underlining — non-continuous — does not underline spaces created by tabs or indents.

If you want the underline to run continuously across the line — including the tab space — you must insert a change in tab style into the document. To change the underline style, you must position the cursor before the beginning of the underline to insert an underline style code; if you don't, the change will affect only subsequent underlines. Move to the beginning of the line by entering

[Enter] [Enter] ←

Underline style options are found on the Format Character menu. Display the menu by entering

[Apple/5]

The lower right corner contains the Underline Style box.

Point at the Continuous button
Click
Click on OK

The underline now includes the space created by the tabs:

Tables and Tabs **3**

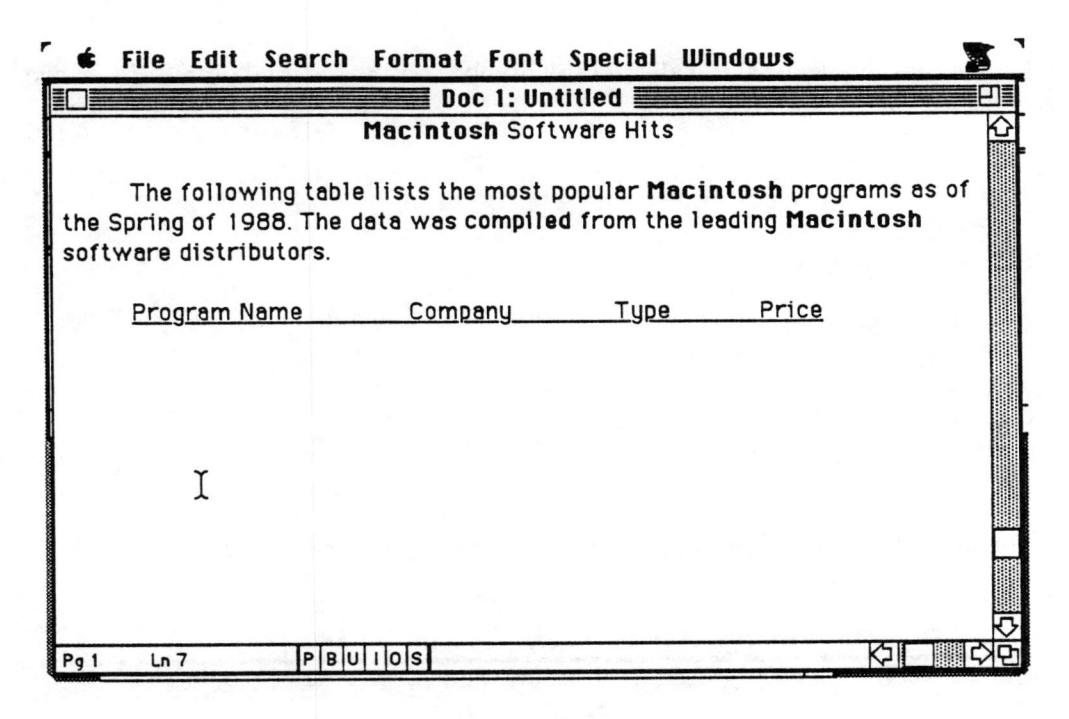

```
 File   Edit   Search   Format   Font   Special   Windows
╔══════════════════════ Doc 1: Untitled ══════════════════════╗
                     Macintosh Software Hits

      The following table lists the most popular Macintosh programs as of
   the Spring of 1988. The data was compiled from the leading Macintosh
   software distributors.

      Program Name          Company           Type       Price




                       I




 Pg 1    Ln 7       P B U I O S
```

Figure 3.9

Table Text

You are now ready to enter the contents of the table. Return the cursor to the end of the document and add a blank line by entering

[Enter] [Enter]↓
[Return] [Return]

Enter the first item on the table:

[Tab]
MacMoney [Tab]
Survivor Ltd. [Tab]
Business [Tab]
119.95 [Return]

105

3 Tables and Tabs

Notice that the decimal tab aligned the number on the decimal point. Enter two more items:

[Tab]
King's Quest I [Tab]
Sierra on Line [Tab]
Game [Tab]
49.95 [Return]
[Tab] Deskpaint [Tab]
Zencor [Tab]
Graphics [Tab]
59.95 [Return] [Return]

The document should resemble the following:

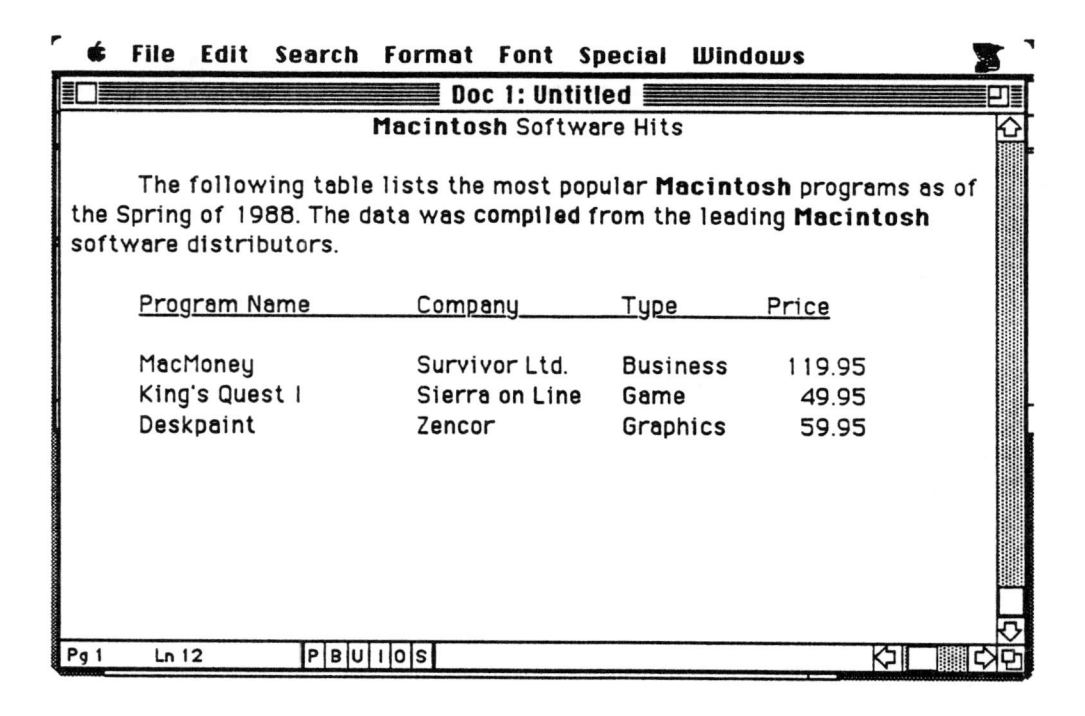

```
 File  Edit  Search  Format  Font  Special  Windows
═══════════════════ Doc 1: Untitled ═══════════════════
                    Macintosh Software Hits

    The following table lists the most popular Macintosh programs as of
the Spring of 1988. The data was compiled from the leading Macintosh
software distributors.

       Program Name        Company          Type        Price

       MacMoney            Survivor Ltd.    Business    119.95
       King's Quest I      Sierra on Line   Game         49.95
       Deskpaint           Zencor           Graphics     59.95


Pg 1   Ln 12    P B U I O S
```

Figure 3.10

106

As a safety precaution, save the text by entering

[Apple/s]
tables [Return]

Deleting Tabs with the Mouse

You can set tabs by using the ruler line and the mouse. Enter a new heading for a table of hardware items:

[Apple/Shift/c]
[Apple/Shift/b]
Hardware Specials
[Apple/Shift/b]
[Return] [Return]

This table requires three columns; two will be decimal-aligned. Display the ruler line. Enter

[Apple/r]

The first step is to delete the left tab aligned at 3.5". To delete a tab, select the tab type by clicking on the corresponding icon:

| **Point** at the left-align tab icon |
| **Click** |

The cursor changes to match the icon by reversing the color (i.e., white on black). To delete the tab, point the icon so that it covers the existing tab. Keep in mind that if you point too far up, the icon will become the mouse arrow again. If that happens, point lower, and the icon will return.

3 Tables and Tabs

> **Point** at tab 3.5
> **Click**
> **Point** anywhere else on the screen

The tab has been removed. Remove the tab at 5" with the same method:

> **Point** at tab 5
> **Click**

You have now removed both left-aligned tabs. To return the mouse cursor to normal, click on the left tab icon again:

> **Point** at the left-align tab icon
> **Click**

The mouse cursor returns to normal. Your ruler line should resemble the following:

Tables and Tabs 3

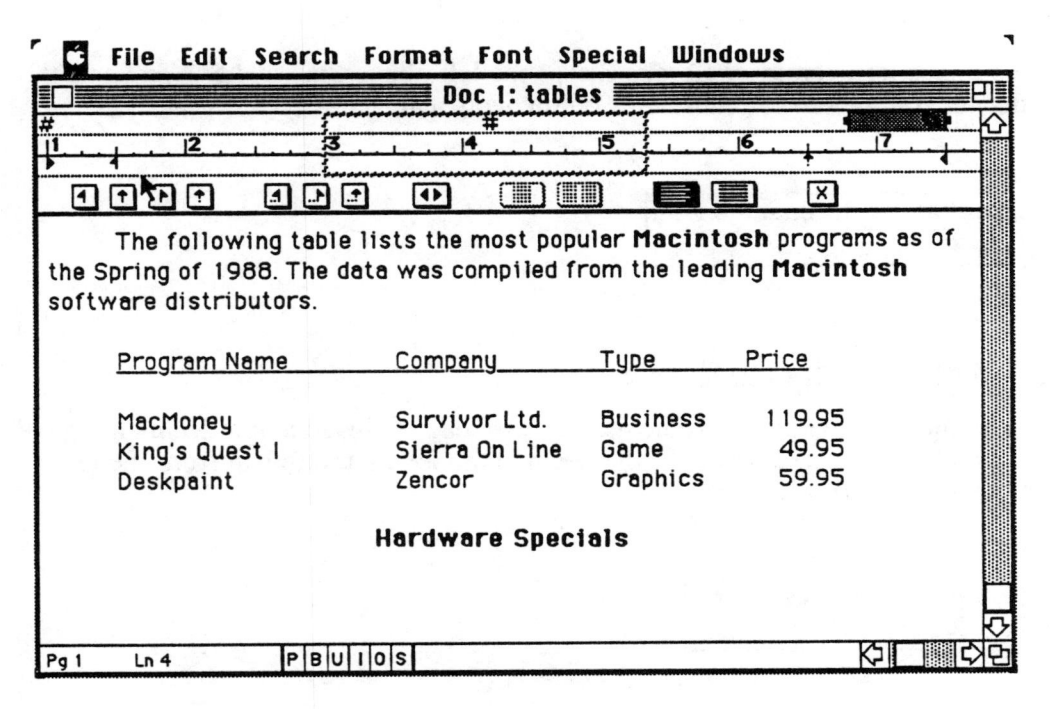

Figure 3.11

To remove the decimal tab at 6.5", you must first select the decimal tab icon:

```
Point at the decimal tab icon
Click
```

The icon changes to indicate that decimal tab operations can be performed:

```
Point at the decimal tab at 6.5"
Click
```

109

3 Tables and Tabs

You have now removed all tabs except the left-aligned tab at 1.5". To leave the decimal tab mode, you must click on the icon again:

> **Point** at the decimal tab icon
> **Click**

Adding Tabs with the Mouse

With the left-aligned tabs removed, you are ready to insert a new decimal-aligned tab. The first step is to select the decimal tab icon — the fourth from the left on the ruler icon display.

> **Point** at the right tab icon
> **Click**

The right icon is darkened, and the mouse changes to a right-aligned tab icon. You can set a right tab by pointing at the position on the ruler line where you want the tab to be placed. In this example, set the tab at 5":

> **Point** at 5" on the ruler line
> **Click**

Move the mouse away from the ruler line so you can see the tabs. Your ruler line should show two tabs:

Tables and Tabs 3

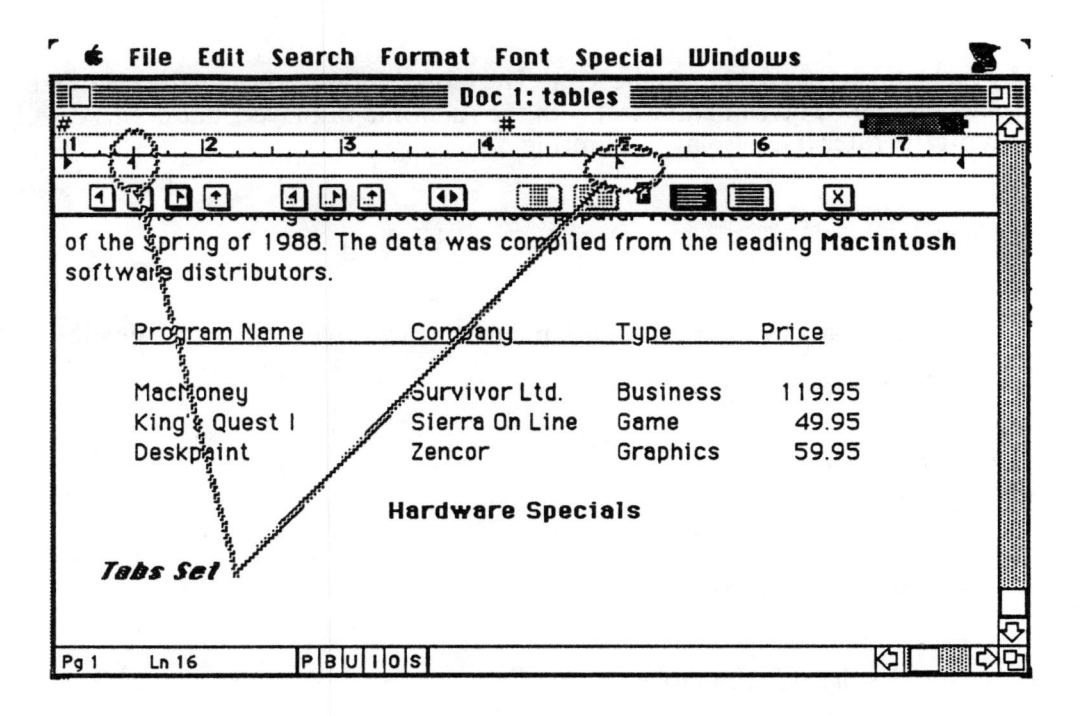

```
 File   Edit   Search   Format   Font   Special   Windows
                          Doc 1: tables
```

of the Spring of 1988. The data was compiled from the leading **Macintosh** software distributors.

```
Program Name        Company         Type        Price

MacMoney            Survivor Ltd.   Business    119.95
King's Quest I      Sierra On Line  Game         49.95
Deskpaint           Zencor          Graphics     59.95

              Hardware Specials
```

Tabs Set

Pg 1   Ln 16   P B U I O S

Figure 3.12

Add another right-aligned tab at 6.5".

> **Point** at 6.5" on the ruler line
> **Click**

To complete the ruler line setting, you must "unselect" the decimal tab icon:

> **Point** at the right tab icon
> **Click**

111

3 Tables and Tabs

The highlight is removed from the icon. The tab locations shown on the ruler line are now active. You can enter text with the ruler line displayed, but in this case, turn off the ruler line display by entering

[Apple/r]

You are now ready to enter information into the new table. Create the headings. Enter

**[Tab] [Apple/Shift/u]
Product [Tab]
List [Tab]
Your Cost
[Apple/Shift/u] [Return] [Return]**

Enter the first item in the table:

**[Tab]
PL 30 Megabyte Hard Disk [Tab]
890.00 [Tab]
629.00 [Return]**

Enter a second hardware item:

**[Tab]
PL 100I Hard Disk - Mac II [Tab]
1899.00 [Tab]
1295.00 [Return]**

Tables and Tabs 3

Complete the table with a third entry:

[Tab]
Memory Upgrade 2 Megabyte[Tab]
495.00[Tab]
279.00[Return]

The document should resemble the following:

```
 File   Edit   Search   Format   Font   Special   Windows
━━━━━━━━━━━━━━━━━ Doc 1: tables ━━━━━━━━━━━━━━━━━
of the Spring of 1988. The data was compiled from the leading Macintosh
software distributors.

    Program Name        Company          Type        Price

    MacMoney            Survivor Ltd.    Business    119.95
    King's Quest I      Sierra On Line   Game         49.95
    Deskpaint           Zencor           Graphics     59.95

                    Hardware Specials


    Product                         List         Your Cost

    PL 30 Megabyte Hard Disk        890.00        629.00
    PL 1001 Hard Disk - Mac II     1899.00       1295.00
    Memory Upgrade 2 Megabyte       495.00        279.00

Pg 1   Ln 21      P B U I O S
```

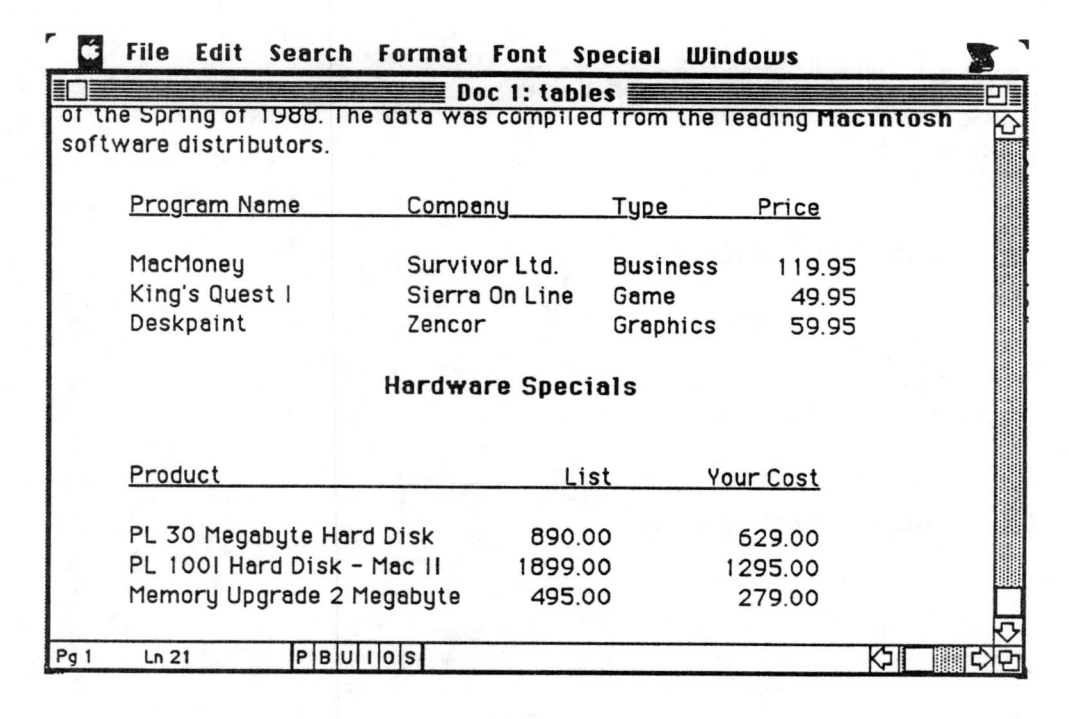

Figure 3.13

113

3 Tables and Tabs

Double Underlines

The next item in the table is a special sale item. To make this item stand out from the others, use WordPerfect's character options. For example, you might want to draw a double line across the table to mark off the special offer. As you saw earlier in this chapter, the appearance of an outline is controlled by the outline style format selected from the Character menu. To draw a double underline, select Double Underline from the Character menu. Enter

[Apple/5]

Point at Double under Underline Style
Click
Click on OK

Draw the underline by entering

[Apple/Shift/u]
[Tab] [Tab]
[Apple/Shift/u] [Return]

Change the font size to 18-point:

Point at Font
Drag to 18
Release

Enter the special offer. Note that you use the underline mode to add an underline below the text to match the double underline above the text. Enter

Tables and Tabs **3**

[Tab]
[Apple/Shift/u]
AST Turbo Laser[Tab]
4699.00[Tab]
4200.00
[Apple/Shift/u] [Return] [Return]

The screen should resemble the following:

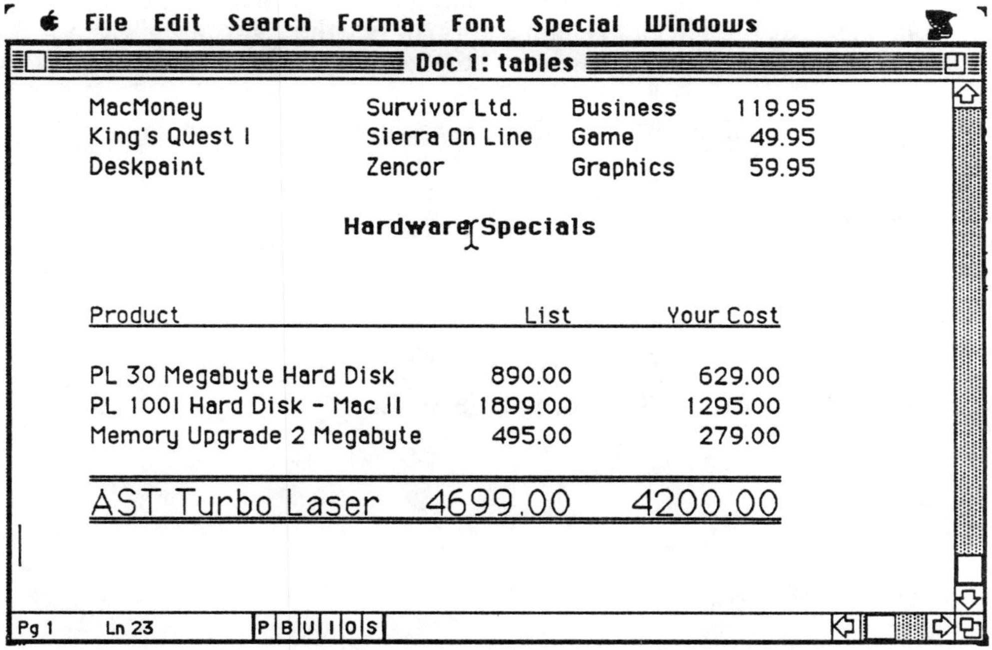

```
 File   Edit   Search   Format   Font   Special   Windows

                        Doc 1: tables

        MacMoney          Survivor Ltd.    Business    119.95
        King's Quest I    Sierra On Line   Game         49.95
        Deskpaint         Zencor           Graphics     59.95

                         Hardware Specials


        Product                        List        Your Cost

        PL 30 Megabyte Hard Disk      890.00        629.00
        PL 1001 Hard Disk - Mac II   1899.00       1295.00
        Memory Upgrade 2 Megabyte     495.00        279.00

        AST Turbo Laser   4699.00     4200.00


 Pg 1    Ln 23       P B U I O S
```

Figure 3.14

115

3 Tables and Tabs

Tabs with Leader Characters

WordPerfect can also create tables in which space between tabs is automatically filled with dots. This format is commonly seen in special tables such as tables of contents. WordPerfect can generate a table of contents from a document. Keep in mind that generating a table of contents is different from typing a table that resembles a table of contents. The most common use of a dot leader is to fill space between a left-aligned tab and a right-aligned tab. For example, if you list products on left-aligned tabs and their respective prices on right-aligned tabs, the term "dot leader" would imply that it is the space between the tabs that would be filled. In this case, you will fill the space between a left-aligned tab and a right-aligned tab, which means that the left tab remains normal, but the right tab is given a dot leader. WordPerfect will fill the space to the left of the right-aligned tab.

To create a sample of this type of table, change the font size back to 12-point:

| **Point** at Font |
| **Drag** to 12 |
| **Release** |

To set the tabs, display the Tab Format menu. Enter

[Apple/4]3

Clear the existing tabs:

| **Point** at Delete |
| **Click** |

Place a left-aligned tab at 2". Enter

2

116

| **Point** at Set
| **Click**

To make a right-aligned tab with a dot leader,

| **Point** at Right
| **Click** on Dot Leader

Now, enter the location:

6

| **Point** at Set
| **Click**

The symbol placed at 6" is a right-aligned tab with a dot to indicate that a dot leader will precede this tab:

3 Tables and Tabs

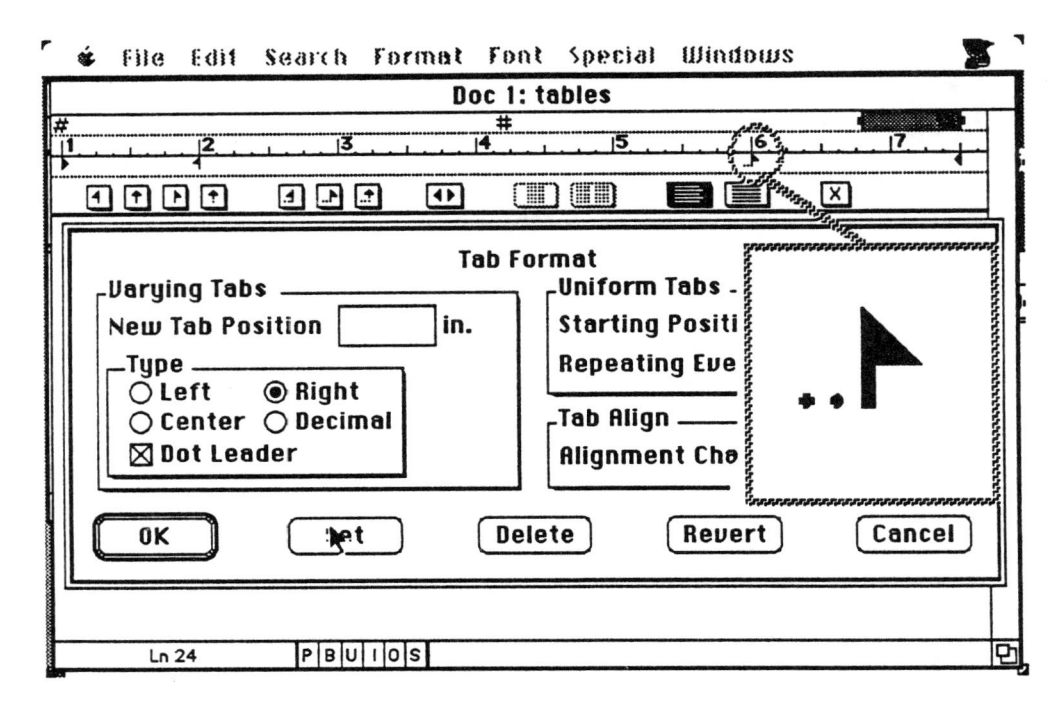

Figure 3.15

```
Point at OK
Click
```

Begin with a heading for the table. Enter

[Apple/Shift/c] [Apple/Shift/b]
Miscellaneous
[Apple/Shift/b] [Return] [Return]

Enter the table items:

[Tab] Surge Suppressor
[Tab] 19 [Return]

Tables and Tabs 3

The second tab generates a series of dots to its left, stopping at the previous tab:

```
┌──────────────────────────────────────────────────┐
│  File  Edit  Search  Format  Font  Special  Windows │
├──────────────── Doc 1: tables ───────────────────┤
│              Hardware Specials                    │
│                                                   │
│   Product                    List      Your Cost  │
│                                                   │
│   PL 30 Megabyte Hard Disk   890.00     629.00    │
│   PL 1001 Hard Disk - Mac II 1899.00   1295.00    │
│   Memory Upgrade 2 Megabyte  495.00     279.00    │
│   ─────────────────────────────────────────────   │
│   AST Turbo Laser   4699.00   4200.00             │
│                                                   │
│              Miscellaneous Items                  │
│       Surge Suppressor.................. 19      │
│                                                   │
│ Pg 1  Ln 27     P B U I O S                       │
└──────────────────────────────────────────────────┘
```

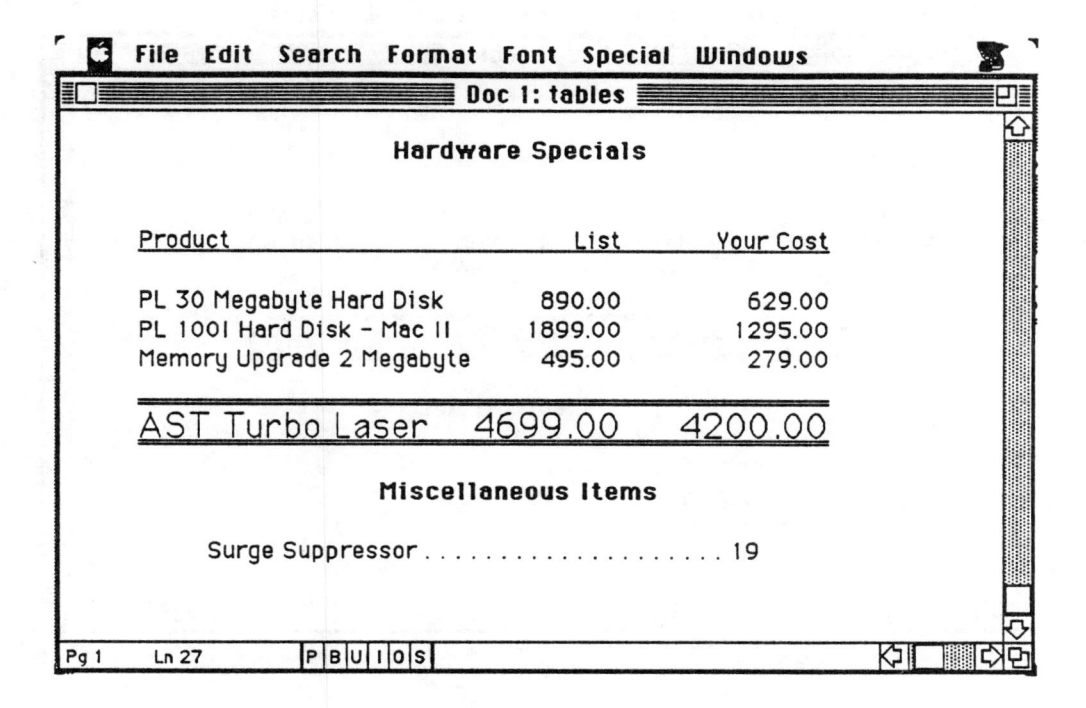

Figure 3.16

Continue entering items into the table:

[Tab]
Mac carrying case[Tab]
65[Return][Tab]
Mac security kit[Tab]
35[Return][Return]

119

3 Tables and Tabs

Your screen should resemble the following:

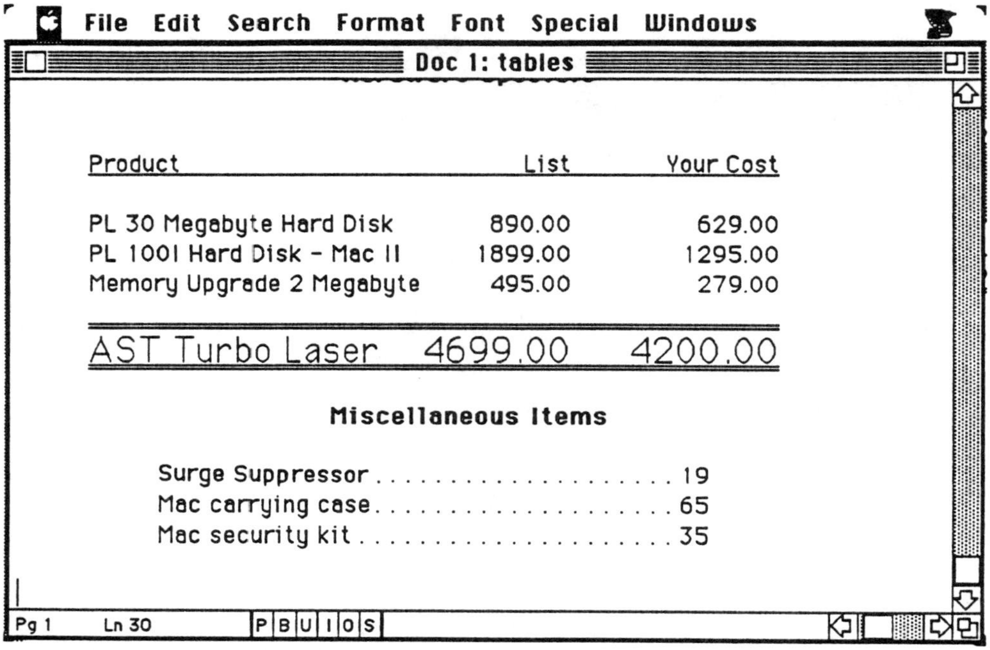

```
┌─────────────────────────────────────────────────────┐
│   File   Edit   Search   Format   Font   Special   Windows │
├═════════════════════ Doc 1: tables ═════════════════┤
│                                                      │
│   Product                          List      Your Cost │
│                                                      │
│   PL 30 Megabyte Hard Disk        890.00      629.00 │
│   PL 1001 Hard Disk - Mac II     1899.00     1295.00 │
│   Memory Upgrade 2 Megabyte       495.00      279.00 │
│   ─────────────────────────────────────────────────  │
│   AST Turbo Laser      4699.00     4200.00           │
│   ─────────────────────────────────────────────────  │
│                  Miscellaneous Items                 │
│                                                      │
│   Surge Suppressor......................19           │
│   Mac carrying case.....................65           │
│   Mac security kit......................35           │
│                                                      │
│ Pg 1   Ln 30     │P│B│U│I│O│S│                      │
└─────────────────────────────────────────────────────┘
```

Figure 3.17

Quick Tables

In the previous table, you set individual tab stops. You selected specific locations for each tab stop as well as tab type: left, center, right, or decimal and with or without leader characters.

WordPerfect allows you to quickly create tables without setting individual tab stops. Enter

[Apple/4]3

First, delete the current tab stop:

120

Tables and Tabs **3**

> **Point** at Delete
> **Click**

The right side of the box displays a section named Uniform Tabs, which refers to tabs placed at regular intervals on the ruler line. To set uniform tabs, you must enter a starting location and the size of the interval. In this example, set the first tab at 2.5" and then set the tabs 1.5" apart after that. Enter

[Tab]
2.5[Tab]
1.5

> **Point** at Set
> **Click**

Tabs are set at 2.5", 4", 5.5", and 7".

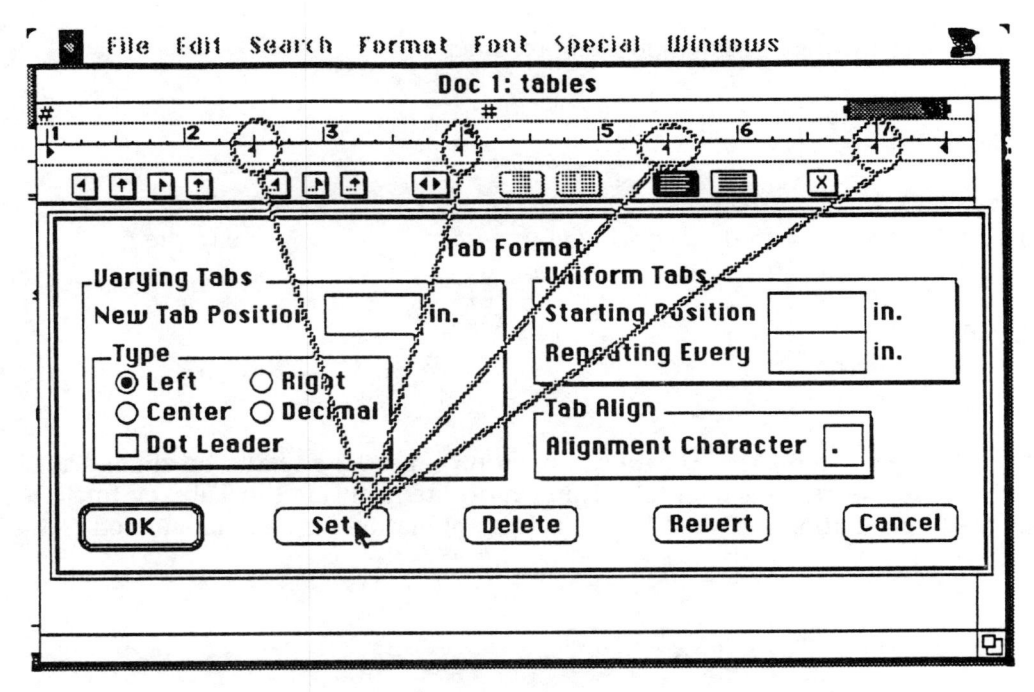

Figure 3.18

121

3 Tables and Tabs

To apply these tabs to the table, enter

[Return]

Create a title for this table. Enter

**[Apple/Shift/c] [Apple/Shift/b]
Software[Apple/Shift/b] [Return] [Return]**

How can you use a table that contains only left-aligned tabs? WordPerfect allows you to use the [Apple/Tab] combination to place decimal-aligned text at left-aligned tab stops. In this way, you can achieve the effects of a fully defined table without defining individual decimal tabs. Enter

**[Tab]
4th Dimension**

To move to the next decimal-aligned tab, enter

[Apple/Tab]

This tab is too close to the text for you to enter the price. Move to the next tab:

**[Apple/Tab]
475.00[Return]**

Note that using the [Apple/Tab] combination caused the text to be aligned as if the tab stop were a decimal tab. Enter more items, using the Tab key for left-aligned information and the [Apple/Tab] combination for decimal-aligned text:

Tables and Tabs 3

[Tab]
Excel[Tab] [Apple/Tab]
228.00[Return]
[Tab]
Focal Point[Tab] [Apple/Tab]
57.00[Return]
[Tab]
[Tab]
Pagemaker 2.0a[Tab] [Apple/Tab]
385.00[Return] [Return]

The new table should resemble the following:

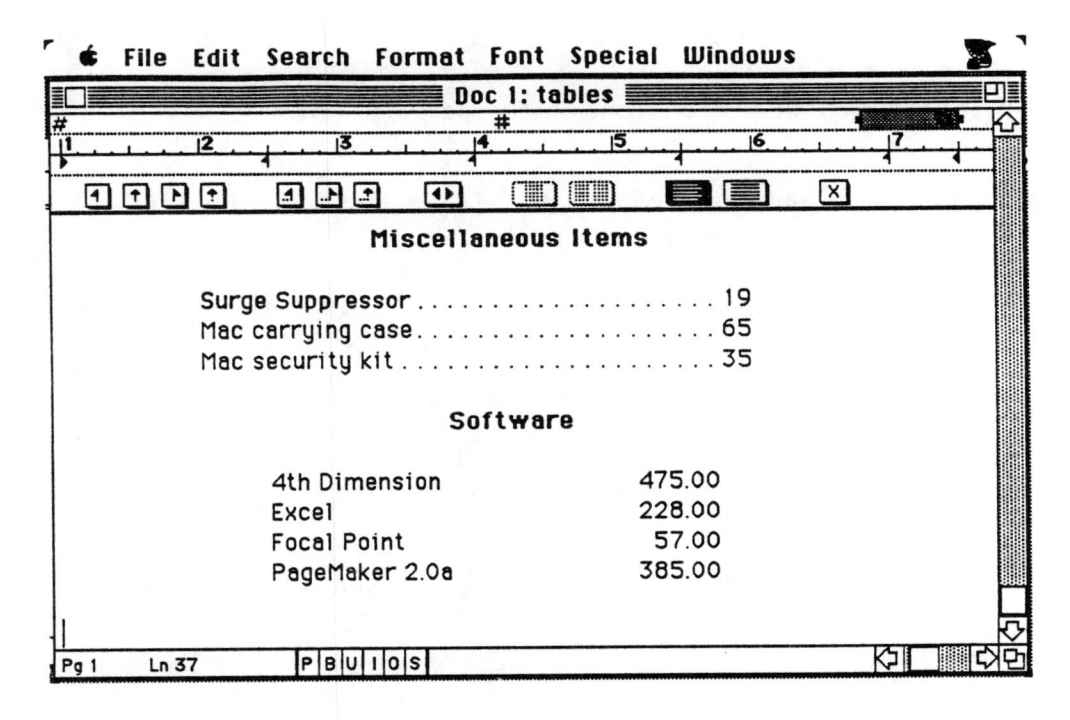

Figure 3.19

3 Tables and Tabs

Cut-and-Paste Tables

When text is arranged in tables, you can easily move items around using cut-and-paste techniques. Suppose you want to move the line containing "Focal Point" to another position. Enter

↑ (3 times)

You can use keyboard commands to highlight specific parts of the text. Display the Select menu by entering

[Apple/6]

This menu allows you to choose one of four specific text items.

Sentence	A sentence in WordPerfect is a group of text ending with a period or exclamation point.
Paragraph	A paragraph is a group of text that ends with a hard return [HRt] code.
Page	A page is a group of text that ends with a soft page [SPg] or hard page [HPg] code.
All	All selects the entire document.

In this case, the correct choice is 3 — paragraph — because each line ended with a [HRt] character. Enter

3

WordPerfect highlights the entire line by extending the highlight to the beginning of the next line. This type of highlight is normal when WordPerfect includes a [HRt] code in a selection block. The highlight on the second line covers the space between the edge of the paper and the left margin. Don't be confused; the only text selected is on the "Focal Point" line.

Tables and Tabs 3

WordPerfect—like most Macintosh applications—includes three basic editing commands for cut-and-paste applications found on the Edit menu: Cut, Copy, and Paste.

Cut The Cut command removes the currently selected text and places it into the clipboard area of memory. Each successive cut deletes the contents of the clipboard; only the most recent cut remains in the clipboard. While the clipboard retains only the most recent cut, WordPerfect provides the Undelete area to retain the last three deletions, cuts, or copies.

The keyboard command for Cut is

[Apple/x]

Copy The Copy command operates much like the Cut command, but the text is not removed from the document when placed into the clipboard. The keyboard command for Copy is

[Apple/c]

Paste The Paste command places a copy of the clipboard text back into the document at the current cursor location. The keyboard command for Paste is

[Apple/v]

In this case, cut the text by entering

[Apple/x]

3 Tables and Tabs

You can move the text to a new location by changing the cursor location and pasting the item into the text at that location. Enter

↑ (2 times)
[Apple/v]

The table should now resemble the following:

```
 File   Edit   Search   Format   Font   Special   Windows
                        Doc 1: tables
         AST Turbo Laser    4699.00    4200.00

                        Miscellaneous Items

              Surge Suppressor . . . . . . . . . . . . . . . . . . . . 19
              Mac carrying case . . . . . . . . . . . . . . . . . . . 65
              Mac security kit . . . . . . . . . . . . . . . . . . . . 35

                              Software

              Focal Point                      57.00
              4th Dimension                   475.00
              Excel                           228.00
              PageMaker 2.0a                  385.00

 Pg 1   Ln 37        P B U I O S
```

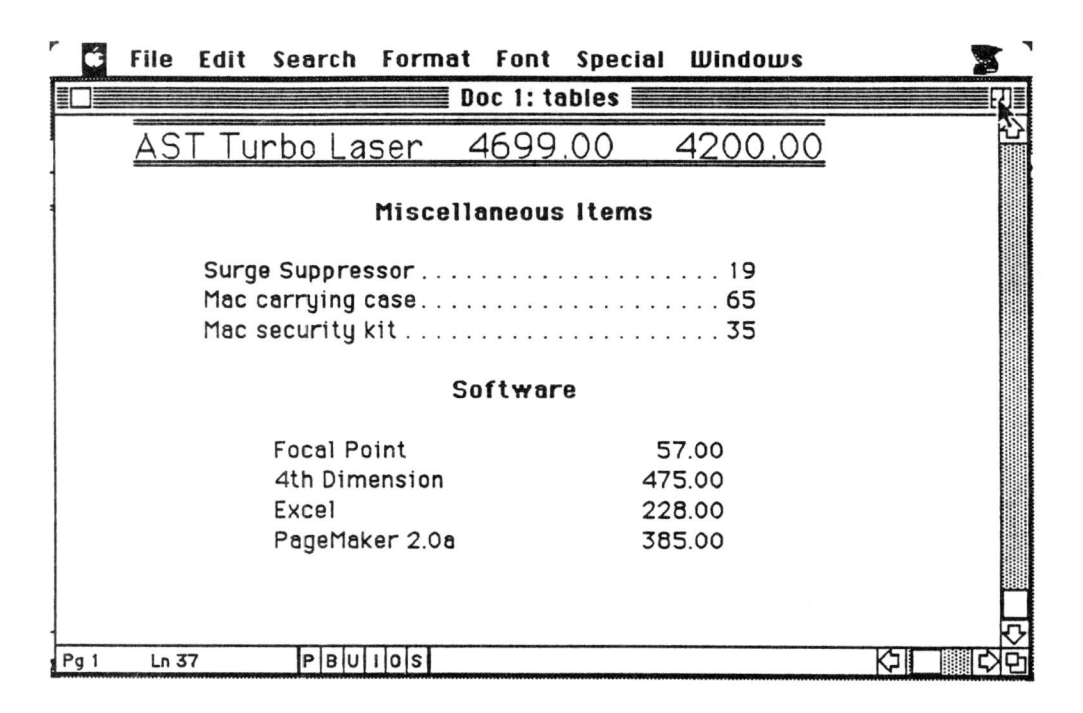

Figure 3.20

Moving from Table to Table

What would happen if you placed a copy of the text, which is still in the clipboard, into another table in the document? Move the cursor to the previous table — Miscellaneous Items — by entering

Tables and Tabs 3

↑ (4 times)

Paste the block into the text by entering

[Apple/v]

The text is inserted, but the alignment is not quite correct:

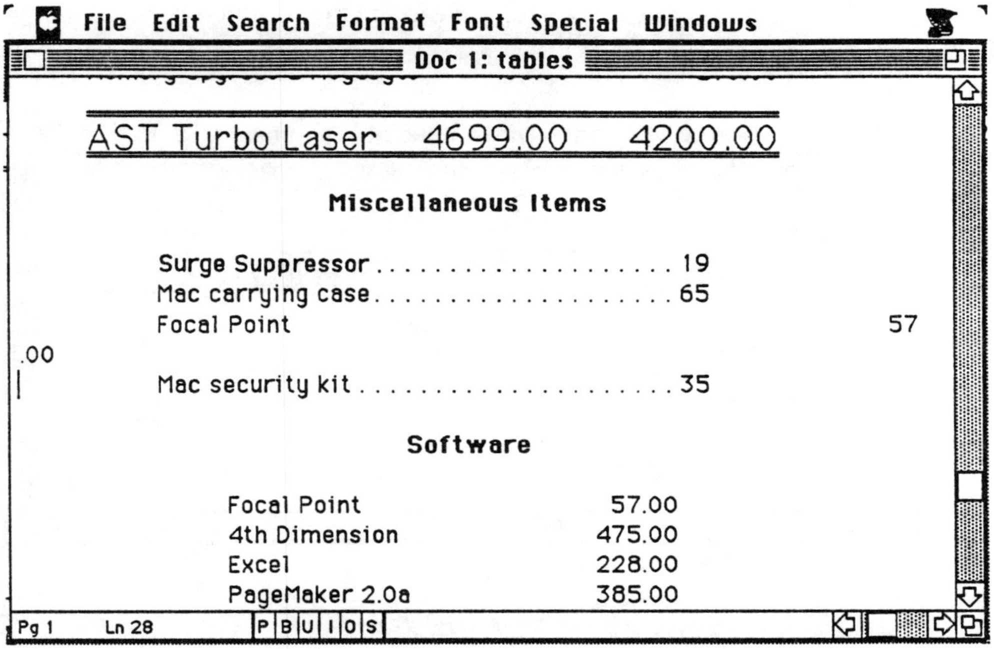

Figure 3.21

3 Tables and Tabs

Keep in mind that when a block of text is pasted, it brings with it the formatting commands—in this case, tab codes—it contained when it was cut. The current table, however, uses a different set of tabs from those in effect in the section of the document from which the text was cut. To achieve the correct alignment, you must display the hidden codes. It may also help to display the ruler line as well. Enter

[Apple/7]
[Apple/r]

With the ruler line and codes displayed, you can see the reason for the poor alignment:

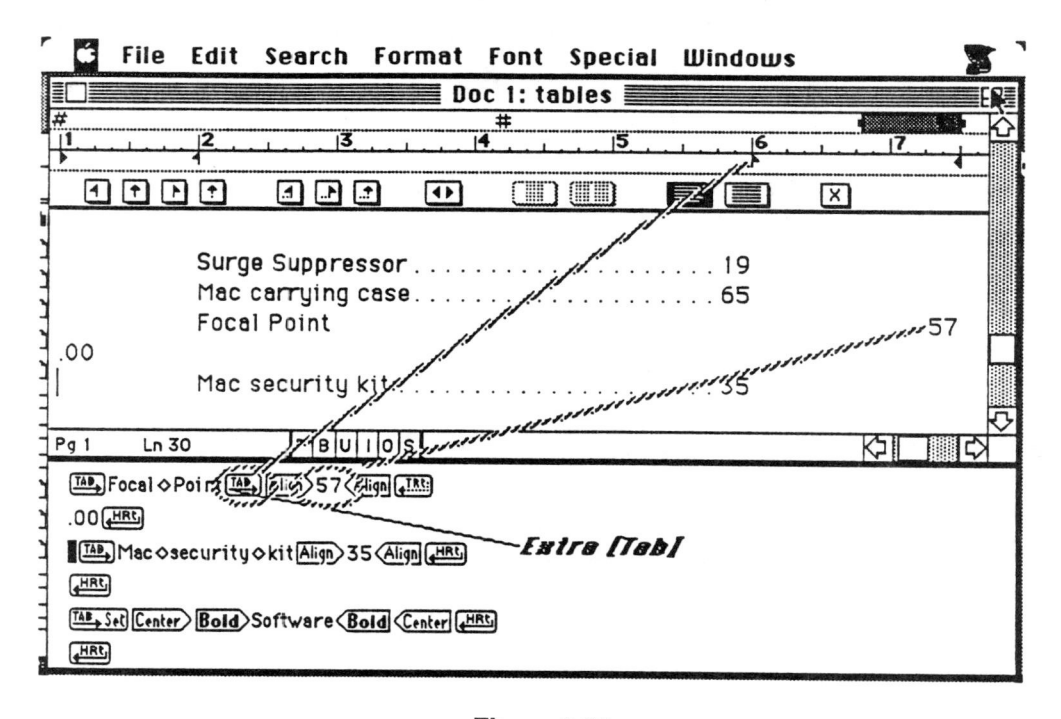

Figure 3.22

Tables and Tabs 3

Note the way WordPerfect employs codes to indicate the type of tab alignment used. If the text is to be left-aligned, a simple tab code is inserted before the text; however, when the text is aligned as a decimal- or right-aligned tab, two codes are used. The [Align code marks the beginning of a decimal or right-aligned block of text, and the Align] code marks the end.

If you look carefully, you can see the difference between a decimal-aligned number and a right-aligned number. When text is right-aligned, the Align] code follows the last character. In a decimal-aligned number, the Align] follows the decimal point, leaving the decimal number to fall after the tab. For example, this code sequence creates a right-aligned number: [Align45.00Align]. On the other hand, this sequence creates a decimal alignment: [Align45.Align]00. Note that in decimal alignment, the Align] falls in between the decimal point and the decimal values.

You can also see why the alignment was not correct. The block of text that was pasted has two tab codes—one normal and the other decimal-aligned. The ruler line shows only two tabs active in this table. The extra tab caused WordPerfect to place part of the text—the 00—on a new line. Note that the line ending is a new code—a [TRt]—temporary return. This return is inserted because the tabs used in the line exceed the number of tabs set on the ruler line.

To correct the alignment, you must delete the extra line. Enter

[Delete] (4 times)

Next, move the cursor to the next tab code. Enter

→ (5 times)
[Delete]

129

3 Tables and Tabs

The screen should resemble the following:

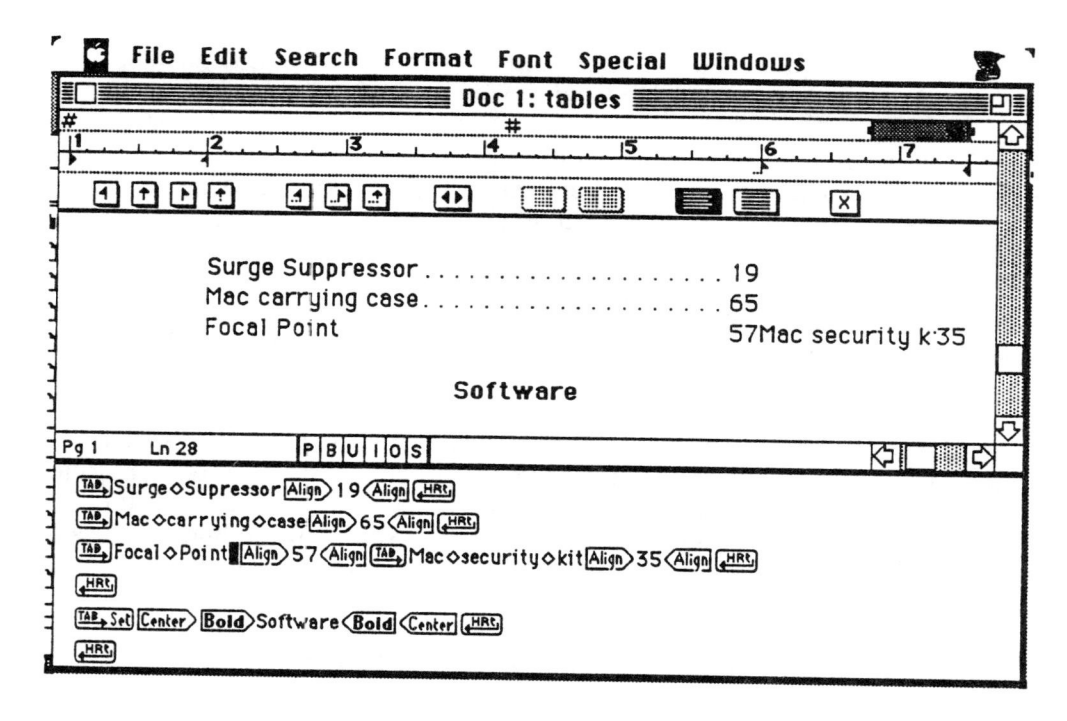

```
 File  Edit  Search  Format  Font  Special  Windows
                    Doc 1: tables

        Surge Suppressor.................19
        Mac carrying case.................65
        Focal Point                57Mac security k·35

                       Software

 Pg 1    Ln 28      P B U I O S

 [TAB]Surge◊Supressor[Align]19[Align][HRt]
 [TAB]Mac◊carrying◊case[Align]65[Align][HRt]
 [TAB]Focal◊Point[Align]57[Align][TAB]Mac◊security◊kit[Align]35[Align][HRt]
 [HRt]
 [TAB,Set][Center][Bold]Software[Bold][Center][HRt]
 [HRt]
```

Figure 3.23

The text still does not look right. In removing the extra tab stop, you allowed WordPerfect to resolve the problem of too many tabs on a line. The program then removed the temporary return code — [TRt] — placing together text that was meant to be on two separate lines. You now must insert a [HRt] code at the end of this line to separate the "Mac security" line. Enter

→ (4 times)
[Return]

Tables and Tabs 3

The alignment is now correct, but something is still wrong with the text. The "Focal Point" line does not display the dot leaders. WordPerfect inserts the leaders at the time the tab is entered. In this case, because the text was copied from another table, leaders are not automatically inserted into this line. To insert the leaders, you must delete the current [Align and Align] codes and enter a new tab. Enter

← (5 times)
[Decimal]
[Tab]

This time, the program correctly inserts the leader dots:

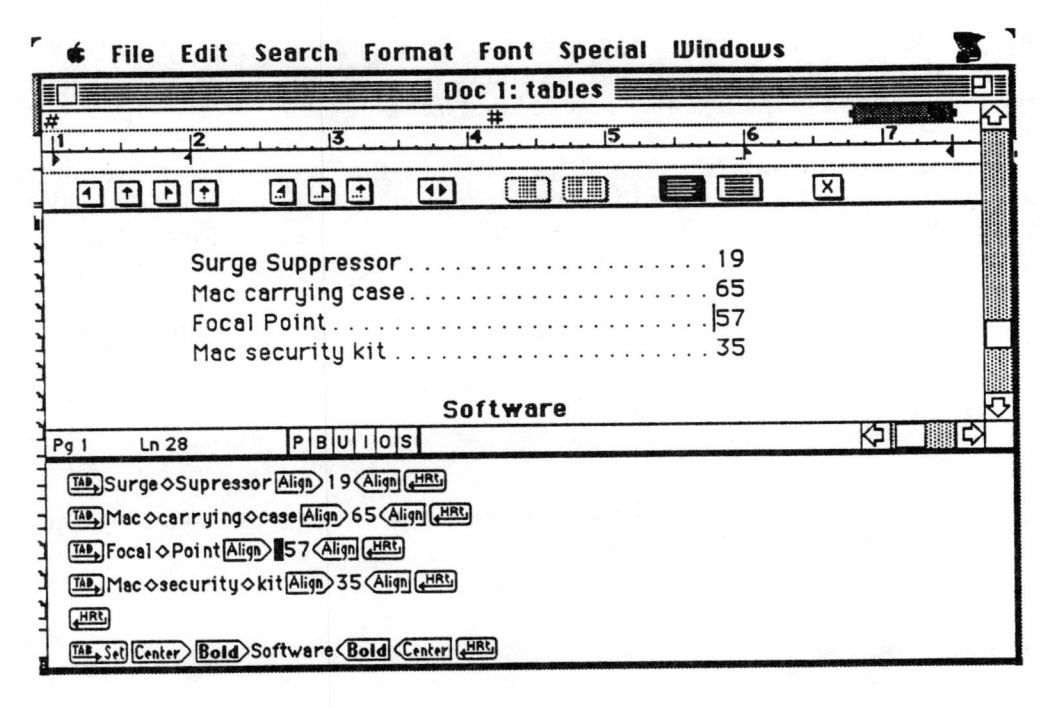

Figure 3.24

3 Tables and Tabs

This exercise shows that when tab-aligned text is moved from one type of table to another, WordPerfect may not be able to automatically adjust the text to its new location. While it is not necessary to delete the text, a number of adjustments in the codes may be necessary. If you pay attention to the codes, you can usually achieve the correct formatting without retyping the text.

Close the codes display by entering

[Apple/7]

Changing Tab Locations

Another type of operation you may want to perform on an existing table is to adjust the location of tabs. For example, the table your cursor is currently positioned in contains two tabs — one at 2" and the other at 6". Suppose you want to change the tab locations so the text aligns on 1.5" and 6.5".

This procedure involves two steps. The first one — the one you might miss most easily — requires you to locate the Tab Set code that controls the tabs for that table. If you do not locate the code, any revisions you make may not be placed at the correct location.

The best way to locate the code is to use the Search command. Enter

[Apple/b]

The Search menu appears. Use the mouse to scroll through the codes list until you see the [Tab Set] code.

```
Point at [Tab Set]
Double Click
Click on Find
```

The cursor is positioned next to the tab set for this table. Begin by changing the tab at 2" to 1.5".

> **Point** at the left-aligned tab icon
> **Click**

To change the position of a tab with the mouse, you must first delete the current tab and then insert a new tab at a different position.

> **Point** at the left tab at 2" icon
> **Click**

The text in the table is scrambled because you have removed the tab; however, this effect is only temporary. As soon as you place a new tab onto the ruler line, the alignment will be corrected.

> **Point** at 1.5"
> **Click**

All text previously aligned at 2" is now aligned at 1.5".

3 Tables and Tabs

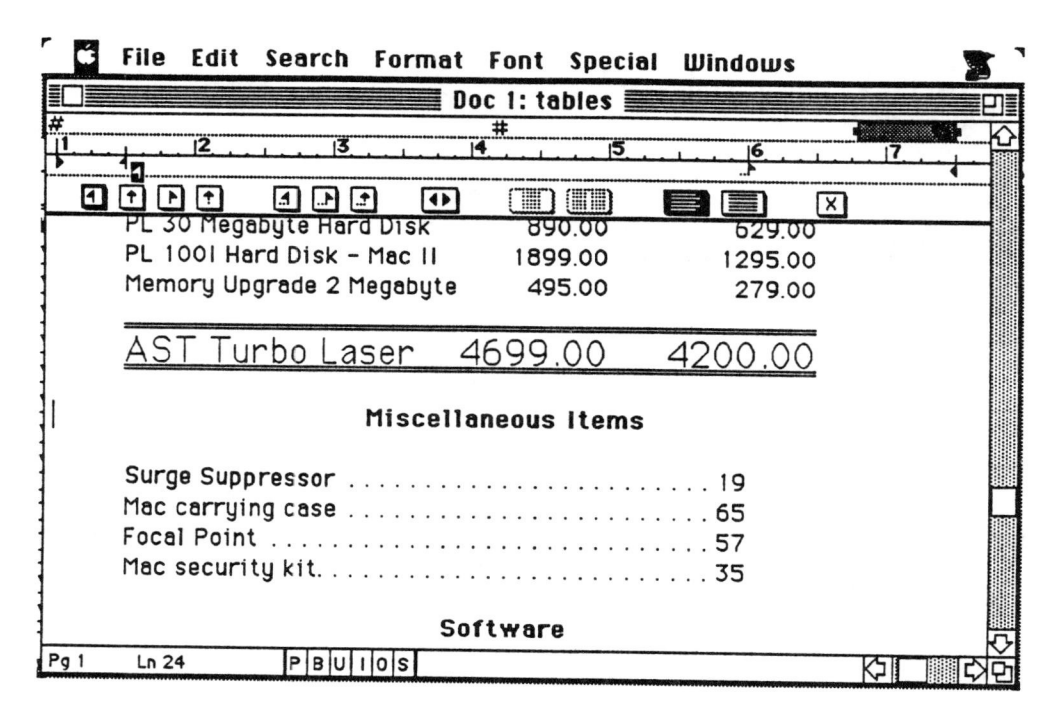

```
 File   Edit   Search   Format   Font   Special   Windows
┌─────────────────────── Doc 1: tables ───────────────────────┐
     PL 30 Megabyte Hard Disk      890.00       629.00
     PL 1001 Hard Disk - Mac II   1899.00      1295.00
     Memory Upgrade 2 Megabyte     495.00       279.00

     AST Turbo Laser    4699.00    4200.00

                    Miscellaneous Items

     Surge Suppressor ......................... 19
     Mac carrying case ........................ 65
     Focal Point .............................. 57
     Mac security kit.......................... 35

                        Software
 Pg 1    Ln 24      P B U I O S
```

Figure 3.25

You can now perform the same procedure to alter the location of the right-aligned tab. First, change the active icon to a right-aligned tab with dot leaders.

Point at the left-aligned tab icon
Click
Point at right-aligned with dots icon
Click

Change the location of the tab:

Tables and Tabs **3**

> **Point** at the tab at 6"
> **Click**
> **Point** at 6.5"
> **Click**
> **Point** at the right-aligned with dots icon
> **Click**

WordPerfect has changed the position of the text aligned on the right tab and filled the wider space between tabs with dots.

Changing Tabs from the Menu Display

You can change values for an existing tab from the Tab Format menu as well as from the ruler line. Close the ruler line display by entering

[Apple/r]

Move to the beginning of this document by entering

[Enter] [Enter] ↑

Locate the tab set code for the first table on the page. Enter

[Apple/f]

Note that the search item — [Tab Set] — is still on the search line. You can search for the same item by entering

[Return]

Now that you have located the code that controls the first table, display the Tab Format menu by entering

135

3 Tables and Tabs

[Apple/4]

Something is wrong with the menu. Option #3 — Tabs — is not accessible at this time.

The problem lies in how the Search command works. When you search for an item in WordPerfect, the program automatically selects the matching item. If you look at the bottom bar, you will see that the words "Select On" appear. This selection is helpful when you want to perform an action on that search text, but it also prohibits you from other operations such as setting tabs. Exit the menu by entering

[Esc]

Before you can change the tabs, you must turn off the selection mode. Enter

[Apple/Shift/n]

The words "Select On" disappear from the bottom bar, indicating that selection has been turned off. You can now display the Tab Format menu by entering

[Apple/4]3

In the Tab Format menu, you cannot delete individual tabs. To set new tabs, you must begin by deleting all existing tabs (there are currently four tabs set).

```
Point at Delete
Click
```

The default settings are for left-aligned tabs. Set three tabs. Enter

1.25

Tables and Tabs 3

> **Point** at Set
> **Click**

3.25

> **Point** at Set
> **Click**

4.5

> **Point** at Set
> **Click**

Now, change the tab type to decimal alignment:

> **Point** at Decimal
> **Click**

Create a tab at 7". Enter

7

> **Point** at Set
> **Click**
> **Click** on OK

The table is reformatted to adjust to the new tab locations. Tables created with tabs have the advantage of being able to adjust to changes in tab location. As shown in the two previous examples, all text aligned on tabs within a table can be moved to a different location by simply changing the location of the tab.

137

3 Tables and Tabs

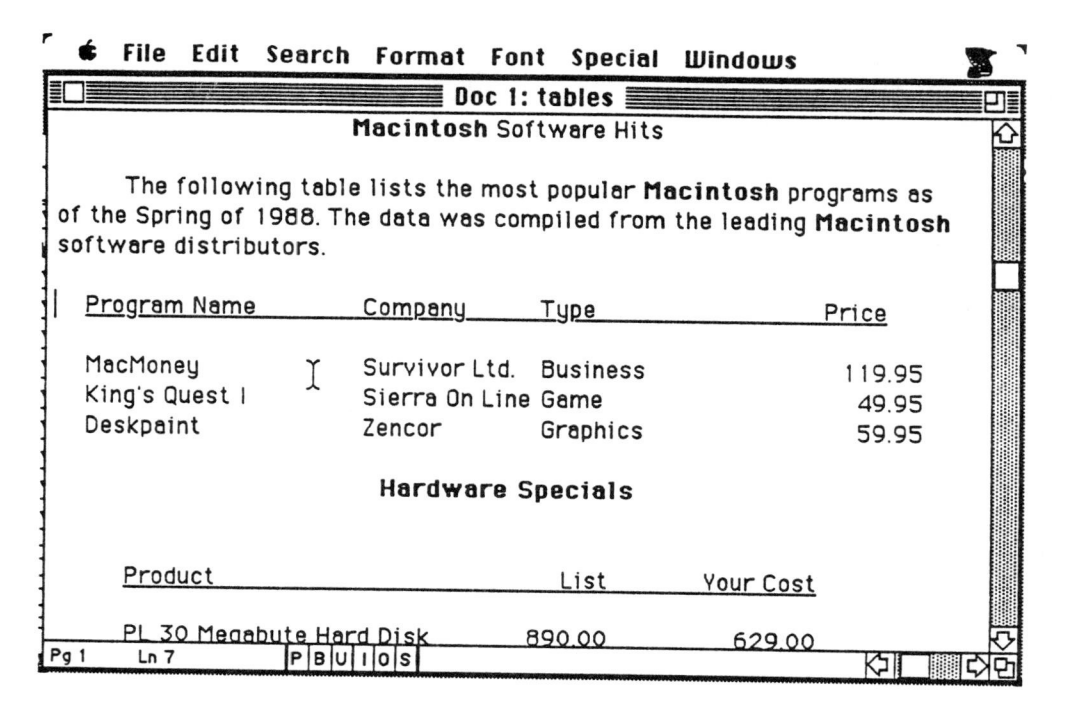

```
  File   Edit   Search   Format   Font   Special   Windows
================= Doc 1: tables =================
                    Macintosh Software Hits

     The following table lists the most popular Macintosh programs as
of the Spring of 1988. The data was compiled from the leading Macintosh
software distributors.

   Program Name         Company      Type              Price

   MacMoney             Survivor Ltd. Business         119.95
   King's Quest I       Sierra On Line Game             49.95
   Deskpaint            Zencor        Graphics          59.95

                       Hardware Specials


   Product                           List        Your Cost

   PL 30 Megabyte Hard Disk          890.00      629.00
Pg 1   Ln 7          P B U I O S
```

Figure 3.26

In this context, WordPerfect tabs are **logical** items, which refers to the idea that the location of text aligned by tab codes — either [Tab] or [Align Align] — is determined by the Tab Set codes that precede that text. If you change the physical location of tab stops set in the Tab Set code, all text aligned in tab codes is re-evaluated to conform to the new settings.

Tabs are logical — not physical — because they can adjust to changes in the environment.

Adjusting for Font Size Changes

Another change that prompts tables to adjust is an alteration in the point size of text. Because tables are logical units, WordPerfect adjusts the point size of text in tables but retains its alignment at tabs.

Tables and Tabs 3

This would not be the case if you created an entry that relied on spaces to separate items. To illustrate this point, add an item to the table using spaces rather than tabs to position the text. Move the cursor to the last line in the table. Enter

↓ (5 times)

Indent the line with spaces. Enter

[space bar] (4 times)

Enter the following items. Note that the [space bar] is used to create the spaces between items. Enter

Ready Set Go 4.0
[space bar] (10 times)
Letraset USA
[space bar] (4 times)
Desktop Publishing
[space bar] (10 times)
279.95 [Return] [Return]

Entering spaces takes a bit more time than entering tabs with the Tab key, but, even more significantly, the spaces represent physical — not logical — spacing. These spaces cannot adjust logically to changes in format, such as a reduction in the point size of the type.

Currently, it is not obvious that the last line of the table has been entered in a different manner from the rest of the table. Making a formatting change will reveal that there is a substantial difference.

Turn on the selection mode by entering

[Apple/Shift/n]

3 Tables and Tabs

Highlight the entire table by entering

↑ (7 times)

Change the point size to 10-point:

> **Point** at Font
> **Drag** to 10
> **Release**

The change in point size of the text did not affect alignment of the tab-aligned text. The last line in the table—which used physical (space bar) spacing—no longer lines up at the proper column locations.

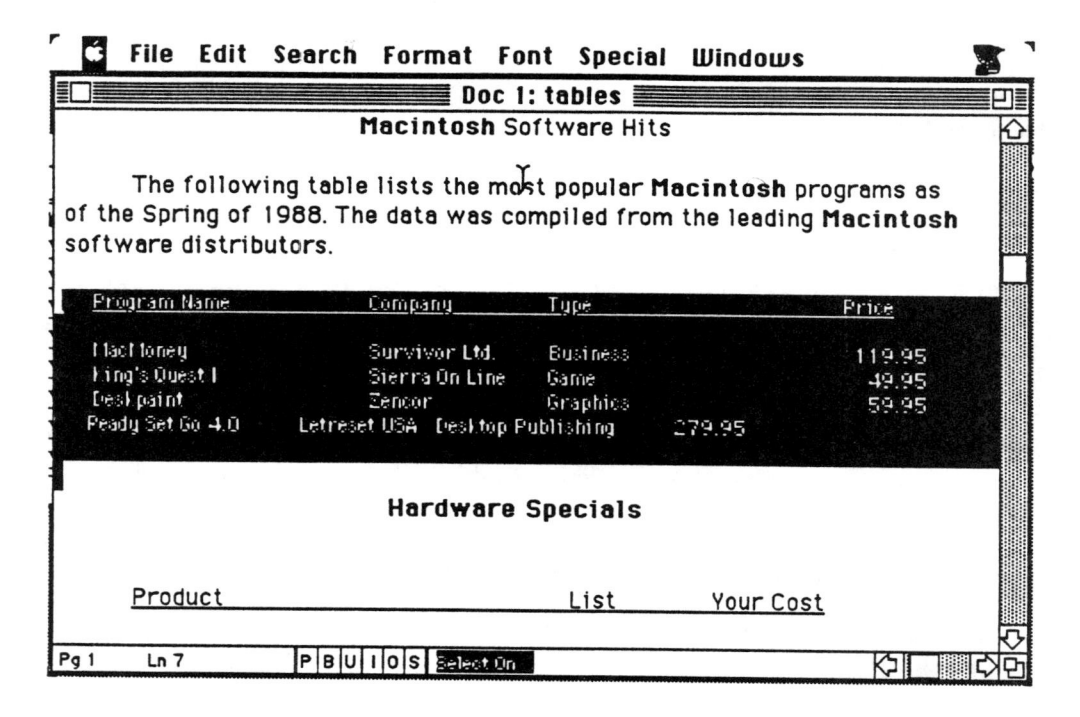

Figure 3.27

Tab alignment is useful because it aligns text in columns and keeps the text in the table properly aligned when you make formatting changes. Entering spaces with the space bar to align text may produce results that look correct in some circumstances, but when you use this method, your spacing cannot adjust to changes in format.

LINE SPACING

Up to this point, you have been concerned mainly with horizontal text spacing. Vertical spacing has been largely left to WordPerfect's defaults.

The height of each line in WordPerfect is determined by the point size of the text in the line. If you mix point sizes on the same line, WordPerfect uses the largest point size as its guide. The height of the line is automatically adjusted in proportion to the height of the characters — i.e., the larger the point size, the greater the line height. Thus, if you change point size and enter blank lines, the blanks will be in proportion to the point size. For example, a blank line entered as 24-point is twice as high as a blank line entered as 12-point.

Line spacing in WordPerfect takes on a slightly different meaning than it does in typewriting or text-based word processors such as those found on the IBM PC (e.g., WordPerfect 4.2 or WordStar). These programs measure pages in terms of the number of lines they contain. (To be fair, WORD for the PC and WordStar 2000 also measure vertical height in inches not lines.) In such cases, each line uses the same amount of vertical space — typically, 1/6".

When all lines use the same height, it is logical to speak in terms of single-, double- or triple-spacing, but when the height of each line can vary with the type size used on each line, the concept of line spacing is more complicated. If you activate double-spaced text in WordPerfect, you are instructing the program to increase the line height to double the normal space for the current font size.

In WordPerfect, vertical spacing is measured in terms of inches. Concepts such as double-spacing are relative to the size of the text involved.

WordPerfect retains the terminology of line spacing, but you should keep in mind that the font-oriented structure of the Macintosh makes the concept of simple line spacing obsolete.

3 Tables and Tabs

While this concept is a bit more complex, the effect can be quite interesting. As an example, take the next table in the document — Hardware Specials. Suppose you want to increase the line spacing in this table. The Spacing menu is found on the Line Format menu. Enter

[Apple/4]

Option #5 controls the line (i.e., vertical) spacing. Enter

5

The Spacing menu appears:

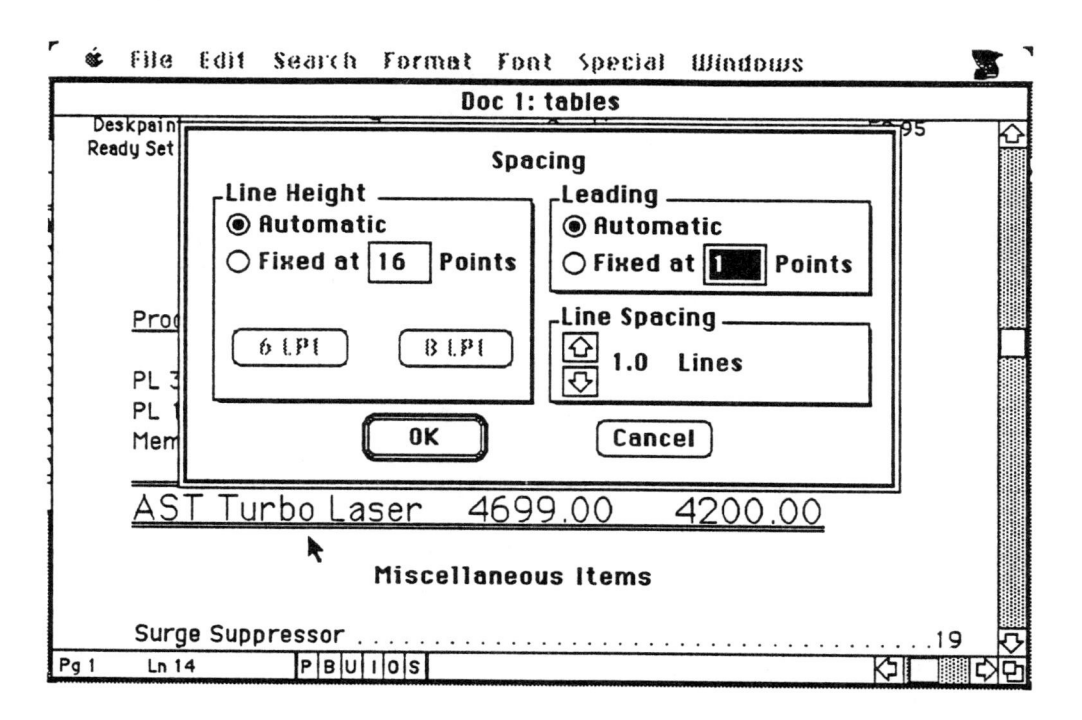

Figure 3.28

Tables and Tabs 3

The Spacing menu contains three options.

Line Height The line height and leading control the height of lines. Line height can be used in two ways. The Automatic setting—the default—adjusts the line height in proportion to the size of the font. If you select Fixed, WordPerfect will keep all lines the same height. The height is entered in points (1/72" increments). There are also two buttons that correspond to common PC line heights: 6 lines per inch (12-point) or 8 lines per inch (9-point).

Leading Leading is the space between the bottom of one line and the top of the next. Leading can be automatic or fixed at a specific point size. The default setting is Automatic.

Line Spacing This option helps you relate the concepts of single-, double-, and triple-spacing to line height calculated in proportion to the font size. You can use line spacing to multiply the automatic line height by specific factors (i.e., 1, 1.5, 2, etc). Each time you click on the large line spacing arrows, WordPerfect increases (Up arrow) or decreases (Down arrow) the line height by a half-step increment.

Suppose you want to create double-spaced text (i.e., double the normal line height). Click on the large Up arrow in the line spacing box.

```
Point at Up Arrow
Click
```

Line spacing is increased by half a step. In this case, the value will show 1.53 because of the automatic calculation of line height.

```
Point at Up Arrow
Click
```

The line spacing is now set as double-spaced (2.06).

143

3 Tables and Tabs

> **Point** at OK
> **Click**

WordPerfect adjusts the text to the new line height:

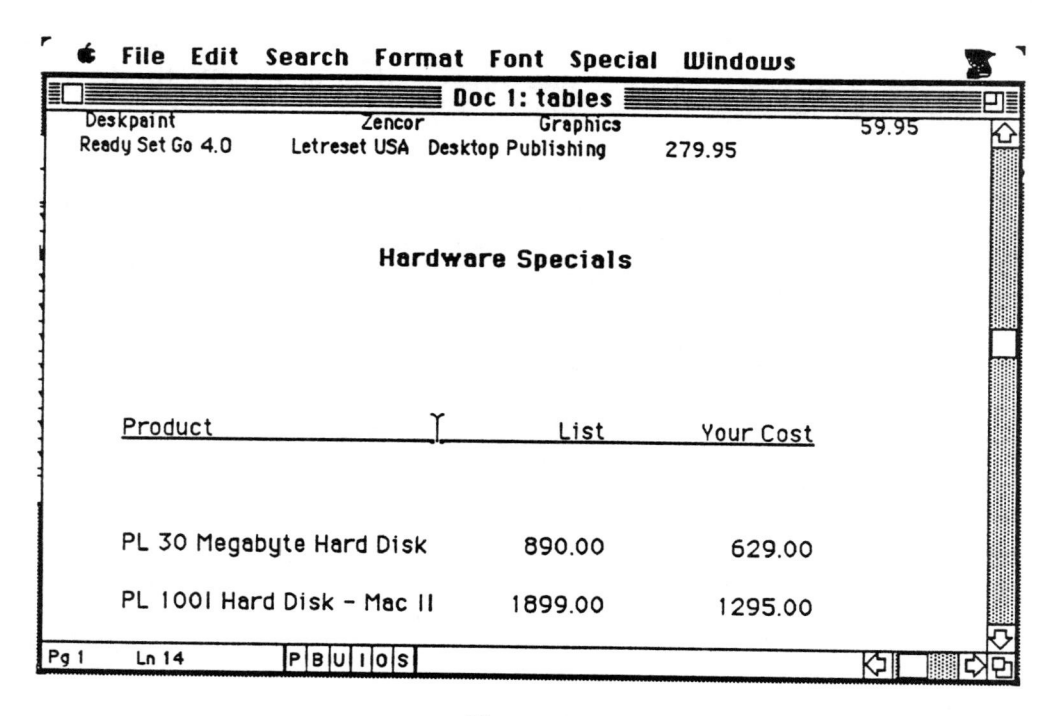

```
 File  Edit  Search  Format  Font  Special  Windows
                     Doc 1: tables
 Deskpaint           Zencor          Graphics              59.95
 Ready Set Go 4.0    Letreset USA  Desktop Publishing   279.95


                         Hardware Specials



          Product                      List        Your Cost



          PL 30 Megabyte Hard Disk    890.00        629.00

          PL 1001 Hard Disk - Mac II  1899.00       1295.00

 Pg 1   Ln 14       P B U I O S
```

Figure 3.29

Scroll down one screen display by entering

[Enter]↓
[Enter]↓

144

Stopping Line Spacing

When you created a new line spacing setting, WordPerfect carried that formatting through the document, beginning at the position where the code was entered and continuing until the end of the document.

Suppose you want to limit the effect of the spacing to just a part of the document — the Hardware Special table. To stop the line spacing from affecting the rest of the document, you must insert another line spacing command following the table. Place the cursor at the title for the next table:

Point before the "M" in "Miscellaneous Items"
Click

Display the Spacing menu by entering

[Apple/4]5

To set the text from this point forward in the document back to single-spacing, you must click on the large Down arrow in the line spacing box:

Point at Down arrow
Click (two times)

The line spacing is set back to 1. Note that your screen may show a slight variation (e.g., 1.02). This is normal. Enter

[Return]

The line spacing for the rest of the document is set back to single-spacing.

3 Tables and Tabs

Keeping a Block Together

At the bottom of the current page, you can see that the Miscellaneous Items table is split by a line. The line represents where WordPerfect will insert a page break. In this case, the table will be split, with part on page one and the rest on page two. WordPerfect normally tries to fit as many lines of text onto any page as the margins permit.

In many instances, you may want to make sure that the table is not split between pages. If WordPerfect cannot fit the text onto the current page, you would want the program to move the entire table to the next page.

WordPerfect provides two ways to protect blocks of text from being split between pages: conditional break and block protect.

Conditional Break   A conditional page break is used to keep a specified number of text lines together on the same page. For example, the Miscellaneous Items table consists of six lines: a title, a blank line, and four items. If you set a conditional end-of-page code for six lines and place it at the beginning of the table, WordPerfect will move the entire table to page 2 if all six lines cannot fit onto the current page. The command for this option is

    [Apple/2]5

Block Protect   The Block Protect feature has the same purpose as the conditional end-of-page command, but it works on paragraph text that includes [SRt] line endings. To use this option, select a block of text consisting of one or more paragraphs. Select Block Protect by entering

    [Apple/2]6

In this case, the conditional end-of-page method will work. Remember, Block Protect will not work on tables because each line in a table ends with a [HRt] code.

Tables and Tabs 3

To create a conditional end-of-page code, enter

[Apple/2] 5

Your screen should resemble the following:

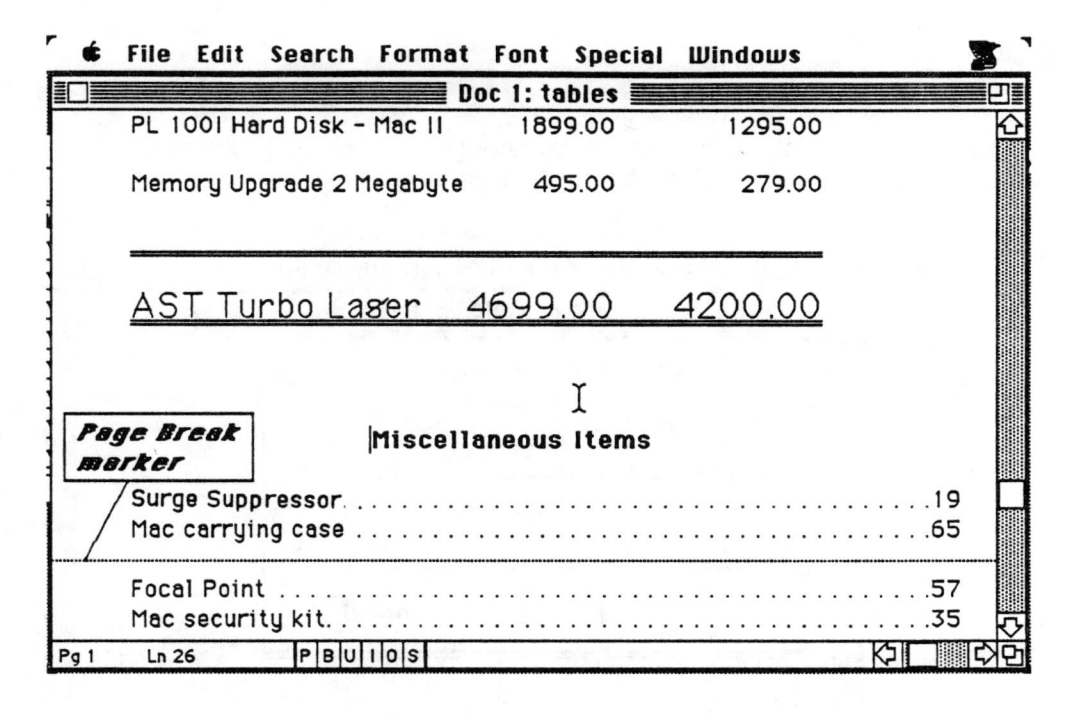

Figure 3.30

You can specify the amount of text you want to protect in terms of lines or inches. The WordPerfect default is lines. Keep in mind that WordPerfect measures the lines in terms of 12-point Geneva text. If you are using larger or smaller type, you must increase or decrease the number of lines to compensate.

3 Tables and Tabs

For example, if you have a table that consists of 12 lines of 10-point text, you must enter nine lines. The calculation would be 10 lines of 10-point text = 100 points, divided by 12 points per line for Geneva 12-point text, which equals 8.4 (i.e., nine) lines of 12-point space.

In this case, you needn't make this type of calculation because your text is entered as 12-point text. Enter

6[Return]

WordPerfect calculates that there is not enough room at the bottom of the page for all six lines and moves the table to the next page.

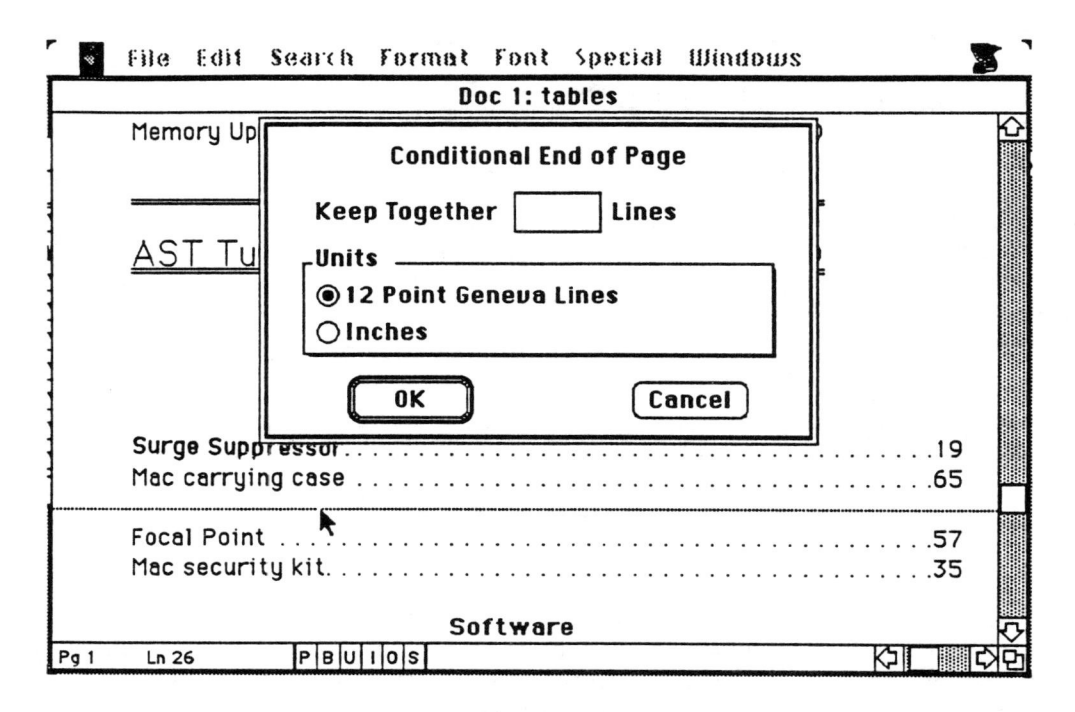

Figure 3.31

Tables and Tabs 3

The advantage of the conditional end-of-page code is that it will adjust to changes in your text and insert the page break only when it is needed to keep the table together. For example, suppose you decide to remove the double-spacing code from the document, which would change the length of the text.

Place the cursor at the top of the document:

[Enter] [Enter] ↑

Use the Search command to locate the line spacing code. Enter

[Apple/f]

Scroll the codes display until you see the Spacing Set code:

> **Point** at [Spacing Set]
> **Double Click**
> **Click** on Find

The program has located and selected the line spacing code that creates double-spacing. Remove the code by entering

[Delete]

The Hardware Specials table returns to single-spacing. Move to the end of the document:

[Enter] [Enter] ↓

You can see that the Miscellaneous table will fit onto the first page, and the conditional end-of-page command removes the page break.

3 Tables and Tabs

You can now print the document by entering

[Apple/p]

Save the document and open a blank document window by entering

[Apple/s]
[Apple/k]
[Apple/n]

SUMMARY

- **Tabs.** Tabs are used to align text at specific horizontal locations. WordPerfect allows you to set four types of tabs: left-, center-, right- and decimal-aligned. You can also choose to fill the space in front of a tab stop with leader dots.

- **Underline Style.** Underlines in WordPerfect are subject to the underline style currently in use. Underlines can be single or double and be displayed as continuous or non-continuous lines.

- **Line Spacing**. Vertical spacing used for line height is calculated based on the point size of the text. You can manually override these settings by entering a line spacing command that increases or decreases the amount of space left for each line.

CHAPTER 4

SPECIAL TEXT FORMATS

4 Special Text Formats

The first three chapters taught you how to use the most common WordPerfect formatting operations. This chapter will teach you how to create special formats to use on documents requiring more than the ordinary level of structure. Included in these special effects are outlines and column-oriented text.

INDENTS

Like tabs, paragraph indents use tab stops to format text. The difference between an indent and a tab is the number of lines that are affected.

If a paragraph contains more than one line of text, the tab affects only the first line. All other lines are formatted by the margin settings. An indent affects all of the lines in the paragraph. All of the lines are indented until you mark the end of the paragraph with a **[HRt]**.

Begin the new document with a line of bold text. Enter

[Apple/Shift/b]
THE PHILOSOPHY OF EDUCATION [Apple/Shift/b]
[Return] [Return]

Instead of typing the next paragraph flush with the left margin, create an indent. The Indent command can be found in the Format Paragraph menu.

> **Point** at Format
> **Drag** to Paragraph
> **Release**

Option #4 creates a paragraph indent. Enter

Special Text Formats **4**

The cursor jumps to the first tab stop. Enter

The quality of learning depends very largely on the quality of teaching. Good teaching guides and inspires learning in the classroom and directs and motivates learning to be done at home.
[Return] [Return]

The indent causes all lines in the paragraph to be indented. When you enter [Return] at the end of the paragraph, the cursor is released from the indent code, and the next paragraph will appear as normal text.

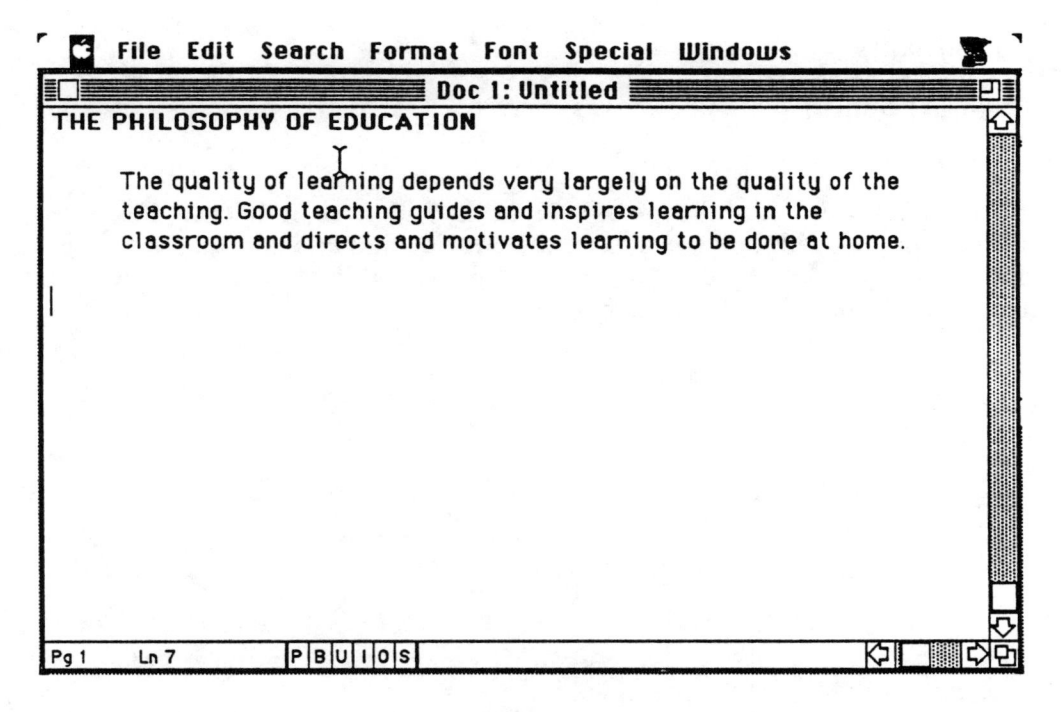

Figure 4.1

153

4 Special Text Formats

The indent sets a temporary left margin at a specific tab stop. The margin stays in effect only until the next [HRt] is pressed and is then released. Continue entering the following text:

The previous words were written by John Dewey, an American educator and philosopher.
[Return] [Return]

To indent the next paragraph, you can use the shortcut keystroke for insert and indent, [Apple/Shift/t]. Enter

[Apple/Shift/t]
Dewey went on to declare:
[Return] [Return]

WordPerfect uses a second type of indent called a left/right indent. This indent formats the text with one tab stop on the left side and one tab stop on the right side. To create a left/right indent, display the Format Paragraph menu. Use the keyboard shortcut, [Apple/3]. Enter

[Apple/3]

To create a left/right indent, enter

5

Then enter the text for the paragraph:

The goal at which any single phase of education should aim is always more education.
[Return] [Return]

Note that this time, the right and left margins are indented. Also note that WordPerfect does not furnish a command that indents only the right margin.

Multiple Indents

WordPerfect allows you to enter more than one indent command before the same paragraph. The effect of multiple indent commands is different from the effect of some other WordPerfect formatting commands, such as [Margin Set]. For example, if you begin a paragraph with two consecutive Margin Set commands, only the last command (i.e., the right-most code) will have a direct effect on the text because WordPerfect assumes that any given paragraph can have only one set of margins. If you insert several [Margin Set] codes before a paragraph, WordPerfect treats the codes as mutually exclusive and ignores all but the last Margin Set command.

However, multiple indents are allowed. WordPerfect adds together the codes, and then formats the paragraph accordingly. For example, if you were to go back to the beginning of line 12 and insert another indent left/right code, WordPerfect would indent the paragraph two tabs from the left and two tab stops from the right. Indent codes are cumulative, not exclusive. Position the cursor at the beginning of line 12 by entering

↑ (3 times)
[Enter] ←

Insert another left/right indent. This time use the keyboard shortcut combination, [Apple/Shift/L]. Enter

[Apple/Shift/L]

The text is indented two tab stops.

4 Special Text Formats

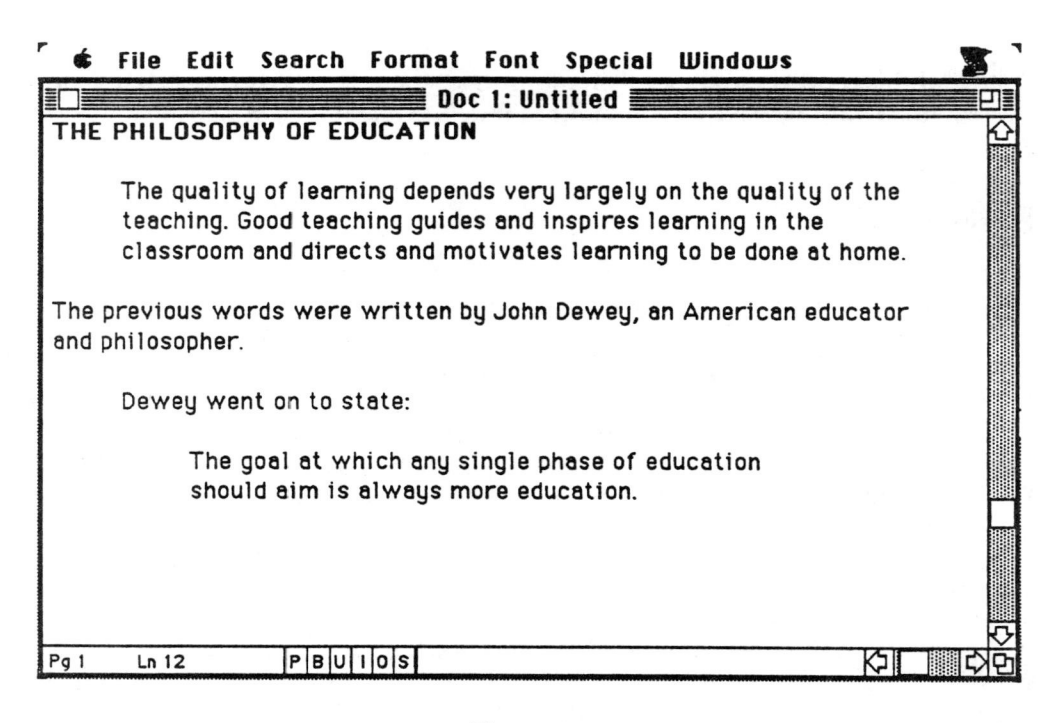

Figure 4.2

You can combine left indents with left/right indents. For example, adding a left indent would cause the left margin to be moved in another tab stop but would leave the right margin as it is. Enter the shortcut key command for a left indent:

[Apple/Shift/t]

The left margin shifts while the right margin remains the same. To see how Word-Perfect records your instruction, display the codes by entering

[Apple/7]

Special Text Formats **4**

Your screen should resemble the following:

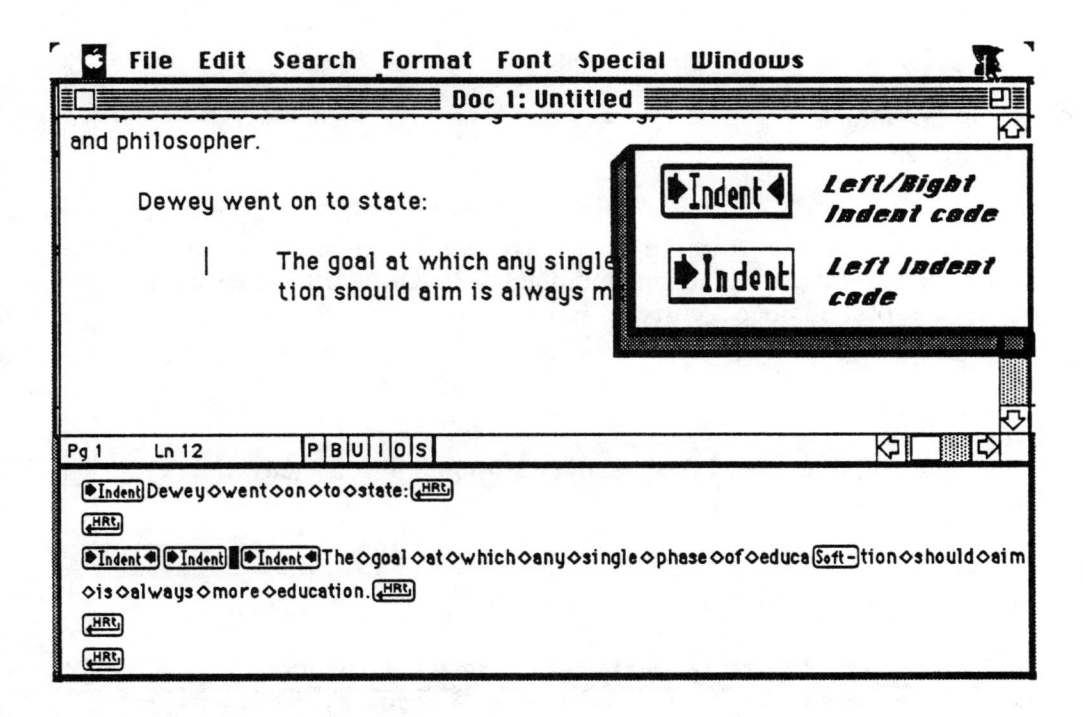

Figure 4.3

The display shows that there are three codes inserted before the text. The final formatting for this paragraph is determined by adding together the effects of all three codes:

(1 left & right) + (1 left) + (1 left & right) = 3 left and 2 right

Close the codes window by entering

[Apple/7]

157

4 Special Text Formats

Continue entering text at the end of the document:

[Enter] [Enter] ↓
[Apple/Shift/t]
Further he added:
[Return] [Return]

To indent the next paragraph so it will correspond to the previous quotation, you must enter two left/right indents and one left indent. Order does not matter as long as the total number is correct. Enter

[Apple/Shift/t]
[Apple/Shift/L] (2 times)
Other goals may surround the goal of education, but it is central.
[Return] [Return]

The text should resemble the following:

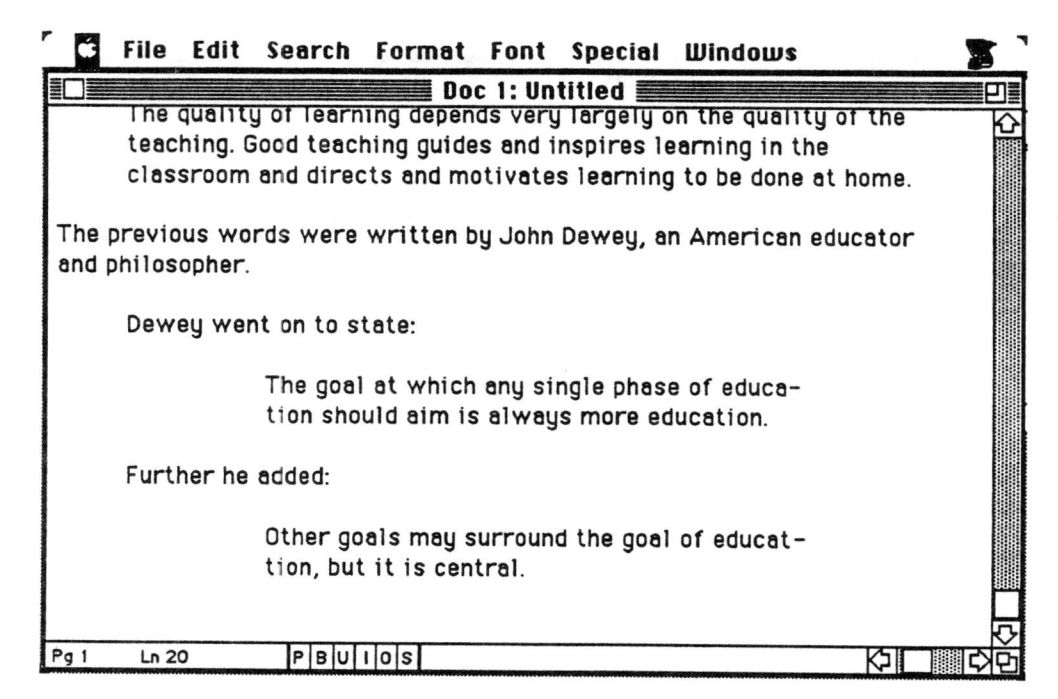

```
 File  Edit  Search  Format  Font  Special  Windows
═══════════════════════ Doc 1: Untitled ═══════════════════════
The quality of learning depends very largely on the quality of the
teaching. Good teaching guides and inspires learning in the
classroom and directs and motivates learning to be done at home.

The previous words were written by John Dewey, an American educator
and philosopher.

     Dewey went on to state:

          The goal at which any single phase of educa-
          tion should aim is always more education.

     Further he added:

          Other goals may surround the goal of educat-
          tion, but it is central.

Pg 1   Ln 20      P B U I O S
```

Figure 4.4

Complete the text by entering another item:

[Apple/Shift/t]
Finally, he concludes:[Return][Return]
[Apple/Shift/t]
[Apple/Shift/L] (2 times)
No adequate system of education can be founded exclusively on the need to dispense technical information. [Return]

Changing an Indent

You may have noticed that the first paragraph in this document was indented as a left-indented paragraph only. All of the other quotations use both left and right indents. To change the format of this paragraph, you can delete the left indent code and insert a left/right indent code. Move the cursor to the top of the document by entering

[Enter][Enter]↑

Open the codes window so that you can look for the [Indent-] code. Enter

[Apple/7]

Remove the code by entering

↓ (2 times)
[Decimal]

Replace it with a left/right indent. Enter

[Apple/Shift/L]

4 Special Text Formats

Close the codes window by entering

[Apple/7]

The document should now resemble the following:

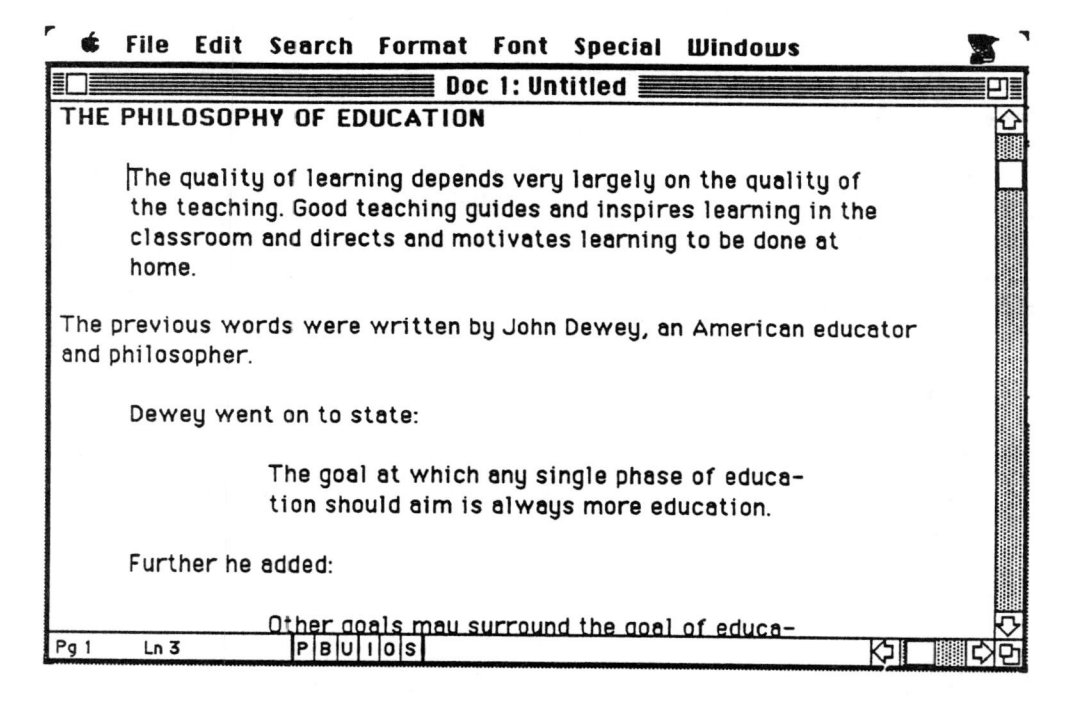

```
  File  Edit  Search  Format  Font  Special  Windows
══════════════════════ Doc 1: Untitled ══════════════════════
THE PHILOSOPHY OF EDUCATION

    The quality of learning depends very largely on the quality of
    the teaching. Good teaching guides and inspires learning in the
    classroom and directs and motivates learning to be done at
    home.

The previous words were written by John Dewey, an American educator
and philosopher.

    Dewey went on to state:

            The goal at which any single phase of educa-
            tion should aim is always more education.

    Further he added:

            Other goals may surround the goal of educa-
Pg 1   Ln 3       P B U I O S
```

Figure 4.5

CREATING A NEW PAGE

In most cases, WordPerfect automatically creates a new page of text when the page you are working on is filled. This technique is called **automatic pagination**; however, there are times when you will want to start a new page even when you have not filled the current page. This technique is sometimes called **manual pagination**, or a **forced new page**. The term "forced" implies that WordPerfect does not normally start a new page at this position.

Special Text Formats **4**

Place the cursor at the end of the document:

[Enter] [Enter] ↓

To create a new page, enter the [Apple/Return] combination:

[Apple/Return]

WordPerfect inserts a line across the bottom of the document, denoting the beginning of a new page. Note that the page counter changes to Pg 2.

OVERHANGS

Indents and tab stops can be used in another way to create paragraph overhangs. An **overhang**, or text that is typed outside the left margin of a paragraph, can be created in two ways.

Indents When you use a paragraph indent, the overhang is created by entering text at the beginning of the paragraph before you insert the indent code. The text entered before the indent creates the overhang effect.

Margin Release In this method, a new margin is set, which indents all of the text. Then a special margin release command is used to allow you to type text outside of the current margins.

To use the indent method, enter a title for this section of the document:

[Apple/Shift/b]
WORDPERFECT 5.0 AND RAM FONT
[Apple/Shift/b]
[Return] [Return]

161

4 Special Text Formats

Creating a Bullet

Bullet refers to a special type of overhang text often found in marketing material. A bullet is a special character, usually a dot or an arrow, that hangs out from an indented paragraph. You can use any keyboard character as a bullet; however, WordPerfect allows you to enter special Macintosh font characters, even though they do not appear on the keyboard. You can insert one of these characters from a special submenu, called Insert Literal, found in the Edit menu.

> **Point** at Edit
> **Drag** to Insert Literal
> **Release**

WordPerfect displays a box in the center of the screen, showing available characters that do not appear on the keyboard.

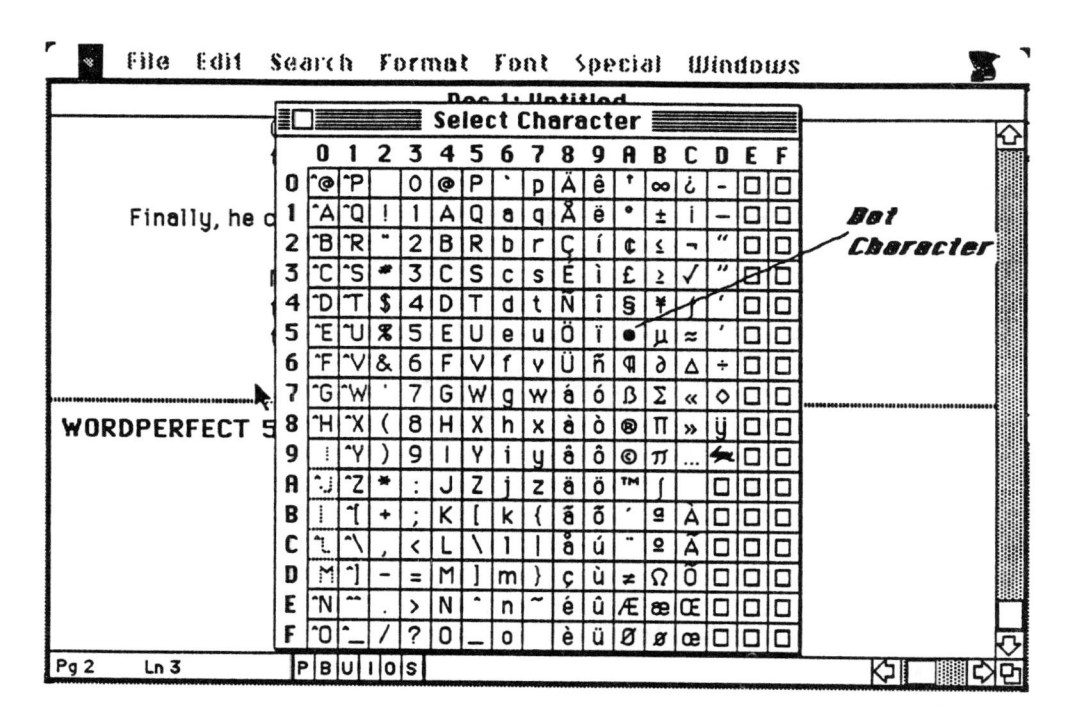

Figure 4.6

162

Special Text Formats 4

You can select any of these characters by clicking on the one you want to insert. Here, use the black dot in column A, row 5.

> **Point** at the dot in A5
> **Click**

The dot is inserted into the text. Before you enter the text, insert an Indent command. Enter

[Apple/Shift/L]

Then enter the following paragraph:

WordPerfect 5.0 for the PC is the first full featured word processing package to utilize most of RamFont's vast potential. [Return] [Return]

Your screen should resemble the following:

4 Special Text Formats

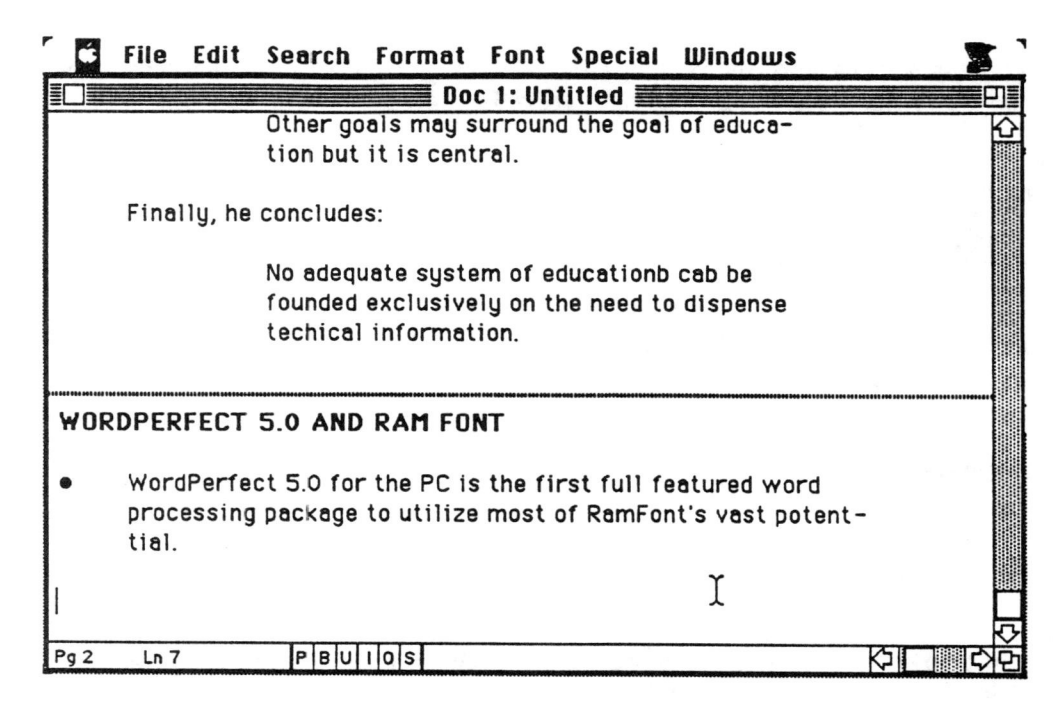

Figure 4.7

You have created the bullet effect by typing part of the paragraph before the indent code and the remainder of the paragraph after the indent code.

To create the next bullet, you can use a keyboard shortcut for typing the dot. The Option key is used in many Macintosh applications to access non-keyboard characters. (You can use the Keycaps desktop accessory program to determine what characters are typed with the Option key in different fonts.) Enter

[Option/8]

Complete the bullet by entering

[Apple/Shift/L]
Provides you with What You See Is What You Get screen display including fonts, attributes and point size. [Return] [Return]

Special Text Formats 4

Add a third bullet to the page. Enter

[Option/8]
[Apple/Shift/L]
Users can edit in twelve different character styles at one time without slowing the program. [Return] [Return]

Enter the final bullet:

[Option/8]
[Apple/Shift/L]
No other graphics card provides as much display flexibility for the WordPerfect 5.0 user. [Return] [Return]

The document should resemble the following:

```
 🍎  File  Edit  Search  Format  Font  Special  Windows
════════════════════ Doc 1: Untitled ════════════════════

 WORDPERFECT 5.0 AND RAM FONT

   •  WordPerfect 5.0 for the PC is the first full featured word
      processing package to utilize most of RamFont's vast poten-
      tial.

   •  Provides you with What You See Is What You Get screen display
      including fonts, attributes and point size.

   •  Users can edit in twelve different character styles at one time
      without slowing the program.

   •  No other graphics card provides as much display flexibility for
      the WordPerfect 5.0 user.

 Pg 2   Ln 16      P B U I O S
```

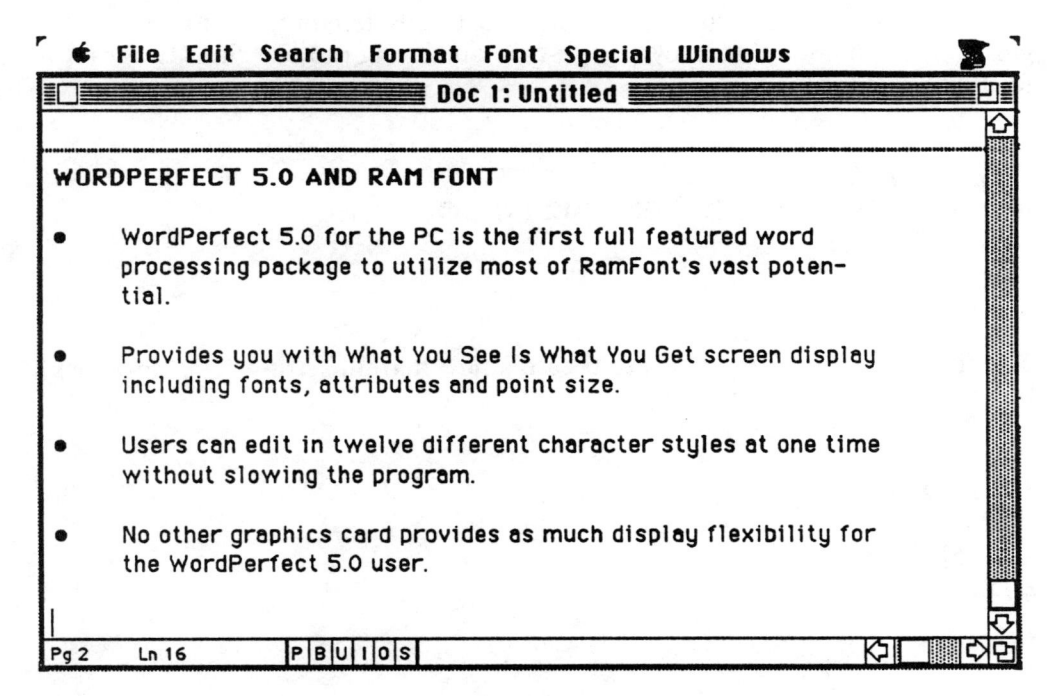

Figure 4.8

165

4 Special Text Formats

As a safety precaution, save the document by entering

[Apple/s]
special formats [Return]

Note that WordPerfect has placed the name of the document at the top of the display window. The next time you enter [Apple/s], WordPerfect will not need to request the name of the document because the name, "special formats," has already been assigned.

Create a new page by entering

[Apple/Return]

Margin Release

Another method of creating overhangs is to set a new left margin and use the Margin Release command to allow you to type outside of the margins. Enter a title for this section:

[Apple/Shift/b]
RUNNING THE IMAGEWRITER SELF-TEST
[Apple/Shift/b]
[Return] [Return]

The first step in this process is to create a new margin setting. For now, use 2" left and right margins. Enter

[Apple/2] 1
[Tab]
2 [Tab] [Tab]
2 [Return]

Special Text Formats **4**

The cursor jumps to the new left margin at 2". To type the overhang portion of the paragraph, you need to release the Margin command. Enter

[Shift/Tab]

The cursor moves back one tab stop to the left of the margin. Entering several Margin Release commands causes the cursor to move one tab stop farther to the left. Enter

[Shift/Tab]

The cursor has moved back two tab stops to line up with the heading. Now enter

Step #1

You can enter the text for Step #1 in paragraph form, allowing the new margins to format the text. Enter

[Tab]
The self test is a repeated printing of the Imagewriter character set.
[Return] [Return]
Turn the ImageWriter II off by pressing the On/Off button. [Return] [Return]

Your document should resemble the following:

167

4 Special Text Formats

```
 File  Edit  Search  Format  Font  Special  Windows
         Doc 1: special formats

 •  Users can edit in twelve different character styles at one time
    without slowing the program.

 •  No other graphics card provides as much display flexibility for
    the WordPerfect 5.0 user.


 RUNNING THE IMAGE WRITER SELF-TEST

 Step #1   The self-test is a repeated printing of ImageWriter
           character set.

           Turn the ImageWriter II off by pressing the On/Off
           button.

 Pg 3   Ln 8        P B U I O S
```

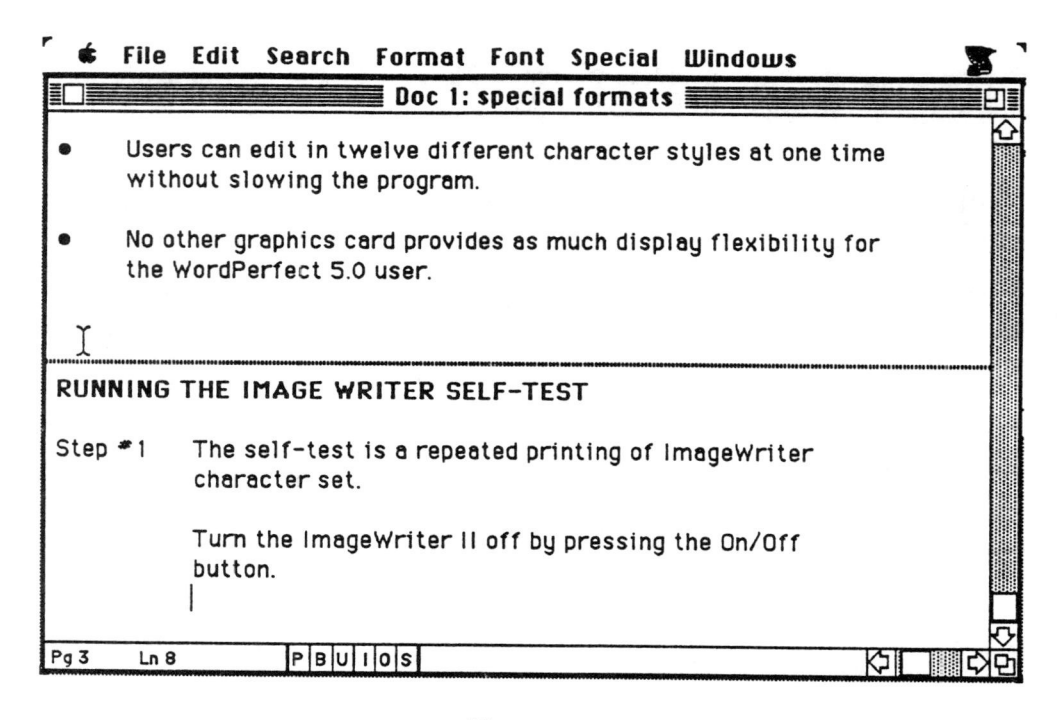

Figure 4.9

In this example, using the Margin Release method makes sense because you are typing more than one paragraph for each overhang. In the bullet entry example, each paragraph had an overhang associated with it. There, it was more efficient to use the paragraph indent method.

To enter Step #2, you must release the margin again. Enter

[Shift/Tab]   (2 times)

Enter the text for Step #2:

Step #2 [Tab]
Press and hold down the form feed button. [Return] [Return]
Turn on the ImageWriter II by pressing the On/off button. [Return] [Return]
When the print head moves, release both buttons. The printing will not begin until you have released the buttons. [Return] [Return]

Special Text Formats **4**

Your screen should now resemble the following:

```
   File  Edit  Search  Format  Font  Special  Windows
┌─────────────────── Doc 1: special formats ───────────────────┐
│ RUNNING THE IMAGE WRITER SELF-TEST                           │
│                                                              │
│ Step #1    The self-test is a repeated printing of ImageWriter
│            character set.
│
│            Turn the ImageWriter II off by pressing the On/Off
│            button.
│
│ Step #2    Press and hold down the form feed button.
│
│            Turn on the ImageWriter II by pressing the On/off
│            button.
│
│            When the print head moves, release both buttons.
│            The printing will not begin until you have released
│            the buttons.
│
│ Pg 3   Ln 18      P B U I O S
└──────────────────────────────────────────────────────────────┘
```

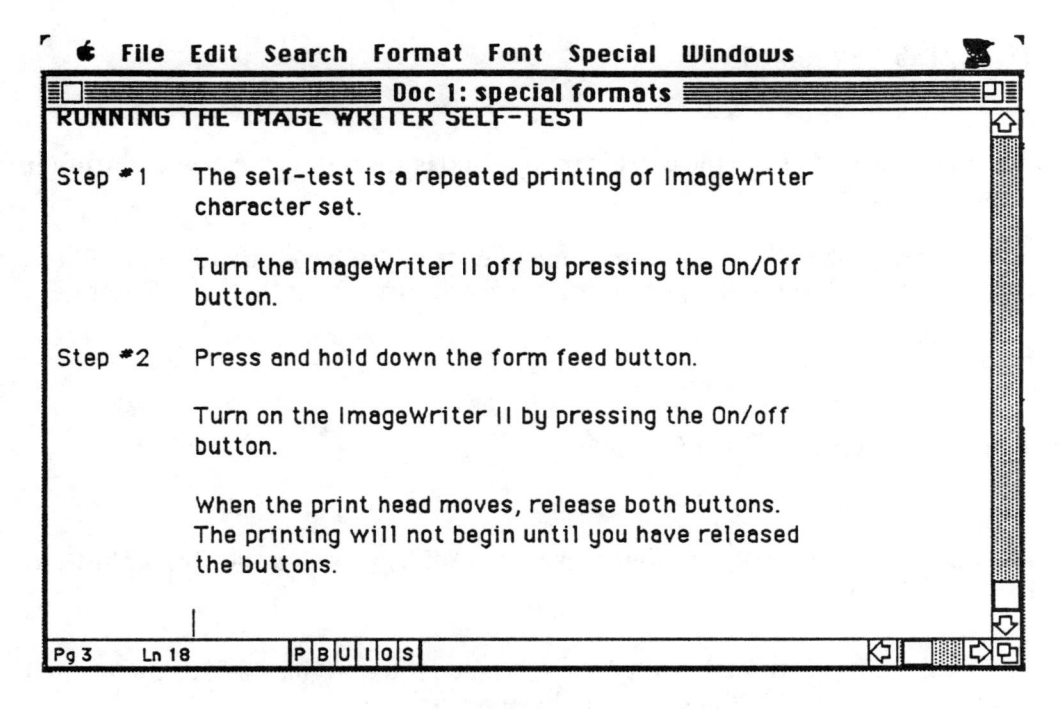

Figure 4.10

Enter the last step in the testing process:

Step #3

A mistake appears because you forgot to enter the Margin Release commands before you entered the overhang text; however, this situation is not really problematic. As with most WordPerfect commands, you can insert Margin Release codes after you have typed the text, as long as you have positioned the cursor in the text where the codes should be placed. Move the cursor to the beginning of this line.

[Enter] ←

169

4 Special Text Formats

Insert the two Margin Release commands. Enter

[Shift/Tab] (2 times)

The text is released from the current margin and is aligned correctly with the other overhang text.

For the next entry, the tactic is to remember that you have already entered the overhang text. To continue, you must move the cursor past that text. Enter

[Enter] →

You can now enter the text for the paragraph:

[Tab]
To stop the self-test, turn the ImageWriter II off by pressing the On/off button.
[Return] [Return]

The final step with this type of entry is to place the margins back to the normal document setting, 1" left and 1" right, by entering

[Apple/2] 1
[Tab]
1 [Tab] [Tab]
1 [Return]

End this page by entering a forced Page End code:

[Apple/Return]

Save the revised document by entering

[Apple/s]

Special Text Formats **4**

OUTLINES

Outlines represent text highlights structured in levels. In most cases, outlines are difficult to type because they require you to pay attention to a complicated method of paragraph numbering. If an outline has many levels (that is, headings, subheadings, sub-subheadings), it can be quite distracting.

To make creating outlines simpler and more accurate, WordPerfect includes a special entry mode in which outlines can be created. It is important to understand that the outline feature in WordPerfect is an entry mode, as contrasted to an entry command. A command is manually entered from the keyboard each time you want that command code to be inserted in the text. The indent command used in the previous section, [Apple/Shift/L], is a typical example.

The term "mode" is used to describe the outline feature because once the outline mode is activated, WordPerfect automatically inserts specific codes into the document. The purpose of these codes is to generate an accurate sequence of numbers for your outline.

The next section in the Formats document consists of an outline structure. Begin with a page heading. Enter

[Apple/Shift/b]
AN OUTLINE OF WORLD HISTORY
[Apple/Shift/b]
[Return] [Return]

Because the outline feature is a mode, it must be turned on. The outline feature is found in the Format Paragraph menu.

Point at Format
Drag to Paragraph
Release

171

4 Special Text Formats

To turn on the outline mode, enter

1

The bar at the bottom of the window displays the word "Outline," indicating that you are in the outline mode.

To begin the outline, enter

[Return]

In response to the entry of the Return key, WordPerfect not only created a new line but it automatically typed Roman numeral I on that new line.

Your screen should resemble the following:

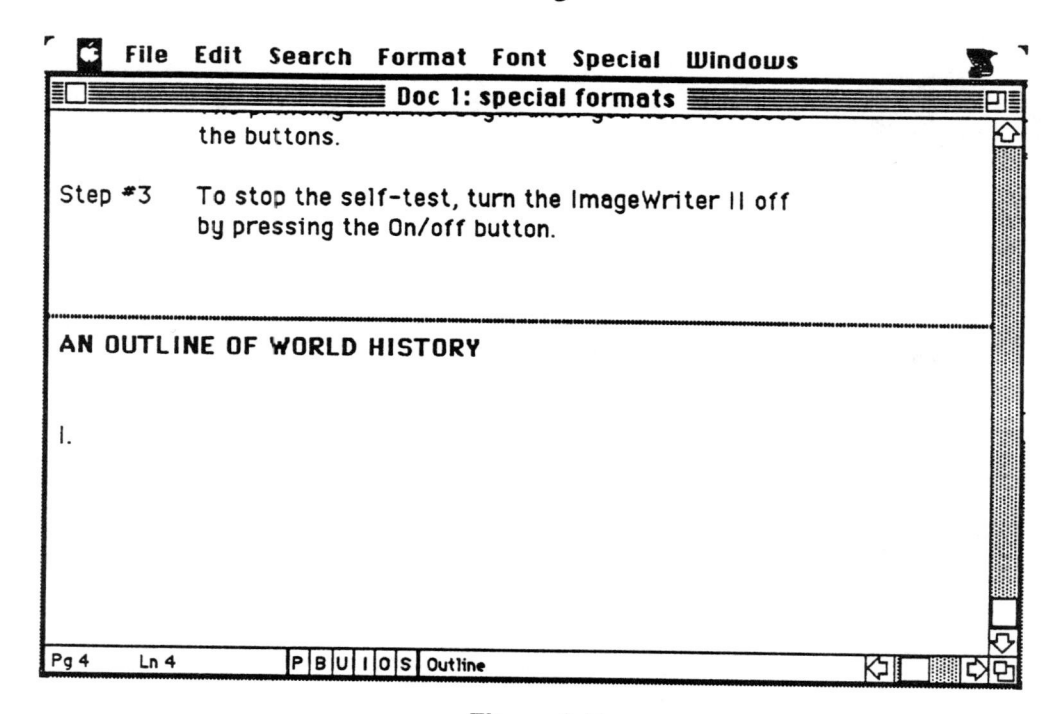

```
 File   Edit   Search   Format   Font   Special   Windows
═══════════════════ Doc 1: special formats ═══════════════════
           the buttons.

 Step #3   To stop the self-test, turn the ImageWriter II off
           by pressing the On/off button.
·············································································
 AN OUTLINE OF WORLD HISTORY

 I.




 Pg 4   Ln 4        P B U I O S  Outline
```

Figure 4.11

172

Special Text Formats **4**

The Roman numeral I stands for the first major heading in the outline. To begin entering text, you must insert a paragraph indent. Note that you can use either a left indent — [Apple/Shift/t] — or a left/right indent — [Apple/Shift/L]. Enter

[Apple/Shift/t]

Then enter the major heading text:

[Apple/Shift/b]
EARLY CULTURES
[Apple/Shift/b]
[Return]

Your document should resemble the following:

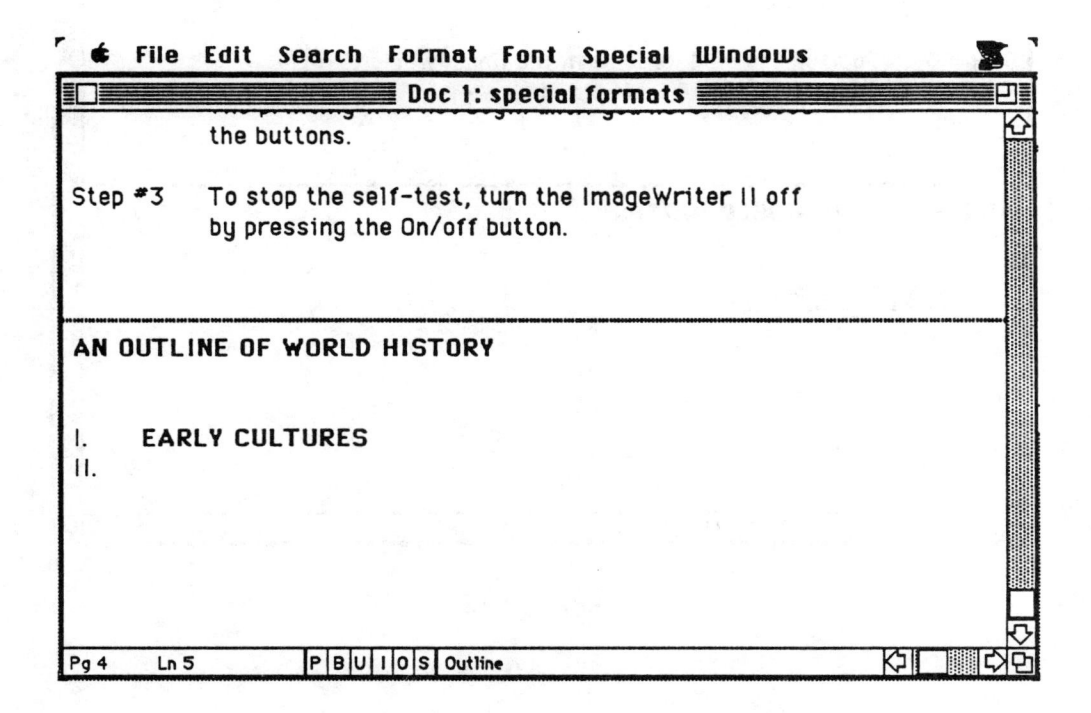

```
                                the buttons.

        Step #3    To stop the self-test, turn the ImageWriter II off
                   by pressing the On/off button.


        AN OUTLINE OF WORLD HISTORY


        I.      EARLY CULTURES
        II.
```

Figure 4.12

173

4 Special Text Formats

Changing Outline Levels

Because the outline mode is active, WordPerfect automatically inserts the next major heading number, II. But suppose that the next item on the outline is a subheading, not a major heading. By using the Tab key, you can tell WordPerfect to change the numbering sequence to a lower level. In the outline mode, the Tab key is used to indent the outline and lower its level by one. Enter

[Tab]

WordPerfect indents the number and changes it to the first subheading under the major heading, A.

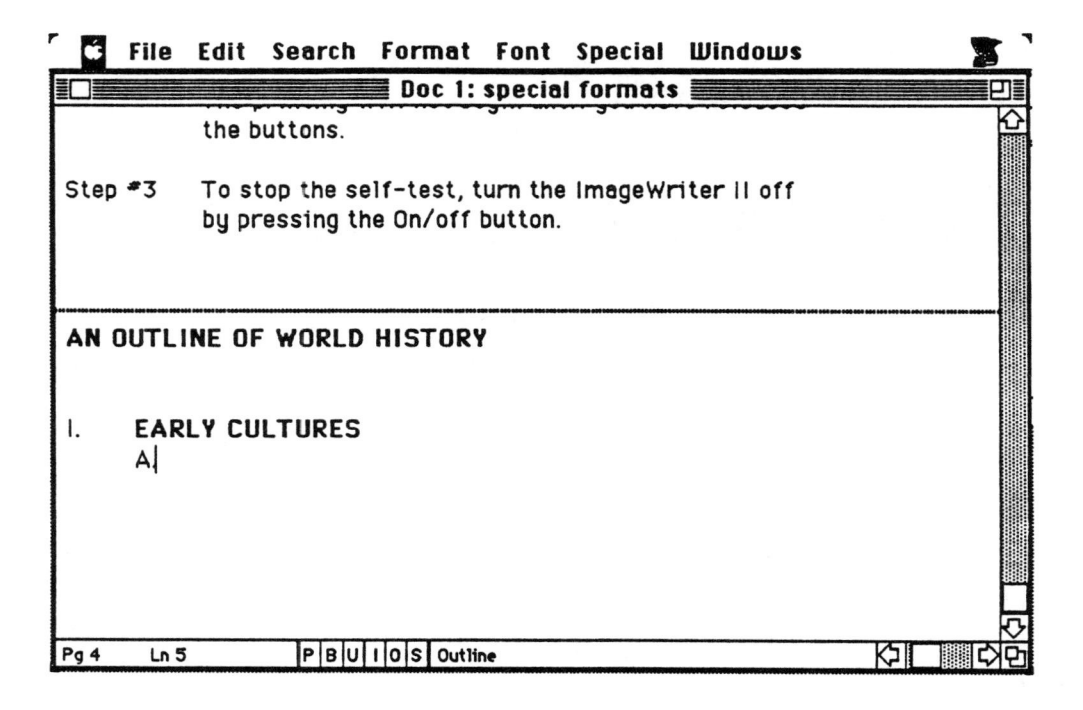

Figure 4.13

Now that the level is correct, save the number at that level by entering

[Apple/Shift/t]

Then enter the text of the subheading:

SUMERIA [Return]

Note that when you press the Return key, WordPerfect reverts to numbering major headings. In this case, you want to create a sub-subheading under SUMERIA. To do so, reduce the number two levels by pressing the Tab key twice. Enter

[Tab] (2 times)

You now have the correct number level. Enter

[Apple/Shift/t]
Begins about 4000 B.C. [Return]

Note that each time you press the Return key, WordPerfect jumps back to the major heading level. Add two more items under SUMERIA. Enter

[Tab] (2times)
[Apple/Shift/t]
Large Cities of Ur and Nipper [Return]
[Tab] (2 times)
[Apple/Shift/t]
Law codified by Hammurabi, 1750 B.C. [Return]

4 Special Text Formats

The next entry is a subheading, which requires only one Tab. Enter

[Tab]
EGYPT [Return]

Enter the next item under "EGYPT":

[Tab] (2 times)
[Apple/Shift/t]
Upper and Lower Egypt United 3300 B.C. [Return]

The next two items are subheadings below "Upper and Lower Egypt," which means that three tabs are needed. Enter

[Tab] (3 times)
[Apple/Shift/t]
Nubia added in 2600 B.C. [Return]
[Tab] (3 times)
[Apple/Shift/t]
Pharaoh Menes rules[Return]

```
     File   Edit   Search   Format   Font   Special   Windows
```
```
================= Doc 1: special formats =================
Step #3      To stop the self-test, turn the ImageWriter II off
             by pressing the On/off button.


AN OUTLINE OF WORLD HISTORY


I.     EARLY CULTURES
       A.    SUMERIA
             1.    Begins about 4000 B.C.
             2.    Larges cities of Ur and Nipper
             3.    Laws codified by Hammurabi, 1750 B.C.
       B.    EGYPT
             1.    Upper and Lower Egypt United 3300 B.C.
                   a.    Pharaoh Menes rules
                   b.    Nubia added in 2600 B.C.

 Pg 4    Ln 13        P B U I O S  Outline
```

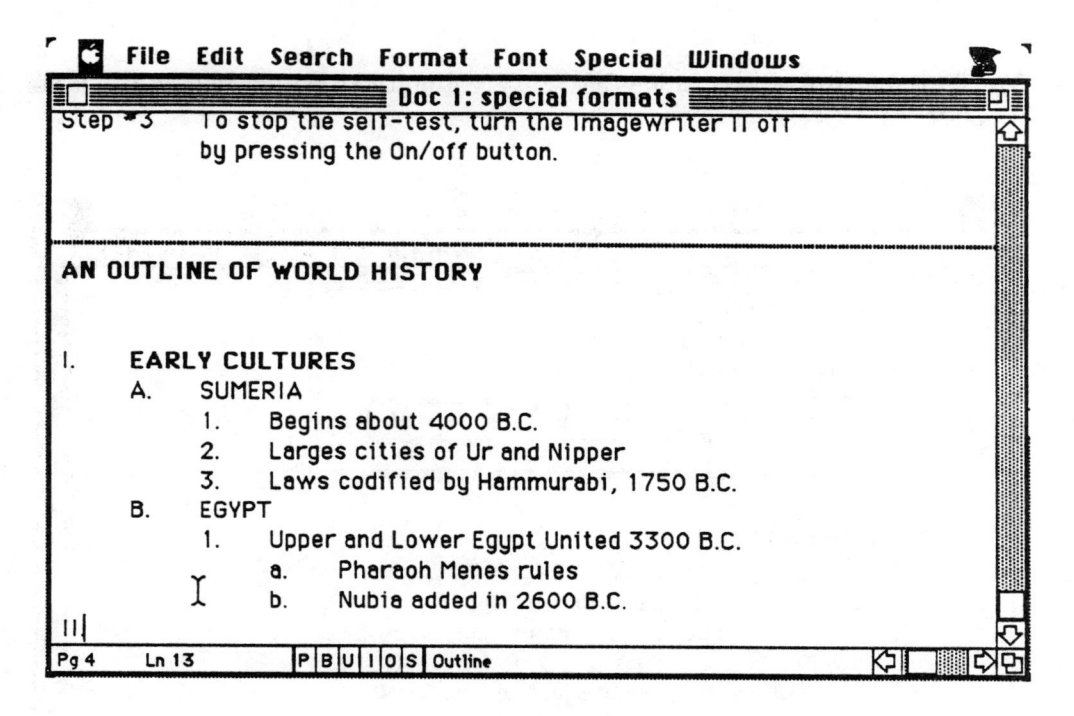

Figure 4.14

Stopping the Outline Mode

You can turn off the outline mode and return to normal text entry by activating the Format Paragraph Outline command a second time. To speed the process, you can use the shortcut keystroke, [Apple/Shift/y]. Enter

[Apple/Shift/y]

The word "Outline" is removed from the bar at the bottom of the screen; however, there is a small problem. The last Return key command in the outline created a number for which no text entry was made. This number can be removed by entering

[Delete]

177

4 Special Text Formats

WordPerfect displays a warning that you are about to delete a Paragraph Number code.

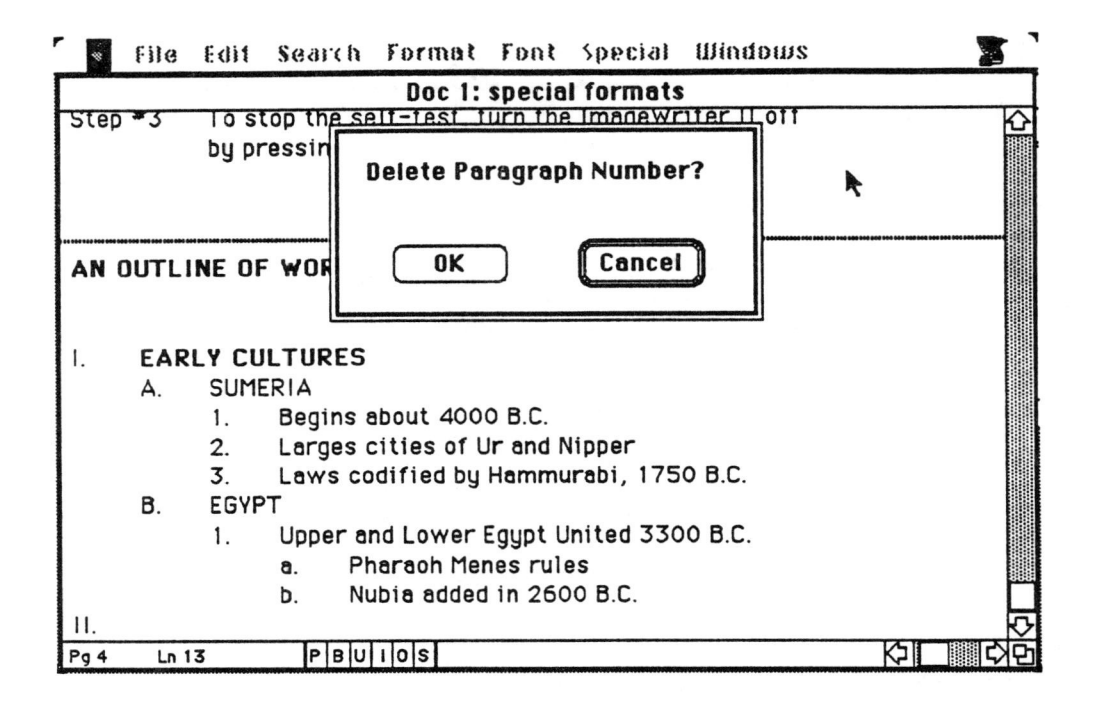

Figure 4.15

This warning indicates that the outline mode inserts codes into the document. When the outline mode is active, every time you enter a Return key command, WordPerfect automatically generates a paragraph number code that causes the display of the outline numbers. Confirm the deletion.

> **Point** at OK
> **Click**

When you delete the code, the number disappears.

Special Text Formats **4**

Revising an Outline

Once you had finished the outline, suppose you realized you had forgotten an item. What would that do to the numbering sequence? There are two methods by which you can automatically update the numbering sequence. You can preserve the sequence by using the outline mode to enter any changes in the outline that affect the numbering sequence. Or you can manually insert in the text the paragraph number code of the correct level.

You will explore both methods. Begin by placing the cursor at the beginning of heading line B. Enter

↑ (4 times)
[Enter] ←

Turn on the outline mode. Enter

[Apple/Shift/y]

Enter a new subheading:

[Return]

This approach to the outline, however, doesn't seem to work. Pressing the Return key is supposed to generate a new item number, but in this case, pressing the Return key placed a new number on a line in the outline that already had a number and left a blank line without any number.

To revise this outline properly, you must position the cursor not at the beginning of the line, but at the end of the previous line. In that way, when the Return key is entered with the outline mode active, you create a new line and number at the correct place.

Delete the unwanted code and blank line by entering

[Delete]

4 Special Text Formats

```
Point at OK
Click
```

And again enter

[Delete]

Place the cursor at the end of the previous line by entering

←

Now enter the new line:

[Return]

This time, the number and blank line are inserted in the proper position. Lower the level of the heading by one level. Enter

[Tab]

Note that WordPerfect automatically updates the number sequence of subheadings to accommodate the new entry. Complete the entry by entering

[Apple/Shift/t]
PHONECIA [Return]
[Tab] (2 times)
[Apple/Shift/t]
Invention of phonetic alphabet

Special Text Formats **4**

Your outline should resemble the following:

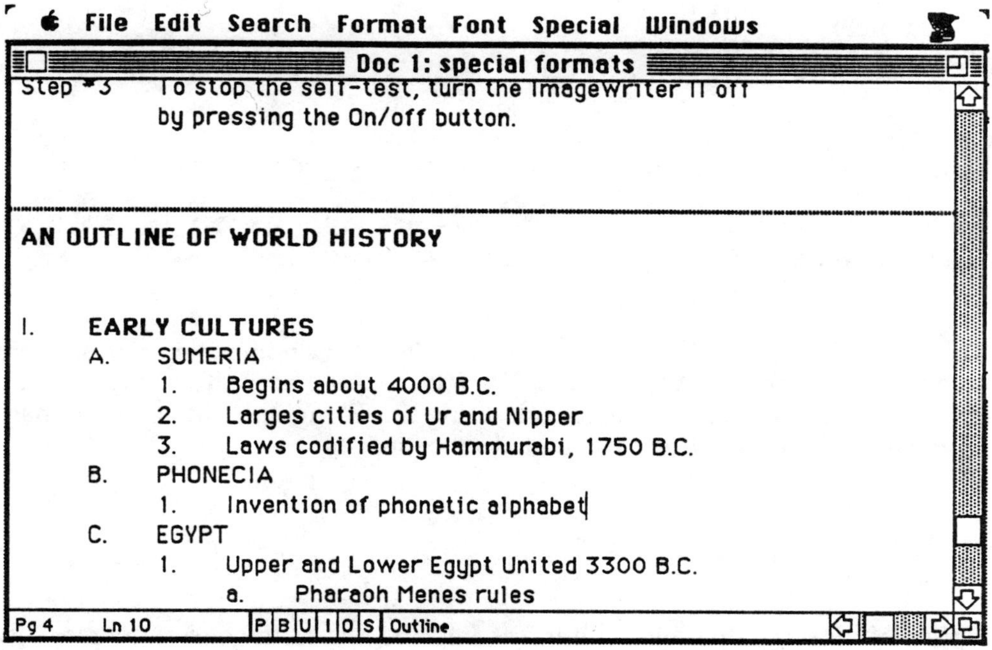

```
 ☀  File  Edit  Search  Format  Font  Special  Windows
━━━━━━━━━━━━━━ Doc 1: special formats ━━━━━━━━━━━━━━
Step #3    To stop the self-test, turn the ImageWriter II off
           by pressing the On/off button.


AN OUTLINE OF WORLD HISTORY


I.   EARLY CULTURES
     A.   SUMERIA
          1.   Begins about 4000 B.C.
          2.   Larges cities of Ur and Nipper
          3.   Laws codified by Hammurabi, 1750 B.C.
     B.   PHONECIA
          1.   Invention of phonetic alphabet
     C.   EGYPT
          1.   Upper and Lower Egypt United 3300 B.C.
               a.   Pharaoh Menes rules
Pg 4    Ln 10        P B U I O S  Outline
```

Figure 4.16

Turn off the outline mode by entering

[Apple/Shift/y]

Inserting Paragraph Numbers

WordPerfect provides another method by which you can insert lines into an outline. This method uses the Format Paragraph Number command.

4 Special Text Formats

Suppose that you wanted to insert a new item under SUMERIA. Enter

↑ (3 times)
[Return]

Press the Tab key to indent the cursor to the proper tab stop. Enter

[Tab] (2 times)

Keep in mind that you do not want to manually enter a number such as 3. Typing an actual number will not help WordPerfect keep an accurate sequence. You must insert a paragraph number code using the Paragraph Number command. Display the Paragraph Format menu by entering

[Apple/3]

Option #2 inserts a paragraph number into the text at the current cursor location. Enter

2

WordPerfect displays a box asking you to enter the level number for the paragraph number.

Special Text Formats 4

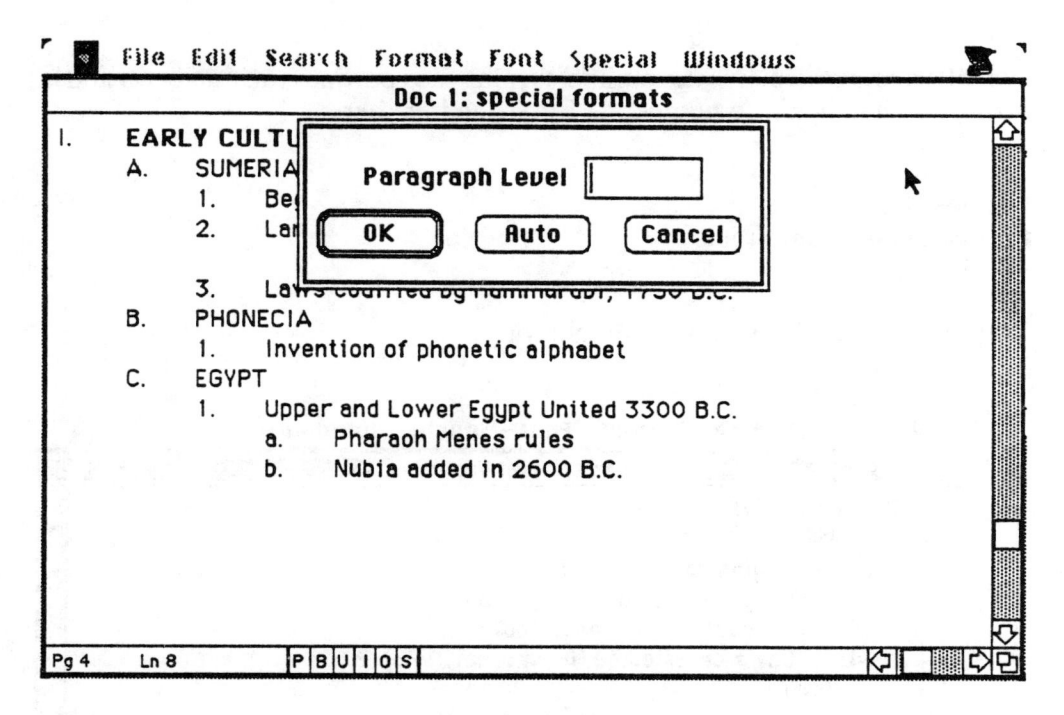

Figure 4.17

You now have two options: You can enter the specific heading level at which you want the number sequenced. Or if you select Auto, WordPerfect uses the number of [tab] codes preceding the paragraph number code to determine the heading level.

In this case, you have already inserted two [tab] codes. Selecting Auto treats the code as a third-level heading. Select Auto.

Point at Auto
Click

183

4 Special Text Formats

WordPerfect recalculates the outline, turning the code into the number 3 and adjusting the line below to number 4. Enter the item here:

[Apple/Shift/t]
Production of bronze tools

Your outline should resemble the following:

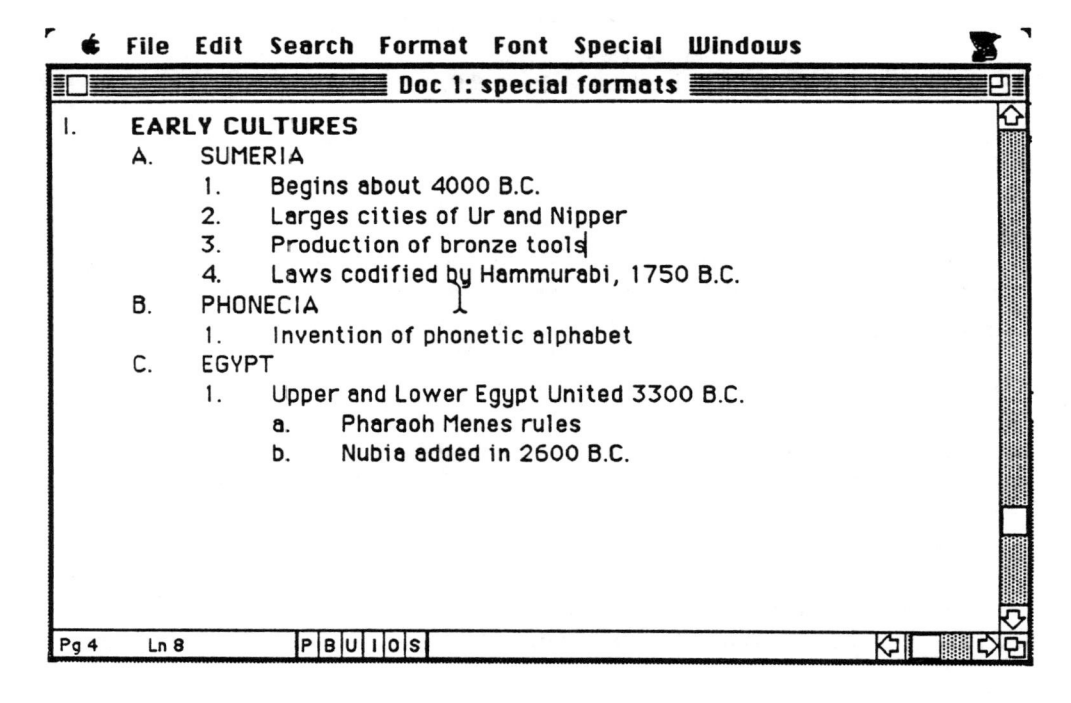

```
 File  Edit  Search  Format  Font  Special  Windows
═══════════════════ Doc 1: special formats ═══════════════════
  I.  EARLY CULTURES
      A.  SUMERIA
          1.  Begins about 4000 B.C.
          2.  Larges cities of Ur and Nipper
          3.  Production of bronze tools
          4.  Laws codified by Hammurabi, 1750 B.C.
      B.  PHONECIA
          1.  Invention of phonetic alphabet
      C.  EGYPT
          1.  Upper and Lower Egypt United 3300 B.C.
              a.  Pharaoh Menes rules
              b.  Nubia added in 2600 B.C.

Pg 4   Ln 8       P B U I O S
```

Figure 4.18

Outline Codes

The WordPerfect outline mode creates a rather complicated codes display. Open the codes window. Enter

[Apple/7]

184

Special Text Formats 4

The codes display shows how WordPerfect implements the outline feature.

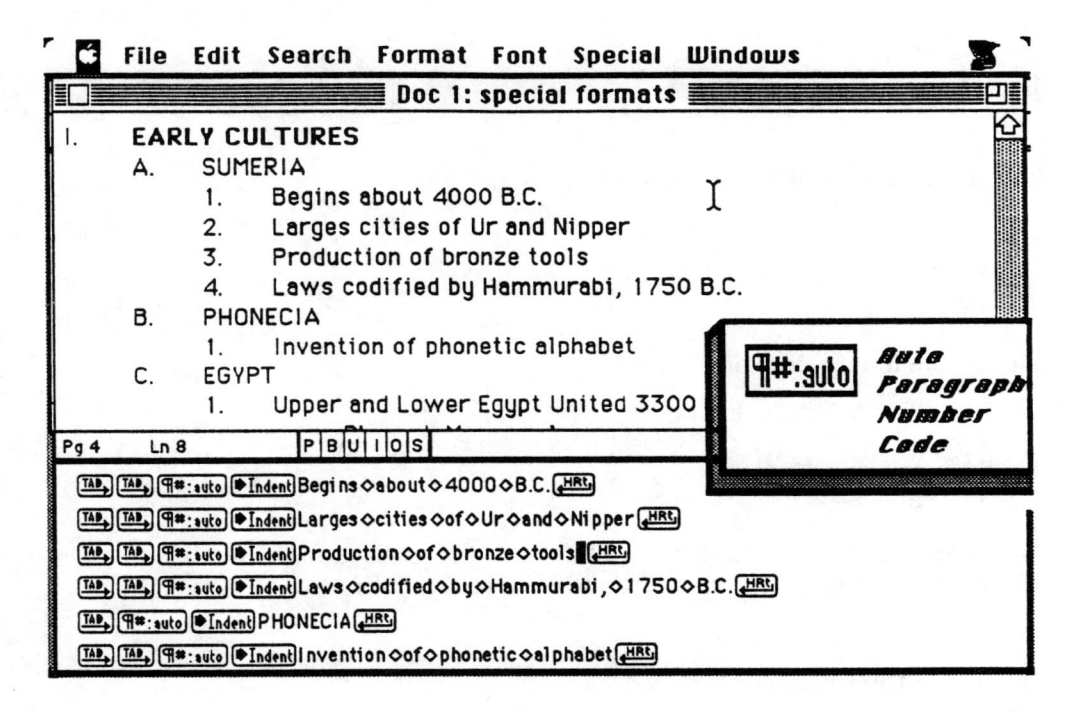

Figure 4.19

Note that the codes do not actually show any number values for the paragraphs. They merely record the location for the numbers and provide WordPerfect with a way to infer what number should appear in the document. Remember that if you delete any of the items, WordPerfect can use the remaining codes to calculate the proper sequence.

Close the codes window by entering

[Apple/7]

4 Special Text Formats

To see what would happen if you removed a line from the outline, enter

↓ (2 times)
[Enter] ←

Select this line for deletion. Enter

[Apple/6] 3

Delete the line by entering

[Delete]

WordPerfect automatically recalculates the correct sequence for the numbers. Reinsert the line in another position in the outline. Enter

[Enter] [Enter] ↓
[Apple/u]

```
Point at Restore
Click
```

If you want to change the level of this item, simply insert or delete the correct number of tabs. Enter

[Enter] ←
[Tab]

WordPerfect is able to instantly update the outline for cut and paste changes that you make to the elements in the outline.

Special Text Formats **4**

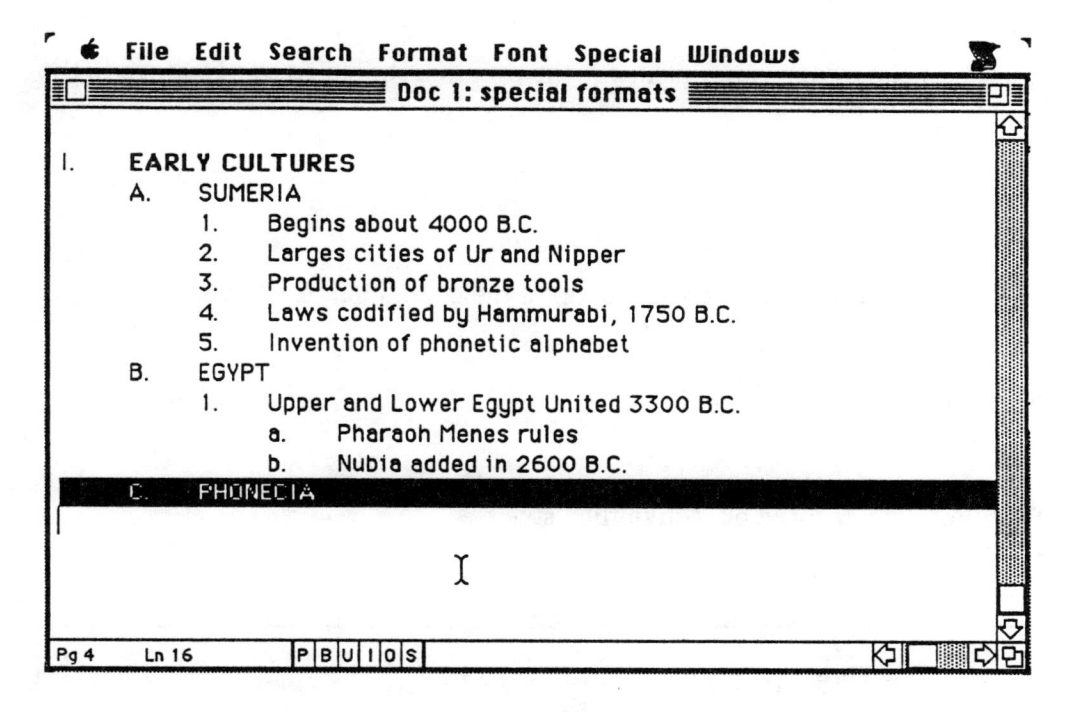

```
  File   Edit   Search   Format   Font   Special   Windows
≡════════════════ Doc 1: special formats ════════════════≡

I.  EARLY CULTURES
    A.   SUMERIA
         1.   Begins about 4000 B.C.
         2.   Larges cities of Ur and Nipper
         3.   Production of bronze tools
         4.   Laws codified by Hammurabi, 1750 B.C.
         5.   Invention of phonetic alphabet
    B.   EGYPT
         1.   Upper and Lower Egypt United 3300 B.C.
              a.   Pharaoh Menes rules
              b.   Nubia added in 2600 B.C.
    C.   PHONECIA

Pg 4    Ln 16        P B U I O S
```

Figure 4.20

Outline Styles

WordPerfect provides a means by which you can alter the style of numbering used in outline or paragraph number codes. The outline style refers to the sequence of letters as well as Roman and Arabic numerals used to number the outline.

To change the style of the outline, you must position the cursor at the beginning of the outline, which can be done quickly by moving to the top of the page with one of the Goto commands. All Goto commands begin with [Apple/g]. Enter

[Apple/g]

187

4 Special Text Formats

A box appears asking you which page the program should go to. To move to the top of the current page, enter

↑

The cursor is now positioned at the top of the document. Enter

[Apple/3]
3

WordPerfect has three built-in outline styles.

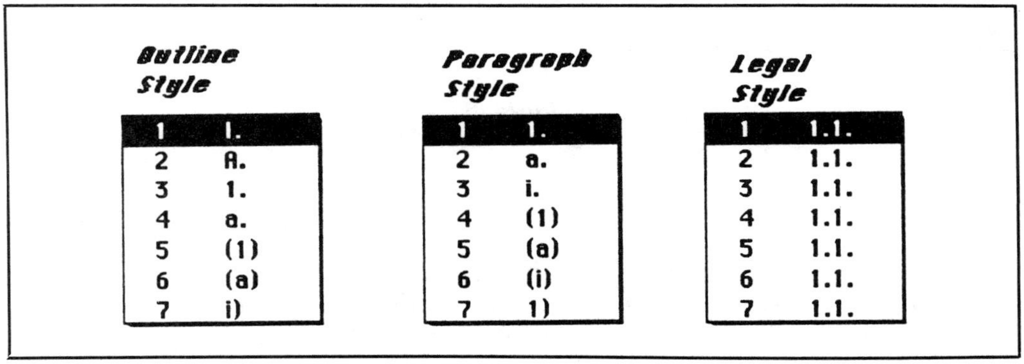

Outline Style	Paragraph Style	Legal Style
1 I.	1 1.	1 1.1.
2 A.	2 a.	2 1.1.
3 1.	3 i.	3 1.1.
4 a.	4 (1)	4 1.1.
5 (1)	5 (a)	5 1.1.
6 (a)	6 (i)	6 1.1.
7 i)	7 1)	7 1.1.

Figure 4.21

You can select one of these styles or create one of your own by using the Custom selection. For example, to display the outline in the legal style, use the mouse to select legal numbering.

> **Point** at the Legal button
> **Click**
> **Click** OK

Special Text Formats **4**

The outline is changed to the legal style.

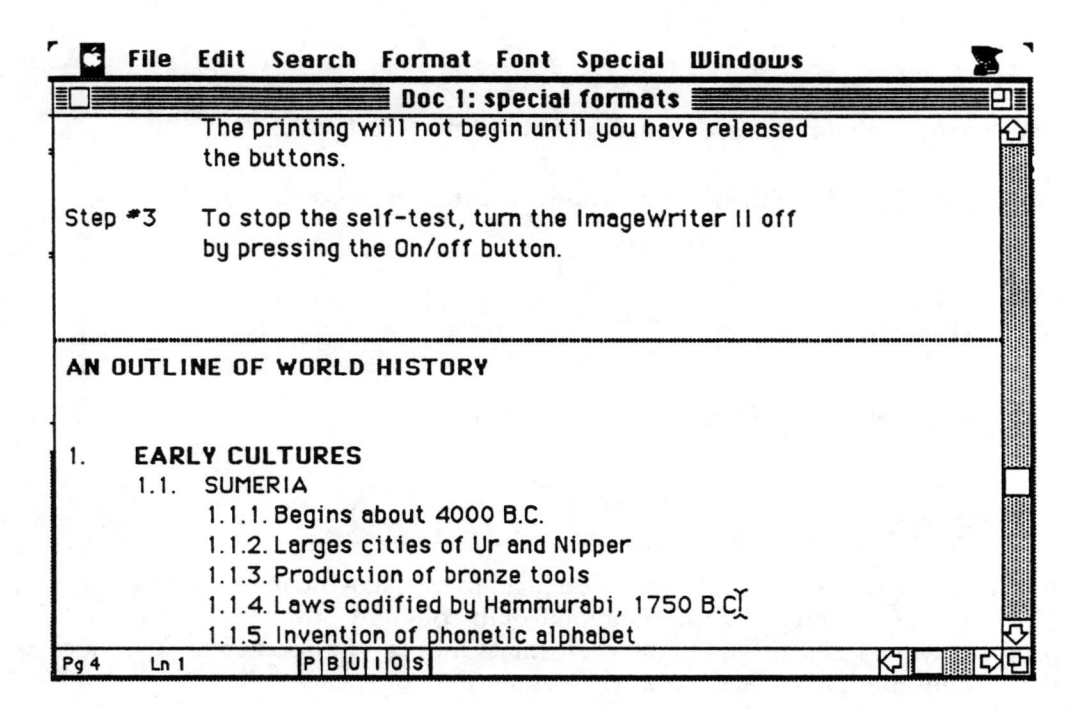

```
 File   Edit   Search   Format   Font   Special   Windows
                    Doc 1: special formats
         The printing will not begin until you have released
         the buttons.

Step #3  To stop the self-test, turn the ImageWriter II off
         by pressing the On/off button.


AN OUTLINE OF WORLD HISTORY

1.   EARLY CULTURES
     1.1.  SUMERIA
           1.1.1. Begins about 4000 B.C.
           1.1.2. Larges cities of Ur and Nipper
           1.1.3. Production of bronze tools
           1.1.4. Laws codified by Hammurabi, 1750 B.C.
           1.1.5. Invention of phonetic alphabet
Pg 4    Ln 1          P B U I O S
```

Figure 4.22

To return to the normal outline style, you can simply delete the outline style code. Enter

[Delete]

Point at OK
Click

Change to the paragraph outline style. Enter

[Apple/3] 3

189

4 Special Text Formats

> **Point** at the Paragraph button
> **Click**
> **Click** OK

Once again, the numbers are recalculated to fit the latest codes.

Move to the bottom of the page and insert another page break. Enter

[Apple/g] ↓
[Apple/Return]

You are now at the top of page #5.

COLUMNS

In Chapter 3, you learned how to create text tables, using the most common type of column operation—aligning items into tab columns; however, WordPerfect provides two special types of column formats that can be used to handle more demanding column layouts: parallel columns and newspaper columns.

Parallel columns are designed to solve one of the basic limitations of tab columns. In a tab-oriented column, you must manually end each short entry and insert a tab. Suppose, however, that you wanted to enter paragraph text that would wrap around at the end of each line in a table rather than enter short phrases or numbers. Parallel columns, such as those used frequently in catalogs or brochures, allow you to make such entries.

Newspaper columns refer to page-length columns of text such as those found in news publications. In some cases, formatting a document into newspaper-like columns allows you to fit more text onto the same page. This situation is true only if the document contains a relatively large number of paragraphs separated by blank lines. Newspaper columns save space because when a blank line is encountered, that line takes up only a column width of space as compared to a page width of space in a normal document.

Next, you will learn how to implement both types of special column formats.

Special Text Formats **4**

Parallel Columns

One of the most useful features in WordPerfect is the parallel column feature. The term parallel is used because these columns are designed to be read from left to right across the page in the same way that you read the tables created in Chapter 3. The difference between parallel columns and a simple tab-structured table is that parallel columns allow you to enter full paragraphs into each column instead of restricting you to short items.

Begin this page with a title. Enter

[Apple/Shift/b]
1988 CATALOG OF NEW PUBLICATIONS
[Apple/Shift/b]
[Return] [Return]

There are two parts to any WordPerfect column operation: defining columns and turning columns on and off.

Column Definition   A column definition tells WordPerfect the type of column layout to use, how many columns to create, and what the widths of the columns should be. You must create a column definition before you can enter text into the column format; however, you can revise the column definition after you have entered the text.

Column On/Off   When you define a column layout, WordPerfect does not automatically assume that you want to enter text in columns. Once you have created a definition for the column layout, you must then turn on the column mode in order to format your text as column text. This extra step has advantages. It means that once you have created a layout, you can choose to format specific parts of your document as columns while formatting other parts as normal paragraph text.

4 Special Text Formats

The first step is to create a column definition. Display the Format Columns menu by entering

[Apple/1]

Note that the Columns On option is not available at this time because you have not created a column definition. Select option #2, Column Options, by entering

2

The Column Options menu appears.

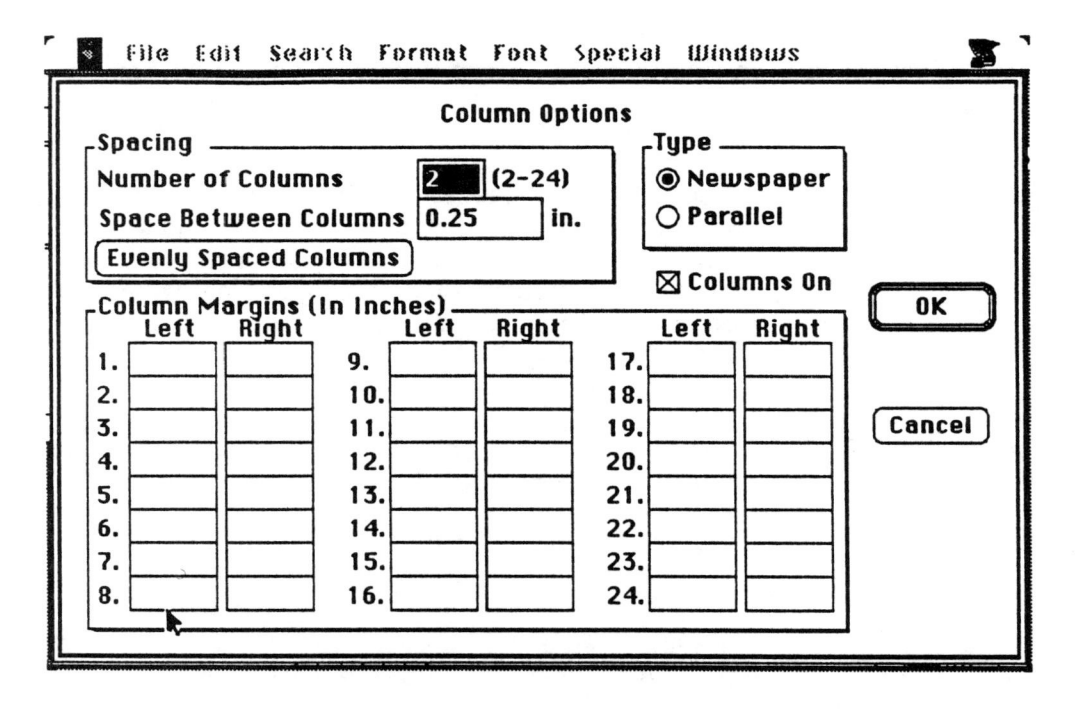

Figure 4.23

Special Text Formats 4

This menu allows you to create a column layout containing two to 24 columns. The first step is to choose the type of column layout you want to create. WordPerfect defaults to the Newspaper-type layout. Change this option to Parallel.

> **Point** at the Parallel button
> **Click**

Next, enter the number of columns you want to create. In this case, you will create three columns. Enter

3

You also must decide how much space is to be left between each column. The default setting is 0.25". Change the spacing to a full 0.5" by entering

[Tab]
.5

The last part of the column definition involves the actual widths of the columns. WordPerfect will evenly divide the available space between the 3 columns if you click on the Evenly Spaced Columns option.

> **Point** at Evenly Spaced Columns
> **Click**

WordPerfect automatically enters left and right margin settings for each of the three columns.

There is one other setting to take note of on this menu, the check box called Columns On. The box is currently checked. If you enter a column definition with this box checked, WordPerfect automatically turns the column mode on so that you can begin to enter column-formatted text. If you do not want to immediately enter column text, click this option box before you complete the definition.

4 Special Text Formats

To accept the current values, enter

[Return]

Begin the text entry by creating headings for the three columns. Turn on the bold and underline text attributes. Enter

[Apple/Shift/b] [Apple/Shift/u]
Publication

Look at the position indicator at the bottom of the window. It shows an additional item, "Col:1." When you are in a column format layout, WordPerfect adds this extra indicator to tell you in what column your cursor is located. To move to the top of the next column, you must enter a Page End command. Enter

[Apple/Return]

The cursor jumps to the top of the next column. Next, enter

Description

To move to the top of the final column, enter

[Apple/Return]

Enter the title for the last column, and turn off the underline and bold attributes:

Pricing
[Apple/Shift/b] [Apple/Shift/u]
[Apple/Return]

194

Special Text Formats 4

After the last column entry, the cursor returns to the first column. You are now ready to enter an item into column #1. The parallel column feature allows you to type as much as you like without having to worry about typing into the second column. Instead, your text will automatically wrap around to another line in the same column. Enter

[Apple/Shift/i]
dBASE III Plus Power Tools by Rob Krumm
[Apple/Return]

WordPerfect wraps the lines into a narrow column on the left side of the screen, rather than letting the line spread across the screen to the next column. When you end the entry with [Apple/Return], WordPerfect jumps to the top of the next column.

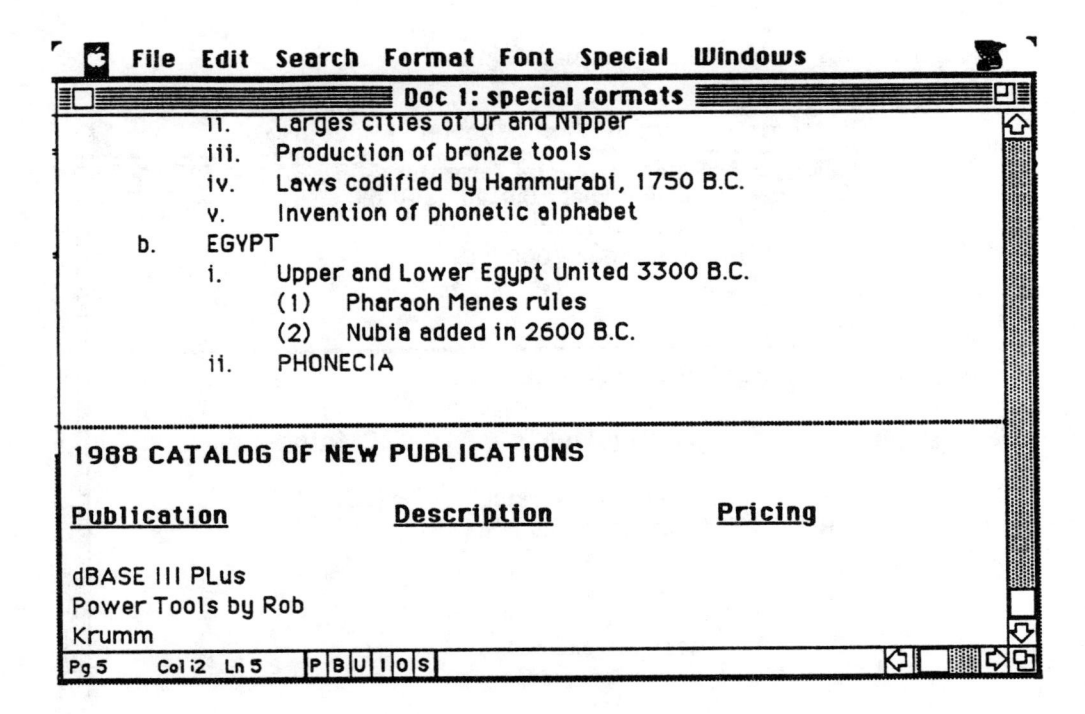

```
  File   Edit   Search   Format   Font   Special   Windows
================== Doc 1: special formats ==================
         ii.    Larges cities of Ur and Nipper
         iii.   Production of bronze tools
         iv.    Laws codified by Hammurabi, 1750 B.C.
         v.     Invention of phonetic alphabet
    b.   EGYPT
         i.     Upper and Lower Egypt United 3300 B.C.
                (1)   Pharaoh Menes rules
                (2)   Nubia added in 2600 B.C.
         ii.    PHONECIA

1988 CATALOG OF NEW PUBLICATIONS

Publication              Description              Pricing

dBASE III PLus
Power Tools by Rob
Krumm
Pg 5    Col i2  Ln 5    P B U I O S
```

Figure 4.24

195

4 Special Text Formats

Next, enter the description of this book:

Covers networking, debugging and file management.
[Return] [Return]

Note that the [Return] by itself simply creates line endings and blank lines. You can type several paragraphs in any given column. Enter

Includes compiled applications and memory resident utilities.

Now, move to the last column by entering

[Apple/Return]

The cursor moves to the top of the third column.

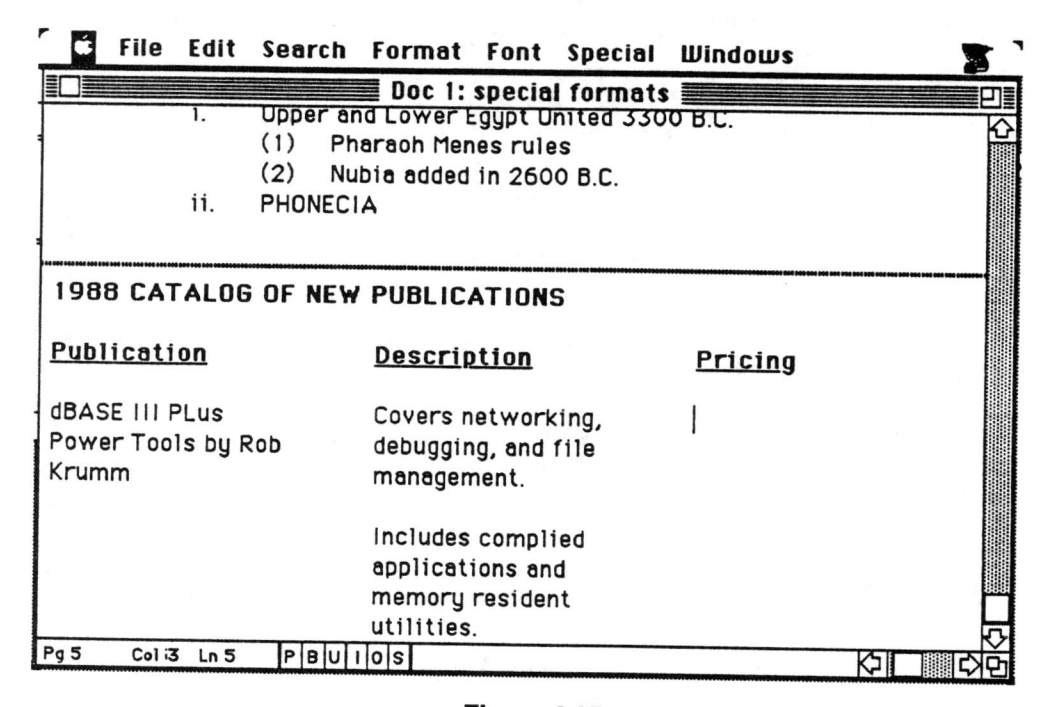

Figure 4.25

196

Special Text Formats 4

Enter the following text into the third column:

List Price $22.95, currently in print.

Complete the entry with another Page End command. Enter

[Apple/Return]

Now, enter another item into the columns:

WordPerfect Power Tools by Rob Krumm
[Apple/Return]
Explores the power of WordPerfect 4.2 advanced features such as macros, merge and math.
[Apple/Return]
List price $19.95, educational discounts available.
[Apple/Return]

The document should now resemble the following:

4 Special Text Formats

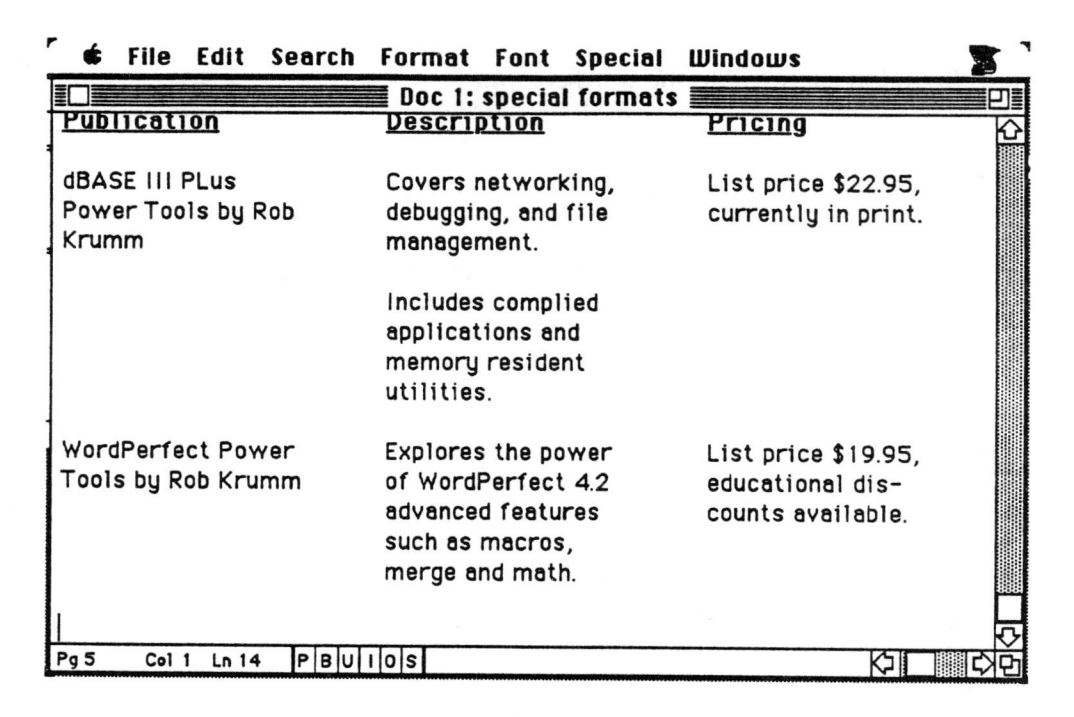

Figure 4.26

To return to the regular text entry mode, you need to turn off the column entry mode. Display the Column Formats menu by entering

[Apple/1]

Option #1 on this menu turns off the column mode. Enter

1

Special Text Formats 4

You can now enter normal paragraph text:

**[Apple/Shift/c] [Apple/Shift/b]
NEW RELEASE FOR FALL 1988
[Apple/Shift/b]
[Return] [Return]**

Whenever you want to start parallel column entry again, turn on the column mode. WordPerfect uses the previous column definition. Note that you must have created at least one column definition in the document to be able to turn on the column mode. You can use the keyboard shortcut to toggle the column mode. Enter

[Apple/Shift/k]

Enter the following text into the columns:

**The Power of WordPerfect for the Macintosh by Walter La Fish
[Apple/Return]
The most popular word processing program for the PC is now available for the Macintosh.
[Apple/Return]
List Price 21.95
[Apple/Return]
[Apple/Shift/k]**

The screen should resemble the following:

199

4 Special Text Formats

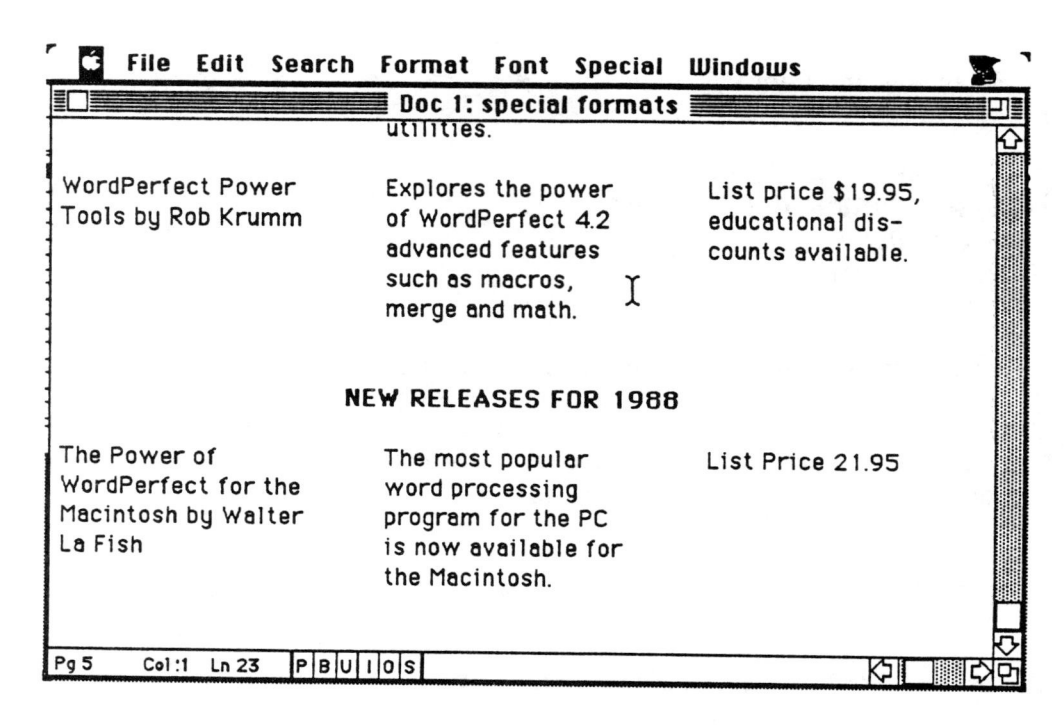

```
    File   Edit   Search   Format   Font   Special   Windows
    ═══════════════════ Doc 1: special formats ═══════════════════
                                  utilities.
    WordPerfect Power         Explores the power        List price $19.95,
    Tools by Rob Krumm        of WordPerfect 4.2        educational dis-
                              advanced features         counts available.
                              such as macros,
                              merge and math.

                           NEW RELEASES FOR 1988

    The Power of              The most popular          List Price 21.95
    WordPerfect for the       word processing
    Macintosh by Walter       program for the PC
    La Fish                   is now available for
                              the Macintosh.

    Pg 5    Col:1  Ln 23   P B U I O S
```

Figure 4.27

Uneven Columns

In the previous set of columns, WordPerfect calculated the margin locations for you. If you want to create unbalanced column layouts, you can enter the values for the column margins yourself. Begin a new page by entering

[Apple/Return]

Keep in mind that when the column mode is *not* active, the [Apple/Return] command creates a new page. When the column mode is active, the [Apple/Return] command creates a new column.

The use of unbalanced columns is typical in documents such as resumes that usually require a narrow column on the left and a wider column on the right. As an example, use a parallel column format to create a simple resume.

Special Text Formats 4

Begin by entering

[Apple/Shift/c]
Resume [Return] [Return]
[Apple/Shift/c]
Walter Q. La Fish [Return] [Return]
[Apple/Shift/b] [Apple/Shift/u]
Work Experience
[Apple/Shift/b] [Apple/Shift/u]
[Return] [Return]

Next change to a column mode of entry. The current column definition uses three evenly spaced columns. For the resume, you must change the column definition before you can turn on the column mode.

Display the Column Format menu by entering

[Apple/1] 2

Change the number of columns to 2 by entering

2 [Tab]

The amount of space between columns is only significant when you are using the Evenly Spaced Columns option to automatically calculate the margins for the columns. In this example, you will be manually entering the value for the column margins.

This document uses a narrow column of 1.5" on the left side of the page and a second column on the right side that uses whatever space is left over. To create this column, you can leave the first column's left margin at 1" and then enter a right margin of 2.5". Enter

[Tab] [Tab]
2.5 [Tab]

4 Special Text Formats

The gap between the columns is determined by the placement of the left margin for the second column. To leave a 0.25" gap, enter the left margin as 2.75":

2.75 [Tab]

For the right margin, enter the value of the current right margin on the page, 7.5".

Note that the use of measurements in the Column Layout menu differs from the way margins are measured in the Page Layout menu. In column layout, both left and right margins are measured by their distance from the left edge of the page. In this case, the right margin is described as 7.5" from the left edge of the page. In page layout, the right margin setting is expressed as the distance from the right edge of the page. On the Page Layout menu, the value 1" for the right margin expresses the fact that the page is 8.5" wide and the right margin is indented 1" from the right page edge. Both menus express the same idea but in different ways.

Enter

7.5

Remove the extraneous value for column #3. Enter

[Delete] [Tab]
[Delete]

Note that the Columns On box is checked, which means that when you enter the new column settings, the screen display will automatically be placed in the column entry mode. Enter

[Return]

Special Text Formats 4

You are now in the left column. Enter the following:

LFT Financial Services, 1985 to 1986
[Apple/Return]

Now type the text for the job description:

Analyzed the operations to create a procedure to produce a manual for the documentation of accounting procedures within the data processing department.
[Apple/Return]

The document should resemble the following:

```
 File   Edit   Search   Format   Font   Special   Windows
================ Doc 1: special formats ================
La Fish              is now available for
                     the Macintosh.
─────────────────────────────────────────────────────────
                        Resume

                    Walter Q. La Fish

Work Experience

LFT Financial        Analyzed the operations to create a procedure to
Services, 1985       produce a manual for the documentation of accounting
to 1986              procedures within the data processing department.

Pg 6   Col 1  Ln 11    P B U I O S
```

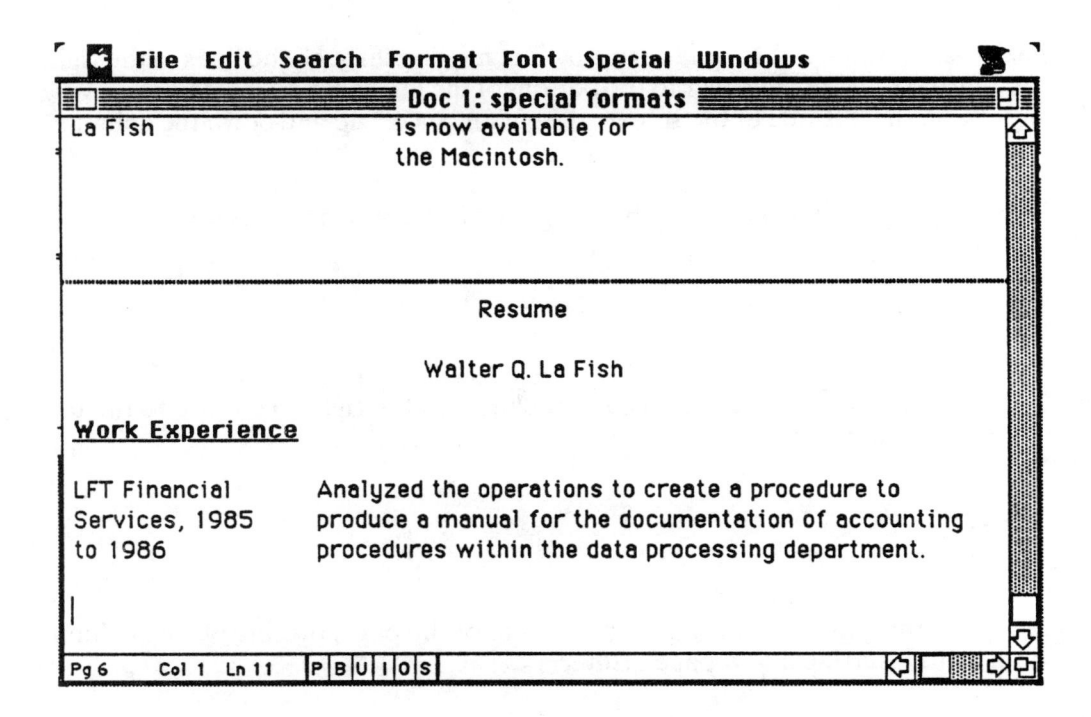

Figure 4.28

4 Special Text Formats

Now enter another job:

Journal Newspapers, 1982 to 1984
[Apple/Return]
Production Assistant in charge of paste up, layout and visual arrangements.
[Apple/Return]

Moving Around Columns

The movement of the cursor will appear different from what you might expect when you are moving through text that is formatted into parallel columns. Enter

↑ (6 times)

The cursor advances through the text by first moving through the lines in the right column and then moving over to the bottom of the left column. Instead of moving directly up the left side of the screen, the cursor snakes up and down the columns.

You can jump between columns by using the Goto commands. Enter

[Apple/g] →

The cursor moves to the top of the next column on the right. To move to the top of the left column, enter

[Apple/g] ←

Complete this entry by moving to the bottom of the page, turning off the column mode, and inserting a new page. Enter

[Enter] [Enter] ↓
[Apple/Shift/k]
[Apple/Return]

Special Text Formats 4

Newspaper Columns

The final format to add to this document is newspaper-style columns. Newspaper columns divide the text on a page into a series of page-length columns. Unlike text in parallel columns, text entered into newspaper columns must fill the entire first column before text can be added to the second column. This format can be used to create newsletters. As an example, create a simple newsletter. Begin with a title. Center the first line by entering

[Apple/Shift/c]

Change the point size to 24.

```
Point at Font
Drag to 24
Release
```

Select Shadow text by entering

[Apple/Shift/s]

Enter the title:

News On The March [Return] [Return]

Change the text back to normal type by entering

[Apple/y] 1

4 Special Text Formats

> **Point** at Font
> **Drag** to 12
> **Release**

To enter text into newspaper-style columns, you must create a new column definition. Enter

[Apple/1] 2

Create a four-column layout. Enter

4

> **Point** at the Newspaper button
> **Click**
> **Point** at the Even Spaced Columns button
> **Click**

WordPerfect automatically calculates the margin settings for the columns. Note that because the Columns On box is checked, you will immediately enter the column mode when you exit from this menu. Enter

[Return]

Centering in a Column

You can center text within a column by using the centering command just as you would do in normal text entry mode. Enter

[Apple/Shift/c] [Apple/Shift/b]
Parking [Return]
[Apple/Shift/c]
Problems [Apple/Shift/b]
[Return] [Return]

Enter the following news item:

Due to the construction of the new hotel, it appears that nonresidents are using our parking lot.
[Return] [Return]
Please make a note of the plate number of any vehicles that you think do not belong in the parking lot.
[Return] [Return]
If the vehicles are not registered to residents we will take steps to have them towed at the expense of the owners.
[Return] [Return]

At this point, you are still entering text into the first column. Add another new item. Enter

[Apple/Shift/c] [Apple/Shift/b]
New Security [Return]
[Apple/Shift/c] Badges
[Apple/Shift/b] [Return] [Return]

Now, enter the text for this article:

Starting on the first of next month, all employees will be required to have new photo ID badges. [Return]

4 Special Text Formats

You are now typing in the second column. Your screen should resemble the following:

```
Parking              be required to
Problems             have new photo
                     ID badges.

Due to the
construction of
the new hotel,
it appears that
non-residents
are using our
parking lot.

Please make a
note of the
plate number of
any vehicles
that you think
do not belong in
the parking lot.
```

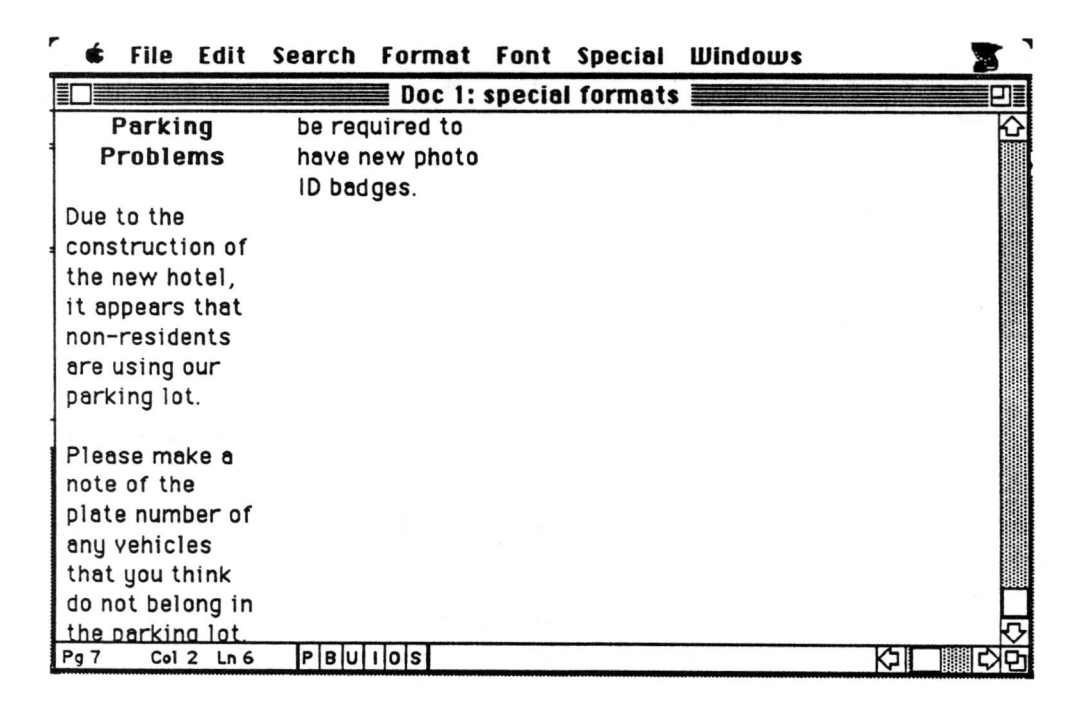

Figure 4.29

Note again that in a newspaper column layout, WordPerfect automatically moves to the next column when the current column is filled with text. Unlike columns in which you manually switch to the next column, you must fill up each column before you can move to the next column.

To save time, assume that you are finished with the newsletter and want to move on to some other project. Turn off the column mode by entering

[Apple/Shift/k]

208

Note what happens. WordPerfect tries to automatically create a new page when you exit the newspaper column mode. The newspaper column format precludes adding non-column text to the same page, which is in contrast to the parallel column mode; it can be turned on and off several times on the same page.

PREVIEWING THE PRINTING

When you have large, complex documents, you may want to preview the document before you send it to the printer. The page preview display reduces the text so you can see the entire page.

To preview the formats created in this chapter, move the cursor to the beginning of the document. You can do so with the [Enter][Enter]↑ command. Another way to move around a document is to use the Goto command to move to specific pages. Enter

[Apple/g]

Your screen should resemble the following:

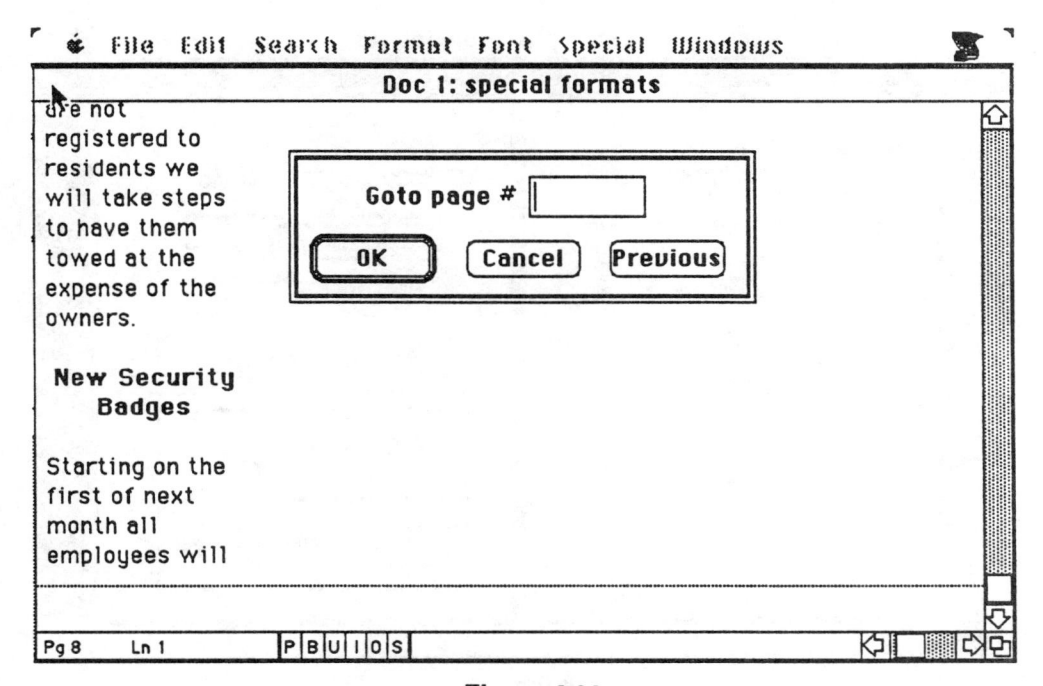

Figure 4.30

4 Special Text Formats

You can go to the top of a specific page by entering the page number. As an example, move to page #5 by entering

5 [Return]

To move to the beginning of the document, enter

[Apple/g]
1 [Return]

To preview the document, enter

[Apple/Shift/p]

WordPerfect changes the display window to the preview mode.

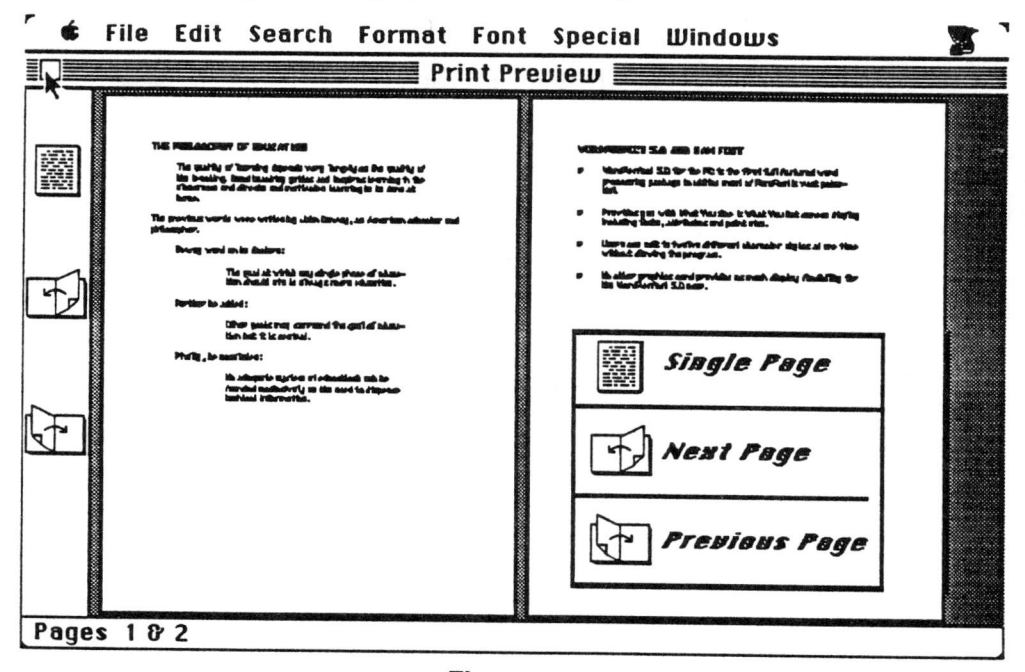

Figure 4.31

210

Special Text Formats 4

The page preview mode displays the first two pages of the document in a reduced view. The icons on the left side of the screen indicate three operations you can perform in the print preview mode. At the bottom of the screen, WordPerfect tells you that you are viewing pages 1 and 2.

Clicking on the Single Page icon changes the view from a double- to a single-page display. Clicking on the Next Page icon moves the display to the next page. And clicking on the Previous Page icon moves the display to the previous page.

Change to the next page:

```
Point at the Next Page icon
Click
```

The display now shows pages 2 and 3.

```
Point at the Next Page icon
Click
```

Pages 3 and 4 are displayed. Finally, change to the single-page display:

```
Point at the Single Page icon
Click
```

WordPerfect displays a single page in the preview mode.

4 Special Text Formats

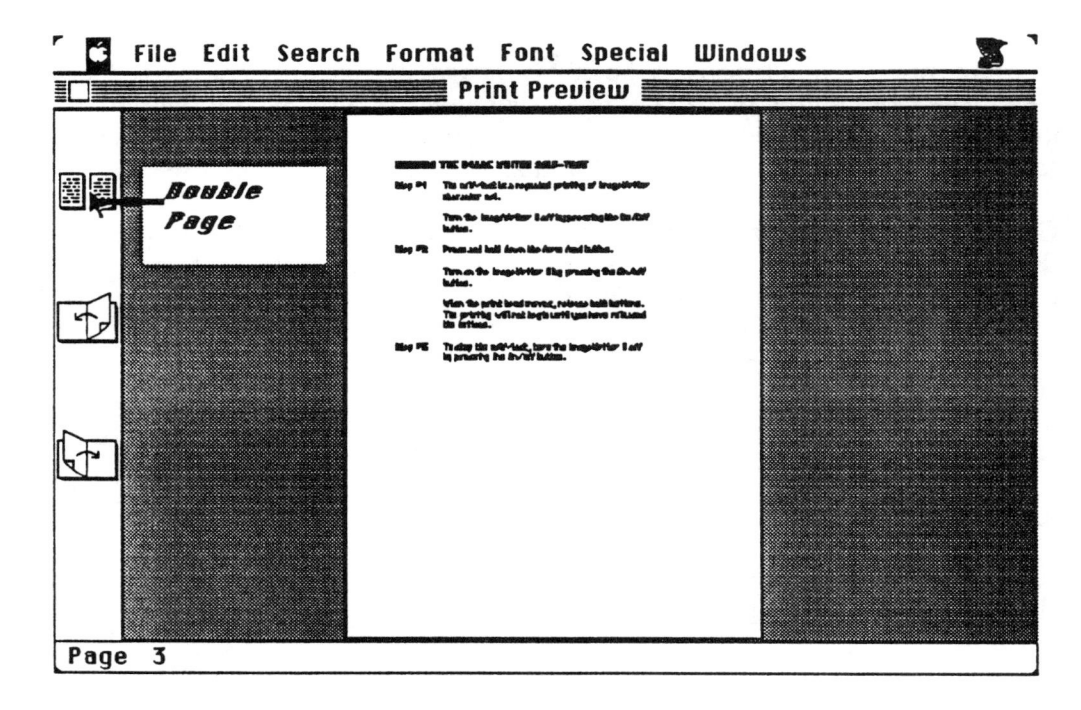

Figure 4.32

Note that a new icon, Double Page, takes the place of the Single Page icon. You can leaf through the document in the single-page mode by clicking on the icon just as you would in the double-page display.

ZOOMING THE DISPLAY

While still in the preview mode, you can zoom in on part of a page and see the character at normal size.

> **Point** at the top of the page

You will see that the cursor appears as a tiny magnifying glass. You can display the section of the document you are pointing at by clicking the mouse.

Special Text Formats **4**

Click

The display zooms in on that area of the document.

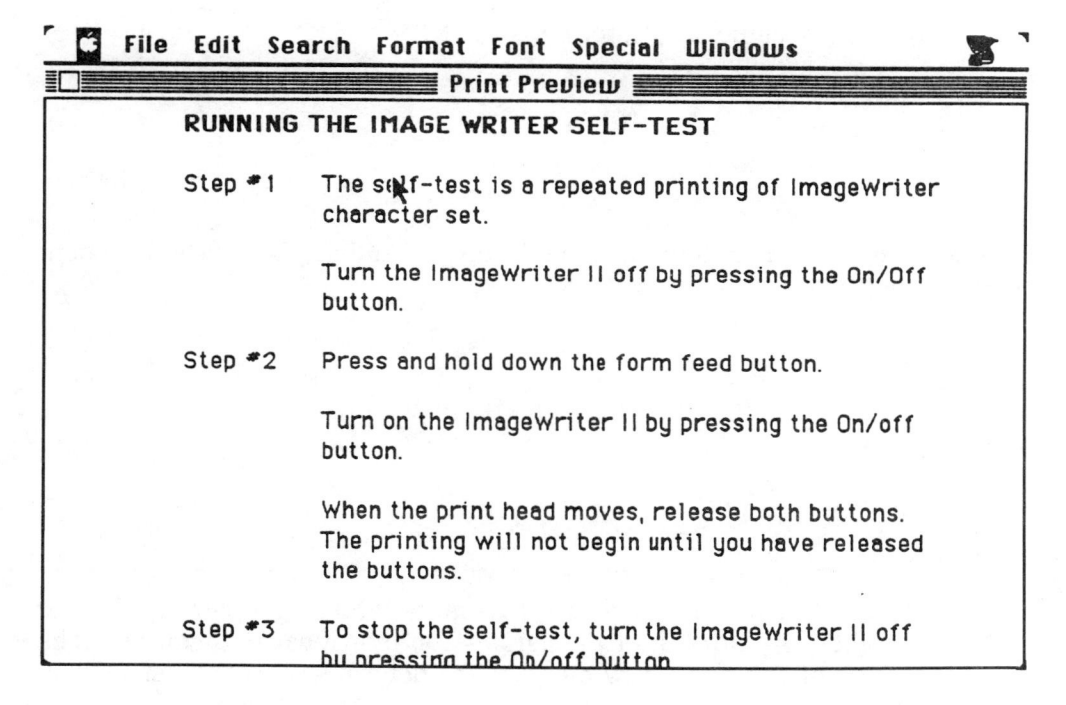

```
 File  Edit  Search  Format  Font  Special  Windows
━━━━━━━━━━━━━━━━━ Print Preview ━━━━━━━━━━━━━━━━━
   RUNNING THE IMAGE WRITER SELF-TEST

   Step #1    The self-test is a repeated printing of ImageWriter
              character set.

              Turn the ImageWriter II off by pressing the On/Off
              button.

   Step #2    Press and hold down the form feed button.

              Turn on the ImageWriter II by pressing the On/off
              button.

              When the print head moves, release both buttons.
              The printing will not begin until you have released
              the buttons.

   Step #3    To stop the self-test, turn the ImageWriter II off
              by pressing the On/off button.
```

Figure 4.33

To return to the full-page display, click the mouse button again.

Click

Use the Next Page and Previous Page icons to inspect all of the pages in the document. These pages show a wide range of formats available in WordPerfect.

To exit the document preview mode, you must click on the close box in the upper left corner of the display.

213

4 Special Text Formats

> **Point** at the close box
> **Click**

You are now back in the normal text mode.

You can print the document by entering

[Apple/p]
[Return]

When the printing is complete, save the document, and display a new document screen by entering

[Apple/s]
[Apple/k]
[Apple/n]

SUMMARY

- **Indents.** Indents are used to set temporary left — [Apple/Shift/t] — or left/right — [Apple/Shift/L] — margins for individual paragraphs. The locations of the temporary margins are determined by the current tab settings. The temporary margins end when a [HRt] is encountered.

- **Margin Release.** The Margin Release command allows you to type outside the current margins.

- **Outlines.** WordPerfect can automatically number paragraphs such as those found in outlines. In the outline mode, the paragraph numbers are added to each new paragraph, following the entry of a [return] character. Outlines can contain up to seven levels, and the style of numbering can be selected by inserting an outline style code in the document text.

Special Text Formats 4

- **Column Formats**. WordPerfect can automatically format text into two different types of column layouts. **Parallel columns** allow you to type short columns of text that wrap at the ends of lines, such as in some catalogs and brochures. **Newspaper columns** format the text into longer columns that snake up and down the page, such as in newsletters.

CHAPTER 5

PAGE FORMATS

5 Page Formats

In the previous chapters, you learned to create a variety of text formats that affected characters, lines, and paragraphs. In this chapter, you will look at WordPerfect features that create entire page effects. These features include headers and footers, page numbering, and footnotes.

OPENING FILES

To begin, load the document you created in Chapter 4, called Special Formats. Enter

[Apple/o]

WordPerfect displays the selection menu for opening a file.

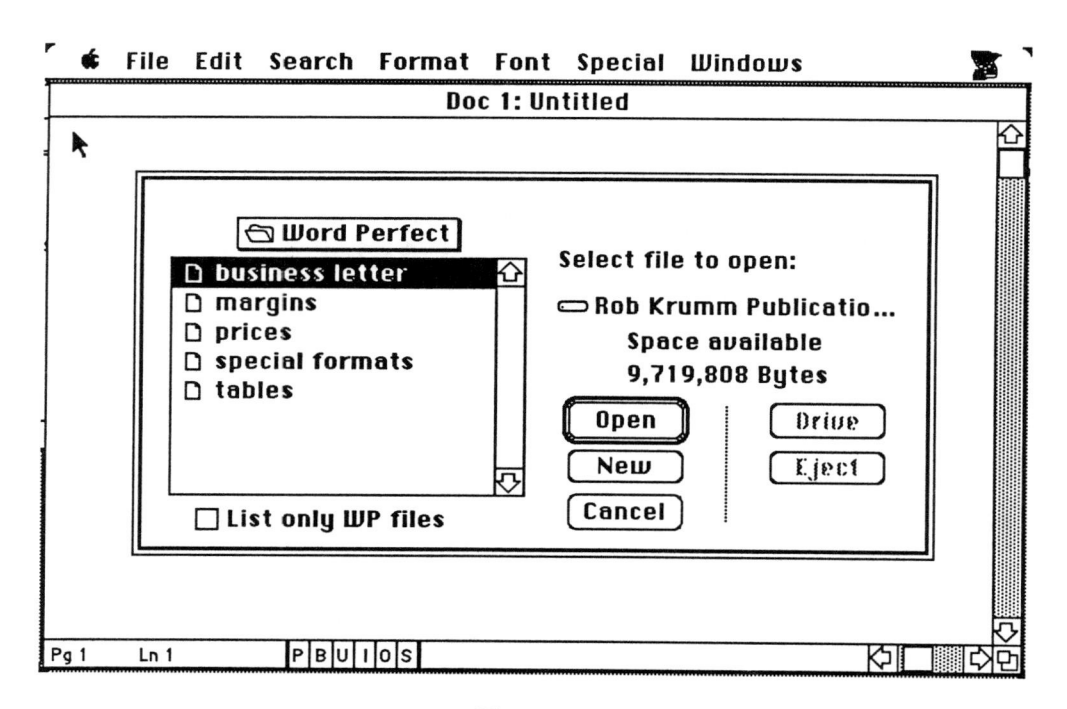

Figure 5.1

Page Formats 5

There are three ways to select a file from this display.

Mouse You can use the mouse to highlight a file name by pointing at the name in the scroll box and clicking the mouse button. If the name you are looking for does not appear in the box, you can scroll the display by clicking on the scroll bar on the right side of the box. To select and load a file in one operation, double click on that file name.

Cursor The ↑ and ↓ (up and down arrow) keys will move the highlight through the file list. If the list is longer than the box, the display will scroll when you move the cursor past the top or bottom of the display. To load a file that is highlighted, enter [Return].

Search You can have WordPerfect automatically search the file list for names that match specific characters. For example, if you typed the letters "sp," WordPerfect would place the cursor on the first file that began with "sp." If no file name began with those letters, the highlight would fall on the name closest in the alphabet to the letters you entered. Pressing [Return] loads the selected file.

For this example, try the search technique. Enter

sp

The highlight jumps to the Special Formats file, which begins with those letters. (If your disk contains other files that begin with the letters "sp," you may find that those files are selected instead of Special Formats.)

Load the file by entering

[Return]

WordPerfect loads the text of the file and displays the top of the first page in a window entitled Doc 2: Special Formats.

5 Page Formats

ADDING PAGE NUMBERS

In large documents, you will probably want to add page numbers. WordPerfect has two ways of adding page numbers.

Page #   The page number feature is used to place a page number at any one of six preselected positions on the page. The print style is always the default, Geneva 12-point.

Header/Footer   You can also add a page number by including it in header and footer text. When a page number is included in a header or footer, you can select the style of text used to print the page number.

As a general rule, if you want only page numbers and no page header or footer text, the first method (Page#) is the simplest to use.

To add page numbering to this document, display the Page Format menu by entering

[Apple/2]

Setting Page Numbers

The Page Format menu displays eight options. Only option #6, block protect, is not available. Block protect is only available when a portion of the text is selected (i.e., highlighted as a block). The second option on the menu is used to set page numbering. Enter

2

The Page Numbering menu appears.

Page Formats 5

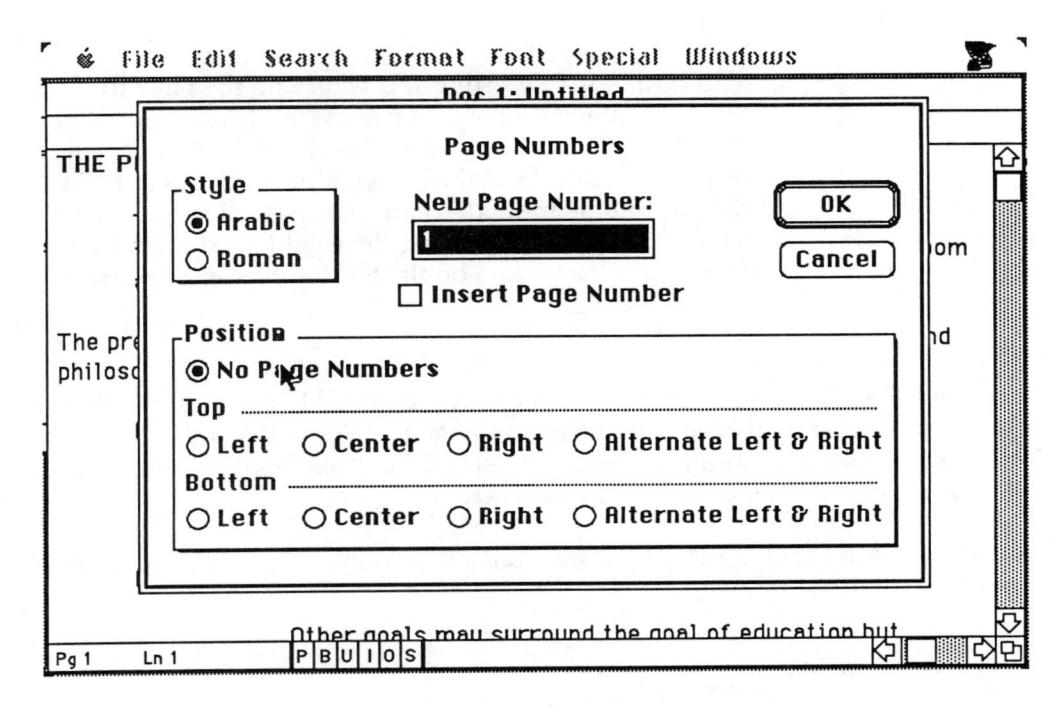

Figure 5.2

The Page Numbering menu allows you to enter three types of information about the page number.

Style This option is used to select Arabic — 1,2,3 — or Roman — I, II, III — numbering.

New Page Number This number selects the starting number for page numbering. WordPerfect automatically places the actual number of the page in this box. Because you are located on page one, the number 1 appears in the box. If you were on page eight, an 8 would appear. Entering a different value will cause WordPerfect to number the pages consecutively, starting with that value.

221

5   Page Formats

Position   This option tells WordPerfect where on the page to place the page number. You can choose to place the number at the top or the bottom of the page and select a left, center, or right horizontal position. Another option is to print the page number on alternate sides, which means that the page number will appear on the right for odd-numbered (right-side) pages and on the left for even-numbered (left-side) pages.

The Insert Page Number option on this menu is used to add a page number to the text of the document. It is unusual to insert a page number in the body of the text. This page numbering option is usually reserved for page headers and footers, which you will learn about later in this chapter.

The default setting is No Page Number. Add a page number by selecting the Bottom Center button.

Point at Center in the Bottom box
Click

Complete the selection by entering

[Return]

Note that adding a page number has no visual effect on the displayed text. The page number will appear only when you print the document or use the print preview display. To make sure that you have correctly entered the command, you can display the hidden codes. Enter

[Apple/7]

222

The screen should resemble the following

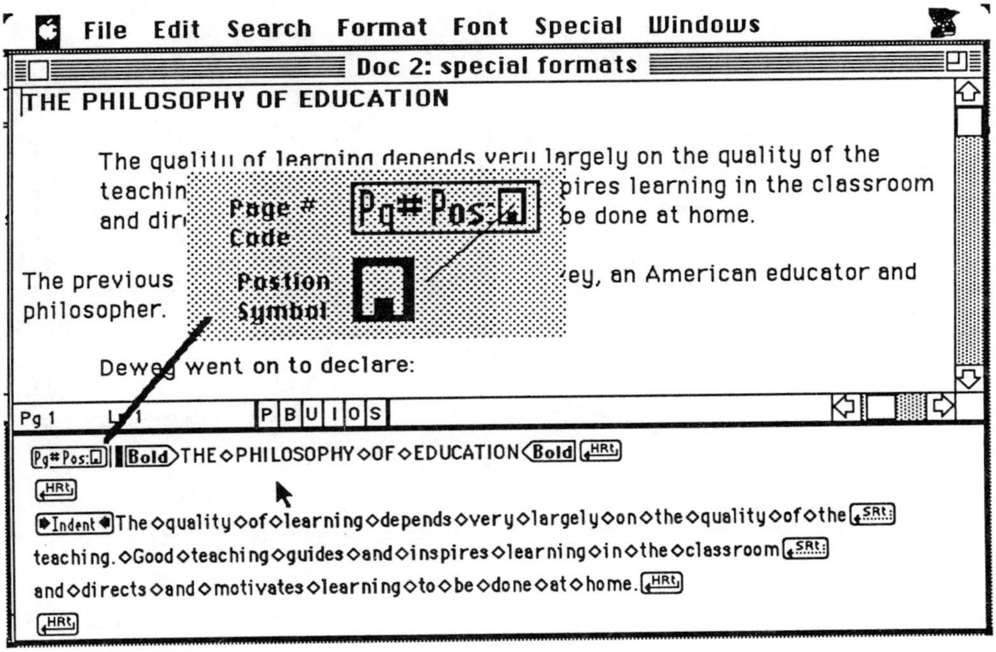

Figure 5.3

The [Pg#Pos] code tells WordPerfect to add the page number to the bottom center of each page when the document is printed. To see how such pages would appear, you can use the print preview mode. Enter

[Apple/Shift/p]

You can see that page numbers are placed at the bottom of each page automatically.

5 Page Formats

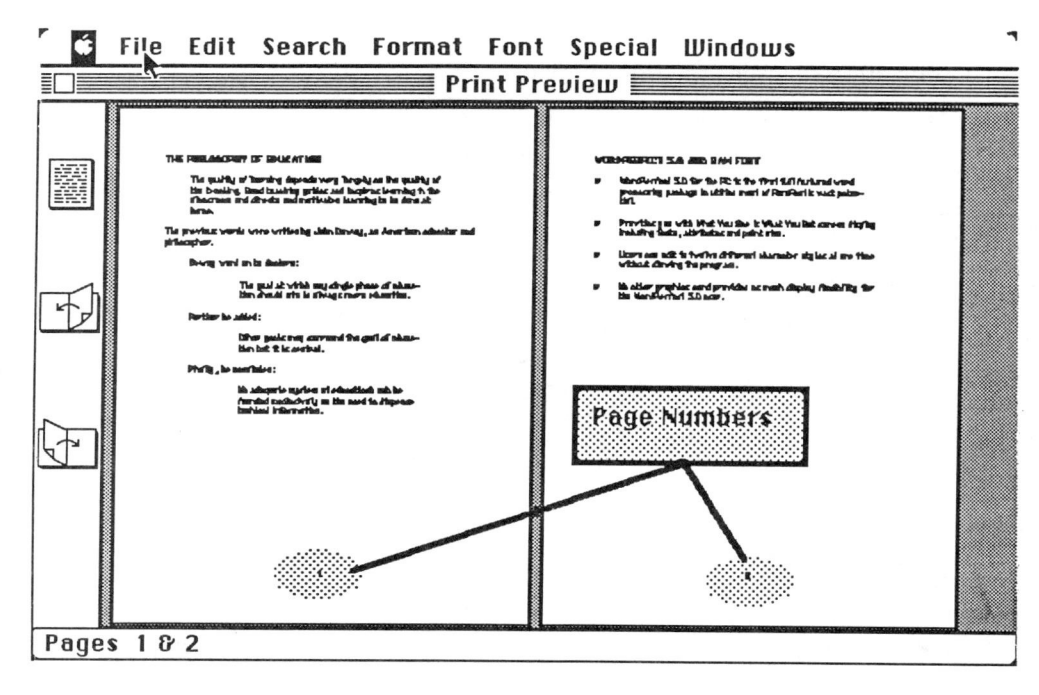

Figure 5.4

You can use the magnifying lens to examine the page number more closely.

```
Point at page number at the bottom of page 2
Click
```

The expanded display shows the number 2 clearly. Return to the normal display.

```
Point at the Close box
Click
```

Suppressing Page Numbers

In this example, you have added page numbers to all pages in the document; however, it is common to begin printing page numbers on the second page of the document. WordPerfect has a special page command that can suppress the printing of the page number on a specific page.

To suppress the printing of a page number, position the cursor on the page that contains the number you want to suppress. The cursor need not be at the top of the page, but it must be somewhere on that page. In this example, the cursor is on page 1, which is the page number you want to suppress.

Display the Page Format menu by entering

[Apple/2]

The third option on the menu, Suppress Format, is the one you want to select. Enter

3

WordPerfect displays the Suppress Format menu box.

5 Page Formats

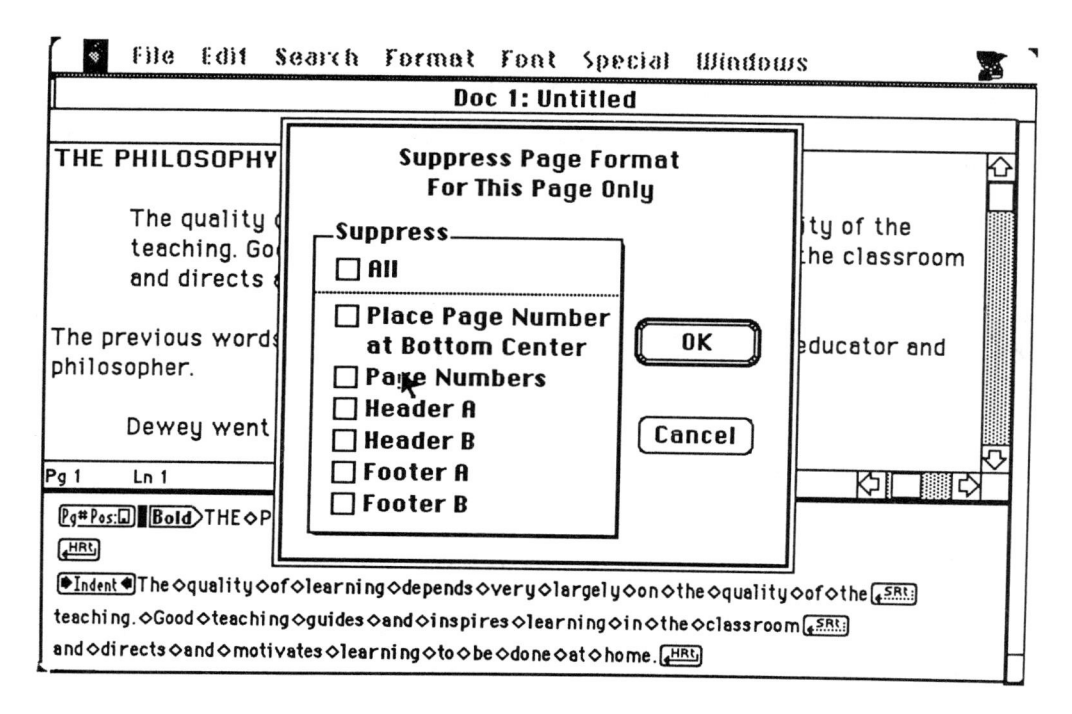

Figure 5.5

The menu allows you to suppress all page formatting or to suppress individual page options, such as headers. In this case, you can simply choose to suppress all page formatting for this page.

```
Point at All
Click
Click on OK
```

WordPerfect inserts a [Suppress:All] code into the text. Use the print preview display to see how this code affects the appearance of the final, printed document. Press

[Apple/Shift/p]

Note that page 1 does not have a page number, but page 2 does.

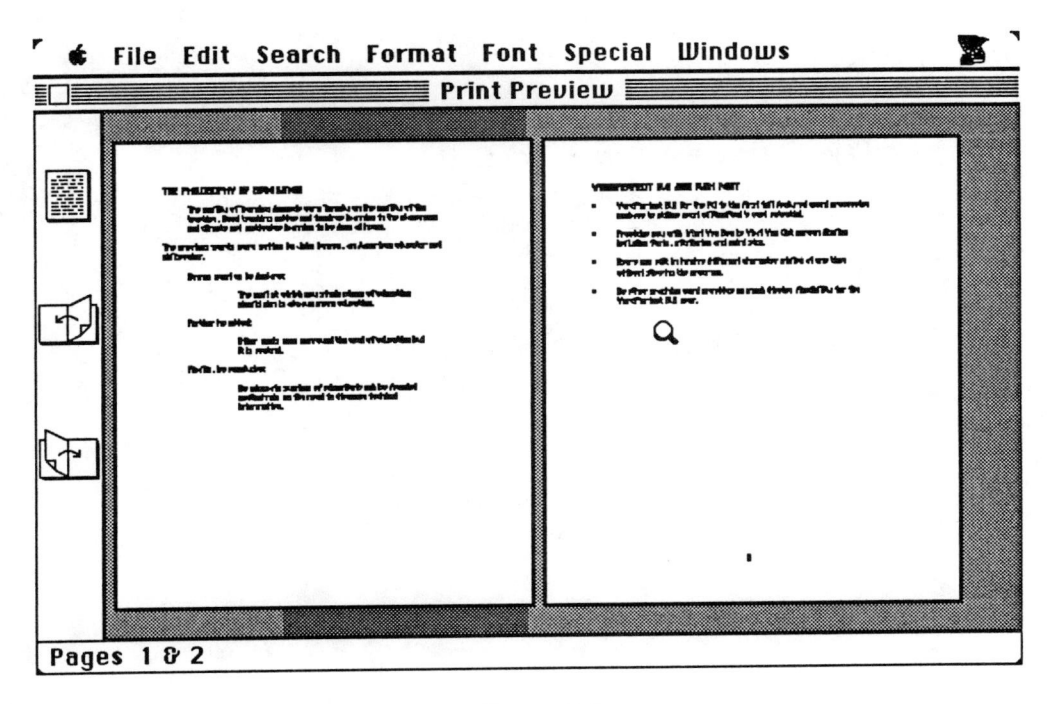

Figure 5.6

Return to the document window.

```
Point at the Close Box
Click
```

Numbering Sequence

You can choose to start or change the page numbering sequence so that Word-Perfect will print page numbers that do not correspond to the actual page numbers. For example, suppose that the Special Formats document is really part of a larger project. The previous section ended on page 129, so you want this document to begin on page 130.

227

5   Page Formats

The first step is to delete the page format codes you have just entered. Enter

[Delete] [Delete]

Display the Page Format menu by entering

[Apple/2]

Select Page Number by entering

2

To set the page numbering at 130, enter

130

Select the position for the page number.

> **Point** at Top Center
> **Click**
> **Click** on OK

Note that WordPerfect inserted two codes, [Pg#:130] and [Pg# Pos:].

Page Formats 5

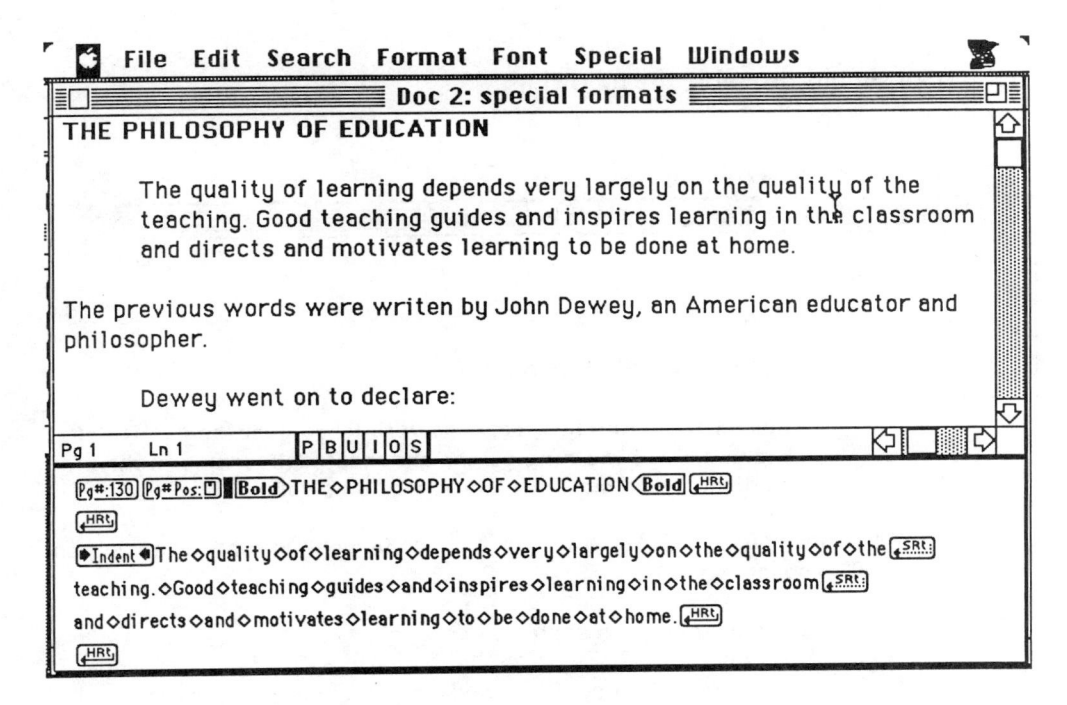

Figure 5.7

Also note that the bar at the bottom of the text window shows the page number as 130, reflecting the value you entered with the code. Use the print preview display to see how the page number will appear on the final document. Enter

[Apple/Shift/p]

Use the magnifying glass icon to examine the top of the first page.

> **Point** at the top of the first page
> **Click**

229

5 Page Formats

The screen should resemble the following:

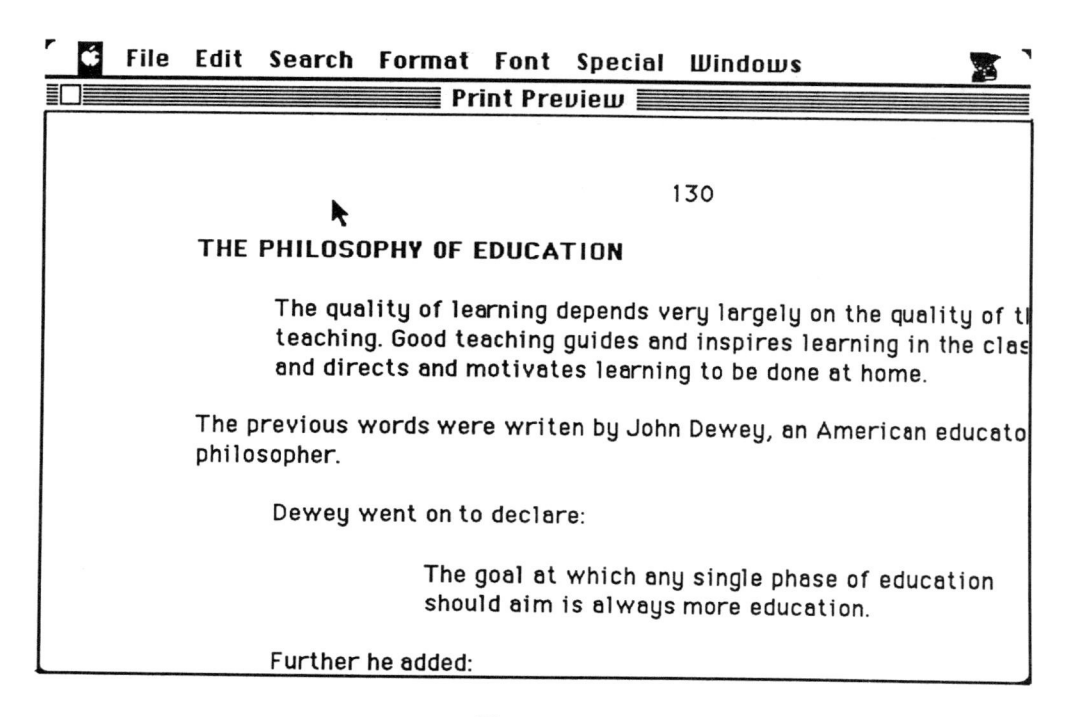

```
 File   Edit   Search   Format   Font   Special   Windows
                        Print Preview
                                                    130
         THE PHILOSOPHY OF EDUCATION

             The quality of learning depends very largely on the quality of t
             teaching. Good teaching guides and inspires learning in the clas
             and directs and motivates learning to be done at home.

         The previous words were writen by John Dewey, an American educato
         philosopher.

             Dewey went on to declare:

                     The goal at which any single phase of education
                     should aim is always more education.

             Further he added:
```

Figure 5.8

The page number 130 should appear centered at the top of the page. Return to the document display.

| **Point** at the Close box |
| **Double Click** |

Mixing Page Number Formats

If you want, you can change the location and the sequence of the page numbers within a document. Suppose you wanted to insert photographs into the document after page 133. The photographs would be mounted on pages 134 and 135. In this case, you would need to change the page numbering sequence so that the page following 133 printed out as page 136.

230

Page Formats 5

To do this, move the cursor to the top of the page currently numbered as 134. Enter

[Apple/g] 134 [Return]

Note that in WordPerfect you use the **logical** page numbers to refer to the pages in the document. Insert a new page number code at this point in the document. Enter

[Apple/2] 2

Enter the new number for this page:

136

You can also change the position of the page number.

```
Point at Bottom Center
Click
Click on OK
```

Preview the pages. Enter

[Apple/Shift/p]

The pages that appear have the page numbers at the bottom of the page. Use the icon to enlarge the page number at the bottom of the left page.

```
Point at the page number on the left
Click
```

231

5 Page Formats

The screen should resemble the following:

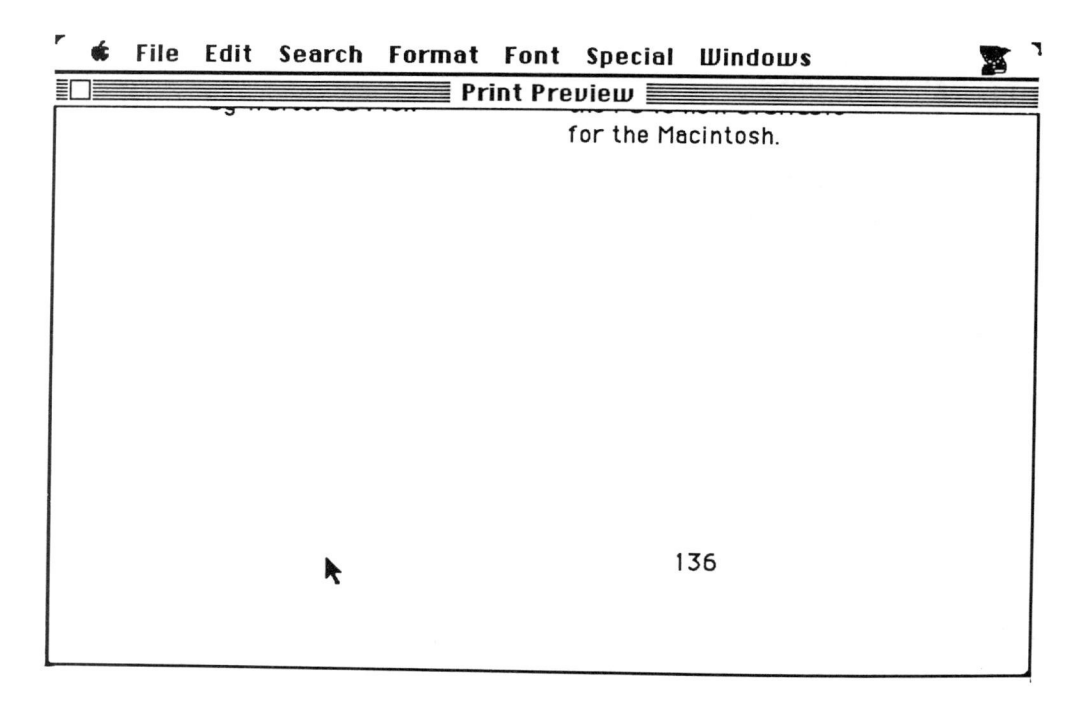

```
 File   Edit   Search   Format   Font   Special   Windows
                    Print Preview
                                              for the Macintosh.




                          ▲                      136
```

Figure 5.9

You can see that this page is correctly numbered as 136.

> **Point** at the Close box
> **Click**

Move back one page in the display.

Page Formats 5

> **Point** at the Page Back icon
> **Click**

You can see that the page number changes from the top on the left page to the bottom on the right page.

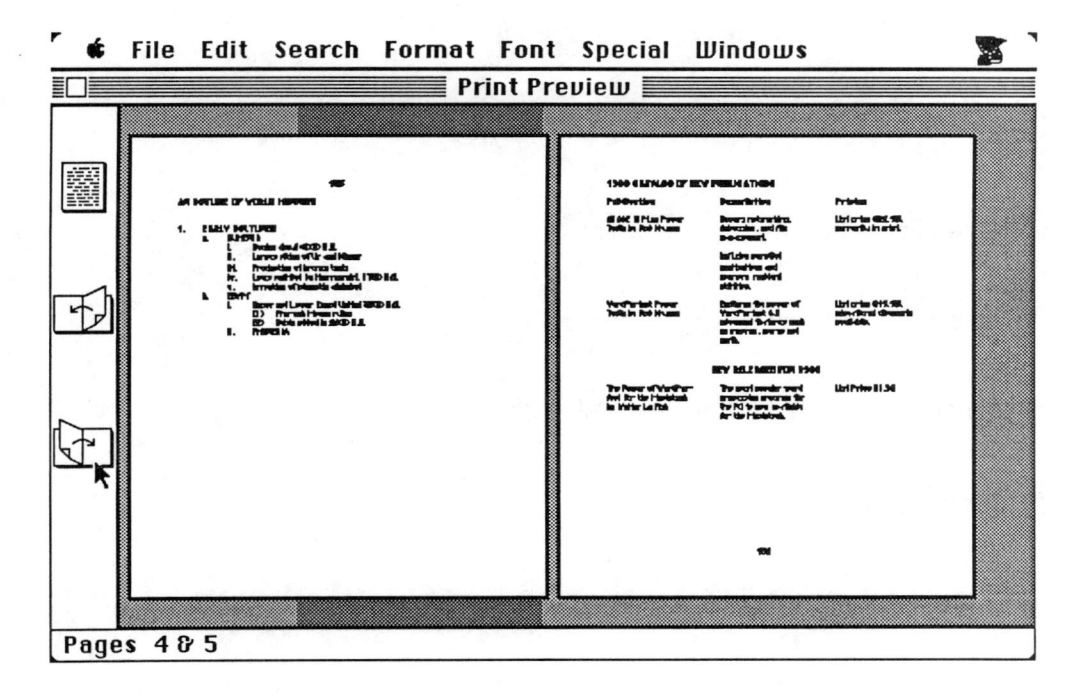

Figure 5.10

Return to the document window.

> **Point** at the Close box
> **Click**

233

5 Page Formats

Alternating Page Number Positions

The last page number effect you will investigate is alternating page number position. Alternate positions are used when you intend to print or copy the text onto both sides of a page. By alternating between left and right sides of the page, WordPerfect positions the page number on the edge of the page that is away from the binding—the same way page numbers are printed in books.

Display the Page Number menu by entering

[Apple/2] 2

> **Point** at Top Alternate Left & Right
> **Click**
> **Click** on OK

Display the print preview once again. Enter

[Apple/Shift/p]

The page numbers should appear on opposite sides of the two pages.

Page Formats 5

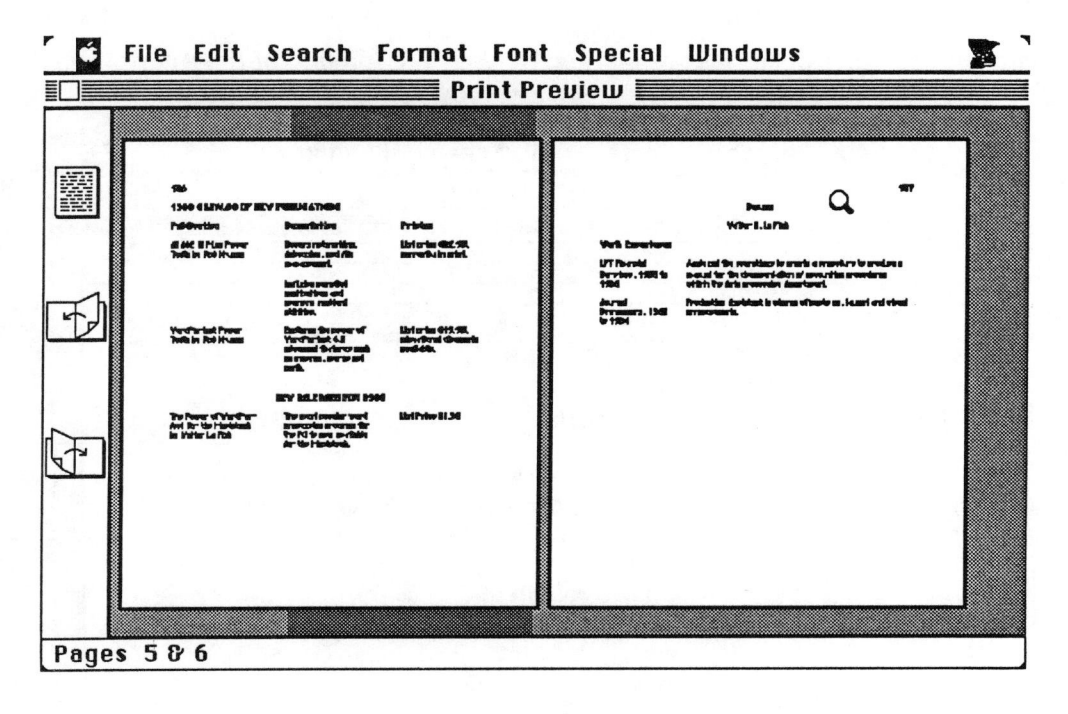

Figure 5.11

| **Point** at the Close Box |
| **Click** |

Modifying Page Number Positions

Page number positions can be modified using the rule line display. Display the page ruler by entering

[Apple/r]

235

5 Page Formats

The page number positions are marked by # on the top line of the ruler display.

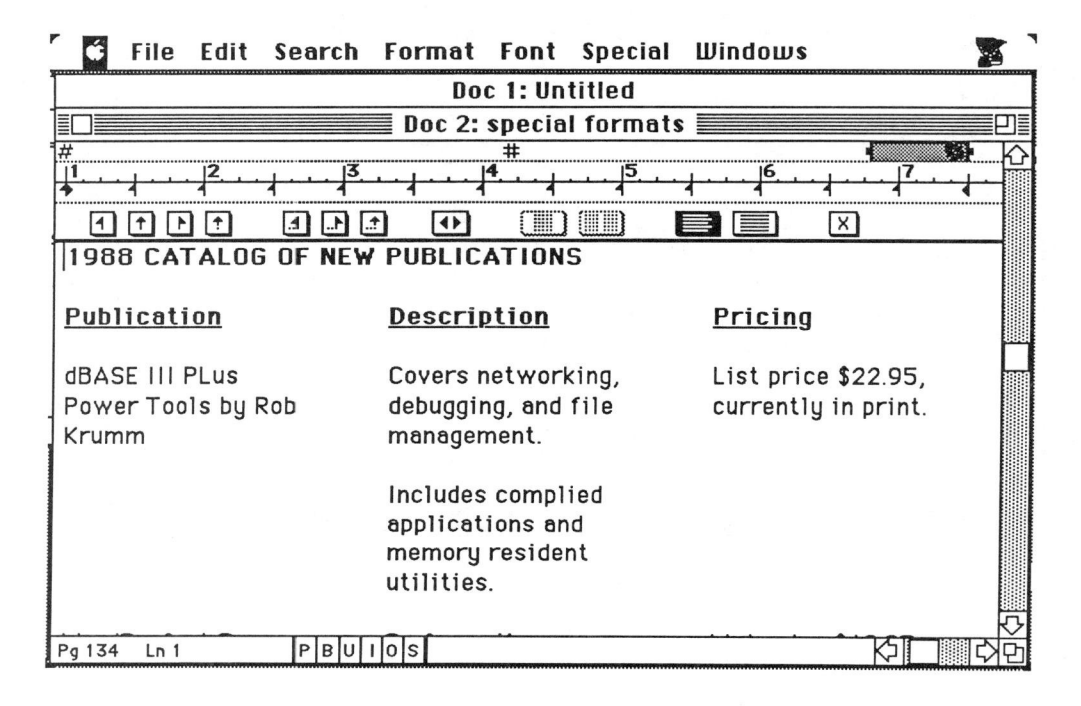

Figure 5.12

You can change the page number positions by dragging the # markers to new locations. **Note:** Imagewriter users may need to scroll to the display to the right to see the right page number marker.

> **Point** at left # marker
> **Drag** to 2"
> **Point** at right # marker
> **Drag** to 6"

236

The screen should resemble the following:

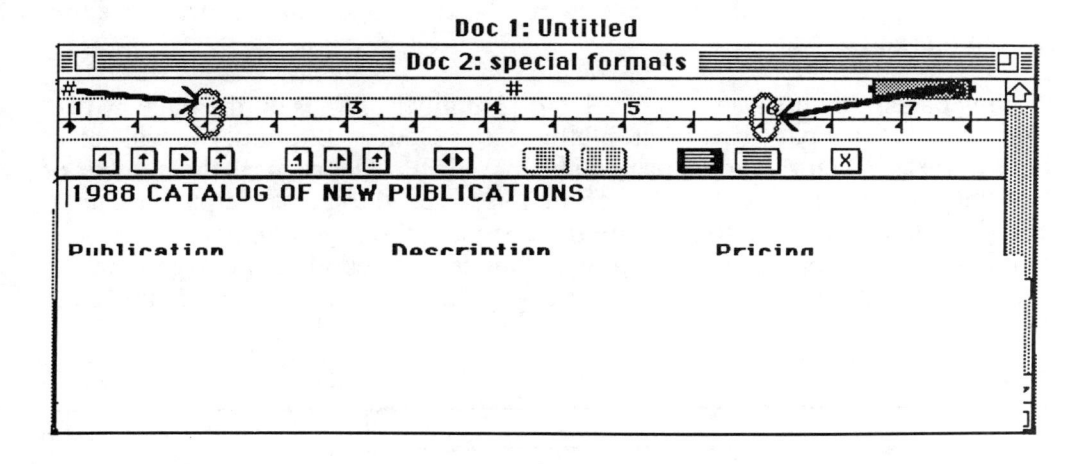

Figure 5.13

To see the effect of this change, place the document into print preview display. Enter

[Apple/Shift/p]

The position of the page numbers now reflects the new positions selected on the ruler line. Note that the change in page number positions inserts a code into the text at the current cursor location, which means that any page numbers printed before the page on which this code appears will still use the default page number positions. In this example, you inserted the code on page #136. Previous pages (e.g. 130, 131) will print the page number at the usual positions. To make a change in position for the entire document, you would enter the new page positions on the first page of the document.

5 Page Formats

How Page Numbers Affect Text

Adding page numbers to a document takes up space on the page that would otherwise be used for text. When a page number is added, WordPerfect places a top page number just below the top margin or a bottom page number just above the bottom margin.

Adding page numbers also reduces the total number of lines on the page by two. For example, on a page that prints all the text as Geneva 12-point, you will get 40 lines of text. When you add a page number, WordPerfect reduces the number of text lines on that page to 38. One of the lines is used to print the page number, and the other is inserted to separate the text from the page number. If the page number is at the top of the page, a blank line is inserted after the page number. If the page number is at the bottom of the page, a blank line is inserted before the page number.

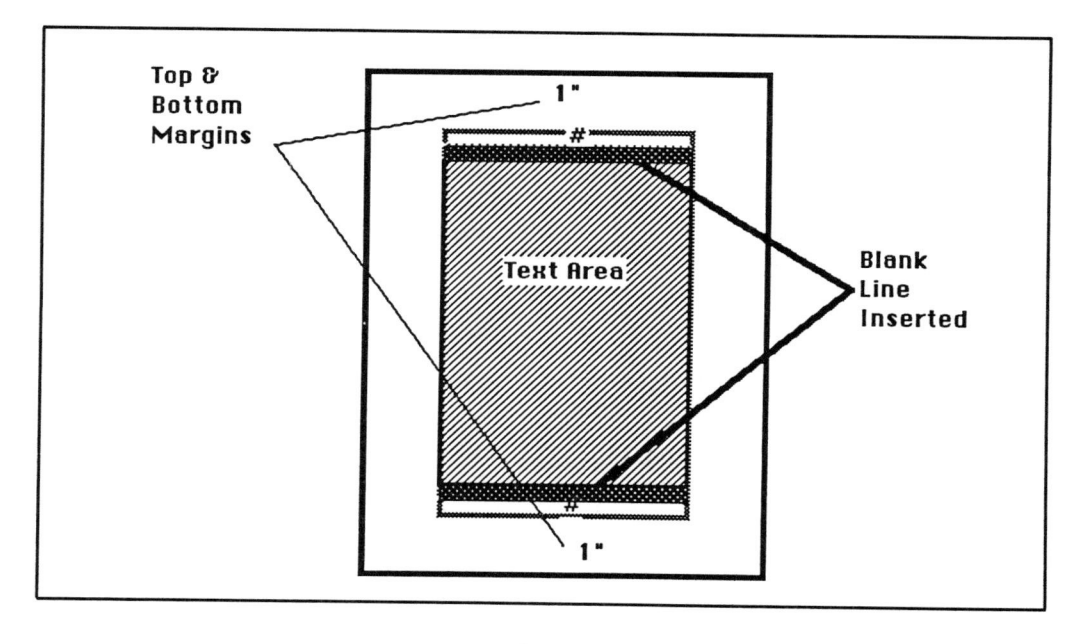

Figure 5.14

WordPerfect supplies a good deal of variation for inserting, sequencing, and positioning page numbers; however, there are some limitations. Page numbers cannot be formatted for special text attributes such as changes in style or font size. Also, the single line for spacing between the number and the text cannot be increased.

WordPerfect allows you to create running headers and footers for a document, which can print page numbers as well as other text that is meant to repeat on each page. In the next section, you will attach headers and footers to the Special Formats document.

Abandon the changes made to this document.

> **Point** at the Close box
> **Click**
> **Click** on No

Load the document a second time by entering

[Apple/o]

> **Point** at Special Formats
> **Double Click**

HEADERS AND FOOTERS

Documents that consist of a large number of pages typically use text that appears at the top and bottom of every page to identify the document and print page numbers or other information. For example, headers in books often print the name of the book or chapter at the top of each page.

WordPerfect allows you to create page headers and/or footers for your documents. The headers and footers can contain any of the text options that you would use in regular text, such as font size, font style, underlines, centering, and tabs.

5 Page Formats

Like page numbers, headers and footers do not appear as part of the normal document window display. They are stored in codes in the text and can be seen only when the document is printed or displayed in the print preview mode.

The advantage of headers and footers is that you do not need to manually insert this text on each page. Because WordPerfect automatically inserts the text, changes made in the document will not affect the location of the header or footer text.

A document may contain a header or footer and a separate page number. Or you can include the page number as part of text in the page header or footer.

To create a page header or footer, you must place the cursor somewhere on the first page that should have a header or footer. The cursor does not need to be at the top of the page.

The command to create a page header or footer is found on the Page Format menu. Enter

[Apple/2]

Option #4 is used to create page headers and footers. Enter

4

WordPerfect now displays the Header and Footer menu.

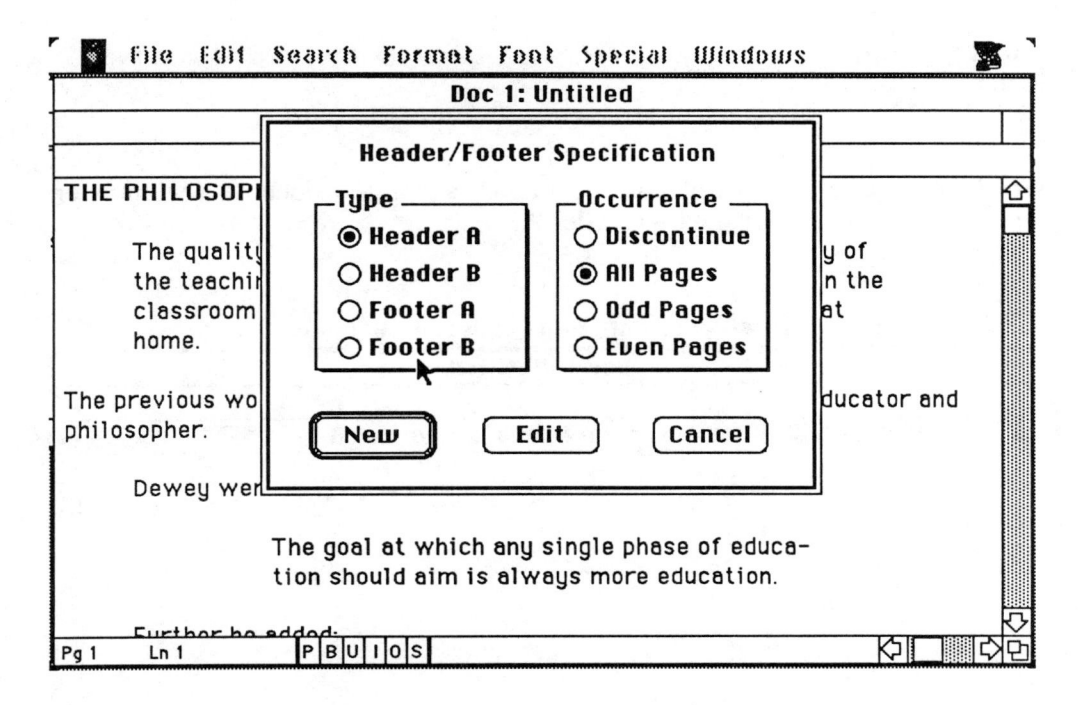

Figure 5.15

This menu is used to create new headers and edit existing headers. To create a new header or footer, you need to make two selections.

Header/Footer   You can choose between headers A and B or footers A and B. The use of both A and B allows different headers or footers on odd- and even-numbered pages.

Occurrence   The occurrence section tells WordPerfect which pages the header or footer should be placed on. The Discontinue option allows you to turn off the header or footer on a specific page.

The default settings are Header A and All Pages.

5 Page Formats

> **Point** at New
> **Click**

WordPerfect clears the display window and loads a new document window entitled Doc 3: Special Formats—Header A.

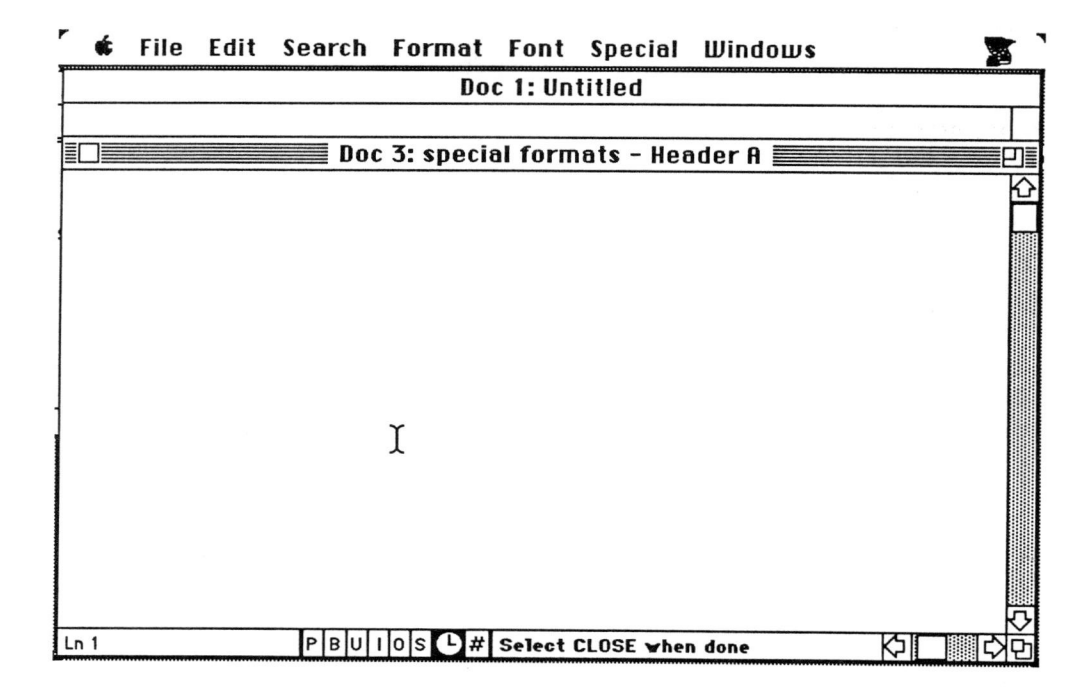

Figure 5.16

The window looks exactly like a document window with the exception of the bottom bar. The bar has two additional icons—one to insert the current date and the other for inserting the page number. It also displays the message

Select CLOSE when done.

The header window allows you to enter almost all of the normal text formatting operations. For example, you can choose the character attributes for the header just as you would for normal text. Enter

[Apple/5]

Select bold, continuous double-underlined text.

```
Point at Bold
Click
Click on Underline
Click on Continuous
Click on Double
Click on OK
```

Center the header by entering

[Apple/Shift/c]

Note that because the underline mode is continuous, the underline follows the cursor to the center of the page.

WordPerfect Text Formats

To run the underline to the right margin, enter a Flush Right command. Enter

[Apple/Shift/f]

The screen should resemble the following:

5 Page Formats

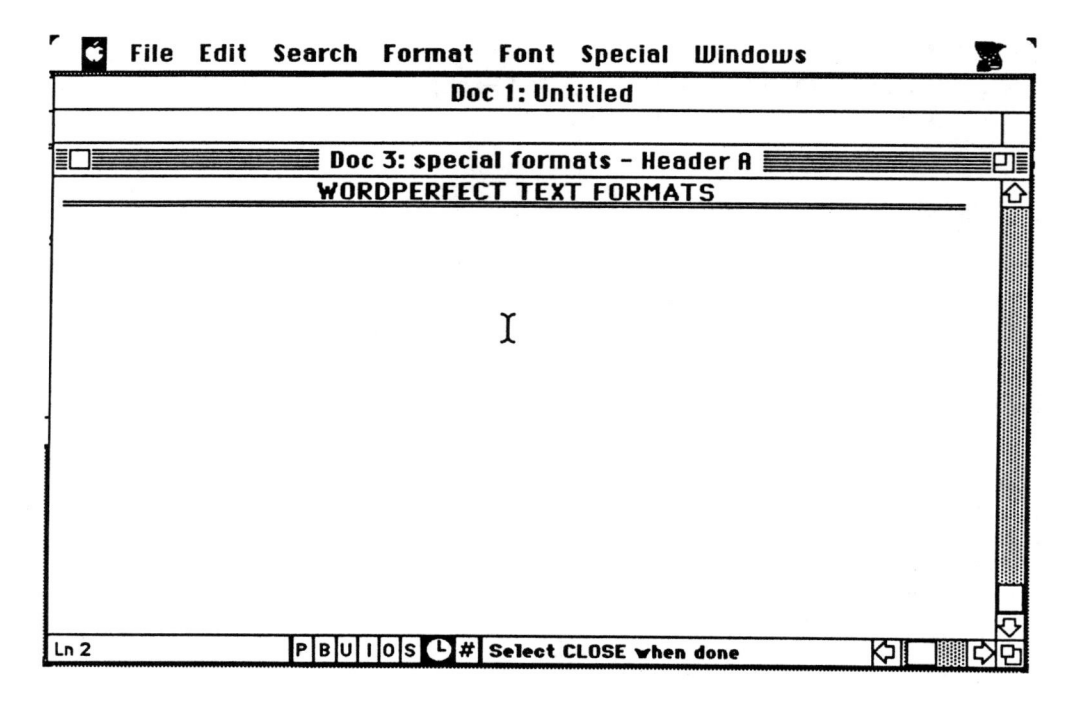

Figure 5.17

The position of headers is similar to the position of page numbers. A page header is always placed below the top margin. Following the header text, WordPerfect skips one line before it prints the text. If you want more than a single line of space between header and text, you can insert blank lines into the headers. For example, if the header consists of one line of text and one blank line, two blank lines will appear below the text line of the header on the final printed copy. The first line will be part of the header itself, and the second line will be the blank line automatically generated by WordPerfect.

To add a blank line to this header, enter

[Return] [Return]

Page Formats 5

You can complete the header by using the Close box or the Close command. Enter

[Apple/k]

The header text is stored as a code in the document. It does not appear in the text window but will be inserted on the printed copy and in the print preview display mode. To confirm the header entry, you can open the codes display window. Enter

[Apple/7]

The screen should resemble the following:

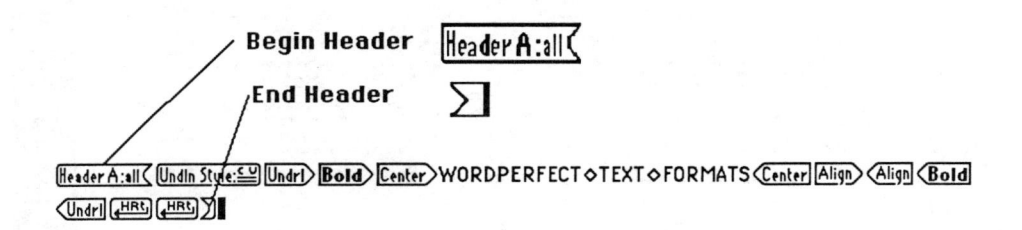

Figure 5.18

5 Page Formats

You can see that the code for headers is quite extensive and explicit. It contains all the codes and text entered in the header. Note that you cannot edit this code directly in the codes display. You must use the Header/Footer command to edit headers and footers.

To see the effect of a header, use the print preview display. Enter

[Apple/Shift/p]

Each page displays a header at the top.

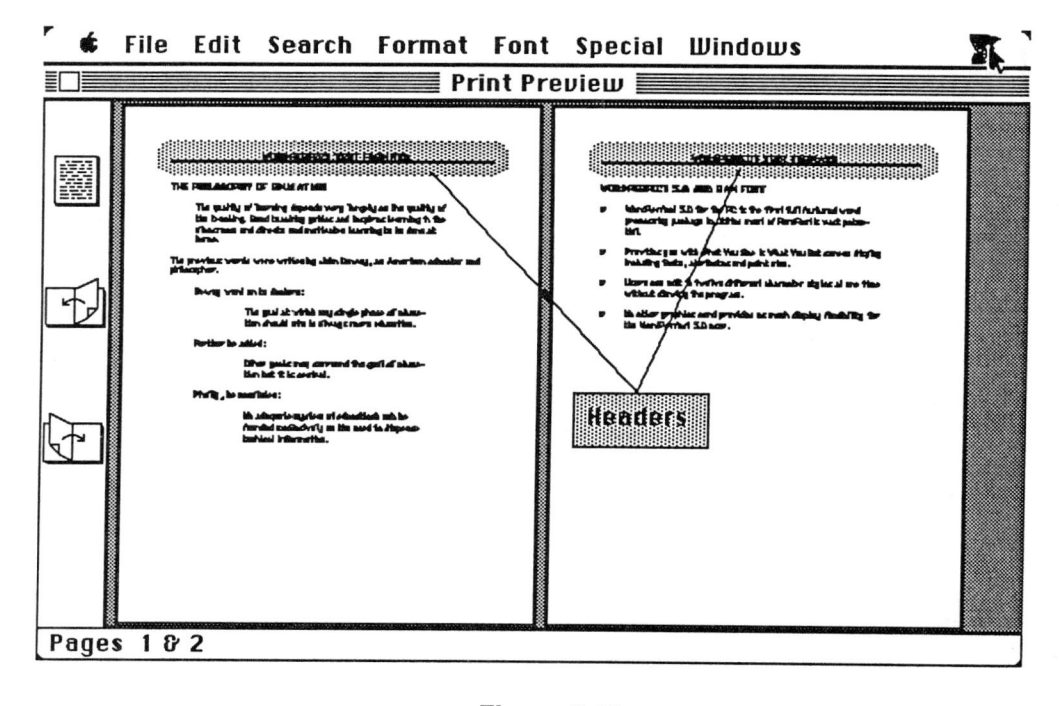

Figure 5.19

Page Formats **5**

Return to the text window.

```
Point at the Close box
Click
```

The next step is to add a footer to the document that will include the page number. You can use the WordPerfect shortcut command keystroke for headers and footers—[Apple/Shift/h]—to bring up the menu. Enter

[Apple/Shift/h]

Select Footer A.

```
Point at Footer A
Click
Click on New
```

Note that because the codes display was turned on while the text window was displayed, a codes display window appears in the footer text window as well. Footers are positioned just above the bottom margin of the page. WordPerfect automatically enters a blank line before the first line of the footer. If you want more than a single line of space preceding the footer, you must enter a blank line at the beginning of the footer text. For example, to create two lines of space between the text and the footer, enter a blank line as the first line in this footer. Enter

[Return]

Center the next line. Enter

[Apple/Shift/c]

247

5 Page Formats

Turn on the bold print. Enter

[Apple/Shift/b]

Then, enter

Chapter 4-

This text will appear on every page of this document. It is the **literal** part of the footer. Turn off the bold setting. Enter

[Apple/Shift/b]

You can now insert the symbol for the page number. Note that a special icon has been added to the bottom bar of the window. You can insert the page number symbol into the footer by clicking on the # icon.

```
Point at #
Click
```

The number 1 appears in the text display, but a [Page #] code appears in the codes window. This code tells you that the 1 is not a literal 1, but the current value for page number, which will change on each page.

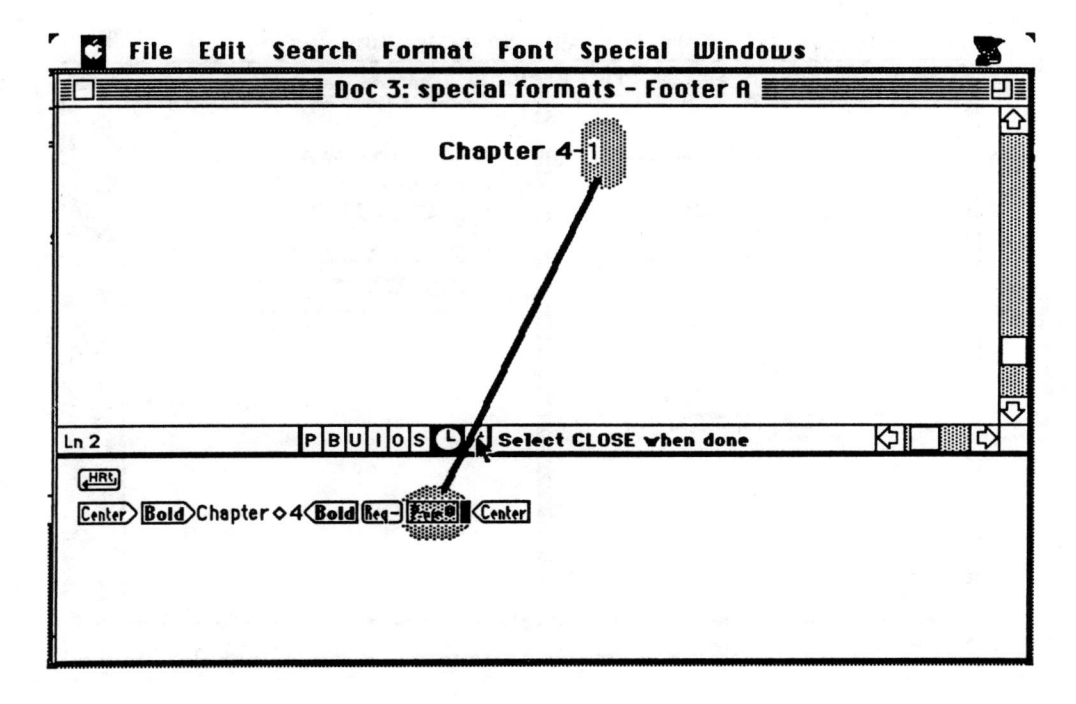

Figure 5.20

Complete the footer entry. Enter

[Apple/k]

In the text window, you can see that the codes display shows both the header and the footer definition codes. To see the effect of the code, enter

[Apple/Shift/p]

The screen displays the image of pages with both the header and footer.

5 Page Formats

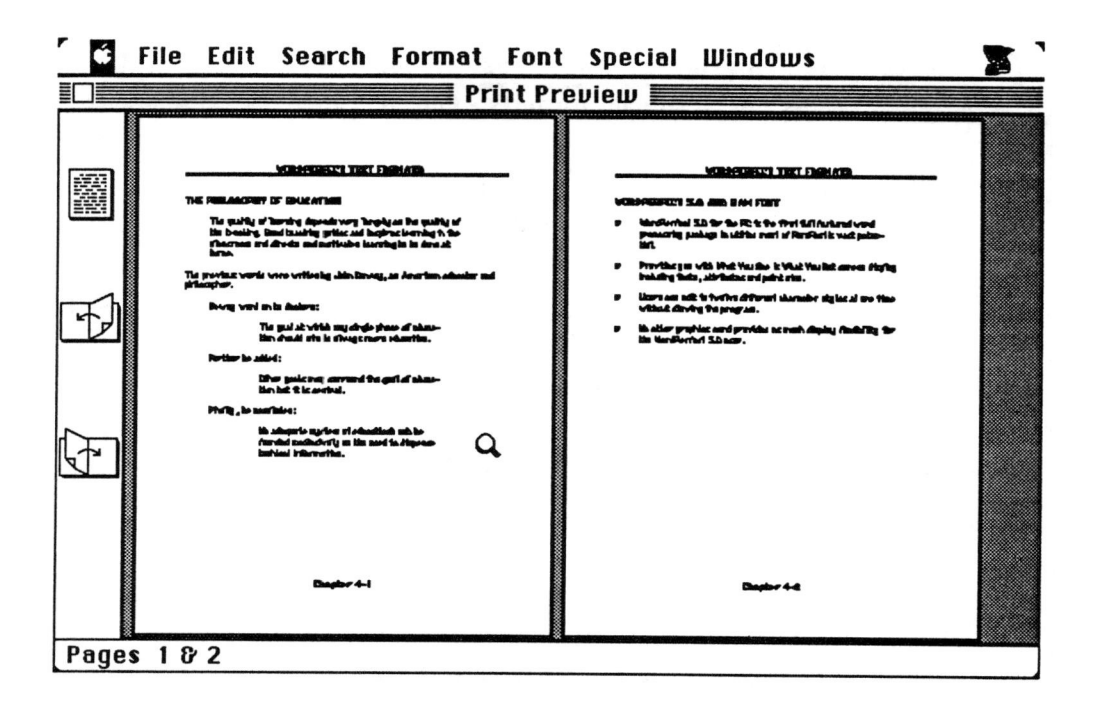

Figure 5.21

Return to the document window.

> **Point** at the Close box
> **Click**

Suppressing Headers

In creating the page headers and footers, you have chosen to place them on every page. It is a common practice to suppress the printing of a page header on the first page of the document. The footer, containing the page number should print. You can achieve this effect by using the Suppress Format command to suppress only the page header. Enter

[Apple/2] 3

Page Formats 5

Note that the Suppress Page Formatting menu has a number of options. In this case, you want to select Header A to tell WordPerfect not to print that header on this page.

```
Point at Header A
Click
Click on OK
```

Use the print preview mode to verify the effect of this command.

[Apple/Shift/p]

The display shows that no page header is printed on page 1 but that the footer and the page number are printed. On page 2, both a header and a footer are printed, along with the page number.

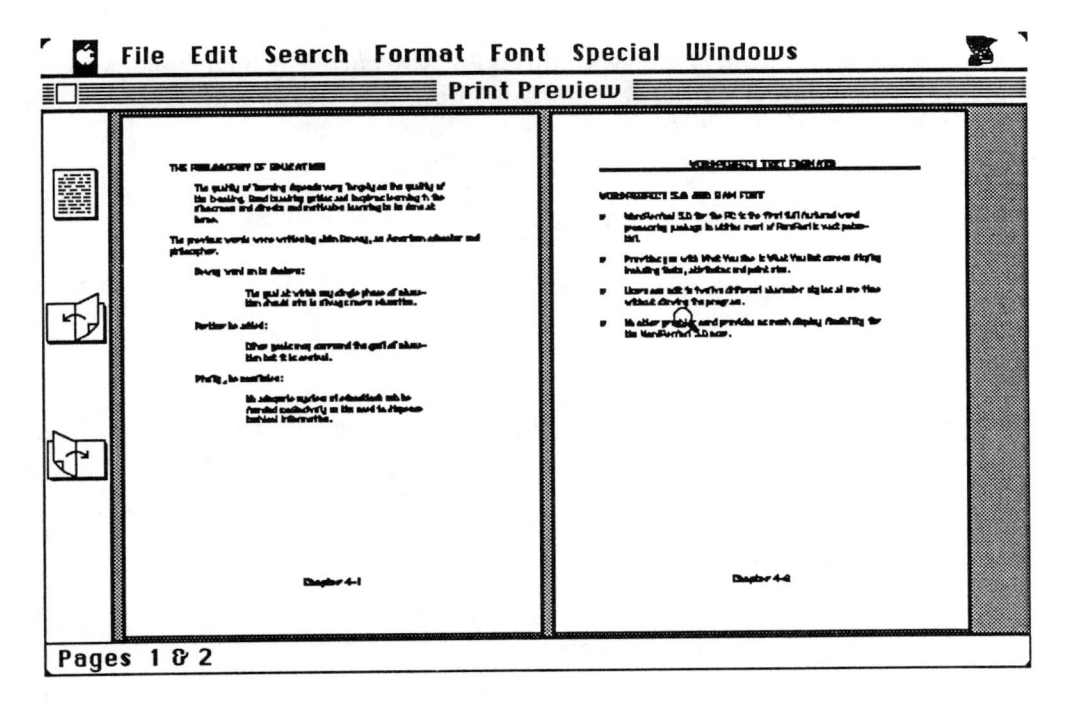

Figure 5.22

5 Page Formats

Return to the text display.

```
Point at the Close box
Click
```

Odd and Even Headers

The headers and footers you have produced so far are appropriate for printing on one side of the page; however, if you plan to reproduce the text by printing on both sides of the paper, you will probably want to create even and odd headers and footers. The purpose of even and odd headers and footers is to position the text differently on odd and even pages. The most common type of positioning is to place header text in the right margin on odd-numbered (right-side) pages and in the left margin on even-numbered (left-side) pages. When text is printed on both sides of the paper, odd-numbered pages go on top and even-numbered pages on the bottom. By alternating the position of the header and footer text, you make sure that the page number always falls on the side of the page that is away from the binding.

If you have been following along with this book, you currently have header A and footer A assigned to every page. To create alternating headers and footers, you can reassign the existing headers and footers to odd pages only. Then, create a new set of headers and footers for the even pages.

Display the Header/Footer menu. Enter

[Apple/Shift/h]

To assign header A to odd pages only, change the bottom setting from All Pages to Odd Pages.

```
Point at Odd Pages
Click
```

To change the contents of the header, select the Edit mode.

```
Point at Edit
Click
```

When Edit is selected, WordPerfect searches forward in the text for the next Header A code, which means that you do not have to position the cursor on the header or footer code to edit it. WordPerfect automatically searches the document for that code when Edit is selected.

You are now faced with an interesting problem. The text in this header is set as center-aligned text. Your goal is to print the header and footer for the odd pages on the right side of the page, so your first step is to delete the [Center] code. Enter

→ (3 times)
[Decimal]

The heading is no longer centered, which causes the text to default to left-aligned. This setting would be correct if this were the header for the even-numbered pages, but the odd-numbered pages require that you align the text on the right side of the page.

Before you proceed to create the correct alignment, you can take advantage of the fact that the text is currently left-aligned. You can use WordPerfect's Delete/Undelete commands to copy the text from this header to make the header you will want for the even-numbered pages. To place a copy of this text into the delete buffer, select the entire header by entering

[Apple/Shift/a]

Place a copy of the text into the memory by pressing

[Apple/c]

5   Page Formats

Remember that WordPerfect's Delete area can hold three deletions at one time, which means you can delete two more times without losing the text you just copied.

Now return to the problem at hand.   Enter

↑   (2 times)
←   (2 times)

You can see that just to the right of the text "WORDPERFECT TEXT FORMATS" is a pair of right-alignment codes, [AlignAlign]. These codes were originally placed into the header to cause the underline to continue to the right margin. If you place the text in between the "S" in "FORMATS" and the [AlignAlign] codes, the text will then be aligned with the right margin. You can use the Cut and Paste commands to accomplish this task.

First, highlight the text. Turn on the Selection mode. Press

[Apple/Shift/n]

Use the right arrow key to place the cursor between the "S" in "FORMATS" and the [AlignAlign] codes.

Page Formats 5

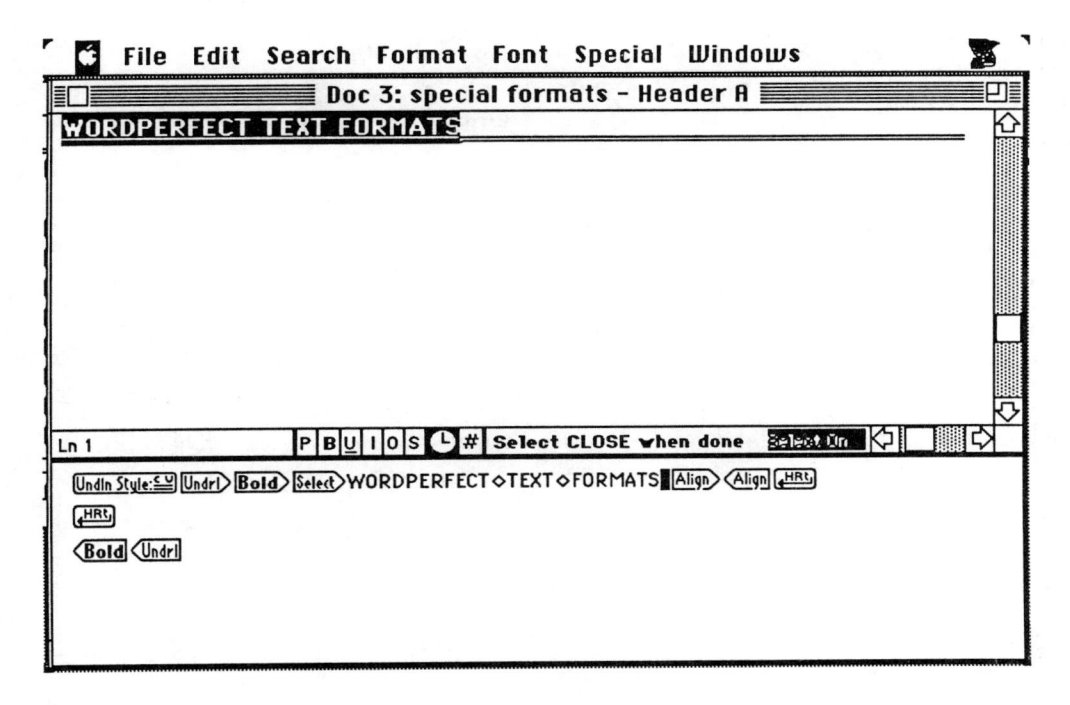

Figure 5.23

Cut the text from the document. Enter

[Apple/x]

Move the cursor in between the codes by entering

→ (3 times)

Now paste the text back into the document by entering

[Apple/v]

The text is pasted between the [AlignAlign] codes, causing WordPerfect to align the text with the right margin.

255

5 Page Formats

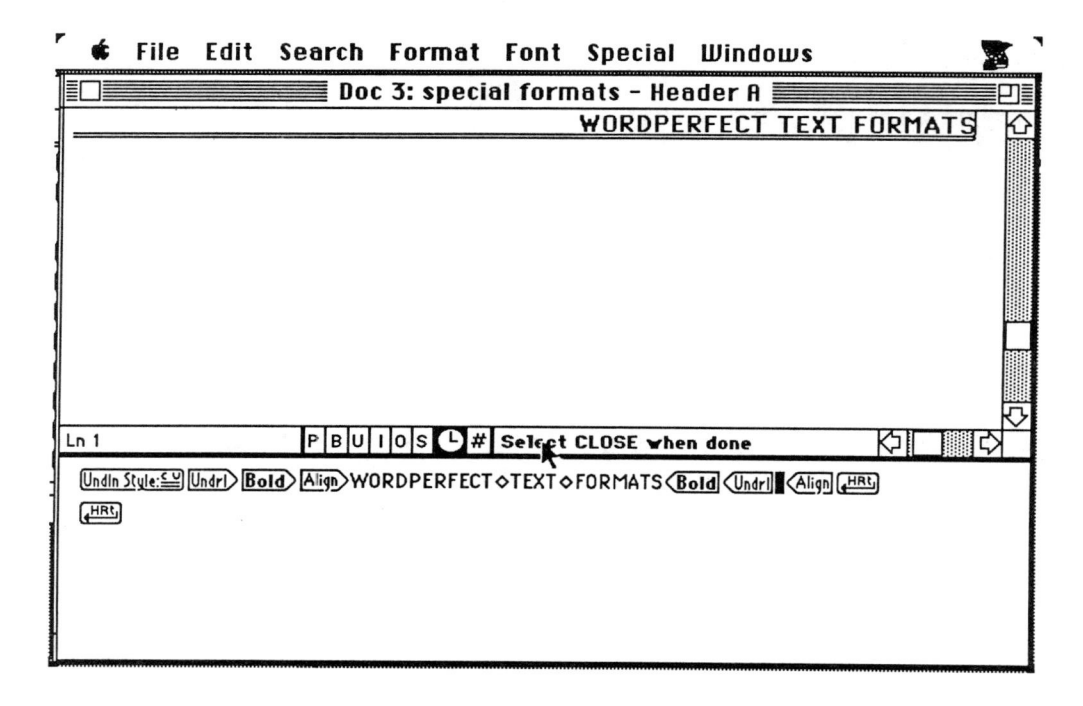

Figure 5.24

Save the revised header by entering

[Apple/k]

You can now create the header for the even-numbered pages by pasting the text stored in memory into a new header. Display the Header menu by entering

[Apple/Shift/h]

Select Header B for the even pages.

Page Formats **5**

> **Point** at Header B
> **Click**
> **Click** on Even Pages
> **Click** on New

To restore text stored in memory, use the Undelete command. Enter

[Apple/u]

WordPerfect displays the last block of deleted text. Your screen should resemble the following:

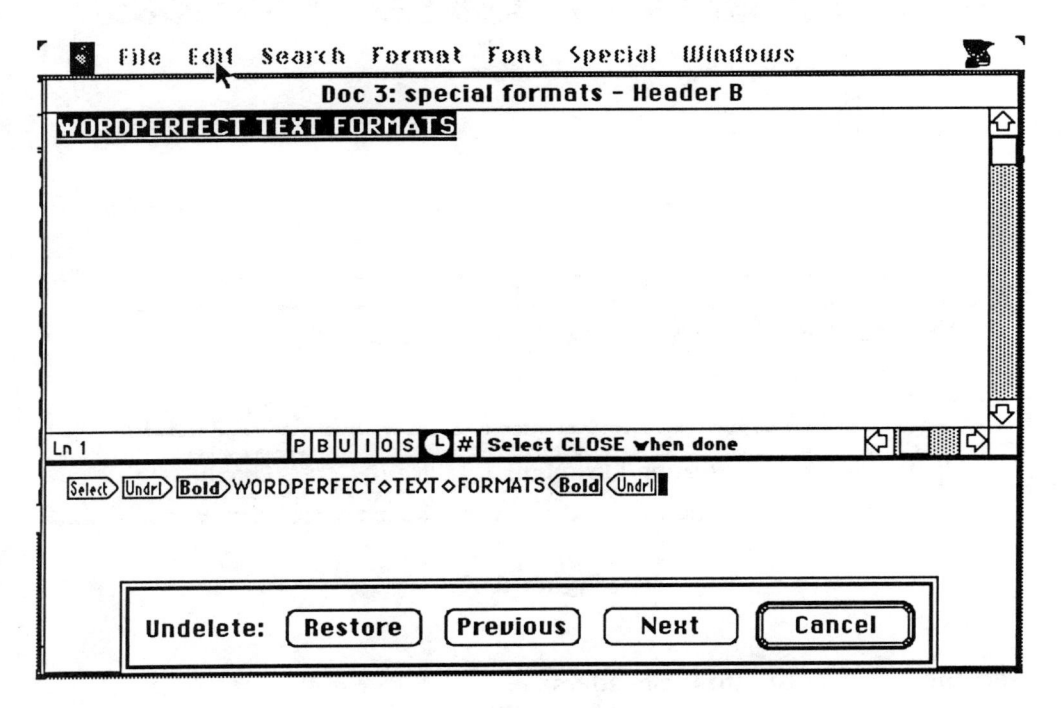

Figure 5.25

257

5 Page Formats

This is not the correct block. Move back to the previous block of text.

| **Point** at Previous |
| **Click** |

The screen now displays the deletion that contains all the text and formatting codes needed for the even page header.

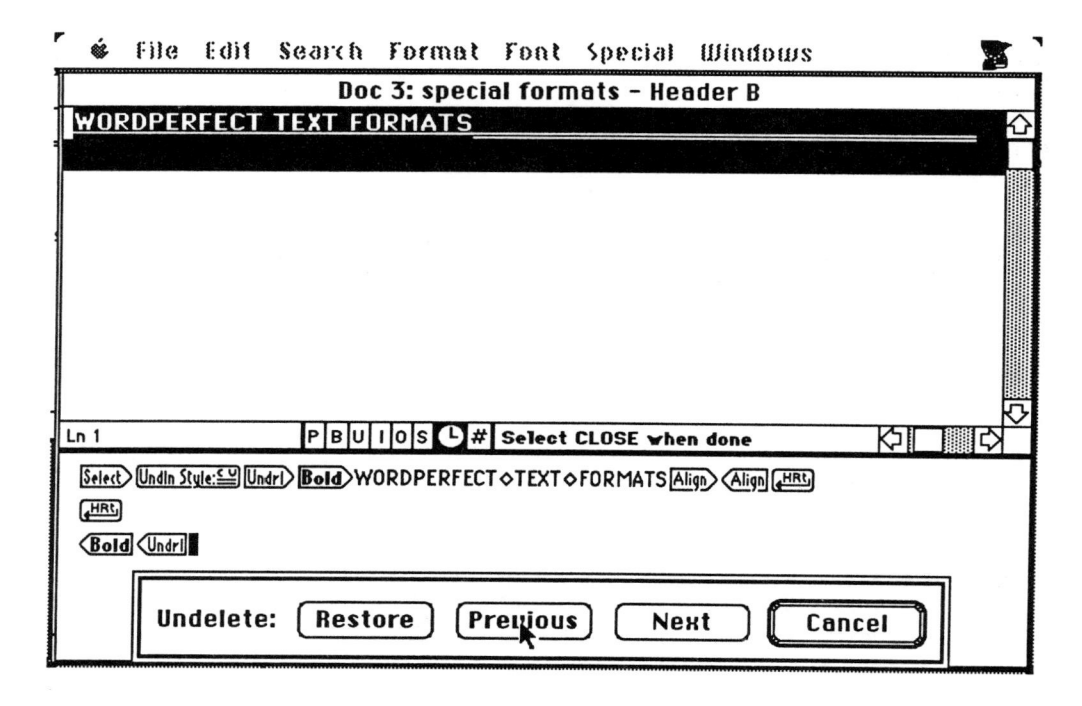

Figure 5.26

Insert the deleted text into the headers.

| **Point** at Restore |
| **Click** |

Page Formats 5

Complete the header by entering

[Apple/k]

Next, set Footer A for odd pages only. Enter

[Apple/Shift/h]

```
Point at Footer A
Click
Click on Odd Pages
Click on Edit
```

If you examine the codes display in the bottom half of the screen, you can see that you need to replace the center code with a right-alignment code. Enter

↓ **[Decimal]**

Align the text on the right side by entering

[Apple/Shift/f]

The odd page footer is now set.

5 Page Formats

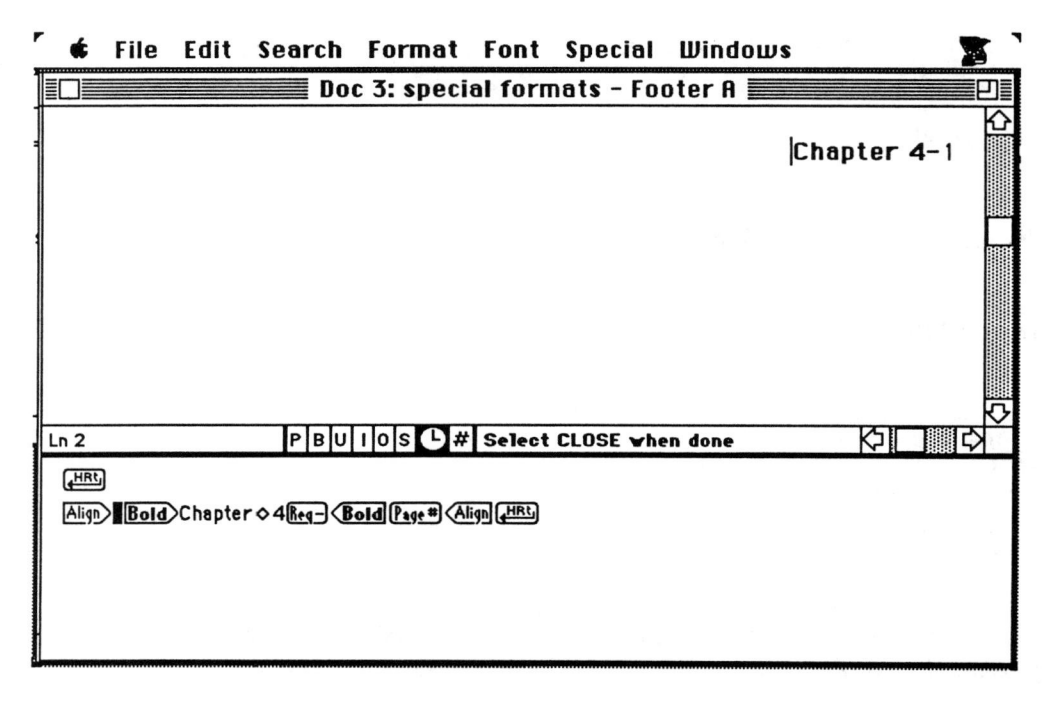

Figure 5.27

Save the header by entering

[Apple/k]

The last step is to define a footer for even pages. Enter

[Apple/Shift/h]

Point at Footer B
Click
Click on Even Pages
Click on New

Enter the text you want for this footer. Then, enter

[Return]
[Apple/Shift/b]
Chapter 4-
[Apple/Shift/b]

To add the page number code,

```
Point at #
Click
```

Save the new footer by entering

[Apple/k]

The codes display shows that the beginning of the document contains a large number of codes, although the text display shows no evidence of their presence (see Figure 5.28).

5 Page Formats

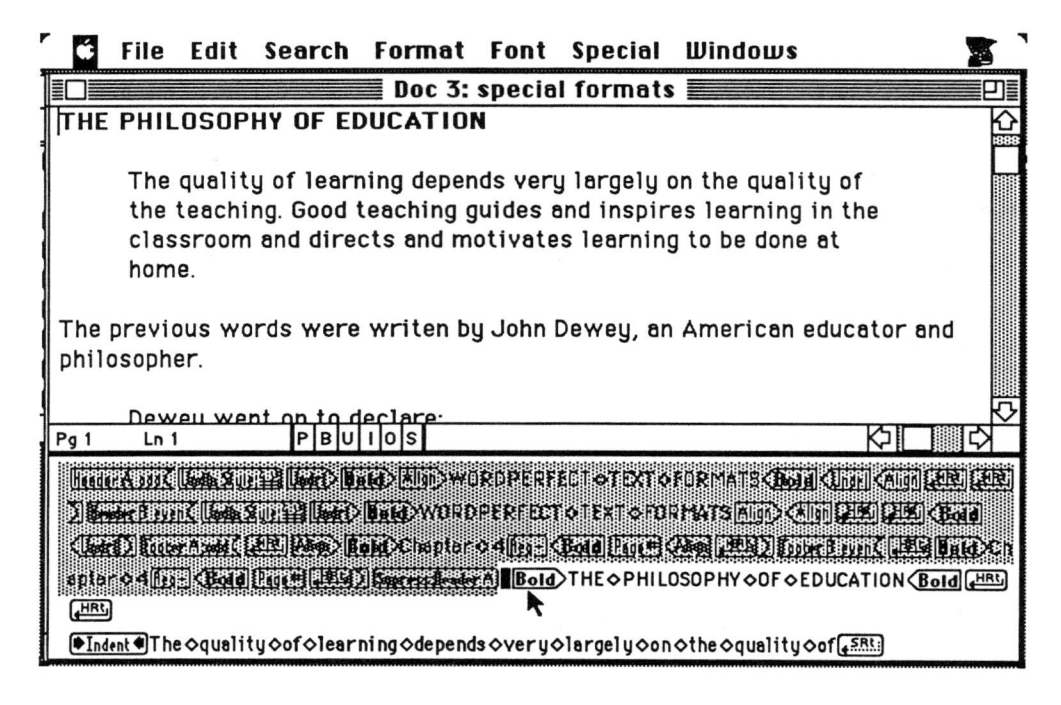

Figure 5.28

To see the effect of the header and footer codes you have entered, display the document in the print preview mode by entering

[Apple/Shift/p]

The display shows that the even and odd pages use different headers and footers. Remember that the suppression of the header on page #1 is still active. Your screen should resemble the following:

Page Formats **5**

[Figure 5.29: Print Preview window showing Pages 1 & 2]

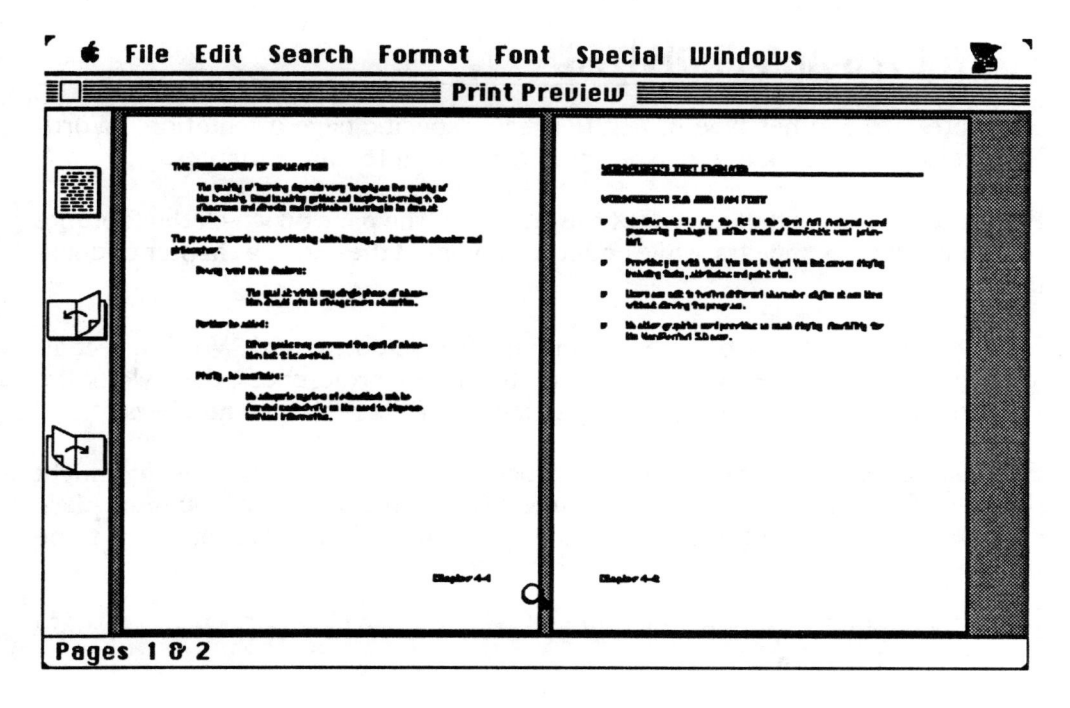

Figure 5.29

```
Point at the Next Page icon
Click
```

You can now see pages 2 and 3, and all four headers and footers are displayed in their proper positions.

Return to the text display.

```
Point at the Close Box
Click
```

263

5 Page Formats

FOOTNOTES AND ENDNOTES

Footnotes are another type of text that has a specific page orientation. WordPerfect can keep track of two types of notes: footnotes and endnotes.

Footnotes are notes that appear at the bottom of the page on which the footnote reference number appears, while endnotes appear at the end of a chapter or document.

You can use either type of note, or both, in a single document. WordPerfect allows you to control the style of the footnote/endnote references, the style of the notes themselves, and the numbering sequence of the reference numbers.

For example, say the first page of your document contains quotations that might require a footnote to explain their source. To create a footnote, you must place your cursor at the point in the text where you want the footnote reference to be inserted.

In this example the reference should be entered after the words "done at home" in the first paragraph.

> **Point** just after "done at home."
> **Click**

Footnote operations are listed under the Special menu.

> **Point** at Special
> **Drag** to Footnotes
> **Release**

The Footnotes menu appears. To create a footnote, select option #1. Enter

1

264

Page Formats 5

WordPerfect displays a new window labeled Doc 3:Special Formats — Footnote #1. The technique for entering footnotes is the same as the one used for entering headers and footers, except that WordPerfect automatically inserts a special code, [#]. WordPerfect uses this code to calculate the footnote reference value. In this case, the first footnote code appears as 1. The 1 is automatically superscript. Your screen should resemble the following:

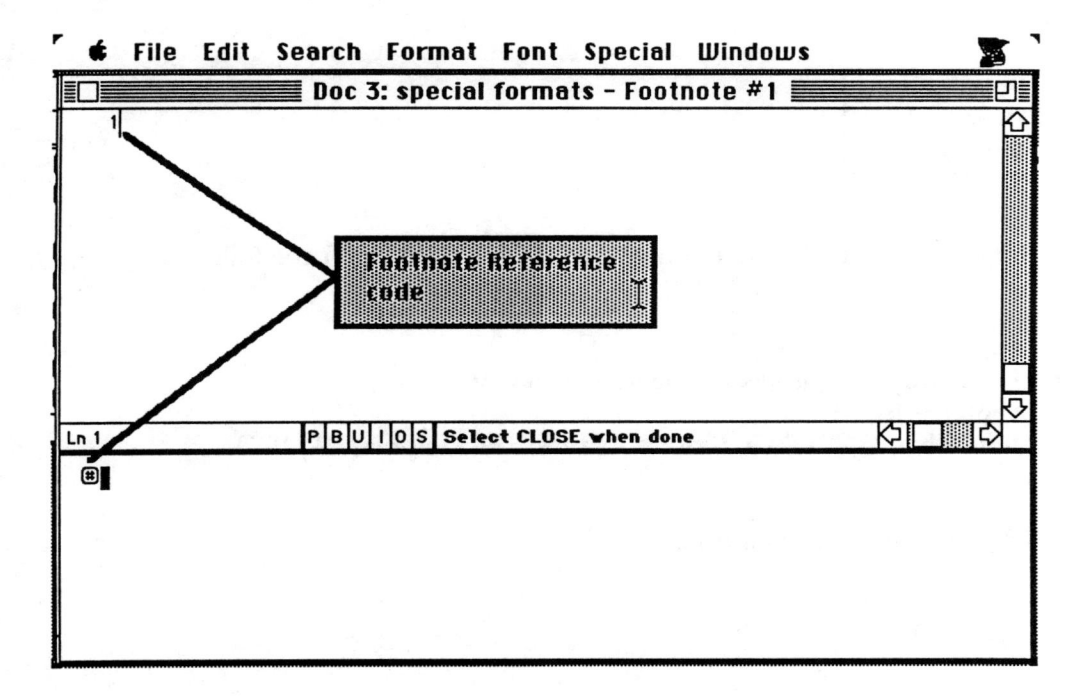

Figure 5.30

You can now enter the text of the footnote just as you would in the text mode. In entering this text, you might want to use formatting commands to make the text appear in a more standard footnote format.

265

5   Page Formats

Set a temporary margin by using the Indent command. Enter

[Apple/Shift/t]

Set the font to 9-point type.

> **Point** at Font
> **Drag** to 9
> **Release**

For this example, to create the text of the footnote, enter the following:

[Apple/Shift/u]
The History of American Education Thought
[Apple/Shift/u]
, Johnathan Q. La Fish, Krummy Press, Philadelphia, PA, 1973

Save the footnote by entering

[Apple/k]

The footnote entry is handled in a manner similar to the way a header entry is handled. A code is inserted into the text that shows the text entered into the footnote. The code appears in the code window; however, the text does not appear anywhere in the document display. Instead, the footnote reference number appears in the text as superscript text.

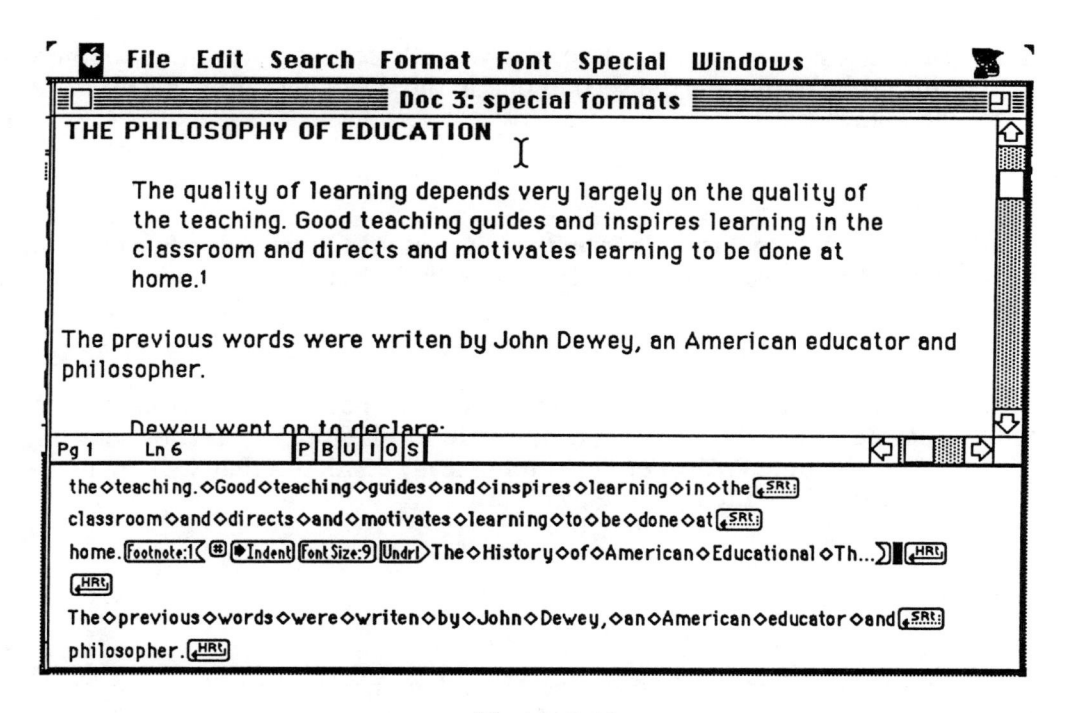

Figure 5.31

Create another footnote at the end of this page. Enter

[Apple/g] ↓
←

The cursor is now positioned following the words "technical information." Display the Footnote menu by entering the command keystroke shortcut.

[Apple/9] 1

5 Page Formats

The footnote window appears. Note that WordPerfect use the name Footnote #2 because this footnote is the second one in the document. For this example, enter the following:

[Apple/Shift t]
The source for this quotation is from the Diary of E.M. Backslide who claims to have attended a lecture at Columbia in April of 1919 where Dewey spoke on education.

Note that this footnote automatically picked up the 9-point text font from the previous footnote code. Once you set a type style for the footnote text by selecting it in the first footnote, WordPerfect automatically continues that style in all the following notes. Save the footnote by entering

[Apple/k]

The footnote code appears in the text. Note that only the first 50 characters of the footnote appear in the footnote code. To see how WordPerfect handles footnotes, examine the document in the print preview mode by entering

[Apple/Shift/p]

The display shows that WordPerfect places the text of the footnotes at the bottom of the page. WordPerfect automatically inserts a line above the first footnote to mark off the footnote text from the rest of the text on that page.

Page Formats 5

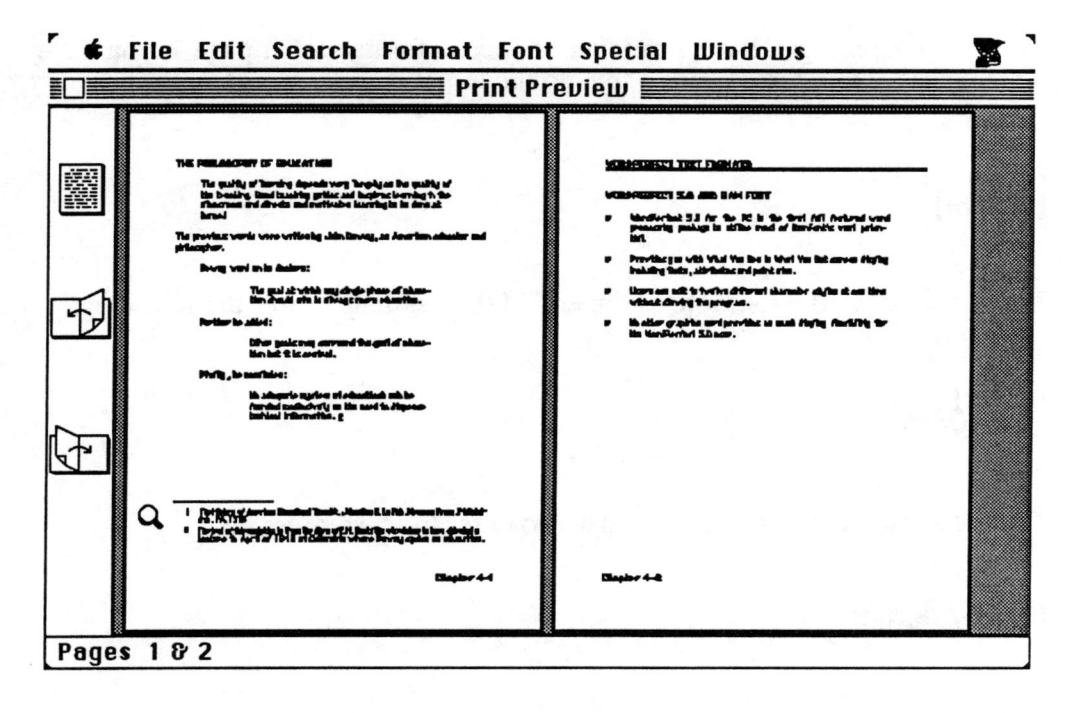

Figure 5.32

Return to the text display.

> **Point** on the Close box
> **Click**

Close the codes display by entering

[Apple/7]

5 Page Formats

In this document, you have a number of special formats. On page 7, you have newspaper column text layout. Move to the top of page 7 by entering

[Apple/g] 7
[Return]

This time, attach the footnote to the end of the heading. Enter the following:

[Enter] →
[Apple/9] 1

The footnote is correctly numbered 3. To enter the text, press

[Apple/Shift/t]

and enter the following text:

This publication is produced by the employees of this company and they are solely responsible for its content.

Close the footnote window by pressing

[Apple/k]

The text shows that the footnote reference number has taken on the font and style of the text into which it was inserted. Your screen should resemble the following:

Page Formats 5

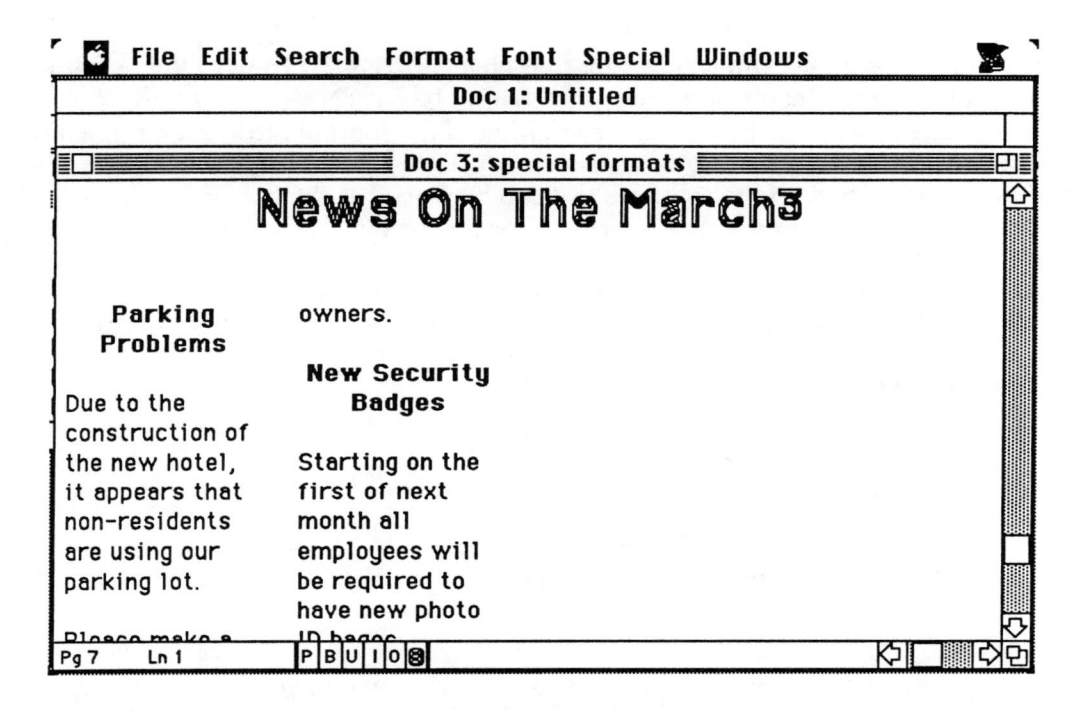

Figure 5.33

In most cases, taking on the current font would be the logical choice, but in this case, you probably want to change the format of the footnote reference to plain text. Enter

[Apple/Shift/n]
←
[Apple/Shift/y] 1
[Apple/Shift/n]

The reference number should now be formatted as plain text.

271

5 Page Formats

If you look carefully, you will see another change. The insertion of the footnote has caused WordPerfect to change the column layout. Note that column #2 no longer begins with the headline; the addition of the footnote text, even though it is not visible at the moment, has caused WordPerfect to shorten the length of the newspaper column so the footnote text can be placed at the bottom of the page. Because the columns are now shorter, WordPerfect was forced to move one of the lines from column #1 into column #2. The addition of footnote text can affect page and column formatting because it reduces the amount of space left on the page for normal text.

Preview the page by entering

[Apple/Shift/p]

The screen should resemble the following:

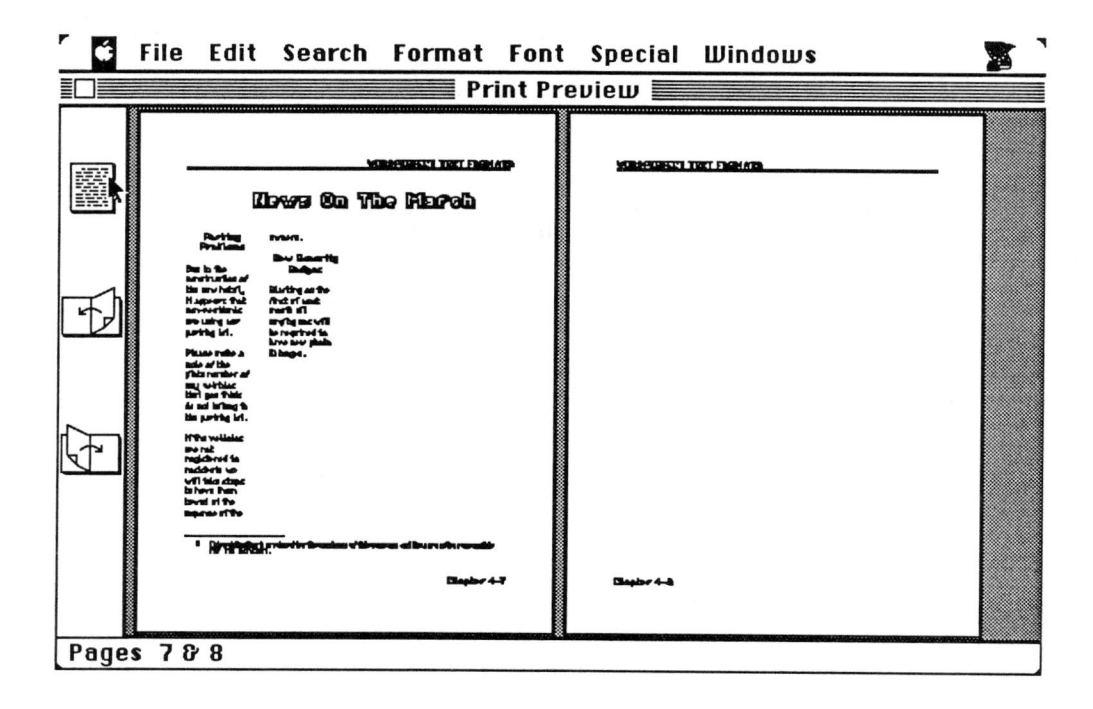

Figure 5.34

Page Formats 5

You can see that the footnote text is inserted at the bottom of this page. Return to the text display.

> **Point** on the Close box
> **Click**

Inserting a Footnote

What would happen if you had forgotten to place a footnote in the document? For example, suppose that you wanted to place a footnote on page 5, between the notes on pages 1 and 7. Move the cursor to the top of page 5 by entering

[Apple/g] 5
[Return]

Place the cursor at the end of the line by entering

[Enter] →

Insert a footnote by entering

[Apple/9] 1

Note that WordPerfect numbers this note #3, which is correct because it is the first note in the text following note #2 on page 1. Enter the following key combinations and text:

[Apple/Shift/t]
Information in this list is subject to change without notice.
[Apple/k]

273

5 Page Formats

You may wonder what has happened to the previous footnote #3 on page 7. Enter

[Apple/g] 7
[Return]

WordPerfect automatically recalculates the footnote numbers to maintain an accurate series. This footnote is now #4.

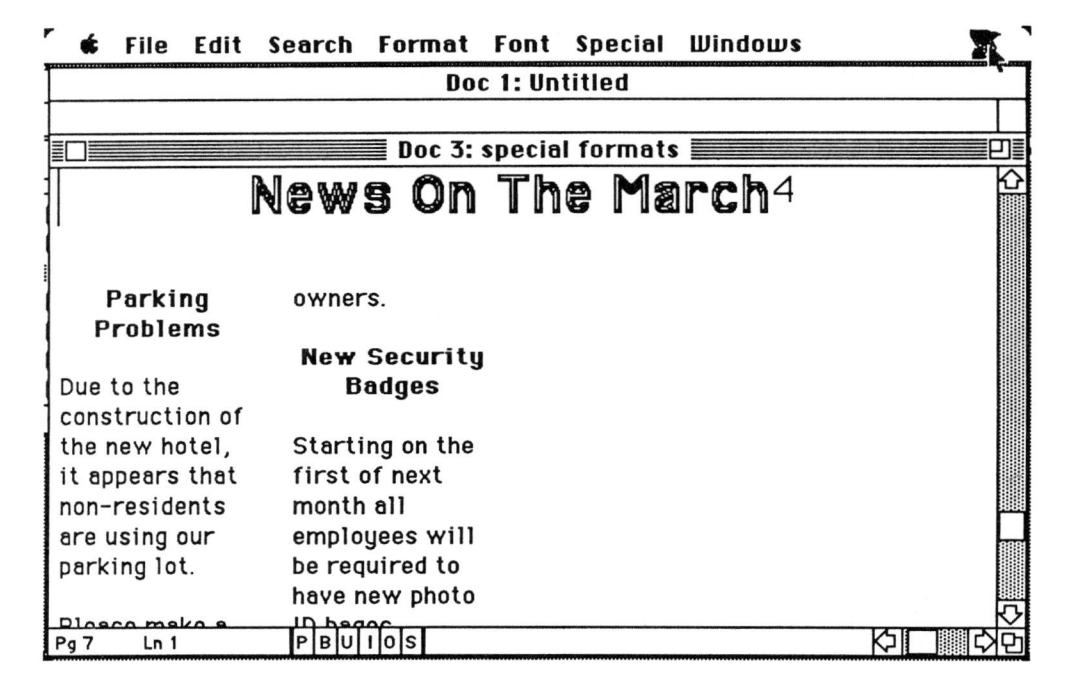

Figure 5.35

Page Formats **5**

Endnotes

Endnotes are text notes that are placed at the end of the document rather than at the bottom of each page. For an example of an endnote, place the cursor on the top of page 4. Enter

[Apple/g] 4 [Return]
[Enter] →

Display the Footnote menu. Enter

[Apple/9]

The endnote commands are options #5 and #6. Enter

5

The endnote window is similar to the footnote window except that the endnote reference includes a period. Note that this is endnote #1. The numbering sequence of endnotes is independent of the footnote numbering sequence. Enter

[Apple/Shift/t] [Apple/Shift/u]
World Almanac
[Apple/Shift/u]
1982

Close the window by entering

[Apple/k]

5 Page Formats

To see the effect of the endnote, enter

[Apple/Shift/p]

Notice that the note does not appear on page 4. To advance to the end of the document,

```
Point  at the Next Page icon
Click  (3 times)
```

The addition of footnotes and endnotes will increase the amount of time WordPerfect needs to format the print preview display. If the display does not appear right away, be patient. You will see that WordPerfect has placed the endnote text on the last page of the document rather than on the same page as the reference. Your screen should resemble the following:

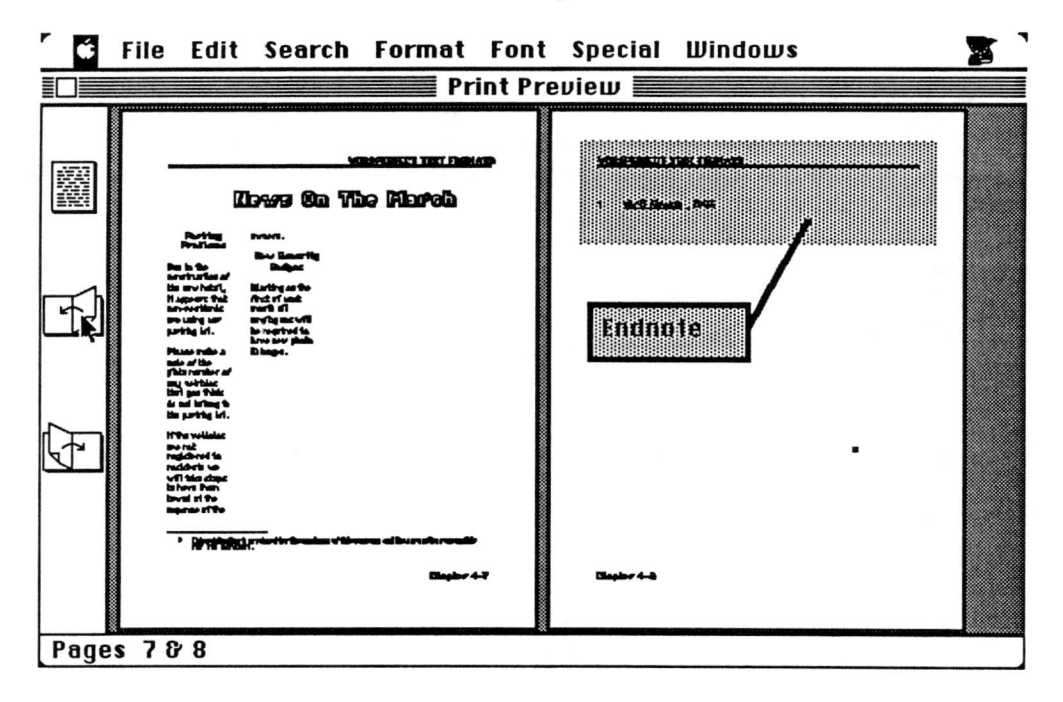

Figure 5.36

Return to the text display.

> **Point** at the Close box
> **Click**

Editing a Footnote

Like all text, footnotes require revision. Unlike normal text, which appears in the text display window, footnote and endnote text is hidden in the codes display. WordPerfect will help you revise footnotes and endnotes by automatically searching for the next footnote or endnote in the document when you select the editing mode. Enter

[Apple/9]

Option #2 allows you to edit footnotes. Enter

2

WordPerfect displays a box on the screen.

5 Page Formats

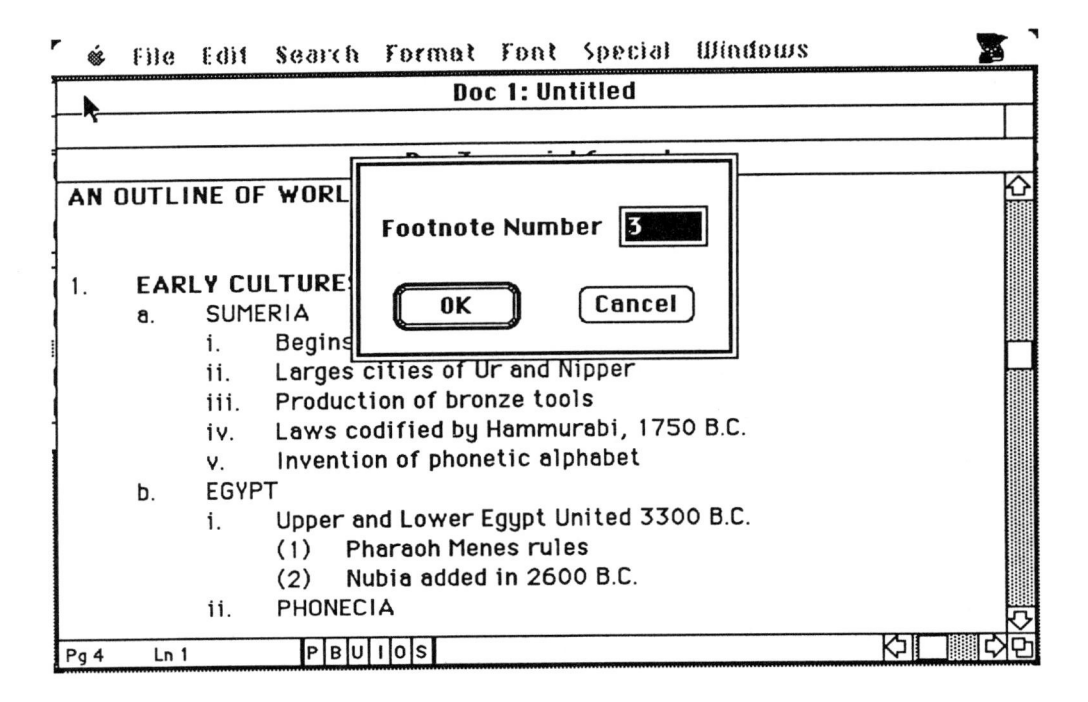

Figure 5.37

The number inserted in the box is the number of the next footnote. You can accept this number or enter another value for the footnote that you want to edit. To edit this note, enter

[Return]

You can now edit the footnote freely. Enter the following:

[Enter] →
[space bar]
Please call to confirm prices.

Complete the footnote revision by entering

[Apple/k]

Note that the cursor is now positioned at the place in the text where the footnote was revised, which was not the cursor's original position. The cursor is placed where the revision occurred because the Footnote Edit command actually contains a search operation that repositions the cursor.

Footnote/Endnote Styles

In creating the previous footnotes and endnotes, you may have noticed that WordPerfect makes a number of assumptions about the way these items should be formatted. One problem you have encountered in this specific case is that your endnotes and footnotes use the same numbering style (i.e., 1, 2, 3, etc.), which makes it hard to distinguish between reference marks for endnotes and footnotes.

WordPerfect allows you to control many of the stylistic features associated with footnotes and endnotes by inserting a special code in the document. In theory, this code can be placed anywhere in the document, but in practical terms, it makes sense to place this code at the beginning of the document so that it precedes all footnote and endnote codes. If you place the footnote options in the middle of the document, some footnotes entered prior to the code may use a different style from the ones that follow the code. Unless you specifically want this effect, always place the footnote options at the beginning of the document.

To create a new footnote and endnote style setting, place the cursor at the beginning of the document by entering

[Enter] [Enter] ↑

Display the Footnote menu by entering

[Apple/9]

5 Page Formats

Option #4 allows you to view and alter the footnote settings. Enter

4

WordPerfect displays the Footnote Option menu. This menu displays a combination of footnote and endnote settings.

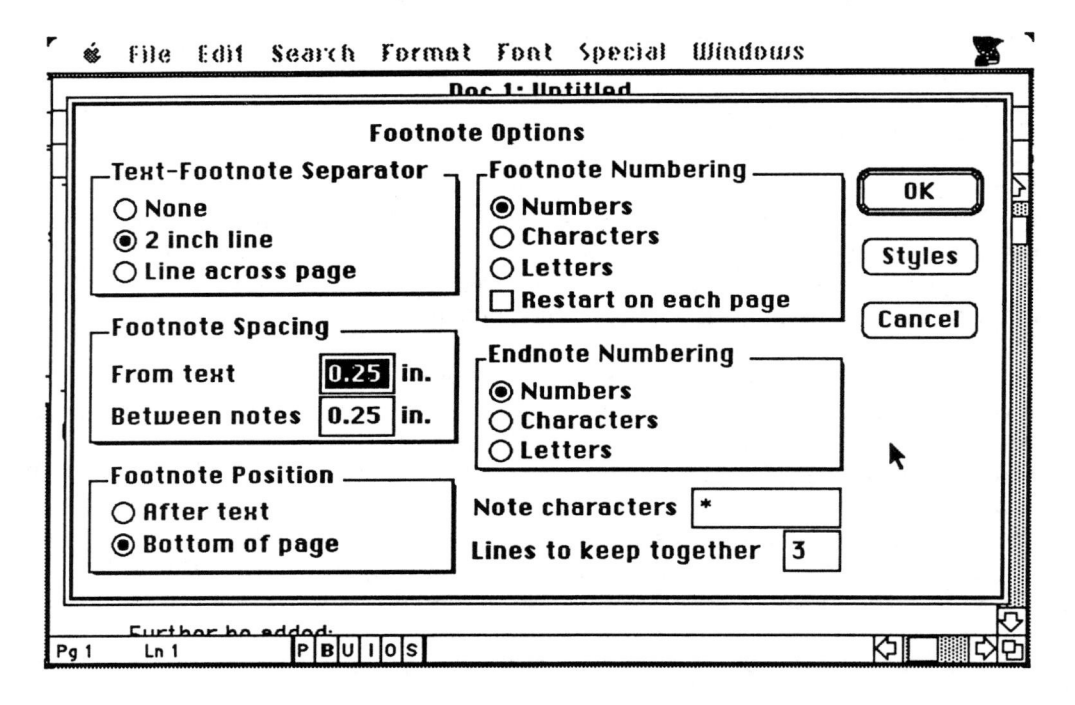

Figure 5.38

Separator

This setting determines whether WordPerfect inserts a line between footnotes and regular text. The default setting creates a 2" line above the footnote text. You can select the None option to suppress the lines or the Line across page option to draw a line across the page from the left to the right margin.

In this example, choose a full page width line.

```
Point at Line across page
Click
```

Spacing

This setting controls the vertical spacing used in the footnote display. The first value indicates the distance between the end of the text to which the footnotes refer and the footnotes themselves. The second value controls how much space will be left between footnotes if more than one footnote appears at the bottom of a page. The default value for both settings is .25".

If you use a small font, as in this example, you might want to decrease the amount of space left between footnotes. To reduce the amount of space to .2", enter

[Tab]
.2

Position

This setting determines how WordPerfect will handle footnotes on pages that are not full. If the After text option is selected, WordPerfect places the footnotes directly after the last line of text. When a page is not full, the After text setting will place the footnotes farther up on the page than it would when the entire page was full. If the Bottom of page option is selected, the footnote text will always appear at the bottom of the page, leaving a gap between the end of the text and the footnotes on pages that are not full. Bottom of page is the default setting.

Numbering

The Numbering setting controls the type of footnote reference entered into the text. WordPerfect allows three types of footnote references: numbers, characters, and letters. The default is to use consecutive numbers. Choosing Letter causes WordPerfect to enter lowercase letters—a, b, c, etc.—as footnote or endnote references.

5 Page Formats

The Character option is used to insert characters as footnote or endnote references. When a character is used, the reference is marked by repeating that character the number of times that will match the footnote reference number. For example, if the reference number is 3, WordPerfect inserts three characters, e.g. ***, to mark the footnote. The character to be used is shown in the Note Character box. The default character is * (asterisk).

You can enter up to five different characters for references. When you enter more than one character, WordPerfect uses the characters in the order they are typed. If the footnote references exceed the number of characters you entered, the sequence is repeated, using double, and then triple, characters. For example, if you entered three characters, #$*, the numbering sequnce would be #, $, *, ##, $$, **, ###, $$$, and so on.

WordPerfect also displays a Restart on each page check box for footnote numbers. If this option is selected, footnote numbering will not be consecutive throughout the document. Rather, the first footnote on each page that contains footnotes will be 1, the second 2, and so on.

The ability to select different numbering styles can help readers distinguish between the footnotes and endnotes. For this example, change the endnote numbering to characters.

Point at Characters under Endnote Numbering
Click

To change the character to &, enter

[Tab]
&

Keep Together

The last option on the menu guides WordPerfect when the complete text of a footnote cannot fit onto the same page as the footnote reference number. The default value for this setting is 3, which means that WordPerfect will print at least three lines of footnote text on the same page as the reference number. The remainder of the footnote text will be moved to the next available page bottom.

Page Formats 5

To accept this setting, press

[Return]

To see the effect of this style change on the endnote numbering, display the text of the endnote by using the Edit Endnote option on the Footnote menu. Enter

[Apple/9] 6
[Return]

WordPerfect displays the text of the next endnote in the document. Note that this time, instead of a number 1, the & appears as the endnote mark. The period following the & is automatically generated by WordPerfect. In the next section, you will learn how to remove that period.

Close the endnote editing window by entering

[Apple/k]

You can see that the & also appears in the text as the endnote reference mark.

Changing Note Styles

In the previous display, you might have noticed that the endnote symbol was automatically followed by a period. This style makes sense when the reference mark is a number or a letter (i.e., "1." or "a."), but not when the reference is a character. WordPerfect provides a means by which you can alter the display style used for footnotes and endnotes. Using this style option, you can specify additional characters or codes that should be included with each reference.

Return the cursor to the beginning of the document by entering

[Enter] [Enter] ↑

283

5 Page Formats

Display the Format Settings menu by entering

[Apple/9] 4

To alter the styles used, you need to click on the Styles button.

> **Point** at Styles
> **Click**

WordPerfect displays another box that shows the current setup for footnote and endnote styles.

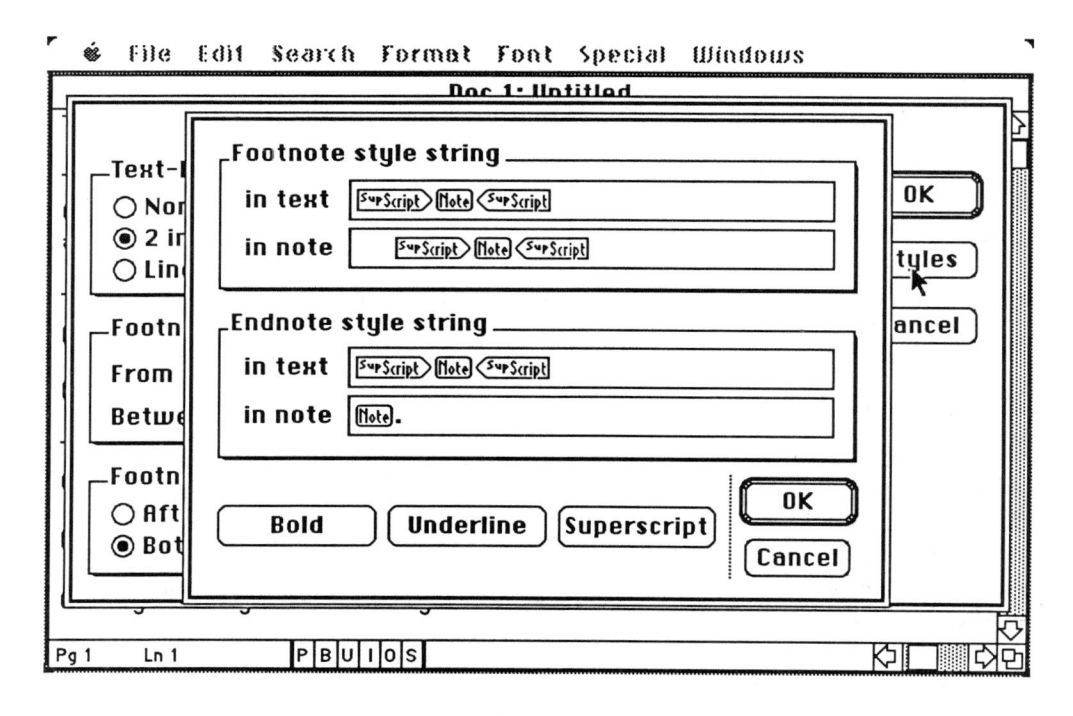

Figure 5.39

Page Formats 5

Both footnotes and the endnotes consist of two parts. The first, **in text**, shows the format used to show the reference in the text. The **in note** layout is the line that appears when the note is printed or displayed in an edit window. WordPerfect allows you to enter any type of text characters and also allows you to enter bold or underline codes.

There is not usually a great need to alter these settings because their default settings are standard footnote and endnote styles; however, in this example, the use of a period following the endnote marker looks odd because you have chosen to use a character as the endnote reference.

Move the cursor to the note section of the endnote style setting by entering

[Tab] (3 times)
→

Delete the period by entering

[Delete]

Replace it with a hyphen (-). Enter

[space bar]-[space bar]

Save the change in the footnote.

> **Point** at OK
> **Click** (2 times)

Apple/9] 6 [Return]

5 Page Formats

The endnote edit window displays the endnote text with the new character, - , in place of the period.

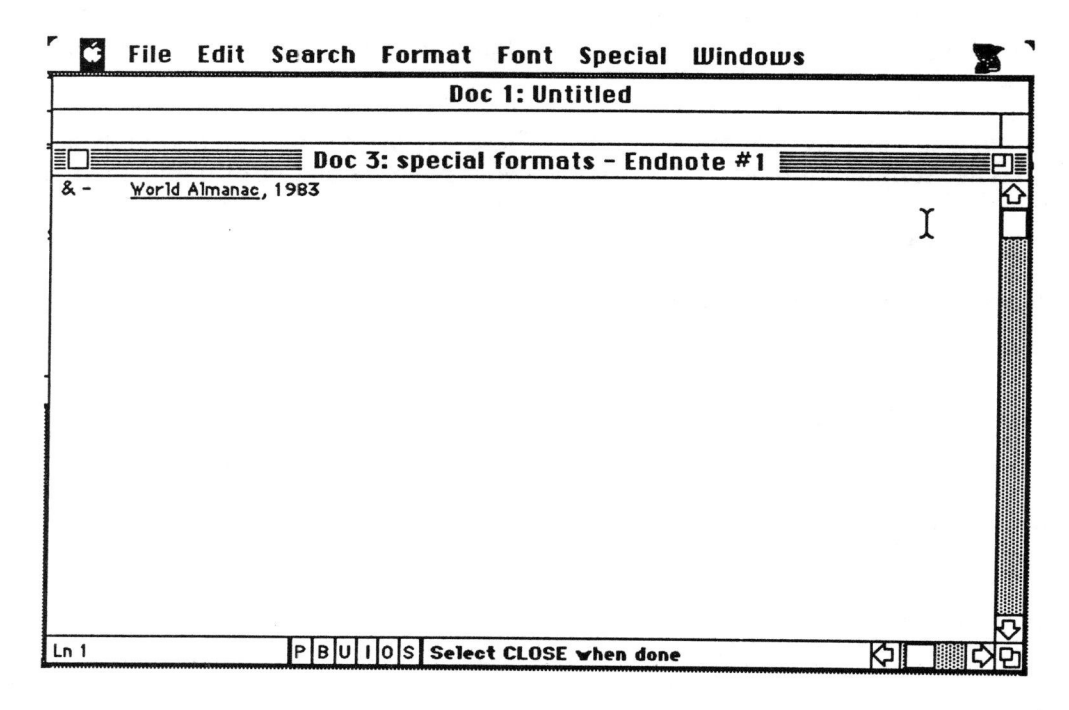

Figure 5.40

Close the window and return to the beginning of the document. Enter

[Apple/k]
[Enter] [Enter] ↑

To see the final effect of your changes, print the document. Enter

[Apple/p]

Page Formats **5**

When printing is complete, save the document and close the window by entering

[Apple/s]
[Apple/k]

PAGE FORMATS AND MARGINS

WordPerfect's method of creating headers, footers, footnotes, and endnotes has one drawback when it comes to changing margins. When margin changes are entered, WordPerfect's reformatting method does not change accordingly the text stored in codes such as header, footer, footnote, or endnote codes.

In other words, when a header, footer, footnote, or endnote is created, WordPerfect uses the current document margins to create the text. If you later change the margins of the document, WordPerfect will not automatically change the text stored in the header, footer, footnote, or endnote codes to match the new margins. There are two options for updating the text in the codes.

One by One   You can use the Footnote Edit command, [Apple/9] 2, and the Endnote Edit command, [Apple/9] 6, or the Edit Header/Footers Text command, [Apple/Shift/h], to update each item. When the item is displayed, WordPerfect reformats the text to the correct margins. Save the reformatted text by entering [Apple/k].

Update   WordPerfect updates the format of coded text when a spelling check is performed. You can update the margin format of all the header, footer, footnote, and endnote codes by using the Spell Count command, [Apple/e] 6. The Count command will search the entire document without stopping. Because words in text codes are also included in the search, those items are automatically updated.

5 Page Formats

SUMMARY

- **Page Formats.** Page formats are commands and options that refer to text operations that affect entire pages or page layouts.

- **Page Numbers.** You can have WordPerfect automatically number your pages by inserting a Page Number command in any one of six preset locations.

- **Suppress Format.** WordPerfect allows you to suppress the page number or other page format option for a specific page.

- **Alternate Page.** WordPerfect page numbering and header/footer commands can set alternating page formats to accomodate documents that will be printed on both sides of the paper.

- **Headers/Footers.** Headers and footers are text lines that are inserted at the top and bottom, respectively, of each page. Headers and footers can contain normal WordPerfect text as well as special codes for dates and page numbers.

- **Footnotes and Endnotes.** WordPerfect is capable of printing footnotes and footnote reference marks on the pages to which the footnotes refer. Endnotes print reference marks on the pages to which the endnotes refer, but those notes appear at the end of the document. WordPerfect allows you to select style and numbering options for both footnotes and endnotes.

CHAPTER 6

MULTIPLE DOCUMENTS AND WINDOWS

6 Multiple Documents and Windows

One of the advantages of the Macintosh user interface is its ability to allow multiple-window operations. In word processing, multiple windows allow you to work on several documents at one time. You can perform copy and cut and paste operations between several documents and include graphics created with programs such as MacDraw and HyperCard in WordPerfect documents. This chapter demonstrates how you can operate multiple documents and windows and how you can use the Macintosh clipboard to insert graphics into WordPerfect.

The assumption is made that you are starting WordPerfect with a blank document—Doc 1: Untitled—on the screen.

OPENING MULTIPLE DOCUMENTS

In previous chapters, you worked with one document at a time. This is the most common approach to word processing, but WordPerfect can take advantage of the Macintosh interface to allow you to simultaneously edit several documents at once—each one in a different window.

When you load WordPerfect, it automatically creates a document window. WordPerfect assigns a number to each window you open or each document you load. The first blank window is Doc 1. When you open a new window, WordPerfect assigns the window the name Untitled to indicate that this window has not been assigned a file name.

You can create another new document by using the File New command. Access this command through the File menu, or use the WordPerfect keyboard shortcut—[Apple/n]. Enter

[Apple/n]

WordPerfect creates a second window, which is assigned the designation Doc 2. Because this new document has never been assigned a file name, it too is called Untitled. Note that WordPerfect displays the windows so that Doc 2 is slightly smaller than Doc 1 and positioned so that the title bars of both windows are visible at the same time.

Multiple Documents and Windows 6

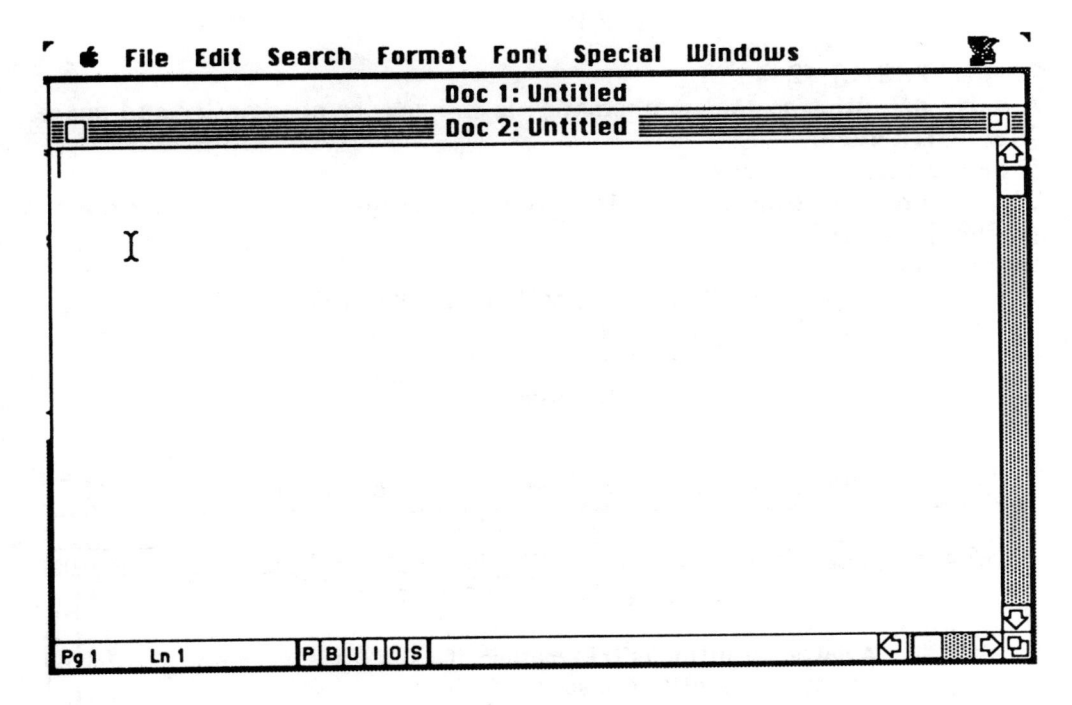

Figure 6.1

Enter text into Doc 2. Begin with a heading in shadow text:

[Apple/Shift/s]
[Apple/Shift/c]
What is Mathematics?
[Apple/Shift/s]
[Return] [Return]

Enter the following paragraphs. The paragraphs will be indented two tab stops (1") from the left and right margins.

6 Multiple Documents and Windows

[Apple/Shift/L] (2 times)
A naive definition is that mathematics is the science of quantity and space.
[Return] [Return]
[Apple/Shift/L] (2 times)
The science of quantity in its simplest form is called arithmetic.
[Return] [Return]
[Apple/Shift/L] (2 times)
The science of space is called geometry.[Return] [Return]

The screen should resemble the following:

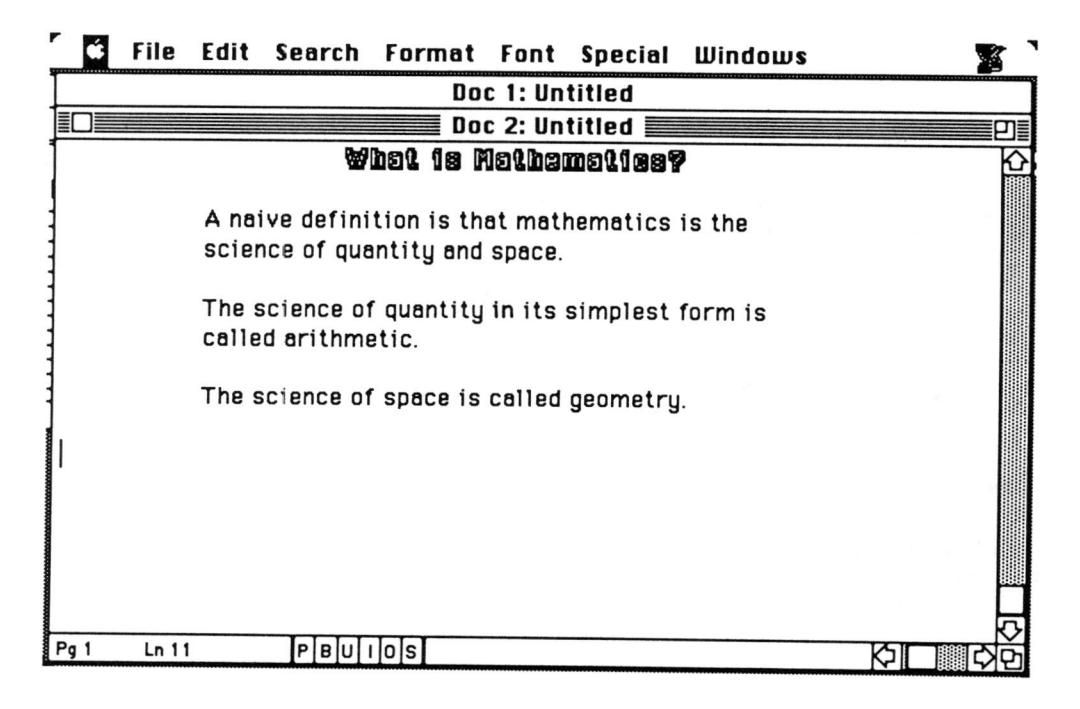

Figure 6.2

Multiple Documents and Windows **6**

CHANGING WINDOWS

Once you have created more than one window, you may want to switch operation from one window to another. The simplest way to do this is to use the mouse to select the window you want to use. To select a window, all you must do is point the mouse at that window's title bar and click. You can point to any part of the title bar including the name of the document. Activate Doc 1 using the mouse.

Point at Doc 1: Untitled
Click

The Doc 1: Untitled window is now **active**, which means that the window is now in the foreground of the screen display, and the cursor is moved to its previous position in this window. Because the Doc 1: Untitled window is larger than the Doc 2: Untitled window, you cannot see the text of Doc 2: Untitled because it is covered by the active window.

Because Doc 1: Untitled is now active, you can edit or add text in this window without affecting the text in Doc 2. Enter the following text:

[Apple/Shift/c] [Apple/Shift/s]
Where is Mathematics?
[Apple/Shift/s] [Return] [Return]
[Apple/Shift/L]   (2 times)
Where is the place of mathematics? Where is knowledge, mathematical or otherwise?
[Return] [Return]
[Apple/Shift/L]   (2 times)
There is hardly a culture, however primitive, which does not exhibit some rudimentary kind of mathematics.
[Return] [Return]

Now that you have created two document windows containing text, you can begin to explore the ways in which WordPerfect allows you to operate on multiple windows and documents.

293

6 Multiple Documents and Windows

The Windows Menu

At this point, you have two documents open in two different windows. How can you be sure? Examining the screen provides no indication that another document window is active or how you might gain access to that window.

The Windows menu can help you access the document windows you have open.

> **Point** at Windows
> **Click**
> **Hold** down mouse button

WordPerfect displays the windows menu, which consists of two parts. The top part contains two commands—Cycle Windows and Show Clipboard—that will always be the same. The bottom part consists of a list of active document windows and their current titles. A check mark appears next to the currently active window—in this case, Doc 1.

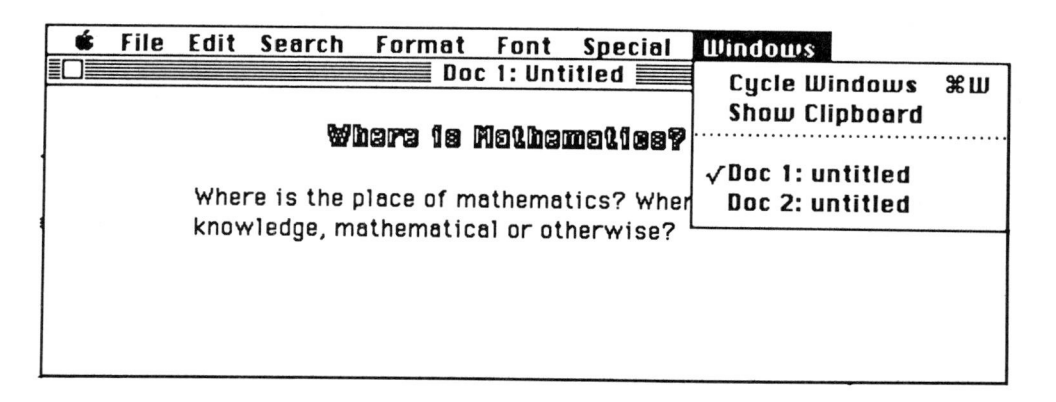

Figure 6.3

294

Multiple Documents and Windows 6

To activate a window from this menu, you must drag the mouse to the name of the window you want to use.

> **Drag** the highlight to Doc 2
> **Release**

Doc 2 becomes the active document; it is placed in front of the Doc 1 window.

The advantage of the Windows menu is that you can select the specific document window with which you want to work. WordPerfect provides a keyboard command to cycle the display through each of the active windows. **Cycle** means that each time the command is entered, WordPerfect displays the next window in the document window list. When the end of the list is reached, WordPerfect returns to the first window. The command to cycle to the next window is [Apple/w]. Enter

[Apple/w]

WordPerfect switches to Doc 1. Create another document. Enter

[Apple/n]

The new window is layered on top of the Doc 1 window:

6 Multiple Documents and Windows

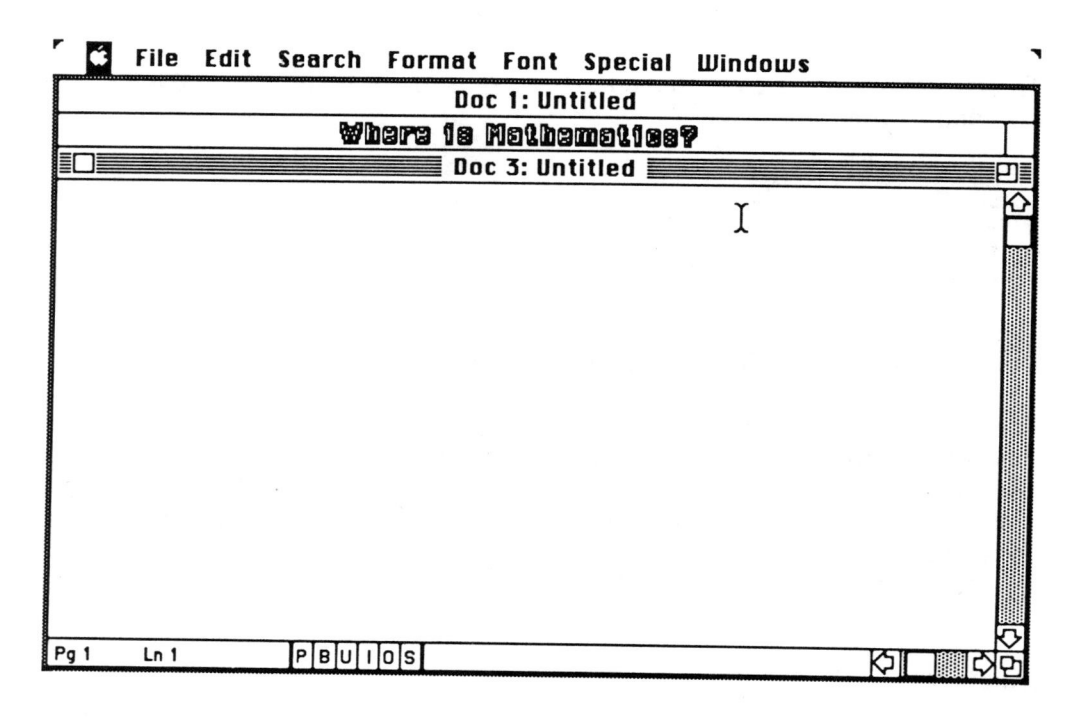

Figure 6.4

In addition to opening new document windows, you can create windows by opening existing document files. Open the file you created in Chapter 1 — Business Letter. (If you have not worked through Chapter 1, substitute any other document.) Enter

[Apple/o]

> **Point** at Business Letter
> **Click**

You now have four document windows; three are visible at this time:

Multiple Documents and Windows 6

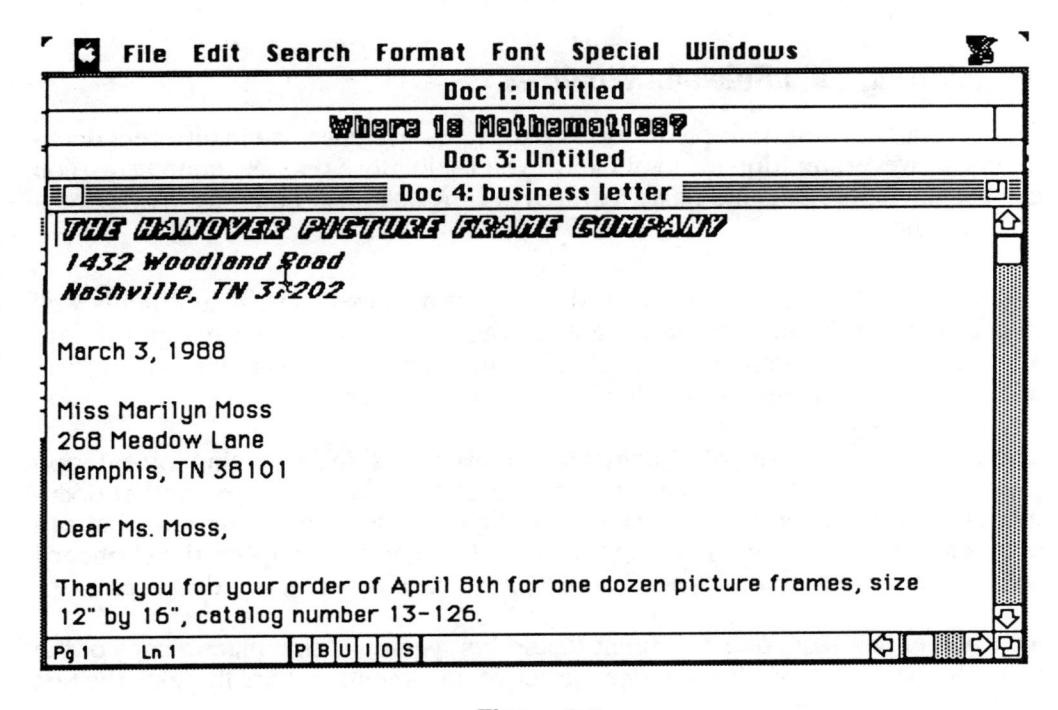

Figure 6.5

You can press [Apple/w] to change the active window between all four windows. Enter

[Apple/w]

Doc 2 becomes active. Enter

[Apple/w]

Doc 1 becomes active.

6 Multiple Documents and Windows

Transferring Data Between Windows

One reason for using multiple windows is to cross-reference text in different documents; however, multiple windows allow you to do more than examine text. You can use the Copy, Cut, and Paste features to copy or transfer data from one document to another.

For example, the last paragraph in the current document might fit equally well into Document 2. Suppose you want to transfer a copy of that paragraph into another document window. WordPerfect uses one of the standard Macintosh concepts — the **clipboard** — to allow this type of transfer.

The clipboard is an area of Macintosh memory set aside for storing information clipped from the active application. Text can then be inserted into another document or another program. In a sense, the clipboard is a "super window" that can be opened in any document or application. Later in this chapter, the clipboard will be used to transfer a HyperCard graphic into a WordPerfect document.

To transfer text from one document to another, you must first place a copy of the text into the clipboard, then change the active document, and finally paste the text into its new location.

The first step in this operation is to use the selection commands to highlight the text to be transferred. To highlight the last paragraph, position the cursor in the paragraph by entering

↑ (2 times)

Select the entire paragraph by entering

[Apple/6]3

Place a copy of the selected text into the clipboard by entering

[Apple/c]

The text is copied to the clipboard.

Multiple Documents and Windows **6**

Showing the Clipboard

Previously, you used the clipboard—without looking at its display—to move and copy text within the same document. You may, however, be unsure about what has been transferred to the clipboard. In such cases, you can display the clipboard's contents by using the Show Clipboard option located on the Windows menu:

```
Point at Windows
Drag to Show Clipboard
Release
```

WordPerfect displays the contents of the clipboard in a window at the bottom of the screen:

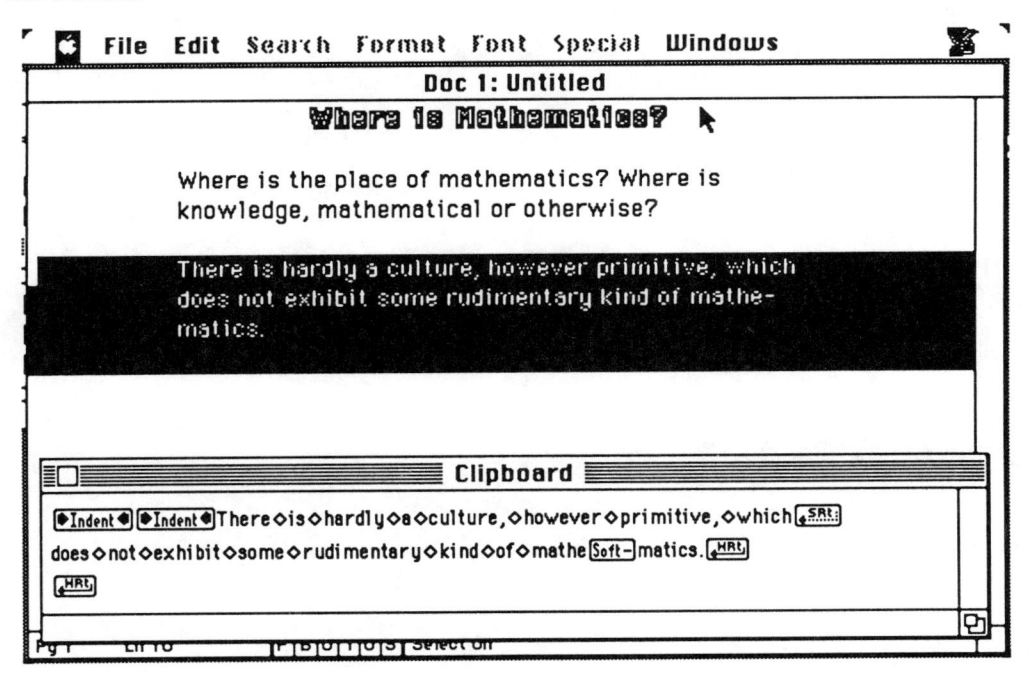

Figure 6.6

299

6 Multiple Documents and Windows

Remember, the clipboard is a feature that works in all Macintosh applications. As such, it is not specific to WordPerfect and does not display the text as a WordPerfect document. The text is displayed with formatting codes—similar to the way the hidden codes display would show the text. You can see that the text of the highlighted paragraph as well as the formatting codes contained in that paragraph have been transferred to the clipboard.

The clipboard is different from other document windows in another respect: you cannot directly edit text in the clipboard. The only way to place text into the clipboard is by using the Cut, Copy, and Append commands.

To return to WordPerfect, close the clipboard window by clicking on the Close box:

> **Point** at the Close box
> **Click**

The next step is to select the document window in which you want to paste the contents of the clipboard. Enter

[Apple/w]

Doc 3—currently empty—appears. Move to Doc 2 by entering

[Apple/w] (2 times)

Paste the text contained in the clipboard into this document by entering

[Apple/v]

Multiple Documents and Windows 6

The screen should resemble the following:

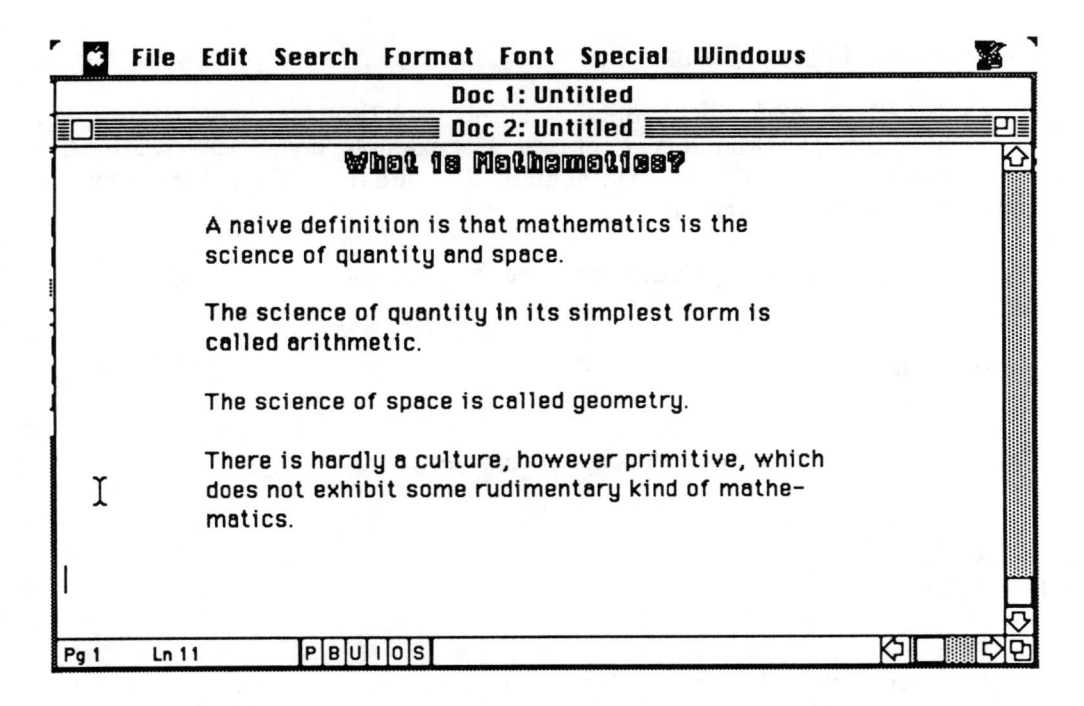

```
 File   Edit   Search   Format   Font   Special   Windows
┌─────────────────────────────────────────────────────────┐
│                    Doc 1: Untitled                      │
│                    Doc 2: Untitled                      │
│               What is Mathematics?                      │
│                                                         │
│     A naive definition is that mathematics is the       │
│     science of quantity and space.                      │
│                                                         │
│     The science of quantity in its simplest form is     │
│     called arithmetic.                                  │
│                                                         │
│     The science of space is called geometry.            │
│                                                         │
│     There is hardly a culture, however primitive, which │
│  I  does not exhibit some rudimentary kind of mathe-    │
│     matics.                                             │
│                                                         │
│ |                                                       │
│                                                         │
│ Pg 1   Ln 11      P B U I O S                           │
└─────────────────────────────────────────────────────────┘
```

Figure 6.7

Once text is placed into the clipboard, you can paste the text as many times as you like into the same or a different document. Paste a copy of this paragraph into Document 3 by entering

[Apple/w]   (2 times)
[Apple/v]

The text is inserted into another document. Return to Document 1 — the original document — by entering

[Apple/w]   (3 times)

301

6 Multiple Documents and Windows

Note that the highlight is still in place on the selected paragraph.

Adding Another Clipboard Item

The clipboard can hold only one item at a time; each time you select a new item, the previous clipboard contents are erased. For example, if you were to place the title of this document — "What is Mathematics?" — into the clipboard, the previous contents would be overwritten.

Move the cursor to the top of the document by entering

[Enter] [Enter] ↑

Place the title paragraph into the clipboard by entering

[Apple/6]3
[Apple/c]

Show the contents of the clipboard:

> **Point** at Windows
> **Drag** to Show Clipboard
> **Release**

The screen should resemble the following:

Multiple Documents and Windows 6

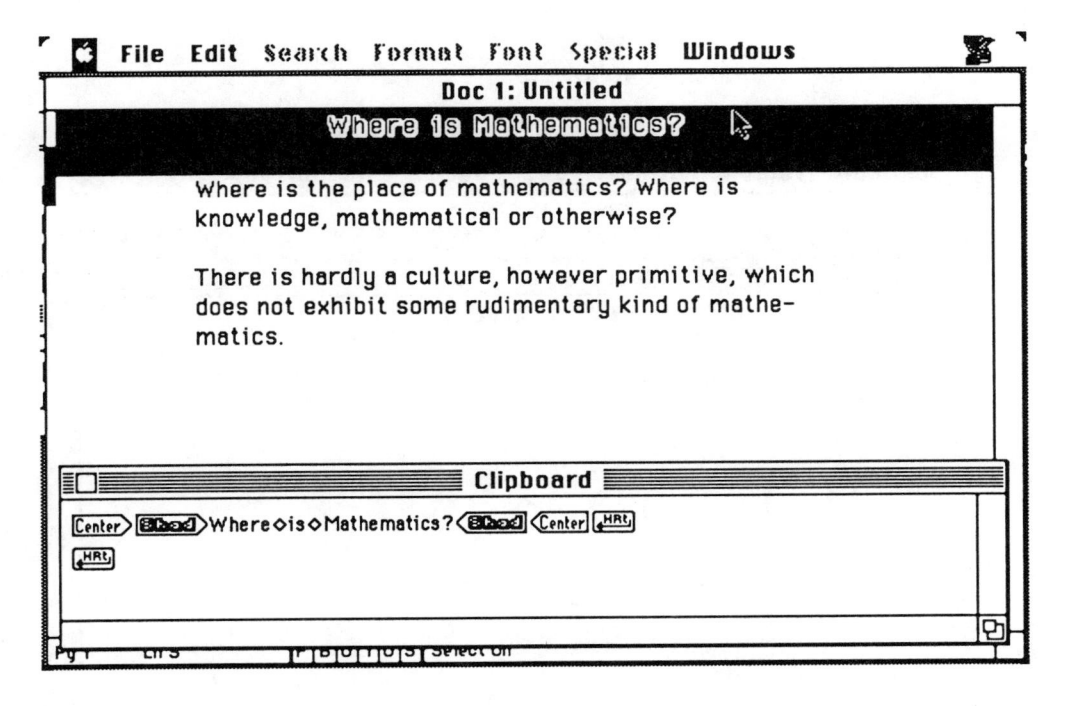

Figure 6.8

This time, you can see that the clipboard contains only the text of the most recent copy. The text of the previous copy was erased when the new text was added. Close the clipboard:

> **Point** at the Close box for the clipboard
> **Click**

Paste this title into Doc 3. Enter

[Apple/w]
[Enter] [Enter] ↑
[Apple/v]

303

6 Multiple Documents and Windows

Doc 3 should now resemble the following:

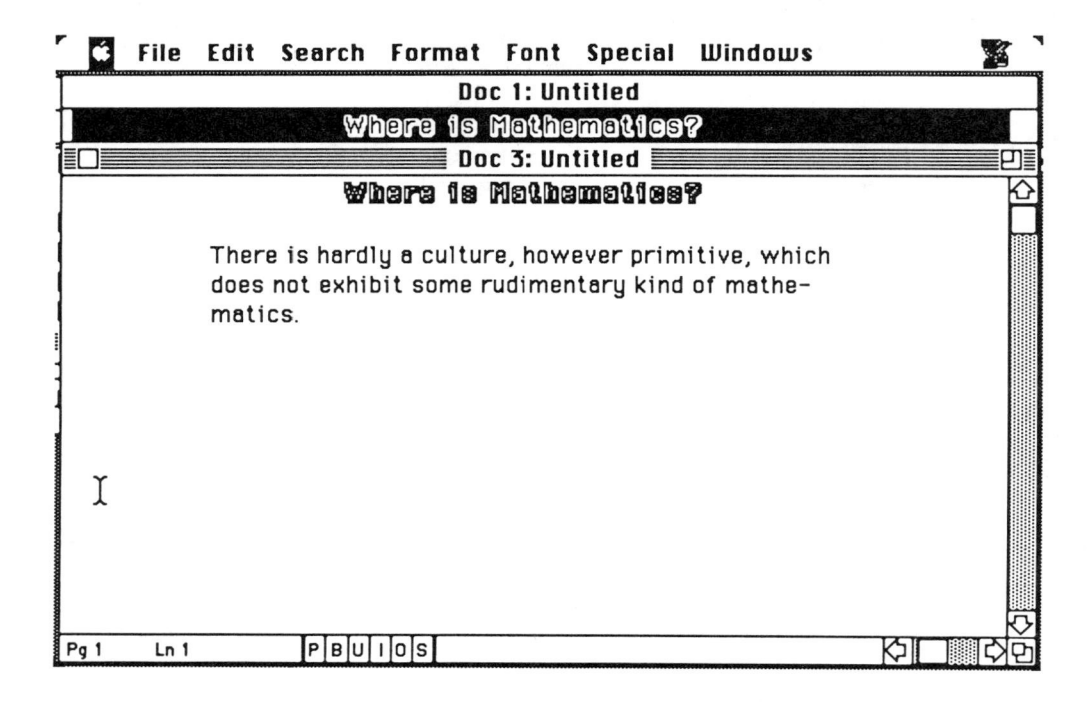

Figure 6.9

Appending Text to the Clipboard

Previously, you learned that when you add text to the clipboard with the Copy or Cut commands, any text previously in the clipboard is deleted before the new text is inserted. The Macintosh clipboard always works in this way, but WordPerfect includes an additional command found on the Edit menu: Append.

The Append command allows you to copy several items into or cut several items from a single clipboard. The Append command does not erase the previous text in the clipboard; it adds new text to the current entry.

The advantage of the Append command is that you can choose several non-contiguous text items and transfer them as a unit with a single Paste command.

Multiple Documents and Windows 6

As an example, change to Doc 2. Enter

[Apple/w] (2 times)

Begin copying into the clipboard from the top of this document. Enter

[Enter] [Enter] ↑

Place the first paragraph in the clipboard:

[Apple/ 6]3
[Apple/c]

Display the clipboard's contents:

```
Point at Windows
Drag to Show Clipboard
Release
```

The clipboard contains *only* the information just copied. The previous contents have been replaced.

6 Multiple Documents and Windows

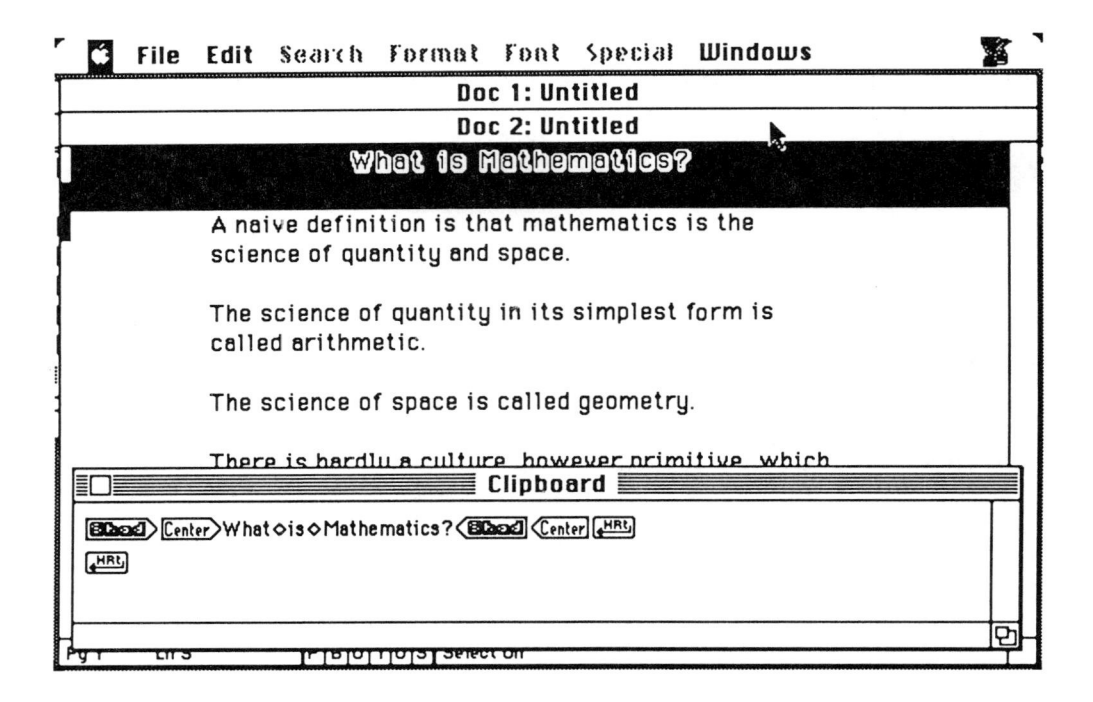

Figure 6.10

> **Point** at the Close box for the clipboard
> **Click**

Move down to the third paragraph by entering

↓ (3 times)

Highlight this paragraph by entering

[Apple/6]3

Multiple Documents and Windows 6

Instead of using the Copy command, use the Append command to place a copy of the selected text into the clipboard, following the current clipboard text but not replacing it. Enter

[Apple/a]

WordPerfect displays the Append menu, which contains two options: Clipboard and File.

Clipboard This option places the highlighted text into the clipboard along with the current text. The new text is always inserted at the end of the current text.

File The File option adds the text to the end of an existing file.

In this case, use the Clipboard option by entering

1

To see the effect of the Append command, display the clipboard:

```
Point at Windows
Drag to Show Clipboard
Release
```

307

6 Multiple Documents and Windows

The screen should resemble the following:

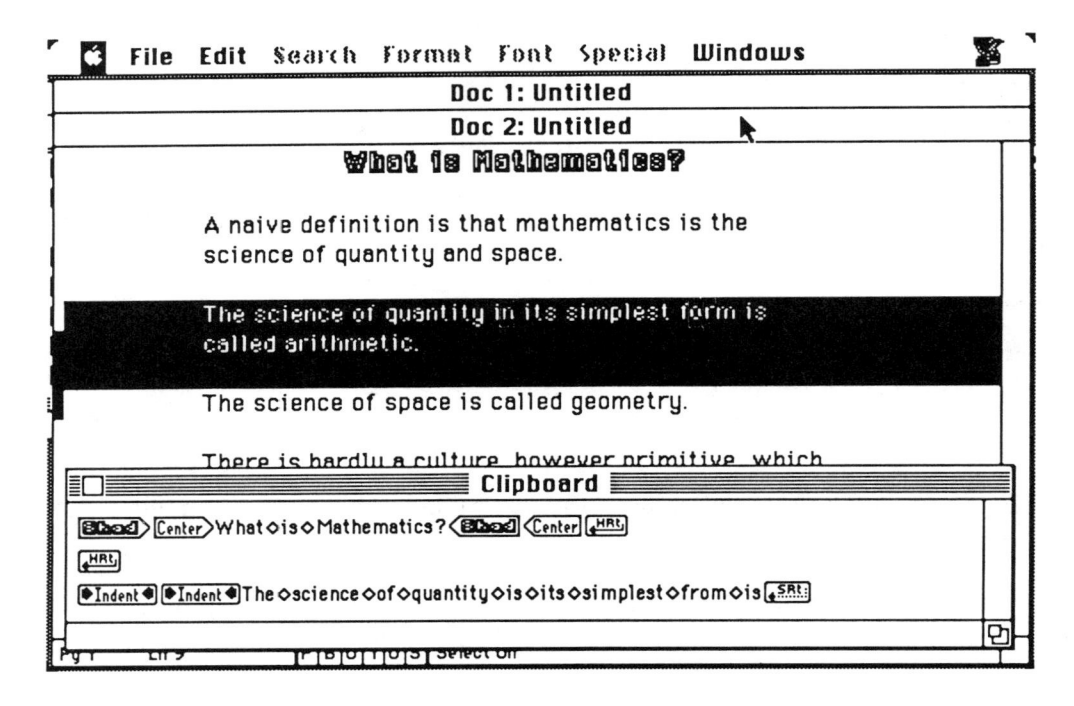

Figure 6.11

The clipboard display shows that the clipboard now contains two items copied from the document.

> **Point** at the Close box for the clipboard
> **Click**

Change the display to Doc 3. Enter

[Apple/w] (2 times)

Multiple Documents and Windows **6**

Paste the items from the clipboard onto the end of the document:

[Enter] [Enter]↓
[Apple/v]

The screen should now resemble the following:

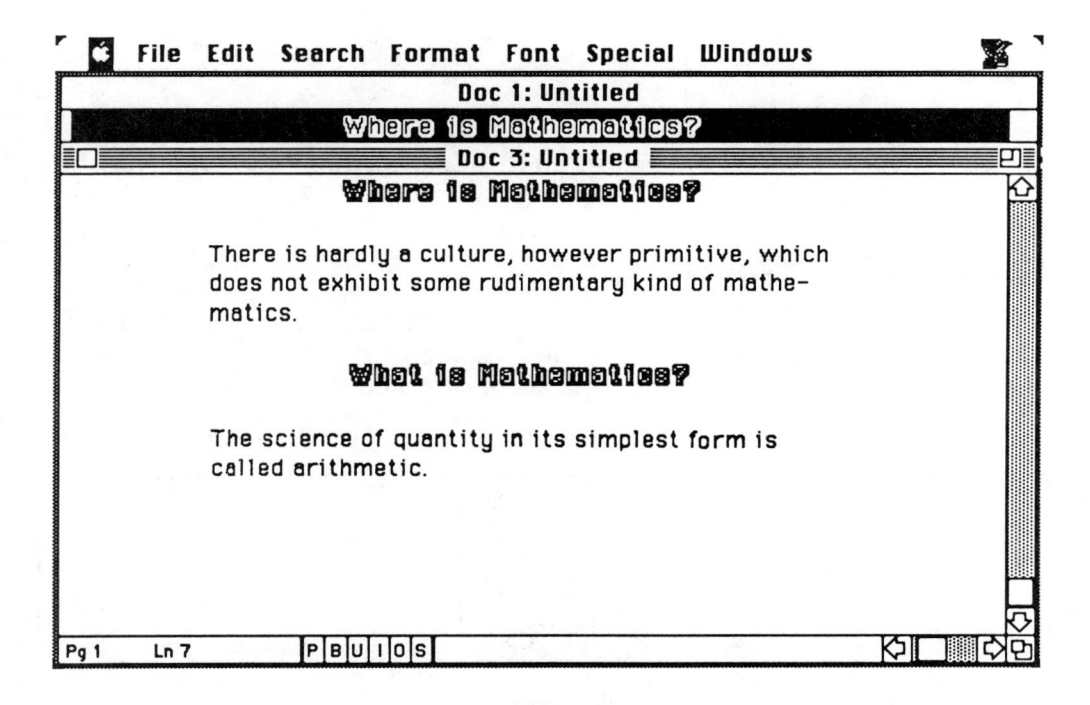

Figure 6.12

Cleaning up the Display

To simplify the next set of tasks, close document windows you don't currently need. Close Doc 3 by entering

[Apple/k]

309

6 Multiple Documents and Windows

Abandon this text:

| Point at No |
| Click |

Close Doc 4. Enter

[Apple/w] [Apple/k]

This process leaves two documents — 1 and 2 — open on the WordPerfect desktop.

Moving and Sizing Windows

If you are familiar with the Macintosh, you know that the size and position of display windows can be changed. Three important areas on the display are used to change display windows: the size icon, zoom icon, and move bar.

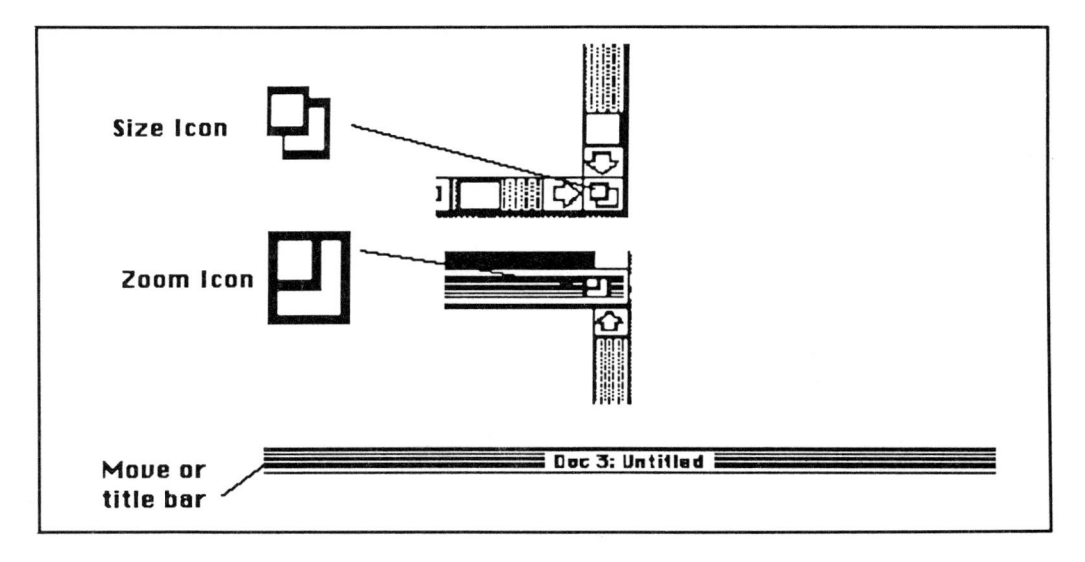

Figure 6.13

Multiple Documents and Windows 6

Size Icon   This icon—located in the lower right corner of each document window—allows you to change the size of the window. To use this icon, point the mouse at the icon and drag the mouse.

Zoom Icon   The zoom box icon—located in the upper right corner of the window—automatically enlarges a window to its maximum size. The zoom box is activated by clicking the icon.

Move Bar   The move bar is the same as the title bar that appears at the top of the window. To move a window, point to a part of the title bar and drag the mouse. The window will follow the mouse cursor to its new location.

In this case, two documents are currently layered on top of one another. You might want to change the size and location of the windows so you can view them simultaneously.

To make the Doc 1 window smaller, drag the size icon straight up the screen to reduce the vertical length of the window by approximately one-half:

Point at the size icon
Drag the mouse halfway up the screen

When you reduce the size of the Doc 1 window, you will see the bottom part of Doc 2 at the bottom of the screen. The screen will resemble the following:

6 Multiple Documents and Windows

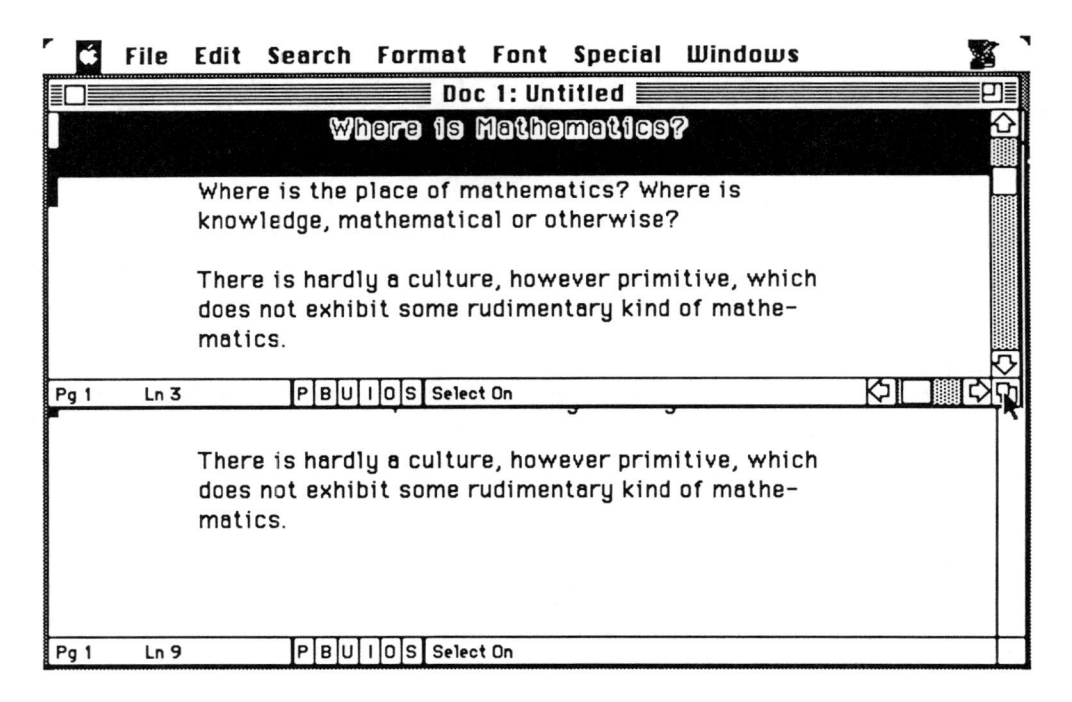

Figure 6.14

The next step is to change the size and position of Doc 2 so you can see both documents at the same time. Switch to Doc 2 by entering

[Apple/w]

Use the size icon to reduce by one-half the vertical size of this window.

Point at the size icon
Drag the mouse halfway up the screen

Both half-size windows occupy the top part of the display.

Multiple Documents and Windows **6**

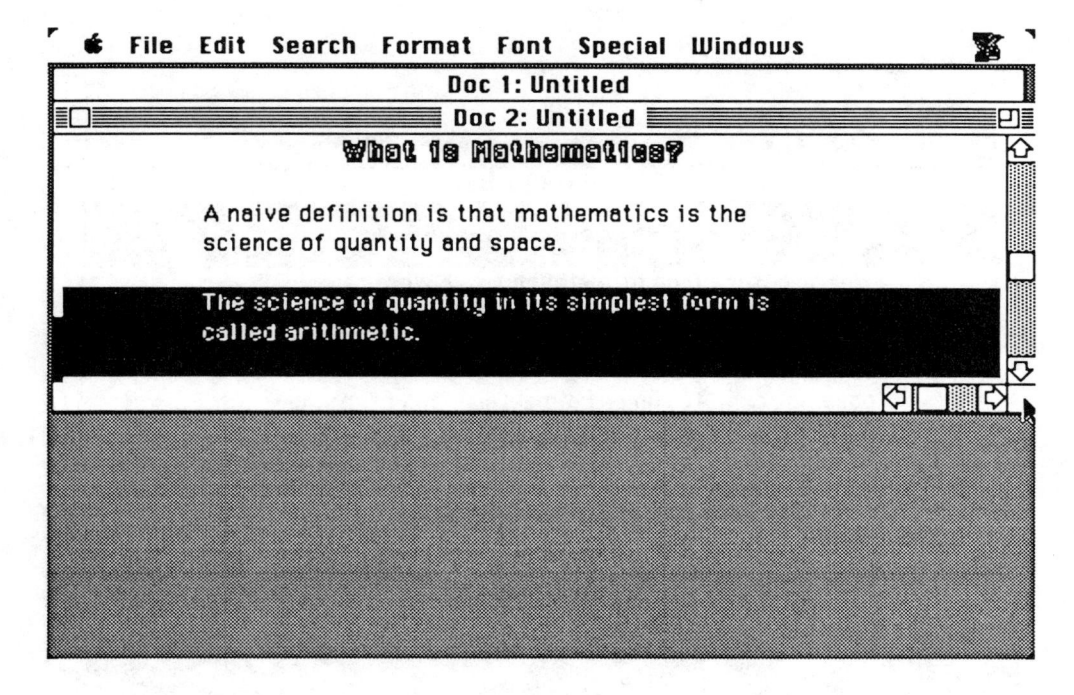

Figure 6.15

The next task is to use the move bar to place the Doc 2 document in the bottom half of the screen.

Point at the move bar for Doc 2
Drag the window down to the bottom half of the screen

313

6 Multiple Documents and Windows

The screen should resemble the following:

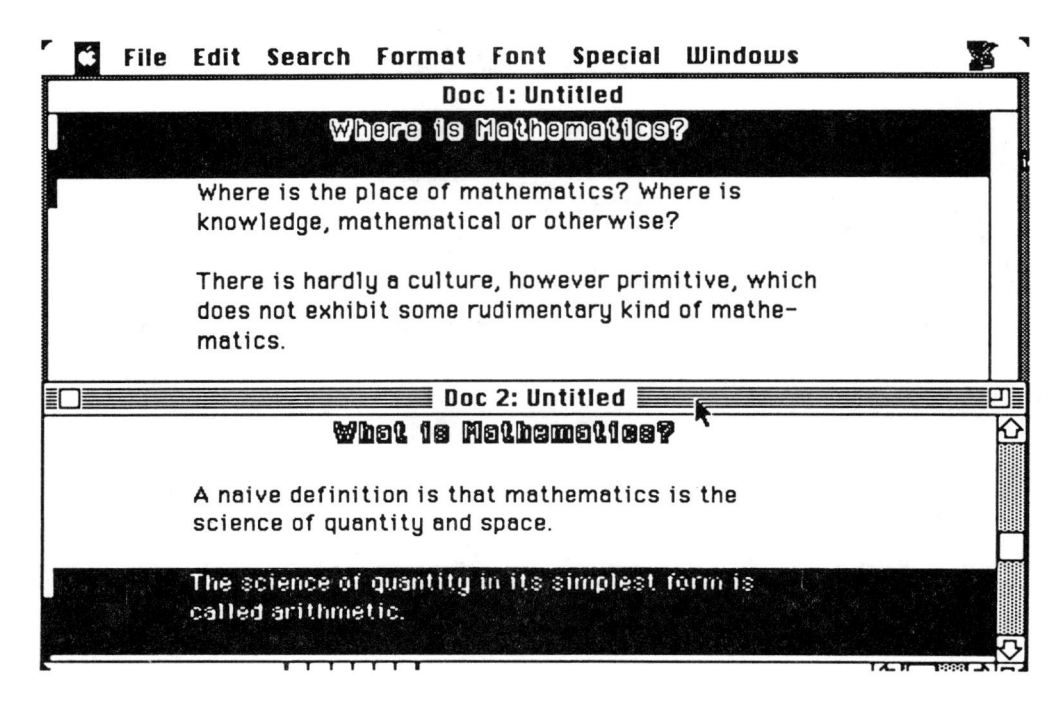

```
 File   Edit   Search   Format   Font   Special   Windows
═══════════════════════ Doc 1: Untitled ═══════════════════════
                    Where is Mathematics?

    Where is the place of mathematics? Where is
    knowledge, mathematical or otherwise?

    There is hardly a culture, however primitive, which
    does not exhibit some rudimentary kind of mathe-
    matics.
═══════════════════════ Doc 2: Untitled ═══════════════════════
                    What is Mathematics?

    A naive definition is that mathematics is the
    science of quantity and space.

    The science of quantity in its simplest form is
    called arithmetic.
```

Figure 6.16

The split screen display allows you to see the text of both documents at the same time. You can also switch quickly back and forth between the documents, using the mouse to activate the document window to be edited. Keep in mind that reducing the size of the document window has no effect on the amount of text you can enter into that document. The reduced window only means that you see a smaller section of each document displayed on the screen.

Move the cursor to the bottom of Doc 2, and enter another paragraph:

[Enter] [Enter] ↓
[Apple/Shift/L] (2 times)
To the extent that all children learn some mathematics, we are all part of the mathematical community.
[Return] [Return]

314

Multiple Documents and Windows **6**

This document is now complete — at least for now. Save the document and close the window by entering

[Apple/s]
math 2[Return]
[Apple/k]

The remaining document window occupies only half the screen. The Macintosh desktop will appear in the bottom half of the screen.

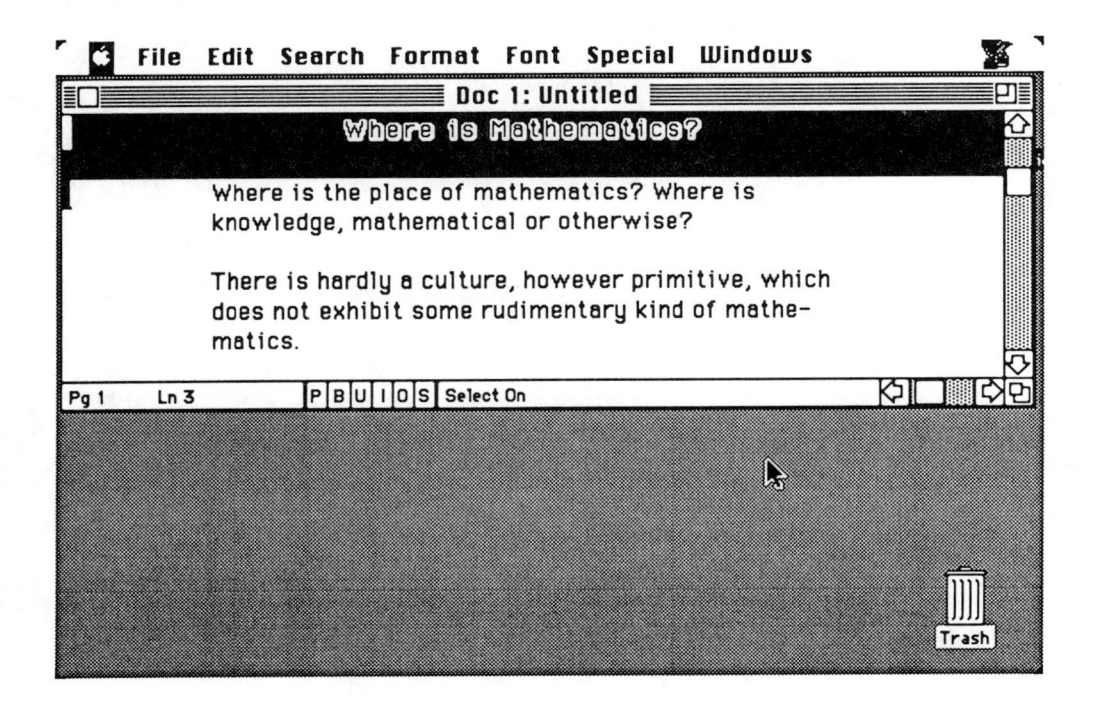

Figure 6.17

Zooming a Window

The Macintosh interface provides a quick way to return any window to full-screen size. The zoom icon — in the upper right corner of the window — will expand the window with a single click.

315

6 Multiple Documents and Windows

> **Point** at the zoom icon
> **Click**

The window expands to full-screen length:

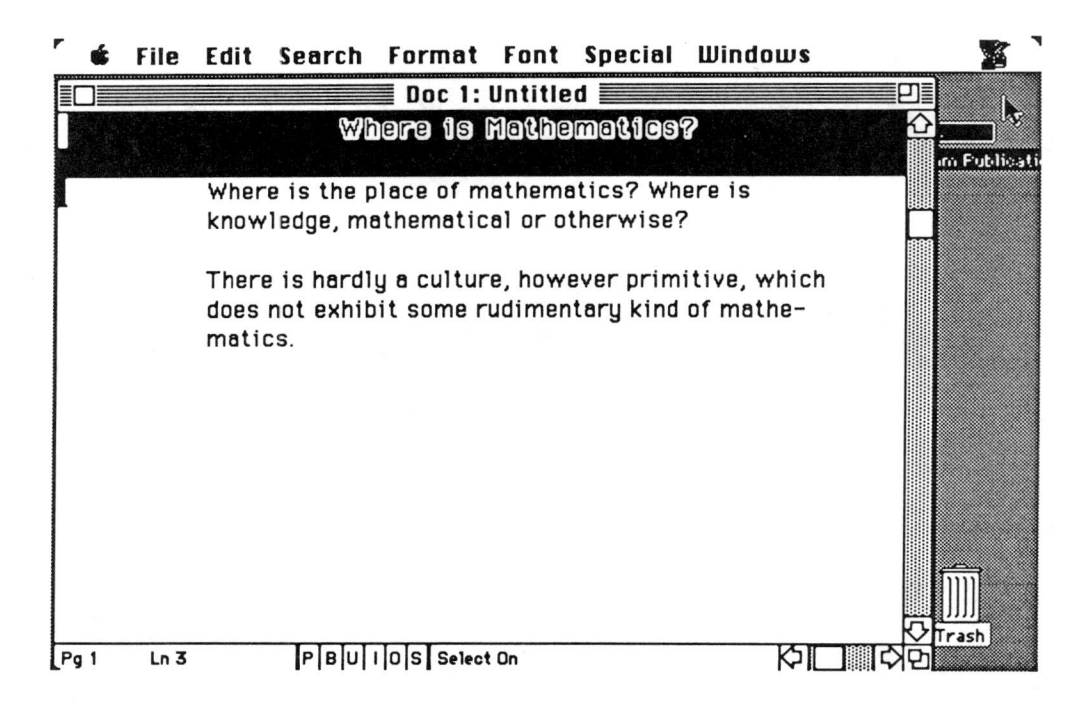

Figure 6.18

If you click on the icon again, you will return the window to its previous shape:

> **Point** at the zoom icon
> **Click**

The screen should resemble the following:

Multiple Documents and Windows **6**

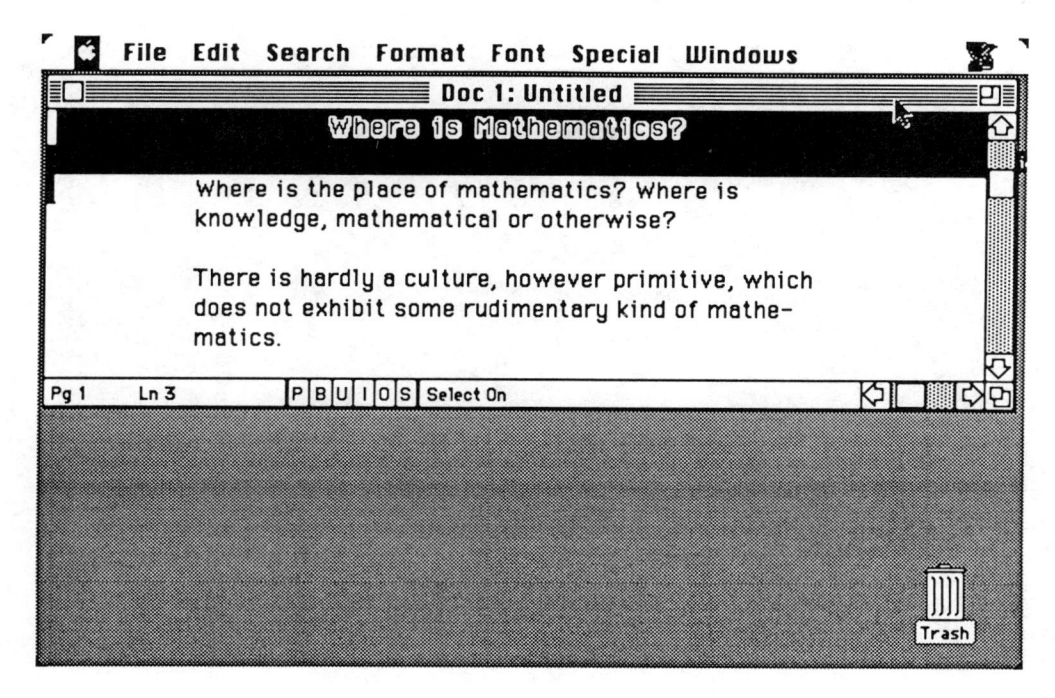

Figure 6.19

Save this document and close the window by entering

[Apple/s]
math 1[Return]
[Apple/k]

When all document windows are closed, close the Macintosh desktop. The exact appearance of the desktop will vary, depending on which document folders will be displayed below the WordPerfect menu bar.

6 Multiple Documents and Windows

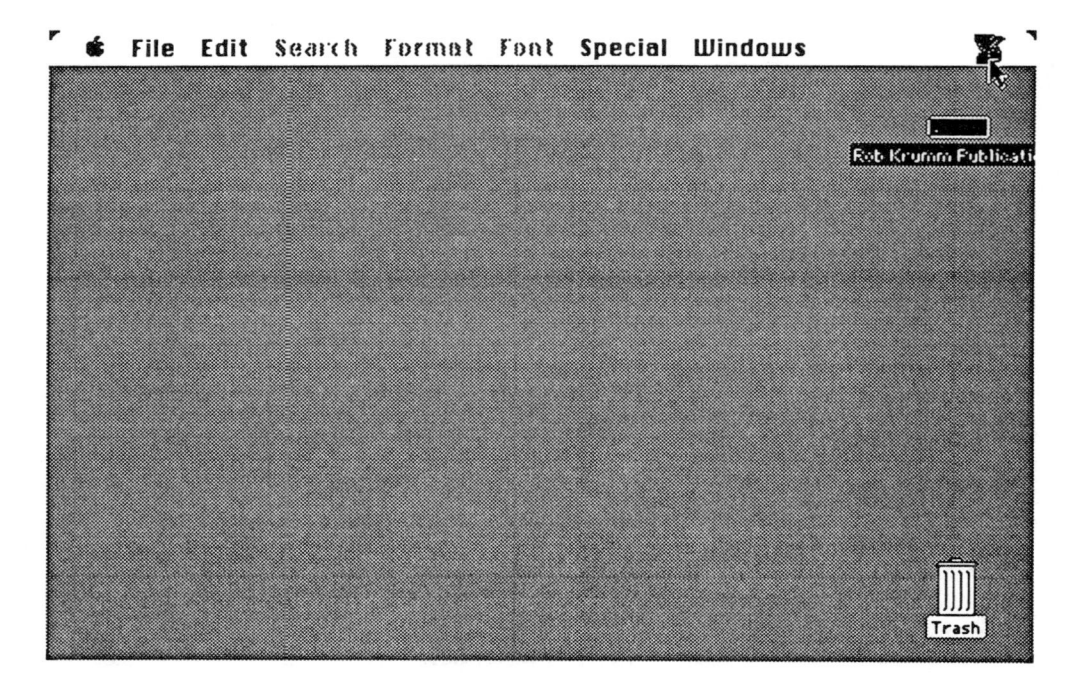

Figure 6.20

Display a new blank document on the screen by entering

[Apple/n]

The document is assigned the name Doc 1: Untitled because it is the first document window to be opened.

RETRIEVING TEXT

You may have noticed that WordPerfect has several menu options that sound like they perform the same operation, such as File Open and File Retrieve. There is an important difference. The File Open command always creates a new document window for the text being loaded. File Retrieve adds the text being loaded to the current document window. The File Retrieve command allows you to insert the text of an entire document at the current cursor position. The text of the current document and the retrieved file are merged into a single document.

Multiple Documents and Windows 6

For example, you currently have two documents stored on disk — Math 1 and Math 2. You can use the File Retrieve command to combine the text stored in both documents with the text of any document you are working on. This technique allows you to prepare a series of small documents that are then combined into a single larger document. The advantage of creating a document in this manner is that it is easy to combine the files in different orders by simply retrieving them in the order you want them to appear, which is usually simpler than cutting and pasting large blocks of text.

Begin by entering some text into the new document window:

THE MATHEMATICAL EXPERIENCE[Return] [Return]
SUMMARY CHAPTER 1[Return] [Return]

Load the contents of the Math 1 file into the current document:

> **Point** at File
> **Drag** to Retrieve...
> **Release**
> **Double Click** on Math 1

WordPerfect inserts the entire text of the Math 1 document at the cursor position in the current document.

6 Multiple Documents and Windows

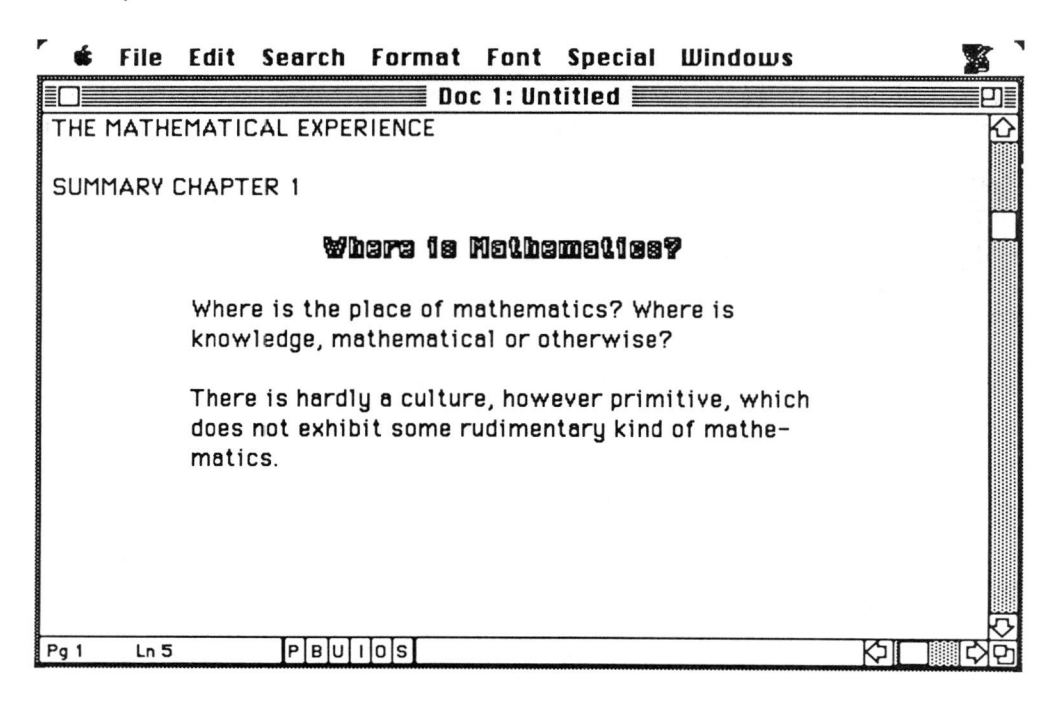

```
 File   Edit   Search   Format   Font   Special   Windows
════════════════════ Doc 1: Untitled ════════════════════
THE MATHEMATICAL EXPERIENCE

SUMMARY CHAPTER 1

              Where is Mathematics?

    Where is the place of mathematics? Where is
    knowledge, mathematical or otherwise?

    There is hardly a culture, however primitive, which
    does not exhibit some rudimentary kind of mathe-
    matics.

Pg 1   Ln 5        P B U I O S
```

Figure 6.21

Move to the end of this document and enter the following text:

[Enter] [Enter]↓
SUMMARY CHAPTER 2 [Return] [Return]

Use the Retrieve command again to add the text of the Math 2 file to the current document:

> **Point** at File
> **Drag** to Retrieve...
> **Release**
> **Double Click** on Math 2

The text of Math 2 is added to the current untitled document:

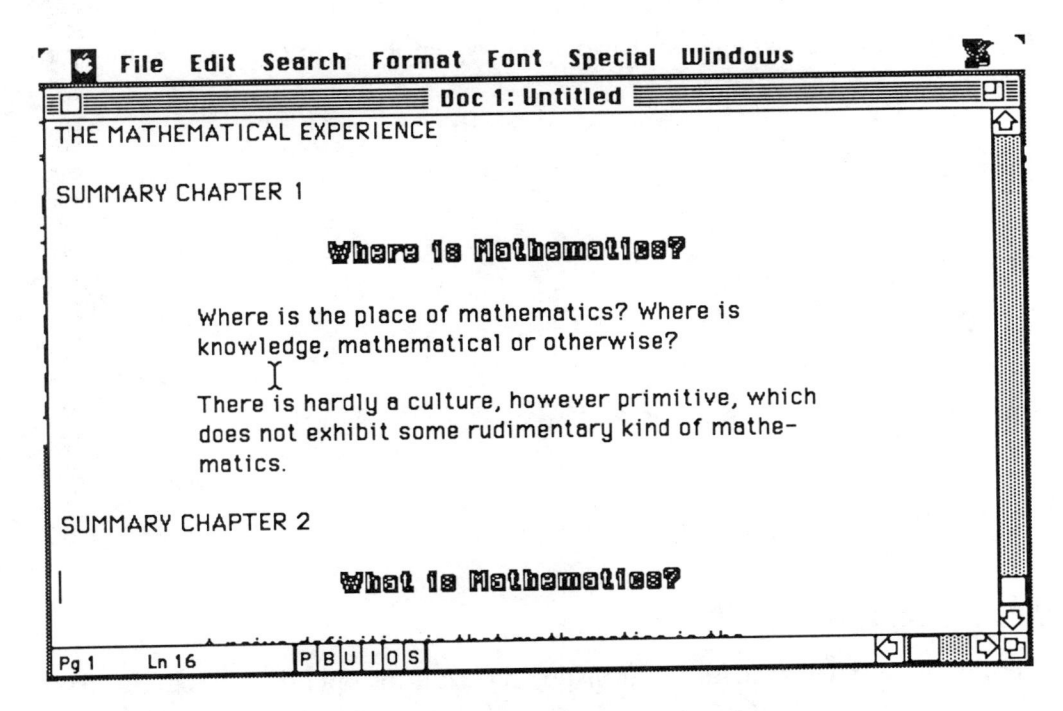

Figure 6.22

The Retrieve command allows you to create a new document by combining smaller documents; it is a type of Paste command in which the text is drawn from a file stored on the disk instead of from the clipboard. Retrieving text from disk files does not require as much memory as an equivalent clipboard operation. For example, if you have two 10-page documents simultaneously open and want to combine them into a single document, you can proceed in two ways.

If you used the clipboard, you would create a new document window and copy and paste the contents of both documents into the new document. This technique would require enough memory for at least 40 pages — 10 for each of the originals and 20 for the combined file. You may not have enough memory to perform this operation. The alternative is to save both documents and close their windows. Then, use the File Retrieve command to combine the two files into a new document. Because the text is copied from disk files and not from memory, you use up only the memory needed to hold the combined document (in this example, 20 pages).

6 Multiple Documents and Windows

The clipboard is appropriate for small blocks of text while the File Retrieve command is more efficient when you have large amounts of text to transfer.

Clear the document window and display a new, empty document window by entering

[Apple/k]

Point at No Click

Enter

[Apple/n]

Appending Text to a File

Another variation on the idea of transferring text is to append a block of text from the active document onto a disk file. WordPerfect allows you to use the Append command to add text to the end of a file that is already stored on the disk. Remember, text transferred to a disk file in this manner can be added only to the end of the file. To insert the text at a specific location within the document, you must load the file and use the clipboard method.

Enter the following paragraph into the current document:

This text was created by Walter LaFish as part of his WordPerfect training course. [Return]

The note you have just typed should be attached to both the Math 1 and Math 2 files because it applies to both of those documents. You can use the Append command to add this text to as many documents on the disk as you like.

Multiple Documents and Windows 6

The first step when appending text to a file — as when appending text to the clipboard — is to select the text you want to append. In this case, the document only contains one paragraph, so you can select the entire document. Enter

[Apple/Shift/a]

To append this text to a file, enter

[Apple/a]

Option 2 on the Append menu is To File. Enter

2

WordPerfect displays the document selector box. The document selected will have the highlighted text appended to it.

```
Point at Math 1
Click
```

To append the same text to Math 2, simply repeat the process. Note that the text remains selected so that you need not select it again. Enter

[Apple/a]2

```
Point at Math 2
Click
```

323

6 Multiple Documents and Windows

To check if this operation was successful, load the Math 1 document. Enter

[Apple/o]
math 1[Return]

The document appears with the new text appended to the end of the document:

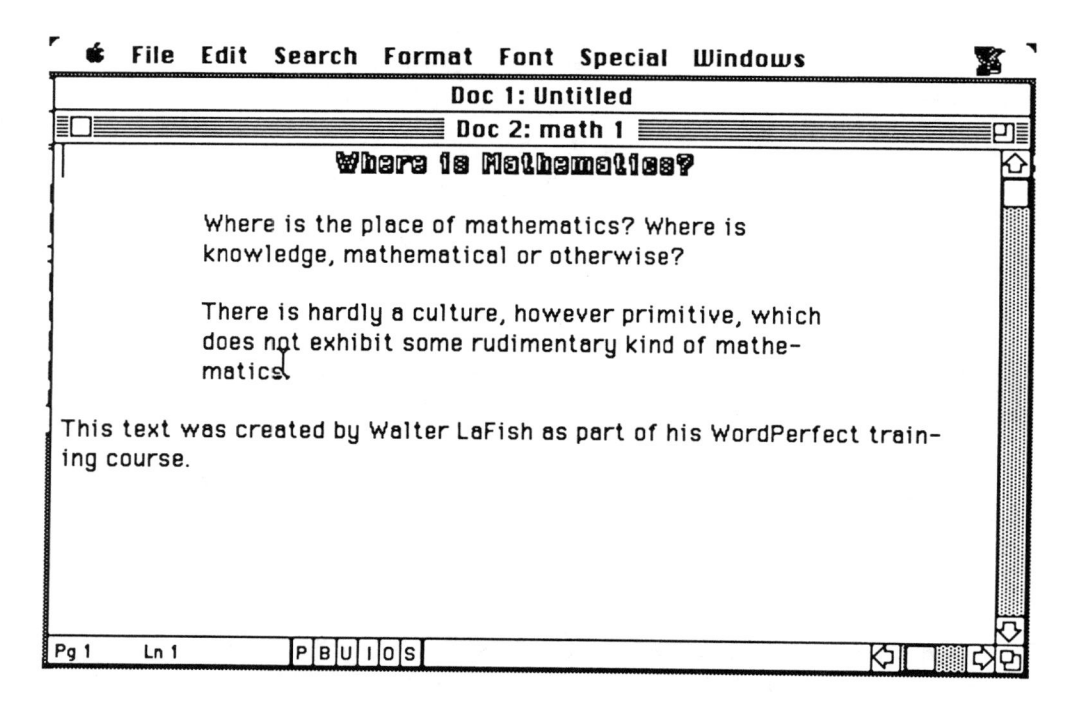

Figure 6.23

Close the documents. Enter

[Apple/k] (2 times)

Multiple Documents and Windows **6**

> Point at No
> Click

INSERTING GRAPHICS

This final section of the chapter describes how to insert graphics into WordPerfect. Graphics for the Macintosh can be produced by a number of available programs. This example uses a copy of a HyperCard graphic and places it into a WordPerfect document. HyperCard was selected because it is furnished with all new Macintosh computers. Of course, the concept of pasting graphics applies to many Macintosh programs—not just to HyperCard. If you do not own HyperCard or are not familiar with its use, you may want to skip this section.

To begin, quit WordPerfect and load HyperCard. When HyperCard appears, you will see the Home Card.

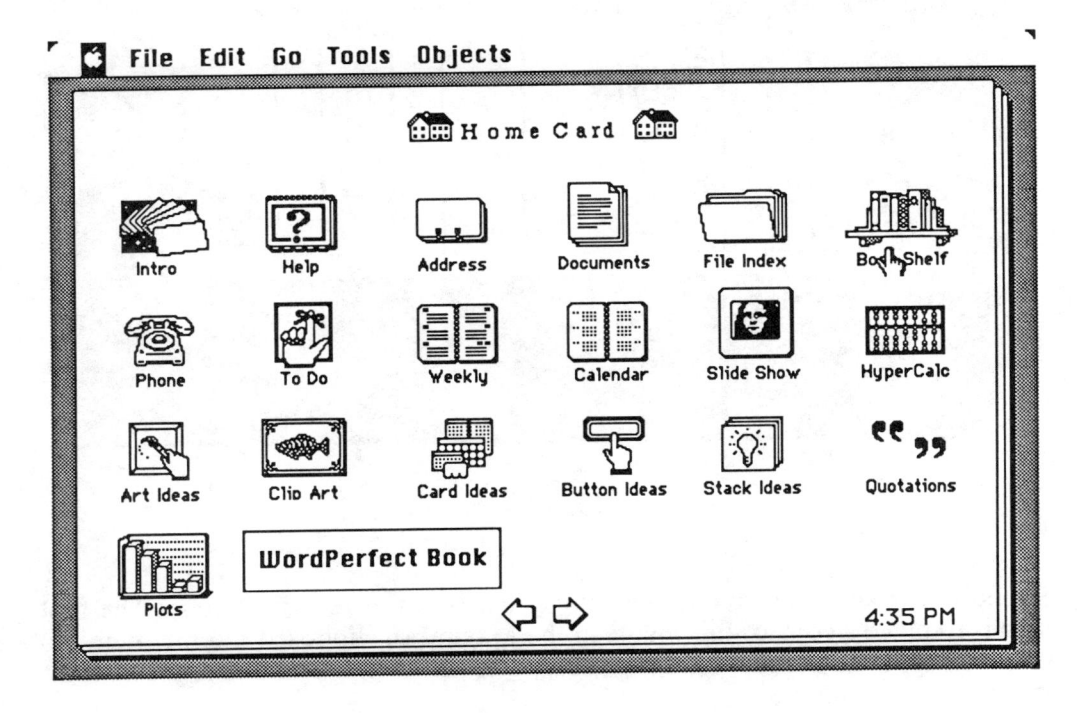

Figure 6.24

325

6 Multiple Documents and Windows

HyperCard contains a wealth of visual images. As an example, display one of the cards in the Book Shelf stack:

> **Point** at Book Shelf
> **Click**

The screen displays a picture of a book shelf:

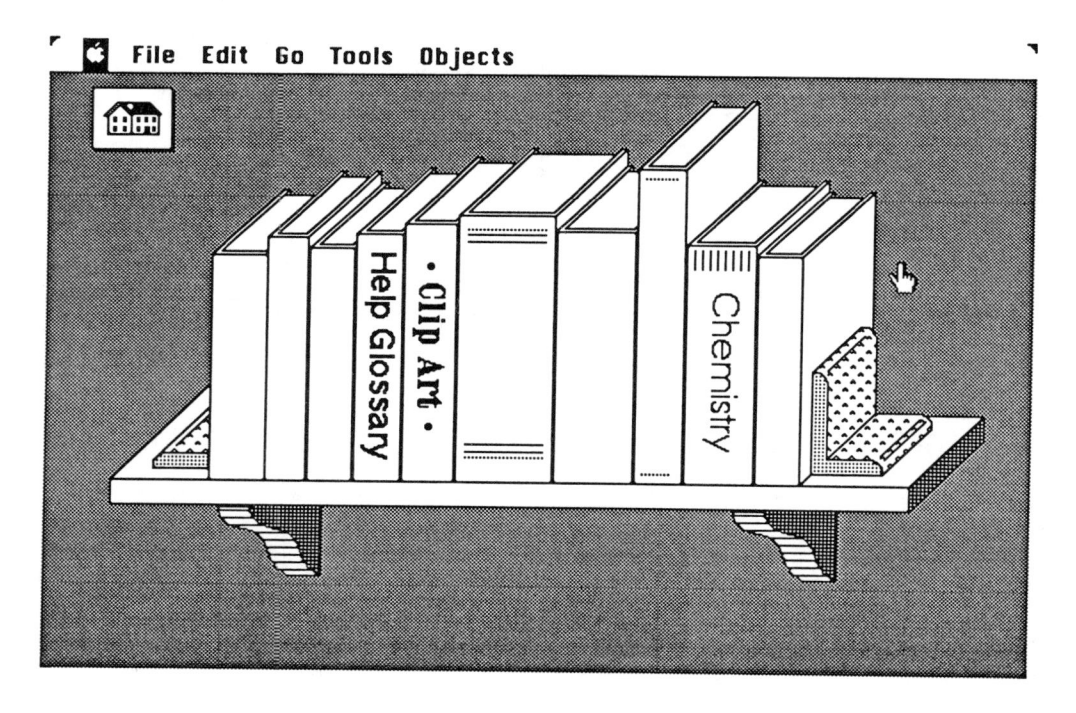

Figure 6.25

Suppose that you want to add this image to a WordPerfect document. The first step is to place a copy of this image in the Macintosh clipboard. Remember, because all applications share the clipboard, you can use it to transfer any data from one program to another.

Multiple Documents and Windows **6**

To copy a graphic, you must select the part of the image you want to copy in much the same way as you select text to copy to the clipboard. To do this, you must select the graphics selection tool from the Tools menu, which appears as follows:

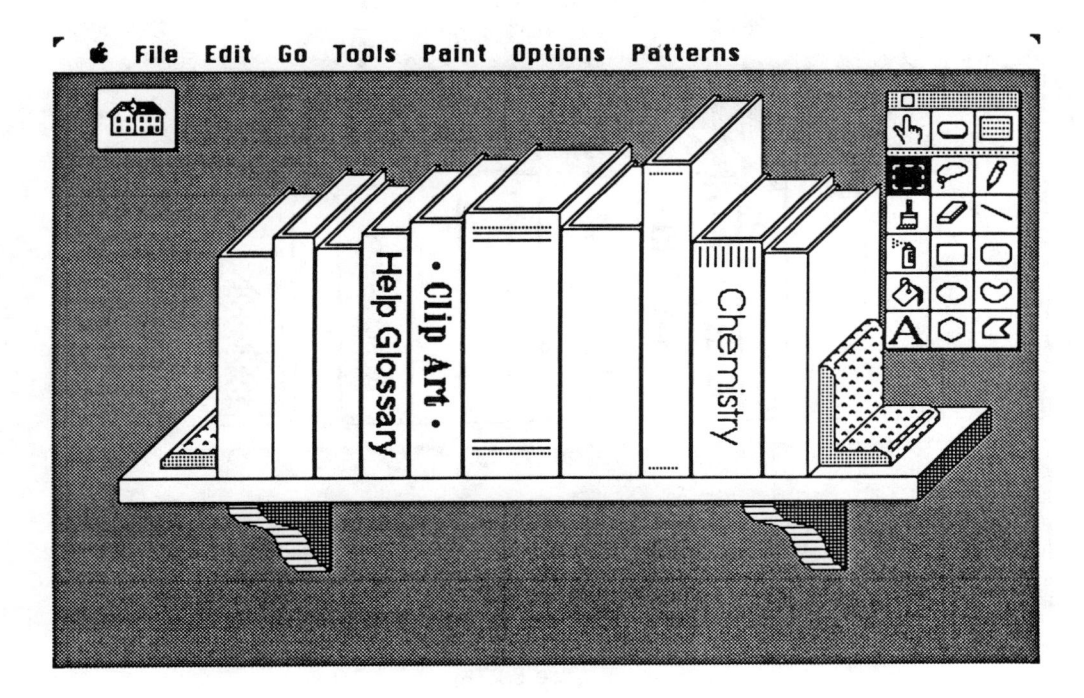

Figure 6.26

```
Point at Tools
Drag to the Selection icon
Release
```

Once you have chosen the selection tool, you must indicate what part of the picture you want to select:

```
Point at upper left corner of the picture
Drag to the lower right corner
Release
```

6 Multiple Documents and Windows

An outline will enclose the picture:

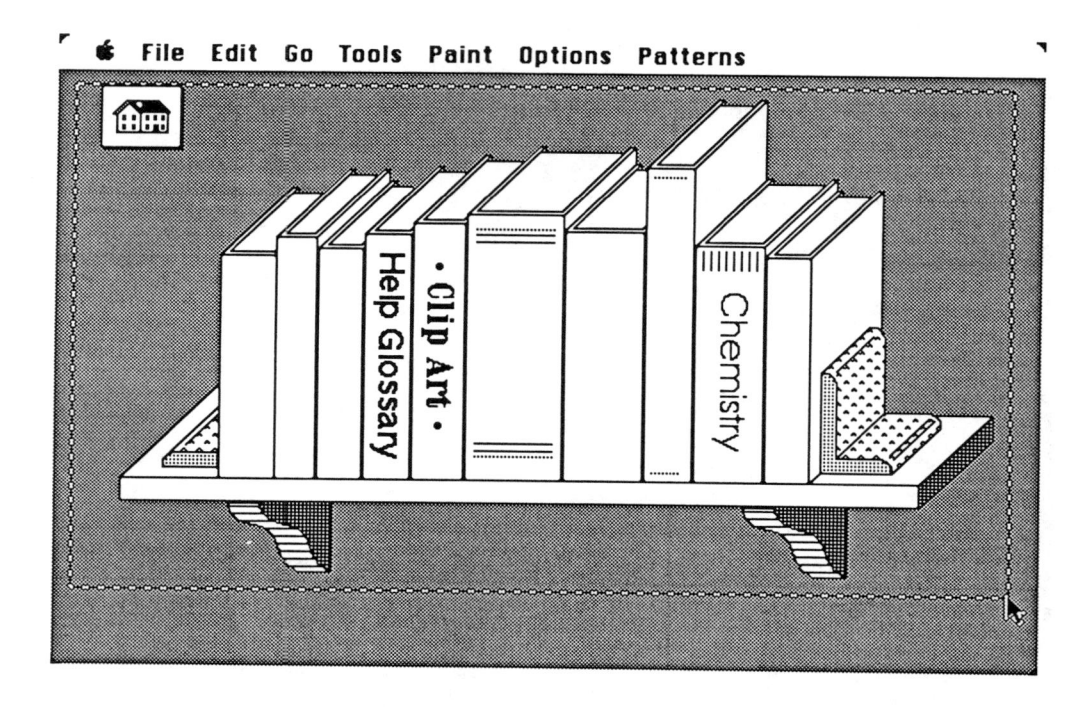

Figure 6.27

With the picture selected, place a copy in the clipboard by entering

[Apple/c]

The graphic is copied to the clipboard. You can now leave HyperCard and return to WordPerfect. Quit HyperCard by entering

[Apple/q]

Multiple Documents and Windows 6

Restart WordPerfect in the usual manner. When the program is loaded, open the Math 1 document by entering

[Apple/o]
math 1[Return]

You will paste the HyperCard graphic into this document. The first step is to decide where in the text the image should be placed. In this case, insert the graphic between the first and second paragraph. Enter

↓ (5 times)

Once the cursor has been positioned correctly, you can insert the graphic into the document by entering

[Apple/v]

The picture appears in the document at the current cursor position:

6 Multiple Documents and Windows

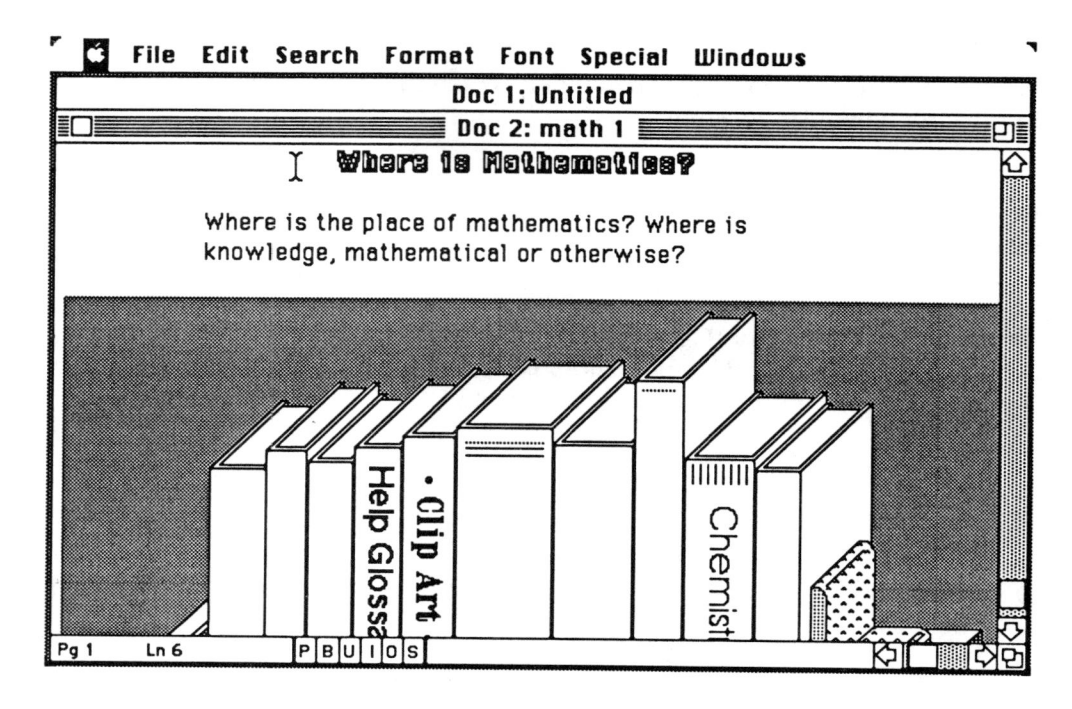

Figure 6.28

When a graphic is placed into a WordPerfect document, the program inserts a [Picture] code into the text. To see how the picture appears in the codes display, enter

[Apple/7]

The screen should resemble the following:

330

Multiple Documents and Windows **6**

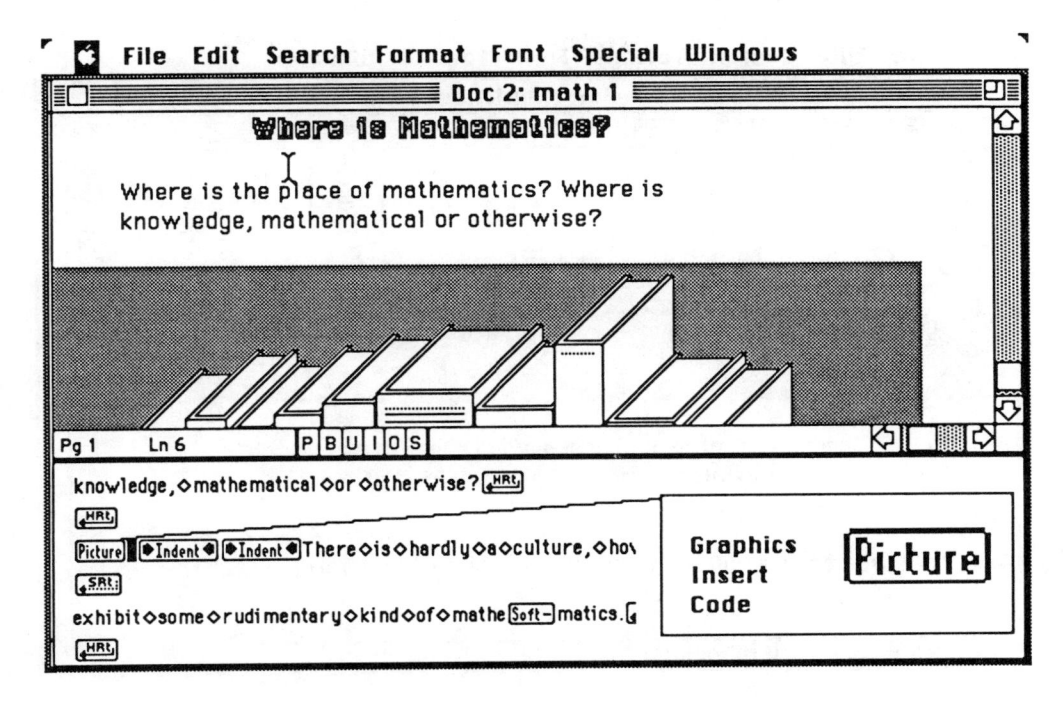

Figure 6.29

You can see that WordPerfect places the graphics code on the same line as the text of the second paragraph. You will not be able to read the text; it will be covered by the graphic. To correct this situation, insert a [Return] to separate the image and text. Enter

[Return]

Close the codes display by entering

[Apple/7]

You can now see the text continue after the graphic. When a graphic is inserted into an existing document, it is important to make sure the image is not covering other text.

331

6 Multiple Documents and Windows

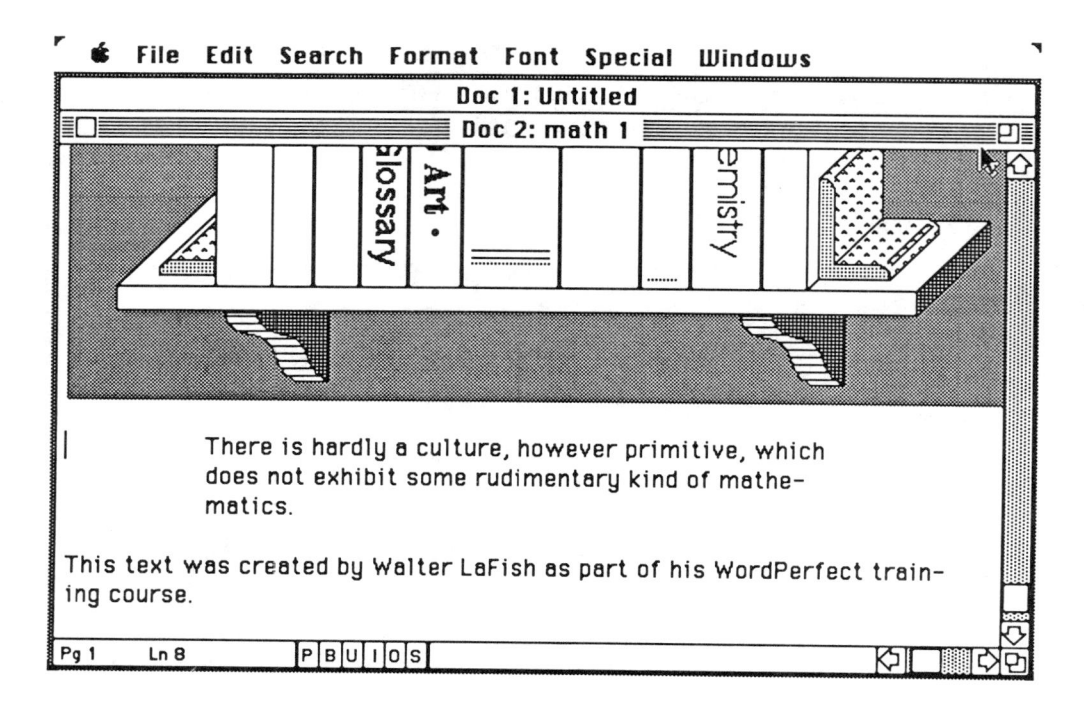

Figure 6.30

Preview the document by entering

[Apple/Shift/p]

The screen should resemble the following:

Multiple Documents and Windows 6

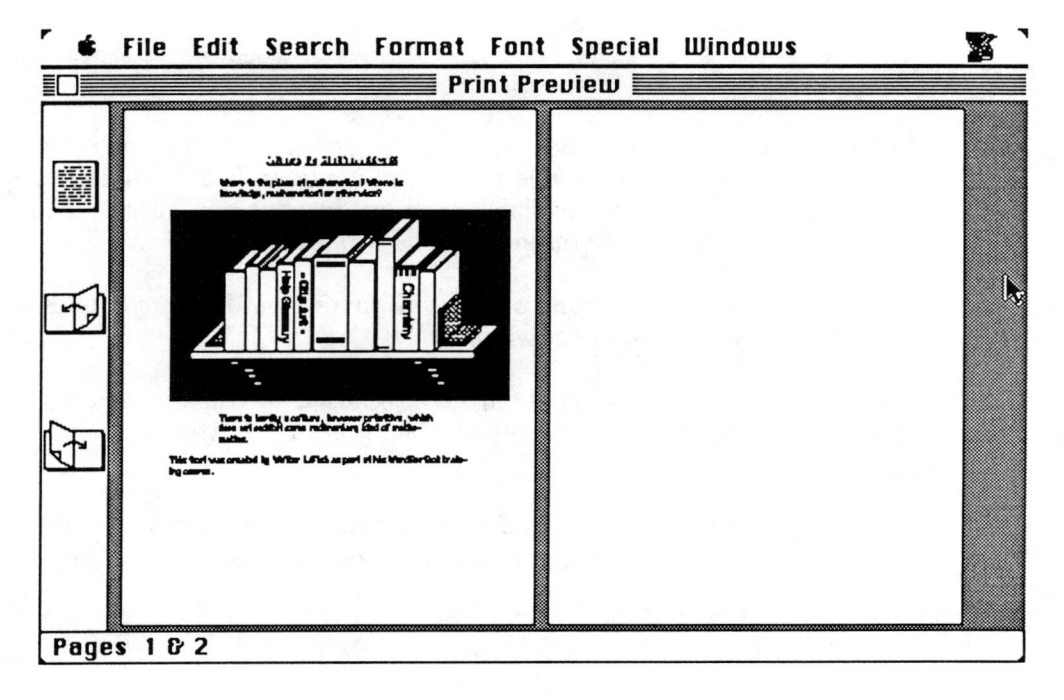

Figure 6.31

Return to the document:

```
Point at the Close box
Click
```

Save the document with the graphic by entering

[Apple/s]
[Apple/k]

333

6   Multiple Documents and Windows

SUMMARY

- **Windows.** WordPerfect can support the editing of multiple documents in different windows. The allowable number of windows is determined by the size of documents and available memory in your computer. The [Apple/w] command cycles you through the windows.

- **Transfer.** You can cut, copy, and paste text from one window into another by switching between document windows.

- **Clipboard.** The Macintosh clipboard can be used to transfer text and graphics between windows and other Macintosh applications, such as HyperCard.

- **Display.** You can change the size and location of the windows on the screen display. The size of the window does not affect document size.

CHAPTER 7

MERGE OPERATIONS

7 Merge Operations

By its very nature, word processing requires a great deal of manual entry. But the real power of the computer comes into play when you can set an activity and let the computer fill in the details automatically. WordPerfect provides a special facility called **merge** that provides a means by which many common document tasks can be automated. The most common use of merge is to print a series of form letters by combining a single letter with a list of people who need to receive that letter. In addition to generating form letters, WordPerfect's Merge commands can be used for a variety of tasks in which you want to use automated processing instead of manual text editing.

In this chapter you will learn how merge is used and what the WordPerfect merge commands can accomplish.

FORM LETTERS

The term **form letter** refers to a standard document, typically a letter, which is used by a person or a company over and over again. Many of these documents are prepared by marketing or legal specialists and are sent in the same form to every recipient. The only changes made to such documents involve specific items such as the recipient's name, address, social security numbers, etc. While merge is often associated with form letters, it is equally useful for legal documents (e.g., wills or pleadings), financial documents (e.g., invoices or statements), and other documents.

The goal of merge is to help you process one or more of these standard forms without having to manually edit each document that follows that standard form. Using merge has several advantages.

Avoid Errors When merge is used, you do not need to manually edit each document in order to insert changes. Because you do not actually change the standard document, you cannot permanently delete or change its text accidentally.

Save Time Even if you don't make any mistakes, manually editing a document takes time. To change a single word, you must still scroll through the document and locate its position. With merge, the computer performs the search and change tasks for you. Merge also saves time when it comes to printing because a single command can print an entire series of forms.

Merge Operations 7

Save Space — Merge saves space on your disks by avoiding saving duplicate copies of similar documents. If the same letter is sent to 25 people, you can save one letter and a list of the specific information that is different for each person.

Mix and match — When working with lists of individuals, you can mix and match letters and lists. For example, you could send two letters — a sales letter and a follow-up letter — to the same people. In that case, you would only enter the names on the list once while producing two mailings. Or, you could create several lists and match those lists with a single letter, sending some mailings out this month and the others the next month, without having to compose another letter.

There are two ways to use merge for filling out forms.

Individual — Individual forms are usually filled out one at a time. For example, you might send a standard letter each time a potential client calls for information. The form letter is filled out in response to each call.

Mass — Mass form processing assumes that you have compiled a list of individuals who should be sent the same letter at the same time.

In this chapter you will learn how merge is used to perform both tasks.

LIST PROCESSING

By far, the most common use of merge is in the area of list processing. The technique of list processing assumes that you have a list of two or more individuals who need to receive the same document at the same time.

Merge allows you to accomplish this task with a minimum of effort by dividing the task into two separate but related documents.

337

7 Merge Operations

The first is called the shell document. The **shell document** is the basic form letter but with specific key pieces of information missing. These key pieces of information are called **fields**. You can create as many fields as you need to fill out a given document. Merge also allows you to use an information field more than once in a document. For example, the clients name might appear more than once in a letter. With the exception of the fields, a shell document can contain any of the formatting and styling commands available in WordPerfect.

The second is the list document. The **list document** contains the specific data with which each copy of the form letter will be filled out (see Figures 7.1-7.4).

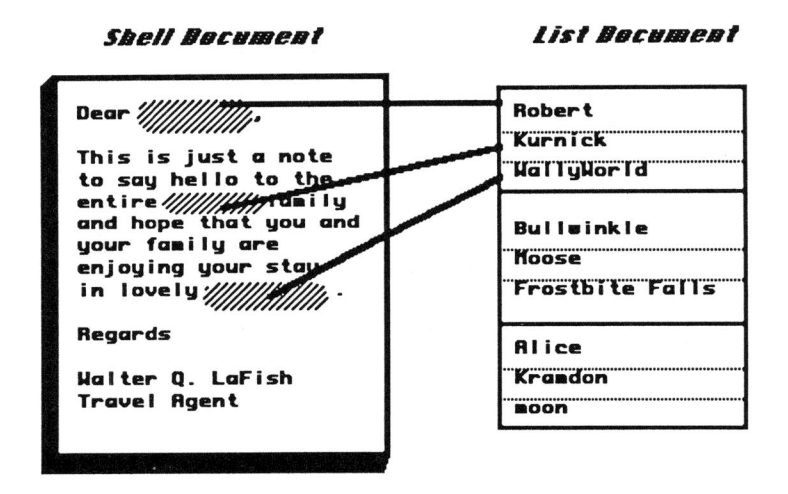

Figure 7.1

Merge Operations 7

Shell Document   *List Document*

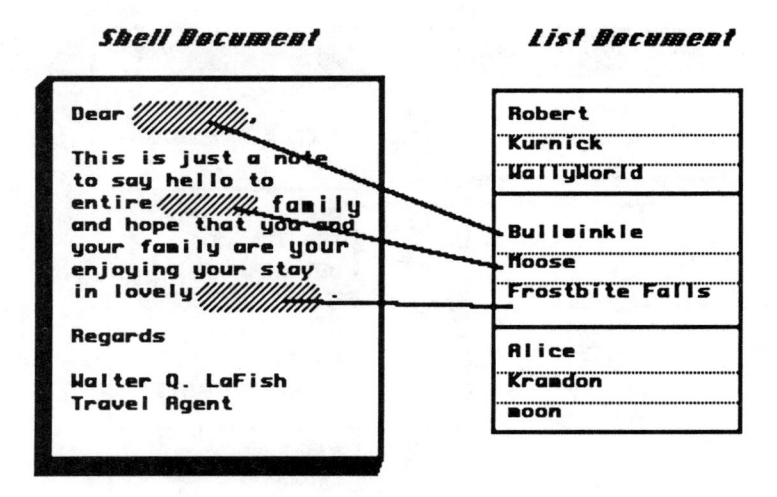

```
Dear ░░░░░,
This is just a note
to say hello to
entire ░░░░░ family
and hope that you and
your family are
your enjoying your stay
in lovely ░░░░░.

Regards

Walter Q. LaFish
Travel Agent
```

| Robert |
| Kurnick |
| WallyWorld |

| Bullwinkle |
| Moose |
| Frostbite Falls |

| Alice |
| Kramdon |
| moon |

Figure 7.2

List Document

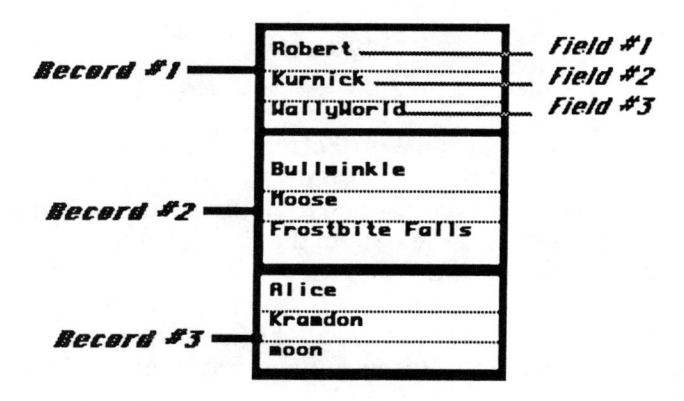

Record #1 — Robert —— *Field #1*
         Kurnick —— *Field #2*
         WallyWorld —— *Field #3*

Record #2 — Bullwinkle
         Moose
         Frostbite Falls

Record #3 — Alice
         Kramdon
         moon

Figure 7.3

7 Merge Operations

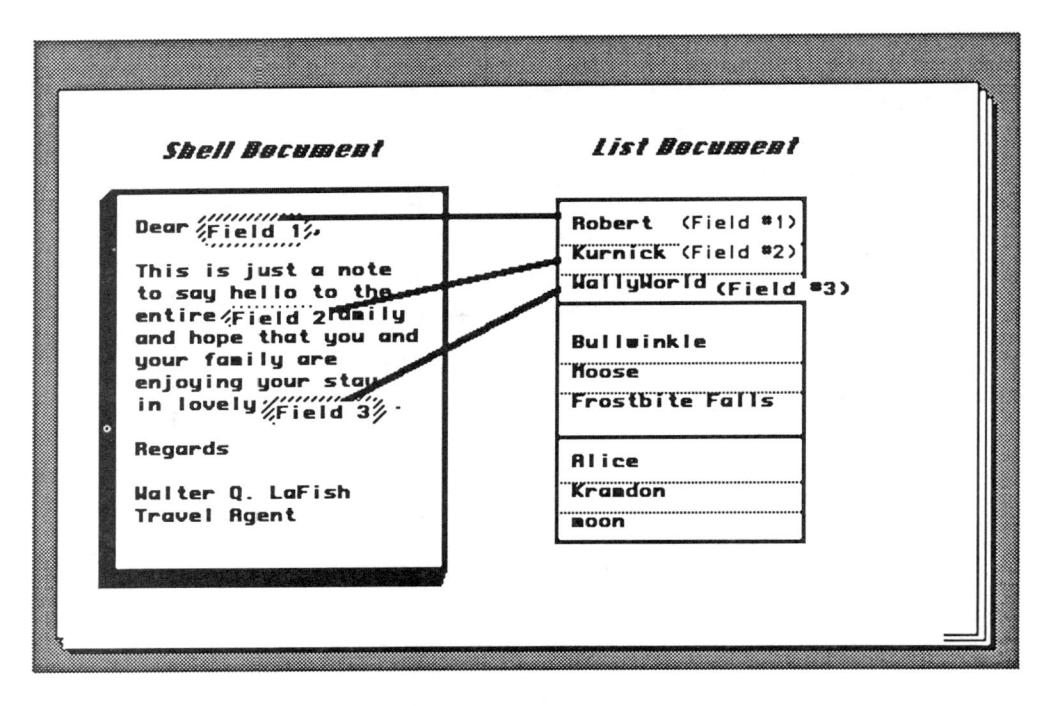

Figure 7.4

The list document is not a typical WordPerfect document. Instead of being organized in lines and paragraphs, a list document is divided into fields and records. The fields in the list document correspond to fields in the shell document. When merged, WordPerfect transfers the data in the list document into the shell letter to produce a complete document.

A **record** is a group of fields that contains all the information needed to complete one copy of the shell document. Because the goal of merge is to create multiple copies, a list document will usually contain more than one record. When the list and shell documents are merged, WordPerfect will produce one unique copy of the shell letter for each record in the list.

To learn how WordPerfect merge operates, begin by creating typical shell and list documents. It does not matter which document you create first; however, you must be sure that the number of fields required by your shell document matches exactly the number of fields in your list document.

Creating a Shell Document

A shell document is prepared in much the same manner as any other WordPerfect document. The only difference is in the insertion of field codes. These codes will tell merge where to insert the information needed to complete the letter when it is merged.

In this example, begin by creating a letterhead for the company. Center the line by entering

[Apple/Shift/c]

Because this example is a letterhead, you will probably want to select a special font. You might find it quicker to use the Format Character display instead of using the Font menu because by doing so, you can select font, point size, and style from a single menu. Select all three for the letterhead. Enter

[Apple/5]

WordPerfect displays the Format Character menu, which includes all the character attributes in a single display.

7 Merge Operations

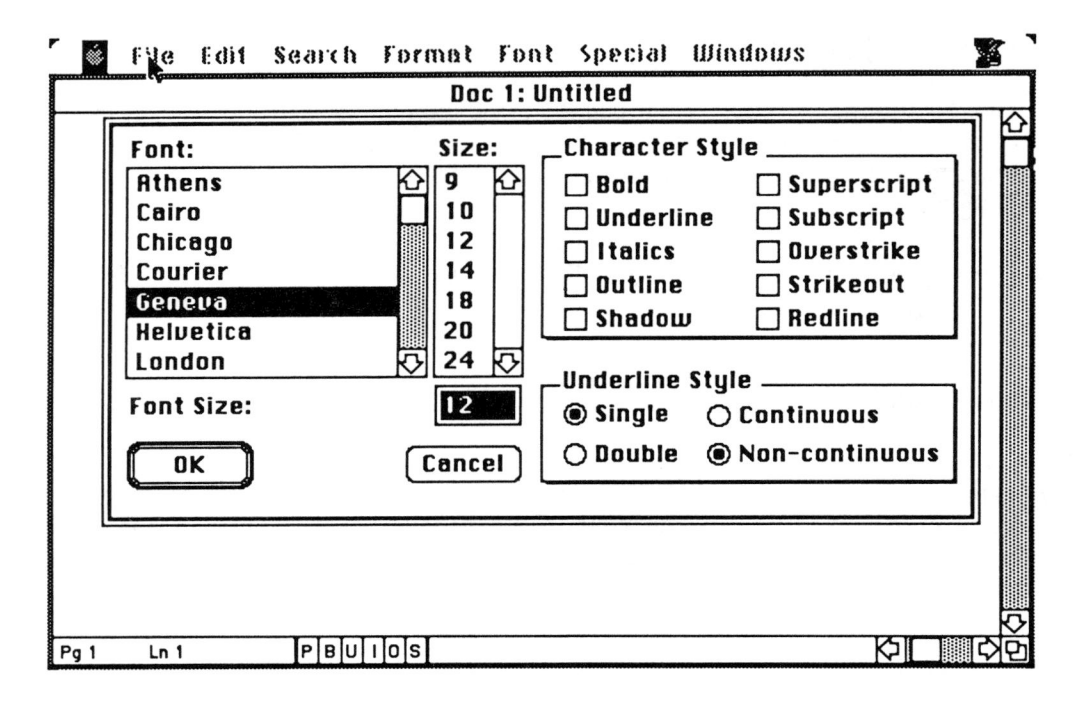

Figure 7.5

The default settings are font = Geneva, point size = 12, and style = plain. In this example, change the font to Athens, 18-point, outline, and underline. If Athens is not available on your system, choose any font you want that allows 18-point characters.

```
Point at Athens
Click
Point at Size 18
Click
Point at Outline
Click
Point at Underline
Click
Point at OK
Click
```

Merge Operations 7

Enter

VAST CONGLOMERATE, INC. [Return] [Return]

Change the font to a smaller, italicized font. Enter

[Apple/5]

> **Point** at Geneva
> **Click**
> **Point** at Size 12
> **Click**
> **Point** at Italic
> **Click**

Turn off the outline and underline printing.

> **Point** at Outline
> **Click**
> **Point** at Underline
> **Click**
> **Point** at OK
> **Click**

Enter

[Apple/Shift/c]
115 Illinois Street [Return]
[Apple/Shift/c]
Worcester, MA 01610 [Return] [Return]

343

7 Merge Operations

Change the font to normal text by clicking on the style buttons at the bottom of the display.

> **Point** at the I button
> **Click**

Insert a **date function** code into the document. The date function will change to match the current system date whenever the document is printed. If you want the date to remain as inserted, use an insert date text rather than a date code.

[Apple/Shift/c]
[Apple/Shift/d]
[Return]

The letterhead should now resemble the following:

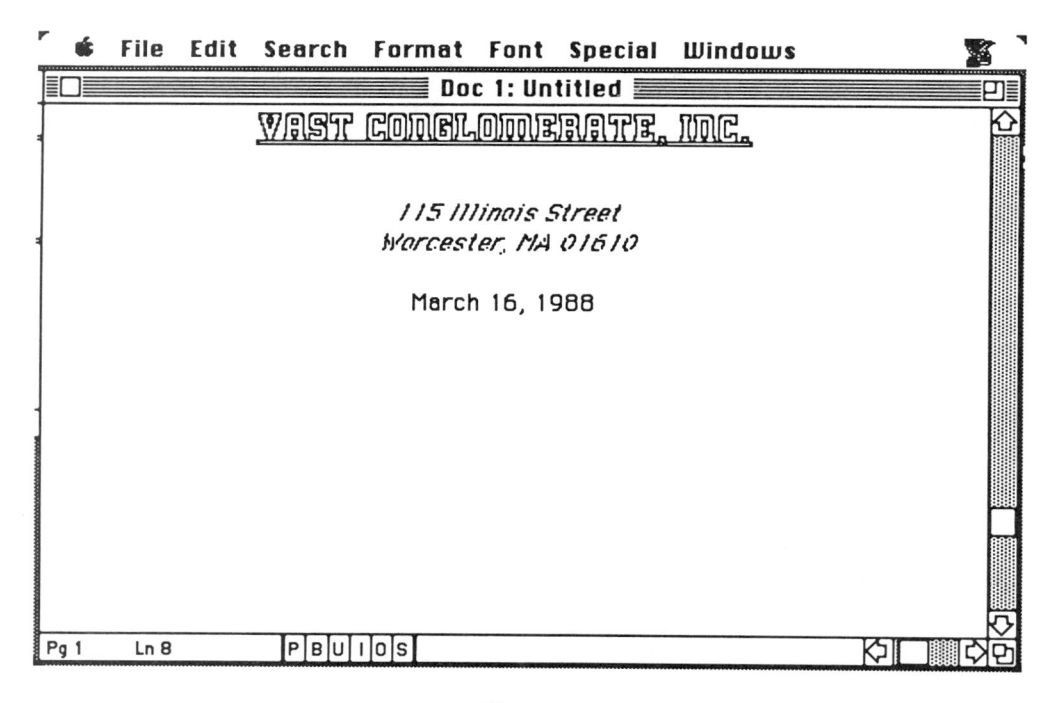

```
 File   Edit   Search   Format   Font   Special   Windows
═══════════════════ Doc 1: Untitled ═══════════════════

              VAST CONGLOMERATE, INC.

                   115 Illinois Street
                   Worcester, MA 01610

                     March 16, 1988
```

Figure 7.6

344

Merge Operations **7**

Creating Field Codes

You have now reached the section of the letter that requires data from the list document. Here, you will insert the field codes to fill out the address block of the letter.

In a shell letter, instead of typing an actual name and address, special codes are inserted called **field codes**. The codes correspond to the information in your data file. Although you have not yet created the list file, you are creating the shell letter in anticipation that you will eventually create a list file to work with it.

The merge codes are listed on the Special menu.

```
Point at Special
Drag to Merge Codes
Release
```

This menu lists 13 merge codes that you can insert into a document. The letters used in this list serve two functions. You can type the letter to select a merge code, and the code will appear in the text as a letter preceded by a ^. For example, the F code, **Retrieve Field**, would appear as ^F in the shell document. Unlike most WordPerfect codes, merge codes appear in the text as a visual aid to the process of merging. Formatting codes, on the other hand, work best when they are invisible and do not interrupt the flow of text. Enter

f

WordPerfect displays a box that asks you to enter the **merge field number** for this code. The merge field number is determined by the order in which information is entered in the list document. For example, suppose that the list document contained the following information:

Mr.
Walter
La Fish

345

7 Merge Operations

The merge field number of "Mr." would be 1 because it is the first item on the list. "Walter" would be merge field number 2, and so on. It is important to remember that if the order of the list data is different, then the merge field numbers will be different. Suppose that the list was entered in the following order:

Mr.
La Fish
Walter

In this case, "Mr." would still be field #1, but "Walter" would now be #3 because it is the third item in the list.

In the current example, the first item in the list document is the title of the person to whom the letter will be sent. Enter

1 [Return]

WordPerfect inserts ^F1^ into the document as an indication of where in the shell letter to insert the first item from the list document. Enter

[space bar]

Remember to treat the merge code exactly as if it were a real text word. If you normally leave a space following a title (e.g., "Mr."), you must leave a space following a code that will insert the person's title. Insert another field — #2 — this time.

You can display the Merge Codes menu by using the keyboard shortcut key. Enter

[Apple/8]

Merge Operations 7

Insert the field code by entering

**f
2 [Return]**

Insert a third code on this line — for the last name of the recipient.

**[space bar]
[Apple/8]
f
3 [Return]**

Complete the first line of the address block by entering

[Return]

The document should now resemble the following:

7 Merge Operations

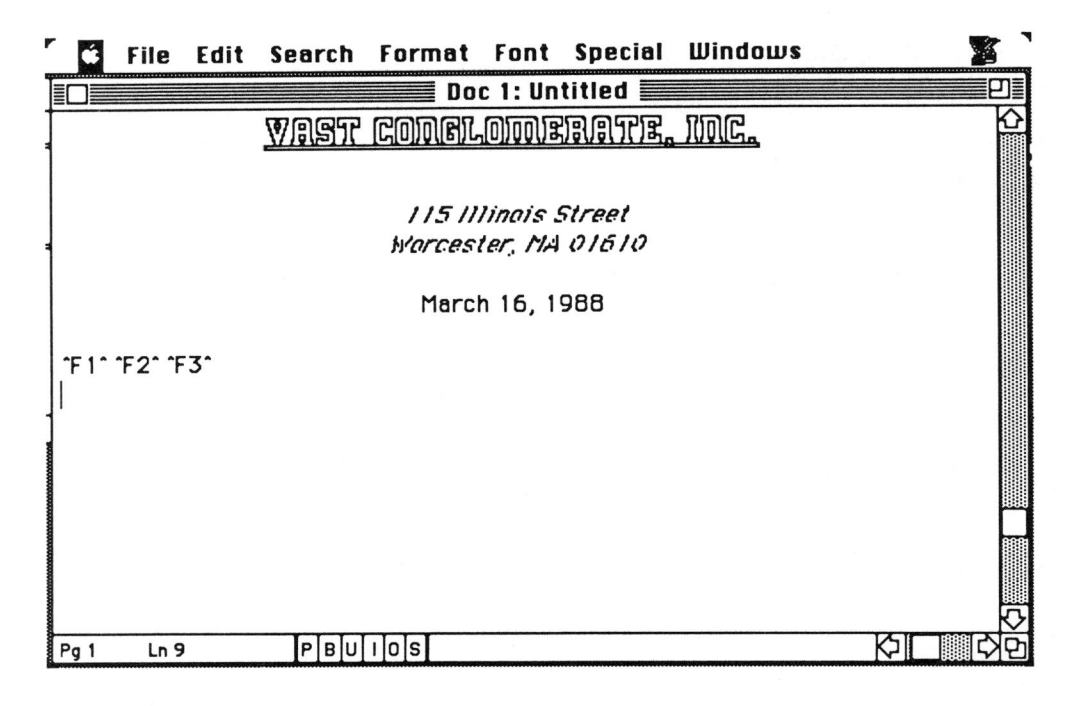

Figure 7.7

Entering Field Codes Directly

You can avoid using the menus entirely when entering merge codes by using the [Control] key in combination with the code letter. For example, the field code "F" can be entered by using the [Control/f] key combination. The [Control] key is used in the same manner as the [Apple] key to create keystroke combinations. Enter

[Control/f]

348

WordPerfect inserts ^F into the document. Remember, you must also include the number of the field, or the code is not complete. To enter the field number, you must type two characters. The first is the actual field number, and the second is the ^ character that marks the end of the field code. The ^ character is found on the upper row of the keyboard, above the number 6. Enter

4^

You have now entered a field insert code without using the menu. Because this method is the fastest, it will be used throughout this chapter; however, if you want, you can use the menu method whenever you need to enter a field code. Complete the address block by entering

[Return] [Return]

Using Fields More than Once

One of the advantages of using field code numbers is that you can use the same field several times in a single document. For example, field #1 is the person's title (e.g., "Mr." or "Ms."), and field #3 is the last name (e.g., "Smith"). In the salutation of a letter, you often use the title and the last name together (e.g., "Dear Mr. Smith"). You have already used field #1 and field #3 in the address block, but this presents no problem for WordPerfect because each field has a unique number, and WordPerfect knows to simply insert the same information a second time. Enter a salutation.

Dear
[space bar]
[Control/f]
1^
[space bar]
[Control/f]
3^
[Return] [Return]

The document should resemble the following:

7 Merge Operations

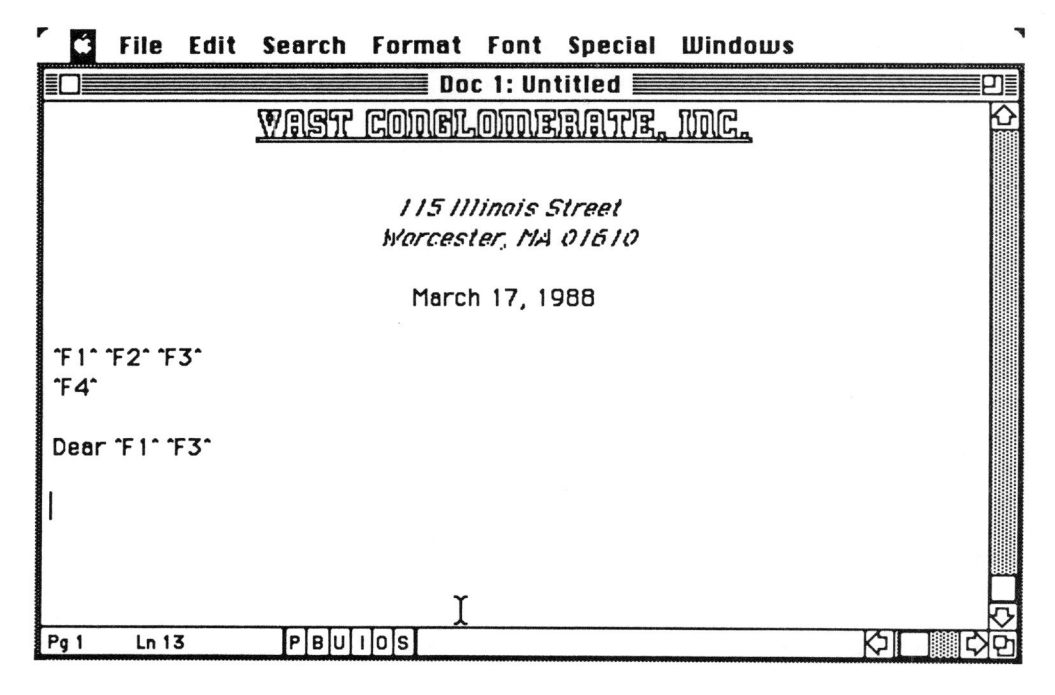

```
 File   Edit   Search   Format   Font   Special   Windows
                        Doc 1: Untitled

                    VAST CONGLOMERATE, INC.

                         115 Illinois Street
                         Worcester, MA 01610

                           March 17, 1988

   ^F1^ ^F2^ ^F3^
   ^F4^

   Dear ^F1^ ^F3^


   Pg 1    Ln 13      P B U I O S
```

Figure 7.8

Inserting Codes in Paragraphs

You can merge codes inside of paragraphs as well as on short lines. Enter the following paragraph text:

Thank you for your purchase of a new

At this point in the paragraph, you are to insert a field code representing the name of the product purchased. The product will be different for each customer receiving a form letter. Assign field #5 to the product. Enter

[space bar]
[Control/f]
5^
[space bar]

350

Now, continue entering the text:

from our

Insert another code that will be used to fill in the name of the store. Enter

[space bar]
[Control/f]
6^
[space bar]

Continue with the text entry:

subsidiary. We at Vast Conglomerate believe that you will get many years of fine service out of the

At this point, you need to insert the name of the product again. Enter

[space bar]
[Control/f]
5^
[space bar]

7 Merge Operations

Continue entering text and codes as follows:

you have purchased. You have a
[space bar]
[Control/f]
7^
[space bar]
guarantee on all parts and labor. Should anything happen to the
[space bar]
[Control/f]
5^
, bring it to our service center conveniently located in
[space bar]
[Control/f]
8^
. [Return] [Return]
We hope to see you again as a customer at
[space bar]
[Control/f]
6^
[space bar]
or any of our other fine stores. [Return] [Return]
Thanks Loads, [Return] [Return]
Walter Q. LaFish [Return]
General Manager [Return]

The document should resemble the following:

Merge Operations 7

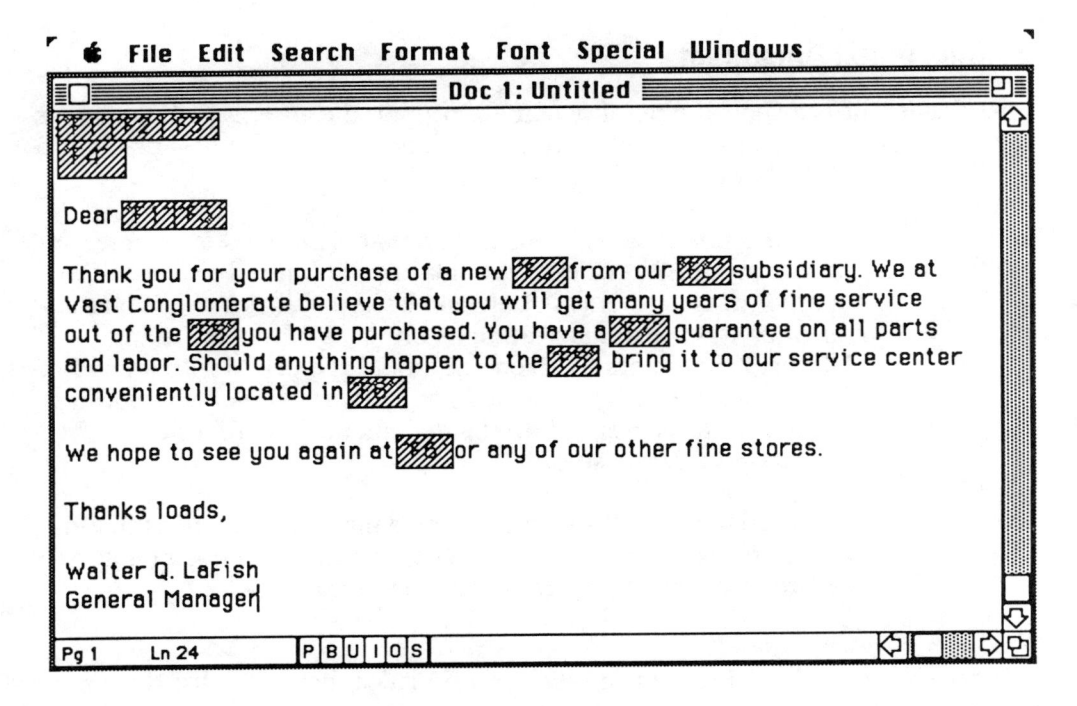

Figure 7.9

Save the document by entering

[Apple/s]
shell letter [Return]

You have completed the first part of the merge setup. The next step is to create a list document to merge with your form letter.

7 Merge Operations

Creating a List Document

A list document is a special type of document prepared expressly to be used for merge documents such as the shell letter. A list document is not organized into lines and paragraphs but into fields and records.

Field A field is one piece of information that is inserted into a merge document. In WordPerfect, fields are not limited to a specific number of characters. A field can be as small as a single character or contain several paragraphs or pages of text including [Return] characters. The end of a field is marked with an **end-of-field** code. Fields are assigned numbers based on the order in which they are entered into the document. The first field is #1, the second #2, and so on.

Record A record consists of a group of fields that make up all of the information needed to fill out one copy of the shell document. A record is marked by an **end-of-record** code.

This system of fields and records implies certain rules that every list document must follow. First, each record should list the information in the same sequence. For example, if the information in record #1 lists Title, First name, and Last name, in sequence, all the records that follow must list the fields in that order.

Second, you cannot skip a field. For example, suppose one of the people on your list does not have a title. You cannot create a record that contains only first name and last name. To preserve the correct sequence, you must enter a **blank** field for the title so that first name and last name will be in the correct position in the record.

To begin a list document, create a new document window by entering

[Apple/n]

Merge Operations **7**

WordPerfect creates a new document window, Doc 2:Untitled. You are now ready to begin entering the list data. Enter the title for the first person on the list.

Mr.

Once you have entered the text for the first field, you must insert an end-of-field code. Display the Merge Code menu by entering

[Apple/8]

The menu shows that the end-of-field code is option R. Enter

r

WordPerfect inserts ^R and moves the cursor to a new line. The ^R symbol indicates the presence of an end-of-field marker. Enter the next field.

Morris

You can mark the end of this field by using the keyboard shortcut command to inserting an end-of-field code. Enter

[Apple/Shift/r]

Enter the last name, field #3:

Finsbury [Apple/Shift/r]

355

7 Merge Operations

Fields with More than One Line

The WordPerfect merge system allows you to create fields that contain more than one line of text. For example, the street, city, state, and zip code comprise one field but must be typed on two separate lines. WordPerfect allows you to insert a [Return] in a field, which means that you can have fields with as many lines as you like. Enter

234 Whiteworm Drive [Return]
Morristown, NJ 08560 [Apple/Shift/r]

Enter the next field:

wolverine [Apple/Shift/r]

Fields with Text Attributes

Although a list document is not organized in standard lines and paragraphs, it is still a document; therefore, you can add text attributes such as italics to the information. To italicize one or more of the words in the next field, enter

The
[space bar]

Turn on Italics.

> **Point** at the I button
> **Click**

Enter

Friendly

Merge Operations **7**

Turn off italics:

```
Point at the I button
Click
```

Enter

Pet Store [Apple/Shift/r]

Now, enter another field:

5 years or 50,000 miles [Apple/Shift/r]

Ending a Record

When you enter the last field in a record the end is marked with an end-of-record marker. Enter the text of the last field:

Frostbite Falls, Minn

Instead of using [Apple/Shift/r], end-of-field, use [Apple/Shift/e], end-of-record. Enter

[Apple/Shift/e]

WordPerfect inserts ^E as the end-of-record marker. All text entered will be used to fill out the first copy of the shell letter when the documents are merged. The list document should now resemble the following:

7 Merge Operations

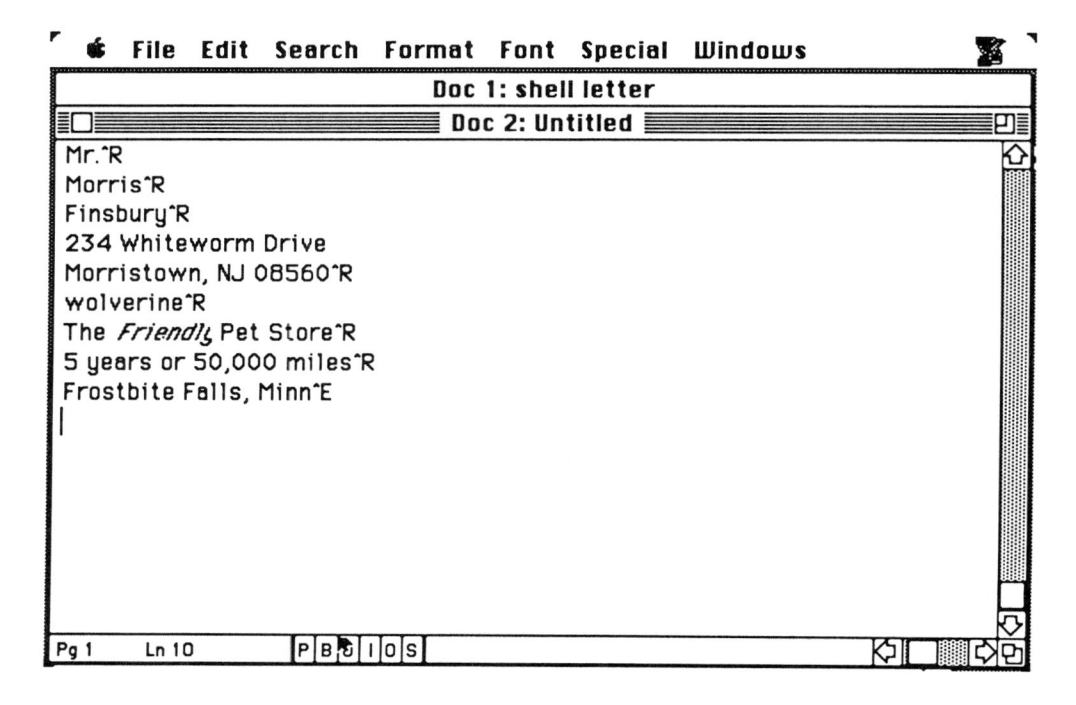

```
 ´  File  Edit  Search  Format  Font  Special  Windows
╒══════════════ Doc 1: shell letter ══════════════╕
│▣═════════════ Doc 2: Untitled ═════════════════▣│
│Mr.^R                                            │
│Morris^R                                         │
│Finsbury^R                                       │
│234 Whiteworm Drive                              │
│Morristown, NJ 08560^R                           │
│wolverine^R                                      │
│The *Friendly* Pet Store^R                       │
│5 years or 50,000 miles^R                        │
│Frostbite Falls, Minn^E                          │
│|                                                │
│Pg 1    Ln 10      P B ▓ I O S                   │
```

Figure 7.10

Add another record to the list document. Enter

Dr. [Apple/Shift/r]
Fredrick [Apple/Shift/r]
Frankenstein [Apple/Shift/r]
1 Creeping Lane [Return]
Mortbury, MA 01610[Apple/Shift/r]
large dead body [Apple/Shift/r]
Mel's Monster Supply Shop [Apple/Shift/r]
lifetime [Apple/Shift/r]
Transylvania [Apple/Shift/e]

The screen should resemble the following:

Merge Operations 7

```
     File   Edit   Search   Format   Font   Special   Windows
╔══════════════════ Doc 1: shell letter ══════════════════╗
╠══════════════════ Doc 2: Untitled ═══════════════════════╣
  Finsburg R
  234 Whiteworm Drive
  Morristown, NJ 08560^R
  wolverine^R
  The Friendly Pet Store^R
  5 years or 50,000 miles^R
  Frostbite Falls, Minn^E
  Dr.^R
  Fredrick^R
  Frankenstein^R
  1 Creeping Lane
  Mortbury, MA 01610^R
  large dead body^R
  Mel's Monster Supply Shop^R
  lifetime^R
  Transylvania^E

  Pg 1   Ln 19        P B U I O S
```

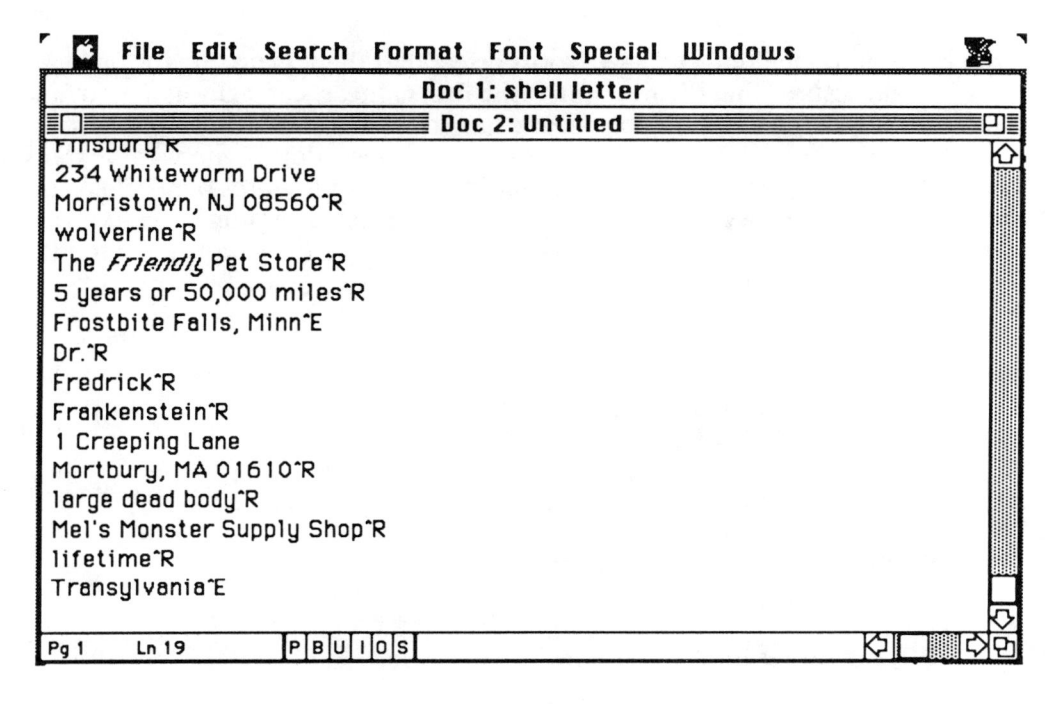

Figure 7.11

Blank Fields

Occasionally, you may need to skip one of the fields in a record because a particular form letter doesn't require information in that field. But skipping a field would play havoc with the field numbering system. For example, if the next record did not have a title (e.g., Mr.) it would be incorrect to begin with the first name instead. If you did, WordPerfect would treat the first name as field #1, the last name as field #2, and so on, placing the items out of sequence in the shell document. The solution is to enter a blank field. A **blank field** is one that consists of an end-of-field code and nothing else. Enter

[Apple/Shift/r]

359

7 Merge Operations

Entering a blank field indicates to WordPerfect that there is no text for field #1. A blank field assures that the next entry, the first name, is correctly assigned field #2. Always make sure that each record has the same number of fields even if some fields are blank. There is one exception to this rule. If you want a blank field or fields at the end of the record, you do not need to enter blank fields because the end-of-record code will cause WordPerfect to automataically insert blanks into any field numbers not assigned to text in the record. Enter the remainder of the record:

Alice N. [Apple/Shift/r]
000 Consciousness Lane [Return]
San Francisco, CA 94546 [Apple/Shift/r]
5000 *Quaaludes[Apple/Shift/r]
Happy Time Drug Store [Apple/Shift/r]
3 hour [Apple/Shift/r]
Ulan Bator, Outer Mongolia [Apple/Shift/e]

The screen should resemble the following:

```
 File   Edit   Search   Format   Font   Special   Windows
═══════════════════ Doc 1: shell letter ═══════════════════
═══════════════════ Doc 2: Untitled ═══════════════════
Frankenstein^R
1 Creeping Lane
Mortbury, MA 01610^R
large dead body^R
Mel's Monster Supply Shop^R
lifetime^R
Transylvania^E
^R
Alice N.^R
Wunderland^R
000 Consciousness Lane
San Francisco, CA 94546^R
5000 quaaludes^R
Happy Time Drug Store^R
3 hour^R
Ulan Bator, Outer Mongolia^E

Pg 1    Ln 28        P B U I O S
```

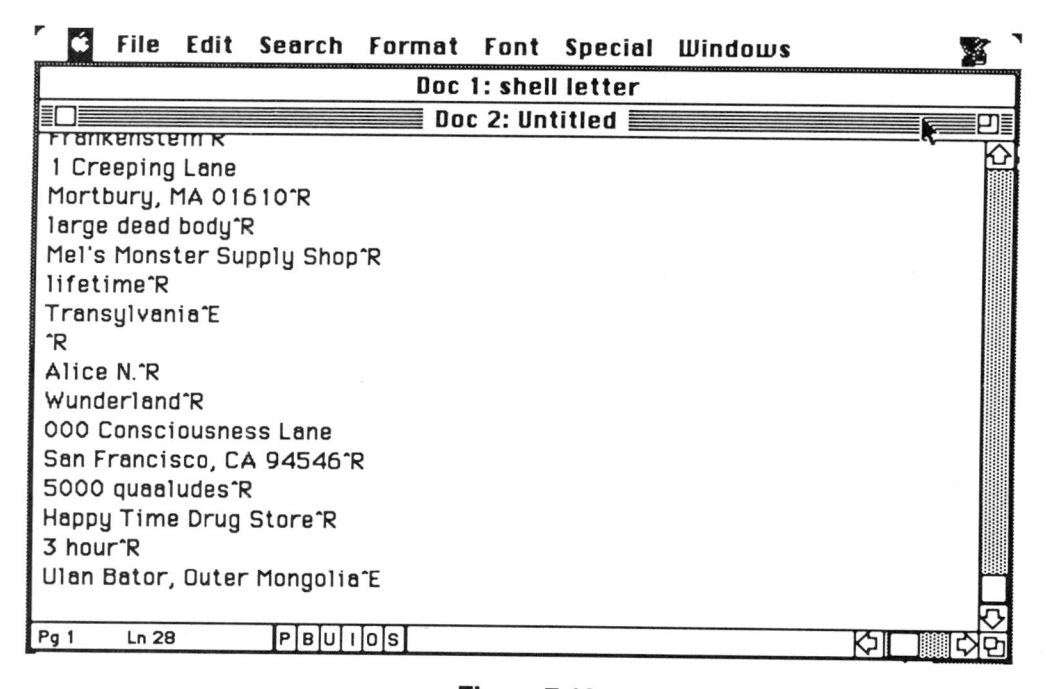

Figure 7.12

Merge Operations **7**

Be sure that you do not enter any text, even a space or [Return], following the last ^E code. Doing so tells WordPerfect that you have started another record and creates an extra copy of the shell letter for that record when you merge the documents. Save the list by entering

[Apple/s]
list document [Return]

Close both document windows by entering

[Apple/k] (2 times)

It is necessary to save both the shell and list documents before you can perform a merge operation. Open a new blank document. Enter

[Apple/n]

The merged letters will be placed in this document.

Merging Documents

When you have correctly prepared a shell document and a list document, you can perform a document **merge**. In WordPerfect, merge operations can be performed on one or two files. The current merge is a two-file merge. WordPerfect calls the shell document the **primary merge file** and the list document the **secondary merge file**.

When the primary and secondary merge files are combined, the results are stored in the active document. In this case, you will merge the results into the blank document window you have just opened.

The Merge command is found on the Special menu.

361

7 Merge Operations

> **Point** at Special
> **Drag** to Merge...
> **Release**

WordPerfect displays a file selection dialog box.

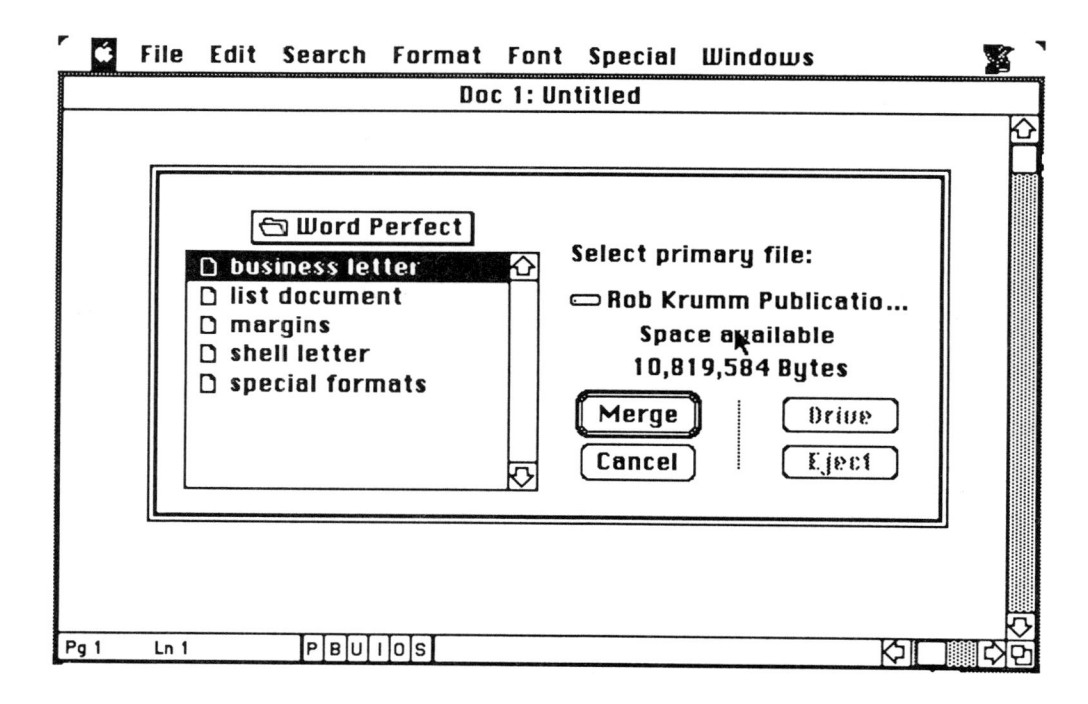

Figure 7.13

Merge Operations **7**

The file selector box on your screen may contain more documents than the one shown in Figure 7.13. In that case, you will need to scroll the files in the box, which can be accomplished in one of three ways:

- Drag the scroll bar with the mouse.

- Use the up and down arrow keys to move the highlight one document at a time.

- Type in the name of the document. Keep in mind that when you type the name of the document, WordPerfect searches for the first name that matches the characters as you type them. For example, typing the letters "REP" will cause the highlight to move to the first file on the list that begins with "REP." Pressing [Return] will select the file with the highlighted document name.

Note that the box contains the heading "Select primary file." In a shell/list merge, the primary file is always the shell document.

```
| Point at shell document
| Double Click           |
```

WordPerfect now displays a dialog box that looks very similar to the previous box. If you look at the heading carefully, you will notice that it says "Select secondary file."

363

7 Merge Operations

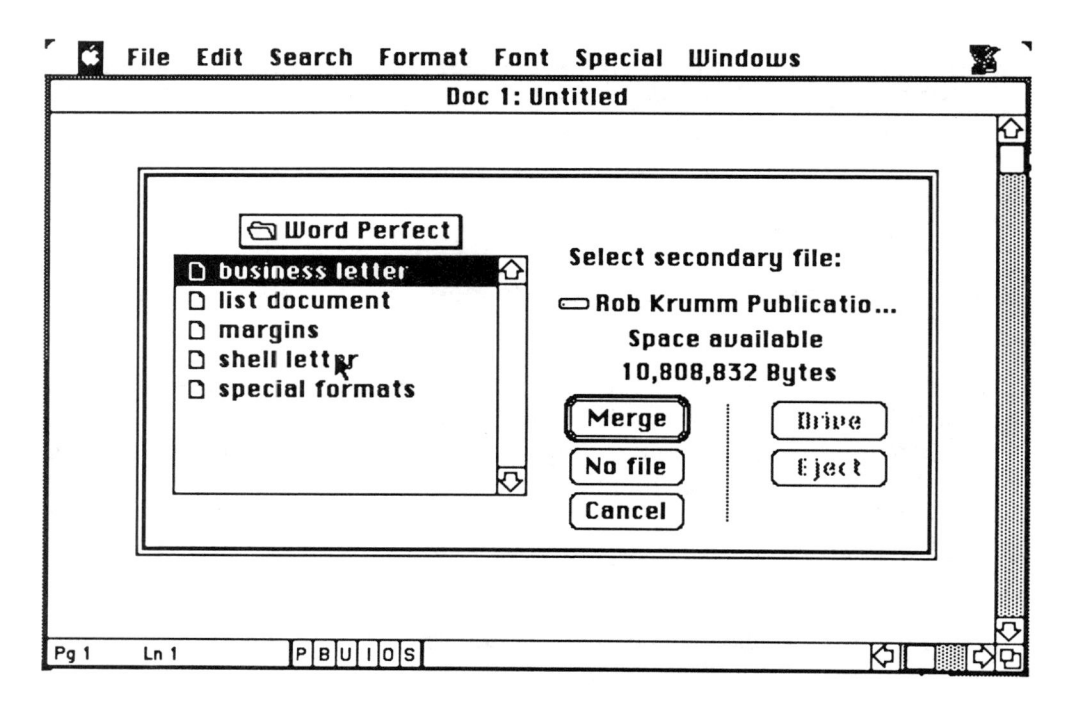

```
┌─────────────────────────────────────────────────┐
│  File  Edit  Search  Format  Font  Special  Windows │
├─────────────────────────────────────────────────┤
│                  Doc 1: Untitled                │
│                                                 │
│        ┌─ Word Perfect ─┐                       │
│        │ D business letter │  Select secondary file: │
│        │ D list document  │                     │
│        │ D margins        │  ⌾ Rob Krumm Publicatio... │
│        │ D shell letter   │  Space available    │
│        │ D special formats│  10,808,832 Bytes   │
│        │                  │   ┌ Merge ┐  ┌ Drive ┐ │
│        │                  │   ┌ No file ┐ ┌ Eject ┐ │
│        │                  │   ┌ Cancel ┐          │
│                                                 │
│ Pg 1  Ln 1    P B U I O S                       │
└─────────────────────────────────────────────────┘
```

Figure 7.14

The secondary file is the list document.

Point at list document
Double Click

WordPerfect proceeds to merge the files into a series of form letters. When this process is complete, the screen should resemble the following:

Merge Operations 7

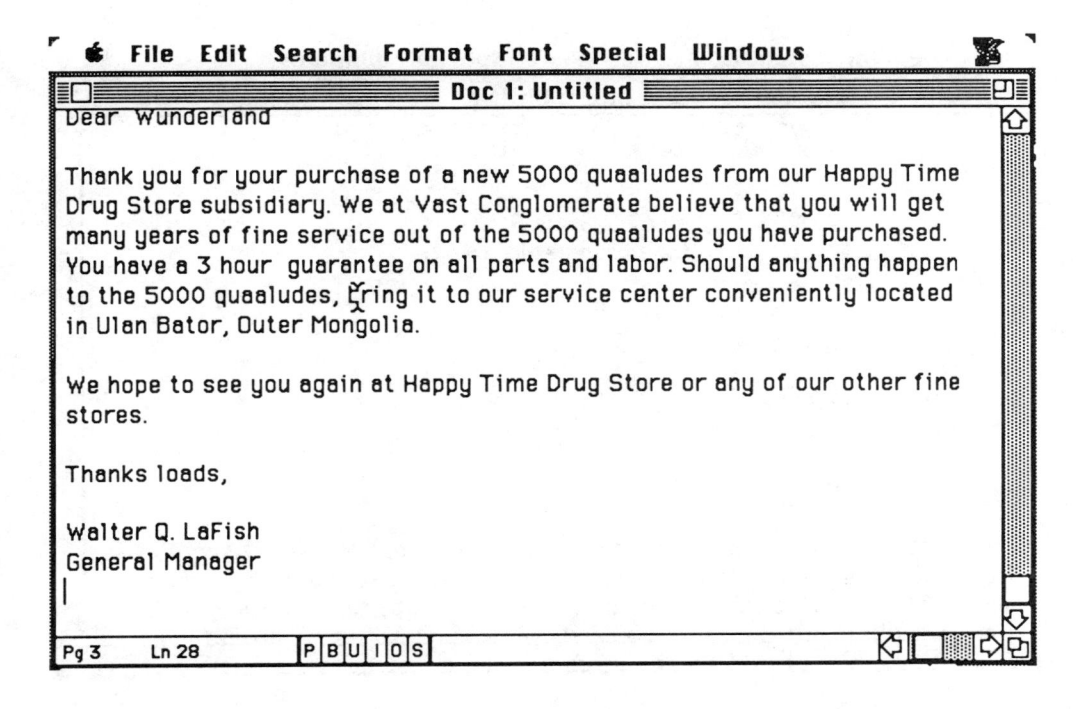

```
 File  Edit  Search  Format  Font  Special  Windows
═══════════════════ Doc 1: Untitled ═══════════════════
Dear Wunderland

Thank you for your purchase of a new 5000 quaaludes from our Happy Time
Drug Store subsidiary. We at Vast Conglomerate believe that you will get
many years of fine service out of the 5000 quaaludes you have purchased.
You have a 3 hour  guarantee on all parts and labor. Should anything happen
to the 5000 quaaludes, bring it to our service center conveniently located
in Ulan Bator, Outer Mongolia.

We hope to see you again at Happy Time Drug Store or any of our other fine
stores.

Thanks loads,

Walter Q. LaFish
General Manager

Pg 3    Ln 28       P B U I O S
```

Figure 7.15

You are looking at the end of the last letter in the merge. Move the cursor to the top of the document to review the letters in sequence. Enter

[Enter] [Enter] ↑

You see the top of the first letter. Note that the word "Friendly" appears italicized. The italics were brought over from the list document as part of the field.

7 Merge Operations

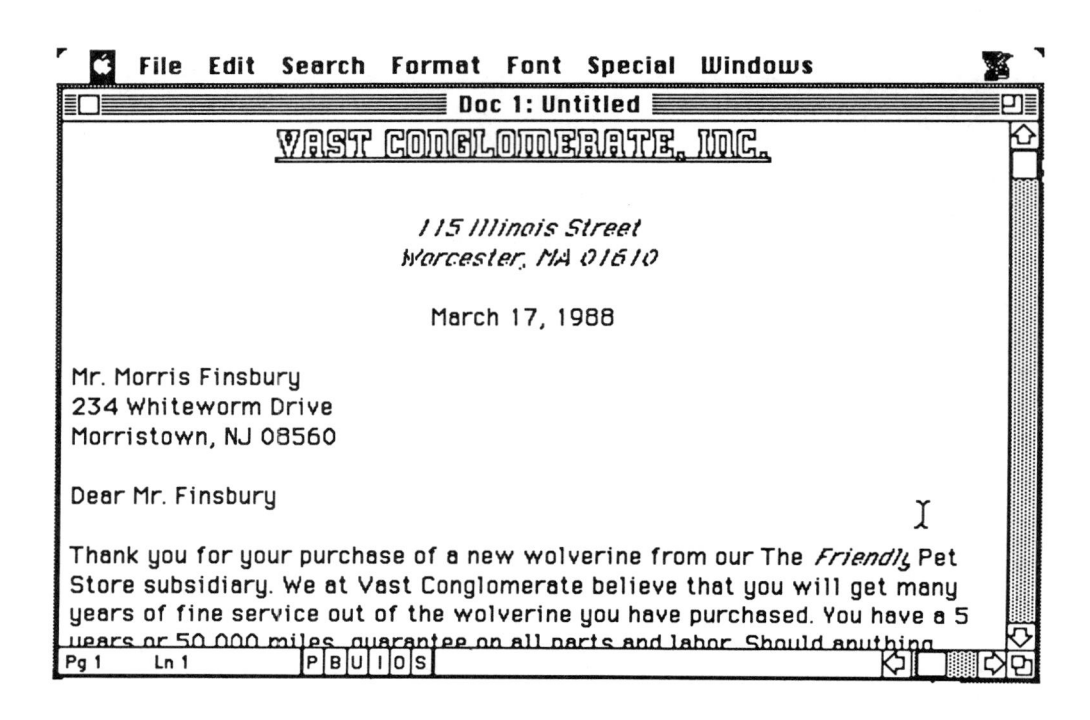

Figure 7.16

You can scroll one full screen at a time by using the [Enter]↓ combination.

[Enter]↓ (2 times)

You can now see the bottom of the first letter and the top of the second. WordPerfect automatically inserts a page end code each time an end-of-record code, ^E, is encountered in the list document. Continue to scroll through the document to make sure that all three letters have been correctly merged.

The current document contains three pages, one for each copy of the shell letter. You can now print the form letters. Enter

[Apple/p]

When the printing is complete, you have the option of saving the merged text. There is little point in saving the merged text because you can always re-create this text by merging the shell with the list again. One advantage of a shell/list merge is that it saves storage space. Saving a shell letter and a list document takes up much less space than storing the full text of all the form letters. Close the window without saving the text. Enter

[Apple/k]

```
Point at No
Click
```

Adding Attributes to the Shell Letter

Suppose that you wanted the name of the product, merge code #5, to appear as bold text in each of the form letters. In the previous section, you learned that you could set text attributes in the list document, and these attributes would be included in the final merged document, which means that you could go through the list document and add bold to all of the product items.

There is another way to attack the same problem. Instead of changing all of the items in the list document, you could add the bold attribute to the merge code ^F5^ in the shell letter, which would mean that whatever text was inserted into that code would automatically appear as bold. This method is much simpler because you need only make changes in a single place rather than search through the entire list document.

Open the shell letter document. Enter

[Apple/o]

```
Point at shell letter
Double Click
```

367

7 Merge Operations

The merge code ^F5^ appears three times in this document, so the best way to change all three is to use the replace command. Enter

[Apple/h]

To insert a merge code, you must scroll the codes list to the bottom of the bar. You will then see the [Control] letter symbols — ^C, ^D, ^E, ^F, etc. — listed.

| Point at ^F |
| Double Click |

The screen should resemble the following:

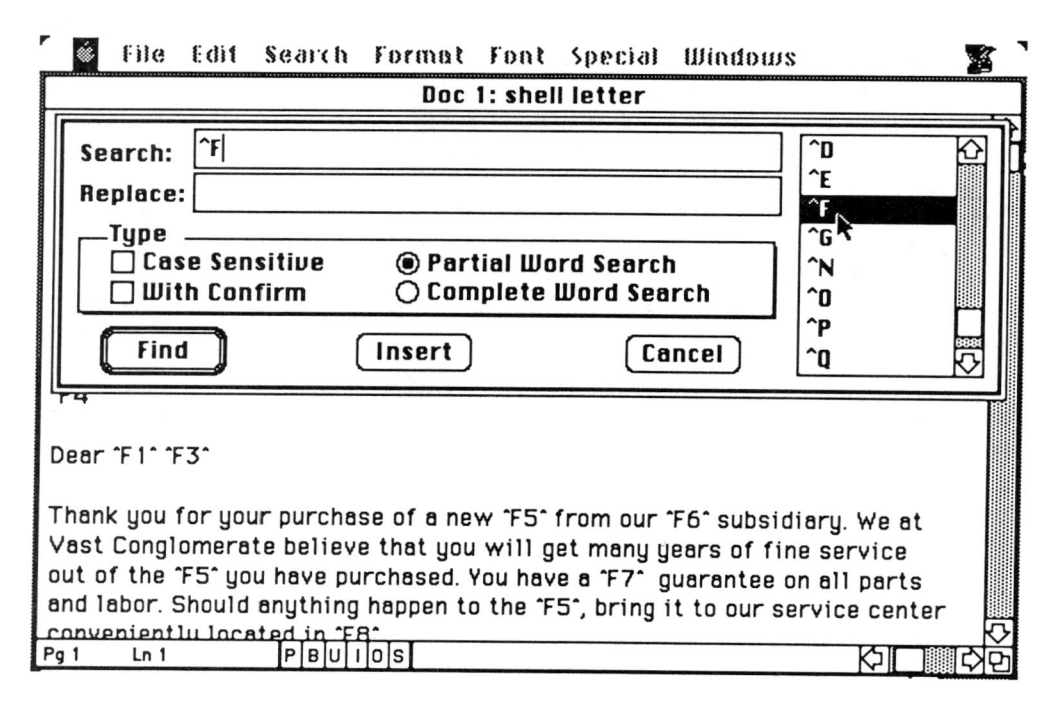

Figure 7.17

Merge Operations 7

A ^F appears in the Search box. Complete the code by entering

5^
[Tab]

To bold the text represented by the field code, you need to bracket the codes with bold codes.

| Point at [Bold |
| Double Click |

Use the scroll bar to locate the ^F code symbol again.

| Point at ^F |
| Double Click |

Enter

5^

Complete the code entry by adding an end bold code. Use the scroll bar to display the top of the codes list where the [Bold and] codes are located.

| Point at] |
| Double Click |

369

7 Merge Operations

You have now set up a replace operation that will bold all the ^F5^ codes.

Your screen should resemble the following:

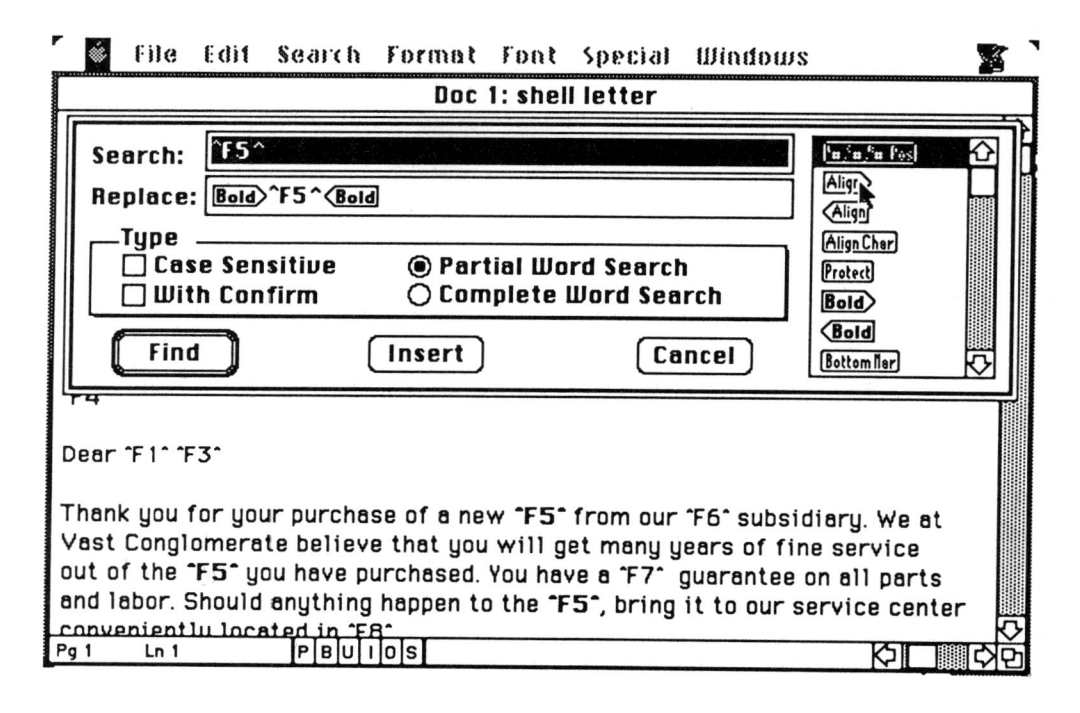

Figure 7.18

Execute the replace operation by entering

[Return]

Save the revised letter by entering

[Apple/s]
[Apple/k]
[Apple/n]

Merge Operations 7

You have saved the revised shell letter and opened a new document window into which you can re-merge the shell and list documents to test your method of adding bold to the product names in all of the letters. Perform the merge.

> **Point** at Special
> **Drag** to Merge...
> **Release**
> **Double Click** on shell letter
> **Double Click** on list document

The letter appears with all product references in bold text.

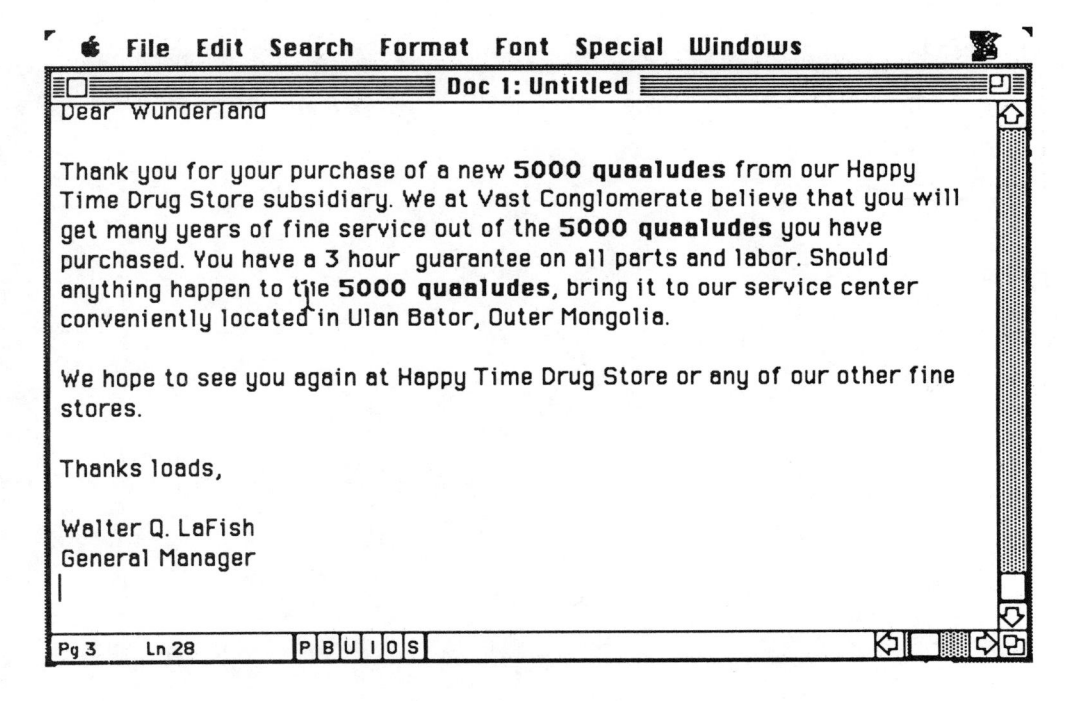

```
 File  Edit  Search  Format  Font  Special  Windows
═══════════════ Doc 1: Untitled ═══════════════
Dear Wunderland

Thank you for your purchase of a new 5000 quaaludes from our Happy
Time Drug Store subsidiary. We at Vast Conglomerate believe that you will
get many years of fine service out of the 5000 quaaludes you have
purchased. You have a 3 hour guarantee on all parts and labor. Should
anything happen to the 5000 quaaludes, bring it to our service center
conveniently located in Ulan Bator, Outer Mongolia.

We hope to see you again at Happy Time Drug Store or any of our other fine
stores.

Thanks loads,

Walter Q. LaFish
General Manager

Pg 3   Ln 28    P B U I O S
```

Figure 7.19

371

7 Merge Operations

When you format a merge code with a text attribute such as bold or italic, or if you change the font or font size, any text inserted in place of that code during a merge will take on those attributes, allowing you to create a more dramatic effect in your form letters by emphasizing key items.

You can print the revised document by entering

[Apple/p]

When the printing is complete, close the window and display an empty document screen. Enter

[Apple/k]

Point at No **Click**

Enter

[Apple/n]

Merge Operations 7

REPORTS

Previously, you learned to create a series of form letters from a single shell document and a list of data that needed to be inserted in each copy of the letter.

You can also produce a report from a list of information. A **report** is a document that places data from as many records as possible on the same page. Reports typically list information from the data file in columns, which is different from a shell letter in which WordPerfect automatically begins a new page for each record.

The key to creating a report is in finding a way to keep WordPerfect from inserting a new page after each end-of-record, ^E, marker is encountered. To see how a report is designed, imagine that you want to create a report that lists the name, product, and store for all the individuals in the list document. Here, you will create a column report. As you learned in the earlier chapters, there are two ways to place text in columns: using tab stops or a parallel column format. Both techniques can be used with merge.

Tab stops are the best choice if the text you want to insert into the columns consists of short items. If you need to insert long items, you can create a parallel column format that will automatically wrap long lines into paragraphs.

As in the first example, use the tab stop method. Limit the report to three of the eight data files. Because you are only including part of the data, you can fit each item at a tab stop. To create the tab stop you need, display the Tab Setting menu by entering

[Apple/4] 3

Clear all the existing tabs.

| **Point** at Delete |
| **Click** |

Set a tab at 3.25" and 5".

3.25

373

7 Merge Operations

```
Point at Set
Click
```

Save the new settings by entering

5

```
Point at Set
Click
```

Save the new settings by entering

[Return]

You can now enter the merge codes for the report. In the left-most column, place the last and first name. Remember that field #2 is first name and field #3 is the last name in the list document file. Enter

[Control/f]3^
, [space bar]
[Control/f]2^

Add the next two fields — #5 for the product and #6 for the store.

[Tab]
[Control/f]5^
[Tab]
[Control/f]6^
[Return]

Merge Operations 7

Get Next Record

Up to this point, the report document has been the same as the shell letter you prepared earlier in this chapter; however, the next step will change the document from a shell (one record per page) to a report (multiple records on a page). In this step, you enter a specific sequence of merge codes, using two new merge codes.

Next Record This command tells WordPerfect to move to the next record in the secondary file. By inserting this command in your document, WordPerfect is prompted to skip the routine it normally follows when the end-of-record code, ^E, is encountered. That routine includes inserting a new page code and recalling a new copy of the primary merge document. The symbol for this command is ^N.

New Primary File The New Primary file merge code tells WordPerfect to use a specified file as the new primary file. The symbol for this code, ^P, is always used in pairs. For example, ^Pletterhead^P tells WordPerfect to select the letterhead file as the primary file.

At first, the New Primary File command seems to have no purpose in this task because you have no intention of using a primary file different from the one you are working on; however, the code serves a very specific purpose. Remember that to keep WordPerfect from creating a new page after the first record is inserted, you would use a ^N merge command. But ^N actually does more than you want. It not only prohibits WordPerfect from creating a new page, but it also prevents WordPerfect from fetching another copy of the primary file. WordPerfect allows you to solve this problem by using ^P^P. The two merge codes entered without a file name tell WordPerfect to fetch another copy of the last primary document.

By entering the codes ^N^P^P into the document, you prompt WordPerfect to repeat the primary document (i.e., print another line of the report) without inserting a page break. To enter the code sequence, display the Merge Code menu by entering

[Apple/8]

375

7 Merge Operations

Insert the next record command by entering

n

Insert the new primary file codes by entering

[Apple/8] p
[Apple/8] p

The document should resemble the following:

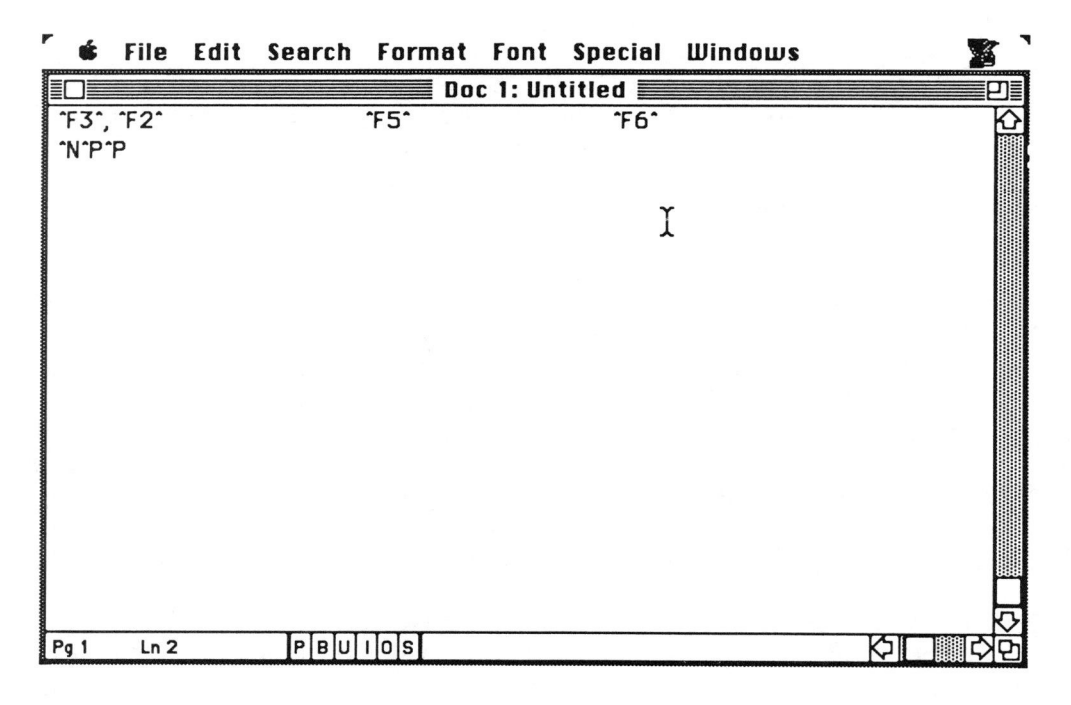

```
 File   Edit   Search   Format   Font   Special   Windows
══════════════════════ Doc 1: Untitled ══════════════════════
^F3^, ^F2^              ^F5^              ^F6^
^N^P^P




                                      I




Pg 1   Ln 2        P B U I O S
```

Figure 7.20

376

Merge Operations **7**

Save the document as "Report." Enter

[Apple/s]
report [Return]

To merge the list with the report document, close the Report file and open a new window by entering

[Apple/k]
[Apple/n]

Begin the merge process by selecting the Merge command.

> **Point** at Special
> **Drag** to Merge...
> **Release**
> **Double Click** on report
> **Double Click** on list document

The merged report appears on the screen.

377

7 Merge Operations

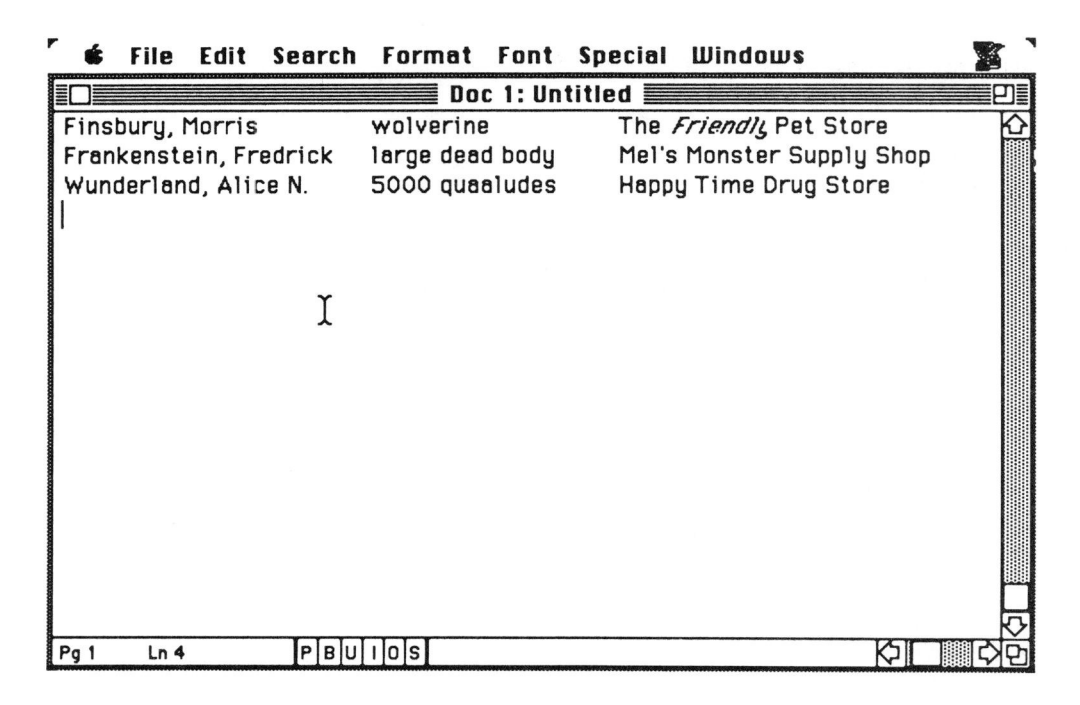

```
 File   Edit   Search   Format   Font   Special   Windows
═══════════════════════ Doc 1: Untitled ═══════════════════════
Finsbury, Morris          wolverine          The *Friendly* Pet Store
Frankenstein, Fredrick    large dead body    Mel's Monster Supply Shop
Wunderland, Alice N.      5000 quaaludes     Happy Time Drug Store
```

Figure 7.21

The report lists on the same page all the names, products, and stores from all of the records in the list document on the same page. Using the ^N^P^P code sequence prevented WordPerfect from creating separate pages for each record.

You can print the results or simply discard the text and open a new window. Enter

[Apple/k]

| **Point** at No **Click** |

Enter

[Apple/n]

378

Merge Operations **7**

Adding Record Numbers

WordPerfect can automatically number each record as it is inserted into the report by adding an automatic paragraph numbering code to the report document. Load the Report file by entering

[Apple/o]
report [Return]

Insert a paragraph number code by entering

[Apple/3]
3

Select automatic numbering.

```
Point at Auto
Click
```

The Roman numeral I appears in front of the ^F3^. Enter a blank space:

[space bar]

Save the revised file by entering

[Apple/s]
[Apple/k]

Merge the revised report.

379

7 Merge Operations

> **Point** at Special
> **Drag** to Merge...
> **Release**
> **Double Click** on report
> **Double Click** on list document

The merged document should resemble the following:

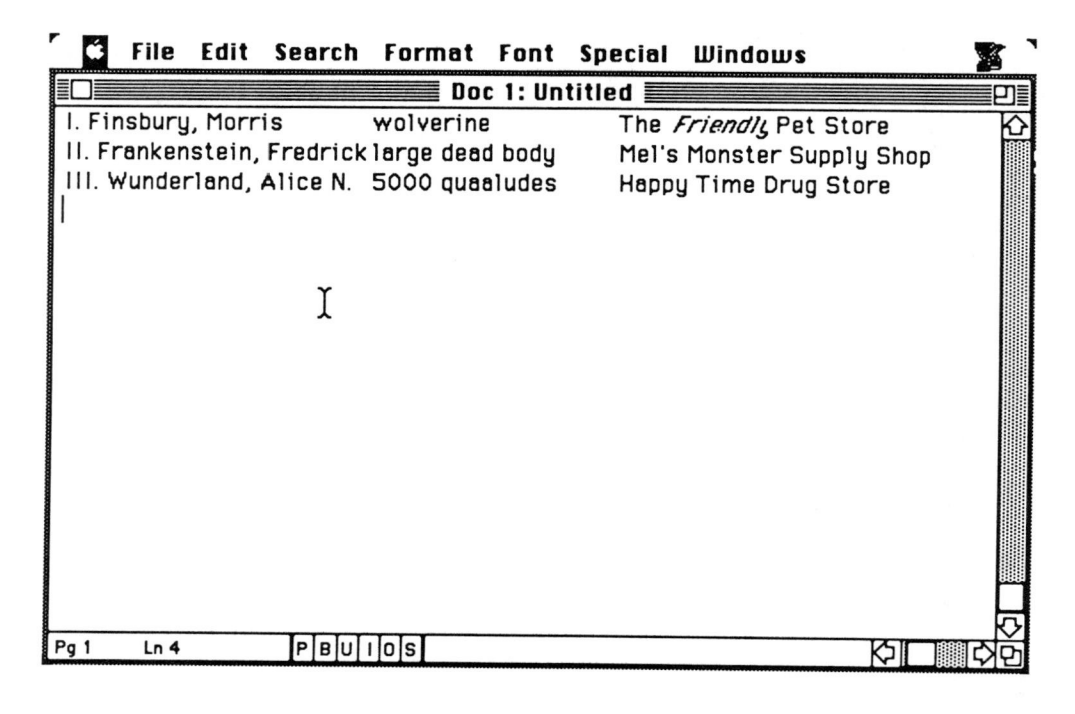

```
 File   Edit   Search   Format   Font   Special   Windows

                        Doc 1: Untitled
I. Finsbury, Morris        wolverine          The Friendly Pet Store
II. Frankenstein, Fredrick large dead body    Mel's Monster Supply Shop
III. Wunderland, Alice N.  5000 quaaludes     Happy Time Drug Store
```

Figure 7.22

Note that the numbers are Roman numerals. If you prefer to use Arabic numerals, a special macro command must be created. Chapter 8 addresses this problem in a discussion on linking macros with merge documents. You could also solve this problem by inserting a level #3 paragraph number code instead of an auto number code.

Clear the work area by entering

[Apple/k]

```
Point at No
Click
```

Enter

[Apple/n]

Parallel-Column Reports

Previously, you saw that you could create column reports with either tabs or parallel text columns. The parallel column format allows you to create a report that automatically wraps long data items into parallel paragraphs. Using this technique eliminates the need to be concerned about fitting the inserted data between tab stops. When you create the report, you do not need to know or consider the actual length of the data in the list document file.

For example, suppose you wanted to create a document that listed the names, addresses, products, and stores for all of the records in the data file. It is obvious that all of that data will not fit into short entries separated by tabs. By creating a parallel column format for four evenly spaced columns, you can generate the report without having to consider the width of the data items. Begin with a column definition. Enter

[Apple/1] 2

7 Merge Operations

Enter the options that will create four evenly spaced, parallel columns. Enter

4

> **Point** at Parallel
> **Click**
> **Click** on Evenly Spaced Columns
> **Click** on OK.

The next step is to enter the field codes into each column. Begin with the codes for the names.

[Control/f]2^
[space bar]
[Control/f]3^
[space bar]   (This extra space is added to help Wordperfect wrap the text in this column. The space marks the end of the column as the end of the word.)

Move to the next column and enter the address field, #4, by entering

[Apple/Return]
[Control/f]4^

Enter the next two fields in the next two columns:

[Apple/Return]
[Control/f]5^
[Apple/Return]
[Control/f]6^
[Apple/Return]

Merge Operations 7

The document should resemble the following:

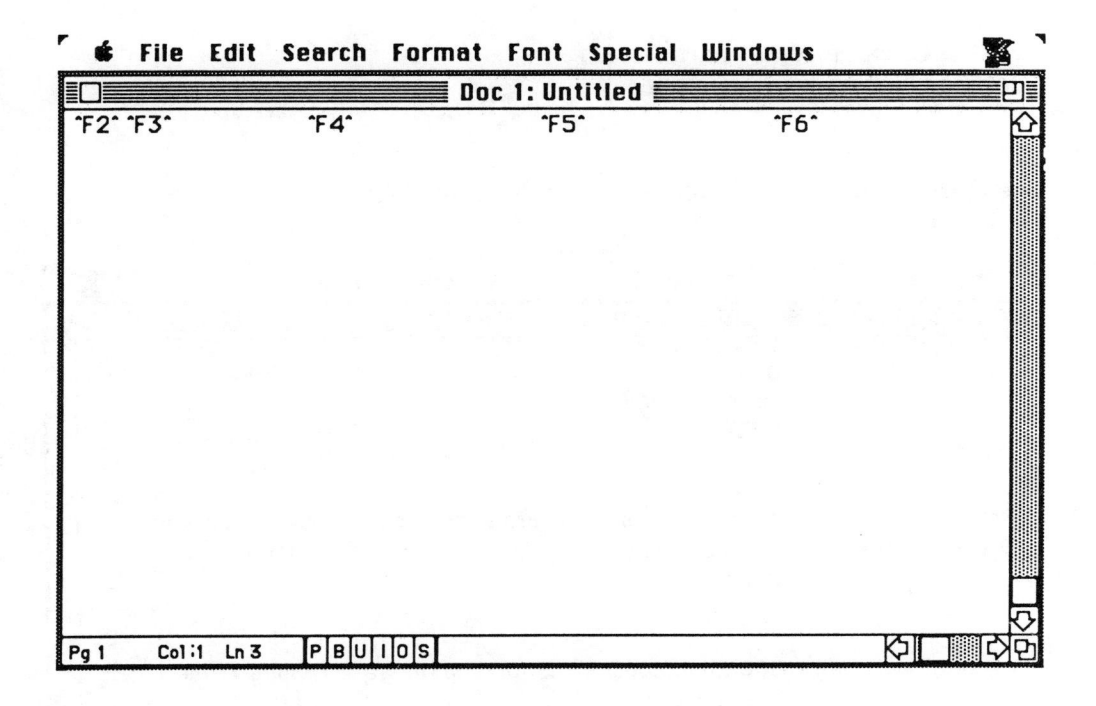

```
^F2^  ^F3^        ^F4^            ^F5^              ^F6^
```

Figure 7.23

Save this new document as "Report Parallel" by entering

[Apple/s]
report parallel [Return]
[Apple/k]
[Apple/n]

Merge the new report form.

383

7 Merge Operations

> **Point** at Special
> **Drag** to Merge...
> **Release**
> **Double Click** on report parallel
> **Double Click** on list document

The merged document should resemble the following:

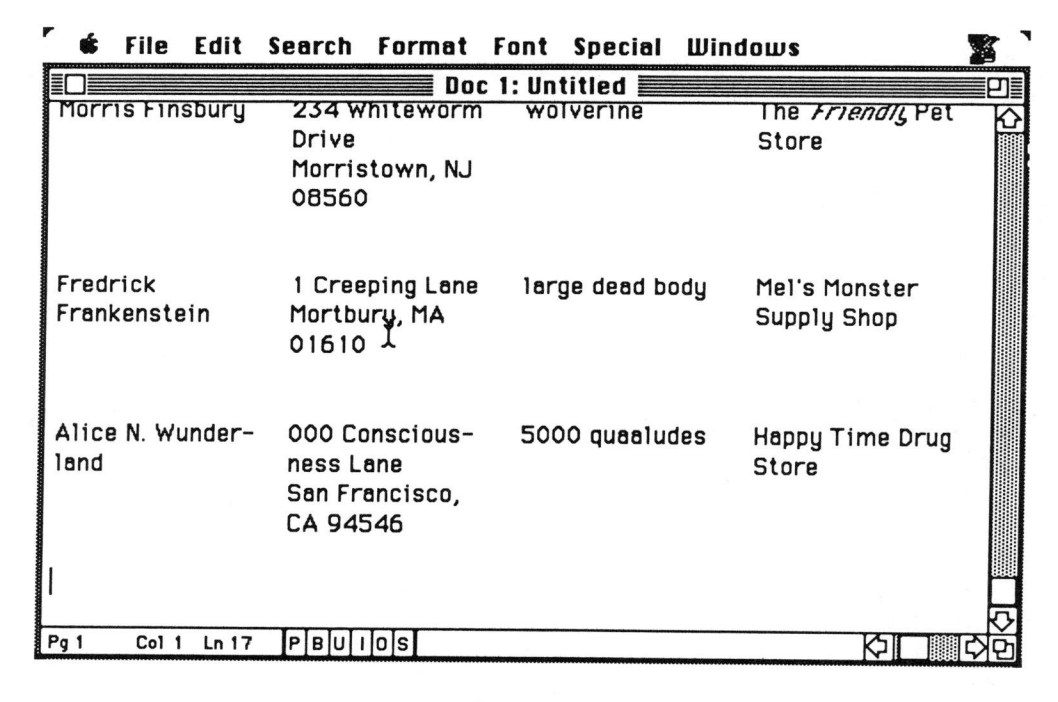

```
 File   Edit   Search   Format   Font   Special   Windows
╔════════════════════════ Doc 1: Untitled ════════════════════════╗
║ Morris Finsbury    234 Whiteworm    wolverine    The Friendly Pet
║                    Drive                         Store
║                    Morristown, NJ
║                    08560
║
║
║ Fredrick           1 Creeping Lane  large dead body  Mel's Monster
║ Frankenstein       Mortbury, MA                      Supply Shop
║                    01610
║
║
║ Alice N. Wunder-   000 Conscious-   5000 quaaludes   Happy Time Drug
║ land               ness Lane                         Store
║                    San Francisco,
║                    CA 94546
║
║ |
║ Pg 1  Col 1  Ln 17   P B U I O S
╚═════════════════════════════════════════════════════════════════╝
```

Figure 7.24

Using parallel columns makes it possible to organize and list information that would not fit between tab stops.

Return to a blank document by entering

[Apple/k]

```
Point at No
Click
```

Enter

[Apple/n]

Adding Headings to Reports

You may have noticed that the reports you created are missing two significant elements that most reports contain: column headings and page numbers.

Normally, adding a heading to a column is a simple matter of entering the text at the appropriate position above the column. But that method will not work in merging primary documents such as Report and Report Parallel because each record added causes WordPerfect to copy the entire primary document. If you include headings directly in that document, you will find that the headings repeat before each record; therefore, you must attack the problem of column headings indirectly, using **headers.**

You can insert the column headings as a page header in the primary document. This method works because it does not matter how many header codes are inserted in the document; only a single header will be printed on any given page. The merge process can copy the contents of the primary document as many times as needed and still produce only a single group of headings on each page.

7 Merge Operations

To understand this method, you will modify the Report document to include column and page headings. Load the Report document by entering

[Apple/o]
report [Return]

You can now add a header to this document that will serve as the header for the report. To make this entry easier, move the cursor to a point in the document under the control of the [Tab Set] code used to align the codes. Display the code by entering

[Apple/7]

The screen should resemble the following:

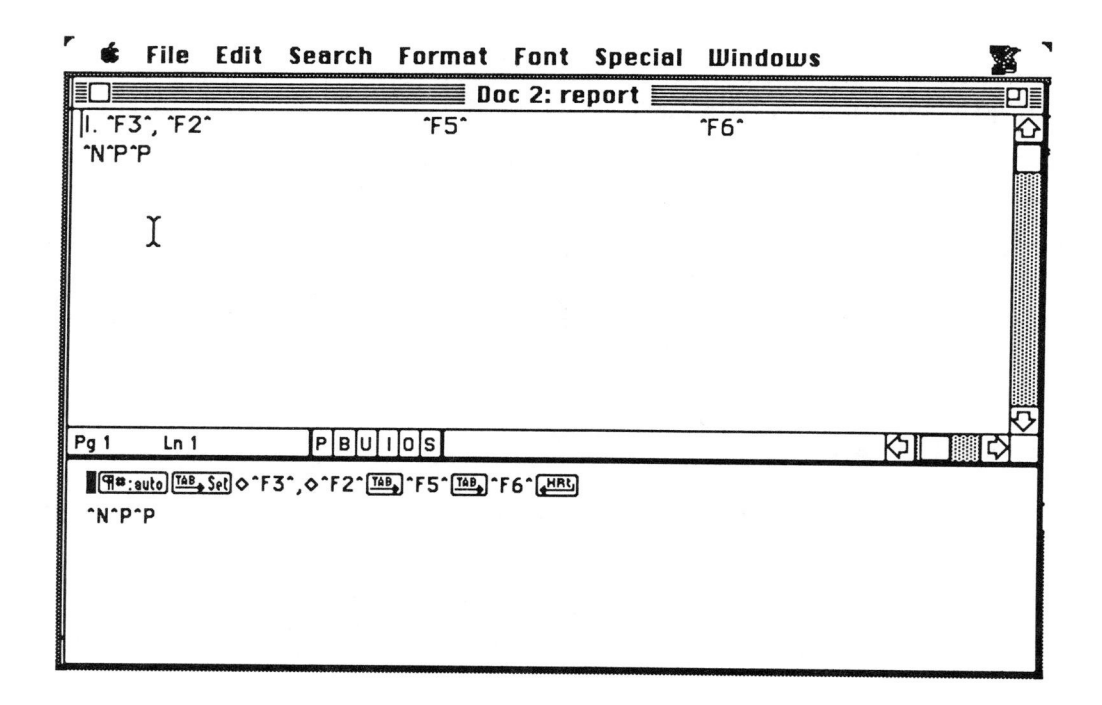

Figure 7.25

Merge Operations 7

Advance the cursor to the area of the document in which the tab set is active. Enter

→ (2 times)

The advantage of moving the cursor to this position is that when you create the header, the header will automatically contain the same tab stops as the document. This makes it easy to align the headings above the columns. To create a header, enter

[Apple/2] 4 [Return]

Note that the codes window stays open, showing the codes display for the header. Add a title for the report. Enter

[Apple/Shift/c] [Apple/Shift/b]
Customer
→
[Return] [Return]

Place a page number on the right side of the header, using the Flush Right command, [Apple/Shift/f]. To insert a page number, click on the # icon or use the keyboard equivalent, [Control/b]. Enter

[Apple/Shift/f]

```
Point at #
Click
```

Enter

[Return] [Return]

387

7 Merge Operations

Now type the headings for each column. Enter

Customer [Tab]
Product [Tab]
Subsidiary [Return]

Complete the entry by clicking on the close box or using the keyboard command [Apple/k]. Enter

[Apple/k]

The codes display shows the header definition, but the text window does not indicate where the column headings will appear on the final document, which is one of the disadvantages of the header method. Save the revised Report document by entering

[Apple/s] [Apple/k]

The screen should resemble the following:

Merge Operations **7**

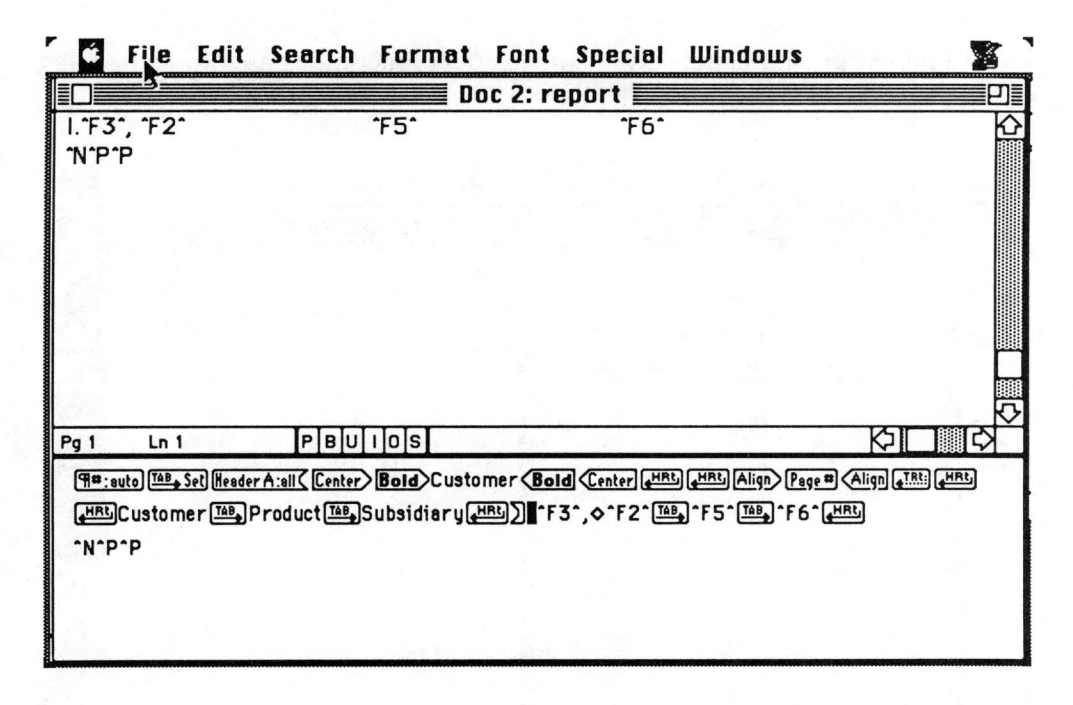

Figure 7.26

Merge the revised Report form:

> **Point** at Special
> **Drag** to Merge...
> **Release**
> **Double Click** on report
> **Double Click** on list document

Remember that the headings are inserted into this merged document as non-displayed header codes. To see the final report, you can use the print preview mode. Enter

[Apple/Shift/p]

7 Merge Operations

The print preview shows the text for the headers functioning as column headings above the records in the report.

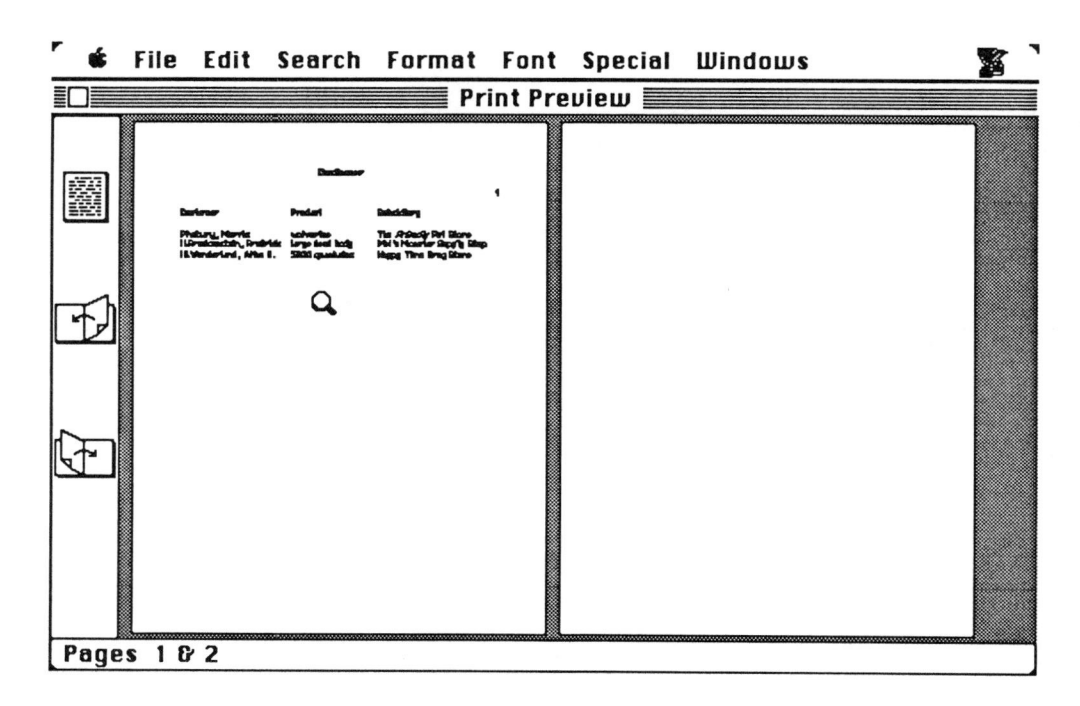

Figure 7.27

Clear the document window. Enter

[Apple/k]

> Point at No
> Click

Enter

[Apple/n]

390

FILL-IN FORMS

Another use of merge codes is to create documents that operate as fill-in forms. A fill-in form is a form letter, similar to the shell letter you prepared earlier in this chapter; however, a fill-in form does not include a list document prepared to supply the missing information. A fill-in document allows you to enter the field information from the keyboard directly into the field codes.

The advantage of fill-in forms is that you do not need to hunt through the document to add the data by editing. Instead, as the document is merged, WordPerfect automatically positions the cursor at specific locations in the text.

The fill-in method makes it much quicker to fill out forms or letters on a per need basis. As an example, you will create a simple form letter that responds to individuals who send in unsolicited resumes. A fill-in form is useful because you never know when you will receive a resume and have no way of assembling a list document.

Create a letterhead for the company. Change the font style to 12-point bold Monaco. Because you need to make several changes, you will want to use the Format Character menu. Enter

[Apple/5]

```
Point at Monaco
Click
Click on 12
Click on Bold
```

Also, select continuous double underlining.

```
Point at Continuous
Click
Click on Double
Click on OK
```

7 Merge Operations

Enter the letterhead information:

The Krummy Bakery [Return]
111 N. Pan Drive [Return]
Concord, CA 94596 [Return]

Turn off the bold type. Enter

[Apple/Shift/b]

To center all three lines with a single command, use the Select All command to highlight the text, and then use the Center command to center all the lines at once. Enter

[Apple/Shift/a] [Apple/Shift/c]

The lines are centered with a single command. Continue with the document and insert a date function. Note that a date function will change to match the current date each time this letter is merged. Enter

[Enter] [Enter] ↓
[Return]
[Apple/Shift/d]
[Return] [Return]

Inserting a Merge Pause

The key to a fill-in document is the use of a **merge pause** code. This code is listed on the merge code display as From Keyboard. This name implies that the information to be inserted in the document will be entered from the keyboard rather than drawn from some file stored on the disk. The symbol for this code is ^C.

In the current document, you have reached the point where you must insert the name and address of the person to whom the reply is being sent. To do so, you must pause the merge with a From Keyboard code. To insert this code, enter

[Apple/8]
c

WordPerfect inserts the ^C symbol into the document. When the document is merged, the cursor will jump to this position in the document, and you can enter the name and address. WordPerfect will then jump to the next merge code, if any, in the document.

You can now enter the rest of the letter:

[Return] [Return]
Dear
[space bar]

Once again you have reached a point where the text will need to be filled in from the keyboard. Enter

[Apple/8]c
[Return] [Return]

7 Merge Operations

The document should resemble the following:

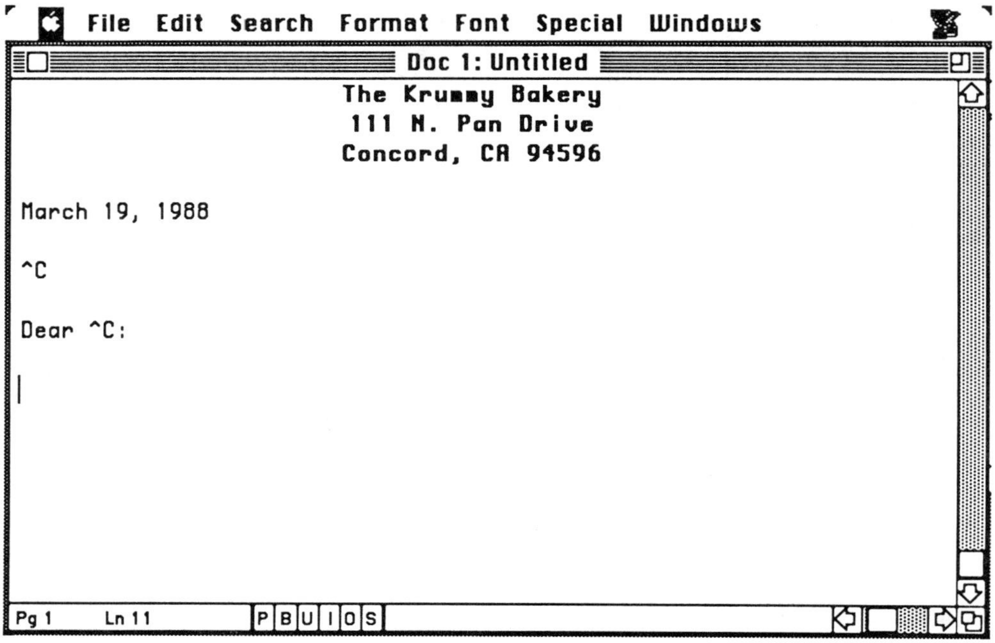

```
 File   Edit   Search   Format   Font   Special   Windows
============== Doc 1: Untitled ==============
                    The Krummy Bakery
                    111 N. Pan Drive
                    Concord, CA 94596

March 19, 1988

^C

Dear ^C:

|

Pg 1   Ln 11        P B U I O S
```

Figure 7.28

Complete the text by entering

Thank you for your interest in a position with our firm. However, at this time we do not have any openings for a

You need another keyboard entry code, here. Enter

[space bar]
[Apple/8]c

394

Merge Operations **7**

Complete the letter as follows:

**. Better luck next time. [Return] [Return]
Regards [Return] [Return]
Sally Fishbine [Return] [Return]
Personnel Director [Return]**

The document should resemble the following:

```
 File   Edit   Search   Format   Font   Special   Windows
═══════════════════════ Doc 1: Untitled ═══════════════════════
                    111 N. Pan Drive
                    Concord, CA 94596

March 19, 1988

^C

Dear ^C:

Thank you you interest in a position with our firm. However, at
this time we do not have any openings for a ^C. Better luck next
time.

Regards

Sally Fishbine
Personnel Director
|
Pg 1    Ln 19         P B U I O S
```

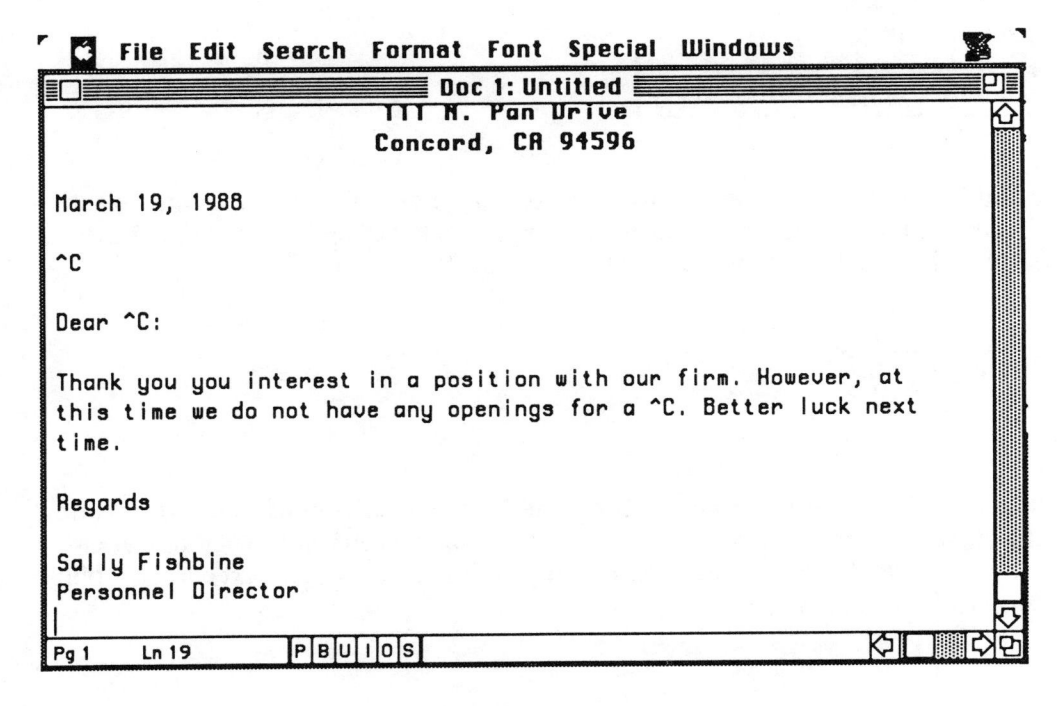

Figure 7.29

395

7 Merge Operations

Save the document. Enter

[Apple/s]
resume reply [Return]
[Apple/k] [Apple/n]

To use the Resume Reply letter, begin a merge.

```
Point at Special
Drag to Merge...
Release
Double Click on resume reply
```

A fill-in form merge does not use a secondary merge file. To skip the selection of a secondary merge file, you must double click on the No file box. Entering [Return] or clicking on OK will select the first file on the list.

```
Point at No file
Double Click
```

The text of the merge document is inserted into the current window. In addition, the cursor moves to the place in the document where you want to begin your entry. Note that the ^C does not appear at that position. Instead, the text cursor is blinking, ready for text entry.

Merge Operations 7

```
 File  Edit  Search  Format  Font  Special  Windows
                    Doc 1: Untitled
                     The Krummy Bakery
                      111 N. Pan Drive
                     Concord, CA 94596

March 19, 1988
|

Dear ^C:

Thank you you interest in a position with our firm. However, at
this time we do not have any openings for a ^C. Better luck next
time.

Regards

Sally Fishbine
Personnel Director
Pg 1    Ln 7      P B U I O S  Merge
```

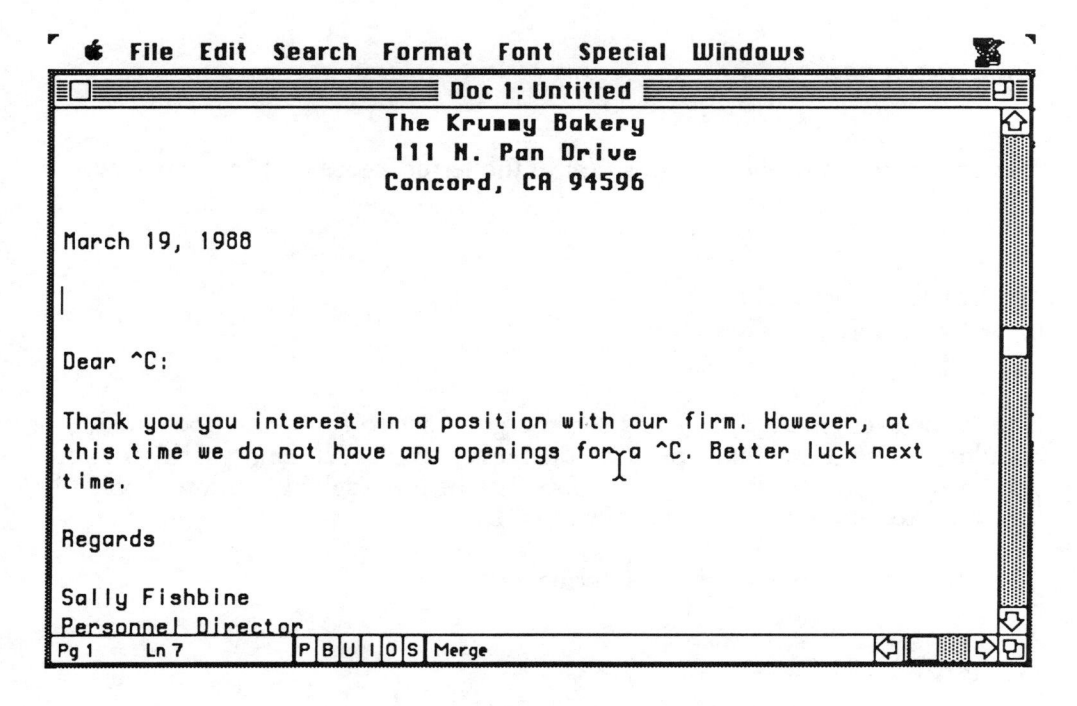

Figure 7.30

Enter the names and addresses. WordPerfect allows you to enter more than one line of text. When the merge is paused for keyboard entry, you can also edit any mistakes you make.

Terry Kamrin [Return]
41 Fishranch Road [Return]
Pleasant Hill, CA 94555

Remember, the pause is not terminated when you enter [Return]. To tell Word-Perfect that the entry is complete, you must enter an end-of-field keystroke — [Apple/Shift/r] — because WordPerfect treats the entry made at the ^C code as a field. Enter

397

7 Merge Operations

[Apple/Shift/r]

The cursor jumps to the next position in the letter where a ^C code is inserted. Enter

Mr. Kamrin [Apple/Shift/r]
Mule Skinner [Apple/Shift/r]

The letter is complete. By using the merge codes to fill in the document, you avoided having to manually position the cursor to fill each empty field. In addition, because you are working on a duplicate of the original Resume Reply file, any mistakes you make will not affect that file.

Clear the document window by entering

[Apple/k]

Point at No **Click**

Enter

[Apple/n]

AUTOMATIC PRINTING

By placing a merge code called To Printer at the end of the merge document, you can get WordPerfect to automatically print the text as part of the merge process. The code inserts a ^T symbol into the text. There are two reasons to use the To Printer merge code.

Merge Operations 7

Auto Print The Auto Print feature allows you to process a series of forms without having to manually enter the Print command. For example, when you are merging a shell letter with a list document, inserting a To Printer code at the end of the shell letter prompts each letter to print as it is merged. The advantage is that you do not need to sit in front of the computer and wait until the merge is complete just so you can manually enter the Print command.

Memory When the To Printer code is used in a merge document, it not only causes the document to be printed, but it also removes the text from the active window once it has been printed, which means that only one letter at a time is held in memory, making it possible to process a large number of form letters using a limited amount of memory.

Keep in mind that when you use the Auto Print feature, you should be fairly certain that your merge list document is correct. Creating a report document is a good way to proof your list document. Because a report places many records on a single page, it takes up much less memory for each record than a form letter.

To see an example of the To Printer command, load the Resume Reply document. Enter

[Apple/o]
resume reply [Return]

The To Printer command is usually placed at the bottom of the merge document. Placing the merge code in the middle of the document is permitted; however, it will cause WordPerfect to print only the part of the document that is entered before the ^T code. Enter

[Enter] [Enter] ↓
[Apple/8]t

7 Merge Operations

Save the revised file. Enter

[Apple/s] [Apple/k]

Merge the Resume Reply document.

> **Point** at Special
> **Drag** to Merge...
> **Release**
> **Double Click** on resume reply
> **Double Click** on No file

Enter the fill-in text as follows:

Fred Q. Jones [Return]
300 Maple Street [Return]
Maple Shade, NJ 08762 [Apple/Shift/r]
Freddy Baby [Apple/Shift/r]
lion tamer [Apple/Shift/r]

After you enter the last code, WordPerfect automatically begins printing the letter. When the printing is complete, the text of the merged letter is automatically removed from memory, and you are presented with a blank screen.

The To Printer merge code adds speed and flexibility to merge options by automatically linking merging with printing.

ASSEMBLING DOCUMENTS

Assembling documents is a method of using merge to combine text from several different files into a single document. Merge assembly can be compared to the concept of cut and paste discussed in Chapter 3. The cut and paste commands were used to compile new documents from pieces of existing text. A merge assembled document uses merge codes to combine small documents into one large document.

Documents often consist of discrete sections combined to make a single document. One part may be a letterhead section that contains the company name and address and the current date. Another section may be the closing part of a letter. In addition, sections of text such as tables or standard paragraphs can be used as existing blocks to fill out a letter.

To demonstrate this concept, you will create three simple documents and then use merge to assemble the documents in different ways.

Begin by creating a document called "Letterhead." Enter

The Computer Corporation of America [Return]
3000 Pine Street [Return]
Philadelphia, PA 19103 [Return]

Change the text attributes of this letterhead by selecting all the text. Enter

[Apple/Shift/a]

Now add the following attributes. Enter

[Apple/Shift/c]
[Apple/Shift/b]
[Apple/Shift/s]

7 Merge Operations

Save the document by entering

[Apple/s]
letterhead [Return]
[Apple/k] [Apple/n]

Create a closing you can use with most letters. Enter

Regards [Return] [Return]
Walter Q. LaFish [Return]
President [Return]

Save the closing as a document. Enter

[Apple/s]
closing [Return]
[Apple/k] [Apple/n]

The next document will be a pricing table. First, set tabs every 2". Enter

[Apple/4] 3

> **Point** at Delete
> **Click**

Enter

[Tab]
2 [Tab]
2 [Return]

402

Enter the following items.

[Tab] 1 to 3 Items
[Apple/Tab] 10%
[Apple/Tab] 5% Freight [Return]
[Tab] 5 to 10 Items
[Apple/Tab] 20%
[Apple/Tab] 3% Freight [Return]
[Tab] 10 and over
[Apple/Tab] 30%
[Apple/Tab] 2% Freight [Return]

Save this document. Enter

[Apple/s]
prices [Return]
[Apple/k] [Apple/n]

Assembling with Merge Codes

The goal of this next document is to assemble the three pieces just created, as well as some additional text, by using merge codes to automatically insert the specified text into the merging document.

The key is to use the ^P, primary document, code to tell WordPerfect which document to insert and in what order. For example, begin with your letterhead. Instead of actually retrieving the file, you can simply insert a merge instruction that will tell WordPerfect to do so automatically. Enter

[Control/p]
letterhead
[Control/p]

7 Merge Operations

Continue entering the text of the document. Enter

**[Return] [Return]
Dear Harry, [Return] [Return]
As of the first of the month we will be using the following rates. [Return] [Return]**

Next, insert the text of the table you created. Enter

**[Control/p]
prices
[Control/p]
[Return] [Return]**

Close the letter by inserting the closing text. Enter

**[Control/p]
closing
[Control/p]
[Return]**

The document should resemble the following:

Merge Operations **7**

```
┌──────────────────────────────────────────────────────────┐
│   File  Edit  Search  Format  Font  Special  Windows     │
│════════════════════ Doc 1: Untitled ═════════════════════│
│ ^Pletter head^P                                          │
│                                                          │
│ Dear Harry,                                              │
│                                                          │
│ As of the first of the month we will be using the following rates. │
│                                                          │
│ ^Pprices^P                                               │
│                                                          │
│ ^Pclosing^P                                              │
│ |                                                        │
│                                                          │
│ Pg 1   Ln 10      P B U I O S                            │
└──────────────────────────────────────────────────────────┘
```

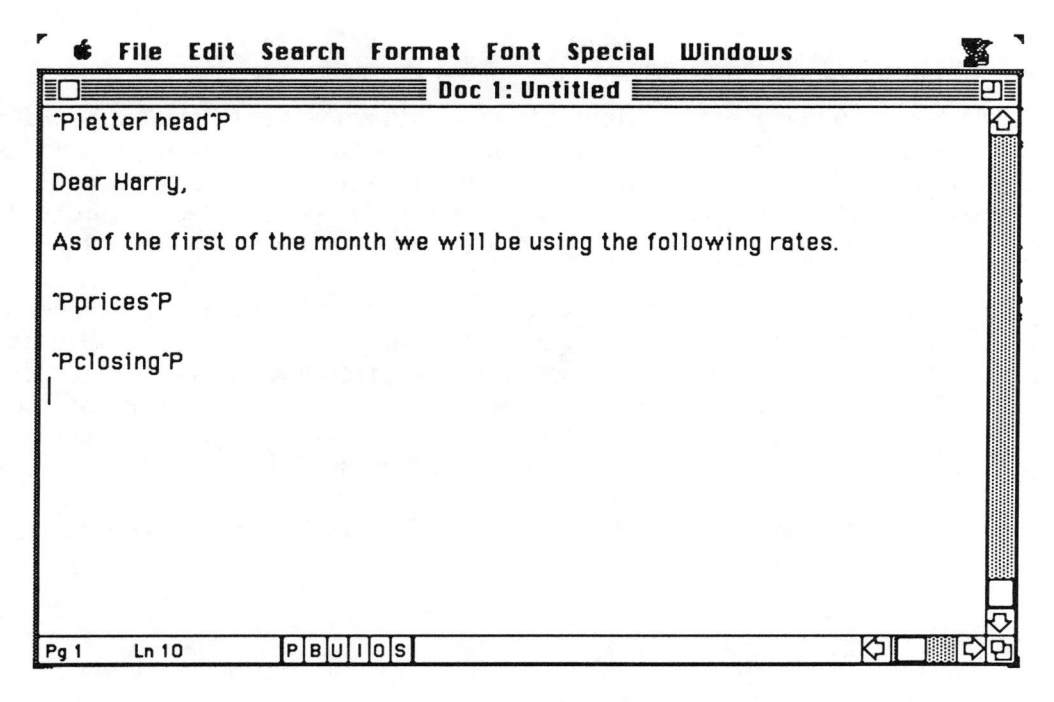

Figure 7.31

This document is a skeleton or outline of the final form. Each pair of ^P commands will be replaced with the full text of the document indicated. Keep in mind that this text will contain all of the formatting codes used in creating the smaller documents it contains. All the font, tab, and margin changes entered in the smaller documents will be inserted into the assembled document. Merge cannot operate on a document that has not been saved, so you must save the assembly document. Enter

[Apple/s]
assembly [Return]
[Apple/k] [Apple/n]

405

7 Merge Operations

Selecting the Work Folder

The assembly document is different from the others you have created because you included in it an instruction that requires WordPerfect to locate and load a specific file. All the other loading operations you performed so far have required you to manually select or type in the name of the file. WordPerfect automatically displayed the default file folder listing each time you wanted to load a file.

In assembly merge operations, WordPerfect will attempt to find the documents automatically, without your assistance. You might assume that WordPerfect looks in the same file folder it displays when you enter a File Open or Merge command, but that is not necessarily the case. When a ^P command specifically includes a file name, WordPerfect searches in the work folder for that document. WordPerfect stores a list of the names of folders in the WP Default file.

You can display and alter those settings using the File WP Defaults command.

```
Point at File
Drag to WP Defaults
Release
```

WordPerfect lists five default options, which are discussed in more detail in Chapter 10. The option you are concerned with is #4, default folders. Enter

4

WordPerfect displays a list of the four locations for which specific folder names can be entered.

406

Merge Operations **7**

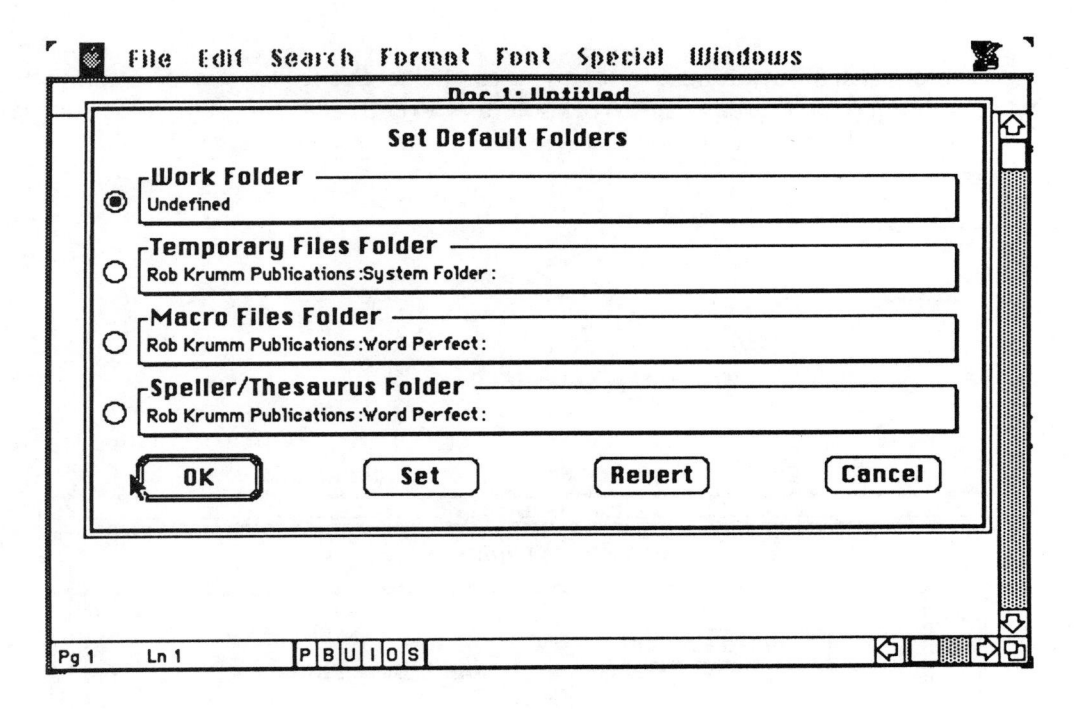

Figure 7.32

Work Folder	This is the folder that WordPerfect uses to locate documents automatically in cases such as ^P codes, which require a specific file to be located.
Temporary	This folder tells WordPerfect where to create temporary files that are used for operations such as automatic backups or memory overflow files. In most cases you are not concerned with these files. The default is to use the Apple SYSTEMS folder.
Macros	This folder determines the location of macro files. The original setting is the WordPerfect folder. You may want to select a separate folder for your macro files so you they won't be mixed up with your documents.
Speller/Thesaurus	This folder determines the location of the speller and thesaurus files. The usual location for these files is in the WordPerfect folder.

407

7 Merge Operations

Each folder has a button next to it so you can select the folder specification you want to change. In this case, the Work folder is already selected. The folder does not currently have a definition. Use the Set option to select a specific folder.

```
Point at Set
Click
```

WordPerfect displays a file/folder selection box.

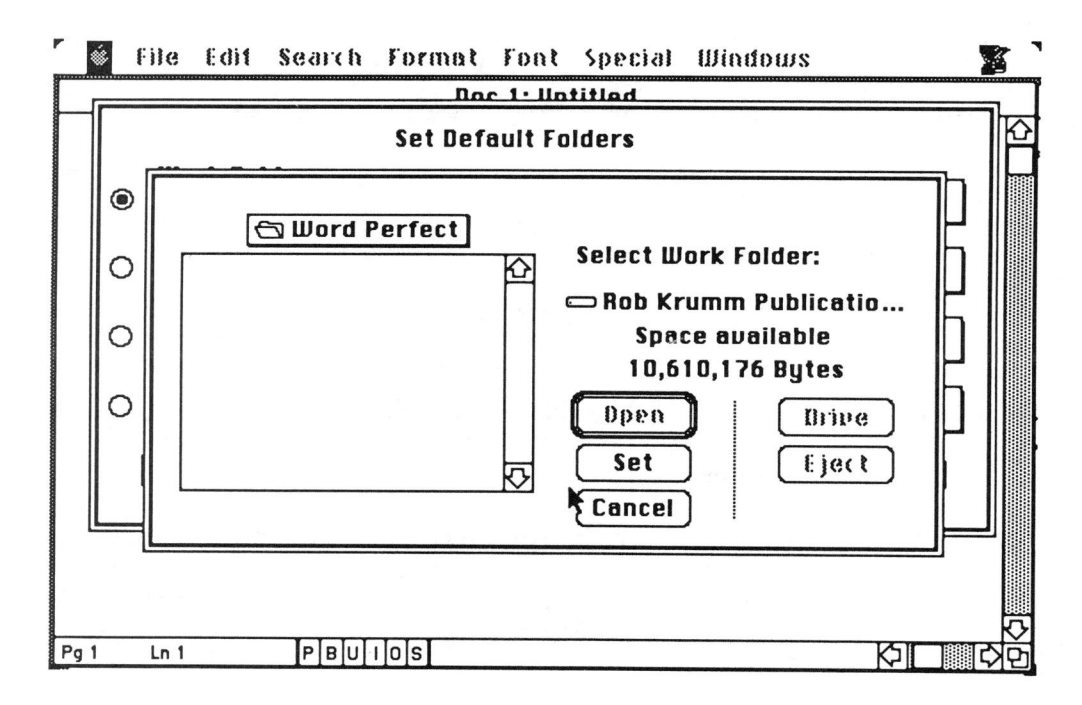

Figure 7.33

The WordPerfect folder is listed at the top of the display because this is the folder you have been working in most recently. If you want to use a different folder, you can use the mouse to navigate to the folder or drive you need. For now, you can set WordPerfect as the Work folder by clicking on the Set option.

Merge Operations 7

    Point at Set
    Click

The menu now shows that WordPerfect has been selected at the Work folder.

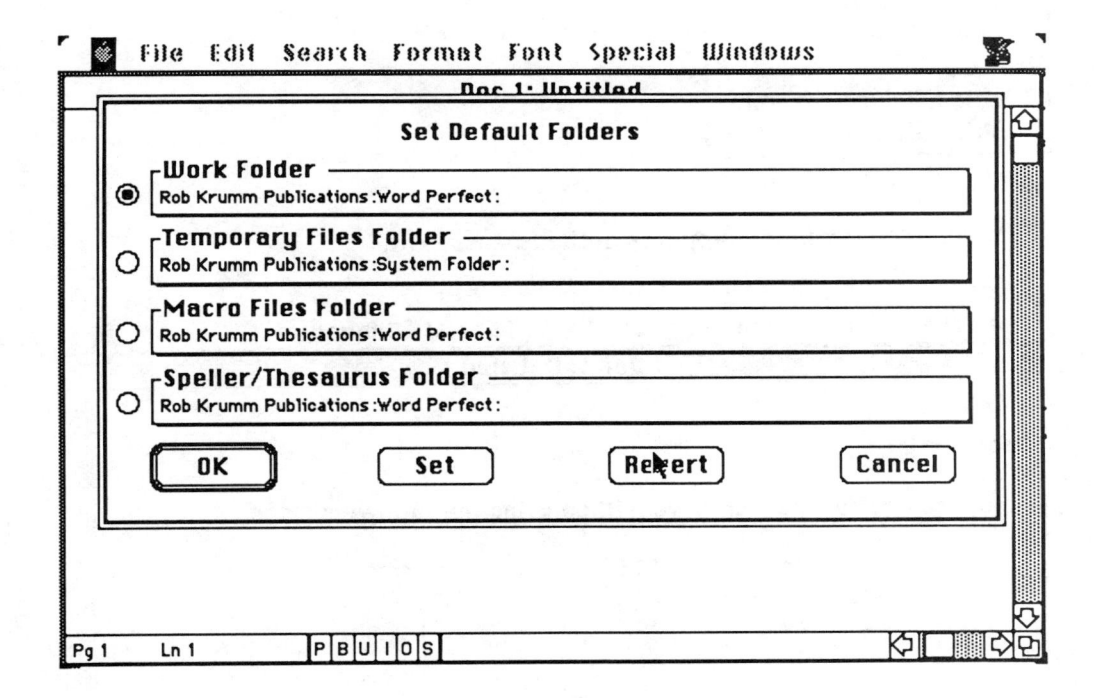

Figure 7.34

    Point at OK
    Click

Your screen should show the document window display.

If you want WordPerfect to default to the folder selections each time you load WordPerfect, you must return to the WP Defaults menu and select option #1, Save Settings; otherwise, the folder options will return to their original settings the next time you run WordPerfect.

7 Merge Operations

Merge Assembly

Now that you have set up the necessary conditions, you can get WordPerfect to complete the job by using merge to assemble the items into a single document.

> **Point** at Special
> **Drag** to Merge...
> **Release**
> **Double Click** on assembly
> **Double Click** on No file

The assembled document appears in the text window.

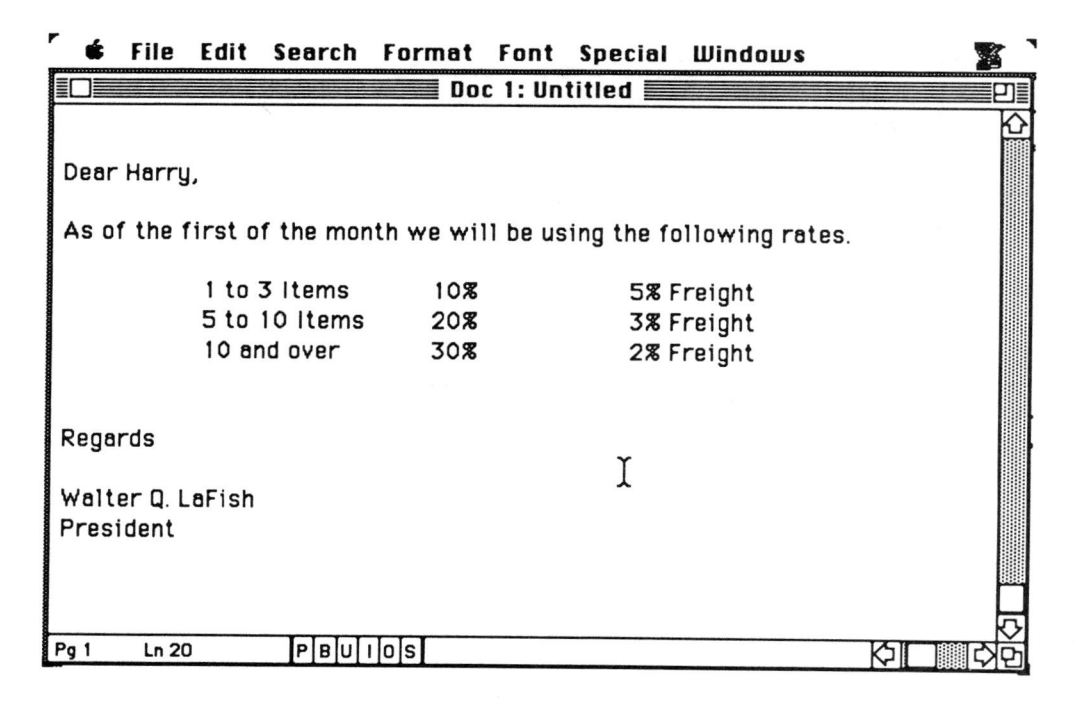

Figure 7.35

Merge Operations **7**

Move to the top of the document to inspect the letterhead portion. Enter

[Enter] [Enter] ↑

You can see that the letterhead section, including its settings, has been correctly transferred.

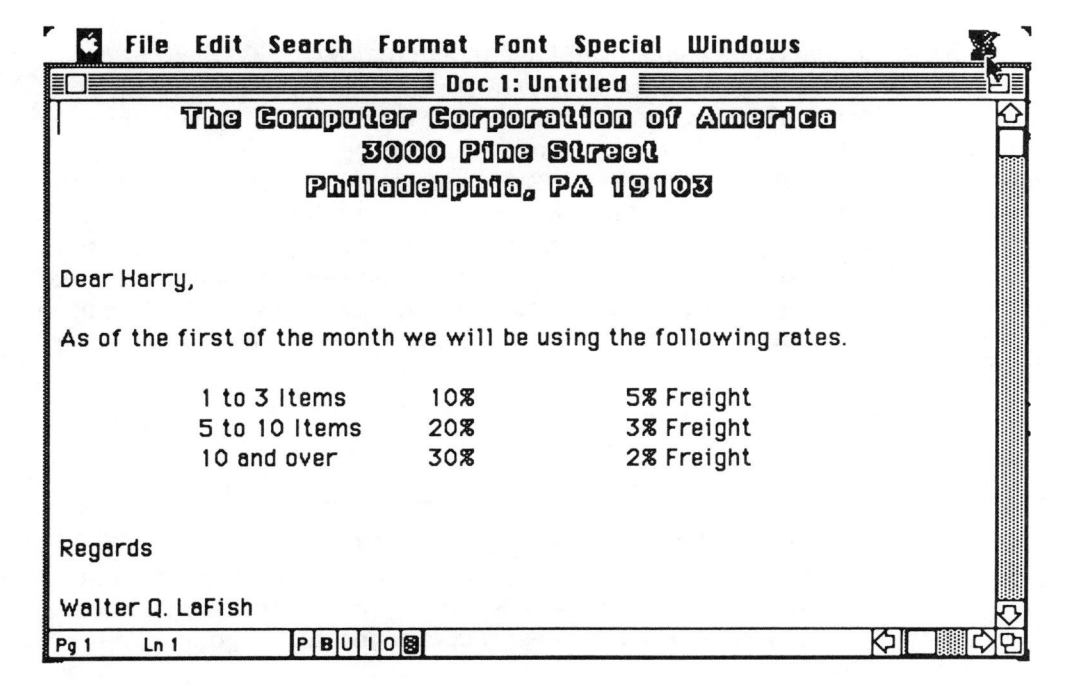

```
┌─────────────────────────────────────────────────────┐
│  File  Edit  Search  Format  Font  Special  Windows │
├─────────────────────────────────────────────────────┤
│                  Doc 1: Untitled                    │
│         The Computer Corporation of America         │
│                    3000 Pine Street                 │
│                  Philadelphia, PA 19103             │
│                                                     │
│   Dear Harry,                                       │
│                                                     │
│   As of the first of the month we will be using the following rates. │
│                                                     │
│           1 to 3 Items      10%      5% Freight     │
│           5 to 10 Items     20%      3% Freight     │
│           10 and over       30%      2% Freight     │
│                                                     │
│   Regards                                           │
│                                                     │
│   Walter Q. LaFish                                  │
└─────────────────────────────────────────────────────┘
```

Figure 7.36

You can now print the document. Clear the work area by entering

[Apple/k]

411

7 Merge Operations

| Point at No |
| Click |

Enter

[Apple/n]

Assembly documents can be very useful if you tend to use specific sections of text in a variety of documents. Using assembly rather than cut and paste in such situations has a number of advantages. It is a quicker method because you need not cut and paste the text each time you want to use those sections. Instead, you simply insert a reference to the text you want to insert. Furthermore, the assembly document is more compact because it is more like an outline of the final document than a full document, which means you are making more efficient use of your disk space if you do not need to save redundant copies of text items. For example, the letterhead file needs only to be stored once on the disk and can be used in any number of documents if you insert the code ^Pletter head^P in the appropriate place.

SUMMARY

Merge operations in WordPerfect can help you perform a number of tasks. The purpose of merge operations is to use merge commands to create new documents by relating stored text to text that is either stored or entered from the keyboard, which is in contrast to the normal editing procedure in which all documents are created from scratch.

- **Shell Documents.** Shell documents typically contain ^F insert field commands. Shell documents are designed to be filled out by drawing data from a list document. WordPerfect refers to these documents as primary merge files.

- **List Documents.** A list document is not organized in lines and paragraphs. Instead, it is divided into fields and records. A field is a block of text to be inserted into a shell document. A record is a complete set of fields that will fill out all of the fields in a shell letter. Each record is marked by an end-of-record code, [Apple/Shift/r], and each field is marked by an end-of-field code, [Apple/Shift/e]. WordPerfect refers to list documents as secondary merge documents.

- **Merge.** The Merge command requires you to specify a primary merge file and secondary merge files to be combined into a series of form letters.

- **Reports.** A report is a special kind of primary merge document. In a report, the goal is to fit as many records as possible onto each page. The ^P and ^N commands are used to suppress the new page normally created by WordPerfect after each record is merged.

- **Fill-in.** Merge can operate without a secondary file. The ^C merge code is used to pause the merge and allow the field information to be entered directly from the keyboard.

- **Assembly.** Merge can also be used to combine a number of individual documents. The ^P^P code operates as an automatic file retrieve command that inserts the specified files into the primary document as it is merged.

CHAPTER 8

MACROS

8 Macros

The basic structure of a program is defined by its menus and command keys. However, as you operate a program, you will find that you often repeat a specific series of commands to accomplish a task. For example, in this book you have frequently been asked to enter a centered, bold heading. Because this command sequence is used so frequently, wouldn't it be nice if you could create a command of your own that automatically carried out all the commands in the sequence for you?

This is the essence of what is meant by a **macro** — assembling a series of smaller commands to carry out one larger command. Macros tend to be sequences that fit closely into specific activities, as opposed to the major commands in a program, which have broader applicability.

Macros allow you to create custom command sequences to fit the way that you work. WordPerfect can create macros that speed up and automate many everyday functions. This chapter demonstrates how to create and use WordPerfect macros.

DEFINING A MACRO

It has been stated that macros enable you to automate command and entry sequences. WordPerfect creates macros by recording a series of keystrokes as you enter them. When the recording is done, WordPerfect stores the keystrokes in a macro file. When you want to perform the same operation again, you enter a command that tells WordPerfect what macro file to read. As the file is read by WordPerfect, each stored keystroke is executed as if you were actually typing it in at the keyboard or selecting it with the mouse.

WordPerfect allows you to create two types of macro file names, which are distinguished by the command you must enter to execute the stored macro keystrokes.

Long Names A **long name** macro can be given any valid Macintosh file name. The macro is executed when you enter [Apple/Shift/x] and then enter or select the name of the macro you want to execute. In addition to normal file names, WordPerfect allows you to use the name **Default Macro**. The Default Macro name can be used for temporary macros to which you do not want to assign a file name.

Macros **8**

Short Names   A **short name** macro can be executed with a single keystroke. Such macros are given single-character names including letters, numbers, or special characters. To execute a short name macro, you use the [Apple/Option] combination with the character. For example, if you name the macro "A," you would enter [Apple/Option/a] to execute the macro.

Short and long name macros function in the same way. The only difference between them is that short name macros can be executed with a single keystroke.

TYPING MACROS

The simplest kind of macro is called a **typing macro**. In typing macros, you record the entry of a block of text and then replay the macro the next time you want that same block entered. For example, you might want to create a macro that sets up up a standard business letterhead. Such a macro would enable you to turn a blank document window into a letterhead with a single command.

To create the macro, you must turn on the macro recording mode. Macros are found on the Special menu.

> **Point** at Special
> **Drag** to Macro
> **Release**

The Macro menu appears. Of the six options, only two are available at this time. Options 3 through 6 can be used only while a macro is being recorded. Option 1 will begin the macro recording process. Enter

1

WordPerfect displays the macro name selection box.

417

8 Macros

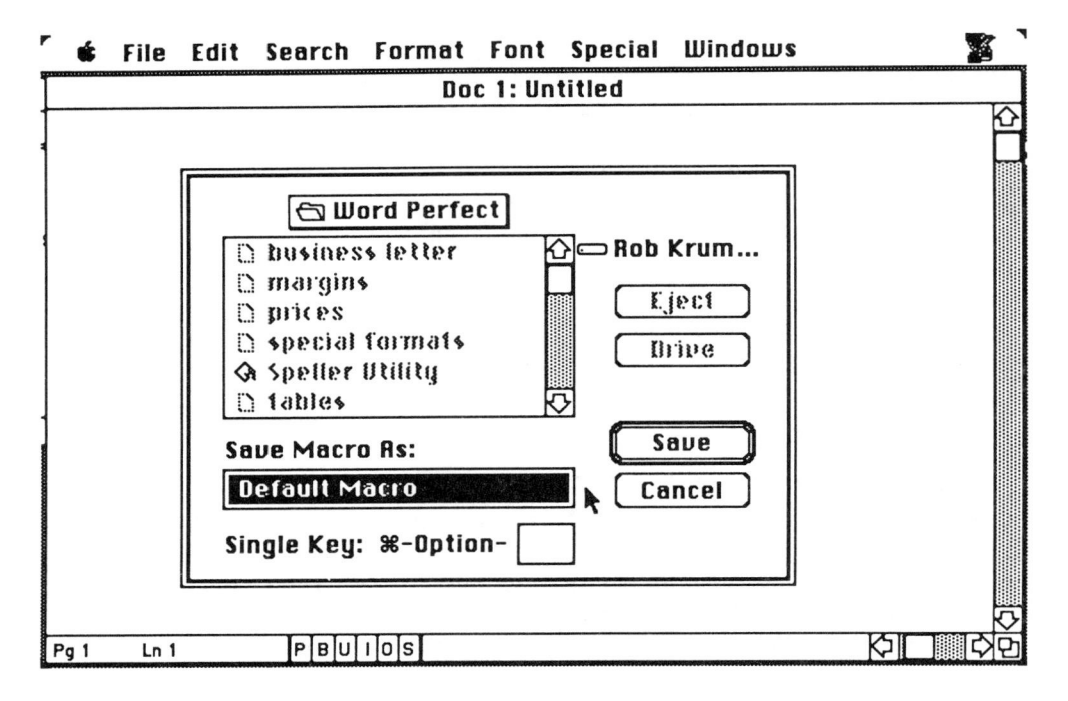

Figure 8.1

At this point, you have three options. You can enter [Return], which will assign the name Default Macro to the macro; you can enter a file name (long name) for the macro; or you can enter a single key character. In this case, enter a file name that describes the purpose of the macro. Enter

letterhead [Return]

WordPerfect returns you to your document window. The only change is that the words "Macro Def" appear in the bar at the bottom of the screen.

418

Macros **8**

You can now begin defining the macro by entering the keystrokes that actually create the letterhead. Enter

La Fish and Associates [Return]
2030 Race Street [Return]
Philadelphia, PA 19103 [Return]
215-888-8990 [Return]

Now that the text is entered, you will want to format the display to look more like a letterhead by changing the type styles.

Move the cursor to the first line by entering

↑ (4 times)

Select this line by using the Select Paragraph command. Enter

[Apple/6] 3

Change the font style by entering

[Apple/5]

Choose 18-point, shadow, italic.

Point at Geneva
Click
Click on 18
Click on Italic
Click on Shadow
Click on OK

419

8 Macros

Center the line by entering

[Apple/Shift/c]

Turn off the selection by entering

[Apple/Shift/n]

Format the address and phone number. Turn on the selection once again by entering

[Apple/Shift/n]
↓ (3 times)

The address and phone number are highlighted. Select bold print and centering. Enter

[Apple/Shift/b]
[Apple/Shift/c]

Turn off the highlighting and bold by entering

[Apple/Shift/n]
[Apple/Shift/b]

You have now completed the macro. To end the macro definition and save the keystrokes already entered, you need to enter a second Macro Define command. WordPerfect provides the keyboard shortcut, [Apple/Shift/m]. Enter

[Apple/Shift/m]

Macros **8**

When you completed the macro, WordPerfect wrote the keystrokes into a file. The words "Def Macro" no longer appear on the bottom bar, indicating that macro recording has terminated.

Now you can put the macro to work. Create a new document window by entering

[Apple/n]

To create a letterhead for this document, you must enter the Macro Execute command. Display the macro menu by entering

[Apple/m]

Choose Execute by entering

2

WordPerfect displays a list of all the macros. Note that if you have created other macros on your disk, they will also appear on this display. The macro name "letterhead" appears in the scroll box.

8 Macros

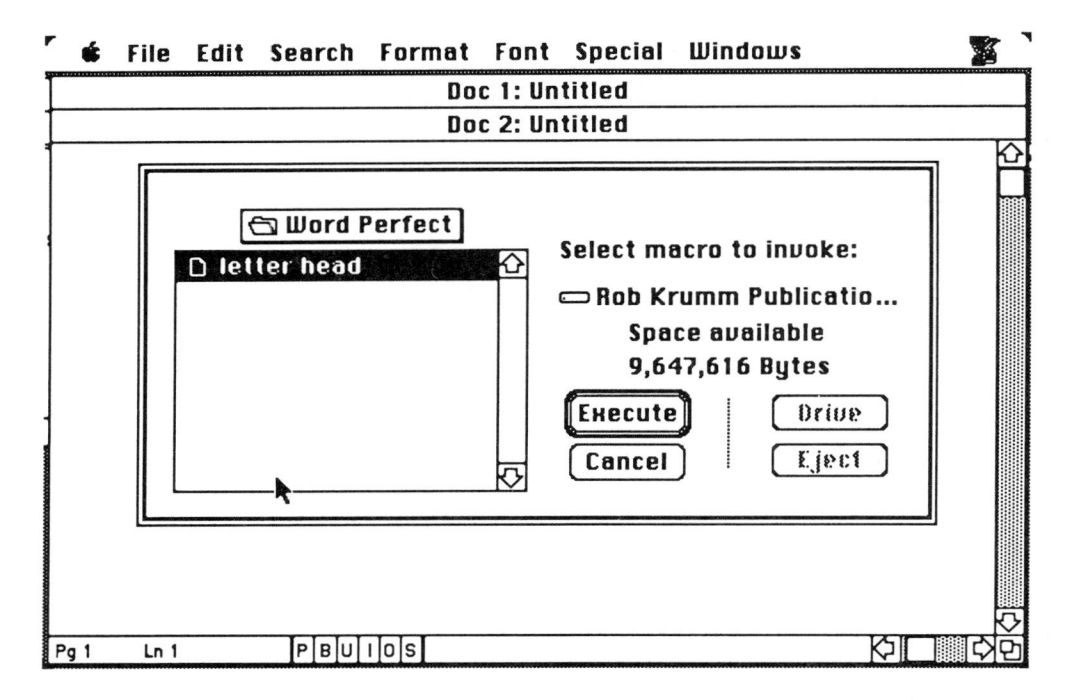

Figure 8.2

To execute the macro, you can double click on the macro name.

> **Point** at letterhead
> **Double Click**

The words "Macro Inv" will appear in the menu bar at the bottom of the screen, indicating that WordPerfect is reading and executing the keystrokes stored in the macro file. The macro will take a few moments to complete its work. When it is done, the words "Macro Inv" disappear from the bottom bar, and the letterhead text appears in the document window.

Macros 8

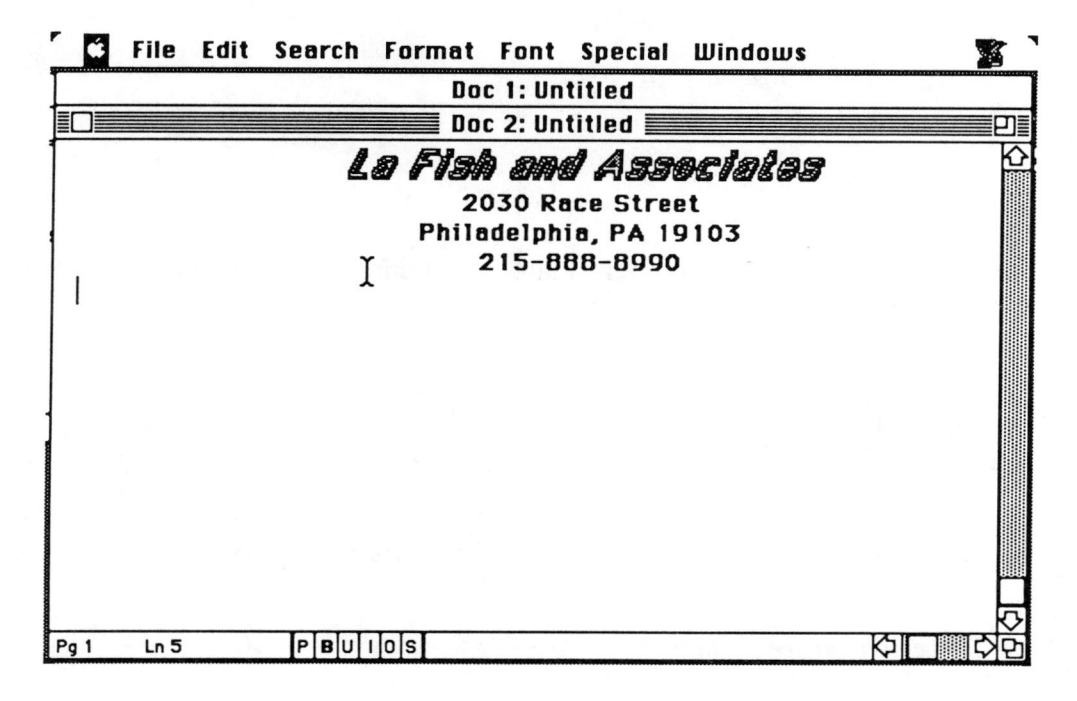

Figure 8.3

"Macro Inv" stands for "Macro Invisible." The term "invisible" refers to the fact that WordPerfect attempts to execute the macro as quickly as possible without taking time to adjust the screen display. When the macro is concluded, WordPerfect adjusts the screen and shows any changes made during macro execution. An invisible macro is the fastest way to execute a stored macro.

MORE MACROS

At this point, you have created a single macro that creates a letterhead; however, you can see that other parts of the letter can be inserted automatically because they remain the same in every letter. For example, the insertion of the date, a salutation, and a closing can also be programmed into a macro. Turn on the macro recording by using the keyboard shortcut command for Define Macro, [Apple/Shift/m]. Enter

[Apple/Shift/m]

8 Macros

Enter the name for this macro:

letter close

The words "Def Macro" appear on the bottom bar telling you that recording is underway. Enter the date with these keystrokes:

[Return] [Return]
[Apple/Shift/c] [Apple/Shift/d]
[Return] [Return]

Continue the macro by entering the salutation and the closing. Enter

Dear [Return] [Return] [Return]
Regards, [Return] [Return]
Walter Q. La Fish [Return]
President [Return]

Conclude the macro by entering

[Apple/Shift/m]

You now have two macros: one that fills out the top of the letter and one that fills out the bottom of the letter. All you need to do is type in the body of the letter.

To test both macros, abandon the current document by entering

[Apple/k]

Macros **8**

> **Point** at No
> **Click**

Open a new document window. Enter

[Apple/n]

You can now run the Letterhead macro. Enter

[Apple/Shift/x]

> **Point** at letterhead
> **Double Click**

Now, run the Letter Close macro. Enter

[Apple/Shift/x]

> **Point** at letter close
> **Double Click**

Both macros fill in the document exactly as you entered the text when you recorded the macros.

Clear the document window by entering

[Apple/k]

> **Point** at No
> **Click**

425

8   Macros

Enter

[Apple/n]

SINGLE-KEY MACROS

Often the most useful macros are not large or elaborate but short, simple macros that carry out common tasks. To make using these macros as simple as possible, WordPerfect allows you to define macros that execute when you type an [Apple/Option] combination with any keyboard character.

For example, you can create a macro that will create an 18-point, shadow print, centered headline out of any line of text that you have just typed. Begin by entering a short line of text.   Enter

Using WordPerfect Macros

Turn on the macro recording mode by entering

[Apple/Shift/m]

The screen should resemble the following:

Macros **8**

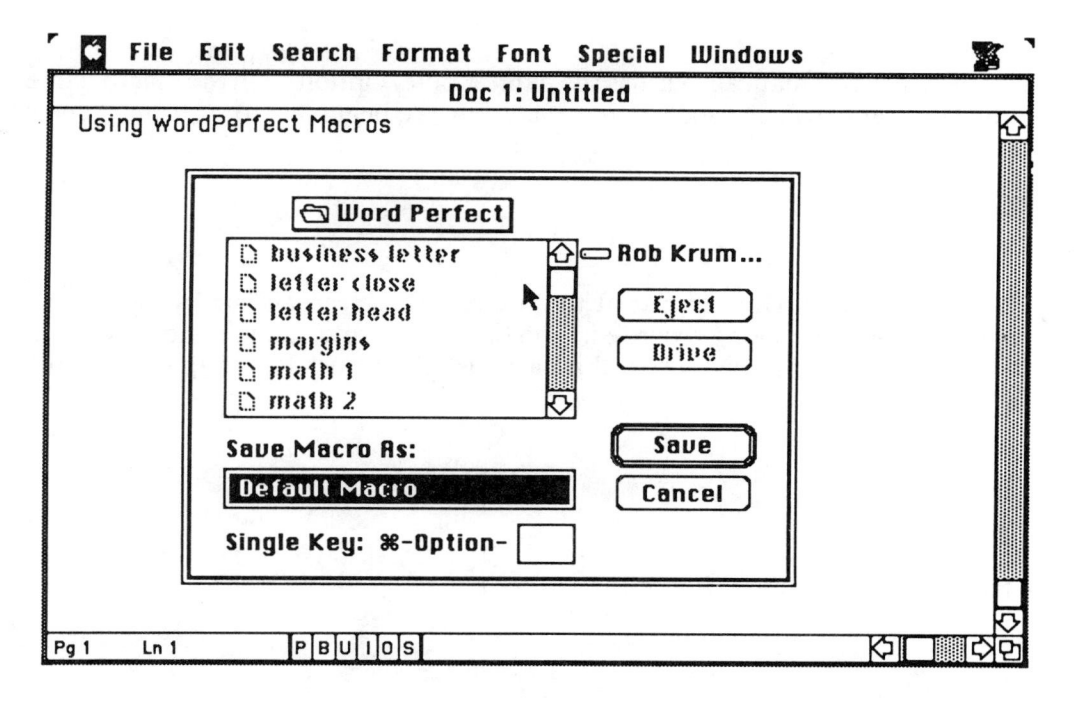

Figure 8.4

To create a single-keystroke macro, you can enter the character you want to assign to the macro in the Single Key option box.

> **Point** at the Single Key option box
> **Click**

Enter

c

8 Macros

WordPerfect automatically inserts the name Apple/Option/C in the macro name line. That name will be used for the macro file. To begin macro recording, enter

[Return]

The words "Macro Def" appear at the bottom of the screen, indicating that all your keystrokes are being recorded. The first step is to select the line of text you want to make into a heading. In this case, use the Select Paragraph command. Enter

[Apple/6]3

Change the point size to 18.

| **Point** at Font |
| **Drag** to 18 |
| **Release** |

Next, select shadow printing. Enter

[Apple/Shift/s]

Finally, enter the text by entering

[Apple/Shift/c]

Complete the line of text by entering

[Enter] →
[Return]

Macros **8**

You have now converted the text into a centered heading.

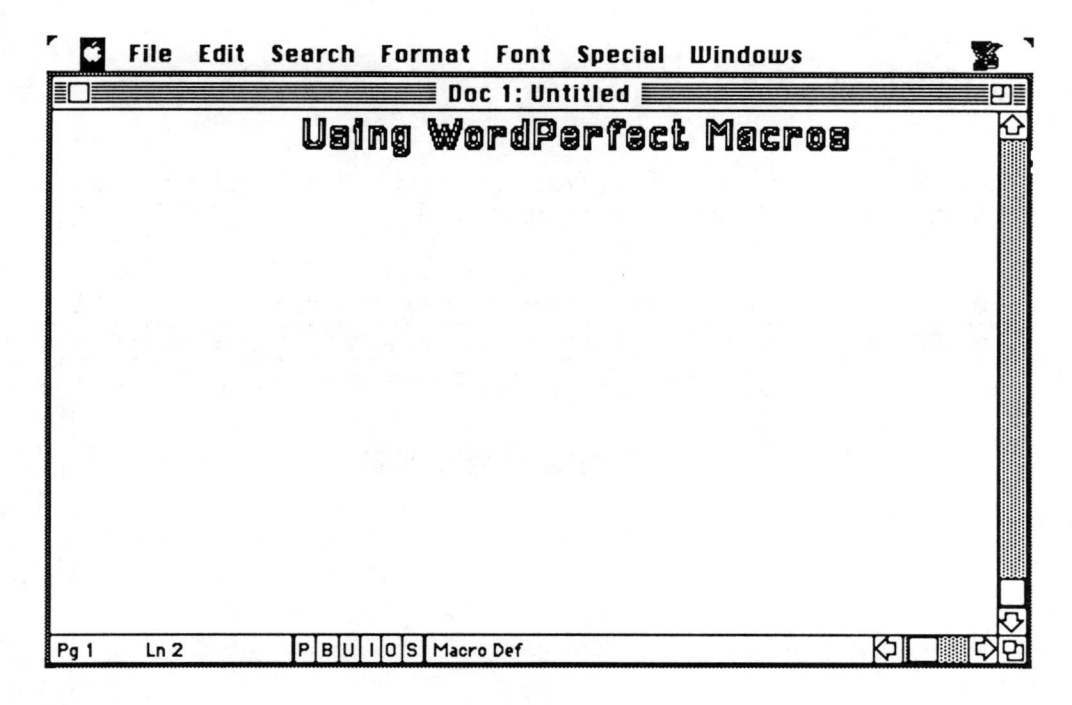

Figure 8.5

Now that the commands are entered, you are ready to conclude the macro. Enter

[Apple/Shift/m]

The macro is stored on disk, ready to be used with any line of text you type. Enter

[Return]
Macro Recording

8 Macros

Use your macro to change this text to a heading like the one in the previous line. Enter

[Apple/Option/c]

There will be a brief pause while the macro plays back your keystrokes, and then the formatted text will appear as a centered heading.

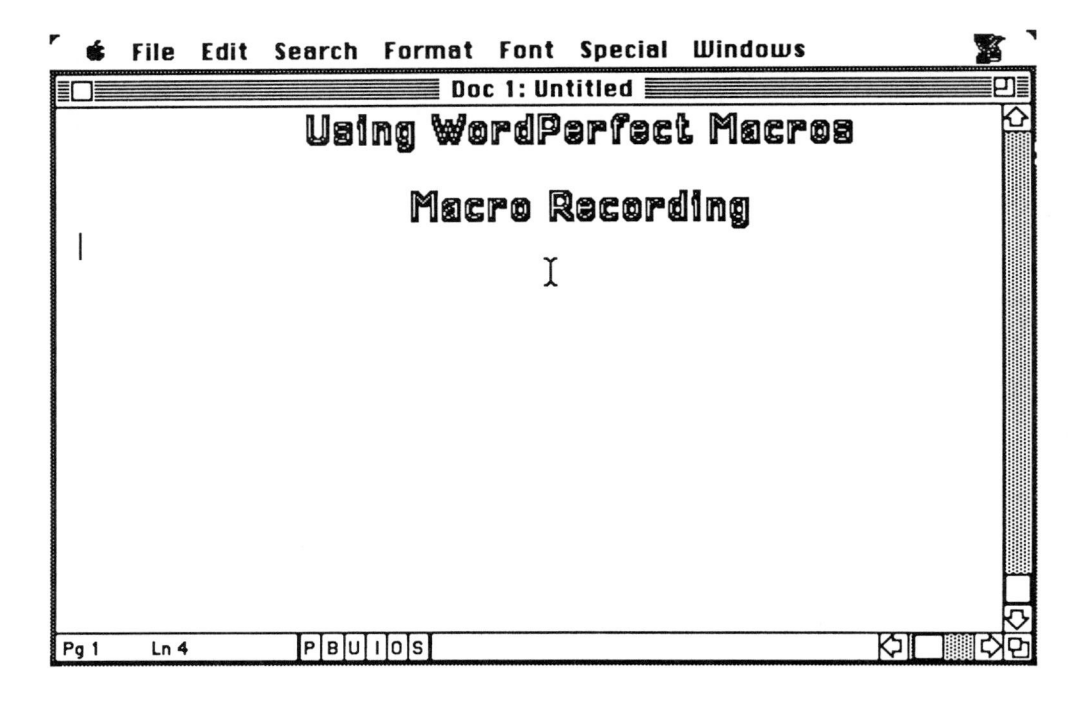

Figure 8.6

Outlines with Formats

One of the chief advantages of using macros is that they allow you to create commands that fit your exact needs. Many of WordPerfect's features are implemented in a general manner so they can apply to many situations, but macros allow you to combine sets of commands to create commands that more closely match your individual work style.

For example, the outline mode is useful because it helps you enter text into a format that is normally difficult and tedious to create; however, the outline mode has certain limitations. It does not provide a way to integrate WordPerfect formatting features into the outline. For example, the outline mode expects you to leave the same amount of space between each level of the outline. The outline would probably look better if you inserted extra blank lines around major headings while using normal spacing for minor headings.

You might also want to take advantage of changes in font style and size to enhance your outline. For example, you might make all the level 1 items 14-point, the level 2 headings 12-point, and so on.

By adding these options to the outline, you will create a much more visually appealing document; however, these additional items would increase the complexity of entering the text of the outline. The solution is to create macros that will automatically format the lines and include blank lines, font size, and style, as well as the automatic numbering.

As an illustration of how macros can combine a number of separate WordPerfect features, you will create three macros, [Apple/Option/1], [Apple/Option/2], and [Apple/Option/3], that will automatically format lines of text as first-, second-, and third-level headings.

Begin by entering a short line of text. This line will eventually become the first major heading in an outline. Enter

What are macros?

The goal is to create a macro, [Apple/Option/1], that will automatically convert this line into a major heading in an outline. In this case, the major heading will have some additional attributes over and above its paragraph number and indent. The major heading should be 14-point, outline style text. In addition, you will want to make sure that there is one blank line before and one blank line after the heading.

8 Macros

The first task is to turn macro recording on. Enter

[Apple/Shift/m]

Enter the character 1 in the Single Key box.

> **Point** at the Single Key box
> **Click**

Enter

1 [Return]

Now, you must enter the commands that will format this line as desired. Begin by inserting the automatic paragraph number for this line, which is done using the Paragraph Number command. Enter

[Enter] ←
[Apple/3] 2
1 [Return]
[Apple/Shift/t]

You have now added the paragraph number for a major heading, level 1, to the text.

Macros **8**

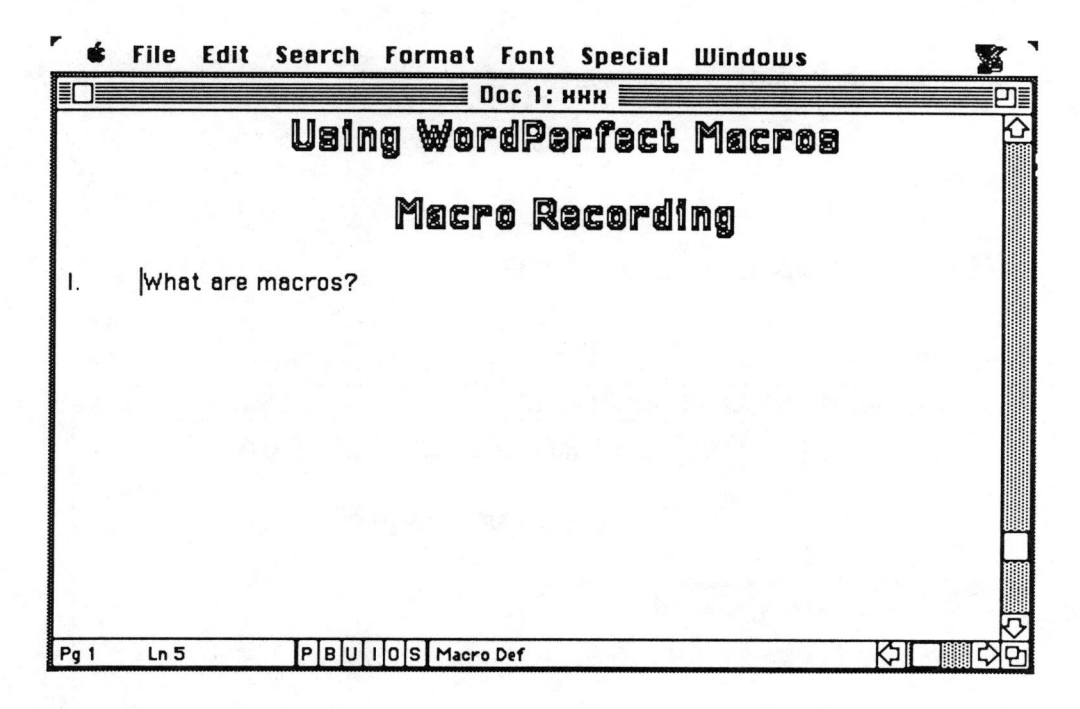

Figure 8.7

The next step is to format the line to the correct style and size of text. Begin by highlighting the line with the Select Paragraph command. Enter

[Apple/6] 3

Change the text to 14-point.

```
Point at Font
Drag to 14
Release
```

433

8 Macros

Change the text to outline by entering

[Apple/Shift/o]

The text now reflects its new size and style.

Figure 8.8

Finally, add the blank lines before and after the line. Enter

[Enter] ← **[Return]**
[Enter] → **[Return] [Return]**

Macros **8**

The macro is now complete. To terminate macro recording, enter

[Apple/Shift/m]

You have now completed the entry for the first-level headings.

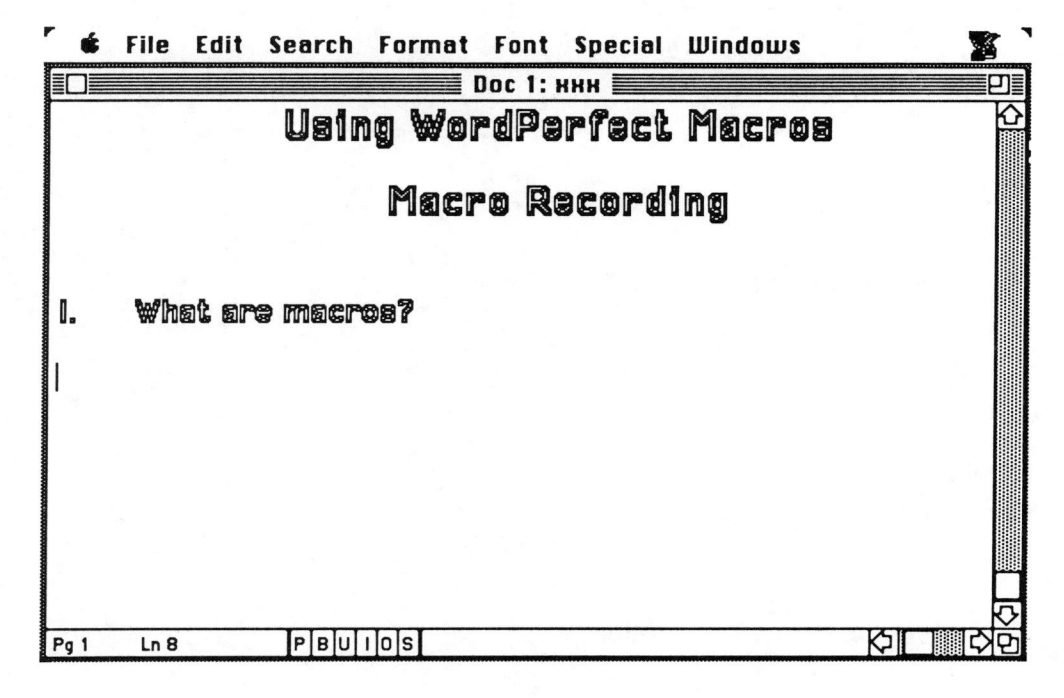

Figure 8.9

Second-level Headings

The basic idea behind this series of macros is the same for the other levels as it is for the first-level heading. They differ only in the specific level, font size, and style you want to use. Create a second-level heading that uses 12-point, bold text. This macro will be [Apple/Option/2]. Begin by entering a line of text that should be formatted as a level 2 heading. Enter

Captures keystrokes in a macro file

435

8 Macros

Turn on macro recording. Enter

[Apple/Shift/m]

> **Point** at the Single Key box
> **Click**

Enter

2 [Return]

You are now ready to format the line. Enter

[Enter] ←
[Tab]
[Apple/3] 2
2 [Return]
[Apple/Shift/t]

Now format the text as bold. Enter

[Apple/6] 3
[Apple/Shift/b]

Complete the macro by ending the line with a single [Return]. Enter

[Enter] →
[Return]

Macros 8

Turn off macro recording by entering

[Apple/Shift/m]

You have now created two of the three macros.

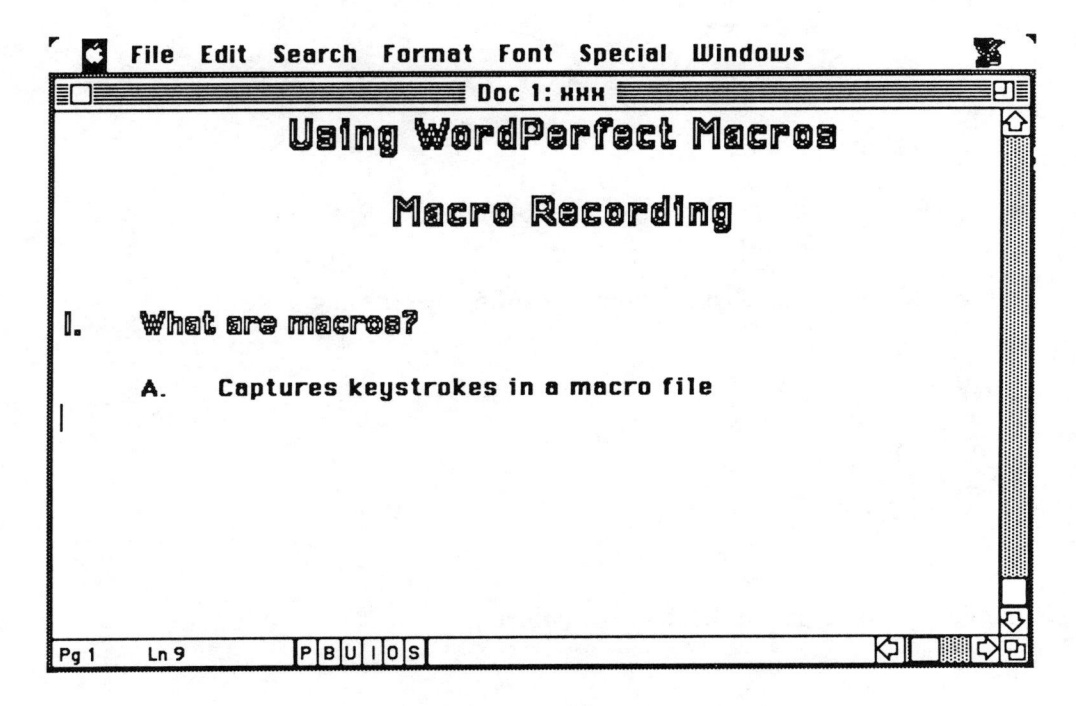

Figure 8.10

Third-level Headings

The last macro in this series will be [Apple/Option/3], the macro for third-level headings. To distinguish these headings from the others, format them as 10-point text. Enter the text for the third-level heading:

Select Define Macro from menu

8 Macros

Begin the recording process by entering

[Apple/Shift/m]

```
Point at the Single Key box
Click
```

Enter

3 [Return]

Format the paragraph as a third-level heading by entering

[Enter] ←
[Tab] [Tab]
[Apple/3] 2
3 [Return]
[Apple/Shift/t]

Change the point size of this level by entering

[Apple/6] 3

```
Point at Font
Drag to 14
Release
```

Macros **8**

Complete the macro by entering

**[Enter]→
[Return]
[Apple/Shift/m]**

You now have a complete set of macros with which to enter fully formatted outlines.

Your screen should resemble the following:

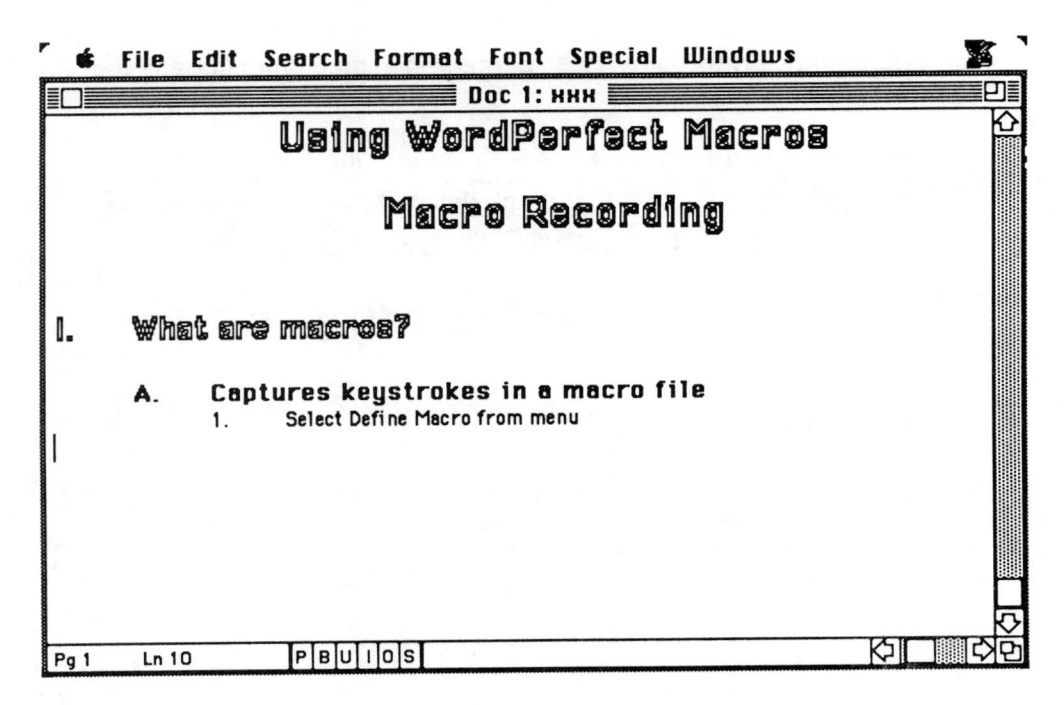

Figure 8.11

8 Macros

Using the Outline Macros

Now that you have created the macros, you can use them to quickly format lines of the outline as you type them. Enter the next line of the outline:

Enter the name of the macro

Note that the text is entered as normal, 12-point text. You can now use one of your formatting macros to style the text into the outline. In this case, make this line a third-level heading by entering

[Apple/Option/3]

The line is automatically formatted with paragraph number, indents, and font size.

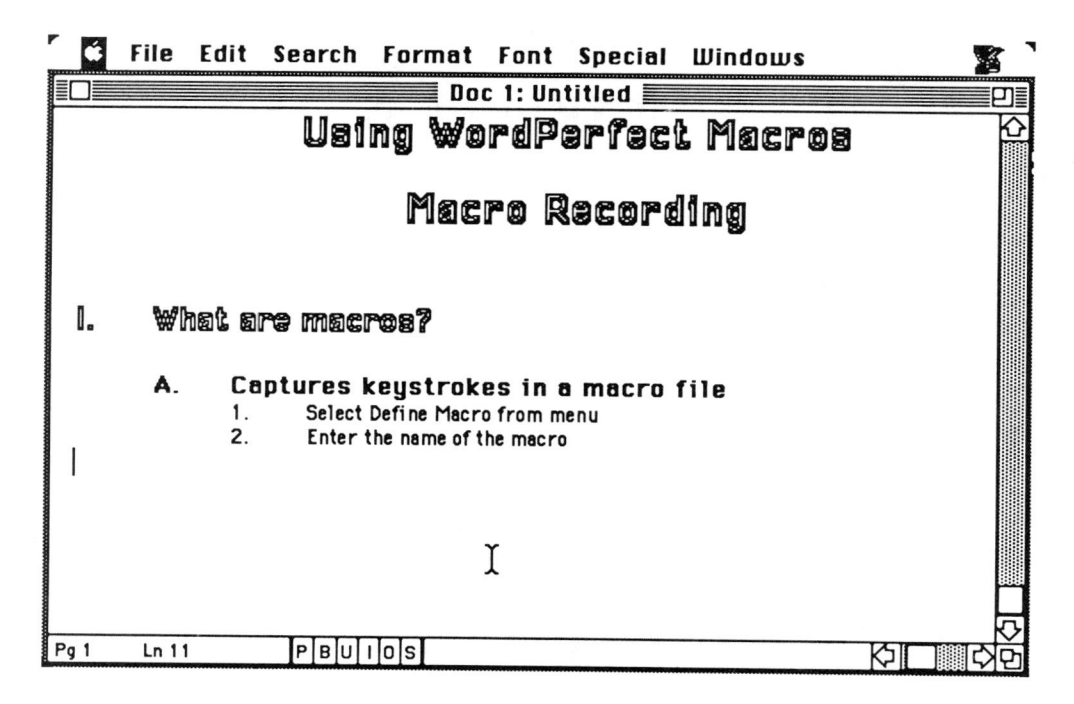

Figure 8.12

Macros **8**

Add another line to the outline. Enter

Ending a macro

Make this line a second-level heading by entering

[Apple/Option/2]

Add two third-level items under this heading. Enter

Select Define Macro from the menu
[Apple/Option/3]
Or use Apple-Shift-m   (type in as text here)
[Apple/Option/3]

The outline should resemble the following:

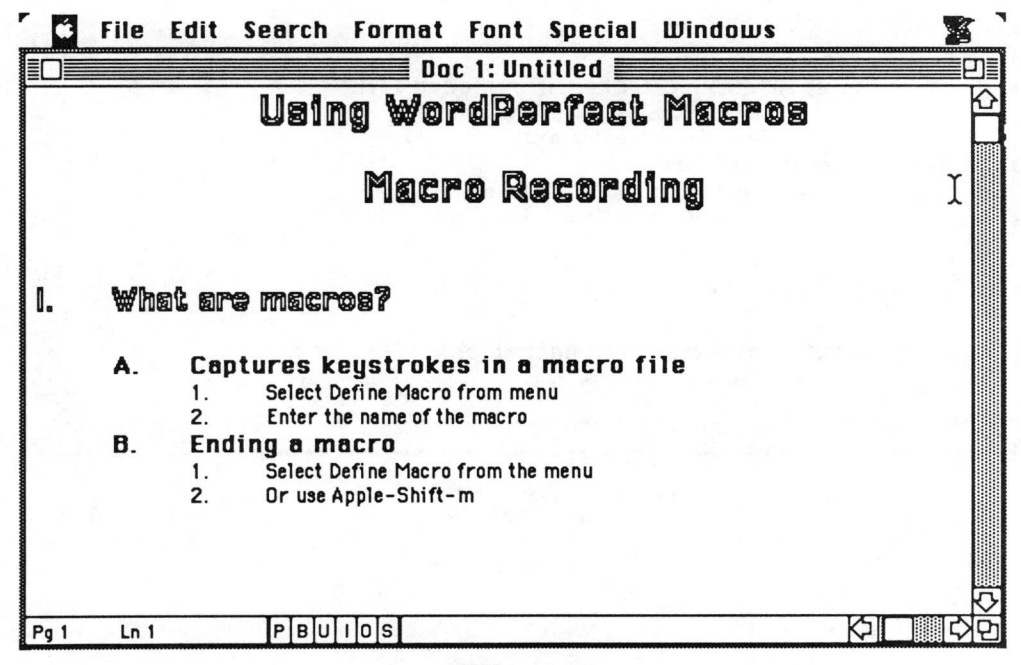

```
 File   Edit   Search   Format   Font   Special   Windows
                    Doc 1: Untitled
              Using WordPerfect Macros

                   Macro Recording

 I.    What are macros?

       A.    Captures keystrokes in a macro file
             1.   Select Define Macro from menu
             2.   Enter the name of the macro
       B.    Ending a macro
             1.   Select Define Macro from the menu
             2.   Or use Apple-Shift-m


 Pg 1   Ln 1       P B U I O S
```

Figure 8.13

8 Macros

Add another major heading with subheadings to the outline. Enter

Macro Features
[Apple/Option/1]
Automate standard operations
[Apple/Option/2]
Enter standard paragraphs
[Apple/Option/3]

The document should resemble the following:

```
 File   Edit   Search   Format   Font   Special   Windows
═══════════════════════ Doc 1: Untitled ═══════════════════════
                    Macro Recording

   I.   What are macros?

        A.   Captures keystrokes in a macro file
             1.   Select Define Macro from menu
             2.   Enter the name of the macro
        B.   Ending a macro
             1.   Select Define Macro from the menu
             2.   Or use Apple-Shift-m

   II.  Macro Features

        A.   Automate standard operations
             1.   Enter standard paragraphs

 Pg 1   Ln 19      P B U I O S
```

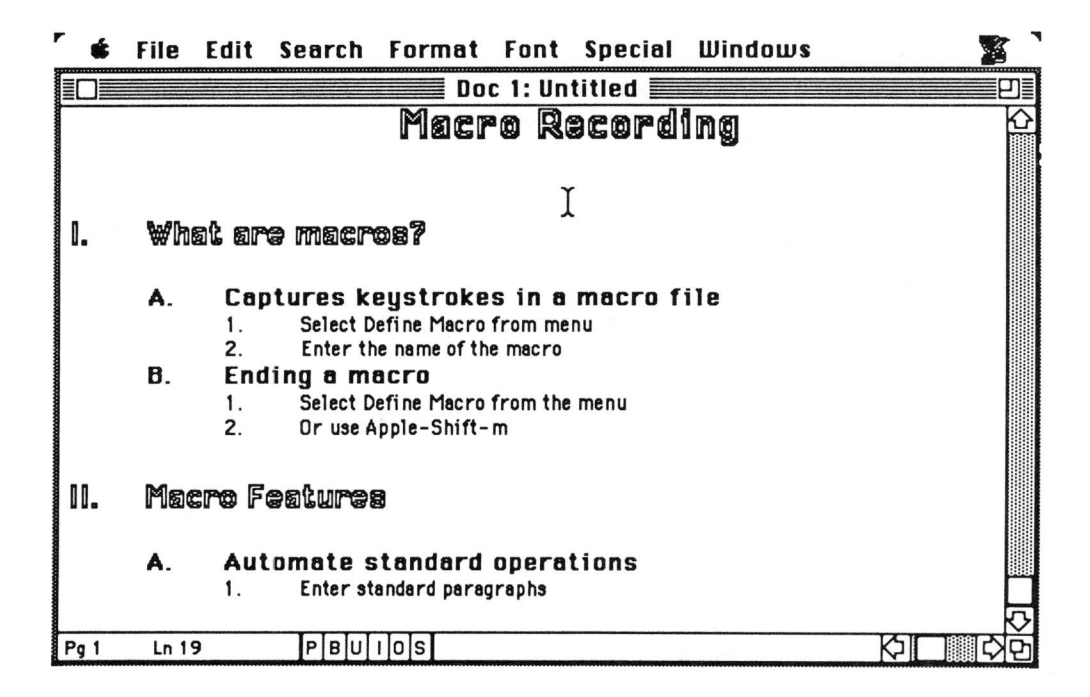

Figure 8.14

Macros allow you to create your own custom versions of standard WordPerfect features. By adding spacing and font style commands to your macros, you can automatically and consistently format documents with the same amount of effort it would take to type them without any special formats.

The single-keystroke macros enable you to execute the macros without interrupting your text entry to search through numerous menus.

ENTER KEY COMBINATIONS

Another way that you can automate operations in WordPerfect is by defining [Enter] key combinations. [Enter] key combinations allow you to assign existing menu options that do not have keyboard keystroke shortcuts to combinations of [Enter] and a letter. For example, on the File menu, most of the commands have key combination shortcuts such as [Apple/o] for File Open and [Apple/s] for File Save; however, the File Retrieve command is not assigned a shortcut key. You could use the [Enter] key feature to assign the File Retrieve command to the consecutive keystrokes [Enter]r. Note that [Enter] key combinations differ from other key combinations in that you must release the [Enter] key before pressing the key that follows it. For example, the [Enter]r key combination would require you to press the [Enter] key, release it, and then press the "r" key.

The [Enter] key combinations are not macros, even though they operate similarly. A macro allows you to combine a number of different commands into a single keystroke command. The [Enter] key combinations will enter only a single menu command (e.g., File Retrieve).

8 Macros

Defining an Enter Key Combination

The [Enter] key combinations are mapped to WordPerfect menu items by using the WordPerfect help display. The help display can be accessed through the [Apple] menu or by using the shortcut key combination [Apple/?]. Enter

[Apple/?]

The WordPerfect help display appears on the screen.

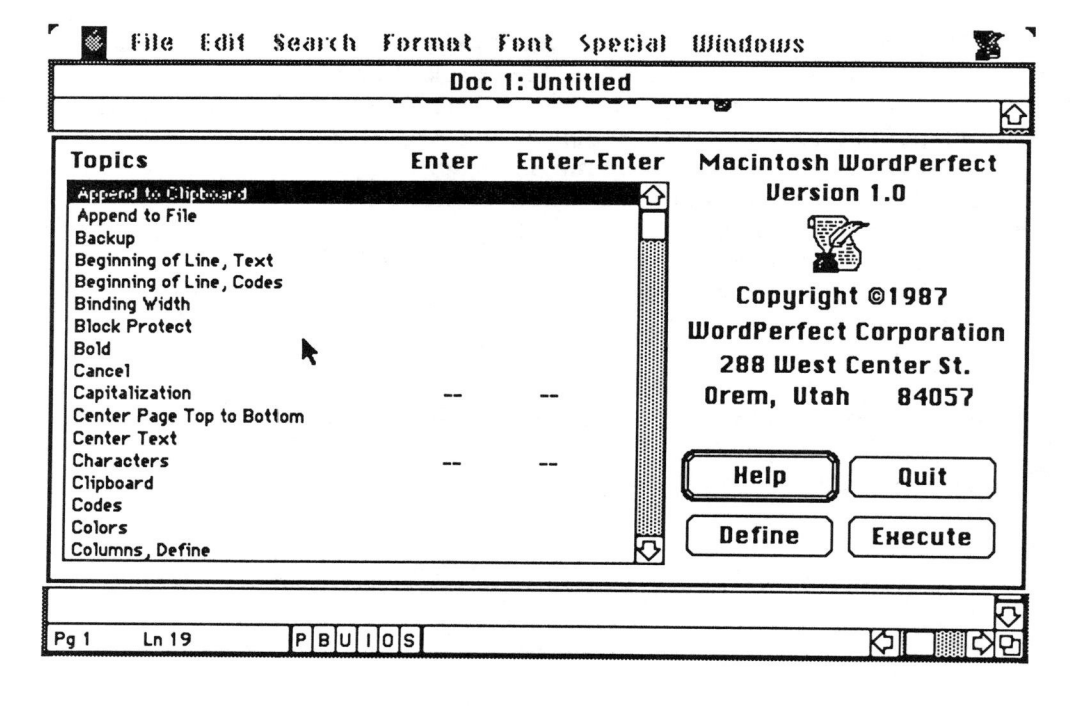

Figure 8.15

The box on the left side of the display contains a list of all of the features in WordPerfect. The list serves two purposes. First, you can select a topic so that you can read an explanation of how it is used in WordPerfect. Second, you can assign that menu option to an [Enter] key combination; however, the items within the Enter columns cannot be assigned to [Enter] key combinations.

Macros **8**

You can select a topic in three ways.

Mouse   You can use the mouse to select an item or scroll the display using the scroll bar.

Keys   You can use the arrow keys to move the highlight down the list of items.

Search   You can search for a topic by entering part of the name. WordPerfect moves the highlight to the first item that matches the search characters.

Once a topic is highlighted, you can display the help screen by entering [Return] or double clicking on the highlight.

For example, suppose you wanted to display help information for the File Retrieve command. Enter

ret

The highlight is automatically positioned on the Retrieve topic. To display the Help menu, enter

[Return]

WordPerfect displays the help screen for Retrieve.

8 Macros

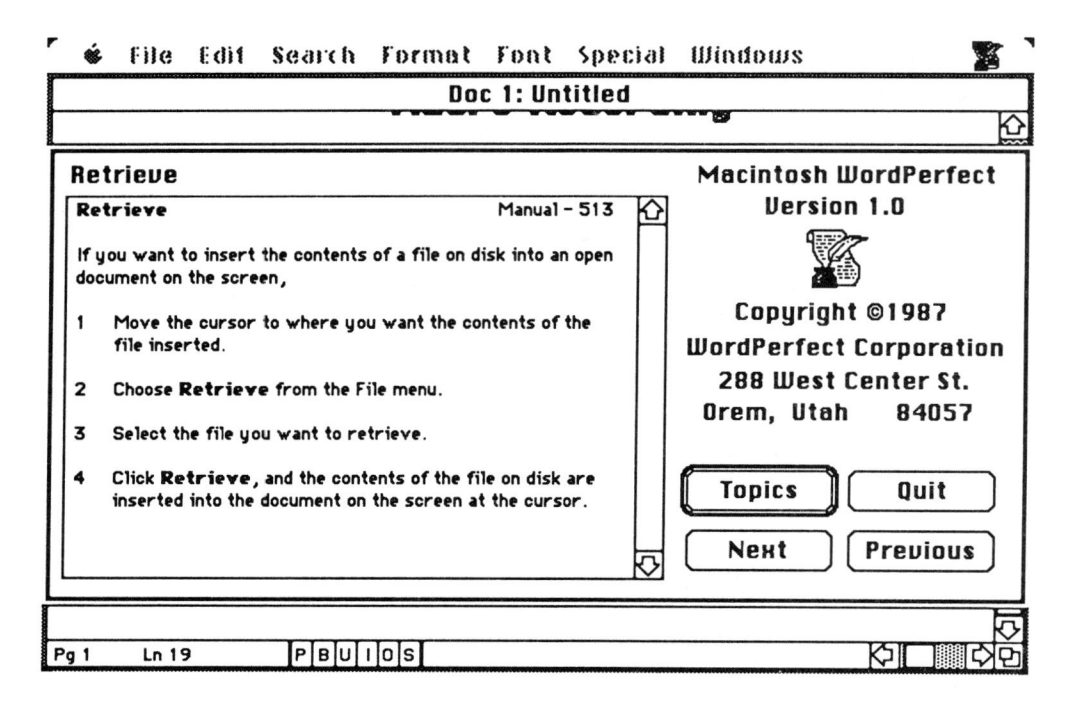

Figure 8.16

To return to the list of topics, enter

[Return]

Suppose you wanted to assign this menu command to an [Enter] key combination. Select Define by clicking on the Define button.

```
Point at Define
Click
```

446

Macros **8**

WordPerfect displays the [Enter] key definition box.

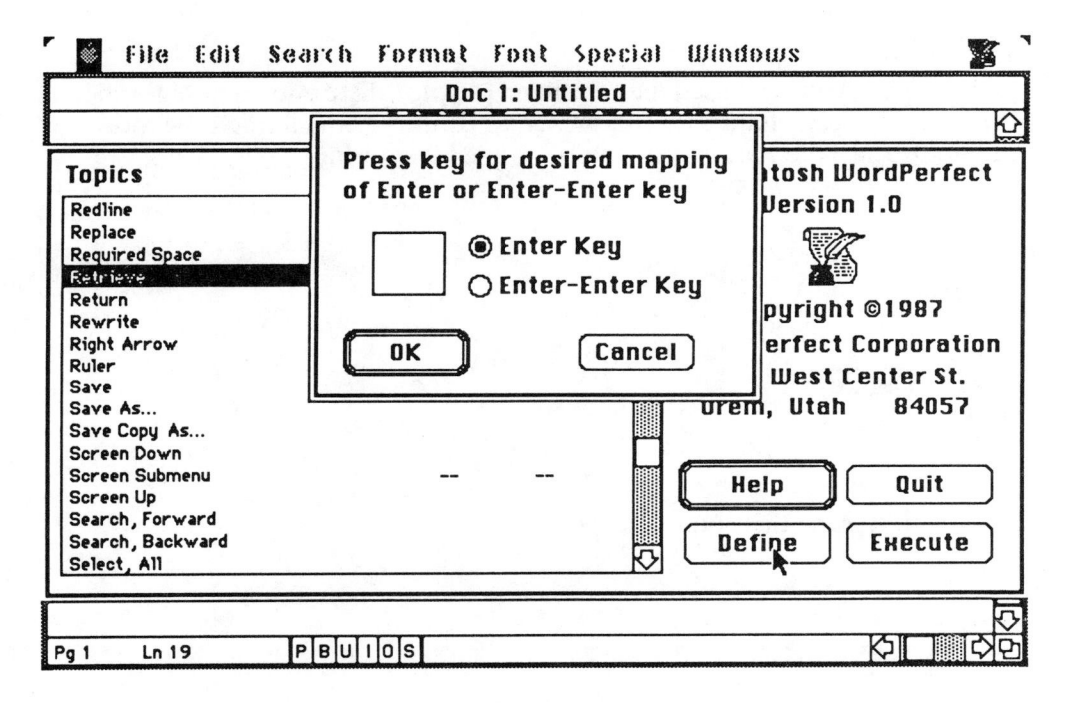

Figure 8.17

WordPerfect allows you to select either an [Enter] or [Enter][Enter] combination for this menu option. The use of [Enter][Enter] in addition to [Enter] provides another set of key combinations onto which you can map menu items. As a general rule, you would probably want to use up all the [Enter] combinations before you move onto [Enter][Enter].

To assign this menu option, File Retrieve, to a key combination, enter the letter. WordPerfect does allow you to enter [Control] key combinations for [Enter] key mapping. For example, if you enter [Control/r] as the character you can use [Enter][Control/r] to execute the command. Using [Control] combinations allows you to extend the number of command mappings by an additional set. Enter

r

8 Macros

```
Point at OK
Click
```

In this chapter, you have used the command [Apple/3]2 to enter a paragraph number code. You can change that sequence to [Enter]n, which might be more convenient. Locate the Paragraph Number topic by entering

par
↓

```
Point at Define
Click
```

Enter the letter for this command.

n

```
Point at OK
Click
```

You can create as many [Enter] or [Enter][Enter] combinations as you need. Return to the document.

```
Point at Quit
Click
```

You can now put the [Enter] key combinations to work. Save the current text. Enter

448

[Apple/s]
outline [Return]
[Apple/k] [Apple/n]

Suppose you wanted to retrieve this document. Use the [Enter] key combination to execute the Retrieve command:

[Enter] r
outline [Return]

The [Enter] key combination executes a command that would normally require a mouse/menu operation.

PAUSING A MACRO

In the previous series of macros you entered the text before you executed the macro. The macro then used the selection features to format the text. Word-Perfect contains a macro command that allows you to attack this type of operation from a different point of view. This feature, called a Macro Pause, can be inserted into a macro. It allows you to enter keystrokes and let the macro continue.

The pause allows you to create macros that can accept user keystrokes before they complete their operation. As an example, create a macro for fourth-level heading. The difference is that this time, the macro will begin by inserting the paragraph number and font size, pause to let you insert your text, and then complete the macro.

Turn on the macro recording mode. Enter

[Apple/Shift/m]

Point at the Single Key box
Click
---

8 Macros

Enter

4 [Return]

Begin by selecting the font size and style. Enter

[Apple/5]

```
Point at  9
Click
Click on Italic
Click on OK
```

Enter the commands that set up a fourth-level heading. Enter

[Tab] (3 times)

Next insert a Paragraph number command. Enter

[Apple/3] 2

Enter the level number and the indent:

4 [Return]
[Apple/Shift/t]

Macros **8**

At this point, you should enter the text of the entry; however, because every item in the outline will be different, this text should not be included in the macro. To exclude the text from the macro, select Pause Macro from the Macro menu. Enter

[Apple/m] 6

The words "Macro Pause" appear in the bar at the bottom of the screen. Enter the text of the heading:

Types in recorded keystrokes

To conclude the macro, turn the recording mode back on so that the change back to normal text will be recorded as part of the macro. When the macro is paused, entering [Apple/m] 6 will execute the Resume Macro command. Enter

[Apple/m] 6

The words "Def Macro" reappear in the bottom bar. Complete the macro by setting the font back to normal. Enter

[Apple/5]

> **Point** at 12
> **Click** on Italic
> **Click** on OK

Complete the line by entering

[Return]

451

8 Macros

The macro is now complete. Enter

[Apple/Shift/m]

Execute the macro by entering

[Apple/Option/m]

The macro sets the font, enters the tabs, and then pauses for the text you want to input. Enter

Carries out pre-recorded commands
[Apple/m] 6

The screen should resemble the following:

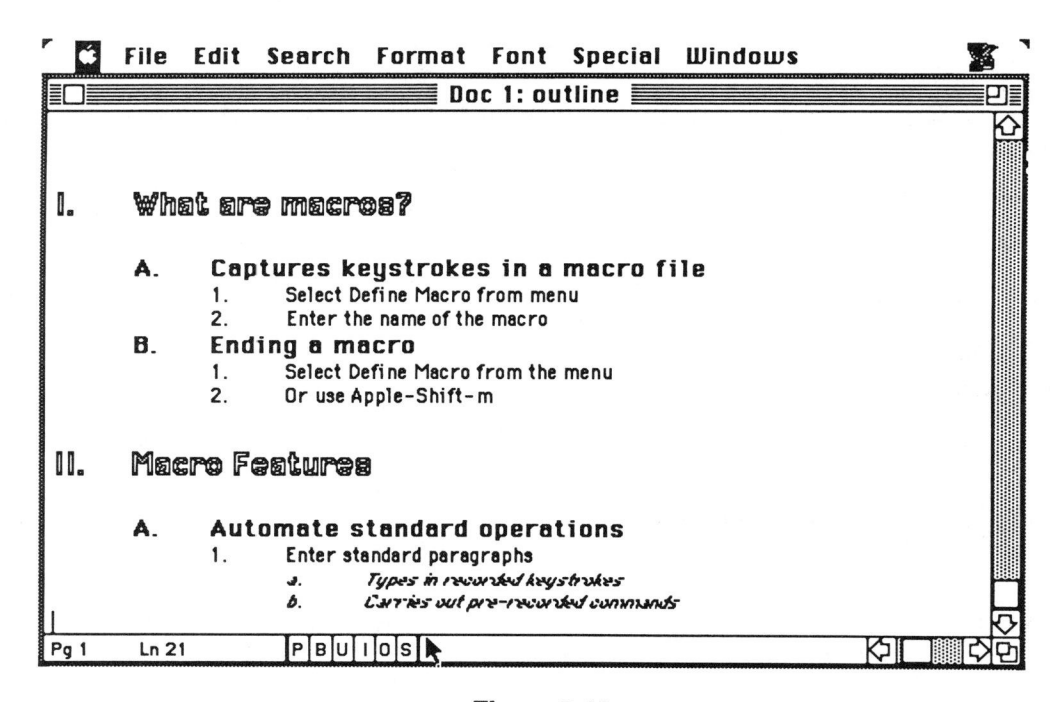

Figure 8.18

Save the Outline document, and open a blank window. Enter

[Apple/s]
[Apple/k]
[Apple/n]

MERGE AND MACROS

One of the most interesting combinations in WordPerfect is putting together the power of merge with the abilities of macros. The combination can create an easy-to-use system that solves some of the limitations imposed by merge.

For the first example of how these two features can be combined, return to the problem left unresolved in Chapter 7. In the Report document, you used the paragraph number code to number the records as they were inserted into the report; however, the numbers were uppercase Roman numerals because Word-Perfect uses the outline style of numbering as the default.

To make the numbers appear as Arabic numerals, you must change the paragraph numbering style in the report. This can be accomplished by creating a macro that will insert the code. WordPerfect provides a special merge command that will automatically execute a specified macro when the document has completed its merge operation.

To see how this type of merge/macro combination can work, create a macro that will change the numbering style from outline to paragraph style. Enter

[Apple/Shift/m]

You can use the name Outline Style for this macro. Enter

outline style [Return]

8 Macros

Enter the keystrokes for this macro. In this case, you want to move to the beginning of the document and insert a paragraph numbering definition style code. Enter

[Enter] [Enter] ↑
[Apple/3] 3

> **Point** at Paragraph
> **Click**
> **Click** on OK

Complete the macro by entering

[Apple/Shift/m]

Note that it is not necessary to have the actual Report document on the screen as long as you know the exact keystrokes that will be needed. Delete the code you just entered as part of the macro; it is not needed in this blank document. Enter

[Apple/7]
[Delete]
[Apple/7]

Attaching a Macro to a Merge Document

The next step is to attach the macro you have just created, Outline Style, to the Report document. Load the file by entering

[Apple/o]
report [Return]

Macros 8

The merge document Report is loaded into WordPerfect. The merge code used to execute a macro is Invoke Macro, ^G. The Invoke Macro merge code is different from other merge codes in that it will operate only once no matter how many copies of the primary merge document are inserted. The Invoke Macro command waits until the merge is complete and executes the specified macros one time.

Macros attached to merge documents in this manner are designed to add the finishing touches to merge documents that would not make sense if they were added after each record was inserted.

You can place the Invoke Macro codes in any part of the merge document. Because the cursor is positioned at the beginning of the document, you can enter the command at that point. Remember, because the Merge command will not appear as part of the text in the merged document, the fact that it is inserted at the beginning of this line will have no effect on the final tab alignment.

An Invoke Macro command consists of the name of the macro surrounded by [Control/g] codes. Enter

[Control/g]
outline style
[Control/g]

The document should now resemble the following:

455

8 Macros

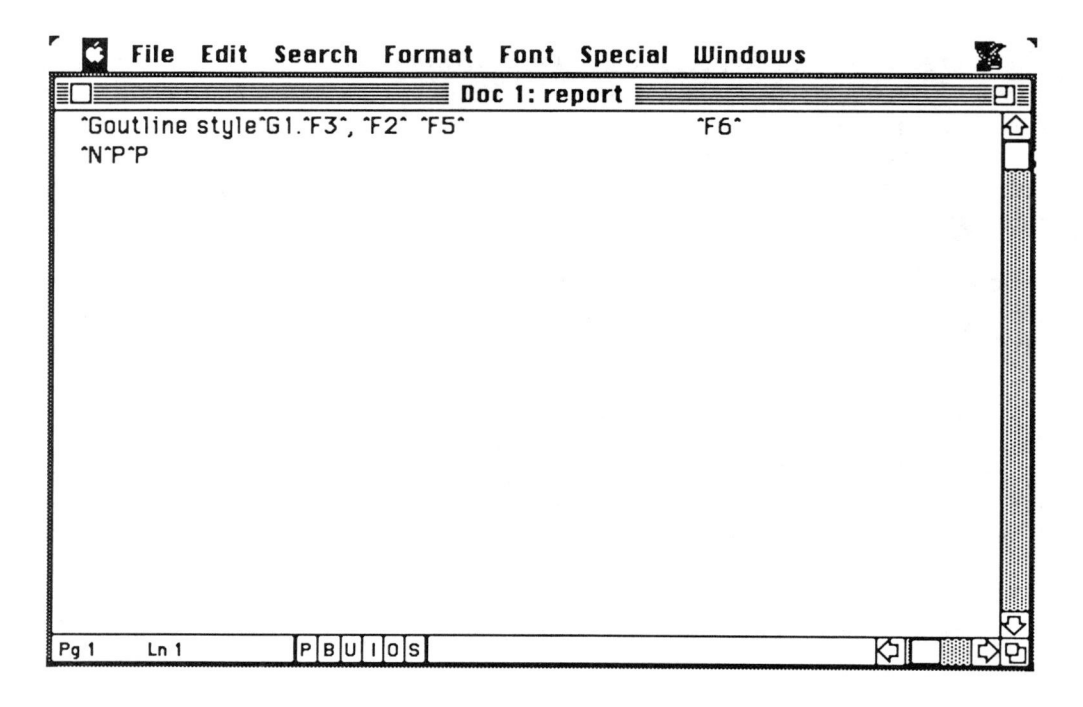

Figure 8.19

Save the revised document by entering

[Apple/s]
[Apple/k]

You can now merge the report with the list document. Note that you will need to scroll the file selection box with the mouse in order to locate the file names.

> **Point** at Special
> **Drag** to Merge
> **Release**
> **Double Click** on report
> **Double Click** on list document

Macros **8**

The report merges as usual, and for a moment the numbers appear in their Roman numeral format. Then, WordPerfect executes the macro, and the numbers change to the Arabic numbering style.

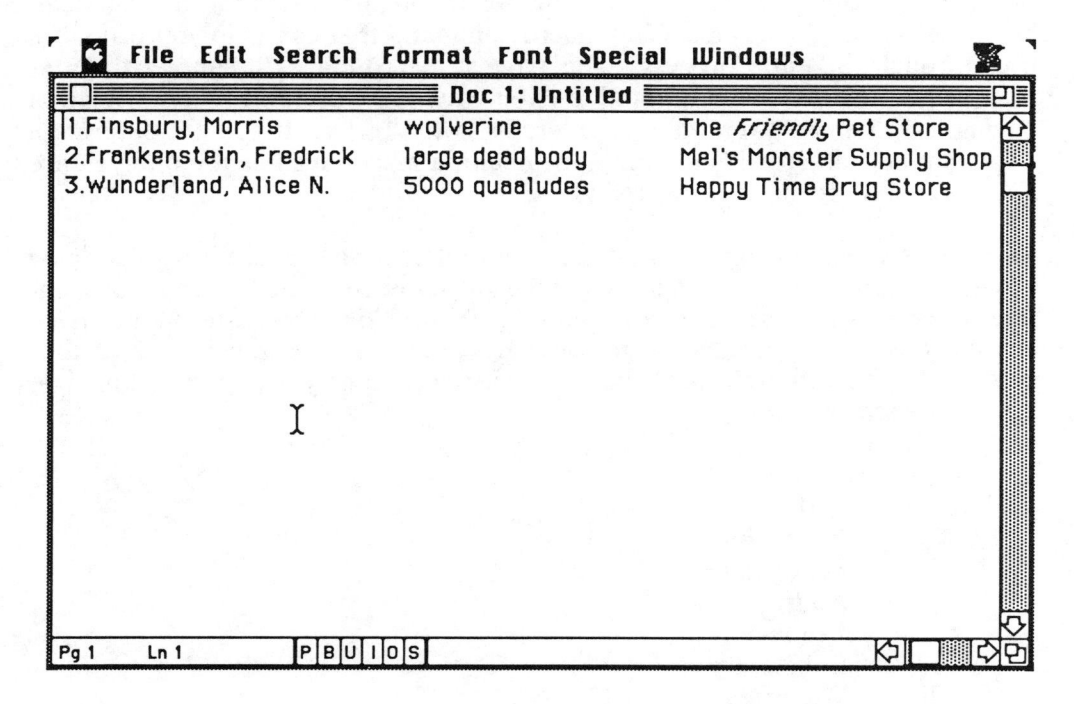

```
 File   Edit   Search   Format   Font   Special   Windows
                        Doc 1: Untitled
1.Finsbury, Morris         wolverine          The *Friendly* Pet Store
2.Frankenstein, Fredrick   large dead body    Mel's Monster Supply Shop
3.Wunderland, Alice N.     5000 quaaludes     Happy Time Drug Store



Pg 1   Ln 1          P B U  I O S
```

Figure 8.20

To print the final report, including page headers, enter

[Apple/p]
[Return]

457

8 Macros

Interactive Macros

One of the key elements in creating a useful merge operation is to enter the data correctly into the list document. In Chapter 7, you performed this task manually, but WordPerfect has a special macro command that can help you prompt a user through the entry process. This type of macro makes it simpler to enter records because you are prompted to enter each piece of information instead of having to remember what data is entered in what order. If you are entering a large number of records into a list document, a macro such as the one you are about to create is almost a necessity.

The macro you are about to create is called **interactive** because it uses a dialog box to prompt the user through each of the entries needed to fill out a record. Interactive macros use the Macro Input command. You can create the macro in any document as long as you remember the items and the order in which they ought to be entered in the data file. In the list document, you need to fill in eight items for each record.

1. **Title**
2. **First Name**
3. **Last Name**
4. **Address**
5. **Product**
6. **Subsidiary**
7. **Warranty**
8. **Service Center**

Your goal is to create a macro or series of macros that will make it simpler and more accurate to enter records into your list file.

Begin by moving to the bottom of the current document. Enter

[Enter] [Enter] ↓

Begin recording a macro. Assign this macro to the [Apple/Option/e] key combination. Enter

Macros 8

[Apple/Shift/m]

```
Point at the Single Key box
Click
```

Enter

m [Return]

You are now ready to create the first part of the interactive macro.

Macro Input Command

The Macro Input command is used to display a dialog box in the center of the screen. Instead of entering the text of the field directly into a document, the user can type into the dialog box, which helps the person entering the data concentrate on what he or she is typing. To create this dialog box enter

[Apple/m]

Option 5 on the Macro menu is Macro Input. Enter

5

459

8 Macros

A dialog box titled "Input" appears on the screen.

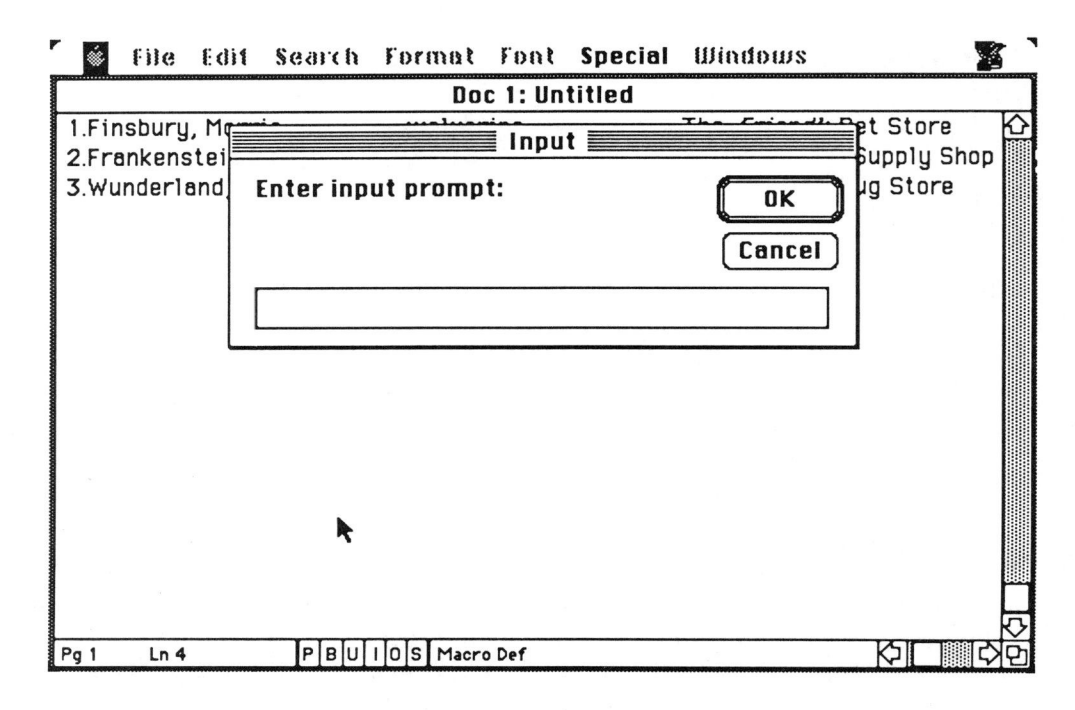

Figure 8.21

Keep in mind that when you are creating this type of macro, you are not actually entering the text; rather, you are entering the prompts that will appear in the dialog box when the macro is executed. For example, this first box should prompt you to enter the title field. Enter

Customer's Title (Mr., Ms., etc.) [Return]

The text that you have just entered will appear as part of the dialog box when you execute the macro. After entering that text, you need to insert the end-of-field code. Enter

[Apple/Shift/r]

460

Macros **8**

Create a dialog box for the first and last names. Enter

[Apple/m] 5
Customer's First Name [Return]
[Apple/Shift/r]
[Apple/m] 5
Customer's Last Name [Return]
[Apple/Shift/r]

Multi-line Entries

The next item is the address. In the list document file, the two-line address is entered as a single field, but the dialog boxes will accept only a single line of text. In this case, you will want to present two dialog boxes but only insert an end-of-field code after the second box. Make sure that you remember to enter the second [Return] after entering "Street Address." Enter

[Apple/m] 5
Street Address [Return]
[Return]
[Apple/m] 5
City, State, Zip [Return]
[Apple/Shift/r]

There are four more fields for which you must create dialog boxes: product, subsidiary, warranty, and service center. Create the dialog boxes by entering

[Apple/m] 5
Product name [Return]
[Apple/Shift/r]

[Apple/m] 5
Purchased From[Return]
[Apple/Shift/r]

[Apple/m] 5
Warranty Period [Return]
[Apple/Shift/r]

461

8 Macros

The last item is service center. This item differs from the others. Because it is the last field in the record, it is ended with an End-of-Record command, [Apple/Shift/e]. Enter

[Apple/m] 5
[Return]
[Apple/Shift/e]

Conclude the macro by entering

[Apple/Shift/m]

Load the list document by entering

[Apple/o]

> **Point** at list document
> **Double Click**

Move the cursor to the bottom of the document. Enter

[Enter] [Enter] ↓

Execute the macro. Enter

[Apple/Option/m]

The macro displays the dialog box.

462

Macros **8**

The macro displays the dialog box.

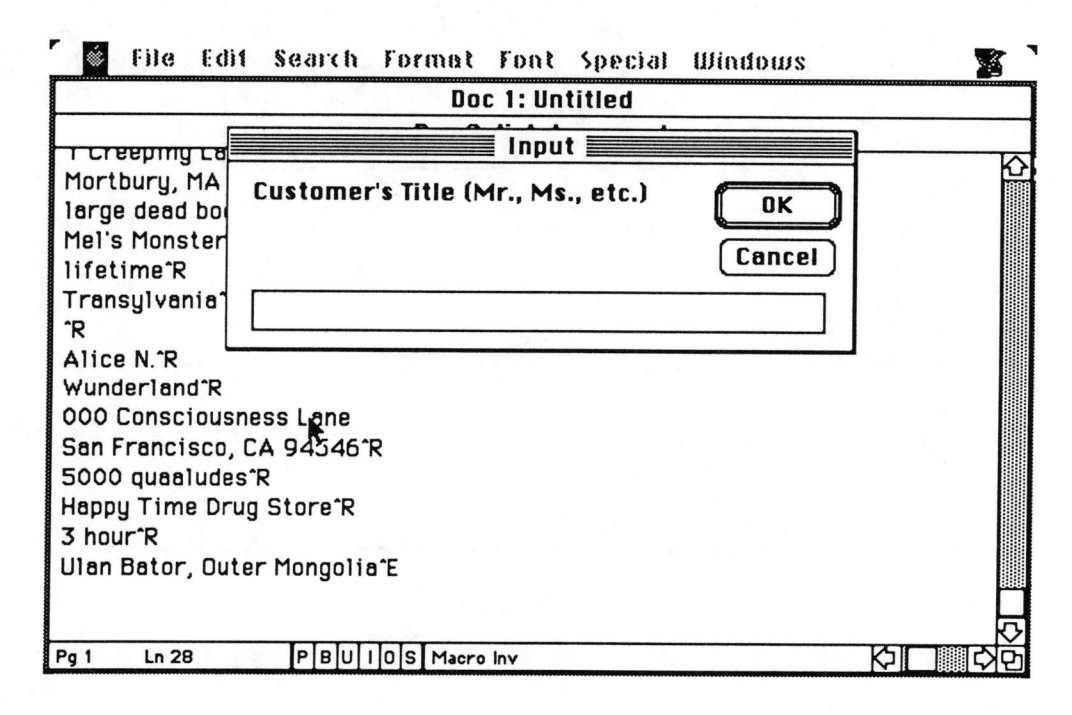

Figure 8.22

Note that the dialog box displays the prompts you created as part of the display. You can now respond to the dialog box by entering the information it requests.

Mr. [Return]

The macro displays the next dialog box

463

8 Macros

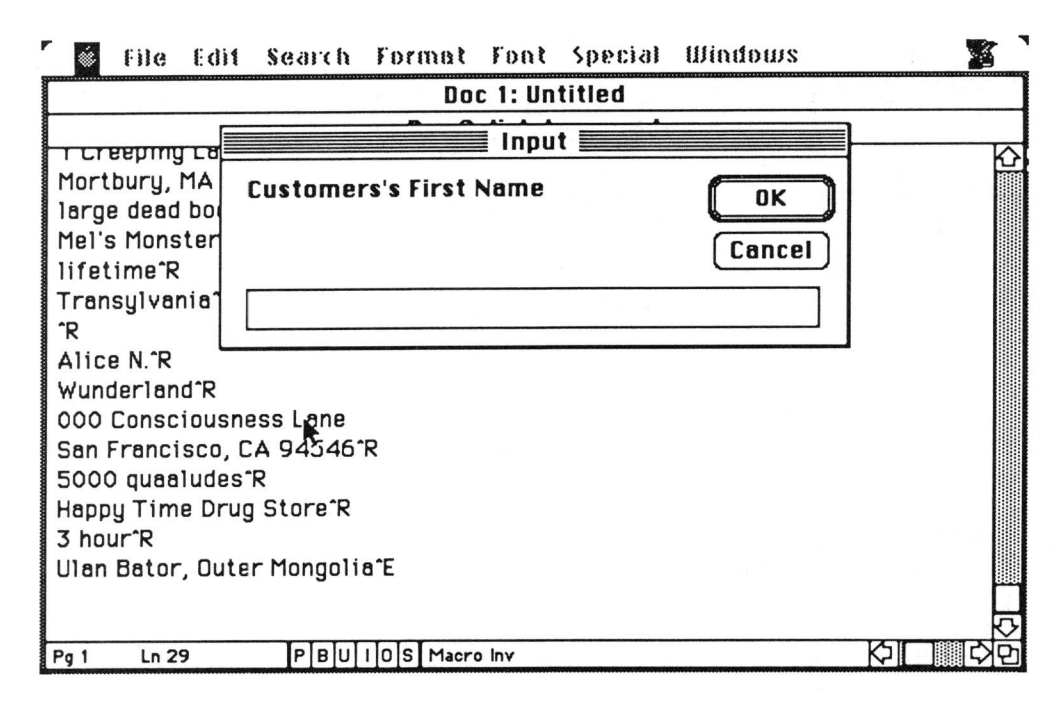

Figure 8.23

Continue the entry:

Pierre [Return]
Fermat [Return]
1250 Pine Street [Return]
Dallas, TX 22333 [Return]
Prime number generator [Return]
The Math Store [Return]
infinity [Return]
Englewood New Jersey [Return]

The macro ends, causing WordPerfect to rewrite the screen display. The text you entered appears as a correctly formatted record.

Macros **8**

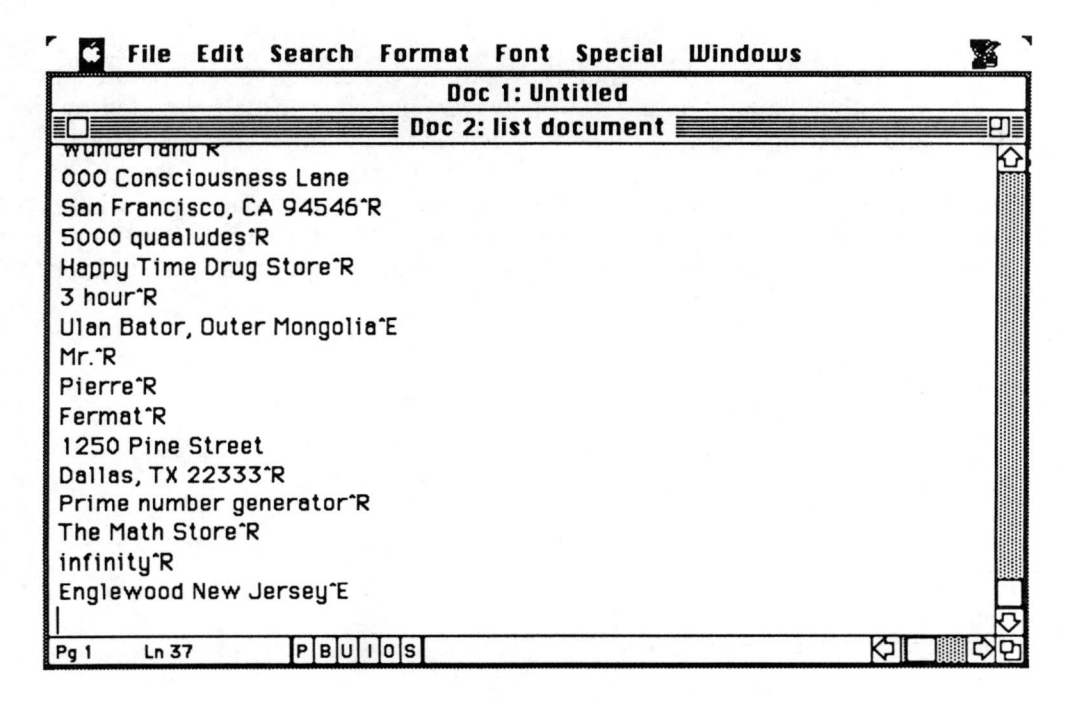

```
 File   Edit   Search   Format   Font   Special   Windows
                     Doc 1: Untitled
                  Doc 2: list document
wonderland^R
000 Consciousness Lane
San Francisco, CA 94546^R
5000 quaaludes^R
Happy Time Drug Store^R
3 hour^R
Ulan Bator, Outer Mongolia^E
Mr.^R
Pierre^R
Fermat^R
1250 Pine Street
Dallas, TX 22333^R
Prime number generator^R
The Math Store^R
infinity^R
Englewood New Jersey^E

Pg 1   Ln 37      P B U I O S
```

Figure 8.24

Save and close the file by entering

[Apple/s]
[Apple/k]

Nesting Macros

The process of adding a record requires a few more steps than your macro actually contains. For example, to enter the new record, you need to open the list document file, move the cursor to the end of the file, start the [Apple/Option/m] macro, and finally save and close the file.

465

8 Macros

One disadvantage of macros is that they cannot be edited (i.e., expanded or revised) after they have been created; however, macros can be expanded by a method called **nesting**. Nesting refers to macros that use other macros as part of their operation. In this example, you might create a new macro that uses the existing [Apple/Option/m] macro as part of its operation. The macro you want to create will include the commands that were not included in the [Apple/Option/m] macro, such as File Open. Call this new macro [Apple/Option/a] ("a" for "add" a record).

Enter

[Apple/Shift/m]

```
Point at the Single Key box
Click
```

Enter

a [Return]

The first step is to load the list document file. Enter

[Apple/o]

```
Point at list document
Double Click
```

Move the cursor to the end of the document by entering

[Enter] [Enter] ↓

466

Macros **8**

At this point, you can nest the [Apple/Option/m] macro inside the new macro you are creating by simply entering the macro command just as you would whenever you wanted to execute the macro. Enter

[Apple/Option/m]

WordPerfect now executes the macro, [Apple/Option/m], which means it will display the series of dialog boxes that create a record.

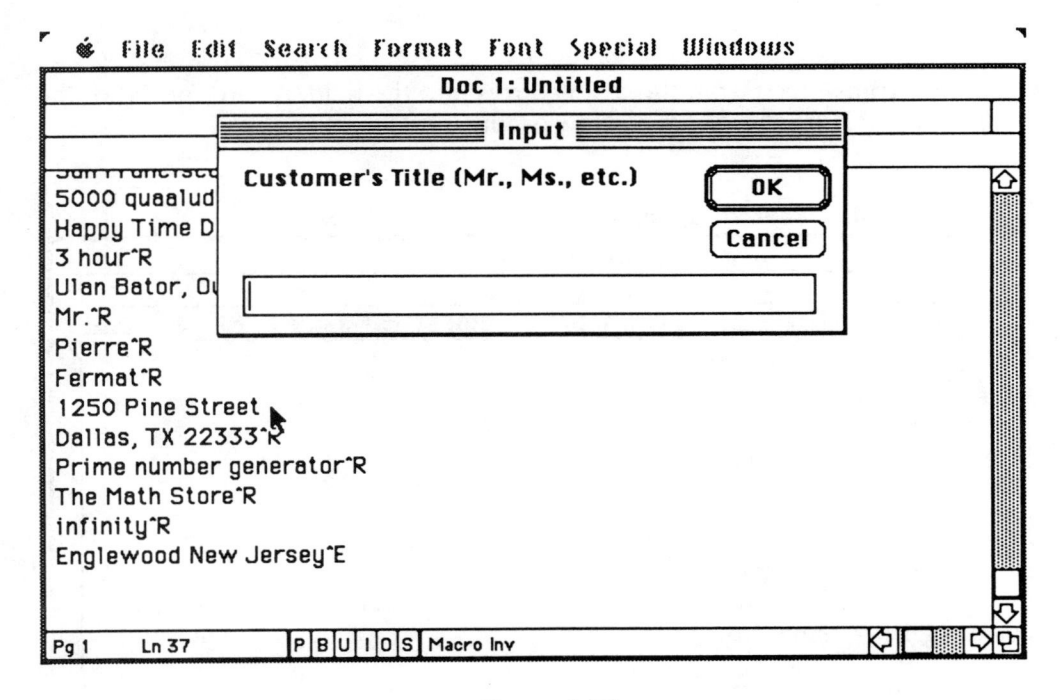

Figure 8.25

467

8 Macros

Enter the following responses to the dialog boxes:

Mr. [Return]
Sally [Return]
Starr [Return]
33 Weeping Willow Lane [Return]
Concord, CA 94555 [Return]
goldfish [Return]
The Friendly Pet Store [Return]
2 day [Return]
Faulkland Islands [Return]

The data is transferred from the dialog boxes into the field/record format of the list document. Note that the macro recording mode is still active.

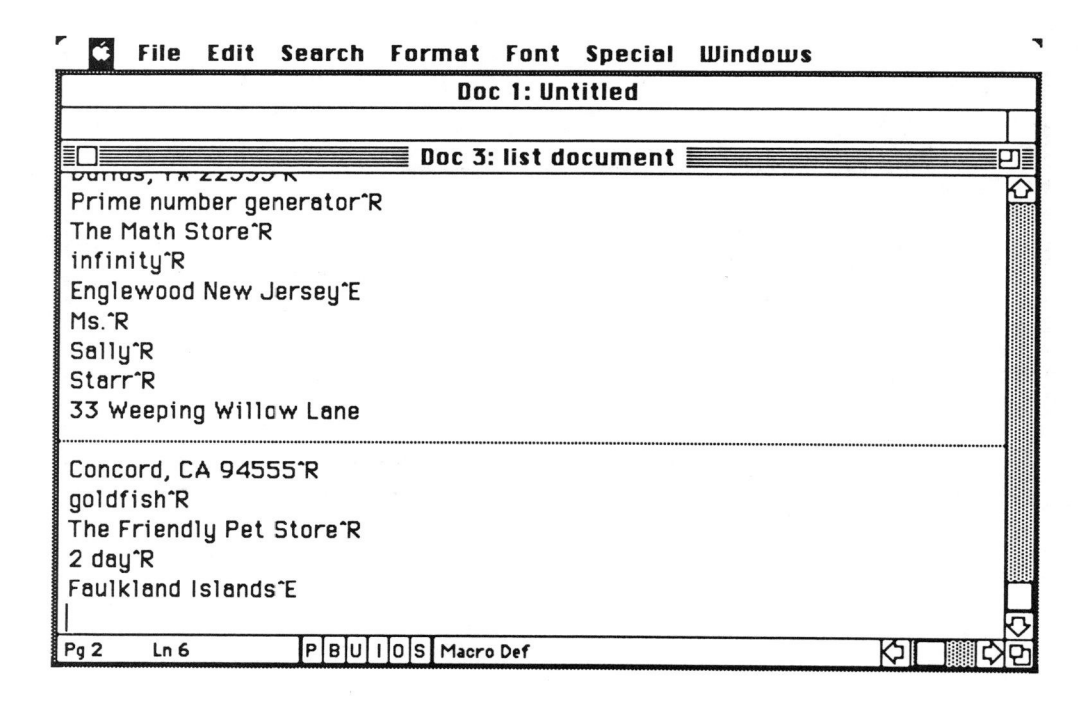

Figure 8.26

Macros **8**

You can now enter the commands needed to save the revised list document and close the file. Enter

[Apple/s]
[Apple/k]

Conclude the macro recording by entering

[Apple/Shift/m]

You have now created a macro, [Apple/Shift/a], that consists in part of the keystrokes entered in a different macro, [Apple/Shift/m].

To test this macro, enter

[Apple/Option/a]

WordPerfect automatically loads the list document and displays the dialog box for entry of a new record. If you look at the background, you will see that the list document appears to be blank because WordPerfect does not stop during an invisible macro to re-draw the screen. The list document is actually filled with text, but WordPerfect will not take the trouble to display that information until the macro is complete. By skipping the screen drawing, WordPerfect executes the macro at the fastest possible speed. You can prompt WordPerfect to re-draw the screen during a macro's execution by inserting a timed delay, [Apple/m] 4, in the macro. When WordPerfect encounters a delay, it will re-draw the screen display.

HALTING A MACRO

Suppose that at this point you decide that you do not want to complete this macro. WordPerfect allows you to cancel a macro by entering [Apple/.]. In most cases entering [Apple/.] will terminate the macro; however, the exception is the situation you have now. At this point, the macro is paused—in this case, with a dialog box input display. If you entered [Apple/.], you would cancel the dialog box but the macro would continue to run.

469

8 Macros

To halt a macro when it is paused, you must enter a double command, i.e., two consecutive [Apple/.] commands. Because timing is important when entering a halt instruction, you can type the double [Apple/.] by holding down the [Apple] key and pressing the period twice. Enter

[Apple/.] (press period twice)

The dialog box disappears, and the macro is halted. You can confirm that you have halted the macro by looking at the bottom bar. The words "Inv Macro" have been removed from the bar, indicating that the macro is no longer running.

Close the document window by entering

[Apple/k]

Note that the window closes with the [Apple/k] command, which tells you that the macro was halted before you entered any new data into your list document.

The concept of nesting is to macros what cut and paste is to text. Nesting allows you to combine several small macros into a larger, more complete procedure. Nesting allows you to develop a large macro out of a series of small operations. Because macros cannot be edited or revised once they have been created, it is always best to develop a large macro out of a series of small macros nested together, which enables you to create and test each part of the macro separately before you combine them into the final procedure. If you encounter an error, you can correct that specific macro without having to re-record the entire procedure.

Another benefit of building large macros from nesting small macros is that you can use the same macro more than once within a nested macro. For example, you might use [Apple/Option/m] several times in a larger macro. Reusing the same macro takes up less disk space then repeatedly recording the same keystrokes over and over in a large macro.

Macros are powerful, but they do require planning. To build an effective macro procedure, you should take some time to think about exactly how the macro should work before you turn on the recording mode. In planning, you should try to break the macro down into a series of smaller macros, each one accomplishing one task in the overall procedure. Create and test each step, and then combine the steps into the final procedure. You will find that the time you take to plan your macro will pay off in time saved tracking down errors.

CHAINS AND SEARCHES

The final topic in this chapter is an example of how macros can be combined with WordPerfect's search abilities to create intelligent macros. The term **intelligent** refers to macros that can perform actions selectively.

For example, suppose that as your customer list grows, you decide that you want to send a form letter or generate a report for a selected group of records. You might want to select only those customers from California or base the selection on some other specific criterion.

You can accomplish this task by creating a macro that will copy the specific records to the clipboard and then paste those records into a new document. In effect, the macro will perform a series of cut and paste operations for you.

The trick is to include a Search command in the macro. The search will cause the macro to locate the items you are looking for — in this example, the state of California.

But such a macro will find only the first matching record. What about the other records that match? The answer lies in the use of a **chained macro**. The trick is to chain the current macro to itself, which means that the last command in the macro is an instruction to run the same macro again.

This strategy appears to make a macro that will go on forever; however, WordPerfect has included an escape clause in the macro chain command. If the search fails to find any more matching items and displays a *not found* message, WordPerfect cancels the macro chain. A chained macro must contain a Search command. If it doesn't, the macro will repeat endlessly until you manually canceled the macro.

8 Macros

You can use this chain concept to carry out your goal of extracting records from the list document. Load the list document file. Enter

[Apple/o]

> **Point** at list document
> **Click**

Turn on the macro recording mode. Assign this macro the name "Select." Enter

[Apple/Shift/m]
select [Return]

The first step is to locate the first record that contains the state abbreviation CA. Use the Search command to locate that record. Enter

[Apple/f]
ca [Return]

The cursor is now highlighting the abbreviation CA in the third record, "Alice Wunderland." You now need to use the Select and Append commands to place this text into the clipboard. Enter

[Enter] ←
↑ (4 times)
[Apple/Shift/n]
↓ (9 times)

472

Macros 8

You have now selected the entire record. The next step is to transfer the selected text to another location. There are many ways to perform this transfer. You can copy it to another document window, place it in the clipboard, or append it to an existing file on the disk. If you believe that the total number of records that will match is small, using the clipboard is the fastest method. If you have a large number of records, you might want to use the Append command and select the To File option to append the records to a disk file. You would need to create a disk file in advance to receive the records. In this example, use the clipboard. Enter

[Apple/a] 1

Turn off the selection mode by entering

[Apple/Shift/n]

You have now completed the cycle for this macro. The rest of the macro is a repetition of this operation until there are no more records left in the file to extract.

To carry out this repetition until no more records are found, chain the macro to itself. Enter

[Apple/m]

Choose the Chain Macro option. Enter

3

The selector display asks you to choose the macro to which you want to chain this macro. To make a repeating loop, enter the name of the macro you are creating.

select [Return]

473

8 Macros

The loop is closed. Turn off the macro recording. Enter

[Apple/Shift/m]

At this point, in recording the macro, you have manually inserted the first record into the clipboard. Run your macro to locate and extract any other records in the file that also match the criterion. Enter

[Apple/Shift/x]
select [Return]

The macro executes, searching the file and extracting the matching records until it reaches the end of the list document.

When the search returns a *not found* response, the looping macro automatically terminates. The clipboard now contains the records you wanted to extract.

Open a new file by entering

[Apple/n]

Paste the records in the clipboard into the new document. Enter

[Apple/v]

You now have a new list document that contains just the selected records. You can use this document as the secondary merge file to produce form letters or reports with only the selected records.

SUMMARY

- **Macros.** A macro is a special user-defined command sequence that is stored on the disk and can be replayed whenever needed. Macros allow you to create customized commands by linking a series of standard WordPerfect commands. Macros are created by recording the keystrokes you enter. Macros are executed by playing those keystrokes back. Macro recording is turned on and off by entering [Apple/Shift/m]. Macros are executed by entering [Apple/Shift/x].

- **Macro Names.** Macros can be assigned two types of names: normal Macintosh file names or single-keystroke names. The macros with file names are executed by entering [Apple/Shift/x] or selecting the file name. The single-keystroke macros can be executed by using an [Apple/Option] key combination with the single letter name of the macro, e.g., [Apple/Option/a].

- **[Enter] Key Commands.** You can increase the number of keyboard alternatives for menu options by assigning the menu options to combinations of [Enter] or [Enter][Enter]. The assignment is made in the WordPerfect help display, [Apple/?]. When the list of help topics is displayed, select the desired menu option, click on Define, and enter the letter key you want to associate with the menu option. Once the key is defined, you can execute the menu option from the keyboard by entering [Enter] or [Enter][Enter] followed by the letter.

- **Macro Pauses.** To create macros with more general utility, you can insert pauses into macros using the [Apple/m] 6 command. When a macro is paused, entering [Apple/m] 6 resumes the execution of the macro.

- **Input Boxes.** Another form of macro pausing can be used to display a dialog box that prompts the user to enter a specific text item. The [Apple/m] 5 command pauses a macro and displays a dialog box during the execution of a macro. The macro resumes when the user enters [Return].

- **Nesting.** Nesting refers to executing one macro as part of another. Nesting allows you to build large macros out of a series of smaller macros.

8 Macros

- **Cancel.** You can cancel a macro by entering [Apple/.]

- **Chains.** By chaining a macro, [Apple/m] 3, to itself, you can create a macro that repeats until a thorough search of the document has been completed. This type of macro must include a Search command, or it will create an endless loop.

- **Invisible.** Macros normally execute in an invisible mode, i.e., WordPerfect executes the keystrokes without pausing to re-draw the screen display. You can prompt WordPerfect to re-draw the screen during a macro's execution by inserting a Macro Delay command, [Apple/m] 4, into the macro.

CHAPTER 9

REFERENCE TASKS

9 Reference Tasks

While most of the documents you create will be simple letters or correspondence, WordPerfect provides some powerful tools for creating large documents such as reports, papers, legal documents or even books. In addition to the text-handling operations needed to prepare these large documents, you may need to prepare reference texts, such as tables of contents, indexes, or item lists, that accompany them. WordPerfect provides a means by which these types of reference materials can be automatically generated from your documents.

The advantage of this automatic generation is that when a document is revised, WordPerfect can update the page references automatically.

This chapter covers how to generate these reference tasks. Also included is the use of special text markings to show revisions made to a document, which is useful when a document is edited by more than one person and changes need to be revised before they are made permanent.

This chapter assumes that you are beginning with a blank document window.

TABLES OF CONTENTS

WordPerfect has the ability to generate lists, tables of contents, and indexes from documents. In order to have WordPerfect generate these lists, you must prepare the document by adding special codes that mark the text to be included in the list, table of contents, or index.

The markings that you place in the text are in the form of WordPerfect codes, which means that they do not appear on the normal text display and have no effect on normal editing or printing.

When the markings are complete, WordPerfect will search the document for markings and then create the appropriate list, table of contents, or index.

The markings (i.e., codes) required for list generation can be entered while you are creating the document, or they can be added after the text has already been entered. Once a document is marked, you can choose to generate a list at any time. You can generate a new set of lists, tables of contents, or indexes after any revision in the document so that the references will be accurate.

The lists, tables of contents, or indexes will show the page numbers for the marked items based on the current version of the document. The advantage of this system is that if you revise the document, and change the position of items in the text, you can simply execute another Generation command and obtain an up-to-date list or table of contents.

To get a clear idea of how WordPerfect creates these lists, you can create a sample document and mark it as you would a document that requires a table of contents. Begin by entering the following:

THE WORLD'S SMALLEST NATION [Return]
[Return]
ANDORRA [Return]
[Return]

Enter the following paragraph:

The nation of Andorra is officially called Valleys of Andorra. The nation is located in the Pyrenees Mountains between the better known nations of France and Spain. [Return]
[Return]

Enter a heading that is meant to be related to an illustration.

RELIEF MAP OF ANDORRA
[Return]

Start a new page by entering

[Apple/Return]

9 Reference Tasks

Enter the next page of text:

POPULATION [Return]
[Return]
The 35,000 people of Andorra live on 188 square miles of land. That is a population density of about 180.85 people per square mile. The United States has an average population of about 65 people per square mile. [Return]
[Return]
POLITICAL MAP OF ANDORRA [Return]
[Apple/Return]

Enter the next page:

COMMUNICATIONS IN ANDORRA [Return]
[Return]
Andorra has about 10,000 telephones, about 6,000 radios and 3,000 televisions. The main economic activity is tourism and some goat herding. [return]
[Apple/Return]

Enter the next page:

GOVERNMENT [Return]
[Return]
HEAD OF STATE [Return]
[Return]
Andorra is ruled by two princes. One is usually the head of state in France and the other is the Bishop of Urgel in Spain. This joint sovereignty has been in effect since 1278. [Return]
HEAD OF GOVERNMENT [Return]
[Return]
Andorra is ruled by a local governor who is appointed by the local council.
[Return]
[Apple/Return]

Reference Tasks 9

Enter the final page:

HEALTH [Return]
[Return]
BIRTH RATE [Return]
[Return]
The birth rate in Andorra is 16.5 per 1000. [Return]
[Return]
DEATH RATE [Return]
[Return]
The death rate is 5.0 per 1000. [Return]
[Return]
NATURAL INCREASE [Return]
[Return]
The increase in population is about 1.2%. [Return]
[Apple/Return]

The entire document should resemble Figures 9.1-9.4:

```
 File  Edit  Search  Format  Font  Special  Windows
═══════════════════ Doc 1: Untitled ═══════════════════
THE WORLD'S SMALLEST NATION

ANDORRA

The nation of Andorra is officially called Valleys of Andorra.
The nation is located in the Pyrenees Mountains between the
better known nations of France and Spain.

RELIEF MAP OF ANDORRA

POPULATION

The 35,000 people of Andorra live on 188 square miles of land.
That is a population density of about 180.85 people per square
mile. The United States has an average population of about 65
people per square mile.

Pg 1   Ln 1       P B U I O S
```

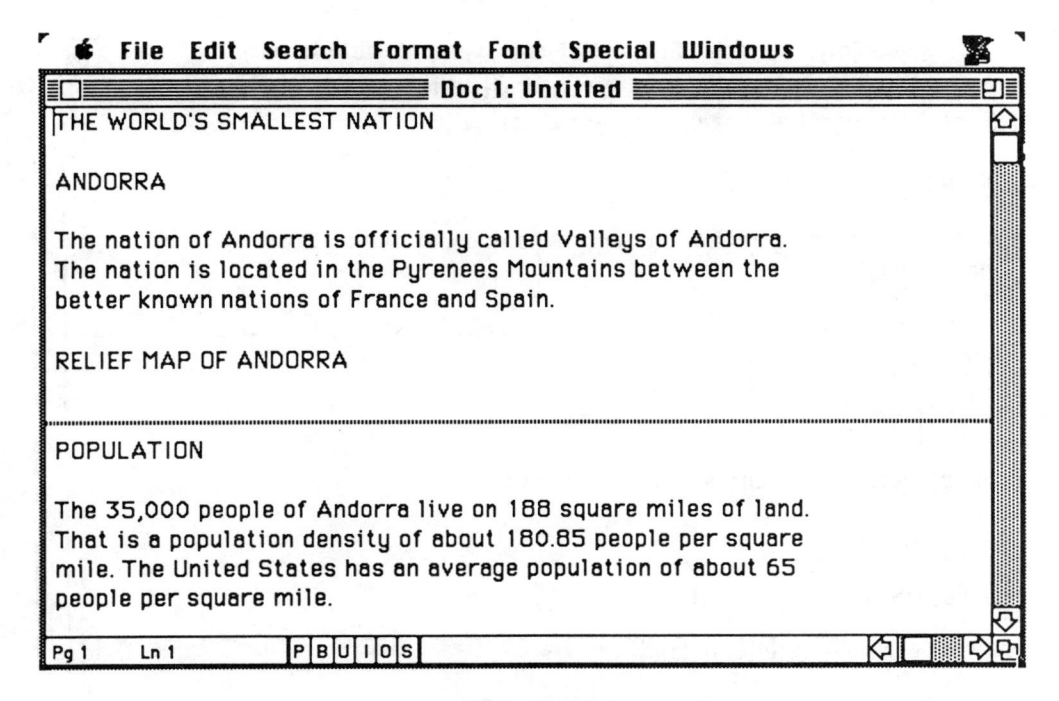

Figure 9.1

9 Reference Tasks

```
 File   Edit   Search   Format   Font   Special   Windows
                        Doc 1: Untitled

POLITICAL MAP OF ANDORRA

COMMUNICATIONS IN ANDORRA

Andorra has about 10,000 telephones, about 6,000 radios and 3,000
televisions. The main economic activity is tourism and some goat
herding.

GOVERNMENT

HEAD OF STATE

Andorra is ruled by two princes. One is usually the head of state
in France and the other is the Bishop of Urgel in Spain. This
joint sovereignty has been in effect since 1278.

Pg 4   Ln 6        P B U I O S
```

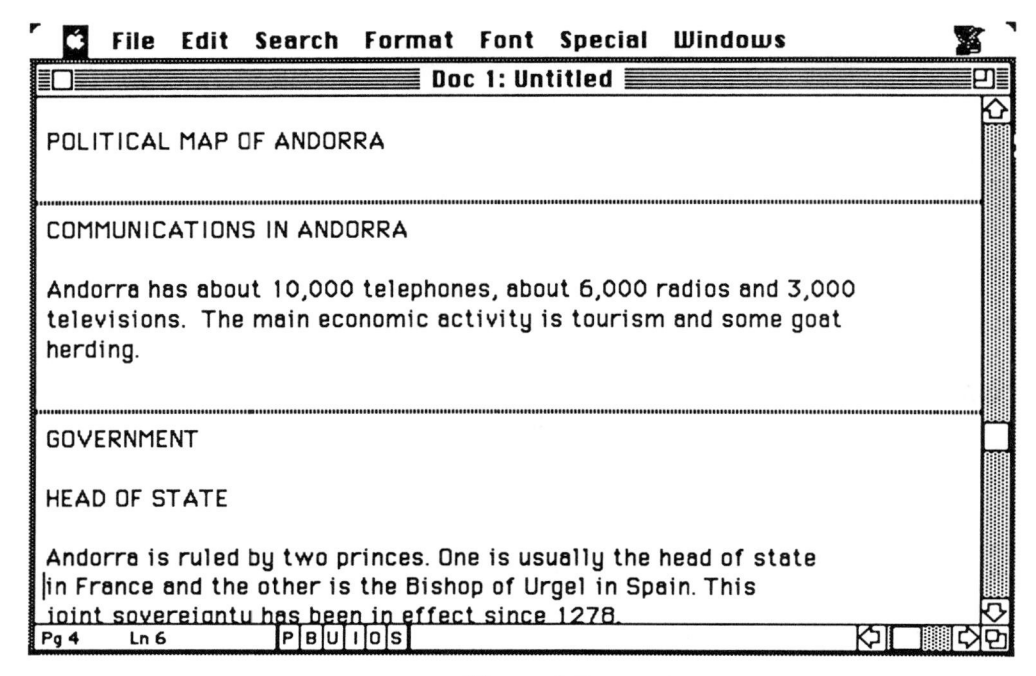

Figure 9.2

```
 File   Edit   Search   Format   Font   Special   Windows
                        Doc 1: Untitled

joint sovereignty has been in effect since 1278.

HEAD OF GOVERNMENT

Andorra is ruled by a local governor who is appointed by the
local council.

HEALTH

BIRTH RATE

The birth rate in Andorra is 16.5 per 1000.

DEATH RATE

The death rate is 5.0 per 1000.

Pg 5   Ln 9        P B U I O S
```

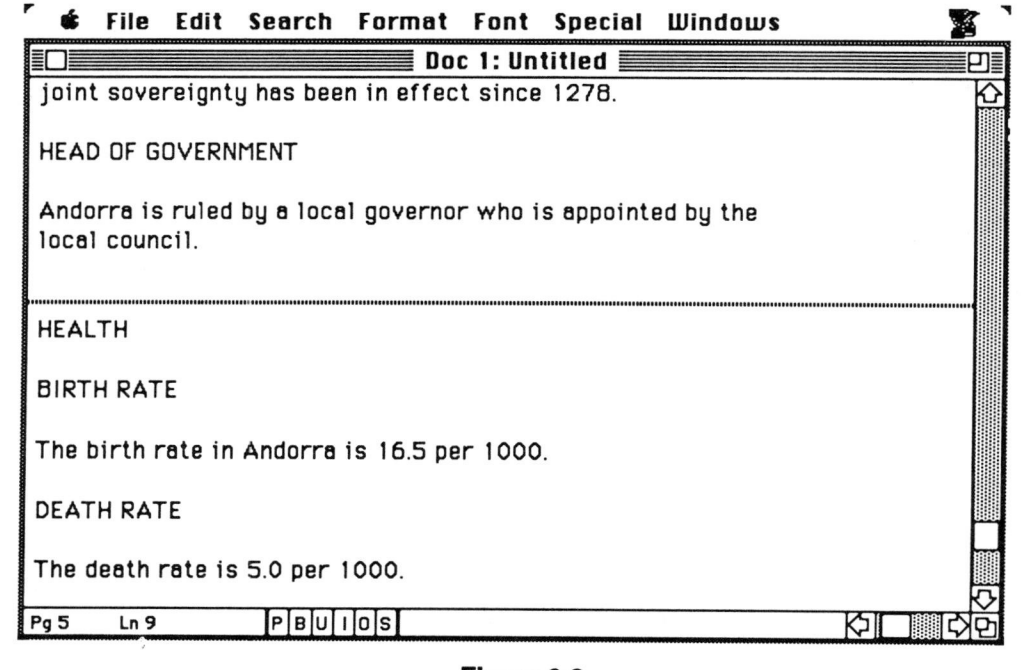

Figure 9.3

Reference Tasks 9

```
 File  Edit  Search  Format  Font  Special  Windows
┌─────────────────── Doc 1: Untitled ───────────────────┐
│ NATURAL INCREASE                                       │
│                                                        │
│ The increase in population is about 1.2%.              │
│ |                                                      │
│                                                        │
│                                                        │
│                                                        │
│                                                        │
│ Pg 5    Ln 14      P B U I O S                         │
└────────────────────────────────────────────────────────┘
```

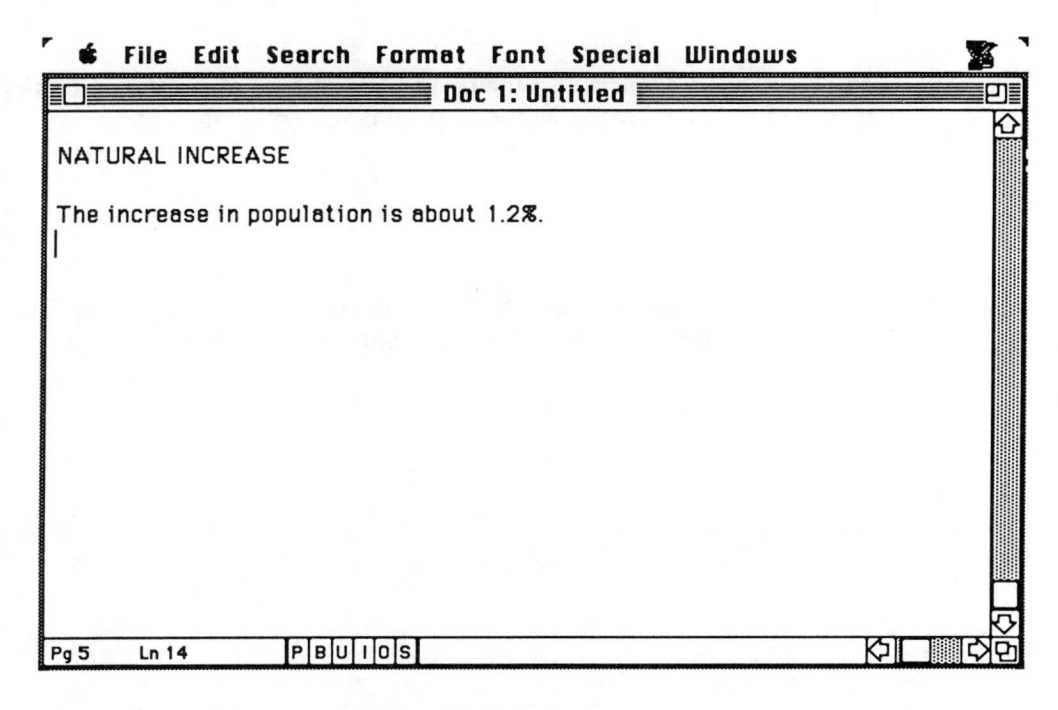

Figure 9.4

Place the cursor at the beginning of the document.   Enter

[Enter] [Enter] ↑

Marking Table of Contents Items

WordPerfect allows you to select lines of text to be included in a table of contents for the document. First, select the text that you want to mark for the table of contents. Then, select the table, list, or index into which this text should be included. Select the first heading in the document.

[Apple/Shift/n]
[Enter] →

483

9 Reference Tasks

Once the text is selected you must tell WordPerfect what type of reference table it should be included in. Display the Mark Text menu by entering

[Apple/j]

The menu will show three active choices: list, table of contents, and index. In this case, the topic should be included in the table of contents. Enter

2

WordPerfect displays a box that allows you to select the level for the text item in the table of contents. For example, major headings are level 1, subheadings are level 2, etc.

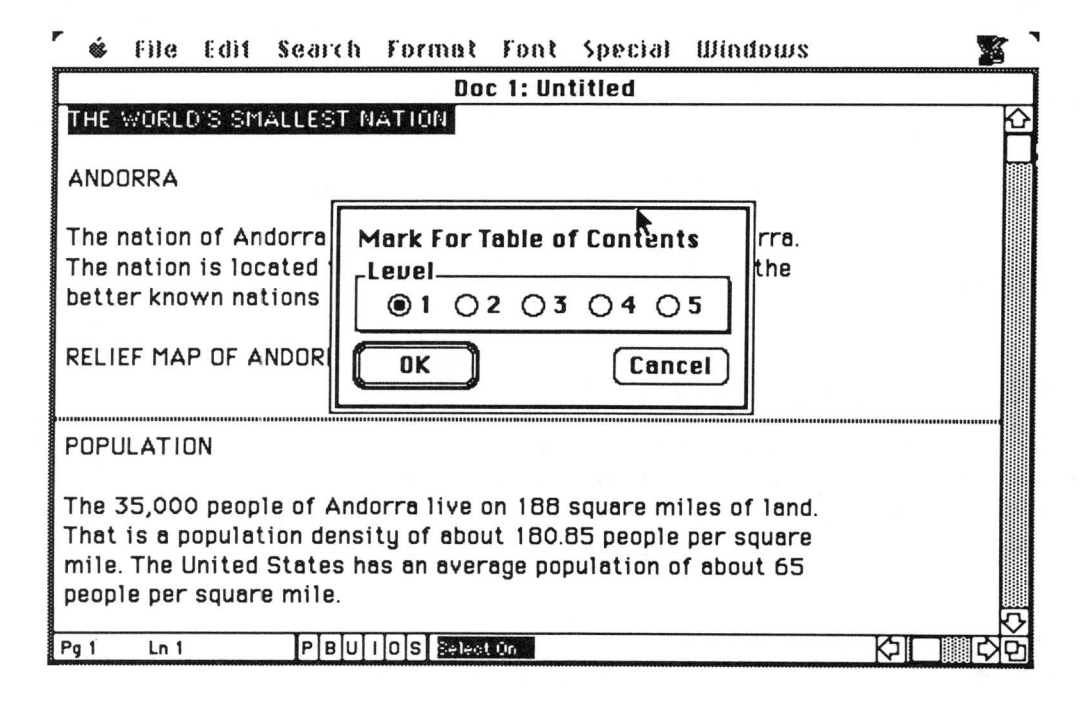

Figure 9.5

Reference Tasks **9**

The default is level 1. Enter

[Return]

The text is now marked as a level 1 table of contents item. Display the codes to see how WordPerfect marks the text.

Enter

[Apple/7]

The screen should resemble the following:

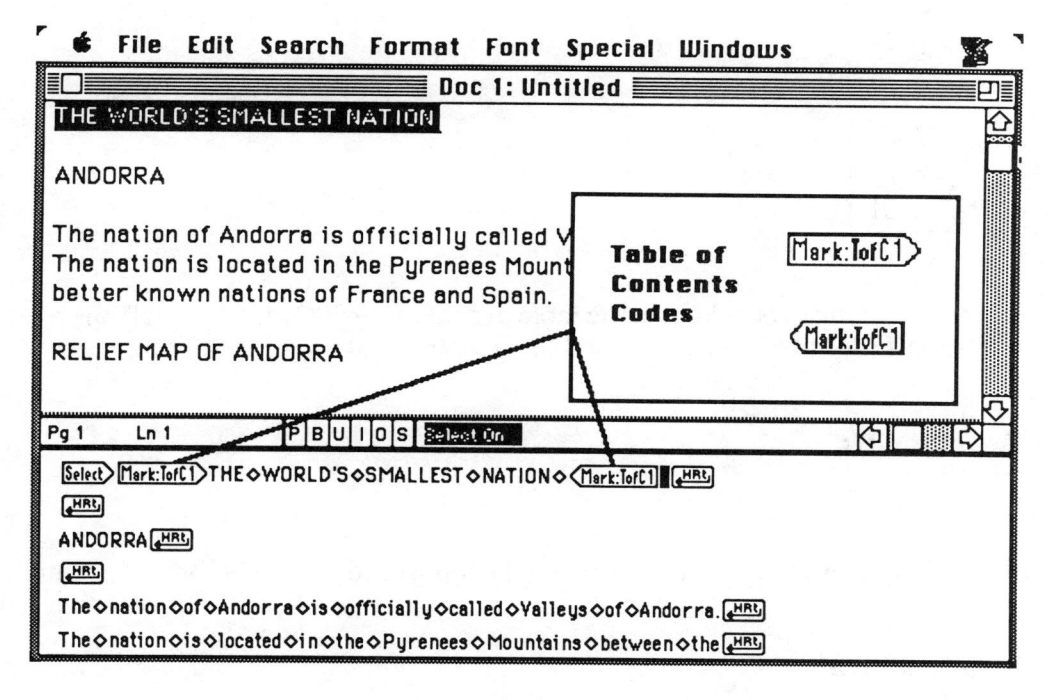

Figure 9.6

485

9 Reference Tasks

Close the codes display by entering

[Apple/7]

Move to the next heading by entering

↓↓

Mark this heading as a level 2 table of contents entry. Enter

[Apple/Shift/n]
[Enter] ←
[Apple/j] 2

> **Point** at 2
> **Click**
> **Click** on OK

The next heading to be added to the table of contents is "POPULATION" on page 2. Turn off the current selection and move to the next page by entering

[Apple/Shift/n]
↓ (8 times)

Mark "POPULATION" as a second-level heading for the table of contents. Enter

[Apple/Shift/n]
[Enter] →
[Apple/j] 2

486

Reference Tasks **9**

> **Point** at 2
> **Click**
> **Click** on OK

Enter

[Apple/Shift/n]

Figure 9.7 shows how the other levels in this document should be marked. Continue the process by marking the items as indicated. You might want to take a shortcut when marking these items by creating macros that select text as first-, second-, or third-level headings for the table of contents—similar to the way you created outline macros in Chapter 8.

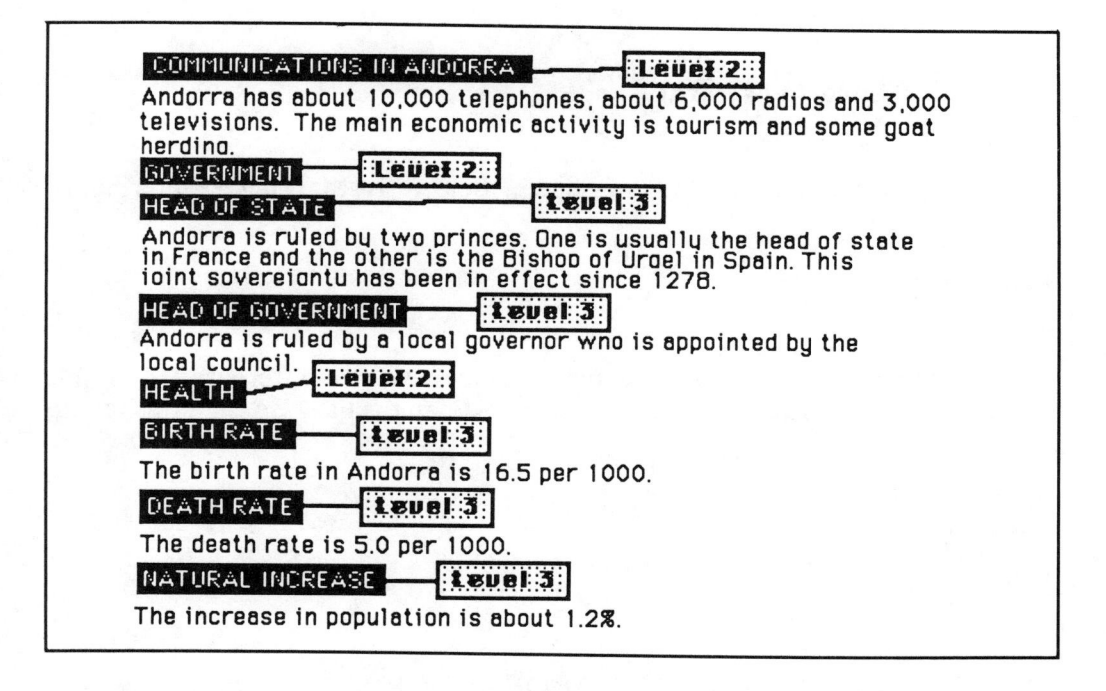

```
COMMUNICATIONS IN ANDORRA ——— Level 2
Andorra has about 10,000 telephones, about 6,000 radios and 3,000
televisions. The main economic activity is tourism and some goat
herding.
GOVERNMENT ——— Level 2
HEAD OF STATE ——— Level 3
Andorra is ruled by two princes. One is usually the head of state
in France and the other is the Bishop of Urgel in Spain. This
joint sovereigntu has been in effect since 1278.
HEAD OF GOVERNMENT ——— Level 3
Andorra is ruled by a local governor who is appointed by the
local council.
HEALTH ——— Level 2
BIRTH RATE ——— Level 3
The birth rate in Andorra is 16.5 per 1000.
DEATH RATE ——— Level 3
The death rate is 5.0 per 1000.
NATURAL INCREASE ——— Level 3
The increase in population is about 1.2%.
```

Figure 9.7

487

9 Reference Tasks

When you have completed the marking, return the cursor to the top of the document by entering

[Enter] [Enter] ↑

OTHER LISTS

WordPerfect also allows you to define items that should be placed on special lists, such as illustrations or maps.

There are two such items in the Andorra document: the relief map of Andorra and the political map of Andorra. To locate and select these items in one step, use the Search command to locate the items. When Search finds a block of text, that block is automatically selected. You can then immediately enter the Mark Text command. Enter

[Apple/f]
relief map of andorra [Return]

The text is located and selected in one step. Select List Marking by entering

[Apple/j] 1

WordPerfect allows you to mark items for as many as five different lists. In this example, you will use one list, for maps. The default is list 1. Assign this text to list 1.

```
Point at OK
Click
```

Move the cursor to "POLITICAL MAP OF ANDORRA," using the Search command.

488

[Apple/f]
political map of andorra [Return]

Mark this item as part of list 1. Enter

[Apple/j] 1 [Return]

INDEXES

Another distinct type of list that can be generated from a document is an index. Index entries are created the same way as list items with the exception that you have the option to manually enter a subheading with the index item.

To illustrate how indexes are created, you will make a few sample entries. To simplify this process, you can use the Search command to find the words you want to add to the index. (Note that searching for a specific word and marking it as an index item could be accomplished by a macro if you perform this task often.) Position the cursor at the beginning of the document by entering

[Enter] [Enter] ↑

Search for the word "Pyrenees" by entering

[Apple/f]
pyrenees [Return]

WordPerfect locates and selects the first match for this word. To mark the word as an index entry, use Option 3 on the Mark Text menu. Enter

[Apple/j] 3

9 Reference Tasks

WordPerfect displays the index entry dialog box.

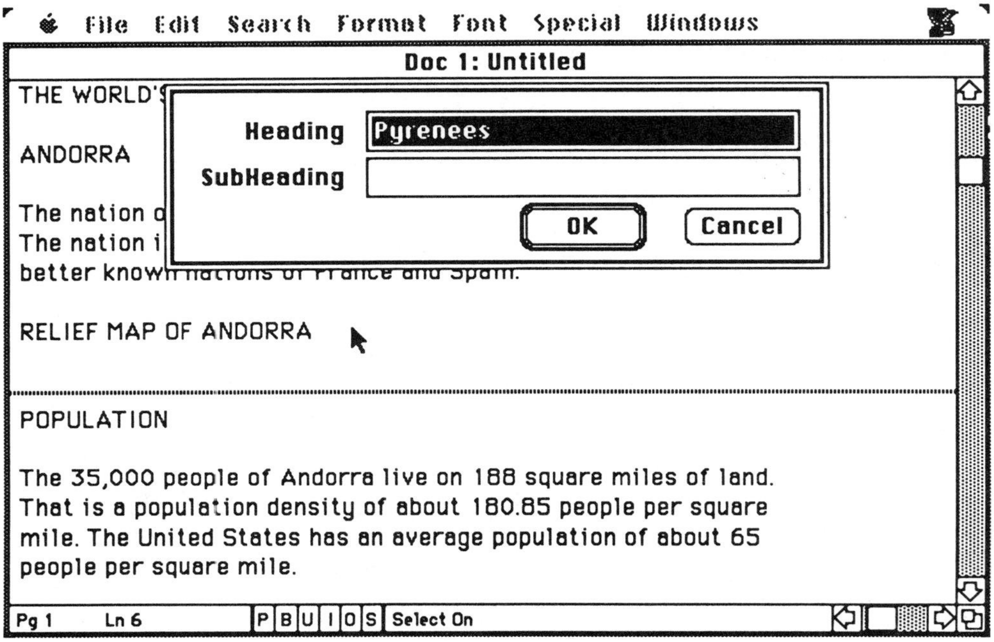

Figure 9.8

This dialog box has room for two entries, the index heading and subheading. The highlighted text is automatically entered as the index heading. You can accept the inserted heading or edit the text. For example, you might want the index entry to read "Pyrenees mountains." In this case, change the heading by entering

→
**[space bar]
mountains**

Reference Tasks **9**

Index Subheadings

You can add subheadings to index items. Subheadings are optional and appear in the index below the main heading. They are used when you have a large number of entries for a given heading and you want to indicate what particular aspect of the subject you are marking. Enter a subheading as follows:

[Tab]
location of [Return]

The index entry is placed into the text at that point. To see the effect of this command, display the codes by entering

[Apple/7]

The screen should resemble the following:

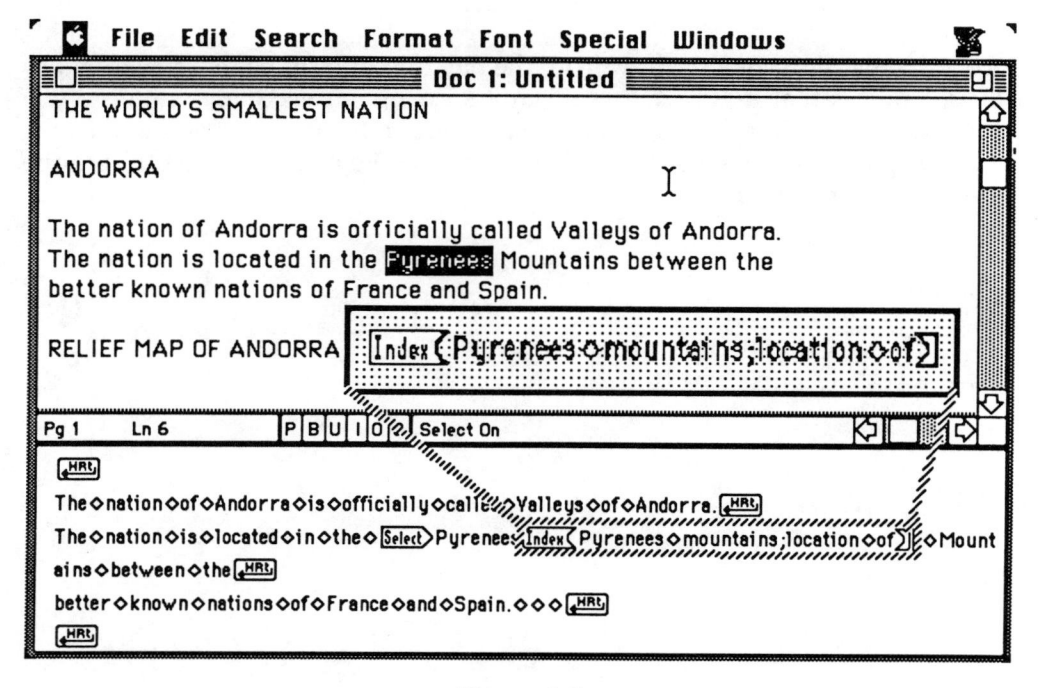

Figure 9.9

491

9 Reference Tasks

The index entry is created by a code that contains the text of the heading and subheading. This code is different from the table and list codes surrounding text that is part of the document.

This difference is significant because it indicates that the table of contents will automatically be updated if you edit the text between the codes; however, you cannot directly change the contents of an index entry when the text is edited, so the index will not automatically be updated.

For example, suppose that you changed the word "Pyrenees" to "Arcadia." The index entry code would still read [Index: Pyrenees mountains; location of]. In fact, you could delete the word "Pyrenees" from this part of the document, and WordPerfect would retain the index entry code.

To update the index entry, you would need to display the codes, delete the outdated index item, and add a new index entry. Note that in the table of contents, that would not be the case with a heading such as "RELIEF MAP OF ANDORRA." If you changed "ANDORRA" to "NEW JERSEY," the table of contents would contain the updated text because the change was entered between existing table of contents codes. Keep this difference in mind when you edit a document in which index codes have already been entered.

Another conclusion you can draw from the fact that indexes cannot be automatically updated is that it is best to wait until a document is complete before you enter index items; however, if you prefer to add index items as you enter text, simply keep this problem in mind when you revise the document. Return to the normal display by entering

[Apple/7]

Search for the word "MAP." Enter

[Apple/f]
map [Return]

Create an index entry. Enter

[Apple/j] 3
Political [Tab]
map [Return]

Enter another index item by finding the word "economic." Enter

[Apple/f]
economic [Return]

Create an index entry by entering

[Apple/j] 3 [Return]

You can continue the indexing process until you are satisfied that the document is adequately referenced. In this example, you can actually generate the lists and indexes indicated by the text marks in the document.

DEFINING LISTS AND TABLES

Before WordPerfect can generate the actual table of contents, list, and index, you must enter definitions for each of the items that is to generate a listing.

The definitions serve two purposes.

9 Reference Tasks

Format   WordPerfect has five styling options for the lists, tables, and indexes produced.

Style	Name	Example
Style #1	No Page number	Pyrenees
Style #2	Page Number Following	Pyrenees 2
Style #3	Page Number in Parentheses	Pyrenees (2)
Style #4	Flush right	Pyrenees 2
Style #5	Flush right with Dot Leader	Pyrenees................2

Lists and indexes can have any one of these five styles. Tables of contents are divided into five levels, and each level can be assigned a style. They can have the same style or different styles.

Location   The text location in which the definition code is entered is also the text location in which WordPerfect will place the generated table or index.

For example, because the table of contents usually precedes the text, the table of contents definition code should be at the beginning of the document. Similarly, because an index usually follows the text, the index definition should be placed at the end of the document.

Begin with the table of contents definition. Place the cursor at the beginning of the text. Enter

[Enter] [Enter] ↑

To make room for the table of contents, enter a blank line.

[Return]
↑

Reference Tasks **9**

Insert a title for this page. Enter

[Apple/Shift/c]
TABLE OF CONTENTS [Return] [Return]

Here, you want to insert the table of contents definition code. The codes are entered from the Define List menu located on the Special menu.

> **Point** at Special
> **Drag** to Define List
> **Release**

WordPerfect lists seven options—lists 1 through 5, plus table of contents and index. In this case, you want to select the location and style of the table of contents. Enter

6

The menu displays the options for formatting the table of contents.

495

9 Reference Tasks

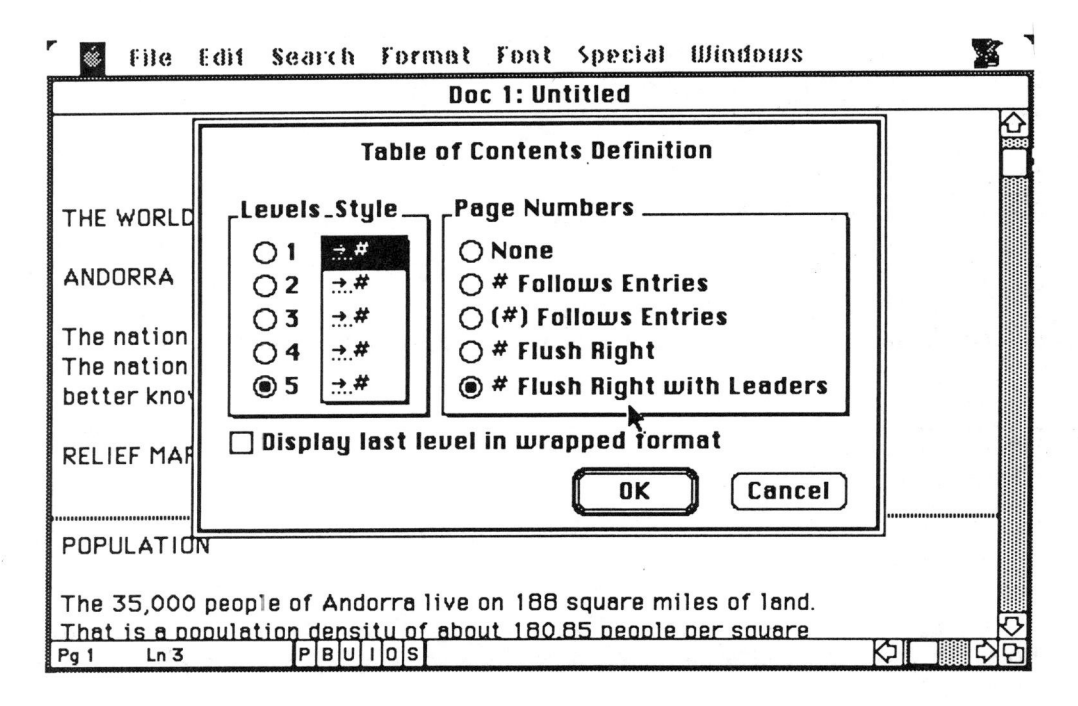

Figure 9.10

Levels

The Levels selection allows you to select how many heading levels should be included in the table of contents. For example, if you have defined three levels of headings in your document, you can choose to include only level 1 and level 2 headings in the table of contents by selecting Level 2. The default is level 5, meaning that all of the marked table of contents items will appear in the table of contents.

Style

The Style selection refers to the placement of the left side of the table of contents entry. The default is to precede each level by an indent followed by a number for the level, similar to the way outlines are numbered. The default setting is 5, indicating that all five levels of table of contents headings should be indented.

Page Numbers

This option allows you to choose the way page numbers are displayed following the table of contents items. The default is to place the page number flush right, and preceded by a dot leader.

Wrapped

WordPerfect provides an option that allows you to suppress the [HRt] following table of contents items of a certain level. When you suppress the [HRt], all headings on that level are wrapped into a paragraph style listing. This option is used when you have a large number of table of contents items and want to conserve the number of pages used in the table of contents.

Figure 9.11 shows the different formatting styles:

```
No Number Style
THE WORLD'S SMALLEST COUNTRY
    ANDORRA
    POPULATION
    COMMUNICATIONS IN ANDORRA
    GOVERNMENT
        HEAD OF STATE

Page Number Follow Entry
THE WORLD'S SMALLEST COUNTRY 2
    ANDORRA 2
    POPULATION 3
    COMMUNICATIONS IN ANDORRA 4
    GOVERNMENT 5
        HEAD OF STATE 5

(Page Number) Follow Entry
THE WORLD'S SMALLEST COUNTRY (2)
    ANDORRA (2)
    POPULATION (3)
    COMMUNICATIONS IN ANDORRA(4)
```

```
Flush Right Page Number
ANDORRA                         2
POPULATION                      3
COMMUNICATIONS IN ANDORRA       4
GOVERNMENT                      5
    HEAD OF STATE               5

Flush Right Page Number w/lead
ANDORRA . . . . . . . . . . . . . . . 2
POPULATION . . . . . . . . . . . . . 3
COMMUNICATIONS IN ANDORRA .  4
GOVERNMENT . . . . . . . . . . . . . 5
    HEAD OF STATE . . . . . . . 5
    HEAD OF GOVERNMENT . . 5
HEALTH . . . . . . . . . . . . . . . . 6
    BIRTH RATE . . . . . . . . . 6
```

Figure 9.11

9 Reference Tasks

In this case, accept the default setting by entering

[Return]

To make sure that there is a page break between the table of contents and text, enter a hard page ending:

[Apple/Return]

Now move the cursor to the end of the document and place the other definition codes in the text, following the document text. Enter

[Enter] [Enter] ↓

Create a page break by entering

[Apple/Return]

You can place the table of maps into the text on this page. Enter a heading:

TABLE OF MAPS [Return] [Return]

The next step is to insert a Define Lists code into the text at this point.

Point at Special
Drag to Define Lists
Release

498

Reference Tasks 9

Select List 1 by entering

1

The screen should resemble the following:

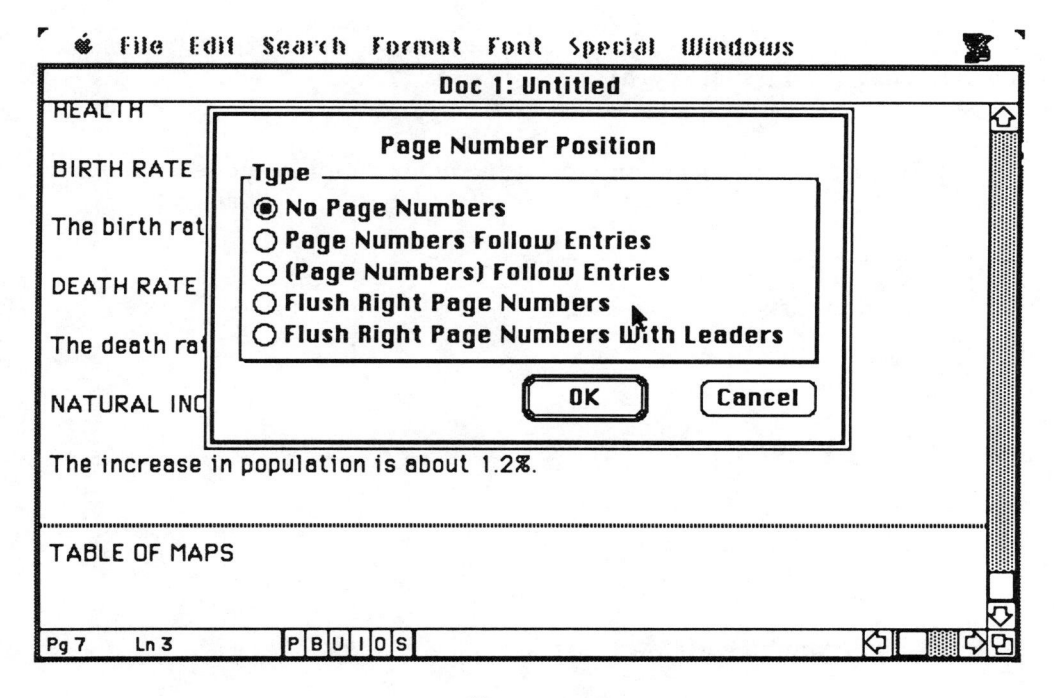

```
┌──────────────────────────────────────────────────────┐
│  File  Edit  Search  Format  Font  Special  Windows  │
├──────────────────────────────────────────────────────┤
│                    Doc 1: Untitled                    │
│  HEALTH                                               │
│                  Page Number Position                 │
│  BIRTH RATE   ┌Type─────────────────────────────┐    │
│               │ ● No Page Numbers               │    │
│  The birth rat│ ○ Page Numbers Follow Entries   │    │
│               │ ○ (Page Numbers) Follow Entries │    │
│  DEATH RATE   │ ○ Flush Right Page Numbers      │    │
│               │ ○ Flush Right Page Numbers With Leaders│
│  The death ra │                                 │    │
│               │      [  OK  ]    [ Cancel ]     │    │
│  NATURAL INC  └─────────────────────────────────┘    │
│                                                       │
│  The increase in population is about 1.2%.           │
│                                                       │
│  TABLE OF MAPS                                        │
│                                                       │
│  Pg 7   Ln 3      P B U I O S                        │
└──────────────────────────────────────────────────────┘
```

Figure 9.12

Again, you need to choose the style for the list. The default is to print the map list with no page numbers. Change this option to page numbers in parentheses.

Point at (Page Numbers) Follow Entries
Click
Click on OK

499

9 Reference Tasks

The last step is to place the index definition code in the document. Begin by creating another new page. Enter

[Apple/Return]

Enter a title for the index:

Index of Topic [Return] [Return]

Display the Define List menu, and insert the index definition code.

> **Point** at Special
> **Drag** to Define Lists
> **Release**

Select index by entering

7

> **Point** at Page Numbers Follow Entries
> **Click**
> **Click** on OK

You have now inserted text codes that tell WordPerfect where to place the lists, tables of contents, and indexes when they are generated.

500

GENERATING LISTS

You are now ready to produce the index, table of contents, and map list. Your current cursor location is not significant when you generate these lists. WordPerfect will scan the entire document for codes and marks that are part of the generation process. The command to generate is found on the Mark Text menu. Enter

[Apple/j]

When the selection mode is not active, only options #4 and #5 are available. To generate the list, enter

5

WordPerfect warns you that any previously generated list, tables of contents, or indexes will be erased by this process. Enter

[Return]

The message box is displayed. WordPerfect will now generate the specified lists, tables, and indexes. You can stop the generation process by entering [Apple/.]

When the generation is complete, move to the beginning of the document by entering

[Enter] [Enter] ↑

9 Reference Tasks

The screen will show the table of contents generated by WordPerfect:

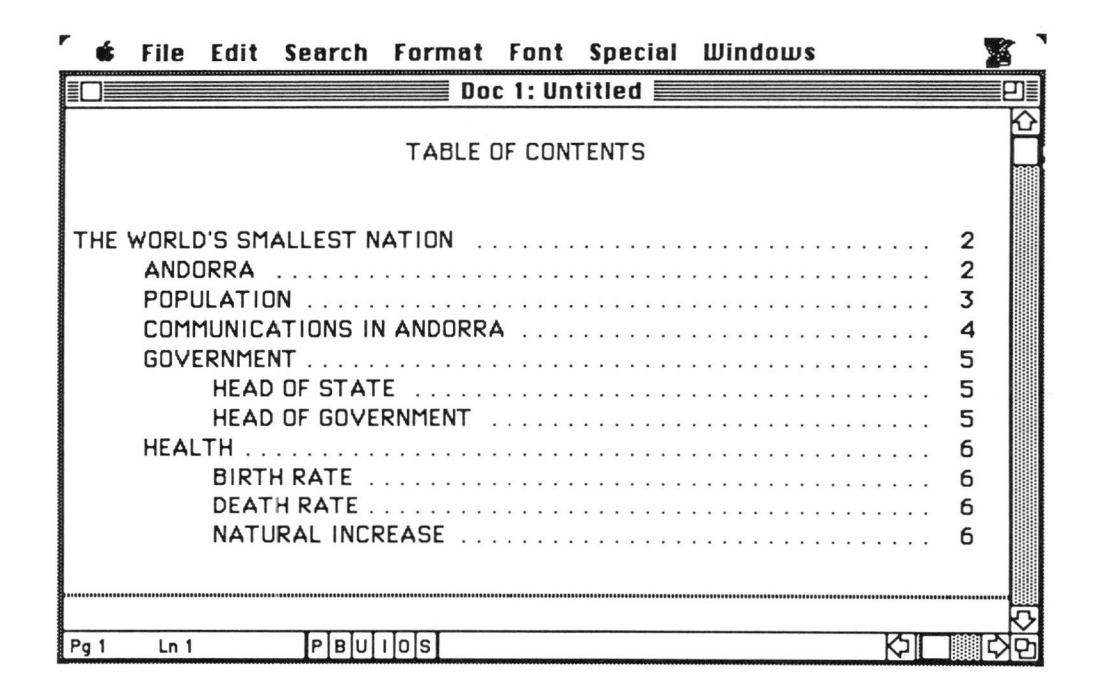

```
 File  Edit  Search  Format  Font  Special  Windows
                    Doc 1: Untitled

                    TABLE OF CONTENTS


THE WORLD'S SMALLEST NATION . . . . . . . . . . . . . . . . . . . . . . 2
     ANDORRA . . . . . . . . . . . . . . . . . . . . . . . . . . . . . . . 2
     POPULATION . . . . . . . . . . . . . . . . . . . . . . . . . . . . . 3
     COMMUNICATIONS IN ANDORRA . . . . . . . . . . . . . . . . . . . 4
     GOVERNMENT . . . . . . . . . . . . . . . . . . . . . . . . . . . . . 5
          HEAD OF STATE . . . . . . . . . . . . . . . . . . . . . . . . . 5
          HEAD OF GOVERNMENT . . . . . . . . . . . . . . . . . . . . . 5
     HEALTH . . . . . . . . . . . . . . . . . . . . . . . . . . . . . . . . 6
          BIRTH RATE . . . . . . . . . . . . . . . . . . . . . . . . . . . 6
          DEATH RATE . . . . . . . . . . . . . . . . . . . . . . . . . . . 6
          NATURAL INCREASE . . . . . . . . . . . . . . . . . . . . . . . 6


Pg 1   Ln 1        P B U I O S
```

Figure 9.13

Inspect the table of maps and the index at the end of the document. Enter

[Enter] [Enter] ↓

The screen will show the table of maps and index generated by WordPerfect:

502

Reference Tasks **9**

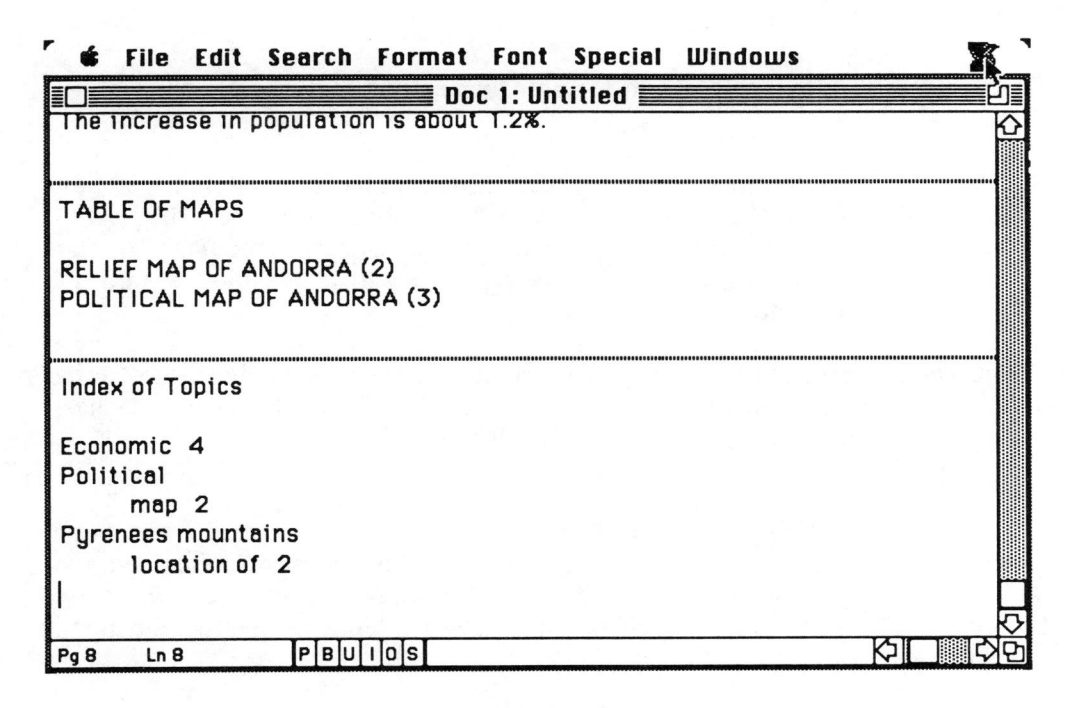

```
 File  Edit  Search  Format  Font  Special  Windows
                    Doc 1: Untitled
The increase in population is about 1.2%.

TABLE OF MAPS

RELIEF MAP OF ANDORRA (2)
POLITICAL MAP OF ANDORRA (3)


Index of Topics

Economic  4
Political
      map  2
Pyrenees mountains
      location of  2


Pg 8   Ln 8        P B U I O S
```

Figure 9.14

Save the document by entering

[Apple/s]
andorra [Return]

REVISION MARKING

Another reference feature in WordPerfect is the ability to mark text that is a suggested addition or deletion to a document. This technique is used to facilitate editing of documents when more than one person is making changes.

Keep in mind that WordPerfect's features are not designed for collaborative writings by large groups of people. The facilities provided furnish limited marking ability appropriate for editing between an author and his or her assistant.

9 Reference Tasks

WordPerfect uses two special text formats for revision marking.

Redline The redline text style places a vertical bar on the left edge of any line that contains redlined text. Redlined text is text that is a suggested addition to the existing text. Beside the bar at the beginning of the line, redlined text appears as normal text in the document.

Strikeout Strikeout text is text that is marked for deletion but is not actually removed from the document. The text is overlayed with dashes, indicating that it is marked for removal.

When the final editing of the document has been performed, WordPerfect can be asked to search the document and remove the revision codes from the document. When this task is performed, the redline text becomes part of the document and the marking bars are removed. Strikeout text is deleted from the text during the same process.

To illustrate how these features can be used, move the cursor to page 2 of the Andorra document. Enter

[Apple/g] 2 [Return]

Suppose that you want to change the word "nation" to "country," but, instead of actually making the change, you want to use the redline and strikeout features to show someone else the change you propose to make. Locate the word "nation" with the Search command. Enter

[Apple/f] nation [Return]

The cursor is positioned on the word "NATION" in the heading. To indicate that you want to remove this word, select the strikeout text style. Enter

[Apple/y]

Reference Tasks 9

Option A is strikeout text. Enter

a

The word that is selected is overlayed with dashes. To enter the replacement text turn off the selection by entering

↓

Turn on Redline text. Enter

[Apple/y] b

Enter the replacement text:

country

Turn off the Redlining. Enter

[Apple/y] b

A bar appears at the beginning of the line, indicating that the line contains redline text.

505

9 Reference Tasks

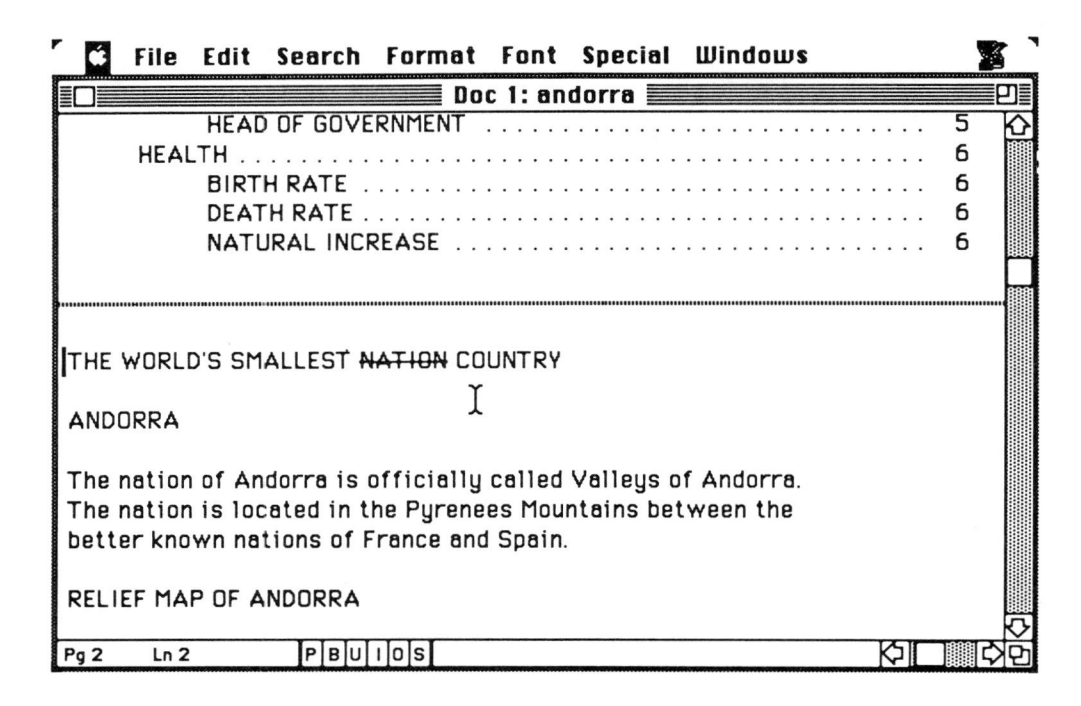

```
 File   Edit   Search   Format   Font   Special   Windows
                       Doc 1: andorra
         HEAD OF GOVERNMENT . . . . . . . . . . . . . . . . . . . . . . . . .  5
      HEALTH . . . . . . . . . . . . . . . . . . . . . . . . . . . . . . . . . . . . .  6
         BIRTH RATE . . . . . . . . . . . . . . . . . . . . . . . . . . . . . . .  6
         DEATH RATE . . . . . . . . . . . . . . . . . . . . . . . . . . . . . . .  6
         NATURAL INCREASE . . . . . . . . . . . . . . . . . . . . . . . . .  6


THE WORLD'S SMALLEST NATION COUNTRY

ANDORRA

The nation of Andorra is officially called Valleys of Andorra.
The nation is located in the Pyrenees Mountains between the
better known nations of France and Spain.

RELIEF MAP OF ANDORRA

Pg 2    Ln 2         P B U I O S
```

Figure 9.15

Perform the same operation on the next two occurrences of the word "NATION." Enter

[Apple/f] nation [Return]
[Apple/y] a
→ ←
[Apple/y] b
country
[Apple/y] b

The screen should resemble the following:

Reference Tasks 9

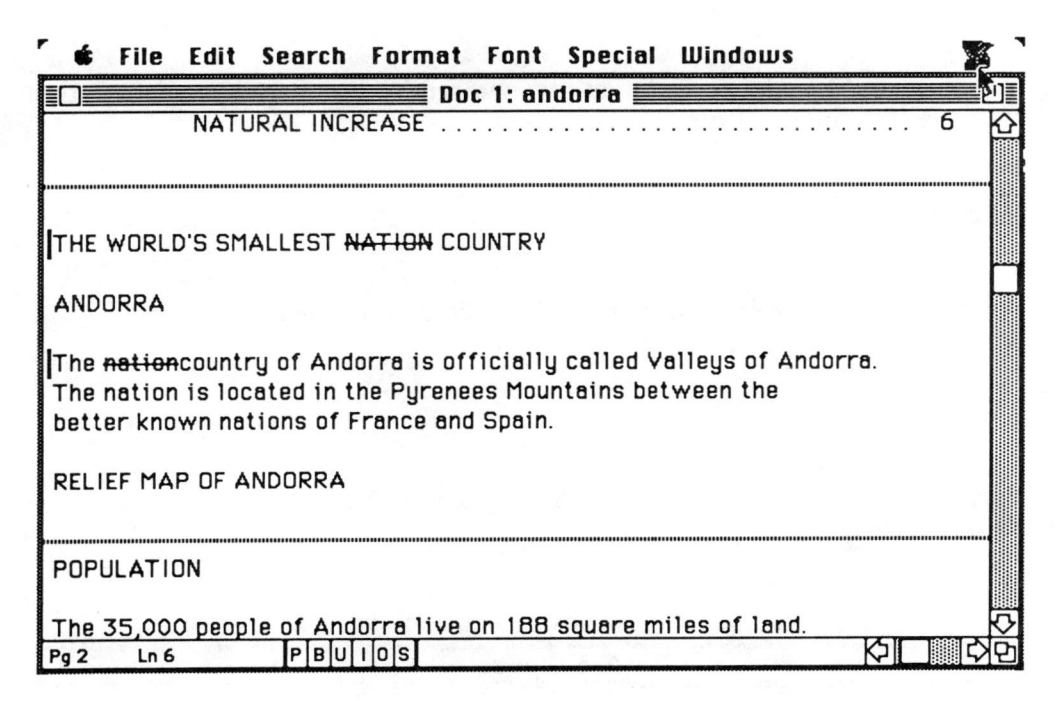

```
  File  Edit  Search  Format  Font  Special  Windows
┌─────────────────────── Doc 1: andorra ───────────────────────┐
│              NATURAL INCREASE . . . . . . . . . . . . . . . . 6  │
│                                                                  │
│ THE WORLD'S SMALLEST N̶A̶T̶I̶O̶N̶ COUNTRY                              │
│                                                                  │
│ ANDORRA                                                          │
│                                                                  │
│ The n̶a̶t̶i̶o̶n̶country of Andorra is officially called Valleys of Andorra. │
│ The nation is located in the Pyrenees Mountains between the      │
│ better known nations of France and Spain.                        │
│                                                                  │
│ RELIEF MAP OF ANDORRA                                            │
│                                                                  │
│ POPULATION                                                       │
│                                                                  │
│ The 35,000 people of Andorra live on 188 square miles of land.   │
│ Pg 2   Ln 6        P B U I O S                                   │
└──────────────────────────────────────────────────────────────┘
```

Figure 9.16

Note that the →← combination was used to make sure that the new text was entered right next to the strikeout text. When entering redline text, do not insert extra spaces because when the strikeout text is removed, these extra spaces will remain in the text and may cause odd spacing in some paragraphs. Entering the redline next to the strikeout with no spaces ensures that only a single space will appear when the strikeout text is removed.

Removing the Revision Marks and Text

When a final draft of the document has been reached, you can have WordPerfect automatically remove all strikeout text and redline codes. This process prepares the final draft for printing. Keep in mind that this process is not selective. All strikeout text will be removed. It is probably a good idea to make a copy of the final draft document before you remove the revision text — in case you have overlooked some strikeout text that should not be removed.

507

9 Reference Tasks

The command to remove strikeout text and redline codes and bars is found on the Mark Text menu. Enter

[Apple/j]

Option #4, Remove, is the one that will affect the revision text. Enter

4

WordPerfect displays a warning box to make sure that you really want to perform this option.

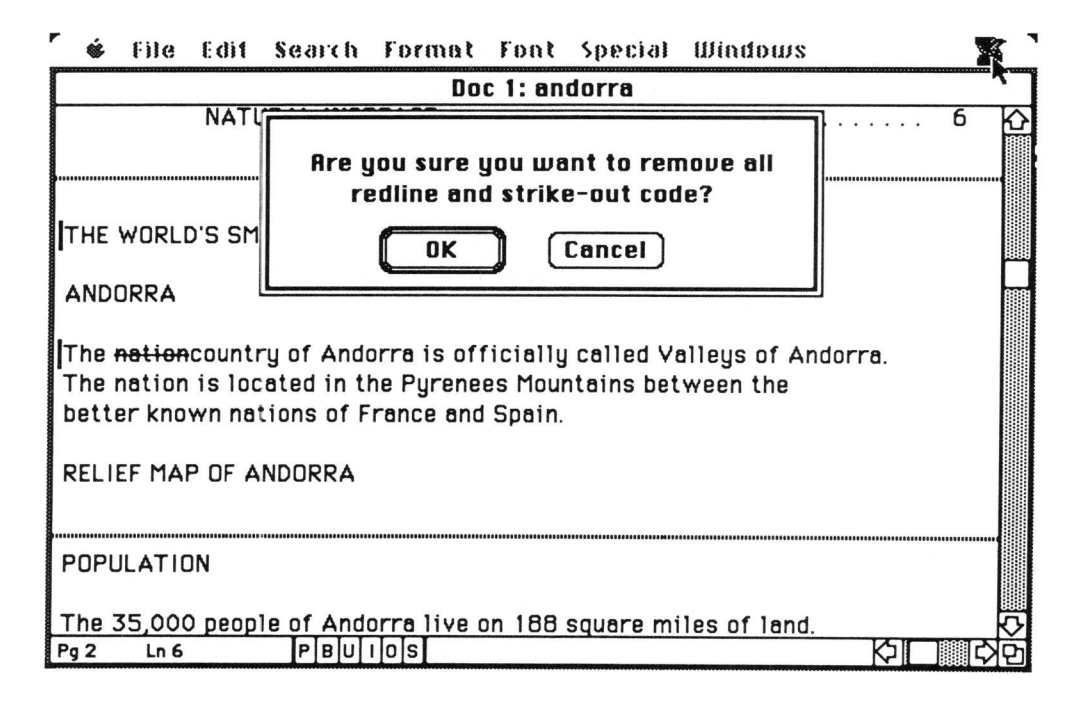

Figure 9.17

Reference Tasks **9**

| Point at OK |
| Click |

WordPerfect scans the entire document for revision codes. Note that the cursor will be positioned at the end of the document. To see the effect of the revisions, return to page 2. Enter

[Apple/g] 2 [Return]

The strikeout text has been removed, and the redline bars no longer appear on the left side of the document.

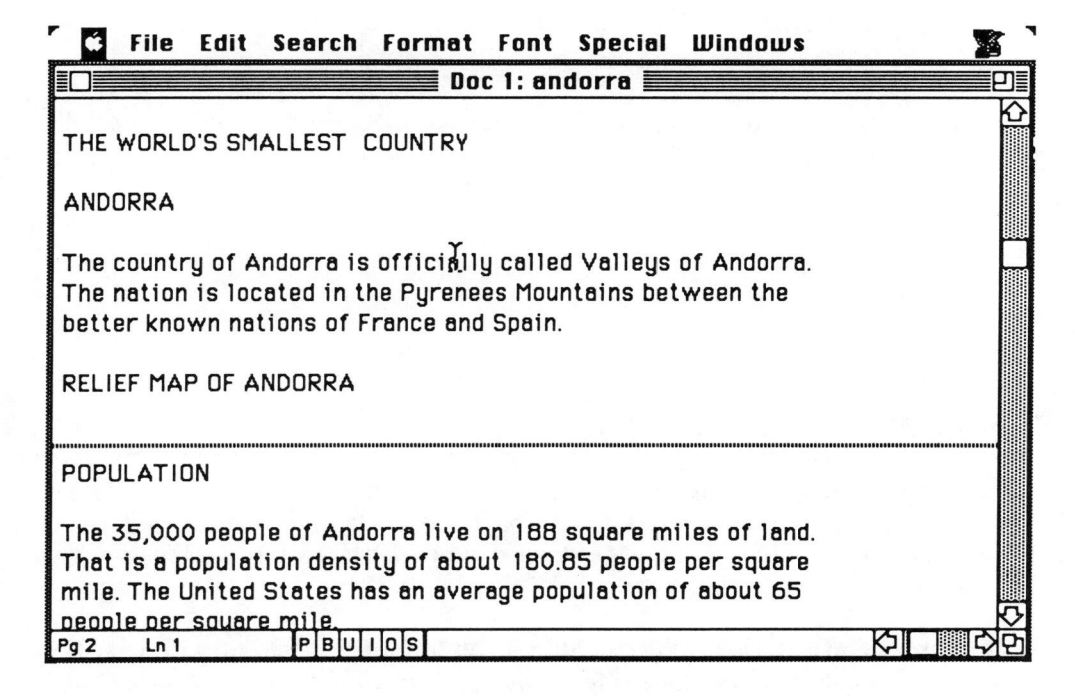

```
 File   Edit   Search   Format   Font   Special   Windows
                        Doc 1: andorra

THE WORLD'S SMALLEST COUNTRY

ANDORRA

The country of Andorra is officially called Valleys of Andorra.
The nation is located in the Pyrenees Mountains between the
better known nations of France and Spain.

RELIEF MAP OF ANDORRA
...........................................................................

POPULATION

The 35,000 people of Andorra live on 188 square miles of land.
That is a population density of about 180.85 people per square
mile. The United States has an average population of about 65
people per square mile.
Pg 2    Ln 1          P B U I O S
```

Figure 9.18

509

9 Reference Tasks

If you look at the heading "THE WORLD'S SMALLEST COUNTRY," you may notice there is an extra space between "SMALLEST" and "COUNTRY." This space occurs because you allowed a space to be inserted between the strikeout text and the redline. This error is very common. You can purge a document of double spaces by using the Replace command. As an example, enter

[Apple/h]
[space bar] [space/bar]
[Tab]
[space bar] [Return]

Return to page 2 by entering

[Apple/g] 2 [Return]

You can see that the extra space has been removed. Save the document and display a new blank window by entering

[Apple/s]
[Apple/k]
[Apple/n]

SUMMARY

- **Mark Reference Text.** You can mark text items for inclusion in tables of contents, or you can mark items for inclusion in up to five miscellaneous lists. The table of contents entries can be marked for 1 to 5 levels within a single table of contents.

- **Index Entries.** WordPerfect allows you to insert index entry items within the body of your document for inclusion into an index at some later point. Each index can contain a heading and a subheading. Entering [Apple/j] will display the Mark Text menu.

- **List Definitions.** List Definition codes must be inserted into the text to tell WordPerfect where the table of contents, index, and lists should be inserted. The codes also tell WordPerfect what style to use in formatting the items contained in the table, list, or index.

- **Generating.** Once the text markers and definition codes have been inserted, WordPerfect can generate the tables, lists, and indexes by searching the document for these codes.

- **Revision Marking.** In situations that require review of proposed editing changes, you can use special text formats—Redline and Strikeout—to mark suggested changes. Redline text is marked by a bar at the beginning of each line that contains Redline text. Strikeout text is overlayed with dashes. The Mark Text Remove command will delete all strikeout text and remove all redline bars from the document.

CHAPTER 10

MANAGEMENT TASKS

10 Management Tasks

By this time, you have learned the major techniques WordPerfect uses for document production. This chapter discusses some of the commands and techniques WordPerfect provides to better organize and manage your system. Most operations discussed in this chapter are optional. For example, WordPerfect provides four different ways to save text. You can operate perfectly well using the [Apple/s] save command; however, the other methods are provided as aids to better document management and, as such, are of concern to you only after you have become comfortable with the basic operations of WordPerfect.

ABOUT SAVING

In working through this book, you have saved many documents. Before you begin to examine alternate saving options in WordPerfect, it might be useful to discuss some of the major ideas related to computers, disks, and programs. If you are an experienced computer user, you are probably already quite familiar with these concepts. In fact, you can use a computer quite well without a thorough understanding of these ideas; however, the following section is provided as background for those who have little or no experience in file management as well as for those who need a refresher course.

Saving Files

Throughout this book, you have used the Save command, [Apple/s], to save the documents you have created as disk files. When you save a document, WordPerfect assumes that you want to replace the file stored on the disk with the newly edited version of the text. Entering [Apple/s] automatically replaces the file on disk with the current version. If the current document is untitled, WordPerfect requests that you enter a name for the document. Once you have done so, that name appears on the title bar of the document window.

WordPerfect provides two alternate forms of Save—Save As and Save Copy As. These commands allow you to save the text in the current document window without replacing the copy of the file on disk.

Save As This command saves the text in the current window to a file with a new name. For example, if you were working on a document called Business Letter and used the Save As command, you could enter a new name (e.g., Letter to Sam). The text would be saved under the name Letter to Sam, and the title bar in the current window would be changed from Business Letter to Letter to Sam. The original business letter file would be unaffected by any changes you made in the active document window.

You could use this option if you decided that the original document you were editing should not be changed and that you wanted to save the changes you made as a new document.

Save Copy As This command performs a similar operation to Save As, except that the current document window retains the original name. Suppose you are editing the file called Business Letter. If you use Save Copy As and enter the name Letter to Sam, you will create a new document with the same contents as the current window but with the name Letter to Sam. The current document window will still retain the name Business Letter, and Letter to Sam will be unaffected by any changes you then make in the active document window.

You could use this option if you decided that you wanted to save the current version of a document under a new name before making further revisions.

File Format

One of the main reasons for using the Save As and Save Copy As commands is to save the text in a format other than WordPerfect Macintosh. In theory, you could also perform a change in format from the Save menu; however, this theory implies that you are creating a document and are immediately planning to save it as a foreign file. It is much more likely that you will create a WordPerfect Macintosh document, save it, and at some later point want to transfer a copy of that file to a different file format. For that reason, it is logical to discuss file formats in terms of the Save As command rather than in terms of the Save command. Select the Save As command.

10 Management Tasks

> **Point** at File
> **Drag** to Save As
> **Release**

WordPerfect displays a file selector box and menu:

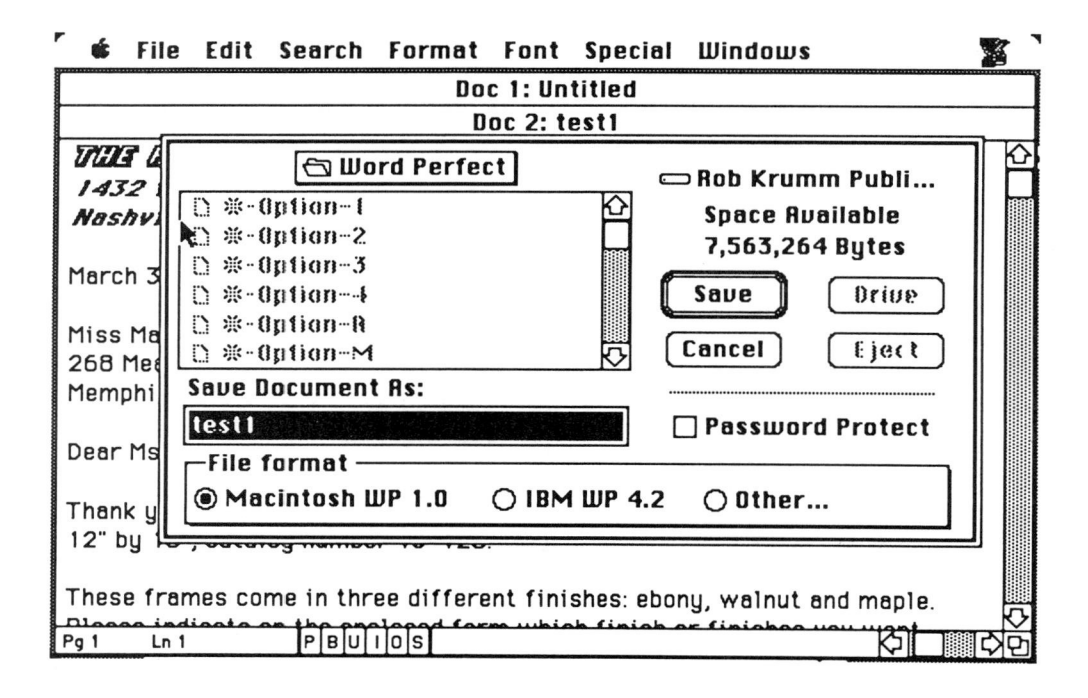

Figure 10.1

As with all File Save menus, with the Save As menu, you can enter the name for the file. In addition, there is a box labeled File Format. The box contains three buttons. The default is WordPerfect Macintosh format. You can also select IBM PC WordPerfect version 4.2 format. The last button is used to display a list of other file formats. If you select this option, WordPerfect displays a format selection box that will list available formats (see Figure 10.2). Currently, only the standard Macintosh Text format is available.

Management Tasks **10**

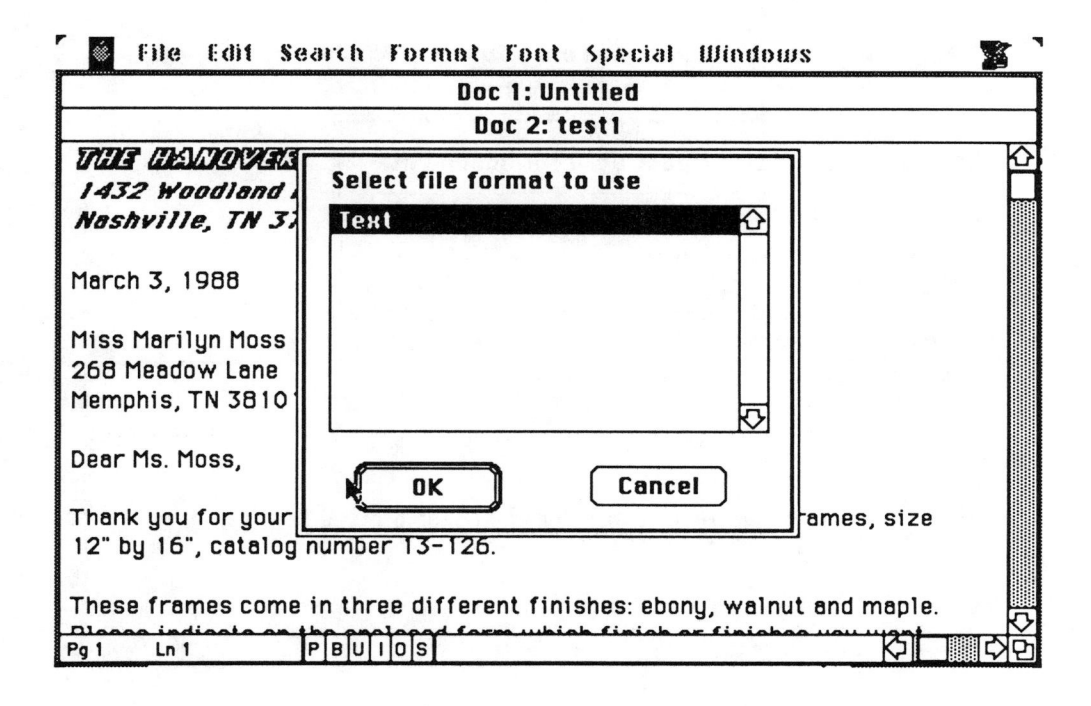

Figure 10.2

Password Protection

Another option available when saving is password protection. You can password protect a document with the ordinary Save command only if you choose to do so the first time you save the document; otherwise, you must use the Save As command and the current file name to add a password to an existing document. If you click on the box labeled Password Protection, WordPerfect will display a box asking you to enter a password (see Figure 10.3).

517

10 Management Tasks

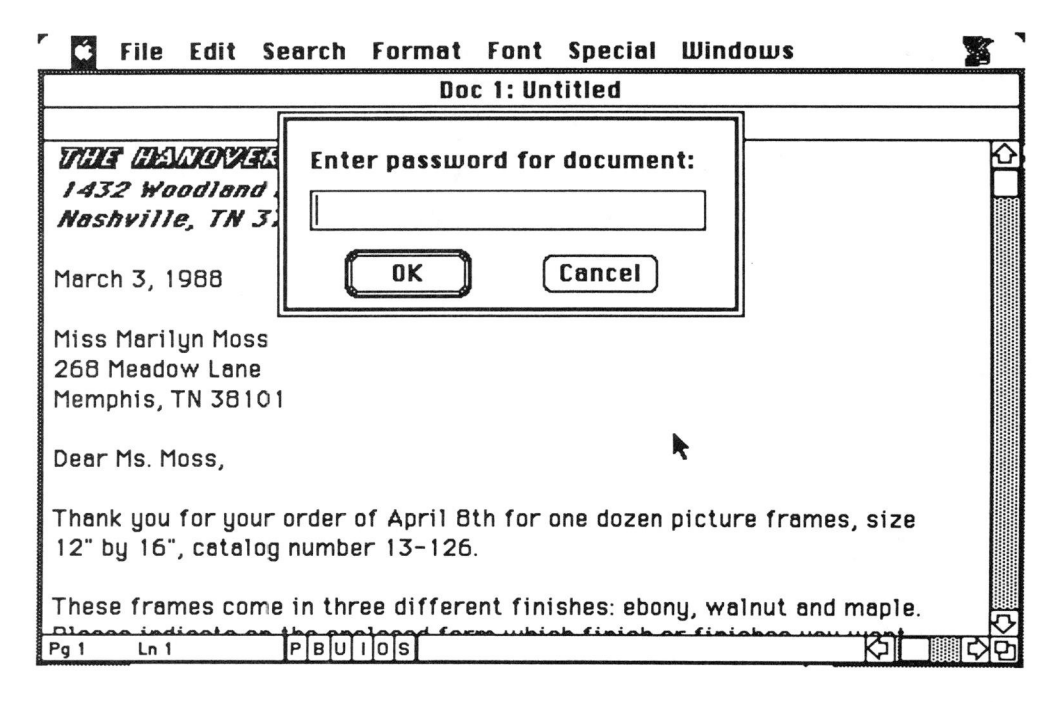

Figure 10.3

When you enter the characters for the password, they will not appear in the box. Instead, an Apple character will be displayed (see Figure 10.4).

Management Tasks **10**

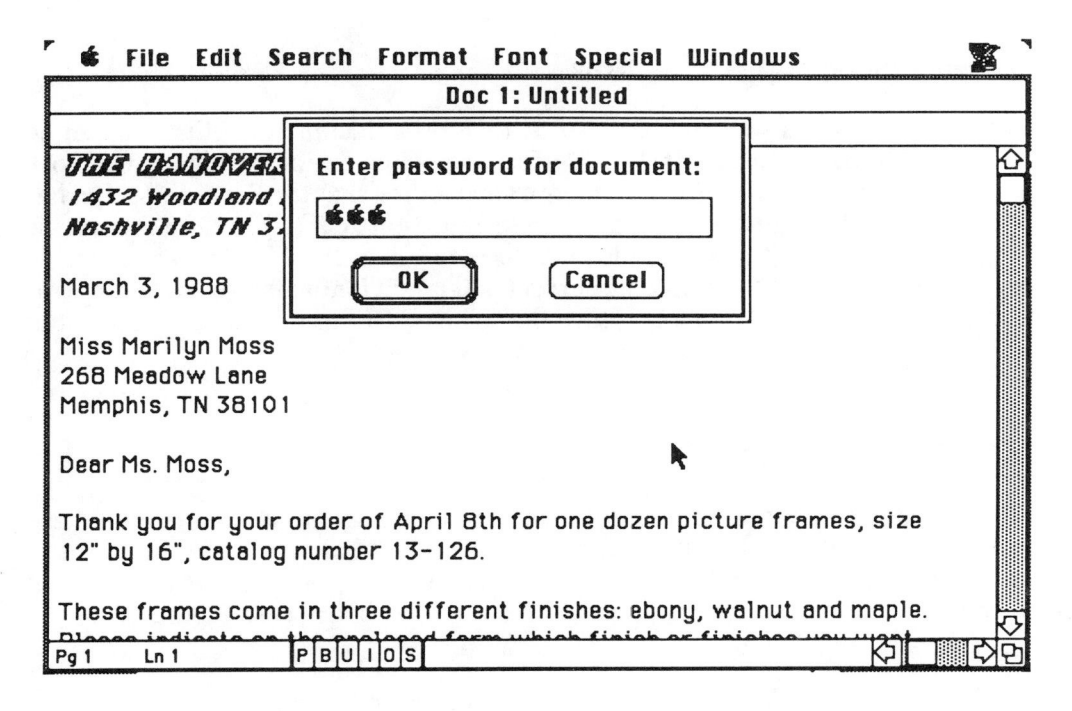

Figure 10.4

You will again be asked to enter the password. This prompt provides you with the opportunity to make sure you have entered the password correctly. After you have completed this operation, you will be asked to enter the password each time you open the document.

To remove the password protection from the document, use the Save As command, and save the file under its original name. WordPerfect will ask if you want to replace the existing file. Clicking on Yes replaces the password protected file with a nonprotected version, thus removing the password protection.

10 Management Tasks

Saving a Block of Text

You can also save a selected block of text within a document. This task can be performed by using any one of WordPerfect's selection options to highlight a block of text. When you display the File menu, you will see that the Save As option has been replaced by a new option called Save Selection As. If you drag the mouse to this option, WordPerfect will allow you create a new disk file from the contents of the selected block. Note that the current document is not affected by this operation. Save Selection As merely copies the selected text to a separate file without deleting the selected text from the current document.

FILE MANAGEMENT

The File menu also contains WordPerfect's file management commands. These commands are grouped around the file management dialog box and file selector. To activate the file management commands, you can choose File Management from the File menu or enter [Apple/L] from the keyboard (see Figure 10.5).

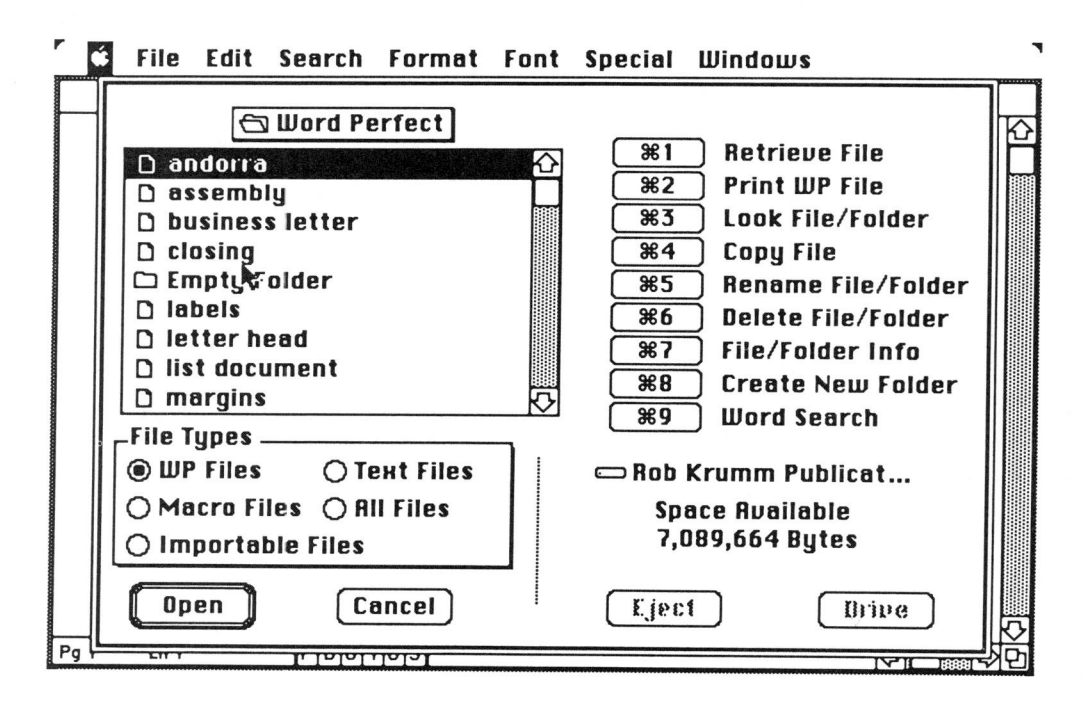

Figure 10.5

Management Tasks **10**

The File Management display consists of a file sector box and ten commands. Nine of the commands are listed on the right side of the box and are assigned to the command keys [Apple/1] through [Apple/9]. The tenth command is Open, which appears as a button at the bottom of the display. Following are descriptions of each option.

Open   The Open command performs the same operation as the Open command on the File menu. When this command is used, the document currently selected will be opened in a new document window.

Retrieve   This command is the same as the Retrieve command on the File menu. Keep in mind the difference between opening and retrieving a file. If a file is retrieved, the text from that document will be inserted into the current document window at the current cursor position. Note that if the current document window is an empty, untitled window, the Retrieve and Open commands are equivalent.

Print   The Print command performs a combination of tasks. If you select and confirm the Print command, WordPerfect opens the selected file and immediately moves to the Print menu. When the document has finished printing, WordPerfect closes the document window and saves the document on the disk. This command acts as a macro that opens, prints, and closes a document.

Look   This command displays the first full screen of text in a selected document. The text is not formatted, but appears as it would in the codes display.

10 Management Tasks

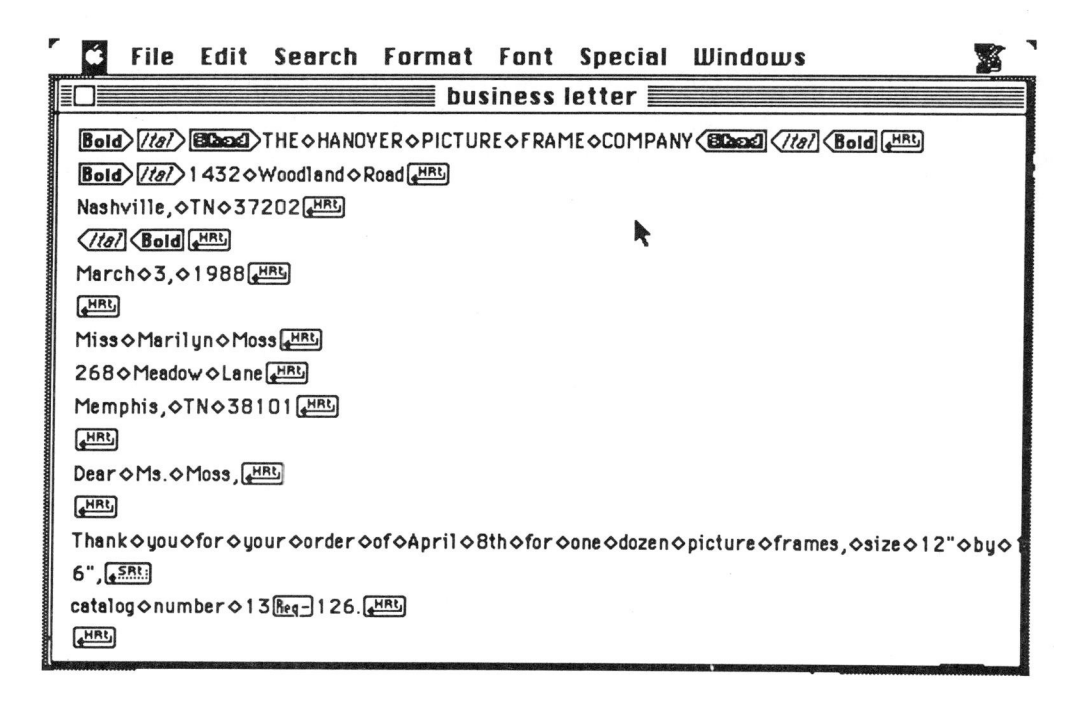

Figure 10.6

The Look command allows you to examine a file to determine whether it is the file you want to work with. Clicking on the close box returns you to the File Management menu.

Copy   This command allows you to create a copy of a document file. The copying process does not require you to load and revise the file and is therefore a faster method to create duplicate files.

Rename   Rename allows you to change the name of the selected file.

Delete   This option deletes the selected file from the disk.

Info   This option displays an information screen about the file or file folder that is currently highlighted.

Management Tasks **10**

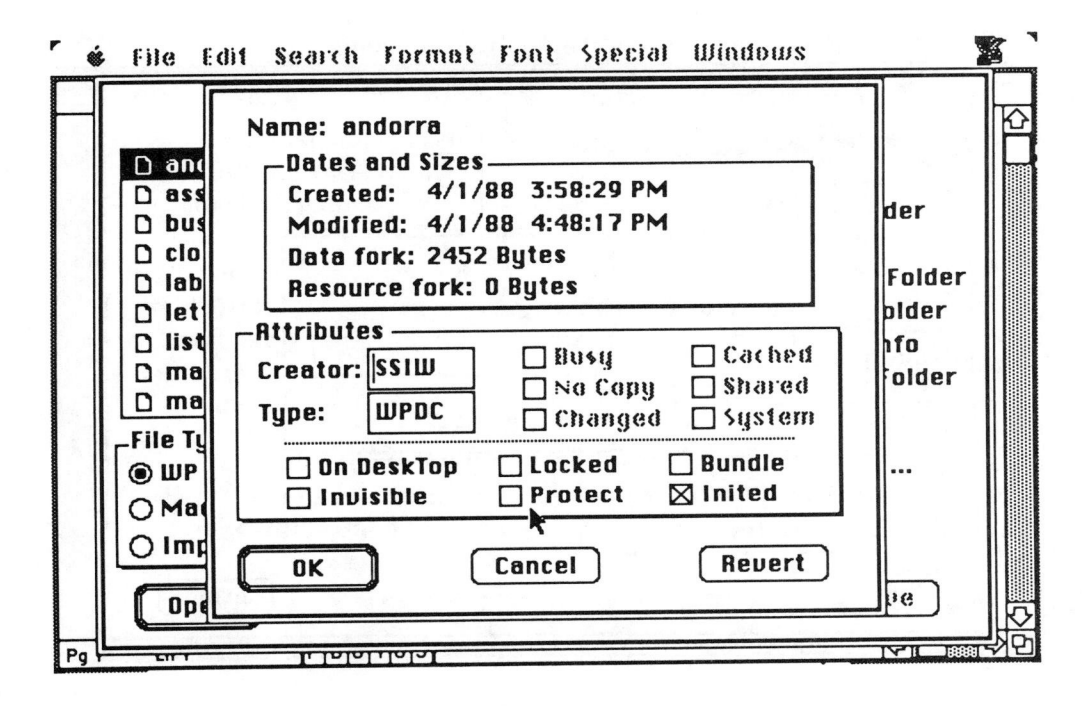

[Figure: dialog box showing file info for "andorra" with Dates and Sizes (Created: 4/1/88 3:58:29 PM, Modified: 4/1/88 4:48:17 PM, Data fork: 2452 Bytes, Resource fork: 0 Bytes), Attributes (Creator: SSIW, Type: WPDC), and checkboxes including Busy, No Copy, Changed, Cached, Shared, System, On DeskTop, Invisible, Locked, Protect, Bundle, Inited (checked), with OK, Cancel, Revert buttons]

Figure 10.7

With the exception of the time and date information, the rest of this display contains data related to the Macintosh file system. For example, each Macintosh application uses an identifier to tell which files belong to which applications. WordPerfect uses WPDC for WordPerfect document files. The information on the screen is of concern chiefly to experienced users with knowledge of the Macintosh operating system.

Create Folder This option allows you to create a new file folder and duplicates the New Folder option available on the Macintosh main system menu.

Search This option is a type of Finder command. When you use the Search command, WordPerfect allows you to enter a word or phrase for which you want to search (see Figure 10.8).

523

10 Management Tasks

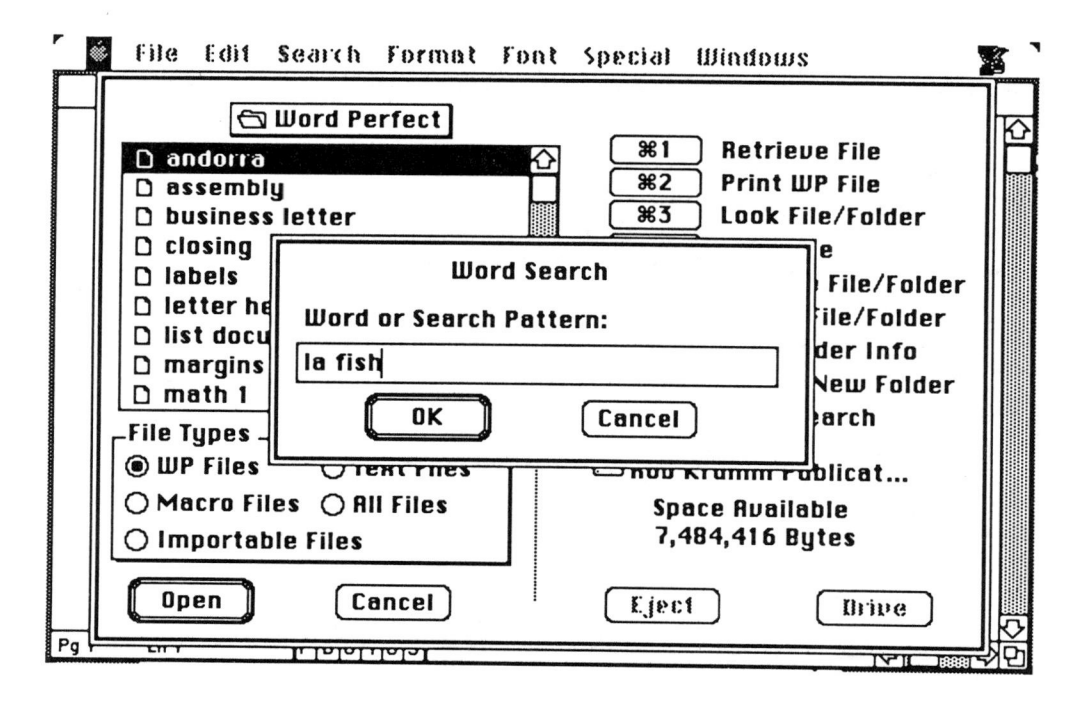

Figure 10.8

WordPerfect then tests all files in the current folder for a match and lists only those files that contain that word or phrase (see Figure 10.9).

Management Tasks 10

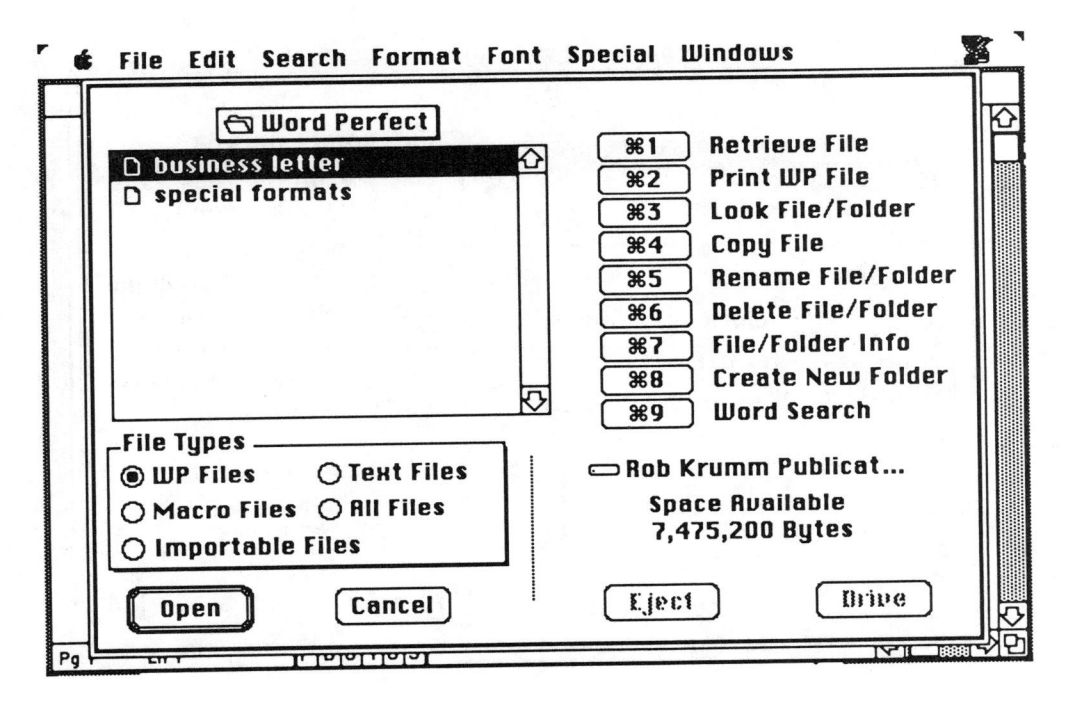

Figure 10.9

WordPerfect also allows you to select the type of files that will be listed in the file selector display.

WP — This option restricts the display to WordPerfect Macintosh document files.

Macros — This option displays WordPerfect macro files.

10 Management Tasks

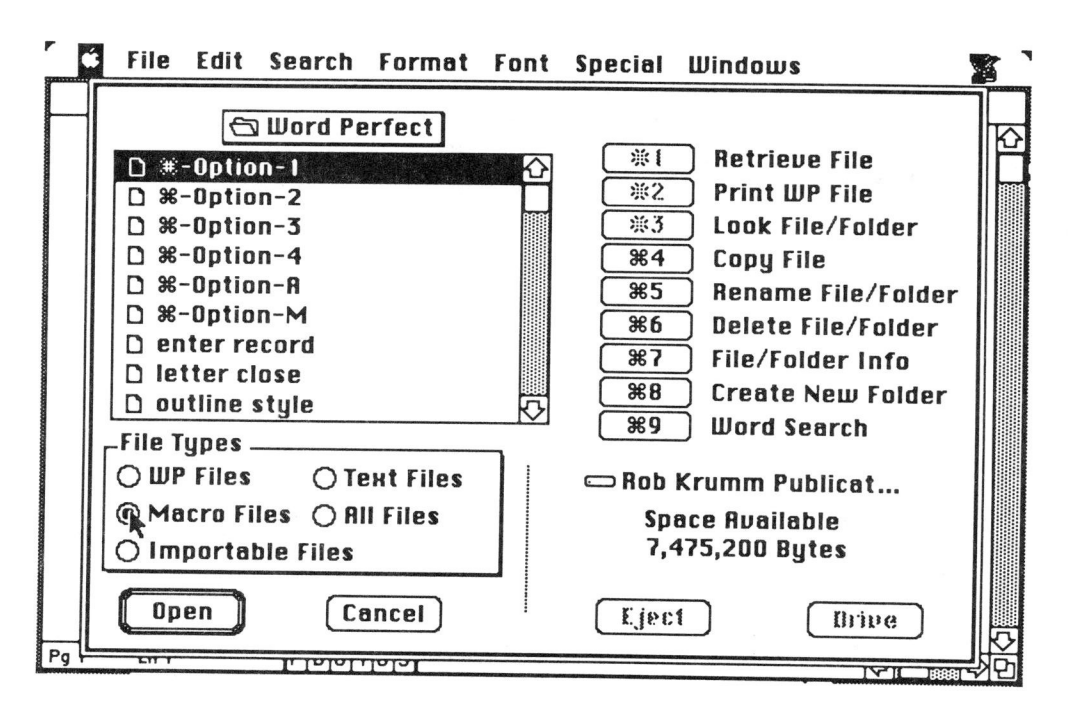

Figure 10.10

Text	This option displays all text files.
All	This option displays all files listed in that folder, including program files.
Importable	This option displays the files that have a type that WordPerfect can load, for example, WordPerfect's IBM PC 4.2 version.

SYSTEM DEFAULTS

WordPerfect allows you to change the system defaults in four areas of operation. To change the defaults, select the WP Defaults option on the File menu.

The default options fall into four categories.

Management Tasks **10**

Backups Backup files are used to protect you from accidental loss of data due to a program error or loss of power. When you open a file, WordPerfect will create a duplicate of it. In addition, you can select a timed backup, which means that WordPerfect will automatically create a backup file every so many minutes. The timed backup will make sure that you can recover most of the changes you have made to a document, in case you lose power or encounter a system error (see Figure 10.11).

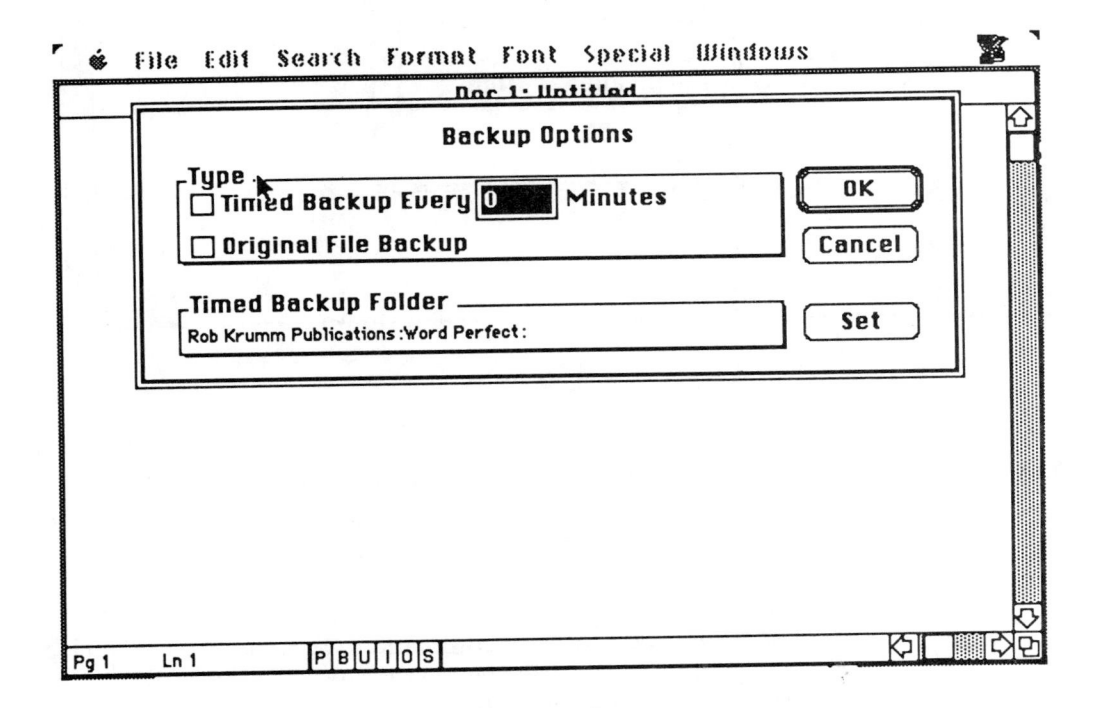

Figure 10.11

Beeps WordPerfect will issue a beep each time one of three events takes place: a search fails to find a match, an error occurs, or a hyphenation point is found when the prompted hyphenation mode is active. You can suppress one or more of these beeps.

527

10 Management Tasks

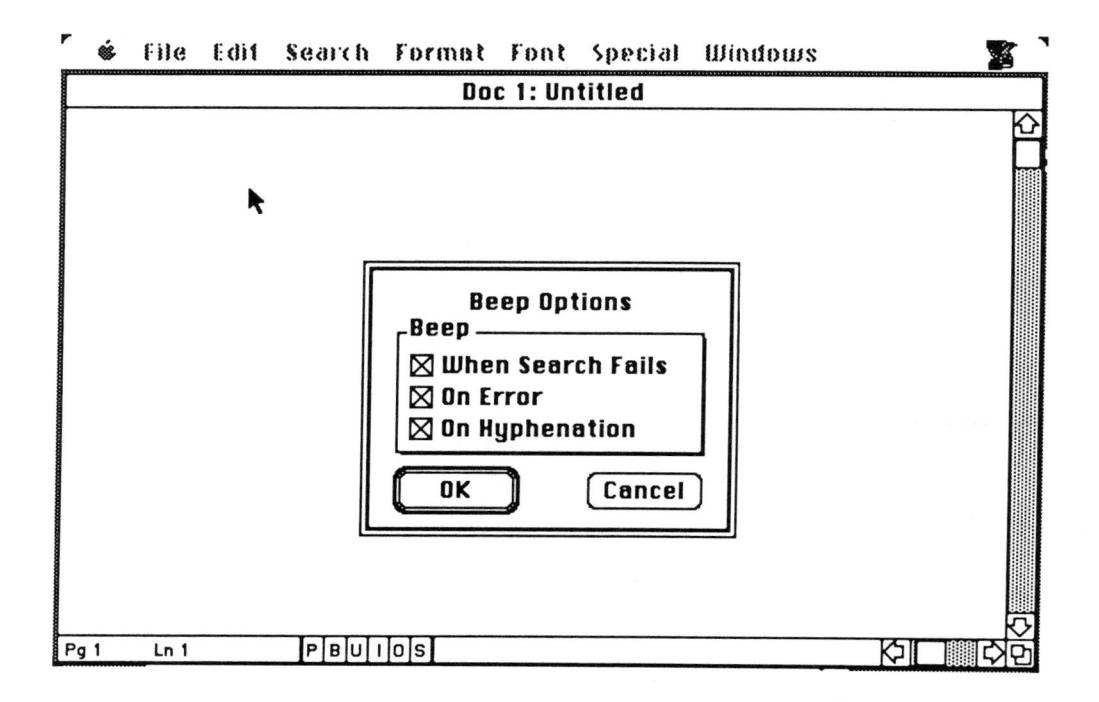

Figure 10.12

Folders

Because many of WordPerfect's operations create files, WordPerfect needs to know which folders on the Macintosh desktop should be used for these files. WordPerfect uses four folders.

The **Work folder** is used for file references. For example, in Chapter 7 you used the ^P^P command to search for a file during a merge operation. WordPerfect always looks in the Work folder for these files. In most cases, the Work folder is the WordPerfect folder.

The **Temporary folder** is used by WordPerfect for files that it needs to in the course of its operation. These files include memory overflow files that are created automatically by WordPerfect when working on large documents. Most users need not be concerned about this folder.

Management Tasks **10**

The **Macro folder** tells WordPerfect where to find macro files when [Apple/Option] commands are entered. The default folder is usually the WordPerfect folder. You may want to designate a separate folder to hold your macro files.

The **Speller/Thesaurus folder** is the folder that WordPerfect looks for when you perform a spell check or a synonym lookup.

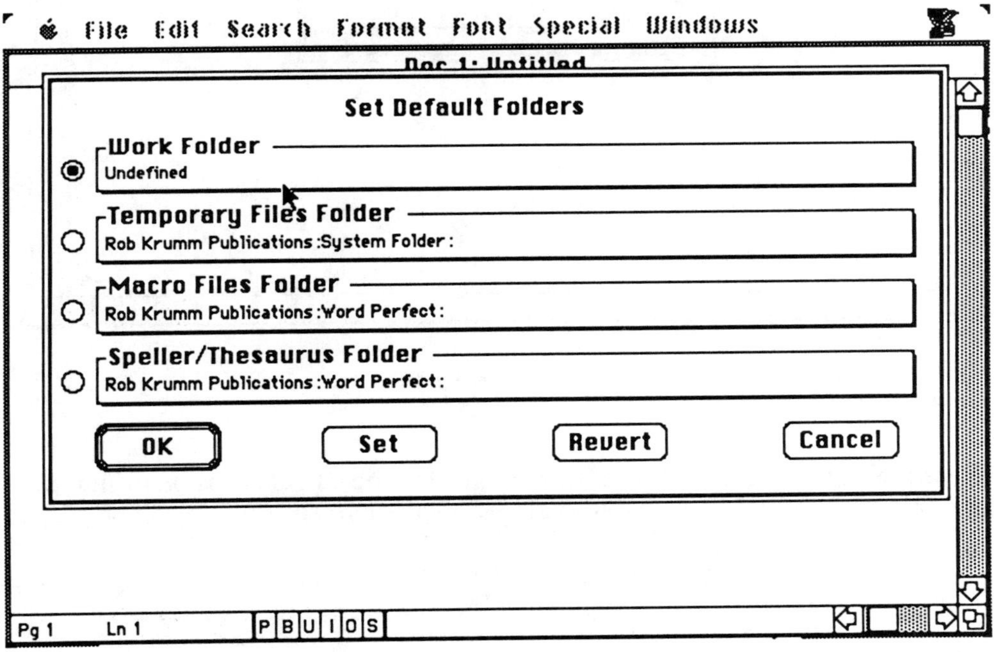

Figure 10.13

Measurement   This option allows you to choose the measurement unit for WordPerfect. The default is to measure in inches. You can choose centimeters, which is the European or scientific style, or points, which is typographers' style. A **point** is a unit of measurement equal to 1/72" that is used by printing professionals.

10 Management Tasks

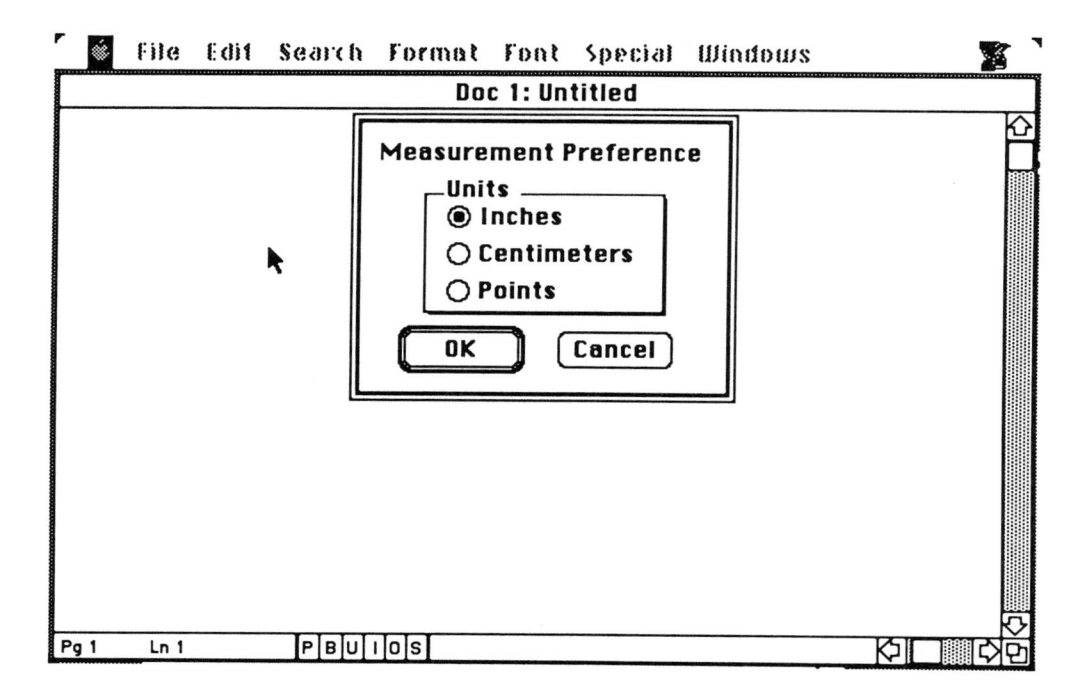

Figure 10.14

These default settings can either be changed for the current session or made permanent. If you change a default setting, only the current session will be affected unless you choose the WP Defaults option #1, Save Settings. This option writes a copy of the defaults onto disk and will set these defaults each time WordPerfect is loaded.

ODDS AND ENDS

So far, the major features of WordPerfect for the Macintosh have been discussed. The following items are features that have not been covered explicitly in the previous chapters but that you may occasionally find useful.

Typeover Mode

WordPerfect normally inserts all text that you enter; however, if you want to type over existing text, you can change the entry mode to typeover by selecting Typeover from the Edit menu. The word "Typeover" appears on the bottom bar to indicate that this mode is active. It is generally best to work in the normal insert mode, so use typeover only for correcting text. Remember to return to the insert mode by repeating the Edit Typeover command.

Widow and Orphan Control

WordPerfect will insert a new page code when you have entered enough text to fill up the current page. This type of system can create widows and orphans.

A **widow** occurs when the first line of a paragraph is separated from the rest of the paragraph. An **orphan** occurs when the last line of a paragraph is separated from the rest of that paragraph. Widow and orphan control is used to suppress these single lines that are considered bad typesetting form. When widow and orphan control is active, WordPerfect will vary the number of lines on each page to make sure that at least two lines of a paragraph are located at the bottom or top of a page.

Kerning

Kerning is another WordPerfect typographical control that is concerned with the amount of space left between characters. Normally, WordPerfect automatically spaces characters according to a proportional spacing table for each character font used by the program.

Kerning allows you to manually alter the amount of space between characters to improve the look of headings that use unusual font or letter combinations. For example, mixing fonts of different size in the same word or phrase may produce odd spacing.

The kerning option found on the Line Format menu has two more options. Kerning allows you to decrease the amount of space between characters, and Letter Spacing allows you to increase the amount of space between characters.

This manual spacing adjustment can be quite tedious. It is usually needed only when you have major headings or titles.

10 Management Tasks

Show Position

WordPerfect normally shows your cursor position in terms of page and line number. Of course line number is relative to the size of the margins and the height of the fonts on the page. If you want to have more exact information about positioning, you can use the Show Position option found on the Special Screen menu.

When active, this option displays the exact horizontal and vertical position of the cursor on the page measured in hundredths of inches.

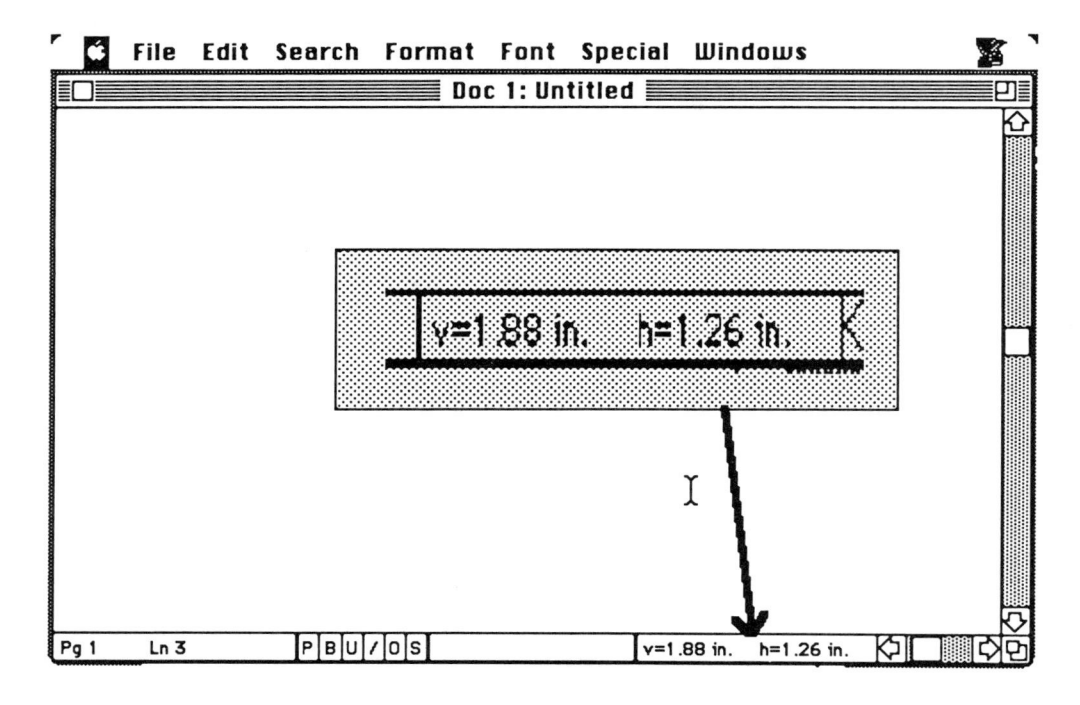

Figure 10.15

Management Tasks **10**

SUMMARY

- **Saving.** WordPerfect allows you to save files and change the document name at the same time. You can also add password protection to files using the Save As command.

- **File Formats.** WordPerfect Macintosh can save files in WordPerfect 4.2 format for the IBM PC or in a generic text format.

- **File Management.** WordPerfect allows you to perform many file operations from a single menu. File management is accessed by using the [Apple/L] key combination. You can open, retrieve, print, copy, rename, or delete a file; display file information; create a file folder; or search files for words or phrases.

- **System Defaults.** WordPerfect allows you to change the default settings for backups, beeps, file folders, and measurement.

INDEX

Special Keys
[Apple] key
move cursor, 3
[Apple-Shift] combination, 25
[Apple/.] command, 40, 469
[Apple/2] command, 46
[Apple/3] command, 154
[Apple/5] command, 243
[Apple/7] command, 67
[Apple/9] command, 279
[Apple/?] command, 443
[Apple/L] command, 520
[Apple/Option] commands, 417
[Apple/Shift/L] command, 155
[Apple/Shift/b] command, 50
[Apple/Shift/c] command, 62
[Apple/Shift/e] command, 357
[Apple/Shift/f] command, 259
[Apple/Shift/h] command, 246
[Apple/Shift/i] command, 50
[Apple/Shift/m] command, 420
[Apple/Shift/n] command, 25
[Apple/Shift/o] command, 50
[Apple/Shift/p] command, 210
[Apple/Shift/r] command, 355
[Apple/Shift/s] command, 50
[Apple/Shift/t] command, 156
[Apple/Shift/u] command, 50
[Apple/Shift/v] command, 50
[Apple/Shift/y] command, 177

[Apple/Shift/z] command, 92
[Apple/b] command, 76
[Apple/c] command, 125
[Apple/d] command, 27
[Apple/f] command, 76
[Apple/g] command, 187
[Apple/h] command, 93
[Apple/j] command, 484
[Apple/k] command, 86
[Apple/n] command, 86
[Apple/o] command, 218
[Apple/p] command, 39
[Apple/Return] command, 161
[Apple/t] command, 36
[Apple/u] command, 257
[Apple/v] command, 125
[Apple/w] command, 295
[Apple/x] command, 125
[Apple/y] command, 49
[Esc] key, 19
[Shift/Tab] command, 167
[control/f] command, 348
[control/g] command, 455
[enter] key, 443
[tab] key, 92
[TRt] code, 129

A
About WordPerfect
  command, 443
Alignment
  center text, 62
  tabs stops, 100
Append to clipboard, 304
Append to file, 307, 322
Assembly documents, 401
Audio control
  beeps, 527
Auto
  automatic paragraph
  numbers, 183

B
Backups
  automatic, 527
Backups
  timed, 527
Beginning of document, 11
Blank fields, 359
Block protect, 146
Bold text, 23
Bullet paragraphs, 162

C
Case
  convert text, 63
Center aligned tabs, 100
Centering in column, 207
Centering text, 62
Change fonts, 62
Character format menu, 243
Clipboard, 299
Clock
  insert date, 27
Close window, 86
Code icons, 68
Codes
  deleting, 76
  display window, 67
  replace command, 95
  search for, 73
Codes display
  cursor, 70
Codes locate, 73
Collaborative writing
  features, 503
Columns
  cursor movement, 204
Columns
  definition, 191
  merge reports, 381
  movement, 204
  newspaper, 205
  newspaper columns, 190
  parallel columns, 190
  parallel columns, 191
  turn on/off, 191
  uneven, 200

535

Conditional page break, 146
Continuous underline, 104, 114
Convert
  case of text, 63
Copy
  between windows, 298
Copy document
  file management, 522
Create folder
  file management, 523
Cursor
  change windows, 293
  codes display, 70
  keyboard movement, 3
  mouse cursor, 2
  move between columns, 204
  move by pages, 187
  movement with mouse, 5
  show position, 532
Customized keys, 443
Cut and paste
  table text, 124
Cut and paste commands, 125

D
Data entry
  with macros, 459
Data files, 337
Date function, 28
Date text, 28
Decimal key, 8
Decimal tabs, 100
Default settings, 526
Define enter key
  combination, 444
Definition
  columns, 191
Delete
  blank lines, 70
  codes, 76
  document, 522
  file management, 522
  tabs with mouse, 107

undelete, 257
Delete codes
  dialog box, 80
Delete codes
  message, 79
Delete key, 8
Delete text, 7
Delete text
  decimal key, 8
Delete words, 11
Dialog boxes
  from macros, 458
Document
  opening, 218
Document information
  file management, 522
Document information
  display, 523
Documents
  format options, 515
  save as command, 515
  save copy as command, 515
  save options, 514
  save part of, 520
Double underlines, 104

E
Editing
  revision text, 504
End of document, 11
Endnotes, 264, 275
Endnotes
  style, 279
Enter key, 4
  define function menu, 447
  defined function, 444
  use function, 449
Enter key combinations, 443
Enter vs. return, 8
Escape key, 19

F
Field codes, 345
Fields, 338

File
  save document, 40
File management
  commands, 521
File management menu, 520
Files
  append to, 307
  document information display, 523
  format options, 515
  management, 520
  opening documents, 218
  partial documents, 520
  retrieve document, 318
  save as command, 515
  save copy as command, 515
Files
  saving options, 514
Find command, 73
First lines indents, 161
Folder
  create new, 523
Folders
  macro folder, 529
  select usage, 528
  select work folder, 406
  temporary folder, 528
  work folder, 528
Fonts
  adjustment for tabs, 138
  changing of, 62
  insert literal characters, 162
Footers, 239
Footnote menu, 264
Footnotes, 264
Footnotes
  change style, 283
  editing of, 277
  insert into sequence, 273
  keep together, 282
  menu command, 279
  number of, 278
  numbering style, 281
  page layout changes, 287
  position of, 281
  reference code, 265

536

separator, 280
spacing of, 281
style string menu, 284
style, 279
update for margin changes, 287
window, 265
Form letters, 336
Format
  tables of contents, 494
Formats
  column layout, 190
Forms
  fill in with merge, 391
Functions
  assign to enter key, 443

G
Generate tables and indexes, 501
Goto command, 187
Graphics, 325
Graphics
  picture insert code, 331

H
H-zone, 84
Hard returns
  delete, 70
Headers, 239
Headers
  even and odd pages, 252
  header code, 245
  header window, 242
  in merge reports, 387
Height of characters, 58
Height of lines, 141
Help
  topic display, 446
  topic list, 445
Help command, 443
Helvetica
  font change, 62
Hot zone, 84
Hypercard, 325

Hyphen zone, 84
Hyphenation, 16
Hyphens, 83

I
Imagewriter
  causing screen scrolling, 14
Inches, 529
Indents
  bullet paragraphs, 162
  change indents, 159
  first line exception, 161
  left indent, 152
  left-right indent, 154
  multiple, 155
  overhangs, 161
  generate, 501
  item entry menu, 490
  mark text for, 489
  sub headings, 491
Info
  file management, 522
Information command, 443
Input boxes
  macros, 459 - 460
Insert date, 27
Insert graphics, 325
Insert literal, 162
Insert text, 7
Italic text, 23

J
Justification, 83
Justification on/off, 85

K
Kerning, 531
Keyboard
Apple key, 3
  change tabs, 135
  enter key, 4
  select text, 25
  text attributes, 25

L
Leaders between tabs, 116
Leading
  between lines, 143
Left & right page numbers, 234
Left aligned tabs, 100
Lines
  height, 141
  height, 143
  leading, 143
  return to normal spacing, 145
  spacing between, 141
List document structure, 354
List documents
  enter data with macros, 459
List processing, 337
Lists
  define style, 498
  define style menu, 499
  generate, 501
  generate from marked text, 488
Locate codes, 73
Locate documents
  file management, 523
Location in document
  tables of contents, 494
Look at document
  display format, 522
  file management, 521

M
Macros,
  attach to merge, 454
  chains, 471
  conditional logic, 471
  define macro menu, 418
  dialog box display, 463
  dialog boxes, 458
  execute, 421
  halt, 469
  input box display, 463
  input boxes, 459 - 460

interactive, 458
introduction, 416
invoke macro menu, 422
invoke macro merge command, 455
invoke macro, 421
long names, 416
nesting, 465
outline macros, 430
pause macros, 449
playback macro, 421
recording of, 417
run macro, 421
searching in, 471
short names, 417, 426
single key menu, 427
single key names, 426
stop execution, 469
style macros, 430
typing macros, 417
user input, 458
with merge, 453
[Apple/Option] commands, 417, 426
[Apple/Shift/m] command, 420
[control/g] command, 455
Margin release, 166
Margin set, 46
Margins
  diagram, 48
  release, 166
  ruler line, 52
  update footnote layout, 287
Mark text
  entry code, 484
  for lists, 488
  for revisions, 503
  index entries, 489
  index item menu, 490
  menu, 484
  redline text, 504
  remove redline, 507
  remove revision, 507
  remove strikeout, 507
  strikeout text, 504

tables of contents, 483
Measurement, 529
Menus
  full screen display, 90
Merge
  [control/f] command, 348
  [control/g] command, 455
  ^C codes, 393
  ^N^P^P sequence, 378
  assembly, 410
  assembly documents, 401
  attach macro, 454
  attributes in shell letter, 367
  auto print code, 398
  blank fields, 359
  column reports, 381
  date files, 337
  end of field code, 354
  end of record code, 357
  end of record code, 354
  field codes, 345
  field codes in text, 350
  fields defined, 338
  fields in list document, 354
  fields with attributes, 356
  fill in forms, 391
  get next record code, 375
  headers, 387
  invoke macro merge command, 455
  list documents, 337
  merge documents, 361
  multiple line fields, 356
  multiple records on page, 375
  new primary code, 403
  next primary file code, 375
  paragraph numbers, 379
  parallel columns, 381
  pause merge code, 393
  primary merge file, 362
  record numbers, 379
  records defined, 340
  records in list document, 354
  report headings, 385

reports, 373
retrieve document, 403
secondary merge file, 364
select records with macro, 471
shell documents, 314
with macros, 453
Merge documents, 336
Merging documents, 361
Mouse
  cursor movement, 5
  delete tabs, 107
  set tabs, 110
Mouse cursor, 2
Move bar, 311
Move by pages, 187
Move cursor
  beginning of document, 11
  end of document, 11
  one word, 3
Move text
  text that contains tabs, 126
Movement
  in column mode, 204
  show position, 532
Moving windows, 310
Multiple documents, 290

N

Nesting
  of macros, 465
New lines, 8
New page command, 160
New window, 86
Newspaper columns, 190
Newspaper columns, 205
Numbering of outlines, 171
Numbering sequence outlines, 187
Numbering sequence outlines, 188

538

Numbers
   automatic paragraph
      numbers, 181
   of pages, 220

O
Open document
   file management, 521
Open files, 218
Options
   default settings, 526
Outline text, 23
Outlines, 171
Outlines
   change levels, 174
   codes used, 184
   numbering sequence, 187
   numbering sequence, 188
   paragraph numbers codes, 185
   revise outlines, 179
   style of outline, 187
   style of outline, 188
   turn off outline mode, 177
   with macros, 430
   with macros, 435
Overhang paragraphs, 161

P
Page break
   conditional, 146
   forced page breaks, 160
   protecting text from, 146
Page end
   conditional, 146
Page endings
   keep lines together, 146
Page format
   footers, 239
   headers, 239
Page layout
   diagram, 48
   even and odd headers, 252
   header code, 245
   margins, 47
   page numbers, 238
   suppress header, 250
Page numbers, 220
Page numbers
   alternating pages, 234
   change positions, 235
   mixing formats, 230
   page number sequence, 227
   position, 221
   position code, 223
   starting number, 220
Page numbers
   styles, 220
   suppress page number, 225
Page number sequence, 227
Pages
   insert page break, 160
   new page, 160
Paragraph numbers, 181
Paragraph numbers
   merge documents, 379
Paragraph numbers codes, 185
Parallel columns, 190 - 191
Parallel columns
   merge reports, 381
Partial
   save part of document, 520
   Password protection, 517
Pause
   in macro, 449
Picture code, 331
Pictures
   insert into document, 325
Plain text, 23
Point size, 58
Points, 529
Position
   cursor with mouse, 5
Preview document, 209
Preview document
   zoom display, 212
Primary merge file menu, 362
Print document
   file management, 521
Print style menu, 49

Print styles, 21
Printing, 39
Printing
   from merge, 398
   preview document, 209
   stop print, 40
Protect blocks
   from page breaks, 146
Protection
   of file with passwords, 517

R
Record numbers, 379
Records in merge, 340
Redline text, 504
Redline text
   remove, 507
Reference tasks, 478
Remove revision marks, 507
Rename document
   file management, 522
Repeat character, 19
Replace command, 93
Replace with codes, 95
Retrieve document, 318
Retrieve document
   file management, 521
Return key, 8
Return vs. enter, 8
Reveal codes, 67
Reveal codes icons, 68
Revision marks, 503
Right & left page numbers, 234
Right aligned tabs, 100
Ruler line, 52
Ruler line
   change tabs, 134
Ruler line icons, 53 - 54

S
Save
   blocks of text, 520
Save
   optional formats, 515

Save as command, 515
Save as menu, 516
Save copy as command, 515
Save document, 40
Save documents
 options, 514
Screen
 full screen display, 90
 move and size windows, 310
 preview printed document, 209
 zoom preview display, 212
Screen scrolling
 imagewriter, 14
Search
 for codes, 73
Search
 in macros, 471
Search backward, 76
Search documents
 file management, 523
Search forward, 76
Search forward command, 73
Security
 passwords for documents, 517
Select
 record from list', 471
Select on/off, 25
Select text
 keyboard, 25
Set
 tabs with mouse, 110
Set tabs
 with mouse, 107
Set tabs
 with mouse, 110
Setup of WordPerfect, 526
Shadow text, 23
Show clipboard, 299
Show position, 532
Size icon, 311
Size of characters, 58
Sizing windows, 310
Soft returns, 83

Sound
 control beeps, 527
Spacing
 between lines, 141
Spacing
 with tabs, 97
Special characters, 162
Spell menu, 30
Spelling
 check document, 30
Spelling
 fix typo, 31
 folder location, 529
 phonetic search, 31
 suggested corrections, 34
 word lookup, 31
 words with numbers, 33
Spelling check, 29
Splitting
 protection from, 146
Stop macro, 469
Strikeout text, 504
Strikeout text
 remove, 507
Styles
 using macros, 430
Styles of print, 21
Suppress header, 250
Suppress page numbers, 225
Symbols
 insert special characters, 162
Synonyms, 35
System date
 inserting, 27
System defaults, 526

T
Tab set icons, 99
Tab set menu, 98
Tab with dot leader icon, 118
Table text
 cut and paste, 124
Tables
 create lists, 488

 define lists, 493
 define tables, 493
 enter text, 103
 index item menu, 490
 index sub headings, 491
 indexes, 489
 mark text menu, 484
 of contents, 478
 set tabs, 97
Tables of contents, 478
Tables of contents
 define menu, 496
 define style, 493
 entry code, 484
 format, 494
 generate, 501
 levels, 484
 location in document, 494
 mark text, 483
 style examples, 497
Tabs, 92
Tabs
 adjustment for font size, 138
 change location, 132
 change with keyboard, 135
 change with ruler line, 134
 evenly spaced, 120
 move text that contains tabs, 126
 multiple setting, 120
 set individual tabs, 97
 types of alignment, 100
 with dot leaders, 116
Temporary return code, 129
Text
 mix with graphics, 325
 undelete, 257
Text attribute buttons, 22
Text attributes
 with keyboard, 25
 with mouse, 22
Text cursor, 2
Text enhancement, 20
Text entry
 wraparound text, 13
Thesaurus, 35

540

Topics
    help list, 445
Typographical controls, 531

U

Undelete text, 257
Underline style, 104, 114
Underlined text, 23
Uneven columns, 200
Upper and lower case
    conversion, 63
User defined keys, 443

V

Vertical spacing, 141

W

Window
    codes display, 67
    full screen display, 90
    open new window, 86
Window and orphan control,
    531
Window close, 86
Windows
    [Apple/w] command, 295
    append to clipboard, 304
    change active, 293
    clipboard, 299
    copying text between, 298
    cycle to next, 294
    moving, 310
    multiple documents, 290
    size window icon, 310
    sizing, 310
    window menu, 294
    zooming a window, 315
Wp defaults
    select work folder, 406

Z

Zoom box, 311
Zoom print preview display,
    212
Zooming a window, 315

RELATED TITLES FROM MIS:PRESS

ordPerfect for the Macintosh
users who want to take full advantage of the power of rdPerfect for the Macintosh, this book documents, in -by-step fashion, all the major features included in Macintosh version of this best-selling word processor. so includes an introductory section for PC and rdPerfect users coming to the Macintosh for the first e from other environments.

Krumm 0-943518-91-1 $19.95

e Power Of: WordPerfect 4.2
gs the powerful features of this best-selling word cessor to the user's fingertips. Highlighting previously ocumented command structures, this book takes the r beyond a working knowledge of WordPerfect, bling the development of specific business lications.

Krumm 0-943518-69-5 $19.95

ordPerfect 4.2 Power Tools
lear and concise explanation of the most powerful ctions of this popular word processing program. udes discussions of financial and statistical boarding, legal documents, desktop publishing, tem configurations, and using WordPerfect with us 1-2-3, dBASE III PLUS, Ventura, and other rdPerfect products.

Krumm 0-943518-30-X $22.95

e Power Of: Microsoft Word 4.0, cluding Style Sheets and Desktop blishing (Second Edition)
es users step-by-step through Microsoft Word 4.0, latest version of this popular word processing gram. Describes how Word 4.0 interacts with desktop lishing in addition to the diverse capabilities of the gram.

othy Perrin 0-943518-31-8 $19.95

Ventura
An easy-to-understand guide for the advanced user, focusing exclusively on Ventura—the best-selling desktop publishing software for the IBM PC. Emphasizing the latest typesetting and design principles, this book concentrates on the aesthetics of desktop publishing in addition to the diverse capabilities of the program.

Rob Krumm 0-943518-37-7 $21.95

Programming Laser Printers
This book describes in a detailed, step-by-step fashion how to create custom fonts, develop macros, design page layout, and output graphics. Also includes specific information on the following products: HP LaserJet Plus, OASYS LaserPro, Mannesmann Tally MT 910, CIE Terminals LIPS, WordPerfect, MS Word 4.0, PageMaker/Windows, Ventura Publisher, GEM, and Harvard Professional Publisher.

Timothy Perrin 0-943518-43-1 $23.95

Running HyperCard with HyperTalk
Shows how to build applications with HyperTalk inside HyperCard, the most revolutionary new development in microcomputer software. Includes a complete HyperTalk reference guide covering the basics of HyperTalk's object-oriented programming principles. Brief examples of HyperTalk scripts are used to demonstrate key points.

Barry Shell 0-943518-79-2 $19.95

*A*vailable where fine books are sold.

MANAGEMENT INFORMATION SOURCE, INC.
P.O. Box 5277 • Portland, OR 97208-5277
(503) 222-2399

free
800-MANUALS

ANAGEMENT INFORMATION SOURCE, INC.